Growing Artists

Teaching Art to Young Children

THIRD EDITION

This book is dedicated to
Matthew and Laurel, my own growing artists.

Growing Artists
Teaching Art to Young Children
THIRD EDITION

Joan Bouza Koster
Broome Community College

THOMSON
™
DELMAR LEARNING

Australia Canada Mexico Singapore Spain United Kingdom United States

Growing Artists: Teaching Art to Young Children, Third Edition
Joan Bouza Koster

Vice President, Career Education SBU:
Dawn Gerrain

Director of Editorial:
Sherry Gomoll

Acquisitions Editor:
Erin O'Connor

Developmental Editor:
Alexis Breen Ferraro

Editorial Assistant:
Ivy Ip

Director of Production:
Wendy A. Troeger

Production Editor:
Joy Kocsis

Technology Project Manager:
Joseph Saba

Director of Marketing:
Wendy E. Mapstone

Channel Manager:
Donna J. Lewis

Cover Design:
Andrew Wright

Composition:
Stratford Publishing Services, Inc.

Library of Congress Cataloging-in-Publication Data

Koster, Joan Bouza.
  Growing artists : teaching art to young children / Joan Bouza Koster.—3rd ed.
      p. cm.
  Includes biliographical references (p.) and index.
  ISBN 1-4018-6561-5
  1. Art—Study and teaching (Early Childhood). I. Title.

  LB1139.5.A78K67 2004
  372.5'044—dc22
  2003068763

NOTICE TO THE READER

Publisher does not warrant or guarantee any of the products described herein or perform any independent analysis in connection with any of the product information contained herein. Publisher does not assume, and expressly disclaims, any obligation to obtain and include information other than that provided to it by the manufacturer.

The reader is expressly warned to consider and adopt all safety precautions that might be indicated by the activities herein and to avoid all potential hazards. By following the instructions contained herein, the reader willingly assumes all risks in connection with such instructions.

The Publisher makes no representation or warranties of any kind, including but not limited to, the warranties of fitness for particular purpose or merchantability, nor are any such representations implied with respect to the material set forth herein, and the publisher takes no responsibility with respect to such material. The publisher shall not be liable for any special, consequential, or exemplary damages resulting, in whole or part, from the readers' use of, or reliance upon, this material.

Contents

Creating Art Guide

Studio Page Guide

Preface

Teaching in the key of life can take many forms, but it always means that one's heart and mind are fully engaged with the hearts and minds of children.

—Mimi Brodsky Chenfeld (2000, p. 2)

INTRODUCTION TO THE THIRD EDITION

Welcome to the third edition of *Growing Artists.* Since this book was first published, many changes have taken place that affect how we approach teaching young children. This new edition reflects continuing growth in our knowledge about the importance of art in developing young minds. At the same time, excellent teaching practice has not changed. Exemplary, art-based teaching continues to be theory driven, shaped by developmentally appropriate practice, and seeped in understanding about how young children from infancy to age eight can be nurtured to reach their creative potentials.

TO WHOM IS THIS BOOK ADDRESSED?

Teachers play a tremendous role in nurturing children's artistic and creative potential. As Christine Marme Thompson points out, "We now recognize that children's art is not an automatic consequence of growth or development but the result of an active process of exploration and inquiry that cannot occur without some facilitation by adults" (1995, p. 82). This book speaks first and foremost to students who are now preparing to work with young children. They, more than anyone else, will most directly influence the young artists of our future. But it is also addressed to anyone, whether practicing teacher, parent, or caregiver, who has ever given a child a

crayon and said, "Draw me a picture"—and then wondered what more they should do.

WHAT IS THE APPROACH OF THIS BOOK?

In order that this relationship between child artists and guiding adults can be deep and meaningful, this book provides a theoretical perspective, grounded in the work of Piaget, Vygotsky, Gardner, and Kindler, and suggests effective practices drawn from the National Art Education Association's National Standards for the Visual Arts and the National Association for Young Children's recommendations for developmentally appropriate curriculum. Together these provide the framework that early childhood educators need in order to design effective art curricula for children from infancy to age eight. Throughout there is an emphasis on understanding how to foster children's artistic development by creating a safe, sensory-appealing environment where art created by diverse people and cultures is valued, where the individual pace of young artists is respected, and where art activities are integrated into the total curriculum in a wide variety of ways.

WHAT IS THE PLAN OF THIS BOOK?

This book is designed to be an easy-to-use resource for both those preparing to be early childhood teachers and those currently working in the field. The ideas, methods, and suggested practices found in each chapter will provide a springboard for readers to design their own curriculum. As such, this book goes beyond the presentation of isolated "projects"; instead, it provides child-tested, traditional, and innovative art experiences that serve as both a resource and a model for those creating their own repertoire of activities.

To accomplish this, the book is divided into twelve chapters, each of which addresses the interrelated areas of knowledge needed in order to successfully introduce young children to art. A series of guiding questions about art education for young children begins each chapter and sets the stage for meaningful reading. In addition, interspersed throughout the book are carefully chosen quotations taken from a wide variety of sources that are designed to provoke, inspire, and introduce the wide range of thought about early childhood art.

The first chapter sets the stage for developing a rich, integrated art program for young children by introducing current research and educational theory as it relates to the development of young children and the teaching of art and includes an example of how such a program would look in an early childhood program. The following chapters delve into topics related to the effective teaching of art to toddlers, preschoolers, and primary school students. Chapter 2 addresses the role of the teacher and positive ways teachers can respond to young artists. Chapter 3 reviews what is known about the artistic development of young children and identifies the factors that influence how children approach art activities. Chapter 4 introduces the creative process as a way of understanding why children create the art they do and as a framework for structuring art activities to allow creative growth. Integrating art into the curriculum is addressed in chapter 5, which provides detailed examples of ways to infuse art across subject disciplines. Chapter 6 presents up-to-date information on how to select safe art supplies for young children and addresses the issue of using food as an art material. Throughout this book, food-based art materials have been marked with an asterisk(*). Chapter 7 shows how visual art can be more than just making something; through the integration of all the arts, it can be a way of perceiving, appreciating, and understanding the meaning of the visual qualities of the world using all of the modalities of learning. Chapter 8 provides exciting hands-on activities that will open up children's eyes to art created by people from many cultures, times, and places. How to create an environment conducive to the growth of children as artists is detailed in chapter 9. Chapter 10 focuses on how art activities can enhance social growth and presents many group art activities. It introduces ways to use the com-

puter as an artistic tool with young children. Chapter 11 sets forth approaches that can be used to accommodate children with special needs, ways to use art to deal with bias, and plans for holiday art activities that are inclusive and open-ended. Finally, chapter 12 suggests ways that teachers can assess the artistic growth of their students and themselves as teachers, such as through the use of process folios and portfolios.

NEW TO THIS EDITION

Topics that have been added to or updated in this new edition include

- a renewed emphasis on developmentally appropriate practice and the role of culture, and its relationship to current learning theory.
- an examination of the implications of the most recent brain-based research as related to the teaching of art.
- an expansion of Howard Gardner's Theory of Multiple Intelligences with the addition of the naturalistic intelligences as a way of expanding the view of children's potential.
- the introduction of the practice of guided discovery and the use of real objects as ways to attract children's attention and nurture motivation.
- an all-new computer art section in chapter 10 that reflects the impact of modern, high-speed computing and more technological sophistication in children, making it easier than ever to add computer art to early childhood programs.
- expanded ways of using art as a way to develop needed physical, language, and social skills in children with special needs.
- an updated, annotated bibliography of children's books that includes the best new books available and provides suggested age ranges for all books.
- more on-line sources of information and materials.

FEATURES

Within each chapter, specific information has been highlighted in order to attract attention to important ideas, present supplementary material, and provide an easy reference for the reader. This featured material follows.

Young Artists at Work

Short vignettes, based on the author's observations of real children in real situations, provide a vivid picture of the kind of child–art interactions most teachers can expect to find in their rooms. These vignettes lead into discussions of the philosophical basis and organizational needs of a creative and an open-ended art program.

Quotations

Interspersed throughout the book are carefully chosen quotations from a wide variety of sources. These are designed to provoke, inspire, and introduce the wide range of thought concerning the topic of early childhood art. The quotations provide a representative survey of the researchers, educators, philosophers, and writers, both past and present, who have been involved with children and their art.

Further Reading

The books listed with annotations at the end of each chapter have been specifically selected either to expand on the ideas and concepts presented in the chapter or to further the reader's personal artistic and creative development. Readers are encouraged to read as many of these books as possible, both to become well grounded in the field and to learn more about themselves as artists. Instructors may choose to use these books as supplements to the text or as recommended reading.

Creating Art

Each of these sections discusses a particular art form in detail. Information on how to present each medium as an integrated, creative, open-ended art activity is organized in the form of a detailed lesson plan that can be used as a guide for teaching. Each section includes objectives, recommended ages, setup, materials, introductory activities, procedures, suggested vocabulary and comments, ways to end the activity, and ideas for follow-up activities. Examples of relevant children's books and integrated language, math, science, and other cross-curricular activities are also provided.

Studio Pages

Each chapter includes activities designed to help readers think further about the information presented in each chapter. These include answering questions about personal beliefs and experiences, applying information from the chapter to real-life situations, and carrying out systematic observations in actual classroom settings. The pages have been perforated so they can become part of a teaching notebook, if desired.

Teaching in Action

A sample lesson that illustrates how the ideas in this book work in the reality of the classroom. It is taken directly from practicing teachers' lesson plans, teaching journals, and taped interviews.

Highlighted Information

In-text icons make the following features easier to find and use.

 Art Words. Interspersed throughout the text are relevant art words and their definitions or examples of how to use them.

 Artist's Tool Box. Art tools and materials that relate to the art activities being discussed are described in terms of age appropriateness, safety, and possible uses.

 Classroom Museum. Ways to introduce young children to artists and their art are presented here.

 Music Box. This offers a lively song or chant to accompany an art activity.

 Safety Note. This provides information on ways to provide safe art activities for children.

 Special Needs. Suggestions are given for adapting art activities to make them accessible to all children.

 Teacher to Family. Sample letters to families are included in many chapters to provide examples of the ways teachers should reach out to the families of the children they teach.

 Teacher Tip. This is a brief, practical idea that may prove helpful to teachers who are just starting out.

Appendices

Appendix A: Teacher Resources. This is a list of sources for the special art supplies, computer software, art prints and artifacts, and recipes mentioned in the text.

Appendix B: Children's Literature on Art. Over 300 children's picture books about art are annotated with suggested uses and cross-referenced by topic. Complete references for books mentioned in the text are found here.

Appendix C: Teacher References. This annotated list will provide further information on art history and approaches to art media for the teacher of young children.

Glossary. A listing of terms used in the text.

Ancillary Materials

Instructor's Manual. Available with this new edition is an updated Instructor's Manual that includes invaluable information for those preparing others to teach early childhood art. The manual contains:

- chapter summaries
- course organizational tips
- motivating, cooperative group activities
- children's literature and questions that support the text
- authentic assessment tools
- short-answer and essay-question test bank
- The Instructor's Manual is available exclusively in electronic format on our Web site. Go to http://www.earlychilded.com, and click on Instructor Resource.

Online Companion™. New to this edition is an integrated Online Companion™ that provides much-needed access to an age-based collection of color photographs that shows the extraordinary range of art produced by young children in exemplary art programs. In addition, there are:

- critical thinking questions and activities related to the text and the artwork
- a sample Web portfolio
- links to art-related Web sites, museums, and articles

The Online Companion™ icon appears at the end of each chapter to prompt you to go on-line and take advantage of the many features provided.

You can find the Online Companion™ at www.earlychilded.delmar.com

WHAT DO THE TERMS MEAN?

Young Artist

In this book, **young artist** (or **child**) is used to refer to children from 18 months to eight years old. This age range is based on the mode of delivery for art education in our society. Most children ages eight and under are in settings such as kindergarten, primary programs, preschool, child care, nursery school, play groups, or at home, where art activities take a wide range of directions depending on the training and knowledge of the adult in charge.

In addition, these years also form an artistically and a conceptually unified whole, because it is during this span that children develop their first graphic symbol system through art. Children in the midst of this process need a nourishing environment in which to create art.

Educational Settings

Programs for young children meet in many different locations, from private homes and church basements to public and private school buildings. For simplicity, **classroom** refers to the inside area used by the children, and **outdoor area** has been used to refer to any contiguous outside play area. Adaptations are included for activities in the home, as are suggestions about when to use the outdoor area.

Guiding Adults

Throughout the text, **guiding adult** is used interchangeably with teacher, parent, aide, and caregiver. The role of the adult in art is to be a guide—someone who selects and prepares the supplies, maps out the possible routes, provides encouragement along the way, takes time for side trips, and celebrates each milepost the child reaches.

ABOUT THE AUTHOR

Joan Koster is an instructor in early childhood education at Broome Community College, Binghamton, New York, and holds degrees in art education and elementary education from Adelphi University and Temple University. She is currently conducting dissertation research under the direction of the Department of Education at Binghamton University on how teachers can use the arts to address racism. She also directs the Talent Development at Homer Brink Elementary in Endwell, New York, where she works daily with prekindergarten through fifth grade students on interdisciplinary projects. Over the past 34 years, she has taught art at all levels, from preschool through college. She is the author of *Bringing Art into the Elementary School Classroom* and *Handloom Construction: A Practical Guide for the Non-Expert.* Her work in early childhood education has been published in various journals, including *Young Children,* and she has presented numerous workshops to teachers' organizations. In addition, with her husband and children she operates a small sheep farm in upstate New York and is a professional handweaver, whose uniquely dyed work has been exhibited and marketed widely.

Acknowledgments

I am deeply indebted to many people who over the years have contributed to the creation of this book. I wish to give special thanks to my husband and family who have provided me the time and space to first write this book, and then to revise it two times. I am also especially grateful to my current young students who willingly posed for the photographs and enthusiastically contributed their artwork to this edition. I also appreciate the continuing kindness of my fellow teachers who have allowed me to photograph in their classrooms, helped obtain permissions, and offered wonderful suggestions.

I wish to acknowledge the critical feedback I have received over the years from my undergraduate students who have pointedly told me what they love about the book, as well as what I should improve. I also want to thank my editor, Alexis Breen Ferraro, and the staff at Thomson Delmar Learning for their support in producing this third edition. In addition, my appreciation goes to all of the members of my publishing team who have seen this work through to completion.

Lastly, the thoughtful and detailed advice of the following reviewers was invaluable in helping me revise this book to make it clearer and more usable.

Carol Anderson
Colorado Community Colleges
    Online
Denver, CO

Elaine Camerin, Ed.D.
Daytona Beach Community
    College
Daytona Beach, FL

Pamela Davis, Ph.D.
Henderson State University
Arkadelphia, AR

Linda Estes, Ed.D.
St. Charles Community College
St. Peters, MO

Mary Clare Munger, M.Ed.
Amarillo College
Amarillo, TX

Art and Young Children

Questions Addressed in This Chapter:

- ✿ Who are the young artists?
- ✿ Why should art be taught to young children?
- ✿ What is the relationship between art and learning?
- ✿ How should art programs for young children be designed?
- ✿ What does a well-designed art program look like?

Young Artists at Work

Maria, age one, pulls her finger through a drop of spilled cereal and then licks her finger.

Steve, age two, amuses himself during his bath by decorating the tub with handfuls of bubbly white soap foam.

Lorna, age four, splashes through a puddle and then with careful deliberation makes a pattern of wet footprints on the pavement. With every step she looks back to see her "trail."

Paul, age six, spends a busy day at the beach building sand mountains and decorating them with broken shells and beach pebbles. Other children join in his fun and watch excitedly as the surf slowly creeps up and then finally washes each mountain away.

WHO ARE THE YOUNG ARTISTS?

Each of these children is a young artist, investigating elements of visual art—line, shape, color, texture, form, and pattern. They are making the same artistic discoveries and decisions that all of us have made in our own lives. In doing so, they are repeating a process that has gone on as long as people have inhabited the earth. Like the circles, swirls, and lines on the walls of the caves and cliffs that were the canvasses of the earliest men and women, the chiseled carvings on temple walls at Tikal, the stone-smoothed satin black pot of a Pueblo potter, and the flowing line of the Chinese calligrapher, the art of young children expresses their personal and cultural history. Their art reflects who they are at that moment in time.

Children between the ages of one and eight are busy discovering the nature of their world. They are not consciously artists in the way an adult is. They do not stop and say, "Now I am creating a piece of art." They are not creating a product—they are involved in a process!

They are at play. They enjoy manipulating the many materials that they find around them and expressing their creative power to change a piece of their world. They are communicating their feelings and what they have learned. As they learn, they grow and develop.

They gain control over their large and small muscles. Their skill in handling different materials improves. They expand their repertoire of lines and shapes and

patterns. They repeat their successes over and over. They learn to use symbols that have meaning not just to themselves but also to the others around them. By the time these young artists reach age eight, they already know a great deal about the world of artistic expression.

But these growing artists are also still very young. They do not yet have skillful control over all their materials. They make messes. They cry if they spill paint on their shoes. Young children have short attention spans and are infinitely curious. They get distracted by a noise and run off, leaving their paintbrush in the middle of their picture. They do not always do things in an orderly sequence. Sometimes they glue their paper to the table. Sometimes they drop clay on the floor and unintentionally step on it when trying to pick it up. Anyone working with these children soon learns that great patience is needed.

But most important, each child is unique. As young as they are, they each bring to the art experience their own personalities as well as their family and cultural heritage. Some are timid. Others are bold. Some have used many art materials and others have used none. One child may have been taught not to get dirty and will not touch fingerpaint, while another child revels in being as messy as possible and smears paint up to the elbows. Children grow at their own pace, but through sensitive planning of art experiences, each child can find his or her personal joy and growth through art.

WHY SHOULD ART BE TAUGHT TO YOUNG CHILDREN?

We need to teach art to young children because it is an integral part of our lives. Visual art is often seen as a pleasant pastime—something to do when the work of the day is over, objects to view in a museum on a Sunday outing, or an activity done by a few individuals for personal pleasure or fame. But if we truly understand what visual art is, we will suddenly discover how deeply it affects us.

Art Is Basic to Humanity

Art exists in all societies and has been created by human beings since prehistoric times. Ellen Dissanayake points out that art creation is taking ordinary things and making them special. She argues that making art is part of being human and is a normal behavior in which all people participate (1995, pp. 222–223).

Art is so much a part of our lives that we can recognize its existence only by imagining its absence. Envision our homes and clothing without patterns, textures, and colors, our books without illustrations, advertisements without photographs, and our homes, furniture, and cars without form. Visual art is the manipulation of the visual and spatial elements of line, texture, color, pattern, shape, and form. Its purpose can be decorative—as in the interior design of a home; communicative—as in an illustration or advertisement; or aesthetically and spiritually expressive—as in a painting of a beautiful sunset.

In the same way, art is a part of every activity we offer children. It is there in the box of blocks we give them to use. It is in the picture book we read to them, or when we ask the child to select the red ball or the blue one. The colors, textures, and forms of the toys we purchase, the pictures we choose to hang on the walls, and the patterns on our floors all form the artistic environment of the child. Art surrounds us constantly. We can choose to ignore it, or we can select activities for children with an awareness of the role art plays in our lives.

Art Stimulates the Growing Brain

The brain is designed for learning. Infants are born ready to make sense of the world. From the begin-

ning, the brain absorbs sensory and spatial information. During early childhood, billions of neural connections grow rapidly as the child interacts with the environment. By adulthood, the connections in the brain number over 100 trillion (Johnson, 1991).

Caine and Caine (1994) have identified the following ways to enhance learning based on recent brain research.

- **Provide multisensory, interactive activities.** Because the brain is capable of simultaneously processing information from many senses, we learn best when sensory, visual, and spatial information are combined. Providing hands-on art stimulates the senses and makes learning more memorable.

- **Create an enriched environment.** Being survival oriented, the brain constantly seeks stimulation and is attracted to novelty—loud noises, sudden movements, bright colors, and unique textures. Unusual events call forth excitement and curiosity. Enriched learning environments have been found to have a positive effect on brain development, actually physically changing the brain. Animals provided with many toys, for example, develop more brain connections than animals in bare environments (Carey, 2002, p. 11). Hanging intriguing artworks on the wall for children to look at and providing colorful, tactile art materials for them to explore are ways to enrich the learning environment and foster young children's brain development.

- **Establish connections.** Searching for meaning is an innate process. The brain constantly processes incoming information, finding and creating patterns as it creates links to previous experiences. We help children learn when we draw on their previous experiences and present new information in integrated ways, such as through thematic units, projects, and cross-disciplinary activities. Art can serve as a vehicle to link ideas and concepts in more meaningful ways.

- **Activate spatial memory.** There are at least two types of long-term memory. Taxon memory is formed over time by rehearsal and repetition, such as remembering phone numbers and the multiplication table. Once in place, these memories become habit and are difficult to change, but they will fade with disuse. An example of this is how hard it is to remember a new phone number. Spatial memory, on the other hand, is more like a map. The brain takes new information and overlays it on previous memories, creating meaningful patterns. This process is quick and flexible. Instead of endless repetition, the information is instantly memorable, because the brain can recall it by remembering the pattern. For example, if you meet someone new, you can remember that person because your brain registers the unique appearance of that individual compared to all of the other people you know. Complex activities that integrate several subjects, expose children to concepts in many different forms and activate spatial memory. Art can be incorporated into such activities as another way to record data and express ideas.

✪ **Build on individual interests.** Every brain is unique. Memories are constantly changing as new connections are made between past experience and incoming information. Making and talking about their art is a positive way for children to share what they know and like. This provides feedback that will allow us to create a more effective, child-oriented curriculum.

Art Improves Well-Being

Physical health, biological needs, and emotional state also affect how well children learn (Goleman, 1995). In situations of stress or threat, the brain is flooded with harmful chemicals, which can impair the ability to think and remember (Jensen, 1998, p. 53). Movement, relaxation, and curiosity promote optimal brain functioning (Hart, 1983). Exploring art materials in nonrestrictive ways can unlock pleasure buttons (Pinker, 1997). Squeezing play dough, welding a paintbrush, and making a handprint allow purposeful physical movement, which causes mood-altering chemicals to be released. These can improve emotional health and attitude. For example, low levels of serotonin are associated with low self-esteem and impulsive, aggressive behavior (Sylwester, 1998). Endorphins, on the other hand, heighten attention and provide a sense of well-being. By creating a positive mental and physical state, art activities can increase children's propensity to learn.

Physically. In addition, art helps children develop physically by improving their ability to control large and small muscles and by refining hand-eye coordination.

Providing a wide range of materials and tools helps young artists improve their ability to control their large and small muscles. Soft, pliable play doughs and clays improve finger strength. Using brushes at an easel develops control of the arm and wrist. Large and small muscles are exercised and challenged through the manipulation of materials and tools when children stack blocks or pick up tiny beads. Cutting a shape from paper or placing a leaf in a dab of glue requires the eye and hand to work together. Creative movement activities, such as imagining one's body as clay that can be made into different shapes, help the child relate physical movement and concepts.

Emotionally. Art helps children develop emotionally by encouraging more self-confidence. Providing a wide range of open-ended, developmentally appropriate art activities allows young children to be successful, to feel pride in their work, and to become more self-confident.

Art also helps children develop emotionally by teaching them to express feelings in a socially acceptable way. Youngsters who know that the adults around them are caring and accepting of their explorations become more open in expressing their feelings through their art. They discover that their art can communicate meaning to others and bring positive attention to themselves.

Children who feel angry or sad or happy will be encouraged in such an environment to show these feelings in their paintings and drawings. Children who act out in inappropriate ways such as pinching or hitting learn to redirect these activities to a lump of clay. Creating art can help children deal with the stress and violence of our society.

Children also learn to see themselves as capable and trustworthy when they successfully manipulate complex and dangerous tools such as scissors.

Art Builds Visual Perception

Art helps children develop perceptually by using their senses to develop concepts about the nature of objects, actions, and events. Children learn through their senses. Arnheim (1969) has shown that visual perception is really "visual thinking," a cognitive process that takes images and gives them meaning. Teachers need to provide experiences that are sensually rich and varied, and that require children to use their perceptual abilities in many different ways. Observational and visual perception skills are heightened as children use their senses to study the patterns, colors, textures, and shapes found in nature and in the artwork of others.

Art also enhances perceptive skills by teaching spatial concepts. Art activities allow the child to play with and use spatial concepts such as big/small, long/thin, and top/bottom, as well as the visual and tactile constructs of color, shape, pattern, form, and placement in space.

Art Creates Community

Art helps children develop socially by teaching them to take turns and share materials with others and to make choices in personal behavior. When children share art supplies and work spaces, they learn to consider the needs of others and to choose behavior that contributes to the harmony of the group.

Art provides opportunities for children to work together to reach a common goal. Art often requires children to work with others to accomplish a project, or to produce a single, unified piece of art. In doing so, they learn to consider the ideas and artistic expression of others. Sharing space and supplies and laughter and tears and working on group projects with other young artists help children learn cooperation and empathy.

Art Develops Thinking

Art helps children grow cognitively by practicing numeration skills. Art supplies invite counting, sorting, and classifying. Through questioning, children can become aware of the number concepts they use in their artwork. They can count the number of flowers they have drawn or how many blue lines they have made. They can graph the shapes in their collages and sort the leftover paper scraps by color.

Art also provides children with practice in developing skill in planning and sequencing. Well-designed art activities require children to make their own decisions and to order their behavior to accomplish a goal. In doing so, they learn that they must put the glue on

the paper first before attaching the piece of yarn. They must dip the brush in the water to clean the paint off of it. They must find a pair of scissors if they want to cut out a shape. When they are done, they must put their materials in the proper place so they will be ready to use again.

Art provides children with experience in identifying how properties change and discovering examples of cause and effect. Handling art materials allows children to explore the properties of different substances—sticky glue, damp clay, shifting sand. Art activities and materials allow the child to observe changes in the physical properties of art supplies, such as drying glue, paint, and clay. Cause and effect is discovered when a child pushes a finger through a piece of play dough and makes a hole in it, or when a painted shape is

Art is more than painting at the easel. Through art, children gain skills and develop concepts that increase their ability to function in their environment.

pressed on a piece of paper and creates a print. Through discussion and questioning, teachers can help children formulate concepts about these changes.

Art Is a Child's First Language

Art is the child's first written language. It reflects how children's minds are groping with and forming a concept of the world long before they can put their constructs into words. The world is touched and tasted and observed. Lines, colors, patterns, and textures are explored as children discover what happens when they smear the paste, put black paint over white, or smash their fist into the clay. It is through this exploration of materials and environment that child artists begin to develop graphic symbols with which to represent their thoughts.

Olson (1992) finds that children learn to write in the same way that written language has developed from pictograph to phonetic script. Drawing on the work of Vygotsky (1978), Olson identifies children's drawings as "first order symbols" that represent objects or actions. She proposes that children be encouraged to draw visual narratives and then engage in dialogues about them as a way to develop language skills.

In this cognitive view of art in general and drawing in particular, visual symbols are seen as intricately tied to verbal ones. Olson provides methods by which learners can be identified as visual or verbal in terms of preferred learning styles. She then offers ways to use this information, combined with art, to improve the children's writing. In order to reach all learners, Olson proposes a joining of art and language instruction.

Viewing art as the beginning of writing has tremendous implications for early art education. If art is related to writing, then preliterate children can use their art to record and "read" experiences and ideas. This moves art from the "make and take" table to the forefront of the entire curriculum. Art can be used to record what happened in a science experiment, to make a notation of the pattern in a musical piece, or to compose a story.

Children's language abilities are enhanced through art when they (1) learn ways to describe and discuss art materials, processes, art forms, and works of art; (2) observe and describe the objects in their environment using art and language; and (3) relate spoken language and graphic symbols. Providing opportunities for children to verbalize about their artwork, and helping them develop a vocabulary for doing so, allows children to develop the relationship between word and picture as a means of communication. Children learn new words to describe what they are doing as they explore new media.

Children share their artwork in a variety of ways—some nonverbally, some through sound effects, and others with intricate oral explanations and stories. The receptive adult who understands that this is an important part of language development—the prewriting stage—will provide many opportunities for the interrelation of art and language. For example, when inspired by the characters, settings, and events depicted in their art, children can make up and tell stories orally, or they can invent new ways of writing them down as they discover the meaning of symbols.

Finally, children develop writing skills by creating a graphic symbol system to record their inner and outer observations. When children are asked to make artwork as a response to an experience, they are being asked to record their ideas and thoughts in a graphic mode. Between the ages of two and eight, children acquire the ability to make symbols and learn that these symbols can communicate to others. Responsive activities, such as making a painting about a visit to the zoo and then talking or writing about it, help them use this developing symbol system and refine the nature of their communication.

Art Nurtures Creativity

The unstructured quality of art media allows children to experiment with familiar materials in new ways. They can use their own ideas and their own power to initiate and to cause change, and to produce original actions and combinations. Paint that drips, paste that does not hold, block towers that fall down, and all of the other small difficulties that art materials present challenge children to find their own solutions to problems.

Torrance (1970) defined *creativity* as being able to see a problem, form ideas about it, and then communicate the results. When children manipulate and explore art materials, they are creating something new and unique; in doing so, they are being creative. As chapter 4 will illustrate, creativity is not something that can be taught, but something that must be nurtured.

Creativity is nourished by providing open-ended activities that allow children to experiment with a wide variety of materials. Art activities should provide challenges and the opportunity for children to solve their own problems. As described in chapter 4, there are many parts to the creative process, and each is vital to the child's learning. Knowledge, motivation, skill development, and the time to immerse oneself in an activity are all essential in solving problems. It is the process through which the child turns random marks into graphic symbols. But children's creativity will flourish or wither depending on the activities offered to the child. The goal should be to create an environment in which creativity can grow.

The well-planned art program provides young artists with adequate time to work, plenty of space, real art materials, and a nurturing environment.

WHAT IS THE RELATIONSHIP BETWEEN ART AND LEARNING?

Young children do not have a set goal in mind as they begin to create with art materials, any more than they start the day with the goal of learning 10 new words. They are caught up in the process of doing and making and responding to and playing with the stimuli around them, such as the way paint drips, the way clay stretches and bends, and the way another child tears paper into little bits.

Adults, on the other hand, see the children growing and developing through the art activities they have designed. They see the changes in behavior that come with increasing experience with art materials—from the first tentative brush strokes of the two-year-old to the colorful lines and symbols of the mature eight-year-old. But it is also necessary that children grow in ways that will make them more successful in their interactions with the world.

The nature of an early childhood art program is determined by a philosophy of how children learn. For the last 60 years, under the influence of John Dewey (1958), Rhoda Kellogg (1969), Viktor Lowenfeld and W. Lambert Brittain (1987), and others, art has had a place in the education of our children. Visits to most preschools, child care centers, and primary school programs will find children drawing and painting and cutting and pasting. However, what the children are

actually making as they draw, paint, cut, and paste will vary widely depending on what the adults in charge believe young children are capable of doing, what they think is the correct way to teach them, and how they interpret the role of art in education.

To strengthen our philosophy and establish our goals, we need to examine learning theories, contemporary viewpoints, current research, and exemplary approaches to art in the education of children. These ideas will provide direction in the creation of a successful and meaningful art program for children.

Piaget and Constructivism

In the early 1920s Piaget, a Swiss biologist, began studying children's responses to problems he designed. Based on his research, Piaget (1959) described how children developed their knowledge of the world. His basic findings include the following:

- Children are active learners. They are curious and actively seek out information that helps them make sense of the world around them.
- Children construct knowledge based on their experiences. Because each child has different experiences, the understandings and misunderstandings acquired are unique to each child and

are continually changing as the child has new experiences.

⟡ Experiences are essential for cognitive development. Children need to physically interact with the people and objects around them.

⟡ Thought becomes more complex as children have more experiences. Although Piaget proposed that cognitive development was age dependent, many researchers today believe that complexity of thought follows gradual trends and may vary in different contexts and content areas (Ormrod, 2003).

Building on Piaget's work, we can see children as self-motivated learners who are responsible for their own learning. We can foster children's thinking by providing hands-on experiences that allow children to explore and develop their own understandings. Open-ended art materials that offer many creative possibilities are ideal for this purpose. Logical thought is developed by asking children to explain why they used the materials in certain ways and helping them discover cause and effect.

Vygotsky's Sociocultural Perspective

Vygotsky (1978), who also did research on children's thinking in the 1920s and 30s, emphasized the importance of adults in cognitive development. He proposed that one way children construct their knowledge is based on past and present social interactions. His major points were the following:

⟡ Complex thought begins through communication with adults and more knowledgeable peers. Watching and interacting with the people around them helps children internalize the thought processes, concepts, and beliefs common to their culture.

⟡ Although children need to make discoveries on their own, they can also learn from the experiences of others.

⟡ Children can perform at a higher cognitive level when guided by an adult or a more competent peer. Vygotsky defined the actual developmental level as what the child can do independently, and the potential developmental level as what the child can do with assistance.

⟡ According to Vygotsky most learning occurs when children are challenged to perform closer to their potential developmental level in what has come to be known as the **zone of proximal development**. It is when they are asked to perform tasks that require communication with more skilled individuals that children experience maximum cognitive growth.

Based on Vygotsky's work, we can see children as members of a social community in which adults are a source of important information about the nature of art. As teachers we can demonstrate how artists think and behave. Art lends itself to what is characterized as the "apprenticeship model" (Gardner, 1993). In an apprenticeship, the child learns not only how to do the task but also how experts think about the task. We can model artistic methods while thinking out loud about the process. We can make well-timed suggestions that guide the child to the next level of understanding, and we can ask children to explain what they are doing so that they make the learning their own. In addition, we can share the world of art with young children by introducing them to wonderful artists from all times and cultures. Doing these things will not only help children grow cognitively but will also nurture their disposition to think and act as artists.

Multiple Intelligences: Multiple Intelligence Theory

Based on cognitive research, Howard Gardner (1983, 1991) has proposed that there are eight intellectual capabilities or **intelligences**. These intelligences represent biological and psychological potentials within each individual. Everyone has capabilities in each intelligence with special strengths in one or more of them. Gardner has identified these intelligences.

1. **Linguistic:** The ability to manipulate the symbols of language
2. **Logical-Mathematical:** The ability to manipulate numerical patterns and concepts
3. **Spatial:** The ability to visualize the configuration of objects in space
4. **Musical:** The ability to manipulate rhythm and sound

5. **Bodily-Kinesthetic:** The ability to use the body to solve problems or to make things
6. **Interpersonal:** The ability to understand and work with others
7. **Intrapersonal:** The ability to understand oneself
8. **Naturalistic-Environmental:** The ability to sense and make use of the characteristics of the natural world.

Traditional educational practice has focused mainly on strengths in the logical-mathematical and linguistic intelligences. Multiple Intelligences (MI) Theory provides a framework upon which teachers can build a more educationally balanced program—one that better meets the needs of children with talents in different intelligences. Art as a learning and symbolic tool is particularly valuable not only because it embraces the intelligences often overlooked in education, but also because it crosses and links all of the intelligences.

Gardner (1993) does not believe that there is an artistic intelligence. Instead, each of the eight intelligences can be used for either artistic or nonartistic purposes. How an intelligence is expressed will depend on a variety of factors, including personal choice and cultural environment. The linguistic intelligence, for example, can be used to scribble an appointment on a calendar or to compose a short story. The spatial intelligence can be used to create a sculpture or to read a map. Conversely, to create a painting, an artist must draw not only on the visual-spatial intelligence

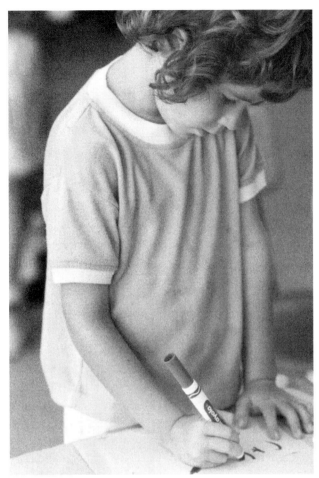

Art is a child's first written language.

in order to visualize the artistic elements in the work but also on the bodily-kinesthetic intelligence in order to control the brush and on the logical-mathematical intelligence in order to plan the sequence in which the paint will be applied.

Multiple Intelligences Theory broadens our view of children's abilities and potentials into a multidimensional view of intelligence. It means that we need to honor the special abilities of every child by creating an early childhood curriculum that includes many opportunities to use all of the intelligences in artistic ways.

Not every activity will engage all of the intelligences, but when activities are chosen that incorporate many of the intelligences, children can learn in whatever way best fits their intellectual strengths. In this book, Gardner's intelligences have been interrelated with the physical, social, emotional, perceptual, and cognitive growth areas in order to create models of such balanced art activities.

"The school bus is flying over the house." Marker—Nick, age 5

HOW SHOULD ART PROGRAMS FOR YOUNG CHILDREN BE DESIGNED?

Based on these ideas about how children learn, various programs and approaches to teaching art to young children have been developed.

Developmentally Appropriate Practice: DAP

A developmentally appropriate curriculum for young children is planned to be appropriate for the age span of the children within the group and is implemented with attention to the different needs, interests, and developmental levels of those individual children.

National Association for the Education of Young Children (NAEYC) (1986, p. 6)

Developmentally appropriate practice (DAP) is based on the idea that teachers need to know how young children typically develop, what variations may occur in this development, and how children's learning and development can best be facilitated. According to the National Association for the Education of Young Children (NAEYC), being knowledgeable about normative development or what children are generally like at various ages allows teachers to make decisions about which activities and experiences will be safe, but challenging, for young children. In designing an art curriculum for young children, DAP guides us to first ask: Is this art activity suitable for children of this age?

Normative Guidelines for Selecting Appropriate Art Activities

The age divisions used in this text follow those of the NAEYC (1986). They are intended to provide general guidelines from which appropriate art activities may be selected.

Toddler. Throughout the text, **toddler** is used to refer to children between the ages of 18 months and three years who may exhibit the following characteristics:

- need to explore with all their senses and may still put objects in mouth
- have limited self-regulatory skills and require close supervision
- engage in parallel play
- show developing control over large muscles in the arm

"I'm writing just like you." Marker—Matthew, age 2¹/₂

- ☺ have short attention spans, usually less than 10 minutes, and need simple materials to explore
- ☺ need to repeat actions
- ☺ say names of objects and understand more words than they can say

Appropriate art activities for toddlers. Appropriate art activities for toddlers allow them to manipulate and explore art materials without pressure to produce a product. Art materials should be simple and direct, with few instructions required. They should be safe if ingested. Explorations must be closely supervised with active adult participation.

Three-year-olds. Most children of this age display the following characteristics:

- ☺ show increasing self-control and can work side by side in small groups
- ☺ usually will not put inappropriate items in mouth
- ☺ show developing control over wrists, hands, and fingers
- ☺ have an increasing attention span and can work independently for 10 minutes or more at a time

Appropriate art activities for three-year-olds. Three-year-olds may be offered more varied materials that require finer muscle control. Representation of actual objects should not be expected, and process must be valued over product. Children of this age can be encouraged to use art materials in self-initiated, creative, and expressive ways. Adult supervision is still required, but the teacher may move away at times to allow children to work independently.

Four- and five-year-olds. Most children in this age range show the following behaviors:

- ☺ show developing control over wrists and hands and exhibit a more mature grip on drawing tools
- ☺ can concentrate for a period of time, 30 minutes or more, on a self-selected art activity
- ☺ can work together in small groups of three to six on common projects and are able to share supplies
- ☺ may dictate or write stories with invented spelling
- ☺ can follow a three-step direction
- ☺ can classify objects and make predictions
- ☺ can use words to describe the qualities of objects—color, size, and shape—and can begin to sort them by those qualities

Appropriate art activities for four- and five-year-olds. Children of this age can participate in a wide range of self-selected individual and group explorations, using a variety of art media. They are ready for aesthetic and art appreciation activities as well. As they develop graphic symbols, they can begin to use art to express their ideas and learning in other curriculum areas. Children can be expected to work on their own and manage their own materials with occasional adult supervision.

Six-, seven-, and eight-year-olds. Most children in this age range show the following behaviors:

- ☺ hold drawing tools with a mature grip
- ☺ can concentrate for an hour or more on a self-selected art activity and can return to an ongoing art project over a period of several days
- ☺ initiate, participate, and assume roles in cooperative group art activities
- ☺ may write stories, inspired by or illustrated with their artwork, with the majority using conventional spelling by the end of the eighth year
- ☺ understand that objects can share one or more qualities and can use this knowledge to make predictions and comparisons and to draw conclusions.

Appropriate art activities for six- to eight-year-olds. Primary-age children continue to need many opportunities to participate in self-selected art explorations using a wide variety of art media. They can also begin to be introduced to art activities that require specialized skills and sequencing behavior, such as papier-mâché, weaving, and pottery making. Children can be expected to use acquired skills and knowledge to respond to experiences and to demonstrate what they have learned in other curriculum areas. As they develop a greater understanding of time, the earth, and its peoples, they can be introduced to the social and historical context of a wide variety of art forms. In the primary years, children can also be expected to take more personal responsibility for initiating, organizing, and carrying out individual and cooperative art activities.

Planning for Individual Needs

At the same time we must be careful not to assume that all children are alike. Children are dynamic and ever changing. The second question we must ask as we design an art curriculum is: Is it appropriate for these particular children at this particular time?

Meeting special needs. Developmentally appropriate practice reminds us that children have individual strengths, needs, and interests. These may be due to maturational differences, developmental delays, or exceptional gifts. Children also differ in the life experiences to which they have been exposed. Lillian Katz and Sylvia Chard (2000) call this the "dynamic dimension of development." Some children may have had negative early experiences that have a delayed impact on later functioning and personality development. In these cases, art materials and activities that allow a wide range of exploration and creative uses should be selected or adapted so that every child can be successful. These then need to be constantly monitored and the level of challenge increased to match the children's developing skill and understanding.

Addressing bias and cultural differences. Children also come from different social and cultural backgrounds. Selecting art activities that show respect for their family backgrounds, home culture, and language can support these children. Activities should reflect appreciation for different cultural beliefs, holiday customs, and family traditions, and they should develop a sense of community. Art materials should reflect the many colors of humanity, and artworks that decorate the walls should represent people from diverse backgrounds. Through seeing, touching, and talking about a wide variety of art forms selected from both their own culture and from different cultures, children learn that art reflects the ideas and feelings of other people, and the experience increases their stores of visual images.

McFee and Degge (1981) have pointed out the importance of culture in determining what kind of art children are expected to produce. Analyzing the cross-cultural studies of children's art done by anthropologists, as well as research by psychologists on how children learn to perceive visual elements, they argue that all studies of children's art must consider the cultural environment in which it is created. In a culture such as that of the United States', in which words are valued over images, beliefs about child art will reflect that value system. The emphasis on using art as another form of language is indicative of this.

All children's art is influenced by the amount and kind of visual stimulation to which they have been exposed, their exposure or lack of exposure to the artwork and symbols of others, and the style of art they have encountered. In cultures in which verbal learning is stressed, child art often shows less attention to visual detail and exhibits more stereotypical symbols. McFee and Degge argue that activities that foster the growth of visual perception skills are vital; they enable children to express their thoughts more clearly with meaningful images. This is best done by including multisensory explorations of the child's environment. Children who have seen, touched, and cared for a rabbit will draw much more detailed and meaningful pictures of a rabbit than children who have only heard a rabbit described.

National Art Education Association Developmentally Appropriate Practices

The National Art Education Association (NAEA) has incorporated the recommendations of the NAEYC in its guidelines for early childhood art education. Colbert and Taunton (1992), writing for the NAEA, recommend the following criteria.

1. Children need many opportunities to create art.
2. Children need many opportunities to look at and talk about art.
3. Children need to become aware of art in their everyday lives.

In designing art programs for children, educators are urged to consider the following aspects.

Curriculum. The art program should foster children's cognitive, social, physical, emotional, and perceptual growth. Developmentally appropriate activities should be based on the children's interests, needs, and abilities. Creativity is nurtured through activities that have no predetermined end product. There is a balance between creating, perceiving, and responding to art that fosters physical, cognitive, and affective growth.

Creativity is nourished by open-ended activities that provide children with challenges and opportunities to solve their own problems.

Art materials. Materials must be safe and easily manipulated and must allow for experimentation. They are organized so that children can independently choose and return supplies. Art materials and art reproductions reflect the diversity of their culture.

Integration. Art and other curriculum areas are interrelated. Art enhances learning in other subjects, and activities in other curriculum areas extend learning in art.

Display. Children should participate in choosing and creating displays. Art should be hung at the children's height to invite children to observe and interact with it.

Responding to art. Children observe and respond to their own work, the work of their peers, and the work created by many other people, in many different times and places. An art program based entirely on making things does not help children develop a sense

of the place of art in their lives and does not prepare them to respond to the art of others. As educators, we need to introduce self-reflection about art and examples of adult art into early childhood programs, not as a replacement for hands-on art but as a way of increasing children's visual-perceptual abilities and aesthetic sense (Mesrobian, 1992; Wolf, 1984).

Anti-Bias and Multicultural Education

Derman-Sparks and the A.B.C. Task Force (1989) suggest ways that art activities can help children accept racial and cultural differences and reject stereotypes. They recommend that art activities should involve using art materials in many colors, and opportunities should be provided to experience art created by people from diverse backgrounds. Educators should provide access to the art of others through field trips, guest artists, prints, and artifacts; they should also initiate discussion about these works.

The Reggio Emilia Approach to Art Education

One of the finest early childhood programs in the world is the pre-primary program of the municipality of Reggio Emilia, Italy. In this program, art is highly valued. Each school has an *atelierista*, or art educator, who works directly with the teachers in designing the program. In addition, each school has a beautiful art room where supplies are arranged by color. This attention to aesthetic qualities carries over to the school itself, which is decorated with childrens' artwork that has been carefully mounted. Light, mirrors, and color produce wonderful spaces in which children can play and create.

In the Reggio Emilia program, children's art is used as one method of recording observations, ideas, and memories of experiences in which the children have participated. The atelierista offers suggestions as the children work. The children also share their art with other children. Unlike in the United States, where artwork is usually sent home at the end of each day, in Reggio Emilia, children are asked to return to their artwork to reconsider, discuss and critique, rework, or repeat their responsive art activities.

Edwards, Gandini, and Forman (1993), New (1990), and Seefeldt (1995), writing in response to observations made at Reggio Emilia, argue that children's drawings and the quality of cognitive growth that they can stimulate have been underestimated in the United States. They believe that visual art needs to be taken much more seriously as a way for children to express what they have learned throughout the curriculum. To bring this level of quality to our art programs, we need to pay more attention to the aesthetic appearance of the environment, to how we display and save children's works, and to how we can create opportunities to share our art with each other. Although a professional art educator may not be available, all of us can learn how to talk to children about their artwork and provide the necessary guidance.

Goals for Learning

What do children need to learn about art? This is a key question in designing an effective art program for young children. According to Lillian Katz and Sylvia Chard (2000), there are four main categories of learning goals.

Knowledge. Knowledge includes the vocabulary, facts, and concepts we want our children to learn. In early childhood art, we expect that children will be learning to talk about and identify art elements, materials, and methods such as shapes and colors, clay and paint, printing, and collage. We then want children to be able to apply this knowledge in the artwork they create. As we have seen, young children construct this kind of knowledge from direct experiences and from interactions with more expert peers and adults.

The knowledge to be imparted can be expressed in the vocabulary words selected, the concepts being applied, and the questions children will be asked, as they are involved in art activities. In the Creating Art sections of this book, examples of these are found under the "What to Say" heading.

Dispositions. Dispositions are patterns of behavior that occur in reaction to specific situations. Examples of dispositions include being intellectually curious,

using the creative process, applying logical reasoning, and being generous and helpful. Another way to view dispositions is to think of them as preferred ways of thinking. We can think and make decisions as would a creative artist, an inquiring scientist, or an observant poet. Dispositions are nurtured instead of being taught directly. They develop best in carefully designed environments that allow exploration and risk taking and where adults model many positive patterns of thinking.

Many different dispositions are developed in the creation of art. First and foremost is the disposition to think and act like a creative artist. This is developed through open-ended art activities using real art materials presented by a teacher who verbally and visually models what artists do. At the same time, thoughtful statements and questions can promote intellectual curiosity, and careful organization of the activity can promote cooperative behavior.

Feelings. Feelings describe how children receive, respond to, and value what they are learning and are reflected in the emotional state of the child. Positive feelings about learning art, or any other subject area, develop when children feel safe, when activities are challenging but possible, when mistakes are seen as positive ways to grow, and when accomplishments are acknowledged.

Children come to value art when guiding adults share with them a sense of wonder and awaken them to the aesthetic qualities of the world in which they live. They learn to respond positively to the art of others when teachers and peers respond to their artwork with heartfelt, thoughtful comments. Most importantly, well-planned art activities allow all children to achieve success, thereby enabling them to see themselves as competent individuals.

Skills. Skills are the observable behaviors, such as cutting out shapes with a scissors or shaping clay into a ball, that children need to create art. Although some skills are learned spontaneously, most develop through use. If we want our children to be able to use paint with control, for example, then we need to give them lots of opportunities to paint. In addition, skills from the different growth areas can be practiced in the creation of art. For example, intentionally having two children use the same glue bottle provides them with an opportunity to practice sharing. Talking about their artwork allows children to develop their oral language skills. In fact, well-planned art activities usually address skill development in all of the growth areas.

WHAT DOES A WELL-DESIGNED ART PROGRAM LOOK LIKE?

The approaches that have been presented here are based on careful and thoughtful observation of real children and their art. All of them give high value to children's artwork and the associated cognitive growth that art creation fosters. The important elements of each can be incorporated into the following goals that can be used to create a successful art program.

An art program for young children should

1. help the child grow—physically, emotionally, socially, perceptually, creatively, and cognitively.
2. educate the whole child through activities involving all of the multiple intelligences.
3. be taught by someone who can model artistic thinking.
4. integrate art into the curriculum.
5. use art as a way for children to express what they know.
6. provide perceptual, sensory, and kinesthetic experiences.
7. encourage self-reflection and responding to the art of others.
8. introduce children to rich visual experiences from a wide range of artistic heritages.
9. provide an environment in which the creative process can flourish.

Art is integrated. In the following "Young Artists at Work," art is inseparable from the total program. There is no art corner or art project of the day. A wide variety of art materials is available in many places in the room. There is the traditional easel, as well as tables for gluing projects, places to draw and cut, art materials for book making, blocks for building, and a computer art program to try. There is a place to work with modeling materials. Children move to these areas when they

have something to express or want to explore. They know where the supplies are located and are confident that they will be there when they need them.

Science, language, and art activities are integrated. The water table activity is both art and science. The children are exploring not just the objects' physical properties but also their visual and tactile qualities. Their observations of the living sea life are expressed through the story that is drawn, the clay snake that is modeled, and the sea creature mobiles. Examples of multicultural fine art are used for card-matching activities instead of stereotypical sea pictures. This increases the visual discrimination skills of the children, and at the same time they are introduced to richer visual images through the art of others.

Integrating art means rethinking the use of the traditional art project where each day a "new" art experience is offered. It means seeing art as more than a way for children to amuse themselves in creating interesting products. It means approaching art as a way children can interact and communicate about their interests and learning. The total educational program must be carefully planned so that art activities are connected to all areas of learning. Chapter 5 presents a variety of ways to use thematic teaching and curriculum connections to accomplish meaningful art integration.

Art is open-ended. Activities are open-ended and developmentally appropriate. Cardboard tubes have been put out for the children to use, but they have not been told what they might make from them. The three-year-old's exploration is just as valid as the more theme-related projects of the older children. The children who are painting the box yellow are exploring the effects of a different kind of brush.

Two children decided that they wanted their paper fish to swim, so they started the idea of hanging them from the ceiling. Other children can now join in their project if they wish, but they are not required to do so. It is not expected that their sea creatures will resemble any real fish. Will it make a difference how many sea creatures are hung up by the end of the week or what they end up looking like?

There is choice. Every child is not expected to participate in theme activities or to produce a project. The children in the block corner and at the computer are

Young Artists at Work

Art is integrated into the curriculum through thematic teaching.

It is a warm spring day, and sunlight streams through the windows of the large bright room. Photographs of fish and sea creatures decorate one wall. Children's books about the sea are on display on the bookshelf. The teacher has already read several books about the sea to the children and talked to the children about experiences they have had during visits to the beach. Seashells, starfish, fishnets, floats, and other sea-related objects are placed around the room. It is easy to tell that the theme of the week is *Under the Sea*.

Children develop socially by working on a group project.

In the center of the room, an aide and several children, ages three and four, are hard at work painting a refrigerator box in which round windows and two doors have been cut. They are using yellow poster paint and large house paintbrushes. Newspapers cover the floor. One child is painting broad strokes of color across the box, while the other child presses the brush down again and again, making rectangular stamp marks in one small section. In the background, a tape of the Beatles' classic "Yellow Submarine" can be heard.

The teacher enthusiastically responds to the artistic elements in the child's work with positive feedback.

While the painters work away on the submarine, other children are playing at the water table, experimenting with a variety of objects in different sizes, colors, and shapes that either sink or float. At an easel, a four-year-old has filled his paper with waving lines using mixtures of blue, green, and yellow paint. The teacher stops to help the painter at the easel remove his smock. "Look at all the blue-greens and turquoises you have made," she tells him, pointing to examples of those colors.

Art activities are open-ended. Children choose to use the art supplies in their own way.

At a round table, three children have taken cardboard paper towel tubes from the supply shelf and are decorating them with paper, yarn, glue, and crayons. One child asks the teacher to attach a piece of blue cellophane to the end of his "scope." A second child puts her tube up to her nose. "I'm a swordfish. This is my sword. I have a beautiful sword," she tells another girl. A three-year-old is exploring what happens when he glues a piece of yarn on the tube and then pulls it off. In another corner, two boys are engaged in noisy, animated play with the trucks and blocks. At the computer, a four-year-old is making a multicolored line travel a wiggly path over the screen.

Visual images from diverse sources enrich the children's experience.

At the game table, two children are matching pictures. The cards have been made from prints of paintings, sculptures, and crafts from many cultures that illustrate subjects about the sea. These have been cut out of museum catalogs,

Young Artists at Work

glued to card stock, and laminated. On the wall behind them is a poster-size print of one of the artworks. One child finds a card that matches the poster and walks over and compares the two pictures. "They're the same, but this one is littler," he notes, holding the picture card up to the print.

Visitors provide real experiences that lead to integrated learning.

Suddenly everyone stops working. A special visitor has arrived! A father of one of the children brings in two plastic buckets, and all the children circle round. In the tubs are saltwater creatures borrowed from the pet store where he works. The children gather about to study a sea urchin, an anemone, and a sea snake. One child looks at the sea urchin through his cellophane-covered tube. "It changes color," he states with wonder. He shares his tube with the others so they can see the change too.

Art and language activities are unified.

When the visitor leaves, some children head off to a table where crayons, markers, and stapled paper booklets are set out. "I'm writing a story about a sea snake and an 'anoome,'" says one five-year-old girl. She draws a long wiggly line on one page. "Here he is very sad." Then she draws a purple circle. "This is his friend, the 'anoome.' Now he is happy!" When she finishes her book, she "reads" it to her teacher, inventing a long, detailed story to go with her pictures. "You made your anemone the same color as the one Sam's father brought to show us," the teacher says. The girl beams with pride and skips off to read her book to her friend.

Children explore sensory experiences.

A three-year-old has settled in with a lump of play dough. He rolls out a long "worm." "Look—I can make it wiggle like a sea snake," he says, as he twists and turns the play dough. Some children take cardboard tubes to decorate. They want to put cellophane on theirs so they can have their own "scopes." Several other children have taken colored paper, markers, and scissors. They talk quietly together as they invent new sea creatures.

"Mine has tentacles like the sea urchin."

"I'm going to give mine a big mouth and teeth," says another. They cut out their creatures and take them to the teacher.

Children initiate and choose what they want displayed.

"Put a string on them and hang them up so they can swim in our sea," says one. The teacher hangs their creatures from clips suspended from the ceiling. They join other paper sea creatures, made by other children, that are already afloat on the air currents.

continued

17

Young Artists at Work *continued*

Meanwhile, several other children have moved into the submarine. They are busy arranging blankets and pillows.

"I think it is softer this way," says Peter. Sam lies down and tries it out. He curls up and sucks his thumb.

"I think we should have a yellow blanket in the yellow submarine," says Sue, bringing in a piece of yellow cloth from the dress-up box. Other children look in through the portholes and make faces at their friends.

Kinesthetic movement grows out of the children's dramatic play and provides a smooth transition to story time.

"We will be the fish swimming around the submarine!" they tell them. The teacher observes the children's play and puts on Saint-Saens's *The Swan*. The music matches the children's actions as they move around the box inventing fish sounds and motions. The teacher joins the dancers and invites the children in the box to come out and swim in the sea with them. Sue swirls the yellow cloth behind her. "This is my tail," she sings.

"Story time!" says the teacher. "Let's swim to the rug." The dancing children and those working about the room move to the rug and settle around the teacher who reads the story *The Rainbow Fish* by Marcus Pfister. The children lie back and look at their floating sea creatures.

"We need a rainbow fish," says one boy.

Children have made plans and look forward to the next day.

"Let's make lots of rainbow fish tomorrow," joins in another.

"I will find some shiny rainbow paper for you," says the teacher. Full of excitement about the next day, the children help put away the materials they have used and then get ready to leave.

pursuing their own interests of the moment. It does not matter if they do not have a sea-related art project to take home or to show their families that day. The teacher, the families, and the children know that learning has been taking place.

The children are not rushed in their work. There is enough time for the children to do several activities. The children have learned that story time is a time for breaking off their activities and coming together as a group. It provides closure to the day. The teacher draws on the children's current interests by asking them to move like fish to the rug for story time. This is an effective, gentle transition. After the story is ended and

the illustrations in the book are shared, there will be time for cleaning up and putting away any materials that are still out.

It all seems so effortless. There is a rhythm and flow to a well-planned program that creates the sense that this is what will happen if the children are just told to have fun with a lot of interesting materials. Nothing could be further from the truth.

Behind that successful program are superb planning and knowledge about how children think, learn, and respond to stimuli in their environment. There are guiding adults who know what to say about art production, how to say it, and when it is best left unsaid.

"The rainbow fish is in trouble. His friend will save him." Crayon and watercolor—*Ben, age 5½*

They know when to interact and when to wait and watch. They are confident that they will be judged not on the children's art products but on their growth. Such teachers are also continually learning and growing along with their young artists from the first contact to the last. They are constantly improving the program they offer, assessing each activity, and noting how the children show growth in relation to the goals they have set for them. It is a program of their own creation, both meaningful and thoughtful.

CONCLUSION: THE WELL-DESIGNED ART PROGRAM

A classroom for young children often looks for all the world like an artist's studio. The products that come out are children's products, but the process that goes on is the artist's process. The rich availability of easels, paints, brushes, paper, clay, and collage materials helps young children live like artists.

—*James L. Hymes (1989, p. 81)*

The stage has now been set for developing a rich and meaningful art program for children. Children are natural artists, in the sense that they play creatively with the elements of art that they find in their surroundings. But those surroundings must be provided, and they are determined by a philosophy of what child art is and what it means. We need to consider why children should do certain art activities, which ones should be selected, how they should be delivered, and what environment is most conducive to their performance.

This chapter has closely examined the why: philosophy and principles. The following chapters will consider the how: how the delivery of art activities affects what children learn, as well as how the way the child learns affects what activities will be successful; the where: the environment in which child artists will work; and the what: the appropriate selection and efficient delivery of art concepts and skills. These ideas and suggestions will help guide the formation of a thoughtful art program for children.

It is the educator's role to nurture the artist within every young child. Although the focus will always be on guiding the artistic development of the child, in doing so the artist within the adult will also be rekindled. Adults and children must become part of the artistic continuum that stretches from our distant human past into the future. To guide young children as they grow through art is a deeply rewarding experience.

FURTHER READING

The books listed below illustrate the place of child art in human experience.

Bredekamp, S. (Ed.). (1987). *Developmentally appropriate practice in early childhood programs serving children from birth through age 8.* Washington, DC: National Association for the Education of Young Children.
This book outlines clearly and concisely what consitutes a developmentally appropriate curriculum for young children.

Fein, S. (1993). *First drawings: Genesis of visual thinking.* Pleasant Hill, CA: Exelrod Press.
Sylvia Fein presents a beautifully illustrated and elegant comparison between the art of our prehistoric past and the first symbols developed by children.

Gardner, H. (1993). *Multiple intelligences: The theory in practice.* New York: Basic Books.
This book presents Howard Gardner's theory of multiple intelligences and how it applies to educating children.

Jensen, E. (2001). *Arts with the brain in mind.* Alexandria, VA: Association for Supervision and Curriculum Development.
Eric Jensen presents current research on the relationship between the arts and the brain and offers reasons the arts should be part of every child's education.

Olson, J. L. (1992). *Envisioning writing.* Portsmouth, NH: Heinemann.
Janet Olson demonstrates the interrelationship between art and writing and details ways to use art to improve writing and to use writing to enhance art.

"I painted lots of animals." Tempera painting—*Vicky, age 6*

Creating Art: Preparation

"It's a pretty day, and the sun is shining."
Tempera painting—*Carmela, age 4½*

CREATING AN ORIGINAL ART PROGRAM

There are many "idea" books on the market that offer all kinds of art projects to do and recipes to try. It is the teacher's role to select carefully from these, and to modify them, in order to create an integrated art program that will work with a unique group of children in a particular educational setting.

This Creating Art section provides a framework for the selection and organization of art activities in a meaningful art program.

SELECTING OPEN-ENDED ACTIVITIES

It is not enough to have wonderful intentions. The art activities and how they are delivered will ultimately determine the children's art experience. Every activity must be carefully designed to meet the needs of each child, to fit the philosophy of artistic growth, and to achieve the learning goals of the total program.

There are hundreds of books on the market describing all kinds of "artsy" projects, such as cutting out a preprinted bunny picture, coloring it, and gluing on a cotton tail. Many of these projects sound like fun and often result in pleasant experiences. Most of them, however, will not encourage the emotional, social, physical, aesthetic, perceptual, linguistic, and cognitive growth of a well-designed art experience, nor will they provide for an integrated and a reflective art program.

Some of them, unfortunately, will even work against the goals of the art program. A child who cannot stay in the lines does not feel successful after scribbling over a coloring book picture. Children who are told, step by step, how to put together precut pieces to make a reindeer have not learned to solve a problem creatively on their own. Worse, they have learned that they are not trusted to make their own choices about how to use the art materials.

Well-planned art activities should fit the following criteria.

They Are Open-Ended

An open-ended activity is one in which there are many possible ways children can approach artwork, and in which children are responsible for making their own artistic decisions. Although children may be influenced by their experiences or by the cultural images around them, they need to be able to incorporate these elements in their own unique way. In an open-ended art activity, the teacher has no preset idea about what the end product will look like. The children choose from the available materials, tools, and techniques, and then decide how they will use them. It is the children who determine what the end result will be and what will be done with any products that might result.

There Is Adequate Time to Explore and Experiment

Young children cannot be rushed. Children who feel pressured to finish in a certain amount of time become frustrated, often to the point of crying. Sufficient time must be planned to allow the child to explore and experiment until satisfied. If it is necessary to end an activity, then the teacher needs to provide a stimulus that will move the children away from their exploration in a gentle and an orderly way. Some projects may require multiple-day access to materials so children can return to their work to add complexity and a sense of closure.

There Is an Ample Supply of High-Quality, Basic Art Materials That Stimulate the Senses and Can Be Used in a Creative and Safe Way

Children need real art supplies and tools—paint, paper, drawing materials, good brushes, scissors that work, and more. Many times because of limited funding, children's art activities have been reduced to creating with the junk of our society. Although there is a place for found and recycled materials in an art program, constant exposure to activities that use such things as paper plates, egg cartons, and packaging materials, which are not the basic materials of the adult artist, trivializes art in the minds of children and their parents.

Art materials need to be varied and must appeal to the senses. For example, paper should be available in different sizes and shapes, and in different colors and textures. Many different sizes of brushes and many colors of paint and crayons and markers should be present. Young artists need clays to mold, materials to build things, and a computer to draw on. Supplies should be plentiful: young children use a lot of paper, glue, and paint!

Materials also should be hazard-free. Children's safety is important above all else. The detailed information about art hazards in chapter 6 will assist in the selection of the safest art materials for young artists.

Activities Should Invite Repetition

Skill development requires that children do similar activities over and over. Basic art materials need to be available at all times, so children may repeat activities in which they have enjoyed success. Children who are allowed and encouraged to experiment with art materials on their own, in a stress-free environment, and on a regular basis, will be willing to take the risks required to find new and creative ways to solve problems.

Activities Should Grow out of the Children's Interests and Needs

Art creation is intrinsically motivating. Often it is enough to put out the supplies and let the children explore them. Drawing, painting, collage, and modeling materials are always popular and should be offered on a regular basis, because they allow children at all skill levels to pursue their own interests. Other, more specific, types of activities should grow out of an experience that has created interest in the children. For example, after a trip to a construction site, an assortment of wood scraps can be laid out for the children to glue into sculptures. If the children need more experience cutting with scissors or working cooperatively, offer open-ended activities that emphasize these skills.

ORGANIZING SUCCESSFUL ART ACTIVITIES

Basic Art Supplies

An excellent art program for children ages 18 months to eight years can be run with the following basic supplies:

Brushes: An assortment of different sizes, including short and long handles, round and flat, housepainting brushes, and foam brushes

Chalk: Blackboard and sidewalk in white and colors

Craft paper: A large roll in basic brown or a color, for murals (24" or 36" in width by 100' or more in length)

Crayons: Both thick and regular size in assorted colors, including various skin tones

Finger paint: Commercial finger paint in a range of bright colors, such as yellow, red, and blue, as well as brown and black

Nonhardening modeling clay

Paper: Large sheets (12" × 18" and 18" × 24") of assorted papers—colored construction, manila, newsprint, white drawing

Play dough: Commercial (Play Doh®) or homemade

School paste

Scissors: Child sized, blunt tipped

Tempera paint (liquid): Basic colors—white, red, yellow, blue, black, and brown (optional: green, violet, orange, gold, and silver)

Water-based, broad-tipped markers

White glue: 4-oz. bottles

Yarn: Assorted colors, thicknesses, and textures

Supplementary Supplies

These basic materials can be supplemented with found materials and special supplies. It is important, however, to make sure that these do not become the focus of the art activity but rather add to the basic media of drawing, painting, collage, construction, modeling, printmaking, and so on. Instead of saying to the child, "Make something out of this egg carton," it is better to say, "How can you use this interesting texture from the top of the egg carton in your collage?"

Examples of supplementary materials include such things as buttons, cardboard pieces, cellophane, cloth, feathers, felt, spools, and wood pieces. Many more suggestions are offered in the Creating Art sections throughout this text.

Food-Related Supplies

Over the years many food items have found their way into art activities for young children. This has become a very controversial issue in early childhood education. Although it is easy to say that such items should never be used, in actual practice educators vary greatly in how they define foods. Chapter 6 presents both sides of this debate. Throughout the book, whenever food items are mentioned that might be used in art activities they have been marked with an asterisk (e.g., rice*). After reading chapter 6, each educator must consider the implications of using such food items in artwork and decide whether he or she feels a particular item is appropriate or not.

Basic Preparation

Although each art medium has its own specific setup requirements, the following general guidelines apply to most art activities.

1. Allow plenty of space for each child to work. The younger the child, the more space is required.

2. Protect any surface or clothing that might be damaged by the material in use. Make sure the protective covering is clearly different from any supplies being used. It is not necessary to cover surfaces that are easily washed.

3. Provide a sufficient amount of supplies so that no more than two children have to share the same resource at a time. Certain supplies, such as scissors, should not be shared, as they can be dangerous when passed from child to child.

4. Have plenty of cleanup supplies on hand for children and adults to use.

5. Activities that make the hands messy should be set up very close to a water supply.

6. Define areas in which certain materials must be kept. This can be done by such things as color coding the tables, hanging signs or symbols, placing

tape on the floor, or teaching simple rules such as "clean hands only" on the rug, at the computer, or in the book corner.

USING THE CREATING ART SECTIONS

The next Creating Art section presents a way to plan and organize open-ended art activities. Succeeding sections describe specific ways to present and use the basic art media using the same activity plan format. These are intended to illustrate the kinds of activities that match the philosophical framework and educational goals discussed in this chapter. They are designed to provide a model for beginning practitioners who have limited experience with young children and their art, and they are full of helpful hints and suggestions that will prove useful to anyone who is teaching art to young children.

Studio Page 1

WHY ART?

All of the following have been suggested as important reasons children should be taught art.

- Think carefully about each item and then rank each by its importance.
- Write a number in front of each, with 1 being the highest rank and 9 being the lowest.
- Based on your ranking, write a statement that explains why you feel art is essential for young children.

- ○ Art is part of being human.
- ○ Art stimulates brain development.
- ○ Art promotes early literacy.
- ○ Art improves physical health.
- ○ Art promotes emotional self-regulation.
- ○ Art develops visual perception.
- ○ Art creates community.
- ○ Art fosters cognitive growth.
- ○ Art nurtures creativity.

_____

_____

_____

_____

_____

_____

_____

_____

_____

_____

_____

_____

_____

_____

_____

_____

HOW TO HAVE A SUCCESSFUL OBSERVATION

Observing children involved in art activities is an invaluable way to learn how children react to various kinds of art experiences. As an observer, you are free of the pressure of performing and can devote your attention to the small details that busy, overworked caregivers often miss.

The following checklist will help you and the participants in the program you are visiting have a pleasant and rewarding experience.

Before the Visit

❍ Call for an appointment and get permission to visit.

❍ Write down the names of the people you speak to on the phone and those of the teachers whose children you will be observing.

❍ If you intend to use a camera or camcorder, make sure you have all the necessary permissions. Parents must sign a release form that allows their children to be photographed. Some schools may already have these on file.

❍ Prepare a form on which to record your observations.

On the Day of the Visit

❍ Arrive on time and introduce yourself to the teachers. If possible, have them introduce you to the children. If asked, give a simple explanation for your visit, such as, "My name is _____. I can't wait to see what you are doing today."

❍ Observe and record carefully. Do not bother the teachers. They are there to work with the children, not you.

❍ When it is time for you to leave, do not disturb the children or the teachers.

After the Observation

❍ As soon as possible, review your notes and add any special details you remember. Some people find it helpful to make an audiotape recording while the experience is still fresh in their minds.

❍ Write a note of thanks to everyone with whom you had contact. A special handmade card for the children is always welcome.

OBSERVATION: ART AND THE CHILD

The purpose of this observation is to observe young children in a typical learning situation. The observation will focus on the artistic behavior of the children in a group educational situation. This observation may be done in an organized school or a child care setting that services children between the ages of one and eight. The observation should last 40 minutes to one hour.

Date of observation: _____   **Length of observation:** _____

Ages of children: _____   **Group size:** _____

Observation

1. What activities are the children involved in?

_____

_____

_____

_____

2. What are the adults doing?

_____

_____

_____

_____

3. How are art activities made available to the children?

_____

_____

_____

_____

4. What is the range of participation children showed in the art activities? (Examples: tried once then left; engaged in nonverbal or verbal interaction with children and/or adults; worked alone; length of time at activity)

_____

_____

_____

_____

Studio Page 4

ANALYSIS: ART AND THE CHILD

Based on your observation, write a response to these questions:

1. How do the activities of the children relate to the areas of artistic growth discussed in this chapter?

_____

_____

_____

_____

_____

_____

_____

2. Which artistic goals for children were being met, and which ones were not? Why?

_____

_____

_____

_____

_____

_____

_____

3. What do you think is the philosophy of early childhood art education of the teachers in this program?

_____

_____

_____

_____

_____

_____

_____

For additional information on teaching art to young children, visit our Web site at http://www.earlychilded.delmar.com

Teaching Art

Questions Addressed in This Chapter:

- What is the teacher's role in early childhood art?

- How does the teacher's behavior affect young artists?

- How should teachers respond to young artists nonverbally?

- How should teachers respond to young artists verbally?

- How should teachers respond to problems?

- How does teaching style affect program delivery?

Young Artists at Work

It was a cold day in February and a small group of four-year-olds was happily cutting and pasting paper shapes. A visitor who was helping for the day walked over to the table and admired the children's collages. She picked up a piece of paper and absentmindedly cut out a heart. "Can I have it?" one little girl asked.

"Sure," replied the visitor. Smugly, the girl pasted it in the center of her paper.

"Make me one!" "Make me one!" came an instant chorus.

"Here, I'll show you how," said the visitor, and she patiently showed them how to fold the paper and cut half a heart shape. But when the children tried it, their hearts did not look like the visitor's; they were jagged and misshapen. One boy crumpled his up in disgust. Another child tried to tear the original "perfect" heart off the first girl's paper. While the visitor tried to quiet the aggressor, the last child at the table began to cry.

Hearing the commotion, the teacher came over to the table. "I don't know how you do this all day," said the visitor. "The children are so demanding. They want their hearts to be perfect."

"I want their hearts to be perfect too, full of joy and hope, but I want their artwork to be their own—each unique and different," replied the teacher. "That's why I don't provide models and patterns."

WHAT IS THE TEACHER'S ROLE IN EARLY CHILDHOOD ART?

Young artists need many things to be successful. They need safe, exciting art supplies, comfortable surroundings, ample space, and time to explore. Most of all, they need a teacher who will enable them to be successful. The teacher is the most important ingredient in allowing children to develop their artistic natures. The teacher is like a gardener, providing the "fertile ground"—the enriched environment—that gives a child a start in thinking and in working as an artist. As the child grows in skill and confidence, enthusiasm and encouragement—the "nutrients" provided by the teacher—allow the child's creativity to flower.

Factors Affecting How Teachers Teach

What are the factors that determine a teaching approach? First and foremost is how teachers view themselves as artists. They must feel comfortable with art exploration before they can lead children's explorations. They must also understand the creative process and have a broad, rich definition of art. In order to increase their ability to guide young artists' growth, they must understand their own art history.

Each of us has had a different experience of art. For some, the word conjures up happy images of fingerpainting in kindergarten. For others, it revives the (memory of a drawing praised by a teacher. Unfortunately, for many adults in our society, the idea of producing art makes them feel incompetent. "I'm not good at art." "I can't draw a straight line." "A child can draw better than I can." These are common statements from adults who have not had a chance to develop their own artistic self-confidence, or who suffered through a poorly taught or highly directed art program.

We need to discover our own artistic natures, no matter how we view our artistic abilities, so that we will be able to model enthusiasm, enjoyment, and competency in art for our young students and thereby facilitate their artistic growth. By understanding the artistic process, we will be better equipped to understand how young children feel as they explore the world of art. Children show more constructive behavior and relationships when their teacher is warm, friendly, and actively and positively involved in their activities (Lay-Dopyera & Dopyera, 1992, pp. 19–20).

How to see oneself as an artist. We are all artists. Art is not limited to the production of a visual product, although that may often be the result. Art is the process of manipulating the visual elements of line, shape, color, pattern, form, and texture. When we choose the colors of our clothing, the style of our hair, or the furnishing of our homes, we are making artistic decisions that are no different from the ones we make when drawing with crayons on paper.

The artist is constantly picking and choosing from the materials available, responding to the effect that is produced when making the next decision. Young children, just like adults, need time and freedom to explore art materials so that they can experience making their own artistic decisions. Activities need to be planned so that children are encouraged and enabled to make as many decisions as possible in each exploration. The activities for children in this book will provide models of open-ended lessons that allow

children to make their own artistic decisions. They are best taught by a teacher who provides guidance but knows when to step back and let the children explore on their own.

Personal "art history." Art is not produced in a vacuum. Art begins as a manipulation of the basic visual elements of line, shape, color, pattern, form, and texture, but once these elements become recognizable as a piece of art to the artists or those around them, they become part of the artists' memories and part of their beliefs about themselves as artistic people. How people feel about themselves as artists is based upon judgments they have made about their abilities because of past experiences.

In the same way, how children feel about themselves is intricately tied to how they judge their own success and how they perceive the response of others. Very young children are often unconcerned about the finished product of their art explorations. For them it is the process itself through which they express themselves. As children grow older, they begin to show pride in their ability to manipulate art materials, the graphic symbols they invent, and the artwork they produce. Teachers need to value all aspects of artistic production. How the teacher responds to the child as an artist, both verbally and nonverbally, is just as important as providing exciting activities for the children.

"Hearts Collage." Cut paper—*Susan, age 5*

There are many ways to respond to children's art explorations. This is a skill that develops with practice. It helps keep one's own art memories fresh, whether happy or frustrating, while creating memories for the children.

How we view our creative natures. Every person has the ability to create something new. People use the creative process daily, whether they are aware of it or not. Any time they have to do something unfamiliar or change a habit, such as when childproofing a room or figuring out how to get to work when the car breaks down, they are using the process. Children are busy learning about a new world and their place in it by following the creative process. Unlike adults, young children do not have a large repertoire of habitual responses to draw on, and so they exhibit high levels of creativity in all areas of learning.

Adults need to provide time, space, and activities to allow children to pursue the creative process. They also need to be prepared for the unique actions and products that may result. Sometimes adults can learn a great deal from young children about how art media can be used! Teachers need to maintain high levels of personal creativity so that they can react and change in response to the uniqueness of the young children with whom they work. No one can plan activities that will work well with all children in every situation. Educators need to rely on their own inherent creative abilities to adapt what they learn and to fit their goals to the reality in which they find themselves.

How we define art. In every culture, people are taught what art is or is not. In some cultures, creative work is viewed differently from our own. An African mask maker takes a piece of wood and waits for the spirit to guide his hands in the shaping of the mask. He has not created a piece of art but has been a tool in the creation of a spiritual item that will be used in ceremony and then discarded. By his definition, the mask is not art, and he is not an artist. But removed from the culture that made it and hung it on the wall of a museum, that same mask becomes art to be studied, judged, and honored.

In this society, people do not always agree on what art is. Their definitions of art are based on what they have been taught by their parents and teachers, what they have experienced in museums and in literature about art, and what they are exposed to from the mass culture, such as on TV and in popular magazines.

Children will acquire their definition of art from the materials to which they are exposed. They need to know that there is more to art than crayons on paper. Their experience will be only as rich as the teacher's definitions and knowledge of art. Teachers need to learn as much as possible about the art of the world. Many activities in this book provide examples of related art forms from a wide variety of times, cultures, and people, as well as ways to present them to young children. Other activities expand the definition of art beyond the bounds of the newspaper-covered table. These will provide the beginnings of an expanded view of art.

HOW DOES THE TEACHER'S BEHAVIOR AFFECT YOUNG ARTISTS?

Children want to be like the adults they admire. They pretend they are grown-ups—a doctor making a sick doll better, a firefighter putting out a fire in a block building, a mom or a dad cooking dinner on the play stove. Most children are not often exposed to adults creating and talking about art. Adults creating art are rarely depicted on TV or in children's books. Art for many young children is something children do at child care or school. Children, not adults, play with play dough; children, not adults, paint at the easel. Because they lacked artistic models, many adults feel art is a childlike activity and of peripheral value to society. It is not enough for teachers to provide wonderful art experiences for children—they must also model artistic behavior.

The teacher can model artistic behavior by exhibiting the following qualities.

Self-Confidence

Teachers must model artistic self-confidence. Would a teacher say to a child, "I'm not a very good reader," or "I can't write the letter 'A' very well," and then expect the child to want to be a good reader or to make a well-formed "A"? But many adults do not hesitate to tell children that they think themselves poor artists, or that they cannot even draw a person. The child may well think that if this important adult who can read so well and knows so much cannot create art, then it must be very hard to be good at art.

If teachers are not self-confident artists, then they need to think about why this might be so. What art experiences convinced them that they could not create art? What do they need to do to increase their self-confidence? Sometimes just becoming aware of the source of their artistic discomfort—a thoughtless comment by a teacher, a rejected piece of work, being laughed at by a friend—is enough to change one's view of one's artistic potential. Taking a drawing course, a painting workshop, or reading about and studying the nature of creativity can change our view of our artistic nature and help us avoid self-deprecating remarks.

Fairness

Adults often say to children, "You're a much better artist than I," even though they would never say to one child that her art was better than her friend's. Putting themselves down in this way does not build up the confidence of children but instead introduces the element of comparative value. The child thinks, "How can mine be better than the teacher's? Can some art be better than others?" Comparing the value of one person's artwork with another's is like comparing apples and oranges. There should be no "better" or "best" artwork in an early childhood setting, for either children or adults.

Enthusiasm

How the guiding adults feel about art will be mirrored by the children. If teachers are fearful and tentative about a project, then the children will react with hesitation. If teachers dislike the feel of a certain material, then the children will sense this and show discomfort. Teachers should avoid using art media or activities that they personally dislike. It is important to be able to express enthusiasm for creating art. Words full of warmth and joy should be used, such as:

> "I can't wait to share this painting with you!"
> "Look at all the bright colors!"
> "Oooo, this play dough feels so smooth!"

Appearance

Personal appearance is a way of showing how people value art and to attract attention to artistic elements and concepts. Dressing in shades of blue when studying the color blue or wearing a wool sweater when talking about fiber art can provide a catalyst for discussion. Appreciation of artwork from other cultures can be shown by wearing African prints, Guatemalan ikat weavings, Indian embroidery, Native American jewelry, and so forth on a regular basis.

Participation

It is important for children to see that adults also use art materials, and that they are not hesitant to touch and play with them. But teachers must be careful to model process and not product. There is a difference between showing children that adults enjoy doing art and providing them with a set model to copy.

When children are just beginning to explore or work with a material, they are unsure of what to do and most vulnerable to trying to imitate what someone

"Me." Crayon—Laurel, age 4

else is doing. At this point, it is extremely important to not overwhelm them with adult-level artwork. Many four- and five-year-olds who are developing symbols of their own are particularly disconcerted when watching an adult they admire draw versions of the same thing they are drawing. Adults should always let children begin first and then draw something completely different.

When adults produce a finished work, it can also overwhelm young artists. An adult can work faster and be far neater and more controlled. It is not necessary to finish the artwork. It is easy to become involved in the children's work or be called away so that there is no need to finish. If reminded by the children to finish, the teacher may say, "I will work on it later, when I am not so busy. I need time to do my best." Later the teacher can share her or his finished work in the same way the children share theirs.

If an activity calls for a simple pattern or method that the children must follow in order to explore the medium, show just that piece of the process while verbally explaining. For example, if the children will be doing sponge prints, say, "Dip the sponge in the paint and press on the paper," while doing so. Do this once or twice but do not continue to produce a finished product. In this book, the word *demonstrate* is used to indicate such simple modeling.

If children are involved in an activity and ask how to do something, or become frustrated because they lack a particular technique, it needs to be explained or demonstrated for them. If it is within the child's ability, suggest a different approach or ask a leading question. For example, if children complain that the paint keeps dripping down their paper, show them how to wipe their paintbrush on the side of the container. If, when using scissors, the children's paper keeps bending and they become frustrated, suggest that they move to a new place to start cutting. A child who is struggling to glue a piece of yarn on paper might be asked, "What is another way you can put glue on the paper?"

New techniques must be within the skill range of the child, and the child must be really interested in learning them. It is helpful to ask, "Do you need help? You look frustrated. Would you like me to show you a way to stop the paint from dripping?" Children learn best when the technique that is being taught is delivered at just the right time—when they need it to solve a problem of their own creation.

It takes a high degree of observational skill to be aware of the technical needs of a group of children all actively involved in art processes. With experience it becomes easier to know which children are ready for a new technique and when they need it. In many cases, a simple pairing of two children of slightly different ages and/or skill levels may be the best way to increase the skill level of a child without direct adult interference.

Teacher Tip

Modeling Process
- ☼ Sit with a group of children involved in an art activity.
- ☼ Handle the materials while the children begin to explore.
- ☼ Start an artwork, but only do a few things to it.
- ☼ Watch the children's motions and use similar or slightly more advanced motions.
- ☼ Avoid doing something well beyond the

children's skill level. For example, rolling balls of clay between the palms is beyond the capability of most two-year-olds and will frustrate them. Cutting out folded paper hearts is too difficult for most four-year-olds.

Modeling Technique (Demonstration)
- ☼ Ask if the child needs help.
- ☼ Ask a leading question or suggest another approach.
- ☼ Show only the part of the process that is needed.
- ☼ Verbally explain as it is being done.

The line between needed intervention and being directive is a fine one. Teachers do not want to miss the "teachable moment" nor interfere with the children's solving of their own problems. This is the art of fine teaching. Teachers must be in tune with their children, understanding their past experiences, sensitivities, and desires. It is not easy. Children are always ". . . dangerously on the brink between presence that they want and repression that they don't want" (Malaguzzi in Edwards, Gandini, & Forman, 1993, p. 58).

HOW SHOULD TEACHERS RESPOND TO YOUNG ARTISTS NONVERBALLY?

Body Language

We speak with more than words. Our whole body communicates our meaning. How close we stand, how we move our arms, and the expression on our faces tell children how we feel about them and their art. It is important for our nonverbal behavior to match what we are saying to children.

Faces are a mirror of our feelings. Smiling at a child tells that child that we are pleased with him or her and that we like what he or she is doing. Frowns and cold stares distance us from the child and show disapproval. Teachers need to be aware of the messages they are sending. If a teacher says to a child, "You used the glue in an interesting way," but frowns at the same time because the glue is dripping on the floor, then the words have no meaning. It is better to react honestly. If the dripping glue is deeply disturbing, deal with the problem first before commenting on the artwork. The teacher might say, "Let's put your collage over here and wipe up all the glue; then I can look at your collage."

How we move and gesture are also strong expressions of our feelings. It is important to remain at the children's level by sitting or stooping when interacting with them as they participate in the art process. Using expansive arm motions can signal enthusiasm or inclusion. More subtly, hand signals and American Sign Language can be used to introduce the children to other ways of communicating, while at the same time providing a quick and nonintrusive way to signal a child without disturbing the other children. A simple "thumbs up" sign, for example, can communicate to a child who is wiping up some paint drips that she is doing something that is appreciated.

Sharing Emotions

No matter how hard we try to cover up our emotions, children seem to sense how we are feeling. It is often better to be open about how we feel. It is hard to shrug off the frustration of a car that would not start that morning or the anger left from sharp words with a friend. Art can provide a way to express such feelings. Share with the children the source of the feeling and then say, for example, "That car is so frustrating, I'm going to make a painting of it and show how it is all broken," or "I am going to draw a whole bunch of angry lines on my paper and get rid of some of this angry feeling." Showing the children that adults use art as a release for emotions lets children know that people of all ages use art for emotional release.

Sitting beside children and using art materials can be a warm, comforting experience.

Active Listening

Active listening is one of the most important ways a teacher or caregiver can respond to a child and should be one of the first responses when children share information about their artwork. Especially with new children, it is extremely important to listen before responding verbally, in order to learn more about the artists' intent before deciding what to say to them. We also need to listen to the children we know well to show that we care about what they are saying. Active listening consists of the following components.

Waiting. Do not always respond instantly and verbally to everything a child says. Establish eye contact, and wait for the child to speak. This will also provide time to formulate a thoughtful verbal response if the child does not offer a comment.

Looking. Maintain eye contact with a child while she or he is talking. Remain at the child's eye level if possible.

Responding. Respond with value-free grunts, head nods, appropriate facial expressions, and "hums" as the child talks.

HOW SHOULD TEACHERS RESPOND TO YOUNG ARTISTS VERBALLY?

Words are powerful. They can transform a humdrum experience into an exhilarating one or destroy a special moment in a second. What adults say to young artists can have a profound effect on how children view art for the rest of their lives. Many adults can trace the origin of their feeling of artistic incompetence to a thoughtless comment by a caring adult. Guiding adults need to take care in offering comments to children. We should not just speak off the top of our heads or repeat the words spoken to us when we were children. What teachers say and how they respond to children is one of the most significant parts of the educational process, and it takes practice to choose words wisely and sparingly.

Research indicates that the younger the child, the more important it is to deliver on a one-to-one basis rather than in a large group situation (Lay-Dopyera &

Dopyera, 1992). Art activities provide significant moments for personal dialogue between a child and a caring adult. This relationship is an important one. Both short-term and long-term studies find that when there are many warm, positive interactions between adults and young children, there is a beneficial effect on social and emotional development.

In addition, by choosing words thoughtfully, we not only help children feel good about themselves but expand their thought processes and make the art experience more meaningful to them.

The Problem with Praise

Probably one of the most common responses to children's artwork is unconditional and false praise. "Good work!" "Great painting!" and "Nice picture!" are said quickly to the child as the teacher scoops up the drippy painting or hustles the child off to the next activity. The intent is to give encouragement and indicate to children that they have successfully used the art medium. However, studies indicate that consistent overuse of such praise actually diminishes the behavior being complimented (Kohn, 1993). Said over and over, the words become empty and meaningless. How can every picture be great or wonderful? The children come to believe that the teachers are not really looking at their work. In addition, unconditional praise does not help children think more deeply about their work or make the experience more educational for them.

Teachers often unintentionally use words that are value laden and judgmental. "That's a pretty picture," "What a beautiful painting!", and "Oh, that's lovely! You made a great project!" are frequently said by well-meaning adults who are afraid of hurting a child's feelings. But not every piece of artwork done by a child is beautiful, pretty, or lovely, and such words introduce the contrasting idea that there must also be child artwork that is ugly or unpleasant, and that adults would not praise. If teachers, in an attempt to be fair, apply such words to all child art, then the terms become more meaningless unconditional praise and convey no information to the children about how they really perceive their work.

When teachers say, "I like it!" or "I like the way you _____ ," they are also making judgments and expressing their personal values. Besides being overused, such terms open the door to more deleterious results. Many adults prefer realistic artwork that is neat and orderly. They are more likely to respond positively to a painting of a house flanked by two trees and overlooked by a smiling sun than to a dripping paper covered in thick swirls of olive-green paint. Expressing adult personal taste in young children's art can lead to some children believing that they are better at art and others feeling like failures. As many art teachers who work with adults have noted (Edwards, 1979; Cameron, 1992), a large number of people have poor artistic self-images because as very young children a piece of their artwork was disliked or compared unfavorably to another's work by a significant adult in their life.

In addition, Marshall (1995, p. 26) and Kohn (cited in Brandt, 1995, p. 16) warn that by focusing the children's attention on whether or not their behavior is likable, they learn that they must perform to please the teacher rather than to successfully accomplish the learning task. The child's joy in self-expression through the art media is then replaced with the child's conscious effort to produce something likable.

Unfortunately, this sort of praise naturally flows from most adults' lips. Arguments can be made that in some sense adults do want children to behave in pleasing ways; telling them we like something may increase the likelihood that they will repeat the action. However, creative art is based on the expansion of new behaviors rather than the repetition of limited actions. Consider what meaningful information a child receives when a teacher says something such as, "I like the way you used green paint today." Does the teacher really want the child to repeat the same use of green paint in every painting, or is there some better way to respond to this child's work?

Positive Feedback

Positive feedback tells children precisely what they did well. Instead of saying "Great painting!" the thoughtful teacher says, "I noticed you wiped your brush on the edge of the paint container so the paint didn't drip." Positive feedback is best used to let children know when they have used a technique well or behaved in a way that will give them further success at the activity.

In order to respond specifically, teachers need to have a clear idea in their minds about what techniques and behaviors are appropriate and possible for the child, and then they must carefully observe the child at work. Positive feedback enhances children's feelings of self-confidence—it provides information on what they have done well, and it communicates to them that adults are personally interested enough in their art activities to observe specific things they have done.

Even though positive feedback seems more like a wordy description than praise, when it is delivered with the same facial expression and the same warm enthusiastic tone of voice that we would use for "Great job!" the child receives it as praise for being successful in a very specific way.

Positive feedback can take several forms, each appropriate in different situations. With practice, this kind of response can become a natural way of talking to children about their art in daily interactions.

Descriptive Statements

A descriptive statement can be used to make children aware of their behavior and of how they solved a problem, or to increase their understanding of art concepts.

Teacher Tip

Alfie Kohn (1993) suggests the following guidelines when praising children:

1. Praise the behavior or product, not the child. Say "That's a very unique brush stroke," not "You're a very original artist."
2. Be specific. Say "I see many red paint strokes," not "That's a nice painting."
3. Avoid phony praise. Use a natural, spontaneous voice.
4. Avoid praise that creates competition. Praise the whole group, not one individual. Say "I see so many of you painting neatly," not "Susie is being such a neat painter today."

How teachers respond to young children will affect how children see themselves as artists.

Such descriptive statements show children that teachers value their individuality, because careful observation is necessary to provide a meaningful description. Often the teacher may give each child at the same activity a different comment.

These kinds of statements refer to how the child is working either with others or with the materials. They are the easiest statements to formulate and can serve as a good entrance into a conversation with children about their work.

If children are working with a material, comment on how they manipulated it. For example:

"I noticed that you rolled the clay into a long snake."
"You moved the (computer) mouse in a circular way to make those curved lines."

When children work well with others, describe their behavior.

"I see that you are sharing your glue with your partner."

"I noticed you gave a piece of your shiny paper to Mike when he couldn't find another one."
"I see that you and Anna have decided who will go first at the computer in a fair way."

Statements can also refer to the amount of effort children have put into an activity.

"You spent a great deal of time working with Allan on your dinosaur project."
"This clay piece represents a tremendous effort on your part."
"You spent almost a whole hour getting the shape just the way you wanted."

Describing Artistic Decisions

Verbalizing the steps children have taken to solve a problem or summarizing their solutions are important ways to make children aware of how they worked through a process.

If the child has struggled to find a solution to a problem, then describe the specific steps taken.

"I noticed that you tried several ways to attach the tubes together. First you tried gluing them, and then you tried bending them. Now you have pushed one inside the other, and they are holding together well."

In responding to a finished piece of work, summarize what choices the child has made. Artistic decision statements often contain the following phrases: "you tried,""you found,""you discovered,""you chose." For example:

"You have chosen to use three different colors of paper in your collage today."
"I noticed you found a way to attach that unusually shaped button to your puppet for its nose."

Describing Art Concepts

Descriptive statements can increase children's vocabulary, further their understanding of the art elements they have used, and make them aware of the sensory qualities of their artwork. This is different from teachers trying to describe what the artwork seems to depict to them. A superficial description of the subject of the picture does not extend the child's learning and puts the emphasis on product rather than process. Everyone who works with children and art should be familiar with the art elements that are found in most artworks. Chapter 7 provides a detailed description of these elements and also of the sensory qualities of art, which should form the basis of this kind of verbal description.

Using art concepts as the basis of descriptions allows higher-level responses to toddlers' scribbles and explorations. For example:

"Look at all the swirling lines you have made!"
"I see many different colors in your painting."
"Your play-dough pancake feels so smooth!"
"Look at the way the wet paint sparkles!"

These same responses can be used even if the child's subject matter seems obvious (about which, see the section, "Expressing Feelings"). If a comment on the subject matter seems appropriate, then focus on the art elements that the child used to express that subject. For example:

"I see you have used many different sizes of rectangles to make your house."
"You used many round yellow shapes to make your flowers."

Paraphrasing

To paraphrase, teachers repeat what children have just said in their own words. This is an excellent way to show children that the teacher has been listening to them. For example:

Child: "I made lots of green lines."
Teacher: "Yes, you did make many green lines."

Expressing Feelings

When teachers respond to a child's artwork on an interpretive level, they model for the child the way art communicates to other people. We can refer to a personal sensation or a visual memory by saying, for example,"The yellows in your picture make me feel warm inside," or "The rectangles in your collage remind me of all the colorful windows in the apartment across the street." The expression of emotions, however, must be done with care. A banal "Your picture makes me feel happy" does not communicate a depth of feeling, nor explain to the child the source of that response. Instead, tie positive emotional responses to the art elements in the work. For example, say, "I feel so peaceful when I look at the blues in your print."

Negative emotional responses must be dealt with differently. We must be careful when responding with the powerful emotions of sadness and anger. We do not want to overwhelm the child with our own negative feelings that can be received as criticism, and yet, we still want to allow the child to express these emotions.

In the case of negative emotions, it is better to put into words what the child is expressing for herself or himself rather than how it makes us feel. In order to do this successfully, it is important to know how the child is feeling and why, and then to tie that feeling into the art elements that the child has chosen to use.

For example:

"You used lots of jagged lines to express your anger at being knocked over by your friend."
"The dark colors you used show how sad you are that your dog ran away."

Interpretive responses based on feelings and memories must be genuine, unique, and thoughtful. They are easily overused and can become as meaningless as "That's lovely," or "Good work." Not every yellow painting should make us feel warm or happy. Teachers' personal interpretive responses to children's artwork should arise spontaneously as part of their interaction with a particular child. They should be carefully phrased so that the interpretation is not imposed on the child but clearly expresses a personal response. Instead of saying "Boy, what an angry (happy, sad) picture you made today!"use words that indicate a personal response, such as "I feel," "I remember," and "I am reminded."

Hall and Duffy (cited in Noyce & Christie, 1989, p. 46) found that when teachers initiated conversations with children by making a statement about their personal feelings or experiences, children gave less stilted, longer, and more spontaneous replies. Used appropriately, such responses can create a wonderful depth of communication between the child and adult.

Describing the Subject

Teachers interpret child art when they assume that they know what the subject of a piece is, as when they respond, before listening to the child's description: "It looks like you painted your family today," or "That must be a picture of your dog."If the child is still at the scribbling stage, attributing a subject has no meaning for the child and serves only to satisfy an adult desire to find reality in all art, instead of appreciating the way the child has used the artistic elements. A better response is to describe the lines, shapes, colors, and other aesthetic elements of the artwork.

Even when children are beginning to develop sym-

Art Words

Descriptive Art Words

☼ **Line**

A continuous stroke made with a moving tool. A boundary between or around shapes.

Straight, curved, wiggly, zigzag, jagged, crisscross

☼ **Shape**

A two-dimensional enclosed area.

Square, rectangular, round, triangular, irregular, oval

☼ **Color**

The different perception of the wavelengths of light by the eye's sensors.

Bright colors: red, orange, yellow, green, blue
Dull colors: gray, olive green, deep brown
Neutral colors: white, beige, gray, tan, brown
Pastel colors: pink, coral, sky blue, lavender, pale green

Intense colors: magenta, purple, fuschia, red-orange, turquoise

☼ **Texture**

The tactile quality of a surface.

Soft, hard, bumpy, rough, jagged, smooth, wet, sticky

☼ **Form**

A three-dimensional object.

Spheres, cubes, pyramids

☼ **Contrast**

An unlikeness in quality.

Light/dark, big/small, top/bottom, front/back, round/square, bright/dull, intense/soft, hard/soft, rough/smooth, patterned/plain, thick/thin, straight/curved

☼ **Pattern**

A design in which art elements are repeated in a regular way.

Plaid, polka dot, stripe, floral, all over, border, checkered

bols that somewhat represent reality, it is difficult for adults to identify the intended subjects with accuracy. A misidentified subject can cause a child to react with anger or disappointment, because children often assume that adults know everything. Although a bold child may reply to the teacher's mistaken, "Oh, you drew your house today," with "Can't you see I made the school?" many children react silently and wonder what was wrong with their artwork that this adult could not understand what they were trying to express. It is easy to avoid this difficulty if we take the time to wait for children to explain their work or ask questions that will elicit a description from them.

However, children like to test adults. With a "Guess what I made?" they challenge us to find their meaning. Even in this situation, it is still better to resort to simple description of media and artistic elements than to risk misidentification and emotional hurt. For example, if the child has made a painting that might show a house, say: "I see you have made a painting using many different colored shapes." Follow this immediately with an open-ended question that will elicit a further description from the child.

Engaging in Artistic Dialogue

Questioning or making a leading statement is one way to learn directly from the artists what their intent was in an artwork. Questions can also be used to further children's understanding of the art process, to help them reflect on the consequences of their actions, and to assess what they have learned from the art activity. By encouraging children to verbalize about their artwork, we also help them develop language skills and clarify their thought processes. Questions must be phrased very carefully so that they are not intrusive, allow many possible responses from children, and make children feel comfortable talking about art.

Creating a responsive atmosphere. Before we can expect a child to respond freely to our questions, we must create an atmosphere in which the child feels safe expressing his or her thoughts and feelings. There are four ways to do this.

First, by providing plenty of opportunities for children to look at art (by displaying art prints and art books) and by talking about artwork regularly, an atmosphere of verbalizing about art becomes a natural part

Teacher Tip

Using Positive Feedback

Typical examples of unconditional praise:

Good glue job!   Nice collage!
Good cleanup!   Super print!

Positive feedback:

I noticed you put the glue on the back of your shapes and then attached them to your paper!
I see you used straight cuts with your scissors to make your shapes!
I saw you pick up all the papers and put them in the right containers!
You made this pattern by pressing the sponge down on your paper over and over!

Typical examples of judgmental statements:
Beautiful painting!
Lovely work!

Positive feedback:
The golds and yellows in your painting make me feel as warm as sunshine.
The lines in your picture swirl in and out like a maze.

Typical examples of imposing statements:
That's an angry picture!
What a happy painting!
It looks like your mother.

Positive feedback:
I see you used lots of black and red and green to show your anger about the accident.
Your painting reminds me of a walk I took in my grandmother's garden.
I see you used many interesting patterns and shapes in this picture. Is there a story to go with it?

of children's experience (see chapter 8). If children are used to asking questions about someone else's artwork, then they will be more comfortable answering questions about their own work.

Second, by expressing our comments about children's artwork in the form of positive feedback, we provide a model of how children can describe their own art.

Third, the style of delivery in asking a question is extremely important. Questions need to be asked in a tone of voice that contains enthusiastic curiosity. Voices need to be soft, eyes need to make contact, and once the child begins to respond, we need to practice active listening.

Finally, questions need to be asked at the right moment. Not every piece of artwork needs to be explained by a child. Choose carefully the moment to elicit a verbal response. If the child has just finished a painting and is eager to join some friends in the block area, do not try to engage the child in a deep conversation about the artwork. At this moment a simple descriptive form of positive feedback will suffice. If a child has been working a long time on a clay sculpture and has stopped for a moment to get another piece of clay, this may provide an opportunity for a discussion about the work.

Take care not to overwhelm children with a long string of questions. They should not feel that they are being grilled. If they must constantly answer questions or explain their art, then they may become resentful and avoid art activities. Use a question to begin a conversation. Continue the conversation only if the child is interested in doing so, and formulate responses based on the direction the child's answer takes.

Phrasing questions. Learning how to phrase questions directed to children takes practice. Although when confronted with a dripping puddle of blue and purple paint, or a much-handled piece of play dough, our initial reaction may be one of "What is it?" or "What is that supposed to be?" such an intrusive, insulting question must be avoided. Not all child art is intended to be something. Much of a child's initial work with a medium will consist of exploration and experiments with the materials and tools and will have no end result. This kind of question is limiting in

that it puts all of the focus on the product and places children in the position of having to give an answer they think will please the questioner.

To learn more about artists' thoughts, phrase questions in such a way that children can give a wide range of answers. Alternatives to "What is it?" ask children to reflect on their artwork in much deeper ways. They allow children to respond with descriptive statements that go beyond subject matter and include thoughts about art processes and artistic decision making. Such questions can take several forms.

Focusing on art elements. Questions can focus the children's attention on the art elements in their work:

> "I noticed you used many different pieces of cloth on your puppet. Do any of them have an interesting texture?"
> "What kinds of lines did you make with the crayons?"

Focusing on process. The child can be asked to explain the process she or he used:

> "You used three different sizes of brushes today. Which lines did you make with the big one?"
> "How did you make the play dough so bumpy?"

Questioning decisions. Artistic decisions can be explained:

> "Where on your collage did you decide to put those interesting pebbles you found?"
> "Which fingers did you use to make your fingerpainting?"
> "How did you make this color?"

Exploring relationships. Questions can be used to focus the children's attention on what they might do next and to see relationships between their behavior and the results. Kamii and DeVries (1993, p. 27) have postulated four types of questions that help children learn about how objects and events are related.

1. Predicting:

> "What do you think will happen when you press your fingers into the clay?"
> "What do you think might happen if you mixed these two colors of play dough together?"

2. Creating an effect:

> "Can you make different kinds of lines with your paintbrush?"
> "What do you think you could do if I gave you these pieces of yarn for your collage?"

3. Connecting events:

> "How did you make all these rectangular shapes?"
> "How did you make this color brown?"

4. Finding the cause:

> "Why don't the pebbles fall off your collage now?"

Integrating art. Questions can also be used to extend the child's learning in art to other curriculum areas:

> Science: "What are the different kinds of leaves you used in your collage?"
> Math: "How many balls of clay have you made so far?"
> Language: "What kind of voice does your puppet have?"

Assessing knowledge. Through gentle questioning, we can assess what the child knows:

> "Which object in your collage is rough (smooth, round, biggest . . .)?"
> "What colors did you use in your painting today?"

Eliciting stories. The relationship between a child's thought processes and the artwork produced is an important one. Many educators advocate using children's art as a springboard for the development of early literacy skills (Cecil & Lauritzen, 1995; Olson, 1992). The Reggio Emilia program (Edwards, Gandini, & Forman, 1993), for example, uses art as a way for preliterate children to document what they know or have learned.

Many teachers commonly ask children to dictate a title or story to go with their artwork. However, before diving into asking all children to provide a detailed explanation of their art, it is important to consider the child's purpose in creating each particular piece of art and what might be the best way to record or recognize the child's verbalizations about it.

Taking dictation. What is the best way to write down a child's comments? Many teachers write the child's dictation about their artwork directly on their pictures. In a busy preschool program or child care facility, this is often the quickest and easiest method to capture the words of many children in a short time. Many children do not seem to mind this, however, there are some who are deeply disturbed by having someone else write on their paper. Most artists do not have someone else's writing across their artwork. Always ask permission before writing anything, including the child's name, on the front of an artwork, and respect the child's right to write her or his own name or words if desired, even if she or he is not yet able to do so precisely. Better yet, write on the back of the piece or on a separate piece of paper. One idea is to write the child's name ahead of time on a self-stick label, which can then be stuck to the back of artwork as needed. Mounting the artwork on a colored paper background provides a space for a title and name in the border. If artwork is being made into a book, then the child's description can be written on the page opposite the artwork.

It is not always necessary to write down a child's words at the time the artwork is done. Saving the work until another day when there is a quiet moment to give the child undivided attention, and really listening to what the child is saying, can make the art-language experience much more meaningful for both the child and the teacher. This same conferencing procedure will be practiced in the writing process in later years.

HOW SHOULD TEACHERS RESPOND TO PROBLEMS?

As children participate in art activities, a variety of difficulties can arise. Some of these are the result of the previous art experiences children bring with them. If a program is designed around open-ended activities that draw on the children's interests, and if the teachers show children that they value their artwork through thoughtful conversation, then many of these problems will slowly disappear on their own.

Others are due to the variety of ways art materials

Teaching in Action

Explorations

When children are first becoming familiar with an art medium, regardless of their age, their focus is not on expressing any deep thoughts. Instead, they are just playing, experimenting, and learning to control the tools and materials. For example, a child handling a pair of scissors for the first time is going to be more interested in how to make them open and close and how to hold them straight and make them cut than in trying to make a particular shape. It would be inappropriate to ask this child to invent a title for the resulting "project" or to make up a story about it. Instead, the child might be asked what he or she learned about using scissors.

One way to use art explorations to build literacy is to create a "work log" for the child. After selected explorations, or when the child requests, record the child's description of what was learned about that particular medium. The log could be illustrated with photographs of the child using the material and/or samples of the child's explorations. The child should be actively involved in deciding what goes in the log, in illustrating the cover and pages, and in giving the log a title, such as *Martha's First Book of Cutting,* or *Kira's Color Mixing Experiments.*

Skill Development or Practice Activities

Once children have developed some control over an art material, they may repeat, with small variations, artistic elements that they have learned to make successfully. A child might make a series of easel paintings that features houses, for example, or a group of collages made from cut-and-glued rectangles.

To provide an early literacy experience using practice activities, save the child's work instead of sending home the finished projects each day. A large piece of folded paper labeled with the child's name can serve as a portfolio. (See chapter 12 for more information about using portfolios.) When several pieces in the same medium have been collected, take some time to sit with the child and talk about each piece using positive feedback and leading questions. Then offer to help the child make a book of her or his artwork if desired. Glue the artwork on a colored paper background, punch holes and tie with yarn, or staple the pages together. Have the child think of a title for her or his art book, such as *My House Paintings,* or *Lots of Rectangles.*

Responsive Activities

Responsive activities done in reaction to an experience are intended to express the children's thoughts about what they have done, and are, therefore, an appropriate place to elicit a description from children. For example, if after a visit to the supermarket, several children have chosen to make collages using pieces of food packaging or have drawn pictures of the stacks of food, then invite them to share their artwork and talk about what they remember about the trip. The children's discussion can be recorded on audiotape or videotape or written on a separate piece of paper to accompany the artwork.

respond to young children's manipulation. In responding to these problems, it is important to keep in mind that children do not develop skills when an adult does the work for them, nor do they develop self-confidence in their own abilities if their project is "improved" by a teacher.

Giving Encouragement

There will always be some children who hold back from participating in art activities. They may be afraid to take risks because they have had a bad experience with that material previously or are uncertain what to do. This fear must be respected. It is important to try to find out why they are afraid and then provide the needed assurance. Children may have been scolded for getting dirty or for drawing on the wall, or they may have been made to copy art projects too difficult for them.

Never force children to participate in an art activity. Allow them to watch others working. If they seem interested, then offer to stay nearby and invite them to investigate the activity. Be subtle and positive. Offer materials to use, and then slowly withdraw.

Children have different tolerance levels for messiness. Some dive into sticky and gooey materials with

Teacher to Family

Sample Letter to Families: Responding to Their Child's Art

Families also need to know how to respond to their child's art. Send home a letter that offers suggestions of ways they can talk to their child about the artwork.

Dear Family,

It is a special occasion when your child brings home a piece of art. Each child's artwork is unique, a special part of him or her. Please take a moment to share the art with your child.

Children have many purposes in creating art. Perhaps today was a chance to explore what happened when blue and yellow mixed together. Or maybe your child practiced using scissors and glue and discovered a new way to make shapes. To our adult eyes, we may see only some mixed-up colors or odd sticky shapes.

- Do not ask, "What is it?" It may not be important to your child that the art be something. Do not guess what it might be. You might be wrong.

- Do ask how it was done. You will help your child use words to describe what was learned.

- Ask if there is a story to go with the artwork. You will learn much more about the artist's imagination and assist in language development.

- Describe what you see in the artwork—the lines, the colors, the shapes, the textures, and the patterns—and ask your child to do the same. You will help your child build her or his vocabulary.

- Share a memory of a piece of art you created or have seen. You will be teaching your child that art has been created by many people.

After sharing a piece of art, hang it in a special place for the family to see, such as on a door or a refrigerator. When a new artwork comes home, remove the old one and store it away. Someday your child will enjoy looking at his or her art and remembering that special moment.

Your child's teacher,

"Caitlin and I like to play with all these toys." Marker and crayon—*Brittany, age 5*

glee, while others hold back. Allow children to explore the material on their own terms. Like adults, each child will like some art materials better than others.

If a child indicates a fear of getting her or his clothes dirty, then provide a smock to wear and discuss with the child's parents that young children do get art materials on their clothes sometimes. Suggest that parents dress their child in simple, easy-to-wash clothing. A note should be sent to all parents asking them to dress their children in clothing appropriate for doing art. (See chapter 5, "Creating Art: Painting," for more detail on appropriate dress.)

Providing Comfort

Children cannot produce art if they are upset or worried. Teachers need to create a calm, accepting atmosphere that allows children to feel free to experiment and explore. This can be done by modeling an accepting attitude when interacting with children and their art. For example, if one child criticizes another's art by saying it is stupid or ugly, then respond immediately with a statement appropriate to the incident, such as in the example that follows:

Start by making a positive statement about the artwork in question, such as, "Michelle has used many different textures in her collage." This provides assurance and comfort to the injured child.

Make it clear that the comment made was hurtful and unacceptable, and that all art is acceptable. For example: "It is hurtful to say that about someone's art. Everybody makes their artwork the way they want."

Providing Direction

If a child is misusing an art tool or a supply or is struggling with a technique, intervene as subtly as possible. A quiet restatement of the directions, repetition of the safety rules, or quick demonstration is usually sufficient when given directly to the child.

Building Self-Confidence

It is surprising that even very young children often exhibit a lack of confidence in being able to create art. It does not take much to make a child afraid to create art openly. When a child uses art materials, a product of some kind results, and even if the child is just exploring, in some sense that product is an extension of the child. An unkind word, an accident, a well-meaning attempt to make the product better, or the presence of a model that is beyond the ability of the child to copy can all diminish artistic confidence.

When children say, "Make it for me," there has been some interference in their natural desire to explore and play with art materials. These children need reassurance that their art is acceptable as they choose to make it. This can be done by eliminating patterns and models to copy and by maintaining a "hands-off" policy. An adult should never work on or "fix" a child's art.

If children insist that they cannot create art, then provide assurance by affirming that difference is valued. For example: "Each artist creates in her own way. Look at all the different ways the other children have used the paint (crayons, paper, boxes . . .)." Then ask a leading question:

"Can you invent a new way to . . . ?"
"What would happen if . . . ?"
"Have you tried . . . ?"

HOW DOES TEACHING STYLE AFFECT PROGRAM DELIVERY?

The Teacher as Facilitator

Children have been creating art on their own long before there were organized methods for the teaching of "art." Scratching lines in the dirt with a stick, building sand castles, and making footprint patterns in the snow are all highly creative, child-initiated art activities. In educational situations, however, the creation of art reflects the interrelationship of the child with the purposes of the teacher.

Providing open-ended activities. An open-ended activity is one in which there are many possible ways the children can approach their artwork, and in which they are responsible for making their own artistic decisions. While children may be influenced by their experiences and/or the cultural images around them, they need to be able to incorporate these elements in their own unique way. In an open-ended activity, the teacher has no preset idea about what the end product will look like. The children choose from the available materials, tools, and techniques and then decide how they will use them. It is the children who determine the end result.

Demonstrating confidence. Teachers who provide open-ended art activities demonstrate a high level of confidence. They do not worry about what the product will look like or how it will be judged. They are more interested in the process the child goes through than in the product that may or may not result. These teachers are highly creative in setting up environments that are safe and interesting for curious artists to explore, and in providing experiences that inspire the children to produce art.

Providing a context. The teacher, as a facilitator, may sometimes provide a context for the art activity. The art exploration that is offered may relate to an experience that the children have shared, such as a book that has been read or a field trip they have taken. The teacher may offer a special selection of materials for the children to investigate, or may model the use of certain materials. In doing so, the teacher must avoid adhering to a preconceived notion about how the activity should progress or what the results will be and must be willing to follow the interests of the children even when they do not relate to the context the teacher has provided.

Product-Oriented Art

Book after book and article after article have railed against the prevailing practices in so many early childhood programs: giving children precut pieces to

Teacher Tip

Qualities of a Facilitating Teacher

1. Displays many examples of artwork in the room, but does not present them as models for the children to copy
2. Provides a choice of materials
3. Allows children to use the materials as they wish
4. Does not require that the artwork look a certain way
5. Provides the children with ample time

assemble, hanging up teacher-made models so the children can "see" how it is done, tracing hands to make turkeys, using paper plates to make lion faces, and giving children preprinted pictures to color, and, perhaps, to cut out and make into bag puppets.

There are many reasons these practices have been so hard to eliminate.

It is safe. Many educators lack confidence in their own art abilities. They feel safe putting together a packaged product and feel they can teach the children how to do this. These teachers need to learn more about their own artistic abilities by doing activities such as those on the Studio Pages that follow.

It pleases families. These educators do not understand child art and are unsure of their goals, so they cannot explain the nature of child art to the families. They think families want to see "recognizable" art products. These teachers need to analyze their goals, study the nature of child art, and develop a program for educating families. (See chapter 12 for guidance.)

It is harmless fun. Children who have experienced these kinds of pseudo-art projects are the ones who say they cannot draw or want the teacher to do it for them. It is not harmless. It takes away children's initiative and artistic self-confidence.

It is traditional. There is a place for tradition in classrooms, but it must have educational meaning.

Easels are traditional in early childhood programs. They provide a wonderful, open-ended painting experience for preschoolers. Gluing eyes on precut pumpkins is not an educational experience. It is restricting and uncreative. It is a tradition children can do without.

It is convenient. Early childhood educators are overworked, have limited time, and have too many children to service. It is easy to grab a commercial pattern for the "art table." This is perhaps a major underlying reason for the prevalence of precut and patterned projects.

To have a truly rich program in any of the curriculum areas takes thoughtful consideration and time. However, educators who hold strong beliefs about what child art should be will never compromise this belief, regardless of the time it takes.

CONCLUSION: DELIVERING THE WELL-DESIGNED ART PROGRAM

The teacher's ways of talking, responding, and acting will reflect both her interest in the child and her belief that the content of the learning experience should be in tune with what is meaningful, important, and pleasurable to young children.

—Barbara Biber (1984, p. 73)

Teacher Tip

Aspects of a Product-Oriented Approach

1. A model made by an adult or a "competent" child is displayed by the teacher to show the children how their projects should look.
2. The teacher gives children only prepared materials such as precut shapes and/or counted-out pieces.
3. The teacher does not allow children to add any other materials to their projects.
4. The teacher gives the children adult-made or commercial stencils to trace or pictures to color.
5. Children complain that they cannot create art. They want the teacher to create their projects for them.
6. The teacher limits the amount of time the children can work on their projects.
7. The teacher fixes, finishes, or changes a child's project so it "looks right."

Art activities provide an opportunity for meaningful dialogue.

Adults working with children and art need to be aware of themselves and what they bring to the interaction. How the teacher chooses to present art activities can result in self-confident, creative children or in frustrated, uninterested ones. If the teacher does not feel comfortable with an art material, then the children will acquire this discomfort. If the teacher limits the children's choices or experiences, then the children will rebel or withdraw. If the teacher provides teacher-made patterns, then the children will be frustrated and feel that they cannot be successful in art.

The following list summarizes the information teachers need to know about themselves in order to understand and develop their skills as nurturers of young artists.

- We are artists when we make artistic decisions.
- Our beliefs about ourselves as artists come from our past experiences.
- Everyone uses the creative process to solve problems and explore ideas.

- Our personal definition of art grows out of our past experiences with art.

It is not just children who need to grow. Teachers and nurturing adults who work with young children need to examine their artistic past and plan their future. Whether teachers are starting out or have been working with children for years, they always need to be changing. Every group of children is different. Every activity will have a life of its own. There will be new art forms, new ways of working, and exciting new media. Traditional media may be found hazardous and fade from use. We will not always say the right thing at the right time. Our philosophy of art education will become more refined. Our definition of art will grow more inclusive. We will have successes, and we will face failure.

There is no need for guilt. We must learn from our experiences, listen to others, and be willing to take risks. With thought and care, we will create the best possible art program for young artists.

FURTHER READING

These books will continue your growth as a creative and an artistic teacher.

Cohen, E. P., & Gainer, R. S. (1976/1995). *Art: Another language for learning*. Portsmouth, NH: Heinemann. Beautifully written vignettes of children and their art are skillfully combined with models of exemplary art teaching.

Edwards, B. (1979). *Drawing on the right side of the brain*. Los Angeles: J. P. Tarcher. This book is a series of drawing lessons designed to increase visual perception and to create an understanding of the drawing process. The exercises are an excellent way for adults to increase their self-confidence in art.

"My teacher." Crayon and marker—*Susan, age 3*

Creating Art: Planning for Art

 THE IMPORTANCE OF PLANNING

Art is a complex discipline involving many skills and processes. There are many influences on teachers' decisions about what art activities they ultimately provide to their students. We have already seen how philosophy, goals, and teacher behavior affect the children's art program. Whether a curriculum is planned around themes, projects, learning centers, or play areas, the individual components are the activities—the specific things the children and the educator will be doing. It is important to plan these activities carefully, to ensure that nothing is forgotten and to provide a measure against which we can assess our delivery.

Activities need to be planned around the specific factors that will affect the dynamics of a particular group of children. The plans need to answer the following questions: who, why, where, when, what, and how? By planning answers to each of these questions ahead of time, teachers are better prepared to guide the art activities they offer the children. In this Creating Art section, each of these components is explained. In later Creating Art sections, specific activities using the basic art media are presented using this same structure.

 WHAT ARE THE COMPONENTS OF AN ART PROGRAM?

An art program for young children is made up of five parts that interlink to form a whole: group composition, goals, environment, delivery, and activities. They answer the corresponding questions: who, why, where, how, and what. Careful consideration must be given to each area in order to design the best possible art program.

 WHO? GROUP COMPOSITION

Every group of children is unique. The following characteristics must be considered when making plans.

What Are the Age and Number of Children?

The age and number of students will affect the amount of time, space, and supervision for which the teacher must plan. Planning an activity with four one-year-olds will require very different decisions than designing a program for 20 five-year-olds. If the children are of mixed ages, will all of them be able to work with the same amount of supervision and be successful?

What Are the Children's Previous Experiences With Art?

The less familiar children are with an art medium, the more exploration they need. If the children are competent with a material, then more responsive activities can be planned. If a group contains children of various ages, developmental phases, and experience with media, then carefully selected open-ended art activities will allow children to work comfortably at their own developmental levels.

Are There Children with Special Needs?

Check that each activity will be able to be accomplished by individual children. Do the activities need adaptation so that a child with special needs can have success? Select art activities that can be done by a wide range of children, and modify the materials, tools, and setup as necessary. (See chapter 11 for suggested ways to modify art activities.)

WHEN? TIME FRAME

Consider the amount of time that will be available for the children to work on their art activities. Make sure that there will be sufficient time to complete an activity, whether on the same day or over a period of days. Will there be enough time for wet projects to dry? Be sure to allow time for sharing, discussing, and mounting finished work as well.

WHY? GOALS AND OBJECTIVES

Goals are the long-term changes in behavior that the activities are meant to foster in children. They are why the activities are selected. These are not changes that will happen after one activity or even two. Children need many opportunities in which to learn and to practice. Self-confidence, for example, comes after many successful experiences. A runner does not try

out for the Olympics after winning her very first race but only after years of learning skills and techniques and after many grueling hours of practice.

An **objective** is a statement describing a behavior that can be accomplished within the time frame of the activity. This is different from a **goal**, which is a statement of the kind of growth in a child's behavior that would be expected over a period of time and after many explorations.

Each objective is ultimately related to one of the growth areas. However, it is important to remember that growth in any of these areas depends on repetition and practice. The experience provided in the activity must be repeated many times in other activities in order to foster meaningful growth. For example, the objective that the child will be able to cut cloth relates to the physical growth of the small muscles of the hand. It would not be expected that after one opportunity a child would be expert in cutting cloth or would have fully developed the small hand muscles.

Writing Skill Objectives

Skill objectives usually consist of two parts. The first describes the growth area and skill to be practiced in the activity. The second describes how we will know that this growth is happening by telling us what we should see or hear. For example, a skill objective for a cutting activity might be written as follows: In this activity the children will develop physically as they coordinate eye, hand, and finger movements while using a scissors. I will know that this is happening when I see the children freely cutting shapes out of the paper. The first part of this objective focuses our attention on the behaviors we need to facilitate so that the child will be successful. The second part of the objective provides a way for us to immediately assess the child's progress. The following sample objectives show how objectives relate to the growth areas discussed in chapter 1.

Sample Objectives and Related Growth Areas

1. In this activity, the children will develop *emotionally* by discovering positive ways to express emotions through art. I will know that this is happening when I hear the children tell me what feelings were expressed in their paintings.

2. In this activity, the child will develop *cognitively* by recognizing cause and effect. I will know that this is happening when the children can explain how they mixed one of their colors.

3. In this activity, the child will develop *linguistically* by learning to match words and objects. I will know that this is happening when I see the child point to the correct shape in the artwork when I say the shape's name.

WHERE? SETUP

One way to foster children's disposition to create art is through how the environment is organized.

Environment

The environment is everything that surrounds children when they create art. It is where the child works and learns. It is the room and any other space used for art—hallways, play areas, and the outdoors. It is how orderly the supplies are and how appropriately sized the furniture is. It is the arrangement of the work space and the other children in it. How this environment is planned and used will determine how much the child can concentrate on learning about and creating art.

Teachers need to consider where the children will be working. How should the furniture be arranged? Where should the supplies be located? What changes will have to be made so that this activity will run smoothly?

Art should encompass the environment in a variety of ways, but the core of the early childhood art program is the provision of play centers where children can choose to explore art materials fairly independently. One art center is not enough. There should be art centers of various kinds, ranging from a collage center with trays of beautiful papers and objects to a puppet-making area. Each should be located in its own special area of the room. Creating an environment in which art is infused is the focus of chapter 9.

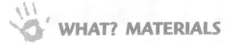

WHAT? MATERIALS

The materials and preparation required for an activity often influence whether teachers decide to offer the activity. It is important to list the supplies needed for each activity. This will quickly indicate which items are on hand and what has to be found or bought. It is often possible, with a little creativity, to make substitutions, but the key to success is to keep the materials basic and safe. The more the children can handle the supplies on their own, without constant supervision, the more they will grow artistically.

Beware of activities that have a long list of required materials, and ones that involve a great deal of preparation, such as cutting certain sizes, sorting objects, or gluing pieces together. None of this is necessary for a great art activity and may, in fact, reflect an overly directed one.

In the long run, the most essential consideration is the creative possibilities inherent in the materials and tools. Some materials allow more exploration than others. For example, the soft flexibility of play dough has made it one of the most popular modeling materials for young children. Precut bear shapes, on the other hand, have only a few possible ways to be used by children.

Use the following materials checklist for judging the materials used in an activity.

Materials Checklist

This material

- allows children to explore independently.
- can be used many times and in many ways by the children.
- is pleasant and easy to use.
- is safe for the children who will use it.
- does not require excessive preparation or cleanup.

HOW? TEACHING PROCEDURE

Delivery

How art activities are offered to young children is as important as which ones are being presented. Teachers need to be aware of how their teaching style, their method of interacting with children, and what they say all affect how much children will learn and grow.

Art activities should be carefully selected in order to foster the most encompassing growth. Childhood passes quickly. Art activities, as engrossing as they are, will only occupy a small part of the total day of an active young child, and it is best not to waste time on activities that do not help the child learn and grow.

Once an activity is selected it is necessary to plan how to present it. First it is necessary to introduce the materials and procedures to the children.

Activity Warm-Up

The warm-up should be designed to get the children interested and at the same time let them know where and how to use the materials. The type of warm-up will depend on the age of the children and their previous experiences.

The real object. For young children who are only just beginning to think symbolically, warm-ups should always include a carefully selected real object and related questions that draw them into the activity. Finding a real object takes extra time, but it is worth it. Presenting something that draws children's attention makes the difference between an ordinary experience and a wonderful one.

A real object should be something that the children can see, touch, and possibly use. In some cases, a new art material or tool can be the real object. For example, a teacher might show the children a large paintbrush at circle time and say:

> **Here is a new brush to try when you go to the easel today. What kind of line do you think it will make?**

In other cases, the real object may be a nature object or a toy.

> **Look at these beautiful shells I found on the beach. What shapes do you see? What colors are they? I am putting these in the drawing center today. Maybe you will want to explore different ways to draw them.**

Although a book may be a part of a warm-up, it should still be accompanied by a real object. Just imagine the difference in the children's interest and artwork between these two examples. In the first, a teacher reads a book about ladybugs and then suggests that the children make ladybug pictures at the drawing center. In the second, a teacher reads a book about ladybugs and then displays a jar of live ladybugs. After the children observe using hand lenses and share what they see, the ladybugs are placed in the drawing center.

In the first warm-up, the children just have the memory of the pictures in the book when they go to the drawing center. Only the second warm-up draws children into the activity and sustains it as they go to the center and reexperience the ladybugs.

Guided discovery. Guided discovery is a form of warm-up that is an ideal way to introduce children to a new material, technique, or center. The purpose is to develop interest and excitement in the children while at the same time establishing guidelines for use. There are three parts to guided discovery.

The unveiling. Wrap a small item related to the activity in gift wrap, or put larger ones in an interesting basket, box, or bag. Centers can be covered with a cloth or blocked with a banner or screen. Ask children to guess what the object is, or what the center might contain. Slowly give clues or unwrap it.

The exploration. Show the object or parts of the center. Ask questions about how it might be used. Focus on what would be careful, safe ways to handle the materials or to behave in the center.

Establish rules. At the end, summarize the children's positive suggestions into easy-to-understand words or pictures, and make a sign to post near the material or in the center. When behavior is inappropriate, refer to the sign as needed.

What to Do

This is a description of what the teacher and children will be doing.

What to Say

Teachers need to consider carefully the kinds of questions to ask, vocabulary to use, and responses to give to the young artists at work. It is through this interaction that knowledge, skills, dispositions, and feelings are acquired.

The Transition Out of the Activity

At the end of the activity, provide the children with closure. This can be a statement that summarizes what the children have been doing, or a question that makes them reflect on their learning. There should then be a procedure for how the child will put away the supplies and finished work. This should be followed by a smooth transition to the next activity.

If the children do not know what to do next, use their interests to draw attention to another area. An example of a closing statement might be: "You had a grand time drawing all those lines! Put your drawing in your cubby, and then maybe you would like to play with the line puzzle on the game table."

WHAT ARE THE TEACHER'S PERSONAL OBJECTIVES?

In every plan, teachers need to establish their own goals for self-improvement. The teacher can put a box of crayons on a table and let the children draw. It happens every day! But a truly inspiring teacher can take a simple activity and, through thoughtful actions and words, increase the children's artistic growth multifold.

Educators need to aim high. At the same time, there is so much to evaluate and do when surrounded by active young children that few activities are perfectly delivered. Choose one area to concentrate on improving during each activity. It could be how to respond to the children's art, the way to ask questions, or how well the supplies are arranged. Teachers need to study the way children respond to their behavior or classroom setup. They are the best indicators of success.

What Has the Teacher Learned?

After presenting an activity to a group of young children, take a moment for quiet reflection. Assess whether or not the activity went the way it was planned. Try to isolate the particular factors that made the activity successful or unsuccessful.

- Were the materials properly presented?
- Did the children become excited about the activity?
- What made the children visibly satisfied?
- Was there a terrible mess to clean up?
- Ask what could be improved or changed to make the activity more appropriate for the children.
- Record these observations on the activity plan. These brief notes will help tremendously the next time a similar activity is planned.

 WRITING AN ACTIVITY PLAN

Figure 2–1 provides an activity plan format that summarizes the above information. This or a similar form can be used whenever a new activity is being considered. The outline provides all of the basic information needed to create successful activities. See figure 2–2 for a sample activity plan.

ACTIVITY PLAN FORMAT

ACTIVITY:

Who?	Group composition age(s): Group size:
When?	Time frame:
Why?	Objectives: In this activity the child will develop . . .
Where?	Setup:
What?	Materials:
How?	Procedure: Warm-up: What to do: What to say: Transition out:

Personal objective:

What I have learned:

FIGURE 2–1 Activity plan format

SAMPLE ACTIVITY PLAN: A Painting Exploration

Who?   **Group composition age(s):** Three- and four-year-olds
            Group size: 2 or 3 at a time

When?   **Time frame:** 3-hour session

Why?   **Objectives:**

In this activity children will develop . . .

1. Emotionally, by using self-regulating skills. I will know that this is happening when I see them waiting patiently for their turn at the center.
2. Socially, by learning how to get along with peers. I will know that this is happening when I see them talking kindly to each other.
3. Physically, by exercising hand-eye coordination. I will know that this is happening when I see them filling scoops, mixing paint with a spoon, and using different paintbrushes.
4. Cognitively, by observing and describing cause and effect. I will know this is happening when I hear them making predictions about what will happen to the texture of the paint and then describing the result.

Where?   **Setup:**
Warm-up on rug. Painting at easel, table, or paint center.

What?   **Materials:**
Containers of tempera paint in a variety of colors
Labeled containers of different materials to add to paint: sand, salt, soap flakes
Small scoops, brushes, and paper at the easel or on newspaper-covered table

How?   **Procedure:**

Warm-up:
Large group: (on rug) Pass around a piece of sandpaper, then a piece of fake fur. Ask children to describe how it feels. Play "Texture Search" game: name a texture; each child has to find something with that texture and touch it. Have children take turns naming textures they find.

What to do:
1. Ask: "What is the texture of paint?"
   "How could we change the texture of paint?"
   "What do you think would happen if you added these things to the paint?"
   "Would you like to add one and see what happens?"
2. Demonstrate how to add one of the materials to the paint. Tell children that they can add any of the materials to their paint when they come to the painting place.
3. As children come to paint, supervise them as they add materials to the color of their choice, and then use it in their paintings.

What to say:
Descriptive: "You are using the large brush."   "You used the textured paint to _____ ."
Questioning: "Which paint did you like using better?"   "Which paint was hard to spread?"

Transition out:
Say: "You had fun painting with the different textured paint. You can add a different texture the next time you paint. Let's put your painting over here to dry. What would you like to do now? I see your friend Ann is having fun with the blocks."

Personal objective:

   I will work on improving my "wait" time. I need to allow the children more time to work before I start talking to them. I will watch for the child to pause before interacting, so that I do not interrupt the creative process.

What I have learned:

   I need to find a better place to set up the paint and texture additions so the children can independently add textures whenever they wish.

FIGURE 2–2 Sample activity plan

Studio Page 5

SELF-EXPLORATION: WHAT SHOULD I DRAW?

Use crayons to draw the first thing that comes into your head. When you are finished, answer these questions.

What was the first color you chose?

_____

Where did you place the first thing on your paper?

_____

Did your ideas change as you worked?

_____

How did you know when you were finished?

_____

What artistic decisions did you make?

_____

How is your art like a child's? How is it different?

_____

SELF-EXPLORATION: MY FIRST ART EXPERIENCE

What is the earliest art experience you remember?

_____

_____

_____

What did you do?

_____

_____

_____

Where and when was it?

_____

_____

_____

What materials did you use?

_____

_____

_____

Who was there with you? What did they say?

_____

_____

_____

Did anyone comment on your work?

_____

_____

_____

What emotions did you feel?

_____

_____

_____

SELF-EXPLORATION: MY PERSONAL TIME LINE OF ART

Fill in all of the art experiences you remember, at about the age you experienced them. You can include such things as art courses you have taken, museums you have visited, a specific artwork you made, an art book you have read, an art movie you have seen, a comment made by a teacher or family member about your art, and so forth.

AGE	EXPERIENCE
Birth to age 5	
5 to 10 years	
10 to 15 years	
15 to 20 years	
20 to 30 years	
30 to 40 years	
40 to 50 years	
50+ years	

What Does My Time Line Tell Me?

Study your time line and ask yourself these questions:

1. Do you remember more experiences from your early childhood or more from your later years?

    _____

2. How many are happy memories?

    _____

3. Do any memories make you feel uncomfortable?

    _____

4. Do you remember any of the adults who participated in creating these memories?

    _____

5. How will these memories affect the way you will approach young children and their art?

    _____

Studio Page 8

SELF-EXPLORATION: DEFINING ART

Close your eyes and picture a piece of artwork you have seen in a book, museum, home, or store. Look at it carefully.

What colors and shapes do you see?

_____

_____

_____

What art media is it made with?

_____

_____

_____

Where did you see it?

_____

_____

_____

Who made it?

_____

_____

_____

Why is it a piece of art?

_____

_____

_____

Where did you acquire the ability to define art?

_____

_____

_____

For additional information on teaching art to young children, visit our Web site at http://www.earlychilded.delmar.com

Artistic Development

❝ The teacher who knows the difference between adult and child world views is likely to communicate and educate more successfully than one not so prepared. ❞

—David Elkind (1974, p. 134)

Questions Addressed in This Chapter:

- ♡ When does art begin?
- ♡ How can children's artistic development be viewed?
- ♡ What patterns can be found in children's art?
- ♡ What social and cultural factors affect artistic development?
- ♡ What do child art development models tell educators?

Young Artists at Work

Andy picks up a crayon and grasps it tightly in his fist. He slowly approaches the large white paper before him. Arm held stiffly, he rubs the crayon on the paper. Lifting the crayon, he looks at the smudge he has left behind. With his other hand he touches it, rubs it, and looks at his fingers. The mark is still there. He bends over and sniffs it with his nose. Cautiously, Andy looks up. Is this all right? Can he do this? But no one is stopping him. He returns to the paper. With broad strokes, Andy makes his first true marks on the world. Broad sweeps of color up and down, back and forth. Again and again, on paper after paper, at the beginning of his second year of life, he draws . . .

WHEN DOES ART BEGIN?

Just as the first sounds that babies make are the same around the world, children's first scribbles are also the same.

—*Elaine Pear Cohen & Ruth Straus Gainer*
(1995, p. 28)

It begins with the line—a line that reflects the child's physical control over the body. The one-year-old is at the beginning of a long and complex process, which in the eighth year of life will end with a mastery of line that is remarkably expressive and controlled. Toddlers do not know that this is where their explorations with line will lead; they only know the moment—this pleasurable and exciting moment in which they have used a tool and produced a result.

All of us were once infants, unable to move on our own. Step by step, we learned to crawl and then to walk. At first we walked unsteadily, clasping a guiding hand. Soon we could take baby steps on our own, and in no time at all we could run, and run we did!

In the same way, each child grows as an artist. Although no newborn is an artist at birth, inside every infant is the potential to grow into an artist. When the time is right, the children start their artistic journey, tentatively making small marks upon the world. These marks enlarge and change from wavy scribbles to enclosed shapes to symbols that encompass the child's experience. This pattern of artistic growth repeats itself in every young child, everywhere in the world. Each child goes through visible stages of artistic growth, reflecting the increasing muscular control and rapid cognitive growth of the very young. This development does not proceed alone but accompanies simultaneous growth in language and reasoning. By viewing artistic growth as a developmental process, one that every human being goes through, guiding adults will be better able to respond to the artistic growth of the young children in their care.

HOW CAN CHILDREN'S ARTISTIC DEVELOPMENT BE VIEWED?

Drawing is only one of many art forms, and yet it plays an overwhelmingly important role in the definition and analysis of children's art. Why is drawing more important than painting, modeling, construction, and designing? An artist would say drawing is the manipulation of lines to create a visual effect. At its simplest, drawing can be done with a finger in the dust or on a frosty windowpane. The tools used for drawing are little more than the extensions of the finger—a stick in the dirt, a pencil, a pen. Drawing is where the toddler's art exploration begins, and where the adult achieves mastery and recognition as an artist. In our culture, which shows less respect than it should for other art forms and artistic abilities, we fully expect that self-proclaimed "artists" can draw well.

But drawing is more than an art form. It is also intimately linked to linguistic growth. The earliest written languages were pictographs. Children's drawings are the beginning of their writing. Artistic growth also reflects the cognitive growth that is necessary for them to become writers. When we place a drawing tool in a child's hand, we are also handing her or him a writing tool. Drawing is important, because it is a tool with which to think and communicate. As the United States Department of Education states, "Children who are encouraged to draw and 'scribble' stories at an early age will later learn to compose more easily, more effectively, and with greater confidence than children who do not have this encouragement" (1986, p. 14).

Young children need many opportunities to draw. They need to hold in their hands a tool that marks and to pull and push it over a variety of surfaces. At first their movements will be aimless, and they will use paper by the mile. But in spurts and sputters, children begin to repeat and vary the marks they have made previously. During this period, children become comfortable with the drawing tools and refine their control over the direction and type of line they can produce. Physical growth of their bodies is reflected in how they hold the drawing tool and in the direction of the lines they make.

The Role of Physical Development in Children's Art

Much of the artwork produced by children is determined by their physical development. This is particularly true in the early years.

One-year-olds. Children develop from the head down and from the center of the body out (Cherry, Godwin, & Staples, 1989, p. 53). At age one, arm movement is undifferentiated. Children grasp the crayon or pencil tightly in their fists and make whole arm movements, up and down, back and forth. They can also lift and drop their arms, stabbing and punching the paper with much gusto and verbal expression. This period has been called by some researchers that of the "random or uncontrolled scribble" (Lowenfeld & Brittain, 1987). Watching the child at work, it does seem at times that the scribble has a mind of its own, careening off the edges of the paper and onto the table or floor. But there is also thoughtful deliberation. Watch the child at work, pausing in midline, expressing delight. The arm and hand may not yet be under control, but a mind is growing there!

Two-year-olds. Between the ages of one and two, toddlers begin to have control over their elbows. This allows them to create new marks. Sweeping arcs are created as children move the lower arm independently. Lines now have curved edges. They loop and swirl across the paper exuberantly. Children may also become conscious of the act of drawing as separate from writing, verbalizing their desire to draw and curiously watching others draw and write.

Three-year-olds. With continued physical maturation, children develop control over their wrists. Now they can control the line that issues from their drawing tools. They can start and stop at will and lift the crayon and place it down again close to where they want it. Scribbles begin to be joined into lopsided geometric figures. Control over the fingers is also slowly developing. The tight fist may be replaced by a looser grip, although some children may still have no particular hand preference.

As children persist in repeating motions and creating the resulting lines and figures, they develop skill and control, but something else is also happening. One day the child will look at the lines, the mess of scribbles, and say, "Look at my doggie," or "I made a bear." And although ten minutes later the child may give a totally different name to the scribble, the lines,

"Mommy yelling." Marker—*Laurel, age 4*

Art begins with a scribble.

still unrecognizable to us, have developed meaning for that child. This development is tremendously exciting. We can "see" and "hear" the child thinking.

Now is when families become enthusiastic. They study the drawings, trying to find what their child sees in the lines. They label the pictures and hang them. Their child is an artist! Their child is communicating! But they are also bewildered, because it will be many months yet before they can find something recognizable in their child's work.

WHAT PATTERNS CAN BE FOUND IN CHILDREN'S ART?

If the observations I have made lead to increased study of children's art, I shall be delighted.

—*Rhoda Kellogg (1969, p. 12)*

In the past 100 years, children's art has attracted the attention of many researchers. Some have collected samples of children's art and looked for patterns (Kel-

logg, 1969, 1979; Schaefer-Simmern, 1950). Others have tried to use it to measure intelligence (Cox, 1993; Goodenough, 1926; Harris & Goodenough, 1963). Many have used it to understand how children think (Gardner, 1991; Golomb, 1981; Winner, 1989). Over the years, several models of artistic development have been created. Each provides important perspectives on the teaching of art to young children.

Stage-by-Age Models

The stage-by-age model is based on the belief that children's art develops in a predictable series of steps that naturally leads to realism. The stages represent the sequence of growth that all children move through and are based on observations of children's drawings.

The work of Rhoda Kellogg. From the 1950s to the 1970s, Rhoda Kellogg (1969, 1979) collected over 1 million drawings done by children from the United States and other countries. These drawings provided the basis for her in-depth analysis of the patterns and forms found in children's art. Today these drawings can be found in the Rhoda Kellogg Child Art Collection in San Francisco. They represent a commitment to the collection of child art unparalleled in early art education research. Kellogg was one of the first to recognize that the scribbles of young children were an important part of the child's development, and that the marks made by young children the world over were more the same than they were different. Based on her collection, Kellogg identified several patterns that were similar in all of the drawings she analyzed.

Basic Scribbles. She isolated 20 kinds of markings (*Basic Scribbles*) made by children age two and under. The Basic Scribbles consisted of all of the lines the children make, with or without the use of their eyes, whether using a crayon on paper, fingerpaint, or scratching the lines in the dirt. She saw these strokes as representative of the neural and muscular system of the child and forerunners of all of the strokes needed to make art and language symbols. Her descriptions of these Basic Scribbles were offered as a way to describe the art of the very young child.

Placement patterns. In addition, she looked at how children under age two placed these scribbles on their paper. She felt that the placement patterns were the

Scribbles. Marker—*various children, ages 1–3*

earliest evidence that the child was guiding the initial formation of shapes. She hypothesized that children react to the scribbles they make by seeing shapes in the drawing itself rather than trying to represent the shapes seen in the world around them, and that visual and motor pleasure was a motivating factor in causing children to scribble.

Diagrams and combines. Between ages two and three, Kellogg found that children began to draw shapes that they then combined into groups. She termed these groups *Aggregates*. At this stage, children move from unplanned scribbling to being able to remember and repeat shapes they have drawn previously. These shapes become the basis of all the symbols later found in children's drawings.

Mandalas, suns, and people. Kellogg was most fascinated by the symbols that often emerged between ages three and four. She noted that the symbols seemed to follow a developmental sequence, and she felt that the mandalas and suns provided the stimuli for the child's first drawings of a person.

Importance of Kellogg's work. At the time Kellogg did her research, most adults considered child art a poor attempt to represent objects and persons in the child's environment, therefore, worthless or in need of correction. Children were discouraged or even forbidden from scribbling and were encouraged to copy adult models. Kellogg felt that drawing was an ex-

pression of the growth of the child's physical and mental processes, that it was the process of drawing that was important. She argued that children need plenty of time for free drawing and scribbling in order to develop the symbols that will later become the basis of all drawing and writing.

The work of Lowenfeld and Brittain. Lowenfeld and Brittain (1987) built on Kellogg's work with young children and expanded the developmental sequence through adolescence. They postulated distinct types of child art for each stage and warned against outside interference in the child's process of self-expression, such as the teaching of specific ways to draw. Instead, children moved through these stages naturally as they matured, and it was the teacher's role to provide the time and materials for children to explore on their own (table 3–1 on p. 66).

The importance of Kellogg, Lowenfeld, and Brittain. The work of these thoughtful educators has had a profound influence on how educators approach the art of young children. The stages they developed are basically descriptive generalizations of the kinds of drawings children make at different ages. Scribbling, shape making, and the development of

Mandalas, suns, and people. Marker—*various children, ages 2–5*

TABLE 3–1	Developmental Stages of Child Art, Based on Kellogg (1969) and Lowenfeld and Brittain (1987)		

AGE	STAGE		CHARACTERISTICS
2–4 years	SCRIBBLING		
A. 1–2½ years	Random Scribbling		Random lines are made using the whole arm Tool held with whole hand Lines may extend beyond paper
B. 2½–3 years	Controlled Scribbling		Begins to use wrist motions Stays on paper, makes smaller marks Controls where lines are placed
C. 3–4½ years	Named Scribbles		Holds tool with fingers Can make many different lines and shapes Names scribbles, but often changes name
4½–7 years	PRESCHEMATIC		Develops a set of symbols to represent concepts May not resemble or be in proportion to real objects Learns pictures communicate to others Begins to value his or her product
7–9 years	SCHEMATIC		Drawing shows concept, not real images Baseline and skyline appear X-ray drawings appear
9–12 years	DAWNING REALISM		Objects are drawn smaller, with more detail Less concern for placement of objects Realizes symbols do not represent real images
12–14 years	PSEUDO-NATURALISTIC/ REALISTIC DRAWING		Detailed figures, cartoon images Shading, proportion, and perspective appear, more or less successfully Spontaneous drawing ends, except for those who go on in art
14+ years	ARTISTIC DECISION: ADOLESCENT ART		Some pursue naturalistic drawing Many copy or imitate various styles before developing their own

graphic symbols were found to be important parts of the normal development of children. Child art also came to be seen as an important facet for understanding how children think.

Gardner's Wave Model

Howard Gardner has led the way in investigations into the cognitive aspects of early childhood art. In general, Gardner (1991) supports Piaget's idea (1959) that sensory learning dominates the first 18 months of life, and that this is followed by a symbolic period during the preschool years, in which children master the symbolic forms of language, number, and art. According to his theory of multiple intelligences, Gardner proposes that cognitive development takes place in waves rather than stages, with burgeoning knowledge developing within a specific intelligence and then overflowing into other intelligences.

The first wave. Gardner believes that sometime between the ages of 18 months and two years, chil-

dren become capable of using symbols to communicate their knowledge that events consist of objects and actions. Although language oriented, this symbolic realization "spills" into other intellectual domains. At this point, if asked to draw a truck, the child scribbles with the marker while making truck sounds.

The second wave. At about age three, a second wave called *topographical mapping* occurs. Now the child's graphic symbols can express the spatial relationships of real objects, such as showing two adjoining circles and identifying the top one as a head.

The third wave. Around age four, the child begins to utilize numerical relationships (*digital mapping*). For example, children may draw four human figures to represent four people in their family, or count the eyes on the drawing of a face.

The fourth wave. The most educationally important event occurs sometime during the fifth, sixth, or seventh year, when children begin to invent their own notational systems. Children now draw pictures using

---

TABLE 3–2	Art and Cognitive Growth, Based on Gardner (1991)

AGE	COGNITIVE UNDERSTANDING		ART PRODUCED
Causal Relationships			
1½–2 years	Discovers relationship between object and event		Draws a cat by scribbling and meowing at same time
Spatial Relationships			
2–3 years	Discovers spatial relationships		Draws cat by putting a circle (head) beside another circle (body)
Numerical Relationships			
3–5 years	Represents numerical concepts		Draws cat with four legs, two ears, and one tail
Notational Relationships			
5–7 years	Invents or learns meaningful symbols of the culture		Draws cat with tail, whiskers, and pointy ears and labels it "CAT"

graphic symbols of their own invention, for such purposes as to remember experiences or to "list" belongings. Gardner, although he points out the influence of seeing adults using notational systems, feels that there is an innate human propensity to create such systems.

Table 3–2 summarizes the relationship between cognitive growth and how it is expressed in children's art.

Symbolic Communication Model

Incorporating these ideas, Kindler and Darras (1994; Kindler, 1997) have proposed a model of artistic development that presents artistic production as a twofold process. One part of the process is comprised of biologically propelled physical and cognitive growth. The other is the social and cultural learning, including the formal teaching, to which the child is exposed. In this model, unlike Lowenfeld's model of linear growth, individuals do not lose their earlier approaches to art pro-

duction but incorporate them or return to them as needed throughout their lives.

Based on the work of these researchers, table 3–3 indicates the possible range of art behaviors that a child might exhibit. Rather than specific ages or levels, artistic production is organized by modes of behavior. During his or her lifetime, an individual may function in one or more of these modes in varying contexts. For example, upon meeting an unfamiliar medium, most children and adults will operate in the exploratory mode, making random movements as they try to assess the nature of the material. Once they have learned to control a material, they will attempt detailed, graphic, and symbolic expression.

This model shows how a child's art is more than the picture on the paper. It is also what the child says and how the child moves. Art production is a multimedia blend of graphic, verbal, and kinesthetic communication that reveals the child's thought processes.

TABLE 3–3	Multimedia Modes of Artistic Production, Based on Kindler and Darras (1994)				
CHILD	**MODE 1**	**MODE 2**	**MODE 3**	**MODE 4**	**MODE 5**
Says:	Random sounds	Words	Matches sound & action	Naming	Story
Draws:	Random marks	Shapes	Action symbols	Object symbols	Pictures in cultural style (understandable without verbalization)
Moves:	Random movements	Conscious control	Self-imitation	Repetition	Imitation of cultural style
ADULT	Media exploration	Simple doodles	Complex doodles	Shorthand symbols (e.g., stick figures)	Detailed, recognizable symbols in style of culture

WHAT SOCIAL AND CULTURAL FACTORS AFFECT ARTISTIC DEVELOPMENT?

An examination of social and cultural context in which young artists function reveals that there are many important ways in which guiding adults and other environmental factors influence young artists—some to good effect and some detrimentally.

Defining Art Materials

Adults determine which art materials are acceptable for children to use. They set the limits on what is creative art and what is not. Smearing fingerpaint on paper is encouraged; smearing cereal on the wall is not. Are egg cartons an art material? Should we use food products in art? The cultural definition of what is and is not an art material will be transmitted to the child. Because of cultural traditions, some art media have higher value than others. For example, an oil painting may be considered fine art, whereas weaving is considered a craft, even though both involve the manipulation of art elements in highly skillful and creative ways.

Experience with Art Media

Adults also determine how much experience children have with a material. The more opportunity to use art media and tools that children have, the more comfortable and adept they will become with those materials. All individuals, regardless of their age, need to spend time exploring a medium before they can use it expressively. Because in our culture young children usually have many opportunities to draw, they usually show their highest level of symbol development in their drawings. The same child may produce much less "competent"-looking artwork if asked to use an unfamiliar material. Children will quickly revert to scribbles in their first finger painting or watercolor. Repetition and practice are the keys to improving skills at any level. Even adults with excellent fine-motor control find themselves scribbling the first time they try to draw freehand with a mouse on a computer.

Availability of Art Materials

Children are influenced by what is going on around them. They are more likely to be interested in creating art if other people around them are as well, and if art materials are visible and easily obtained. Young children may make drawings in mud and soap foam on

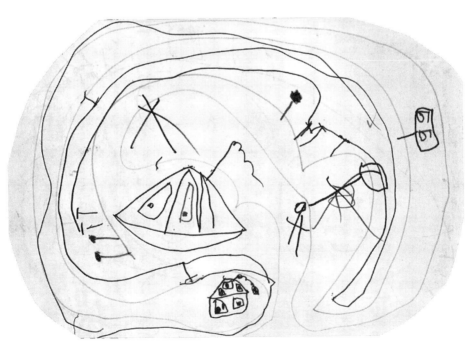

"Route 79 going from my house to town." Marker—*Matthew, age 5*

69

their own, but they are not going to choose formal drawing, painting, or modeling activities unless guiding adults have offered such opportunities to them.

The Environment

Young children may not see the world in the same way adults do, but they are influenced by the pictures they see, the kinds of objects that surround them, and the artistic reactions of their guiding adults to these things. Children who grow up in places where most houses have flat roofs draw house symbols that have flat roofs. Children who have seen that people come in many colors, whether in their community or in pictures, and are comfortable with that fact, are more likely to include skin color in their art. Exposure to a wide variety of interesting objects challenges the child to invent new symbols or refine existing ones. For example, after viewing a live bird, children may add more details to their symbols for a bird.

Children who have seen examples of a variety of art forms and are taught to value them are more likely to incorporate elements from these examples into their own art. Dennis (1966) found that children raised in environments with plentiful visual imagery, surrounded by many drawings of people, had higher scores on the Goodenough Draw-A-Man Test. McFee and Degge (1981, p. 334) cite studies that indicate that children from cultures with stylistic drawings will learn to draw in that style.

Emotional State

How a child feels will greatly influence the artwork the child produces. A child who has just experienced a traumatic event may use art as a way to express deep feelings. Tornados, earthquakes, accidents, and death often elicit scribbling, stabbing at the paper, and splashing of paint from people of all ages. Art can serve as an emotional release. As guiding adults, we need to bring sensitivity to the artistic interaction. With understanding and encouragement, we can allow the child to work through these deep feelings.

Teachers also need to understand how their own actions and those of a child's family can influence how a child feels about art. Children who are pressured to make their art match an adult "ideal" or are frustrated by an art material that is beyond their physical ability to control it may develop feelings of failure. Such feelings may lead to a reluctance to participate in future art activities. Similarly, children who feel that their artwork is rejected or unacceptable also retreat from art activities. That is why it is equally important that teachers show their acceptance of the child's work and teach families how to encourage their young artists.

Seeing the Whole Child and the Child's Art

All of these factors interact with the physical and cognitive development of the child in order to produce the resulting art (see figure 3–1 on p. 72). Each child is a unique combination of these factors. We can never assume that because a child is a certain age, or is offered the same materials as another, we can predict exactly what that child will do with them. This is what makes teaching art to children so exciting. Every day is full of fresh, new graphic images for the teachers to enjoy.

Within an age group, children will be found who are working in all of the modes. (1) Exploration. Marker—*Andrew, age 3;* (2) Initial shapes. Crayon—*Kelsey, age 3;* (3) Action symbol. Marker—*Ross, age 3;* (4) Story symbols. Pencil—*Michelle, age 3.*

WHAT DO CHILD ART DEVELOPMENT MODELS TELL EDUCATORS?

One has to respect the time of maturation, of development, of the tools of doing and understanding, of the full, slow, extravagant, lucid and ever-changing emergence of children's capacities; it is a measure of cultural and biological wisdom.

—Loris Malaguzzi (in Edwards, Gandini, & Forman, 1993, p. 74)

The growth of young children from exploring scribblers to symbol-creating artists is an amazing journey. Guiding adults need to provide art experiences that will enhance the child's journey. These models of children's artistic development have been provided to help teachers better understand the art behavior of young children so that they can offer the most appropriate art experiences.

Four Ground Rules

From these models, four ground rules emerge for teaching art to young children.

Set realistic expectations. These models enhance understanding of why children's art looks the way it does. Among young children, expect to see scribbling, named scribbles, and simple and complex graphic symbols. Within an age cohort, the type of art produced by children may vary widely, depending on the mode of drawing being demonstrated, the children's

"A flower." These 12 pictures, done by the same five-year-old, show how skill and familiarity with media affect how the resulting artwork looks. The pencil and crayon drawings are far more controlled than the cut paper, yarn and collage pictures—Laurel, age 5.

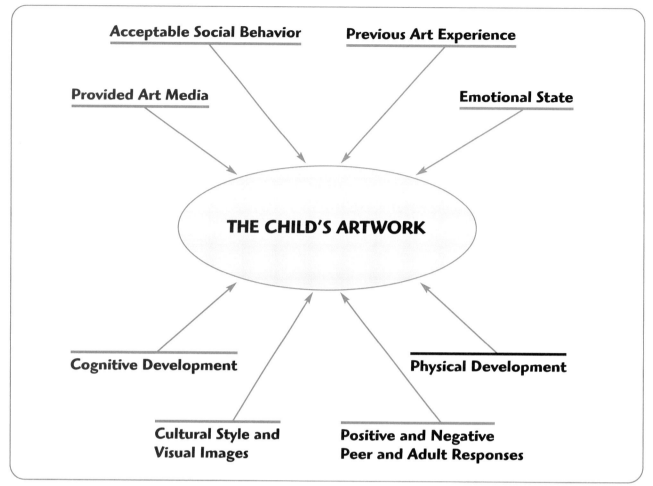

FIGURE 3–1 Influences on children's art

cultural and visual perception experiences, and their familiarity with the media. For example, it is not at all unusual in a group of four-year-olds to have some children scribbling, some using a limited number of symbolic forms, and some drawing complex graphic symbols. We must accept the scribbler's approach to drawing as being just as valid and important as the more adult-pleasing graphic symbols and select open-ended activities that allow all participants to be successful.

Value child art as a developmental process, not as a product. Teachers must find ways of recording and presenting not just the final static product, but the whole process of creation. Anyone who has watched and participated in a child's art activity knows that the final product is almost a letdown. Artwork needs to be accompanied by what the children said, the stages the works passed through, and how the children moved as they worked. This is a challenge for a busy, overworked teacher, but it is not impos-

sible. (See chapter 12 for suggested ways to do this.)

Understand better what the child is thinking. Knowing the physical, social, cultural, and emotional factors affecting a child helps us better understand and accept the young artist's behavior and resulting artwork. For example, a child banging and stabbing the paper with a crayon is probably not being aggressive but more likely exploring the possibilities of the crayon. We can also view the art process as another way to assess what children know. A child carefully counting out loud each finger as it is drawn is demonstrating an understanding of numerical relationships.

Select activities that are suitable for particular children. The art activities that teachers select must be open-ended ones. There must always be room for exploration as well as for symbol production.

Types of Art Activities

Based on these models, there are three kinds of art activities that are most suitable for children under age eight.

Exploration activities. The base of all production, the first phase of development is the exploration of the medium. *Exploration,* therefore, must be the mainstay of early childhood art programs. Children need a multitude of opportunities to play with art media—to "scribble." Children who are scribbling, no matter what their age, need open-ended activities that allow them to learn about the medium. No one can be expected to produce wonderful artwork with an unfamiliar material.

The first phase of artistic development never disappears. Even accomplished artists spend time exploring a new material before using it in a piece of artwork. Children need to know that it is okay to explore, and that these explorations will not be judged.

Practice activities. Exploration must be followed by *practice.* Children need to be given many opportunities to use the same material over and over in order to develop control. The common practice of putting out a new art material or "project" each week does not help children develop their ability to use art materials to express their thoughts. Only after children are comfortable with an art medium, whether pencil, blocks, or paint, do they have the control needed to use the medium to express their thoughts.

Responsive activities. Once children are competent with an art medium, they need to be provided with thought-provoking experiences, visual stimulation, and multisensory happenings, followed by opportunities to use art in all of its multimedia dimensions. *Responsive* activities stretch children's thought processes as they try to represent what they know using graphic symbols of their own invention. Another name for responsive activities is *representation.*

Providing a Continuum of Art Activities

The Creating Art sections that follow each chapter present ways to guide children's experiences with the common media of early childhood art education. Each

Children need to know that their drawings are valued.

Creating Art section begins with an exploratory activity intended for children who have had little or no experience with that medium. Following this are suggestions for practice activities using the same or similar materials. When children are skillful and confident in their use of a material, they will begin on their own to use the medium to respond graphically to their experiences.

Responsive art activities can be encouraged by making sure that familiar art materials are readily available, following such events as visitors to the class, stories that are read or told, science experiments, exciting field trips, and all of the other daily experiences of a young child. Providing time to discuss the children's responsive art and recording their verbal descriptions will also encourage children to move from basic explorations to expressive, graphic responses.

It is important to remember, however, that this is not an orderly progression from simplest art production to most complex. Exploration is as important as graphic representation. Children will vary in their need to explore, practice, and respond. Some children will require longer periods of exploration. Others will move quickly from one mode of working to another. The same child may explore one day, create a detailed, responsive artwork the next, and return to media exploration the following day.

Regardless of the children's ages, always present a new medium as an exploration, and allow time for practice before presenting it as a responsive activity. For example, give children many opportunities to freely explore drawing with chalk before asking them to use chalk to record their reaction to a walk in the woods.

Remember that although the children's artwork is starting to contain somewhat recognizable images, teachers must not demand that children produce a particular image. Activities that require the children to produce turkeys or rabbits or Christmas trees set both teachers and children up for failure. The fact that most young children cannot successfully produce such items is what leads well-meaning teachers to provide patterns, coloring-book pictures, or precut shapes to "help" the children. But they do not help. Instead, they tell children that their symbols and explorations are unacceptable and not valued.

Development does not proceed at a regular pace. Teachers need to be sure that every art medium and activity they offer provides opportunities for each child to work in the way that is most appropriate for her or him at that particular time.

COLLECTING CHILDREN'S ART

Seeing a piece of art being created helps a teacher better understand how and why child art looks the way it does. Everyone who works with young children should keep a collection of children's artwork. Use these guidelines in making your own collection.

Collect work that

1. comes from a wide range of children at different ages.
2. represents different art media.
3. contains examples of what children are capable of doing in a variety of learning situations.
4. comes from the same child over a period of time.

Book

File

Portfolio

Organizing the collection

5. includes exploration, practice, responsive, and instructive activities done both individually and in group situations.
6. shows both typical and unusual approaches.

Respecting the Artist

If you would like a particular piece from a specific child, you must obtain the child's permission. You may not be able to get every piece that you would like, but remember that children are prolific artists; over time, you will be able to build up a wonderful collection. Some artwork, particularly drawings, can be successfully photocopied rather than keeping the child's original. The easiest artwork to obtain is that of your own children or that of other family members. After it is displayed, you can add it to your collection or create a separate portfolio that may become a treasured keepsake in later years.

Organizing the Collection

To be useful, the collection needs to be organized in an orderly way. Three useful storage systems are the portfolio, the oversized book, and an oversized file box. Make sure to label each work with the child's age and a description of how the work was done. Photographs of the child working can also make the collection more descriptive.

CONCLUSION: THE CHILD ARTIST

Once put down a line provokes thought.
—*Sylvia Fein (1993, p. 16)*

Child art development models provide educators with a more encompassing view of the child as an artist. Contemporary research and thought (Gardner, 1991; Kindler & Darras, 1994; Wolf & Perry, 1989) emphasize that artistic development is not a separate process but part of the total growth of the child. This development is a combination of the biological maturation patterns of the body and brain, mediated by social and cultural behavioral expectations and education.

Kinesthetic movement, language, and graphic images occur in unison as children create their own graphic symbol systems. Gardner visualizes this as a spilling over of symbol making from one intelligence to another. Kindler and Darras use the term *multimedia* to describe this simultaneous process, and this is the way early childhood educators must think about children's art. It is not the product that matters but the process the child went through to make it.

Drawing is not simply the creation of a static image but a "multimedia" event.

Art creation for the child is more than the simple manipulation of materials at an art table. It is a culminating moment of kinesthetically, vocally, and symbolically defined action that expresses the child's thoughts. Child art is not the static image on paper so carefully described by the early researchers and so often displayed on the refrigerator door. Nor is it the same as adult art, in which artists skillfully manipulate the symbolic images and accepted media of their culture. Rather, it is a multimedia, multifaceted growth process in which teachers, with all of their cultural and educational beliefs, participate along with the individual responses of the child. It is our challenge to create the environment, to select the activities and delivery system that nurtures this multimedia event.

FURTHER READING

These books will provide further insight into the artistic development of young children.

Cherry, C., Godwin, D., & Staples, J. (1989). *Is the left brain always right? A guide to whole child development*. Belmont, CA: David S. Lake.

This book details the physical and mental development of young children and suggests a wide variety of appropriate activities.

Fein, S. (1984). *Heidi's horse*. Pleasant Hill, CA: Exelrod Press.

This beautiful book presents the drawings of a young girl, from infancy through early adulthood, with descriptions that place the drawings in the context in which they were created.

Gardner, H. (1980). *Artful scribbles: The significance of children's drawings*. New York: Basic Books.

In this book, Gardner presents examples of child art and analyzes the nature of their creation.

Kellogg, R. (1969). *Analyzing children's art*. Palo Alto, CA: National Press Books.

This book presents Kellogg's descriptions of child art and is illustrated with hundreds of children's drawings.

Lowenfeld, V., & Brittain, W. L. (1987). *Creative and mental growth*. New York: Macmillan.

In this textbook for art teachers, Lowenfeld and Brittain present their philosophy and the developmental stages of child art production.

Creating Art: Drawing

"Elephants." Marker—*Joey, age 4*

THE DRAWING EXPERIENCE

Children vary greatly in maturity level and ability to concentrate on an activity. The appropriateness of an activity should be based on each child's day-to-day behavior rather than on chronological age. Drawing can be done by children of all ages, but in order for the experience to be meaningful, teachers need to set up the drawing activities to match the children's developmental levels.

How Children Grow through Drawing

In this and subsequent Creating Art sections, the descriptions of the growth areas addressed by the activity are followed by a parenthetical reference to Gardner's "intelligences," when such a connection is appropriate.

Children will develop

1. physically, by using the large and small muscles of the arm and hand to draw. (Bodily-Kinesthetic)
2. socially, by working alongside other children and sharing art materials. (Interpersonal)
3. emotionally, by learning to enjoy the act of drawing and the ability to control a part of their environment. (Intrapersonal)
4. visual perception skills, by exploring new ways to make marks and responding to the visual effects they have created. (Spatial)
5. language skills, by learning a drawing vocabulary and using sound and language in combination with graphic production. (Linguistic)
6. cognitively, by seeing that their motions can cause the effect of making visual lines. (Logical-Mathematical)
7. art awareness, by becoming familiar with the ways drawing and lines are used in books and in the artwork of others.

INTRODUCING DRAWING: AGES ONE AND UP

Toddlers need many opportunities to make their important marks. The introductory "Drawing for Toddlers" presented here would be appropriate for children from ages 18 months to three years who have had little experience with drawing materials, still put objects in their mouths with regularity, or have short concentration spans no matter what their age or experience.

The following activity describes how to introduce drawing for the very first time.

Group Composition

Work with one to three toddlers at a time. If there are more than that number, provide other activities that will allow the remaining children to play safely on their own, or have another adult help.

Setup

Provide a low table for the child or children to sit or stand at while working. They may also work on the floor. Surfaces should be easy to clean. There should be a place for the teacher to sit comfortably, as close to their level as possible.

Materials

Crayons. For introductory explorations, choose washable crayons in the thickest sizes. Crayons are durable and stand up well to the exuberant pushing, pulling, and pummeling of a toddler's first explorations.

Paper. Paper should be fairly large, at least 12 inches by 15 inches or larger. Large newsprint also works well, although it tears more easily. Whatever you choose, have a large supply on hand so the children can use as much as they like.

Warm-Up

For children this young, just putting out the drawing supplies may be enough to get their attention. If needed, personally invite a child to come over to explore: "Judy, would you like to draw with this red crayon?" If children seem interested, place the crayons in their hands, and show them the paper. It is not necessary to make every child draw. If children are not in-

 ## Safety Note

Handling Crayons Safely

Although crayons are a relatively safe art material, children must learn from the beginning that art materials never go in the mouth. For their own safety, be ready to gently move their hands away from their mouths if they attempt to taste the crayon. If children refuse to do more than put the crayon in their mouths, then distract them and move them away from the drawing activity to one that will allow them to use the sense of taste to explore.

terested, do not force them. They will draw when they are ready. Just keep providing the opportunity.

What to Do

At this stage do not be surprised if one child draws for only a few seconds and then wanders away, whereas another child makes 20 drawings. Some will draw without even looking at the paper. Others will put their faces right up to the paper or look at the back to see if the lines went right through. Children will react in their own unique ways to the drawing stimulus.

What to Say

Sit with the children while they are working; smile and point to the lines and marks they have created. It is not necessary to talk constantly while the children are working, but occasional statements or questions can increase the toddler's enjoyment and learning.

1. When speaking, be enthusiastic and descriptive:

    "Look at that red line!"
    "What a long line!"
    "What kind of line will you draw next?"
    "That's an up and down line!"

2. Use drawing as an opportunity to develop the child's vocabulary. Words to use include: draw, drawing, write, writing, line, lines, long, short, thick, thin, dark, light, colorful, the color names, crayons, dots, marks, paper.

3. Toddlers love songs and rhymes. Make up little poems, using the descriptive words, to go along with their art explorations, and sing them to traditional tunes. (Consult Music Box for a possible idea.)

4. To build vocabulary, look for examples of lines in the environment, such as cracks in the pavement or veins on a leaf. Use the same terms to describe their drawings.

Transition Out

At this young age the children will spend only a relatively short time, by adult standards, drawing. When the child loses interest, let him or her wander off to the next activity. If the drawing activity must end, do so by providing an attractive alternative, such as "Let's read a story now."

More to Do

Continue to provide similar drawing explorations for toddlers daily or as often as possible.

Offer variety. Vary these initial explorations of drawing by offering different colors of crayons and different types of paper.

Artist's Tool Box

Drawing Materials

Crayons. Crayons have been the mainstay of early childhood drawing for many years. Their durability, relative safety, and ease of use will continue to keep them popular. The thick kindergarten size will prove most sturdy for grasping fists. However, other shapes and sizes can be slowly introduced over time. Breakage is to be expected, and removing the paper wrappers expands their creative possiblities. As the children gain better finger control, provide regular-sized crayons as well. Children can also be offered a much wider variety of colors. Fluorescent crayons, metallic crayons, and multicolored crayons will provide great enjoyment for children at this level. Two or three notches can be cut in the side of a large unwrapped crayon. Rubbed sideways on the paper, it will produce an interesting effect.

Markers. Unscented, water-based markers should be the backbone of the drawing program. The smooth, fluid nature of markers allows a level of detail not possible with other drawing materials.

Markers are much loved by toddlers. Choose water-based, broad-tipped markers. They create broad sweeps of vibrant color with little pressure. Taking off and putting on the caps provide small muscle practice, although some youngsters may need help doing this for a while.

Pencils. Look for pencils with very soft leads. Using pencils makes young children feel grown up and lets them draw finer lines than they can with the other materials.

Chalk. If the children are able to keep their hands out of their mouths while working, thick sidewalk chalk used outside on the pavement will provide an interesting color and texture change from using crayons and markers. Avoid the use of chalk on paper or any other surface when working with toddlers. The dust created is hazardous to their health.

Three and up. Regular white and colored blackboard chalk can be offered but only if the children draw outside or on wet paper. Liquid starch, milk,* water, or thinned white glue can be used to dampen the paper. Alternatively, the chalk can be dipped into the liquid and then used for drawing. Do not use dry chalk or artists' pastels. (See chapter 6 for a discussion of health hazards related to chalk use.)

Allow independence. As the children mature and gain experience, allow them more independence. Move away from the artists for short periods of time. Offer more choices of colors of crayons and times and places to work.

Special combinations. Offer a combination of markers, crayons, and pencils in the same color range, such as all reds or all blues. Talk about dark and light and dull and bright.

Read about lines. All children enjoy simple, humorous stories about drawing, such as *The Line Sophie Drew* (Barrett & Barrett, 1972), *The Chalk Box Story* (Freeman, 1976), *Harold and the Purple Crayon* (Johnson, 1955), and *A Very Special House* (Krauss, 1953). (See appendix B, Children's Literature on Art, for more suggestions.)

Music Box

My Lines

(To the tune, "Are You Sleeping?")

I like drawing.
I like drawing.
Yes I do! Yes I do!
Long lines and short lines.
Red lines and green lines. (substitute any colors)
Lines and lines. Lines and lines.

Artist's Tool Box

Drawing Surfaces

Paper. There are many ways to vary the paper offered to children. The size and shape of the paper will affect how the child uses it. Generally, the younger the child, the bigger the paper should be, because smaller paper requires more muscle control to stay within its borders. Newsprint and 50-lb. manila and 50-lb. white drawing paper should be provided for basic drawing activities. Used computer printout paper can also be used for economy. Paper can be cut into squares, rectangles, triangles, and circles. Use paper of different colors and textures as well.

Mural paper. Long, rolled paper can be hung on a wall, inside or outside, to create a "graffiti" mural. A large sheet can also be laid on the floor, and several children can draw together. At this age, toddlers are not fully aware of each other when they are drawing, but it is good to encourage the beginning of cooperative behavior by providing opportunities to work side by side at the same activity. (See chapter 10 for more mural and cooperative ideas.)

Boxes. Four children can work together drawing on the sides of a large box. To withstand the pushing of the artists, the box should be securely fastened to the table or floor, either with tape or by putting a heavy weight inside. A smaller box can be drawn on by one child. The decorated boxes can then be used for all kinds of play: as beds for dolls and stuffed animals, as a pull toy by attaching a string, and as furniture in a play corner.

Sand. If a sandbox or sand table is available, provide the children with tools such as sturdy, smooth twigs or thick, stubby wooden dowels for drawing in the sand. The experience can be varied by wetting the sand. A thin layer of sand (or a similar material such as rice*) can also be placed in a shallow plastic dishpan or tray. Children can make marks in the material with their fingers or with a tool such as a craftstick.

Other surfaces. Children will enjoy drawing on rocks, and cardboard boxes and in sand and rice. With increasing fine motor skills, they can also work on materials with more confining shapes and sizes, such as strips of adding machine tape and sandpaper. Scrap pieces of wood that have been sanded on the edges make an interesting drawing surface. Small decorated pieces may then be used in wood sculpture constructions.

EXPLORING DRAWING AGES THREE AND UP

Once children begin to use graphic symbols, the nature of their artwork changes. No longer is drawing solely for the purpose of exploring the media and refining physical control, although these aspects will always continue to play an important role. Now drawings become a form of communication as well. Children at this stage are able to use drawing tools to express their feelings and ideas. They can also use their drawings to tell stories and to show their reaction to experiences. These new skills, plus the child's increasing independence and conformance to rules, will allow the introduction of more complex drawing activities.

Group Composition

Children can now work side by side in larger groups. Four to six preschoolers or even larger groups of primary children can draw together if the table or paper is large enough.

Setup

Provide flat drawing surfaces, such as child-height tabletops or easels. A small, individual-sized chalkboard makes a portable drawing surface. Children can also work on a smooth floor.

Because they are less likely to misuse the art materials, children can also spread out more and do not need an adult hovering over them. Some children prefer to draw in more private spaces. (See chapter 9 for ideas on space usage.)

Drawing centers should be well stocked with paper, and all drawing materials familiar to the children should be available daily. To spark interest and to provide ideas for their drawings, display interesting objects, perhaps related to the topics being studied, such as goldfish in a bowl or a growing plant. For older children, combining a science and drawing center encourages young artists to record their observations through drawing.

Materials

There are many possible choices; see the drawing Tool Box. All should be presented for exploration and practice before they are used in responsive activities.

Teacher Tip

Avoiding Misleading Shapes

Avoid offering paper cut into the shapes of animals, plants, or other "real" objects. Besides taking up preparation time, such shapes, which have a right and wrong way to be held, are often confusing to young children. An adult-created silhouette or symbol for something such as a car may have very little in common with the child's concept of a car. A child who does not "see" what the shape represents may draw tires or other details in the wrong place.

Even if teachers are open to a wide range of "decoration" by the children, remember that often parents judge their children's intellectual ability by how well they have decorated such shapes. Parental comments such as "Why did you put the eyes on the duck's feet?" or "Don't you know the rabbit's tail belongs here?" are not beneficial to the growth of self-confident young artists.

Warm-Up

Wrap new drawing materials in colorful giftwrap and use guided discovery to introduce them. Follow up by reading a book such as *Harold and the Purple Crayon* (Johnson, 1955), or do a kinesthetic activity such as drawing with an imaginary crayon (see chapter 7).

What to Do

Drawing materials with which the children are familiar should be made available at all times. Children should know where these are stored, how to obtain what they need, and how to put them back when finished.

What to Say

When children share their work, provide supportive, descriptive comments, such as, "You made many circular shapes!" and "The bright colors in your picture really show how you felt."

Transition Out

When children indicate that they are finished, offer a descriptive comment, remind them to replace the materials, and direct them where to put their pictures if this has not been done already.

More to Do

There are many ways to vary drawing. Try the following practice activities.

Draw with wet chalk. Draw on colored construction paper with chalk dipped in water or a thin glue solution.

Use contrasting colors. Use dark-colored paper with light-colored or metallic crayons.

Draw on textured surfaces. Try paper plates and other textured drawing surfaces.

Classroom Museum

There are many fine prints that illustrate drawings in all styles. Durer's Rabbit (Metropolitan), Van Gogh's Harvest (Take Five: Drawing), and the cave art of the Paleolithic (Modern Learning; Take Five: Horses) are all appealing to young artists.

Use shaped paper. Paper can be cut into a variety of geometric shapes, but keep these large and simple. Squares, long, thin rectangles, and large triangles are easy to prepare. A paper cutter is invaluable when working with a large number of children.

Art Words

Kinds of Paper

○ **Bogus drawing paper**
A heavyweight, gray paper (80 lb.) with a rough-textured surface that provides a contrast to the smoothness of most other papers.

○ **Construction paper**
A medium-weight paper that comes in a wide variety of colors. It is available in the same standard sizes as white paper.

○ **Kraft paper**
Medium-weight brown paper like that of grocery bags. It is often sold in rolls. It is a sturdy paper for drawing and other art activities. Rolls of colored kraft paper are also available.

○ **Manila paper**
A medium-weight paper in a pale, golden beige, with a slight texture. Comes in the same sizes as white drawing paper and is less expensive. A durable paper for children's drawings.

○ **Newsprint**
A lightweight, inexpensive paper, slightly gray in color. It can often be purchased from small local newpapers at low rates.

○ **Tag board**
A stiff, smooth, bendable board, also called "poster board" or "oaktag." Available in many colors, it makes a good surface for drawing but is relatively expensive.

○ **White drawing paper**
A sturdy paper with a smooth surface. Standard sizes are 9 by 12, 12 by 18, and 18 by 24 inches. Although more expensive than newsprint, it offers a durable surface for active drawing. Purchase 50-lb. weight paper.

Teaching in Action

Introducing Crayon Drawing

WEEK 1: On the first day of class, sit on a rug and open a brand-new box of crayons. Have children name their favorite color. Ask: "How do we use crayons?" Talk about how, when, and where they can be used. Show children where crayons are kept. Have children model getting crayons from the supply area and going to a work table and then putting them away. Keep this brief—no more than five minutes. For the rest of the week, have white paper and crayons on the storage shelf. Encourage children to get them and draw. Monitor proper use. Save their drawings for the next lesson.

WEEK 2: Start the week by reviewing what the children did with the crayons. Sitting together on the rug, sing the song "Lines." Say, "Last week you learned how to get and use the crayons. Here are some drawings you made. What do you see? Do you see lines? What colors do you see?" Let children respond.

"I will be putting different kinds of papers on the shelf this week. Do you think the crayons will work the same way on them?" Each day put out a different color or texture of paper. Encourage children to compare these to drawings on white paper. Save their drawings.

WEEK 3: Work with a different small group each day. Begin by looking at their drawings. Ask, "What was your favorite paper?" Then say, "Now you know how to get crayons and choose paper. Today I will show you our drawing boards. You can use the drawing board to draw anywhere in the room. You could draw a picture of your block tower. You could draw the fish. You could find a quiet place to draw an imaginary picture. This is how you get a board (demonstrate). Take a crayon container and find your very own drawing place. Draw a picture, and then put away the board and crayons. Gina, can you show us how to put the board and crayons away? Now let's have everyone try it. Find your special place to draw." During the week, encourage children to use the drawing boards.

WEEK 4: Start the week by introducing drawing outside. Say, "Today when we go outside, I will take the drawing boards and crayons. Maybe you will find a special place to draw outside." Continue to encourage children to draw inside and outside. By the end of the week, children should be able to get their own drawing supplies and find a place to draw. Now they will be able to do responsive drawings or keep journals as part of thematic units or in the project approach.

Connections

Language. Booklets can be made either from 9-by-12-inch paper or in "Big Book" size from 12-by-18-inch sheets. Staple the paper together on either the long or short side. Start with two pages; as the children develop their story-making skill, increase the number of pages. Tell the children that pages can be added if they need more to complete their story. Show the children how to fold back the pages so the booklet lies flat while they are drawing.

Read books that feature lines in playful ways, such as *Simon's Book* (Druscher, 1983), and *Monsters* (Hoban,

1989). *My Map Book* (Fanelli, 1995) will inspire children to draw maps of their special places, and *How is a Crayon Made?* (Charles, 1988) will fascinate children as it illustrates how crayons are manufactured.

Math. Have children draw self-portraits or personal symbols on small squares of paper. Laminate them, and use them to create pictographs reflecting the children's interests.

Science. Draw pictures of plants, animals, and insects that have been observed in the classroom and on nature walks. Have children draw pictures that show their ideas about science experiments.

Studio Page 9

LOOKING AT CHILDREN'S ARTWORK

Based on the models of artistic development described in this chapter, how would you describe the following examples of child art?

DRAWING 1

DRAWING 2

DRAWING 3

DRAWING 4

DRAWING 5

DRAWING 6

DRAWING 7

DRAWING 8

Studio Page 10

DESCRIBING CHILDREN'S ARTWORK

For each drawing write a description based on the work of Kellogg, Lowenfeld, Gardner, and Kindler and Darras. What culture influences do you see?

DRAWING 2

Kellogg:

Lowenfeld:

Gardner:

Kindler/Darras:

DRAWING 1

Kellogg:

Lowenfeld:

Gardner:

Kindler/Darras:

DRAWING 4

Kellogg:

Lowenfeld:

Gardner:

Kindler/Darras:

DRAWING 3

Kellogg:

Lowenfeld:

Gardner:

Kindler/Darras:

DRAWING 6

Kellogg:

Lowenfeld:

Gardner:

Kindler/Darras:

DRAWING 5

Kellogg:

Lowenfeld:

Gardner:

Kindler/Darras:

DRAWING 8

Kellogg:

Lowenfeld:

Gardner:

Kindler/Darras:

DRAWING 7

Kellogg:

Lowenfeld:

Gardner:

Kindler/Darras:

Studio Page 11

OBSERVATION: TODDLER DRAWING

1. Plan a drawing exploration or practice activity suitable for a toddler between the ages of one and three.

2. Obtain permission to work with one toddler, either at home or in a child care setting.

3. Set up your activity and observe the toddler at work. If possible, take photos or videotape the activity (get permission first). With the child's permission, save one or more of the drawings for your own collection.

Age of child:

Setup of materials:

Length of time of observation:

---

1. What did the child do first?

2. What did the child say?

3. How did the child manipulate the drawing tool(s)? (For example, describe position of arm and hands, grip, any other body parts involved.)

4. How long did the child work? (Measure periods of concentration. If child stopped, why? How did the child let you know he or she was finished?)

5. Describe the art produced. (What did the child draw first? How many drawings were made? What was repeated?)

6. Compare your observations to the developmental models of Gardner and Kindler and Darras. What behaviors did you see that support their ideas?

OBSERVATION: CHILD DRAWING

1. Plan a drawing exploration or practice activity suitable for a child between the ages of three and eight.

2. Obtain permission to work with one child, either at home or in a school setting. If possible, take photos or videotape the activity (get permission first). With the child's permission, save one or more of the drawings for your own collection.

Age of child:

Setup of materials:

Length of time of observation:

1. What did the child do first?

2. What did the child say?

3. How did the child manipulate the drawing tool(s)? (For example, describe position of arm and hands, grip, any other body parts involved.)

4. How long did the child work? (Measure periods of concentration. If child stopped, why? How did the child let you know he or she was finished?)

5. Describe the art produced. (What did the child draw first? How many drawings were made? What was repeated?)

6. Compare the art activity of this child to that of the toddler you observed. What similarities and differences did you notice?

7. How did this child's behavior fit Gardner's and Kindler's and Darras's models?

For additional information on teaching art to young children, visit our Web site at http://www.earlychilded.delmar.com

Nurturing Creativity

> *Encouraging a person to discover their uniqueness and helping them develop its expression can be one of the greatest gifts we can ever give.*
>
> —Fred Rogers (1982, p. 10)

Questions Addressed in This Chapter:

- How are young children creative?
- What is the creative process?
- How do teachers foster the creative process?

Young Artists at Work

Several four-year-olds are busy using paper and glue. The teacher has put out a tray of precut yellow squares. Stephen spreads glue all over his paper and then slaps on several yellow squares haphazardly. He pokes at one square, sliding it around in the glue. Maryanne carefully makes small dots of glue. Then she selects a yellow square and places it over the glue dots. With a crayon, she draws eyes, a nose, and a mouth. Keith watches his friends at work, then picks up the glue bottle and makes a line of glue in the center of the paper. He chooses a square from the tray and sticks it in place. Then he adds more glue and another square. Soon his paper is covered with a line of gluey yellow squares.

HOW ARE YOUNG CHILDREN CREATIVE?

Creative thinking is not a station one arrives at, but a means of traveling.

—Mary Mayesky, Donald Neuman, and Ronald J. Wlodkowski (1975, p. 6)

Even though children may be the same age and are working with the same materials, the artwork they will produce is undeniably unique to each child. It is not enough to understand how a child grows developmentally. Adults who work with young children must also understand, and value, the nature of the creative process and how it is expressed in the art of each child.

Defining Creativity

Creativity has been the subject of much research and analysis, yet there is no generally accepted definition. A creative act can be viewed in many ways. What is thought creative in one time and place may not be thought creative in another. Different researchers have pointed out important characteristics of creativity.

Uniqueness. Creativity is inventing something so unique that it is astonishing to the viewer or user and produces "effective surprise" (Bruner, 1979, p. 12). Thomas Edison's invention of the lightbulb or Georges Seurat's use of tiny dots of color to create the style of pointillism are examples of unique products that are considered highly creative.

Rule breaking. Creativity is doing something that goes beyond the accepted rules but in a new way that is understandable and acceptable to a wider audience (Boden, 1990, p. 12). Jackson Pollack's drip paintings used familiar art materials in an unconventional way that grew out of the artistic trends of his time.

Problem solving. Torrance (1970) described creativity as the ability to see a problem, form an idea to solve it, and then share the results. Frank Lloyd Wright thought houses should be inexpensive and fit their environment, so he developed slab construction and designed the "prairie home," which became the prototype for the contemporary ranch-style home.

Personal characteristics. Some researchers have concentrated on studying the lives and works of people who are considered highly creative and identifying those qualities to make them exceptional. Amabile (1983) identified these basic characteristics of creative people.

1. They are skilled in a particular area of learning, such as science, art, or writing.
2. They have the ability to imagine a range of possibilities. They are flexible thinkers and can generate many possible ways of doing something or of solving a problem.
3. They are highly persistent and do not give up, even if they fail many times.
4. They set high personal standards for themselves and push themselves to learn more and work harder.

5. They are intrinsically motivated, finding great pleasure and satisfaction in the act of creation.

Divergent Thinking. Guilford (1986) has proposed a model of intelligence that includes divergent thinking as one of the basic thought processes. Divergent thinking can be defined as the ability to generate many different solutions to a problem. It is characterized by

- ✿ fluency—being able to generate a multitude of diverse ideas or solutions.
- ✿ flexibility—being able to see things from alternative viewpoints.
- ✿ originality—being able to think of ideas or solutions that have never been thought of before.
- ✿ elaboration—the ability to improve ideas by adding on or expanding them.

Thinking process. Malaguzzi (Edwards, Gandini, & Forman, 1993, p. 70) views creativity not as a particular way of doing something but as an integral part of how all people think about and process information. Creativity is the human ability to see a problem or need, to use one's knowledge and skill to make plans, to try out ideas, and to come up with a solution. This "creative process" or set of behaviors can be seen operating whenever someone solves a problem or produces a unique product.

Creativity in Children

Most animals have inherited reflexes and responses that enable them to survive from birth. Human beings, on the other hand, must learn almost everything starting in infancy. The creative process can be seen as the mechanism by which people use past knowledge and learned skills to meet the needs of a new situation or to solve a problem. Young children are constantly dealing with fresh circumstances and "creating" a unique response to the situation. The infant finds a dab of spilled milk and creates a design by swirling little fingers through it. The toddler rolls clay into a long, thin cylinder, wraps it around a wrist, and creates a body ornament. The preschooler finds a stone, adds some crayon marks, and creates a "creature."

The nature of the creative artistic responses the child makes will depend upon many factors. The infant does not yet have the ability to create a landscape painting. The toddler cannot produce silver jewelry.

"Shapes and a House." Mixed media collage—*Jenna, age 6*

The preschooler cannot carve a marble monument. Nevertheless, even though the children's responses are limited by their skill level and stage of physical growth, their artworks are still highly creative. At any moment, each child is at a precise point in development, has a unique set of experiences, and has a personal base of knowledge and skills. These combine to produce a particular set of responses to each stimulus that the child confronts. We should not find it surprising that a one-of-a-kind child produces one-of-a-kind art!

Nurturing Creativity

As the process of creativity is discussed in this section, it is important to remember that the behaviors being described come from within the child. These behaviors are not distinctly separate from each other, but are elements of the individual's whole approach to learning. They are not taught directly but are dispositions nurtured through the presentation of carefully designed, open-ended art activities.

Children need an environment that is conducive to the creative process. It is easy for habit-bound adults, intentionally or unintentionally, to react negatively to creative behaviors, or for helpful adults to want to "solve" children's problems for them. One of the more difficult things for adults to learn is when to set limits, when to offer direction, and when to stand back and let children do it by themselves. Guiding adults must constantly set themselves the task of providing safe stimuli and a nurturing environment to allow creative learning in young children.

In the following discussion of the creative process, we will see how teachers' behavior and attitude, and the decisions they make, affect the creative behavior of children. Activities focused on the art medium of collage provide examples of how teachers can foster creative expression through art.

WHAT IS THE CREATIVE PROCESS?

The creative process can be viewed as being composed of a combination of mental processes that will lead to the final creative product or action. It consists of the following:

Knowledge: what individuals already know about what they are exploring

Motivation: the inner drive to accomplish something

Skill acquisition: the development of expertise

Immersion: being intensely focused on creating something unique with this knowledge and skill

Young Artists at Work

"Look!" said the teacher after sharing the book *Planting a Rainbow* (Ehlert, 1988). "Here are some pictures of beautiful spring flowers." He places on the table a basket of magazine clippings showing flowers. The children gather around and begin to cut and paste enthusiastically, while the teacher imagines a beautiful garden of finished collages to hang in the hall.

When the children are done, they hurry to share their creations with their teacher.

"Oh," said the teacher, seeing the finished collages. Where were the gardens? Instead of flowers, each child held a unique artwork. Some had irregular shapes covered with print or a lopsided face encircled with pieces of an advertisement.

"Each one of you used the clippings in your own creative way," said the teacher. "That is what makes art so exciting. You never know what will happen."

Incubation: a period of time in which individuals think and process what they know and what they wish to do

Production: the tangible expression of the creative process

Knowledge

Whenever people face a new stimulus or problem, the first thing that comes into play is their previous knowledge. Young children have a much more limited knowledge base than adults, so their responses are often wildly different from those we might expect. The amount of knowledge children have about an art material or a concept will influence what their creative response will be. For example, before expecting children to create collages using only flower pictures, they must first have many opportunities to identify and to sort mixed clippings of flowers and other subjects by type. Only after the children can do these activities successfully can they be expected to make a collage on such a specific theme.

How do children gain artistic knowledge? Children gain knowledge that will enable them to be creative in art by exploring art materials, physical objects, graphic images, and art concepts. Teachers help children gain knowledge in several ways.

Providing time to explore materials. In designing collage or other art activities, provide time for exploring the basic materials individually before they are used together in a piece of art.

Talking about art concepts. Use a vocabulary rich in artistic language and point out examples of the art elements in children's artwork. Children who know they are making a line, and know that there are many different kinds of lines, will be able to choose the particular line they want to use in their art.

Presenting the art of others. Knowing what other artists have done provides a basis from which children can take a new direction.

Accepting individual differences in knowledge. In some cases, a limited or different knowledge base will cause the child to use the offered art materials in a very unexpected way, as when children take the wadded-up paper towel they used to wipe their fingers and add it to the collage. Although adults may find the addition "unpleasant" from their personal aesthetic viewpoint, it is important to view children's work in terms of what they know.

In this case, the children have demonstrated that they have learned that collages are made from a variety of textured papers glued onto a base paper. Incorporating the used paper towel demonstrates the child's ability to categorize it as a piece of textured paper and represents a highly creative action, equivalent to Picasso's using a piece of real newspaper to represent itself in his early Cubist painting—the result of which was equally unpleasant to art connoisseurs of the time.

Sometimes the child's creative solution will challenge the adult's tolerance for messiness and disorder, such as when children take a glue bottle and "frame" their pictures by squeezing glue on the table all around the outside of the collage. At other times, the inventiveness of a young child will fill us with awe. When selecting and designing art activities for young children, remember that they will each respond creatively, based on their personally unique previous knowledge, not the teachers' preconceived idea of what they will do.

Motivation

Motivation is the inner drive that causes an individual to want to do something. Young children are naturally motivated by intense curiosity about the world around them. Everything is new and exciting to them. They want to touch everything, see everything, and try everything. How wonderful for the teacher!

Often the guiding adult has only to present the art materials and to give a few simple instructions, and the children's natural motivation to explore will do the rest. When motivation is at work, smiling, laughing children gather excitedly around us. They ask curious questions and cannot wait to get started. They spend a great deal of time on their explorations, and they want to do more and more.

How is motivation nurtured? In order to create a motivating environment, teachers need to be as creative as their students.

Provide open-ended activities. Motivating activities are always open-ended, with a multitude of possible end results and ways of getting there. When children

"A Flower." Paper and fabric collage—*Mackensie, age 7*

choose what material they will use or what idea they will express, they take interest in and feel ownership of their work, which will heighten their motivation.

Be stimulating. Motivation happens when the mind is active. Get children thinking and asking questions by making sure something new or surprising is always happening in the room. Display new artworks, introduce new materials, play unfamiliar music, wear unusual clothing, and constantly discuss new ideas and experiences.

Be flexible. Motivation develops from within. Create child ownership of problems and ideas by being willing to change direction and follow up on new ideas and interests that they have.

Be encouraging. Expect failure to occur more often than success. Establish an environment in which mistakes are part of the learning process. Be willing to try a child's idea even if it seems it will not work. Teach children to respect the differing ideas and work of others in an atmosphere where insults and ridicule are forbidden.

Be playful. Create opportunities for everyone to laugh, play, and have fun together. Creativity happens when children are relaxed and happy.

Be on the lookout for emergent problems. Problems that bring forth the most creativity are those that arise in the process of doing something. A problem that happens when a child is trying to accomplish a task, such as mixing just the right color paint for a painting or attempting to glue a large object to a small one, is far more motivating than solving a problem assigned by the teacher.

Show support for creativity. Cherish, honor, and display the creative ideas, actions, and works of the children. Instead of stereotypical commercial bulletin board patterns and ready-made pictures, document in words and pictures the children's creative efforts, both failures and successes, and create visual displays that inform parents.

How is motivation stifled? Unfortunately, motivation is a delicate force. It may be easily stifled by inappropriate organization or presentation of art ac-

Motivation cannot be taught. It must be inspired.

tivities. Overly restrictive art activities quickly dampen a child's natural curiosity.

Restricting choice. Self-motivation in children is diminished by materials that can be used in only one way, projects that must match a model, or actions that must conform to a fixed standard.

Boredom. Boredom arises when the child is constantly offered the same materials with little or no variation. For example, as wonderful as drawing with crayons can be, this cannot be a total art program for young children.

Competition. Rewards such as prizes or stars for "good" work or competition among students replace internal motivation with external motivation and do not belong in an art program for young children.

Conformity. Anxiety about making a mistake can prevent children from fully exploring an art material.

The pressure to conform and to be like everyone else can make children afraid to be different and to express themselves in a new way.

Fear. Fear of getting dirty or ruining something can cause children to be unmotivated to try the messier art materials. To discourage this, encourage parents to dress their children in easily cleaned clothing, provide smocks, and offer damp paper towels for wiping hands. Protect surfaces and offer only supplies that can be easily cleaned up.

Overcontrol. If children feel that they are constantly being watched and evaluated, they may be less willing to take risks and try new ideas. If they think the teacher is going to interfere with their investigations, they will hesitate to pursue their own interests. If teachers solve the problem for them or do the work for them, they will expect that adults always will.

Skill

The more skillfully children can handle an art material, the more they can concentrate on using the artistic elements of line, shape, color, and texture in a creative way in their artwork. A child using a new material or tool is often tentative and focused on controlling this new experience. The process of creating becomes secondary. As children gain skill, their approach changes. They dive into the materials, no longer worried about how they will control them but excited instead by the new way they can play with the artistic elements.

Designing art activities to develop artistic skills. Art activities need to be carefully organized so that the skills required to accomplish them are appropriate for the skill level of the young child. If skills are new to the child, they must be within the physical and mental capabilities of the child to learn. Initial skills need to be presented in a structured format.

1. Materials should be aesthetically interesting and limited to those that can be easily handled by inexperienced children.
2. Children should be closely supervised when they are first introduced to new materials, tools, or techniques. Make sure the children are comfortable and understand what they will use, and how to do so safely.

3. Activities need to be carefully set up so that after new media and techniques are introduced, children can then easily continue exploring and practicing with the materials and tools on their own.

Selecting practice activities. Successful initial explorations motivate the child to want to create again and again with those tools and materials. At this point, practice activities are extremely important in building up skill levels. At the same time, they allow the child to expand creatively.

In selecting practice activities, make sure that they do, in fact, require the same skills that were introduced in the explorations, so that children develop confidence in their own abilities. Children who are able to attach paper to the collage base may be able to glue down similar sizes and shapes of fabric as well, but they may find that the much-different qualities of yarn make it more difficult to glue. In this case, it is not enough to know how to apply the glue and place an item in it.

For example, picture a toddler who is trying to stick down a piece of string, but every time he lifts his gluey fingers the string is still stuck to them. He quickly becomes frustrated. He is no longer thinking about the creative fun of making a collage and how the different textures can be put together. He just wants the sticky string off his fingers. His frustration may grow to the point of furiously shaking his hand until the string goes flying across the room to stick to the wall or floor—a creative way, to be sure, of dealing with his problem, but one that is sure to bring repercussions from the nearest adult. For this toddler to be success-

ful gluing string, he also needs to know how to wipe excess paste or glue from his fingers. Gentle guidance from an aware adult can help this child develop that skill as he creates.

Balancing skill development and creativity. Skill development is often confused with creative processing, because they are so interrelated. Skills are needed to be artistically creative. At the same time, creative activities enable a child to develop skills. If activities are carefully thought out, children will develop the needed skills with a minimum of interference from adults, and they will be unhindered in their creative processing.

Activities that exist solely for the purpose of teaching or practicing skills, such as cutting along predrawn lines, coloring in teacher-drawn pictures, or gluing together preformed pieces from a kit, are not creative art activities. These same skills can be developed through open-ended art activities that allow for the expression of individual creativity. Children can draw their own lines and cut them out. They can color their own drawings, and they can cut out pieces and put them together in their own way.

The teacher's goal should be to offer only those activities that develop skills without dictating the end result.

Immersion

Immersion is the state of being so completely focused on creating something that the passage of time is forgotten, as are personal needs and what is happening

Young Artists at Work

A young child dabs some paste with her fingers and then begins to rub it across her paper in a swirling pattern. Although she is usually easily distracted, at this moment she pays no attention to the other children working beside her at the table. Instead of her perpetual chatter, she is silent. Her tongue projects slightly from her mouth as her eyes follow the movement of her hand. If we speak to her at this moment, she may not even hear us, and if she does, she may jump slightly or hesitate before responding to us. In the simple act of spreading the paste in a new way, this child has become immersed in the process of creation.

around us. In this state we feel relaxed and calm. Our ideas seem to flow effortlessly from our mind to our hands. We are not concerned with the end product but only with the pleasure of the process itself. Creativity is at work! All of the knowledge, skill, and motivation of the individual have come together to make this moment possible.

It is much easier for children to enter this state than adults. Adults rarely have uninterrupted, unlimited time in which to create. Some people, such as artists and writers, find that they have to go off by themselves to a "studio" or "garret" in order to work. Most people, however, spend their days surrounded by the pressure of social ties and job commitments and tending to basic human needs, with only rare moments to become immersed in the creative process. But adults must be careful not to impose such restraints upon children.

Providing time. Anyone who has ever worked with young children knows that unlike adults, young children have little concern for time. Left on their own, children will immerse themselves for as much time as they need on a creative activity. In designing activities and interacting with the children, teachers must always be aware of the time factor in order to best meet the children's creative needs. Before children start an art activity, be sure that there will be sufficient time for them to become immersed in it. Especially when offering an art activity or center for the first few times, and it is unclear how long the children will need, present it at the beginning of the session. If children want to start an activity when they will not have sufficient time, it is better to redirect them to something that will involve less time.

Avoiding interruptions. It is extremely frustrating for a child to be interrupted when immersed in the creative process. Unfortunately, our society runs by the clock. It will happen, despite the best planning—children in the act of creating will need to be interrupted. If an individual child must be interrupted, do so gently. Try to make eye contact before giving a direction. Offer the assurance that the child can continue the activity at another time. It is essential to keep such interruptions to an absolute minimum. If this happens often enough, the child will eventually lose the motivation to create art.

Skill develops with practice.

Incubation and Production

The creative process is like a stew in which knowledge and skill are the raw ingredients that are brought together by motivation and immersion. Incubation is the slow simmering of this rich mix, which produces the creative ideas and products. During the incubation stage, young artists are actively engaged in trying out ideas, asking themselves questions, and evaluating their actions. Outwardly, they may study the materials or handle them playfully. They may experiment with an idea and then cover it over or take it apart. They may test the limits of the material, or the rules, or the teacher's patience. At other times, they may sit quietly and stare off into space or concentrate intently on what they are creating. Inside they may be thinking such thoughts as, "What will happen if I do this?", "How will these things go together?", "Wow, I didn't expect that to happen!", and "I never saw anything like this before."

All of this leads to production, when the ingredients in the stew blend together to form something new, a flavor that has never existed before. At this point, the children have become their creations. For each child's knowledge, skills, and motivation are uniquely different from every other child who has ever existed. Children's artwork is an extension of all that they are at that moment.

HOW DO TEACHERS FOSTER THE CREATIVE PROCESS?

Adults will always be outside of the child's very personal creative process. However, the role they must play is crucially important. Because it is so easy for a child's creativity to be stifled, it is the teacher's task to establish an environment in which the creative process is nurtured.

First, children's personal needs must be met so they will be ready to create. Sick, tired, or hungry children will not be able to concentrate. If children are worried or nervous, they will be unlikely to take the

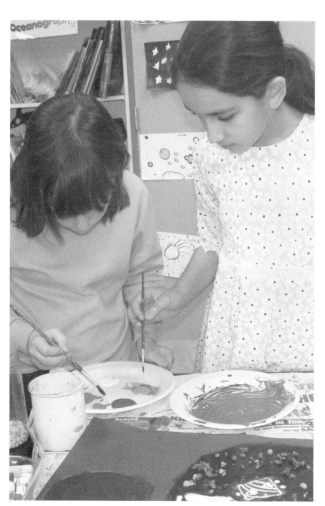

Intense concentration shows creativity at work.

TEACHER TIP

How to Help Children Be Creative Artists

Teachers nurture children's creativity when they help them:

1. accept change.
2. meet their physical needs.
3. learn that some problems have many solutions.
4. accept their own feelings and those of others.
5. appreciate themselves and others for being different.
6. develop perseverance and the courage to take risks.
7. feel safe and relaxed while working.
8. enjoy the creative process.

kinds of risks that creativity requires. Second, teachers need to value curiosity, exploration, and original behavior. Allow children to go at their own pace, to figure things out for themselves, and encourage them to try new things. Refrain from making models, from using children's materials in an expert, adult way, and from requiring children to produce artwork that fits an adult idea of what it should look like. Listen to the children, and pay attention to what they are thinking. Observe the process that children go through in dealing with problems, and pay less attention to the product of this process.

Finally, provide the children with many opportunities in which they can safely explore and pursue creative activities without interruption.

How to Choose a Creative Activity

When selecting activities for young children, consider how they will allow the child to be creative. All activities need limits, but always make sure that the limits imposed on the children will foster creativity, not confine it. Preventing a child from eating paste will not stop him or her from making a creative collage. Offering a set of simple, precut shapes that children can arrange any way they want allows them to create an original collage. There are infinite ways they can arrange those shapes on the base paper, but offering precut shapes that can only be made into a clown face does not allow children any freedom to try something new.

Remember that young children usually try to please the adults around them. They do not want to be yelled at or embarrassed. They will do their best to follow directions. It is certainly possible, with enough preparation and structure, to get a group of children to make paper-bag elephant puppets, cotton-ball rabbits, and folded paper reindeers with antlers made of hand tracings, or whatever the teachers have in mind. Such activities are found in far too many books and magazines and paper the walls of many early childhood classrooms. Young children will work hard on such projects and are happy that they can please their teachers and parents, but producing pseudo-art projects that please adult eyes is precious creative time wasted.

"Lady Cat." Collage—*Laurel, age 5*

Teaching in Action

Choosing Creative Activities

When choosing art activities for young children, ask these questions:

1. Can children explore on their own?

2. Can children go at their own pace?

3. Can children figure out their own ways to do things?

4. Are there many possible ways to do this activity?

5. Are the rules based on safety and management, not on the product desired?

6. Is it challenging?

7. Can children set their own goals?

8. Will it be fun—will they laugh, imagine, and play?

CONCLUSION: CREATIVITY IN TEACHING

When a child is being creative he is fluent, flexible, original, confident, and adventuresome. He can redefine situations, is willing to work at things for a long time, will work hard, and can produce many possible answers to a single question.

—*Mary Mayesky, Donald Neuman, and Ronald J. Wlodkowski (1975, p. 4)*

Creativity is different from the other areas of growth that teachers try to develop in children. It is not something we can teach directly, but we must foster it through our attitude, behavior, and activity choices. The entire learning environment must be designed around the elements that nurture creative processing. Teachers need to provide opportunities for children to gain knowledge and skill by exploring art media. Children need time to immerse themselves in art creation, motivated by their boundless curiosity and the search for solutions. Creativity is found not just at the art table but also in the block corner, the dramatic play area, and on the playground.

Children need time to immerse themselves in creative activities.

It takes a creative person to fashion such an environment. It takes knowledge, skill, and a great deal of motivation to fully bring out creative behavior in children. Like the child, the teacher will say:

"What will happen if I do this?"
"How will these things go together?"
"Wow, I didn't expect that to happen!"
"I never saw anything like this before."

No two individuals approach this task in the same way. This book and experience will provide the knowledge and the skills; teachers must provide their own motivation.

FURTHER READING

Caine, R. N., & Caine, G. (1994). *Making connections: Teaching and the human brain*. New York: Addison-Wesley.
A brain-based approach to cognitive functioning, learning, creativity, and teaching methods that will help teachers design creative art programs.

Cameron, J. (1992). *The artist's way: A spiritual path to higher creativity*. New York: G. P. Putnam's Sons.
A step-by-step process of discovering and nurturing one's own creativity is presented in this book.

Edwards, B. (1986). *Drawing on the artist within.* New York: Simon & Schuster.
Personal creativity can be developed in many ways. Betsy Edwards uses art as a way to break out of habitual thinking patterns.

Goleman, D., Kaufman, P., & Ray, M. (1992). *The creative spirit*. New York: Dutton.
This inspiring book presents the thoughts of many people on the topic of creativity. It offers guidelines for developing personal creativity and includes examples of creative activities currently being used in business and education, including the Reggio Emilia preprimary program.

Creating Art: Collage

"Look at all my shapes." Precut paper and fabric collage—
Joey, age 3

 ## THE COLLAGE EXPERIENCE

Every art program for young children includes the art activity called "collage." Children are offered various papers, magazine pictures, and small objects to glue onto their pictures. Collage has become one of the most popular art forms for young children. It is also one of the most creative. There is no limit to the ways young children can arrange their bits and pieces of collage materials. Adults do not expect children to produce "realistic-looking" collages and do not evaluate them in the same way as drawings. Teachers and parents are often more accepting of the exploration process and the resulting products in collage than they are in drawing or painting. Children are extraordinarily free of restraints as they become immersed in the creative process of making a collage.

How Children Grow through Collage Creation

Children will develop

1. physically, by using the large muscles of the arm to apply paste and tear paper, and by using the small muscles to use scissors and to pick up paper and objects to give them a set place. (Bodily-Kinesthetic)

2. socially, by working alongside others, sharing materials, and learning to use scissors safely around others. (Interpersonal)

3. emotionally, by learning to enjoy the act of collage making as a means of self-expression, and by gaining self-confidence through being able to control a dangerous tool—scissors. (Intrapersonal)

4. language skills, by learning a vocabulary of size, shape, color, and placement and describing the artwork they make. (Linguistic)

5. cognitively, by observing that paste and glue change over time, and that materials have different textures and can be sorted in different ways. (Logical-Mathematical)

6. visual perception skills, by manipulating a variety of textures and shapes and observing them from different points of view, by planning a shape and how to cut it out of a larger shape, and by placing smaller shapes in different positions on larger shapes. (Spatial)

7. art awareness, by gaining familiarity with the way other artists have created collages.

INTRODUCING COLLAGE AGES ONE AND UP

The toddler has limited knowledge of paper and paste and its use to create art forms. Many preschoolers may also have had little opportunity to use paste and glue. As with drawing materials, introductory collage activities need to allow the child to explore the nature of the materials and to learn what can be done with them. In the beginning the child's focus will be on that wonderfully sticky, gooey paste.

Group Composition

When first introducing pasting activities, limit the size of the group to one or two toddlers or four to six three- to eight-year-olds. Of all the art materials, paste and glue are the ones most commonly eaten by young children, probably because they closely resemble the texture of some foods. Until the children can be trusted not to put the paste into their mouths, provide constant supervision.

Setup

Provide a low table at which the children can comfortably stand or sit. The tabletop should be bare and easy to wash. If the table must be covered, use an old shower curtain or a plastic tablecloth rather than newspaper, which can stick to the projects. A laminated sheet of construction paper also works well.

Because pasting and glueing with young children is a "messy" activity, and one that can be confused with food, it is important to set up a place where collages can be done away from food areas. This can be a special table that is near a water source. If working in a kitchen area, a large plastic tray or plastic tablecloth can be designated for collage activities, and pasting and glueing can be done only when that surface is set

Classroom Museum

Share the work of Picasso's Cubist period, in which he used collage, such as *Three Musicians*. Children like to hunt for the different materials, such as pieces of newspapers, that he used in his work.

up. Have on hand an ample supply of damp paper towels so children can wipe sticky fingers before moving away from the work area.

As children gain skill, set up a permanent collage center with attractively displayed paper and objects grouped by texture and color. (See chapter 9 for more ideas.)

Materials

For initial activities, offer each child

- a small amount of paste, such as school paste or the homemade cornstarch paste described in appendix A, a small dab of white glue, or a glue stick.
- a small shallow container (such as a plastic lid from a margarine container) for each child's paste or glue. The small jars and applicator lids in which paste is often sold and give bottles are too hard for toddlers and many preschoolers to use.
- only about a tablespoon of paste or glue at a time. (It is easier to keep refilling the container than to clean up excess.)
- a base such as a sheet of manila or white drawing paper, about 12 inches by 18 inches in size, and a few simple, precut, construction paper rectangles in two or three sizes and colors.

Warm-Up

Collage can be introduced by sharing some of the materials or objects children can use.

With toddlers, sing a pasting chant to attract their interest while showing them the paste. Older children

may enjoy a story that features collage, such as *The Mixed-Up Chameleon* (Carle, 1984) or *Imani in the Belly* (Chocolate, 1994).

What to Do

The basics of collage consist of attaching paper or objects to a base using an adhesive of some kind. This action requires skill in hand-eye coordination. Children's first attempts at managing this complex coordination—putting the paste or glue on their fingers, wiping it on the base, and picking up an item and placing it in the glue—will often result in misplaced glue and papers and will require a great deal of patience on the teacher's part. It is important that children be allowed to develop their own independent skill in handling the paste, and teachers must be careful to provide enough supervision, carefully chosen supplies, and room for children to try out their own ideas. Young children are fascinated by paste and glue the first time they encounter it. It is so similar in texture to food and soap, and yet it is used in such a different way. Their knowledge base may already include the "rule" that food is not smeared on paper.

It is the teacher's task to differentiate paste and glue and their use from that of food. In the initial exploration, concentrate on the paste or glue rather than on the papers that will be glued. Later, in the practice activities, help the children explore the textures, colors, and shapes of the collage items.

What to Say

Use this activity to talk about the texture of the paste or glue and the shapes and colors of the papers. Use a vocabulary that describes the materials the child is using.

> **"Does the paste feel smooth and sticky?"**
> **"You used a red square!"**
> **"You put the green shape next to the blue one."**

Words to use include collage, paste, glue, stick, stuck, attached, wet, gooey, sticky, smooth, cool, cold, damp, squares, rectangles, triangles, circles, and the color names.

As with drawing, make up songs and rhymes about the activity, and sing them while toddlers are working. Preschoolers can sing when they are done working and are busy cleaning up (invent a cleanup song), or they can sing and mime the collage activity during circle time.

Transition Out

When the children are finished with their collages, help them wipe their hands on a predampened paper towel, and then go to the sink to wash off. This prewiping removes any excess paste and also makes it quicker to wash off the remainder. As the children become more independent, the habit of prewiping will prevent items from sticking to their fingers instead of the paper. It will also help keep paste and glue from getting on their clothing and the furniture as they move to the sink. Knowing that they can quickly and easily get the paste off makes many children more comfortable investigating such sticky stuff, and it may also help discourage children's "automatic" wiping of their hands on their clothing.

Music Box

"Pasting"

(To the tune, "Mary Had a Little Lamb")

I am busy pasting, pasting, pasting. [or gluing]
I am busy pasting,
Pasting all day long.

Watch me paste a triangle, triangle, triangle.
   [Substitute other words for triangle—rectangle, yellow square, etc.]
Watch me paste a triangle,
On my paper now!

Now I wipe my fingers, fingers, fingers.
Now I wipe my fingers,
On my paper towel!

Now I wash my fingers, fingers, fingers.
Now I wash my fingers,
My collage is done!

Place the finished collages in an out-of-the-way place to dry. Chapter 5 outlines plans for a drying box that is very convenient for collages as well as prints and paintings. Paste does not hold very securely, so handle the dried collages with care.

More to Do

Every collage experience can be new and different. It is easy to vary the materials that are offered so the children's motivation to explore and practice will remain high. Children will steadily develop more control over the paste and glue if they are given many opportunities to make collages. The challenge of applying paste to objects of different textures and forms will help develop their hand-eye coordination.

Vary the paper. Offer shapes made from different textures of paper.

Explore on their own. Young artists can also tear or cut their own shapes. (See the section on cutting that follows.)

Try different pastes. Offer paste with different consistencies and textures.

Introduce glue. When children can control paste, glue sticks, and dabs of glue add bottled white or gel glue to the collage experience. These glues will enable children to use heavier and irregularly shaped objects in their collages.

Learning to wipe fingers after pasting is an important skill for collage making.

Teacher Tip

Brushes and Glue

Do not use paintbrushes for glue. The glue stiffens up the brush, making it unusable for painting; more important, it confuses the children. If they see a brush being used in the glue, they think all brushes can be used in glue, which can lead to the ruin of many good paintbrushes.

The four-ounce size works well. Glue can be bought by the gallon to refill the smaller bottles.

Introduce new materials. In the beginning, offer only limited types of materials at a time. Slowly, as the children grow in skill, introduce materials that are more difficult to paste or glue. Once they can paste down stiff materials, such as construction paper, oak-tag, posterboard, and cardboard, offer some pieces of lighter paper, such as magazine clippings, newsprint, newspaper, white tissue, and paper doilies.

Irregular objects, such as leaves, yarn, and string, can be added once the child can position these items fairly accurately in the paste or glue. Remember that young children often put a large quantity of paste and materials on a single collage. If the glued items will end up being somewhat heavy, provide a stiff base such as cereal-box–type cardboard, chipboard, or corrugated cardboard. If a base proves too light, it is easy to slip a piece of cardboard under the child's finished collage and staple it to provide support.

Try magazine clippings. Initial selections should focus on color, texture, or pattern rather than on objects. Precut them into simple shapes. Be prepared for the children to paste them down with either side facing up. Because the paper is lighter, some children may have more difficulty picking the pieces up, especially if they are lying flat on a table top. Place the

Artist's Tool Box

Recommended Commercial Adhesives

Glue Sticks

Advantages: Large glue sticks are easy for young toddlers to use. Children can grasp them in one or two hands and easily rub the glue on the backing paper. Disappearing-color glue sticks help the child see where the glue has been put. Glue sticks work best for most paper and fabric.

Disadvantages: One major difficulty is that caps are difficult for young children to remove and put back on. Often the stick of glue is damaged in the process. This is a skill that needs to be taught and practiced. In addition, children often push up the stick more than needed and overapply the glue. Glue sticks do not work well for three-dimensional objects, so they are limited to only certain types of collage. Compared to bottled glue, they are also expensive.

White Glue (also called School Glue)

Advantages: This is a strong, durable adhesive that can be used to glue all kinds of objects. Choose only the type that indicates it washes out of clothing. White glue can be thinned with water and spread on a base to provide a preglued surface for collage. It will stay wet five to ten minutes. It easily cleans up with water, and it is available in a wide variety of sizes and bottle designs. It dries clear.

Disadvantages: The runny consistency makes this glue more difficult for young children to control. When applied heavily, it wrinkles the paper. Its major disadvantage is that it dries very slowly. Projects must be dried flat for at least 30 minutes before they can be handled. (Tacky or craft versions of this glue can be used in specific situations when instant adhesion is required, but it does not wash out of clothing.)

Gel Glue

Advantages: This glue is transparent and may be lightly colored. It dries clear, leaving a shiny mark on the paper. It is strong enough to hold a variety of lightweight- and medium-weight objects. It cleans up with water and does not stain clothing. It is available in bottles similar to that of the white glue, as well as in roller and tube forms.

Disadvantages: This glue is runnier than white glue and is hard for children to control. When glueing fabric, for example, the glue quickly comes right through and wets the fingers. It dries slowly and wrinkles the paper.

Other Adhesives

There are many other pastes and glues on the market. Many of them are not safe for young children (see chapter 6). Others are difficult for the children to handle, such as the mucilage, cellulose, and wheat pastes, which are very sticky or runny. Glue pens and rollers are much more expensive (often three times the cost of white glue!) and work best with children who are skilled in handling drawing tools. See appendix A for recipes for homemade pastes.

Tape

Avoid masking tape and transparent tape. Even though tape is easy to use, it is neither a permanent nor an artistic way to hold art materials together. Unfortunately, once children become accustomed to using tape, they do not want to use the messier and more challenging paste and glue.

pieces in a flat, low-sided basket to make them easier for the children to manipulate them.

Create theme collages. Young children can be offered simple pictures on a theme. Before they begin collage making, however, take time to introduce the pictures. Play simple guessing or identifying games with them, such as "Can you find a yellow flower?" or "Put your finger on the blue car." It helps if the pictures relate to the children's interests. For example, if at the moment they are very involved in car play, then pictures of cars would be a good choice for a theme. Once the children are successful at identification, invite them to use the theme-related pictures in a collage.

Regardless of how competent the children are at identifying the pictures, expect some to be placed on "upside down" or "backward." It is an advanced skill for a child to turn a picture over and put paste on the back. Limiting picture selection to a theme is also a very dif-

Safety Note

Crepe paper and colored tissue paper are not recommended. When wet, the color bleeds out of them and may stain skin and surfaces.

ficult concept, requiring sophisticated sorting skills that should not be expected in children under age four.

Try textured paper. Keep the children interested in making simple collages by offering shapes cut from a variety of papers. Look for papers that are brightly col-

Teacher to Family

Sample Letter to Families: Requesting Collage Materials

Collage supplies can be contributed by families. Send a letter home (such as the one below), or post a sign in a place where parents congregate. Change the list of items to match what is needed. Have clearly labeled containers ready so children can practice sorting when they bring in supplies.

Dear Family,

One of the children's favorite art activities is making collages. Could you please check around your home and see if you have any of the following materials that we can use in making collages?

Bottle caps

Buttons

Cloth scraps

Ribbon

Spools

Styrofoam packing beads (any shape)

Wood shavings

Wrapping paper

Yarn

All contributions are greatly appreciated!

Your child's teacher,

ored or with interesting patterns. Unusual papers are often found in packaging or in advertising brochures. For young children just learning how to paste, select stiffer papers. Corrugated paper, oaktag, and cardboard all work well for beginning independent pasting. Textured paper can be offered mixed with construction paper or on its own. Make up an attractive basket of papers that will relate to each other in some way, either by shape, color, or pattern. For example, offer squares of yellow construction paper, with a yellow-patterned wallpaper and a gold metallic giftwrap.

Occasionally offer a textured paper, such as a paper placemat, as a base for the collage. If the paper is flimsy, such as giftwrap, glue it to a piece of construction paper or thin cardboard first.

Offer cloth and yarns. Textiles make interesting additions to collages. Most young children cannot cut such materials, so precut them into simple shapes. In addition to fabric, offer ribbon pieces, rickrack, lace, thick yarns, and strings. Cut all of these linear items into short lengths, no longer than six inches, to make them easier for young children to handle.

Glue sticks will not hold these items very securely.

Safety Notes

Make sure objects offered for collage are safe for children under age three. Use the choke test to be sure (see chapter 6).

Glitter and metallic confetti are not recommended for young children. These items stick to children's hands and can get rubbed into the eyes.

Lick-and-stick papers should also be avoided. They give the children the impression that it is all right to put art materials into the mouth.

This may be the time to introduce white glue with these new materials. White glue is much messier for children to handle than glue sticks, because it is runnier. Always choose the washable type. Put a small amount on a plastic lid and allow children to use their fingers. Provide a damp paper towel for wiping fingers clean. Demonstrate how to dab the glue with fingers.

Include assorted objects. Many three-dimensional items can be added to collages once white glue has been introduced and handled successfully. Items for children under age three must pass the choke test. Be on the lookout for collage materials both inside and outdoors.

Making Connections

Language. Read a book illustrated with collages such as: *My House* (Desimini, 1994), *Where the Forest Meets the Sea* (Baker, 1987), *Window* (Baker, 1991), and *Mole's Hill* (Ehlert, 1994). *Lucy's Picture* (Moon, 1994) describes how a little girl chooses to make a collage instead of a painting by collecting objects in her schoolyard. Have the children identify the different materials used by the artists in their collages. (See appendix B for more books illustrated with collage.)

Read a book illustrated with collages by Eric Carle, such as *The Tiny Seed* (1987) or *The Grouchy Ladybug*

Special Needs

Other Ways to Paste

Some of the youngest children who have undeveloped small muscle control, or children with special needs, may have difficulty handling paste or glue.

Another way to make collages is to use a piece of cardboard as a spreader to coat a base paper with thinned white glue. The children can then arrange their shapes by placing them on the sticky paper.

A different method is to remove the backing from contact paper and staple it, sticky side up, to a heavy piece of construction paper. Both paper and small objects can then be placed on the sticky surface.

Artist's Tool Box

Suggested Collage Objects

(White glue is recommended for most of these items.)

From Nature

acorns, feathers, flowers, leaves, pebbles, sand (under special conditions), seashells, seeds, stones, twigs, walnut shells

From Home

aluminum foil, bottle caps, cardboard, carpet pieces, cork pieces, cotton, cotton balls, dried beans,* jar lids, macaroni, nails and screws, tubes from paper toweling or toilet paper (cut into short, one-half-inch to one-inch slices), rice,* string, Styrofoam packing beads

From Crafts

beads, buttons, cotton and polyester batting, craft sticks, fabric, foam pieces, fun fur, giftwrap bows, jewelry pieces, leather scraps, paper confetti, pompons, ribbon, rickrack, sponge pieces, spools, stuffing (polyester), tiles, wood scraps, wood shavings, wooden ice cream spoons (also called craft spoons), wool fleece, yarn

---

(1977). Paint, print, and draw on colored paper, and then use these to create a class Big Book illustrated with collages made by the children.

Math. Have children freely cut out shapes from a piece of paper. Collect everyone's shapes. Describe their characteristics, such as size, color, and shape, and then have children work together to sort them. Use the sorted shapes for collages.

Science. Read the book *Paper, Paper Everywhere* (Gibbons, 1983), and explore how paper is made.

Artist's Tool Box

Suggested Collage Papers

Advertising brochures
Binders' board
Candy wrappers
Cereal-box cardboard
Chipboard
Computer paper
Corrugated cardboard
Doilies
Fluorescent paper
Fadeless construction
    paper

Art boards
Blotter paper
Cardstock
Charcoal paper
Coffee filters
Construction paper
Corrugated paper
Drawing paper
Foil paper
Giftwrap
Graph paper

Holographic foils
Magazine pages
Marble paper
Metallic paper
Newspaper
Oaktag
Paper plates
Photographs
Rainbow construction
    paper
Shelf paper
Tracing paper
Velour paper
Watercolor paper
White tissue paper

Kraft pages
Manila
Mat board
Napkins
Newsprint
Paper placemats
Paper towels
Poster board
Rice paper
Sandpaper
Tag board
Typing paper
Wallpaper
Waxed paper

EXPLORING SCISSORS AGES THREE AND UP

Young children are not ready to use scissors until they have control over their wrists and fingers. Children who are not physically able to use scissors find trying to cut extremely frustrating. Within a normal group of young children, there may be children who may not yet be ready to cut, some who may be just beginning to develop sufficient control, and some who are expert cutters. It is important to design open-ended activities in which cutting always remains an option. Collage activities provide a wonderful way to slowly introduce cutting-skill practice.

Group Composition

Depending on the skill level of the particular children, they can work in groups of four to six. Choose a smaller group size if most of the children are just beginning to cut and a larger one if most of the children are competent with scissors.

Setup

The collage area can be a low table with or without chairs. The surface should be bare. Have a wastebasket, paper recycling bin, and/or paper scrap box nearby, along with a dustpan and broom for quick cleanups.

Materials

Choose one of the kinds of scissors listed in the Artist's Tool Box on p. 113. In the beginning, provide construction paper cut into rectangular strips about 1 by 12 inches. Regular construction paper is the easiest for children to learn to cut. Lighter papers, such as newsprint, are more difficult, because they bend easily, and heavier papers, such as tag board, require more hand strength. Individual allotments of glue and base paper (such as manila or white, about 12 by 18 inches) should be set out on the table. Have damp paper towels readily available.

Warm-Up

The children should have had some experiences tearing paper before they are offered scissors. They should be familiar with the collage process and how the ma-

Classroom Museum

Use the book *The Block* (Hughes, 1995) to introduce the collage art of African-American artist Romare Bearden.

terials are set up for their use. When they are comfortable making collages on their own from precut and torn paper, introduce the scissors.

The book *Let's Make Rabbits* (Lionni, 1982) is a good introduction to the idea of cutting paper for artwork. Talk about how drawing is different from collage, but how both are ways to create art. Leo Lionni uses collage for many of his illustrations. Display several of his books, and challenge the children to find the different kinds of paper he used. Other books that feature torn- and cut-paper illustrations are *The Grouchy Ladybug* (Carle, 1977) and *The Snowy Day* (Keats, 1962).

What to Do

When a number of the children seem ready to manipulate scissors, introduce them as a tool that will be available for their use. Show the children where the scissors will be permanently stored. Scissors can be hung on a peg board with other tools or placed in a storage rack or in an attractively decorated can or box. Explain that scissors can be used for cutting paper and collage materials. Set up clear safety rules for using the scissors, including keeping them in a designated area, moving safely with them, and cutting only collage materials with them.

Demonstrate how to handle the scissors safely by always holding them with the hand clasped around the closed blade. Have the children practice handing plastic or model scissors around a circle with the blade closed and tipping the handle toward the next child. The child receiving the scissors should also grasp them by the closed blades. Make up a scissors rhyme such as "The Scissors Passing Song," and sing or chant it while they practice. Once the children are familiar with the location of scissors and the safety rules, begin an introductory cut-paper collage exploration. Once scissors are introduced, the children will naturally be motivated to try out this new tool. There is a fascination with the cutting process, as the children derive a real sense of power from being allowed to handle a (somewhat) dangerous tool.

1. When helping children learn how to hold scissors, it is useful to understand the position of the hand when cutting. Take a scissors and open and close it as if to cut something. Notice that just to use the scissors requires a turn of the wrist. The fingers move in opposition to the thumb. Try cutting a piece of paper. The hand muscles tighten to hold the scissors steady. Children may need assistance in positioning the scissors. If necessary, gently guide their hands into the proper position.

2. Initially most young children will cut with just the tip of the scissors, which is why narrow strips are offered at the start. When the children are more competent, offer other shapes for them to cut up. At this stage, most children will be able to cut short, straight cuts. Being able to cut curves and along drawn lines are advanced skills that many children will just be approaching by the end of their fourth year. They will also not yet be competent at coordinating both holding and turning the paper, which is necessary to cut out shapes. Do not plan activities that require children to cut out teacher-specified or predrawn shapes. If, on occasion, the children choose to cut out something they have drawn on their own, then that will serve as a more creative way to learn these more advanced skills.

3. Closely supervise the initial cutting activities of each child. Because the children will be at various stages, they will need different kinds of help.

4. Demonstrate for the more advanced cutters how to make simple shapes by cutting off the corners of a piece of paper using a straight cut, and how to make a "fringe" effect by making a row of straight cuts along one side of a paper.

5. As they gain hand strength, encourage them to open the scissors wider with each cut so that they can cut a longer snip with each hand motion.

6. Make sure to give general reminders to everyone that they can tear paper as well, so that children

Teacher Tip

Dealing with Cutting Problems

Hesitancy. If children have been forbidden to use scissors in the home, they may be hesitant to begin at first. Give them gentle encouragement to try the scissors.

Difficulty holding scissors. Watch for children who are having difficulty holding the scissors vertically to the paper. Check that they are using the thumb and index fingers to hold the scissors. If they are, gently guide their scissors into the correct position. It may help to hold the paper for them to practice the first few snips. There are also trainer scissors that can be used to give them a start. Sometimes the scissors are too heavy for the child's hand. In this case, the scissors will tip or wobble unsteadily, and the child will not be able to cut paper. Light plastic scissors should be made available to the children.

Hand position. Some children may need help positioning the hand that is holding the paper. Make sure that they learn to keep their fingers out of the path of the scissors.

Paper bends. One of the most frustrating things for a young child is when the paper bends instead of being cut. This often indicates that they are not exerting enough pressure as they close the scissors. If they keep trying to cut in the same spot, they will never succeed. Suggest that they try cutting in another place or using a different piece. Check that the child is holding the scissors in the correct position, as poor hand position often causes the paper to bend.

Using scissors is a complex skill.

who have not yet mastered cutting understand that tearing is also appropriate.

7. Most children will be so involved in cutting the first few times that they will put little time into the actual collage. Once they become confident in their cutting skills, they will go on to create their collages again.

8. Although this sounds like constant interaction with the children, actually this assistance only takes a brief moment or two. Move from child to child, giving help as needed. There will be plenty of time

Working with different kinds of materials requires serious concentration.

Music Box

The Scissors Passing Song

(To the tune, "My Bonnie Lies Over the Ocean")

Scissors are made for cutting,
And handle them safely I must!
When passing the scissors to others,
I must always be holding them shut!

"I cut out shapes to make my dancing man." Cut paper collage—*Colin, age 4½*

Introduce sorting the paper into good scraps that can be used again and sticky ones that have to be thrown away, but do not expect perfect sorting at this age. The scrap box that is created in this exploration can become a regular offering for collage activities. When the scraps are picked up, the children can rinse their hands at the sink.

More to Do

Continue to make the scissors and paper to cut available on a daily basis. Cutting is a skill that only improves with practice.

Cutting in other activities. In addition to cutting shapes for their collages, children can also practice cutting in a variety of other activities, such as puppet making, mask making, printing activities, and constructed sculptures.

to step back and observe the children working. Make sure the children are given time to explore and learn on their own. Step in to help only when the child asks for help or is obviously frustrated.

What to Say

When children need help, quietly show them how to do it, while saying, "It might be smoother if you did this," or "Let's drive your scissors this way."

Vocabulary to use with cutting activities: cut, snip, divide, side, edge, pieces, change, larger, smaller, jagged, sharp, straight, half, and all of the shape names.

Transition Out

When children are done cutting and pasting their pieces down on the base paper, they should clean up the leftover paper clippings. Remind the children to wipe their fingers on a wet paper towel before they handle the scraps.

Special Needs

Other Ways to Cut

Children who have difficulty using their fingers, hands, or wrists will find cutting with a traditional scissors difficult. Scissors that are squeezed together between the thumb and all of the opposing fingers, and that open automatically with a spring, work well for some children. These are often called "snips." Try to select the lightest-weight pair with the bluntest point.

Another option is the use of a rotary cutter, similar to that used by quilters. Look for ones designed for use by children that have a protective cover over the blade. A cutting mat to protect the surface is needed. This mat should also provide a gripping surface to hold the paper still while the child cuts. This setup will allow a child who can only grip with a fist to become quite proficient at cutting. But since the blade is very sharp, provide watchful supervision.

Artist's Tool Box

Cutting Tools

Scissors. Select scissors that are lightweight and move easily at the pivot. They should be sharp enough to cut paper with very light pressure. They should have a blunt tip. Scissors should be designed for use in either the left or right hand.

All-plastic scissors are best for toddlers and younger preschoolers. These scissors will not cut hair, skin, or fabric. Older children can use pairs with lightweight stainless steel blades with plastic handles. They can also use the new children's scissors that make decorative cuts.

Training scissors. For toddlers or children with impaired finger dexterity, select training scissors that have blunt tips and spring-apart, plastic-coated handles.

Double-ring training scissors. These scissors have a pair of outer rings so that as the child holds the scissors, you can guide the actual cutting. They are most useful for children who have dexterity and strength but do not turn the wrist enough to hold the scissors vertically to the paper. This problem is usually manifested when the child tries to cut, but instead the paper folds. Usually the child only needs to use them once or twice. If there continues to be a problem, have the child try the training scissors.

Rotary hand cutter. This cutting tool is very sharp and must be used with close supervision, however, it may be the only way some children can cut. Make sure the blade is covered and the handle easy to grasp. Look for ones with an automatically closing cover. It must be used with a cutting mat underneath at all times.

Teacher's scissors. Adults are always cutting many unusual items for collages. Invest in the best quality, all-purpose snips to be found. These usually have stainless steel blades, spring-apart blades, and a lock mechanism, which makes them safer to have around young children. They should be able to cut through heavy cardboard, all fabrics, carpet, leather, branches, pipe cleaners, wire, and more.

Offer other papers. Once the children have become competent using the scissors to cut construction paper, offer different weights of paper for them to try. Drawing paper, manila, wallpaper, and kraft paper are in the same range as construction paper. The lighter papers, such as newsprint, tracing paper, and metallics, are a little more difficult.

Cutting special materials. Many young children cannot cut papers as light as tissue paper, and they also have great difficulty with cardboard, fabric, and yarn. To cut these items, the children need to open the scissors as wide as they go, and the scissors need to be sharp. If children become frustrated, assure them that special scissors are sometimes needed to cut such materials.

Always have precut pieces available in a variety of sizes and shapes. If any children are having trouble cutting, help them find other pieces that they can use.

Making Connections

Language. Read these books, illustrated with cut-paper collages: *At the Beach* (Lee, 1994), *The Lion's Whiskers* (Day, 1995), and *Sea Shapes* (MacDonald, 1994).

Teaching in Action

Introducing Collage to Toddlers

Who: Toddler group 1½–2 years

When: Fall day

Why:

Language: Children will develop vocabulary by describing leaves.

Cognitively: Children will develop patterning, sequencing, and computation skills when they compare, order, and count leaves.

Physically: Children will develop small motor skills by handling and gluing down leaves.

Socially: Children will develop social skills by participating in a group experience.

Perceptually: Children will develop skill at identifying leaf shapes.

Emotionally: Children will develop self-confidence by successfully making a collage.

Where: With assistants holding their hands, toddlers will go outside under the big maple tree in the yard.

What: Need a basket, leaves, paper, and glue (or contact paper with the backing peeled off).

How:

Introductory experience: Take toddlers outside on a fall day. Try to have one adult or older child paired with one or two children. Together, collect leaves.

What to do: As children find leaves, help them name the colors and describe how beautiful they are. Put the leaves in an attractive basket. Inside, put the basket of leaves on a table. Have the children come to the table one at a time. Spread glue on a piece of paper, or use sticky-side-up contact paper. Have children select several leaves and place them on the paper.

What to say: Talk about the colors and shapes. Count them. Help children remember how it felt to collect them. Ask them why they chose the leaves they did.

Transition out: When all children have made a collage, read the book *Red Leaf Yellow Leaf* (Ehlert, 1991). Have children point out the leaves in the pictures.

SELF-EXPLORATION: WHAT IS IN A NAME?

In this box, write your name in as many different ways as possible. When the paper is full or you run out of ideas, make a list of all the ways they are different in terms of color, size, and thickness.

How many different ways did you invent?

_____

How many look similar to your signature?

_____

How many look different?

_____

How did you use your creativity to invent new ways to write your name?

_____

_____

_____

_____

_____

Studio Page 14

CREATING AN ART NOTEBOOK

In order to develop a creative art program for young children, you need to have knowledge and skill. No one, however, can carry everything about teaching art to young children around in his or her head. By creating your own original notebook on how to teach art to young children, you will build a personal knowledge base that will guide you in a way that no commercial book can. At the same time, creating such a notebook will allow you to personally experience the same creative process that your young artists do, as you develop your own art skills.

Some ideas for your notebook:

1. **An attractive, durable cover:** You will probably be using this notebook for many years. You may want to share it with other teachers or parents. Make sure you have plenty of room for expansion, for it will never be done!

2. **A table of contents:** Before you begin, prepare a list of what you want to include in your notebook. As you put the book together, you will be able to see which areas you know a lot about and which you need to study more.

3. **A way of organizing the information:** Design some kind of divider that clearly marks off each section. The knowledge in your notebook is useless if you cannot find it readily.

4. **Information from books and magazines on art for young children:** Make a collection of ideas, research, and new techniques that relates to teaching art.

5. **Observation notes:** Any observations that you make about children should be saved in your notebook. Also, record anecdotal accounts of your interactions with children and parents. These will form a comparative base from which to design plans and determine your future behavior.

6. **Unit plans and activity plans:** It takes a lot of time to write plans. Save all of your plans, as they will guide you in writing the plans for the next group.

7. **Recipes:** In this section, make a collection of recipes that you have tried and that worked well for you.

8. **Sample projects:** If you try out any activities or materials, save the samples in this section. You can also include children's work. Make sure you label these samples—how, when, what—or they will be useless as a reference.

9. **Illustrations:** Words are fine, but pictures can often say more than words. Sketch, photograph, or clip illustrations for all sections from magazines and catalogs. Art supply catalogs are a good source of material.

10. **Bibliography** Record the bibliographic information for any books or articles you have found helpful. You never know when you will need them again.

11. **Personal diary of experiences:** You will be creating this notebook for yourself. It will be only as useful as you make it. If you do not write down the great rhyme about glueing that you just made up, or note how many minutes it took to wash the hands of 20 three-year-olds, then you may lose that knowledge.

Studio Page 15

OBSERVING THE CREATIVE PROCESS IN YOURSELF

After you have worked on your notebook for several weeks, answer these questions.

1. What knowledge do you need to create this notebook?

   _____

   _____

   _____

2. What is motivating you to make this notebook?

   _____

   _____

   _____

3. What skills do you have that will help you create this notebook? What skills do you need to learn?

   _____

   _____

   _____

4. When do you find is the best time to work on this book? How do you feel if you are interrupted?

   _____

   _____

   _____

5. How do you feel when you figure out how you will include something in your book? Did you have fun designing a cover and making the illustrations? Did you include anything funny—cartoons or anecdotal stories? Did you include anything about which you care deeply?

   _____

   _____

   _____

6. How do you feel about your notebook? Would you like it to be graded or compared to someone else's? Why or why not?

   _____

   _____

   _____

Studio Page 16

DEFINING CREATIVE BEHAVIOR

Just how broadly creativity is defined is critical to any program planning, for far too often creative ideas are ignored, or worse yet, actively squelched when well-meaning educators are only watching for a creative product that matches their aesthetic standards.

—Nancy Lee Cecil and Phyllis Lauritzen (1995, p. 28)

Analyze each of the following behaviors in terms of whether or not you would consider it creative, and what action you would take, if any, to change or control the behavior.

☼ A child eats a piece of play dough, because "it looked like a banana."

_____

_____

_____

☼ A child glues his paper to the table, because he "didn't want it to slide off the table."

_____

_____

_____

☼ A child runs around the room biting everyone with his paper "snake."

_____

_____

_____

☼ A child pours glue into a box of collage papers.

_____

_____

_____

☼ A child uses a scissors to cut the hair of another child.

_____

_____

_____

For additional information on teaching art to young children, visit our Web site at http://www.earlychilded.delmar.com

Integrating the Curriculum

> " Through the multiple threads of many activities, learning can be woven into a whole cloth. "
>
> —Pearl Greenberg (1972, p. 85)

Questions Addressed in This Chapter:

- ✿ How can art activities be integrated throughout the curriculum?
- ✿ What is an introductory experience?
- ✿ What is the thematic approach?
- ✿ What is the project approach?

Young Artists at Work

Dennis has found a dead butterfly in the grass by the swing. He bends over and picks it up gently. "Look!" he says, "I've found a butterfly." Several other children gather around.

"I've seen one like that."

"My sister caught a butterfly."

"Can I have it?"

The teacher notices the group of children and approaches. "Look at my butterfly," Dennis says proudly.

"It has so many colors!" responds the teacher. "I see gold and blue. What do you see?"

"Here's some red and yellow," answers Dennis.

"It has lots of feet," Tomas adds.

"Wow, there is so much to see! Why don't we take it inside and look at it with the magnifying glass?" suggests the teacher.

Inside, Dennis places the butterfly on a soft cushion of paper towels, and the children take turns looking at it through the magnifying glass. Some children begin to pretend they are butterflies fluttering around the room. The teacher says invitingly, "Would you like to paint with butterfly colors?"

"Yes," say the children.

Gold, blue, red, yellow, and black paints are put out at a table. A group of children begins to paint enthusiastically. One paints a huge head and body with many legs and swirls of color around it. Another dabs his brush up and down lightly across his paper. "My brush is a butterfly flying from flower to flower," he says.

Another girl studies the butterfly, then runs over to the table. She makes a tiny dab of paint on her paper. Then she goes back and observes again. Back and forth she goes, choosing each color and stroke with deliberation. "My butterfly is the same size," she states with assurance.

Dennis is painting too. His paper is covered with bold strokes of lines and colors. "This is a butterfly day," he declares.

HOW CAN ART ACTIVITIES BE INTEGRATED THROUGHOUT THE CURRICULUM?

Art is a powerful learning tool. It develops fine motor skills and hand-eye coordination. It activates the spatial domain and stimulates the senses. It is a creative playground for the growing mind. Young children need to use the power of art to express their ideas and knowledge and to respond to their experiences. An integrated art program provides children with the opportunity not only to explore art materials in open-ended ways but also to express what they are learning using visual and spatial symbols. In such a program, art activities expand from the art center and radiate into all areas of learning.

Steps toward Integration

Integrating art into the curriculum requires the teacher to approach art in different ways for distinctive purposes. Lessons must be intertwined, so that children acquire art concepts and skills, use art to connect learning across the disciplines, and respond to experiences through art. Building an integrated art program takes time and effort.

Step 1: Teaching about art. Teachers can begin by teaching art as a discrete subject area with concepts and skills unique to it. A lesson in which the teacher presents a new art medium and then asks children to explore it, or one that has children look at a sculpture and then asks them to imagine how the artist made it, is a lesson about art, addressing the skills, tools, and work of artists. Children must have artistic skills and knowledge in order to use art effectively and creatively in other subject areas. Teachers must plan thoughtful, well-organized lessons with clearly stated objectives that focus directly on art and artists and that provide many opportunities for art exploration and practice. Chapters 7 and 8 suggest ways to teach about art concepts, artists, and their work.

Step 2: Connecting art. Next, art can be connected with learning in other subject areas. A lesson that has children sketch the parts of a flower or that has children draw a picture to illustrate their journal entry is a lesson that uses art to enhance learning in another subject area. This is learning with art. These

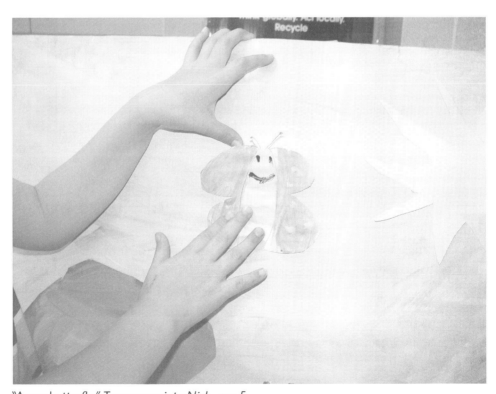

"Angry butterfly." Tempera paint—*Nick, age 5*

kinds of lessons allow children to use art materials to create visual and spatial symbols that express concepts and ideas in other subject areas. Connecting art in this way enriches the learning experience, because it provides multiple pathways for children to make what they are learning about more meaningful. Art can be connected in this way to math, science, social studies, literature, and the other arts. The Making Connections suggestions found in each Creating Art section provide many examples of ways to connect art with other subjects.

Connected art lessons can develop in several ways. They may be carefully planned as part of the curriculum. Children studying trees as part of a unit of study may be given clipboards to use in making labeled sketches of the trees on the playground. On the other hand, sometimes a wondering question may set the stage for an activity. For example, children measuring water at the water table wonder aloud what happens when different amounts of water are added to paint. The alert teacher quickly sets up a paint and water mixing activity and invites the young scientists to explore.

Art activities can also lead to lessons in other curriculum areas. The butterfly painting activity described at the beginning of the chapter could be connected to reading books about butterflies, dramatizing their life cycle, hatching a cocoon, or creating a graph of the different butterflies observed by the children on the playground.

Step 3: Learning through art. In a fully integrated art program, art is found everywhere in the classroom. Art pursuits flow into and out of the daily classroom activities as children need them. Instead of children passing through the art center, each taking a turn at the art medium being offered that day, they are offered a well-stocked art supply center from which they can select familiar tools and media that best meet their expressive needs at that moment. In such a classroom, children studying about homes, for example, may choose to draw "blueprints" of their block constructions or make crayon sketches of the houses near the school. One child may spend several days building a complex house of Styrofoam pieces, while another paints houses at the easel one day and creates a house from collage materials the next.

Ways to Integrate

In order for this level of integration to occur, children must have ideas and experiences to express. There are several ways to provide unifying experiences that inspire children to communicate their ideas artistically.

Cross-curriculum introductions. Introductory experiences are short, attention-getting activities, drawn from different areas of learning, such as reading a story or singing a song, that lead into an integrated learning experience. They work well with toddlers who have short attention spans and in situations where children attend a program for only a few days a week. Because new introductions can be given each day, this also works well for groups with changing membership, such as child care situations.

Thematic approach. The thematic approach unifies the skills, knowledge, and concepts to be taught under a common theme. Because thematic teaching requires sufficient time to develop in-depth knowledge, it works best when the same group of children attends on a regular basis for a significant length of time.

Project approach. The project approach starts with a topic and then fosters the children's exploration of that topic as they apply already acquired knowledge and skills in making sense of new material. The project approach can be used with a group of children that shares a common interest. It is particularly designed to meet the needs of children in prekindergarten, kindergarten, and the primary grades, and it can be very effective in multiage classes, because it draws on the differing skills and knowledge of each child.

WHAT IS A CROSS-CURRICULUM INTRODUCTORY EXPERIENCE?

The purpose of the introductory experience or warm-up is to help children get ready to learn. The experience should unify the information being presented so that it is more understandable and can smoothly transition children's thinking into the topic being discussed. Using Gardner's multiple intelligences (MI) as a guide can be an effective way to organize information to be taught. Figure 5–3, on p. 129, provides an example of an MI planning web. This kind of web can used to plan either a one-day group of activities or a unit that will span several days or weeks. From a web such as this, one attention-grabbing activity can be selected as the introductory experience to the topic of the day or to a unit of study.

Selecting an Effective Warm-up

An effective introduction builds interest and activates curiosity. Depending on the purpose of the learning, the age of the children, and the time frame, warm-ups can take many forms. An exciting cross-curriculum introduction could be listening to a story, drawing a picture, singing a song, or engaging in a movement activity. Science experiments, nature walks, and special events can all lead into responsive art activities.

In selecting the warm-up, look for one that meets the following characteristics:

It nurtures creativity. A perceptually rich warm-up does not determine what the resulting artwork will be. Instead, it encourages a wide range of artistic response. Singing a song about a bird and then having the children cut out preprinted bird shapes does not foster creativity. Instead, after singing the song, challenge children to imagine that they are flying birds, and then paint, draw, or make collages that show what it feels like to fly like a bird.

It develops understanding. A successful warm-up increases children's perceptual awareness and cognitive understanding. Reading a story, for example, about how different colors mix to form new ones, such as *Colors* (Felix, 1993), will entrance toddlers with the idea that certain colors can be combined to make new ones. Then, when they paint, they will relate what happens on their paper to what they heard in the story.

It matches needs and interests. Successful warm-ups fit the needs and interests of the children. Sometimes the best ones are those that occur at the spur of the moment. For example, a group of children is excitedly watching what happens when some paint mixes with water in the sink. An introduction can be as simple as asking them what would happen if they put water on paper and then painted on it. At other times, a carefully planned introduction can spark or renew a less outwardly visible interest, such as sharing the story *Galimoto* (Williams, 1990), and then wondering aloud what kind of toys could be invented from things in the collage center.

It matches the ages and attention span of the children. The younger the child, the less time should separate the warm-up from the activities, and the more directly it must relate to the present interest of the child. Brief introductory experiences, such as sharing a short poem or chant, painting with an imaginary paintbrush, and pointing out a pattern on a piece of clothing, take only a few minutes and are suitable for the short attention span of toddlers. They can also be used with older children when time is limited.

With older children and more time, warm-ups can be more complex. For example, a unit on line can be introduced by reading a story about lines, such as *Billy and the Magic String* (Karnovsky, 1995), then moving kinesthetically in lines, and finally taking a walk and finding lines.

There are many possible ways to integrate art into the curriculum by connecting art activities with learning in other disciplines. Connected learning experiences set the stage for using the language of art. Responsive art activities grow out of such experiences.

Designing Wonderful Introductory Experiences

In order to produce meaningful art, young artists need to participate in experiences that will give them ideas for their work. These experiences must be rich in sensory and visual stimuli. They should be memorable—full of opportunities for asking questions and making observations. Most important, the experience should flow directly into the art activities that are offered to the children.

Be alert. Listen closely to what children are talking about to each other. Be on the lookout for that special event that precipitates children's interest. Have a reservoir of ideas, books, songs, and art materials on hand that can be drawn upon on a moment's notice.

Create enthusiasm. The teacher increases the children's interest by modeling enthusiasm and wonder. Tantalizing questions can make children look more closely or think more deeply. Instead of dismissing

(1)

The children in this kindergarten class made a special visit to their playground. Together with their teacher, they looked carefully at the different shapes and forms and noticed the spaces as well. Then they came back to the classroom and drew pictures in response.

1. "I'm going down the twisty slide." Marker—*Jamie, age 5*
2. "My friends and I like to ride the swings." Marker—*Brittany, age 5*
3. "I like to run and jump all over the playground." Marker—*Joe, age 5*

(2)

(3)

Dennis's discovery of the butterfly with a "That's nice," the teacher draws the children in by pointing out the colors and asking questions about what they see.

Extend the experience. Once the group of children is excited, the teacher needs to build on the experience. If the experience has been planned, the art supplies may already be in place, a book may be set out to be read, and a song prepared to be sung. If it is unexpected, the sensitive teacher discards the plans for the period and instead puts out some familiar art materials and encourages the children to express their observations, reactions, and feelings through art.

Curriculum Connections

Connections are activities in other curriculum areas that can lead into or occur simultaneously with related art activities. For example, if children are experimenting with measuring water at the water table, they can also see what happens when they add different amounts of water to the paints. Cross-curriculum connections are a way of using the experiences gained in one area as a transition into another.

Planning activities that connect across the curriculum helps children appreciate the interconnection of all knowledge and learning. Connections are a simple way to start to form an integrated curriculum. They can be created by focusing on the common elements in two or more areas. For example, both art and science require fine observation skills. Identifying patterns plays an important role in art, math, music, science, and literature. These simple connections are built upon to create an entirely integrated curriculum through the thematic approach.

WHAT IS THE THEMATIC APPROACH?

Life should be a single whole, especially in the earliest years, when the child is forming himself in accordance with the laws of his growth.

—*Maria Montessori (1967, p. 164)*

Many educators would agree that learning is best accomplished when children are surrounded by activities, objects, and active experiences that relate to each other in a meaningful way. Caine and Caine (1994) find that when a thematic approach is used, conditions are created that match optimum requirements for "brain-based" learning. As thematic-based curricula have become widely accepted in early childhood education, more teachers have found that unifying the activities presented to young children is both challenging and very rewarding. The use of themes stimulates both children and teachers to look at the environment around them in new ways.

Planning a Thematic Unit

A thematic curriculum is one in which many different subject areas are integrated by relating them to a carefully selected, broad-based concept. The idea should be expressed in the form of an overarching question or a metaphor that ties together the learning areas. For example, if the chosen theme is "What is water?" then books about water will be read. Children will experiment with water. They will paint with water, wash the dolls and toys in the play area, and splash in water at the water table. They may take a field trip to a stream or lake and talk about the animals that live in the water.

Setting up a thematic unit such as this can be quite time consuming for the teacher. It takes time to locate the books, set up the activities, and plan the field trips. This has led to a profusion of books that present ready-made thematic units, complete with patterns for bulletin boards and ideas for projects, which are often then carried out in lockstep fashion, week by week or month by month.

Rather than following the thematic plan found in a book, a successful and meaningful theme must grow out of the teacher's knowledge of the interests and experiences of the children and must represent a significant element in their lives. Just because there is a wonderful unit on penguins does not mean that this topic will interest a particular group of children, none of whom have ever seen a real penguin.

Selecting a Theme

The following guidelines will aid in the selection of appropriate themes.

What interests them? Begin by learning about the children and their interests. Watch them as they play and interact with each other. What do they talk about? What are their favorite things? Has someone gone on a trip or, like Dennis, brought in something to share that elicits enthusiasm from the others?

Is the concept broad based? Decide if the theme is one that is rich in possibilities for expansion to the different curricula or growth areas. Are there wonderful books to read? Are there related songs and poems? Will there be things to explore through science, art, drama, and play? Will children be able to use skills from all of the multiple intelligences to explore this theme? Some themes have more potential than others (see figure 5–1).

What resources are available? Are the needed supplies available for certain activities? Are there places to visit or people who could talk to the children about this theme? Where can books be found on the theme?

How much time is there? The theme should be open ended enough so if the children's interest wanes it will be easy to move on to something else. There should be sufficient time, however, so if the children become highly interested they do not have to be cut off to "move on." It is not the specific content that teaches. The goal in early childhood education is not to make children experts on the theme. The theme should be a vehicle that allows children to explore and learn about their environment within a meaningful context.

Art in Thematic Units

Thematic teaching provides an excellent way to unify the child's art experiences with the rest of the curriculum. However, it is very important to make sure that the art activities are open ended. It is a real temptation for teachers to want to give the children thematically related pictures to color and patterns to follow, but it must be remembered that such directive activities do not foster artistic growth, no matter how attractive the results may be.

Do not expect or demand that every child make the same theme-related art project to take home. Art allows each child to express a unique view of the thematic experience. Open-ended art activities can be integrated into thematic units in many ways.

Through everyday art. Make sure basic, familiar art supplies are always available. During a thematic unit, children should be free to choose to draw, paint, make a collage, or create a puppet, whether as a personal exploration or as a reaction to a thematically related experience.

Through special materials. Thematically related materials can be offered as a choice. For example, for the thematic unit "What is a tree?" pressed leaves can be added to the collage area, and twigs for painting can be placed alongside brushes at the easel.

Through responsive activities. Encourage children to use drawing as a way to record special events and experiences by providing a special time during which the children "write" and share their ideas. For example, make individual journals by stapling together several sheets of blank or partially lined paper. Then set aside a daily five minutes for children to graphically record their ideas about what they are learning. Have children share their journals with a partner or a small group.

Through group activities. Plan one or more group activities that relate to the theme. Quilts, murals, and box sculptures can be designed to relate to many theme concepts.

Organizing Theme-Related Activities

Once the thematic unit is chosen, brainstorm possible activities. It is important to see beyond the individual activity. Skills and processes in art, as in all subject areas, build on each other. Visualizing the possible directions a thematic unit might take over a period of time enables teachers to see beyond the isolated art activity of the day and allows art materials and techniques to be introduced, explored, practiced, and mastered.

The activities selected should also span the range of developmental growth areas and tap into all of the domains of the multiple intelligences. Consider questions to be addressed, explorations and experiments to be done, vocabulary to use, and assessments to be made. One way to organize this material is to use a planning web or grid (see figures 5–2, 5–3).

Flexible planning. A flexible plan is essential for organizing and carrying out an integrated thematic

Questions for Thematic Units	Possible Topics	Related Art Activities (Note: See Creating Art sections for more details)
How do animals live?	Habitat, shelter, food, food chains, behaviors	Sketch live animals, clay animal models, paint animals. Group: create a zoo, animal habitat mural. Art to view: Edward Hicks's *Peaceable Kingdom* and the art of Henri Rousseau
How do our bodies work?	Body parts, exercise, jobs	Draw people, draw playgrounds, build model of imaginary playground, cut out people pictures from magazines and make collages, puppets. Group: mural of people doing things. Art to view: paintings of people doing things, such as those by William Johnson, Jean Millet, and Edgar Degas
How do we get there?	Transportation: boats, cars, trucks, maps, bridges, stairs, ramps	Draw vehicles, build vehicles from boxes, toy car wheel prints, draw maps, blocks. Group: build model of local roads and places. Art to view: *California Crosswalk*, by Outerbridge (MAPS)
How did these buildings get here?	Architecture, construction equipment, building materials, carpentry, mapping	Blocks, box/papier-mâché buildings, wood sculptures, sketch houses. Group: build city or town model. Art to view: cityscapes by Romare Bearden, Childe Hassam, and Edward Hopper
What can we see?	Eyes, colors, shapes	Paint with different colors, shape/color collages, gadget prints, paint on wet paper, color mixing experiments, sensory experiences, peek boxes. Group: shape or color mural/quilt. Art to view: works by Stuart Davis, Paul Klee, Hans Hofmann, and Piet Mondrian, Amish quilts
What is a family?	Family members, foods, customs	Draw family, make collages of foods/family photos, special objects, puppets. Group: quilt, mini-box or plastic bag mural. Art to view: family portraits by Mary Cassatt and John Singer Sargent, folk art from many places
What is water?	Water sources, uses	Watercolor, sketch pond/puddle/creek, make water creature mobiles, nature collages, boats, pipe maps. Group: box submarine or boat. Art to view: works by Winslow Homer, Claude Monet's *Waterlily* series
Where do we live?	Community, mapping, homes	Sketch stores/houses (inside and outside), draw signs and maps, build box buildings and houses. Group: model community, box house, or store. Art to view: interiors by Albrecht Dürer, Vincent Van Gogh, and Henri Matisse, housing in other cultures
Who are we?	Personal information, portraits, measurement	Self-portraits, masks, costumes, jewelry, collage of favorite things, puppets. Group: portrait mural. Art to view: portraits by Rembrandt Van Ryn, Amedeo Modigliani, and Pierre Renoir

FIGURE 5–1 Sample thematic unit ideas

Language Objectives

These are behaviors and skills that help children receive and communicate ideas through listening, speaking, reading, and writing.

Cognitive Objectives

These are behaviors and skills that help children develop the ability to reason, to think logically, to organize information, to understand mathematical relationships, and to solve problems.

Emotional Objectives

These are behaviors and skills that help children develop independence, understanding, and confidence in their own feelings, preferences, decisions, and abilities.

Social Objectives

These are behaviors and skills that help children get along better with others by showing appropriate reactions to others, such as kindness, acceptance, respect, and affection.

Linguistic Activities

Naming, telling, discussing, describing, defining, retelling, answering, matching lettters to sounds and words, using handwriting, using correct language forms, writing stories, poems, and reports, using the writing process—drafting, editing, and revising own writing and that of others

Logical-Mathematical Activities

Identifying properties of objects, predicting, researching, using and manipulating number concepts, measuring, ordering, comparing, contrasting, finding patterns, using graphic organizers, making graphs, planning and carrying out tests

Intrapersonal Activities

Identifying and expressing personal feelings and preferences, controlling one's feelings and behavior, setting a goal or making a plan and then working to accomplish it, assessing or judging one's own work or efforts

Interpersonal Activities

Sharing, helping, taking turns, performing a role in a cooperative activity, using manners, making moral decisions, settling conflicts, making rules, playing games, and learning about other people and cultures

Thematic Question: A broad, overarching question that addresses an important idea
Concepts: The specific ideas and information children learn through this thematic unit

Musical/Rhythmic Activities

Identifying and using rhythmic and musical elements, critically listening to music, solving aural problems, singing, playing, and composing music, participating in musical performances

Visual/Spatial Activities

Identifying and using the art elements, looking closely at and evaluating artworks, creating original drawings, paintings, sculptures, and so on, reading and making maps, solving spatial problems and representing ideas using graphic images

Naturalistic Activities

Observation, classification and grouping, expressing feelings about nature based on sensory perceptions and outdoor experiences, taking action to protect and care for living things, natural resources, and the environment

Bodily/Kinesthetic Activities

Sensory activities, exercising, doing physical work, using tools, dancing, moving creatively, dramatizing, cutting, pasting, painting, playing an instrument, doing puzzles, block building and other constructions, driving, playing sports

Musical Skill Objectives

These are behaviors and skills that help children express their ideas through rhythm and music.

Art Skill Objectives

These are behaviors and skills that help children express their ideas through visual imagery, two-dimensional graphic images, and three-dimensional forms.

Environmental Skill Objectives

These are behaviors and skills that help children understand, appreciate, and care for the natural world.

Physical Objectives

These are behaviors and skills that help children develop their coordination, physical strength, balance, and use of the sense organs for taste, smell, touch, sight, and sound.

FIGURE 5–2 Sample MI planning web

Language Objectives

Children will
- Increase their vocabulary
- Improve their writing skills
- Improve their listening skills
- Improve oral language skills

Cognitive Objectives

Children will
- Learn to measure using body parts
- Practice counting
- Practice telling time
- Compare and contrast sensations
- Learn to classify based on

Emotional Objectives

Children will
- Become more confident in their movements
- Feel more relaxed moving
- Be more self-aware

Social Objectives

Children will
- Improve ability to wait turns
- Improve ability to share space and materials
- Know safe ways to move around others

Verbal/Linguistic Activities

- Name parts of body and describe use
- Listen to stories about the body
- Dramatize their own body stories
- Write a class Big Book

Mathematical/Logical Activities

- Measure tracings of their bodies
- Count and graph different body motions
- Time races
- Explore textures, different temperature liquids, and so on at sensory center
- Classify bones using bone puzzle

Intrapersonal Activities

- Practice movements until they can perform them expertly
- Do many movement activities and talk about how they make us feel
- Draw pictures of the insides of our bodies and minds

Interpersonal Activities

- Play group games
- Take turns telling body stories, adding to class book, making measurements, and so on
- Work together on hand-footprint mural
- Act out safe ways to behave on field trip so no one is hurt

---

Thematic Question: How Do Our Bodies Work?

Theme-related concepts and facts: Our bodies can move in different ways. Our bodies bend at the joints. Inside our body is a skeleton made of bones. Muscles help our body move. Skin protects our bodies. Our bodies can sense temperature, hunger, thirst, tiredness, texture, and so on. Body parts have special names. We can do work with our bodies. Exercise makes our bodies strong.

Musical/Rhythmic Activities

- Sing body-related songs
- Add own words
- Move to music in different ways
- Paint to music

Visual/Spatial Activities

- Draw people moving
- Make paper fastener "joint" art
- Trace body and paint
- Make hand-footprint mural
- Make stick puppets
- Look at X-rays
- Look at full-length portraits
- Look at Mexican Day of the Dead sculptures

Naturalistic Activities

- Take a "Watch Your Step" walk in the woods
- Observe animals' movements, bones, and body structures

Bodily-Kinesthetic Activities

- Sensory table experiences
- Move to music
- Daily exercising
- Relay races
- Acting out stories with movements
- Watch gymnastic demonstration
- Trip to museum—Inside the Body exhibit

Musical Skill Objectives

Children will
- Improve ability to identify sound patterns
- Improve ability to match rhythms

Art Skill Objectives

Children will
- Visualize the shape and form of the body
- Use the creative process to solve open-ended problems
- Practice mixing paint colors
- Appreciate how other people represent the body

Environmental Skill Objectives

Children will
- Learn how to control body so as not to disturb natural environment
- Appreciate similarities in human and animal bodies/movements

Physical Objectives

- Use senses to gather information
- Perform coordinated body movements
- Strengthen muscles
- Develop safe control over body in space and around others

FIGURE 5–3 Sample thematic unit MI planning web

unit. The practice of writing plans enables teachers to use their knowledge and experience more effectively. Having a plan in place enables teachers to be *proactive* rather than *reactive*. This does not mean that teachers should be inflexible in adhering to the plan, but rather that they should have a basis from which to make decisions. Having a plan is like traveling with a road map. It keeps us from getting lost, and it lets us make side trips with the confidence that we will find our way back to the main road.

One way to create a plan that is responsive to the changing needs of young children is to use cards or sticky notes on which are written the different activities being considered for the unit. Categorize each art activity as introductory, exploratory, practice, and responsive. Lay out the activity cards on a calendar or grid. Figure 5–4 shows how art could be integrated into one week of a thematic unit focusing on the question, "How do our bodies work?"

As the unit progresses, move the cards to extend or repeat activities as needed. At intervals, take time to revisit the plans and notice what is going well. Do not be afraid to discard some activities or add others to better match the needs of the children. The goal is to produce a thematic unit that flows across the disciplines in concert with the children's developing skills and interest.

The Thematic Unit in Action

Thematic units consist of the following components:

Setting the stage. Before beginning the unit, allow the children to become familiar with how the work space or room is organized, what behaviors are expected of them, and how the time is divided during the day. Once the thematic unit begins, the children will already know where the basic supplies are and which areas are used for certain activities. Taking time

Teaching in Action

Thematic Unit: What do we see?

Topic: The color red

Plan: Each week put out materials in a featured color, such as red.

Sand Play: Put out red containers and shovels, and/or hide red blocks or red plastic objects in the sand.

Block Play: Put out pieces of cardboard that have been covered on both sides with red paper or contact paper, and/or add red plastic toys to the block area.

Dramatic Play: Offer red dress-up clothes. Put out red play food, dishes, or art prints.

Easel: Put out red paint, plus white and black.

Thematic Unit: Who are we?

Topic: Faces

Plan: Integrate pictures of faces and photographs of the children into play areas.

Sand Play: Photocopy photographs of the children's faces. Mount the photocopies on cardboard, and hide them in the sand for the children to find and play with.

Block Play: Put out people blocks or plastic people.

Dramatic Play: Put out masks and mirrors, and hang portraits on the wall.

Easel: Put out a variety of skin-colored paints.

MONDAY	TUESDAY	WEDNESDAY	THURSDAY	FRIDAY
Introductory experience Demonstration by gymnast.	**Introductory experience** Display photos of gymnastic demonstration.	**Introductory experience** Display paintings showing people in action, such as Homer's *Crack the Whip* or a Degas ballet scene.	**Introductory experience** Have children show actions using their puppets.	**Sharing** Have children put on playlets using their puppets. Videotape them.
Language Discuss how he moved. Imitate motions. Ask: How do our bodies move? Chart their ideas.	**Language** Talk about photos. Name body parts, and tell how they move. Review visit. Write thank-you note together.	**Language** Look at paintings. Ask: What are the ways we can move? Add ideas to word chart.	**Language** Describe ways the puppets moved. Find the ways on the word chart. Look for word patterns such as *-ing*.	**Language** Show tape and have children identify movements.
Journal time Record what they saw.	**Journal time** Draw thank-you pictures.	**Journal time** Show yourself moving in a special way.	**Journal time** Show how the puppets moved.	**Journal time** Show your favorite part of the show.
Read-aloud *Head to Toe* (Carle, 1997, Scholastic) Do motions.	**Read-aloud** *Me and My Body* (Evan & Williams, 1992, Dorling Kingsley)	**Read aloud** *The Skeleton inside You* (Balestrino, 1990, Scholastic)	**Read aloud** *All about My Skeleton* (Black & Ong, 1995, Scholastic)	**Read-aloud** *I Can Be the Alphabet* (Bonini, 1986, Viking) Do motions.
Art center Put out bendable materials such as chenille stems, yarn, and cardboard strips. Encourage children to compare the different ways these bend. Ask: How can you make art that moves? (Exploration)	**Art center** Put out materials for making stick puppets. Set up puppet theater. (Exploration)	**Art center** Introduce paper fasteners. Show how to use to make a bendable "joint." Encourage them to make moving parts on their puppets. (Practice)	**Art center** Encourage puppet making to continue. (Practice) Add other materials for puppets such as yarn, foils, sports insignia clipped from magazines. Invite interested children to create a play using their puppets. (Responsive)	**Art center** Put out paint and play music. Encourage children to move their brushes in different ways as the music changes in pitch, speed, and rhythm. (Exploration)
Music Teach the "Hokey Pokey." Do motions.	**Music** Review "Hokey Pokey." Do motions.	**Music** Add children's own words and motions to song.	**Music** Use word patterns from word chart to make up a chant. *Example: Running, jumping, hopping, skipping, bending, stopping* Clap the rhythm, and add body movements.	**Music** Recite chant from yesterday. Have children substitute other words and movements. Sing "Hokey Pokey."
Math center Put out light and heavy things to explore and move.	**Math** Add scale to center. Sort items by weight (*small group*).	**Math** Have children select object, weigh it, and record it on chart (*small group*).	**Math** Have children select objects of different weights from chart, push them on flat surface, and describe how it feels and the motion they see. Add information to chart (*small group*).	**Math** Offer a new set of objects. Have children sort them by what they predict they weigh, then weigh them.
Science center Put out bendable model skeleton, X-rays, and drawing materials.	**Science** Have children match skeleton's bones to their own bodies (*small group*). Ask children to describe motions of figures.	**Science** Have children find their joints and bend them. Draw pictures of the skeletons inside them. (*small group*).	**Science center** Add boiled chicken bones. Provide mat for sorting bones by size and shape. Ask them to guess what part of a chicken they come from.	**Science center** Put out drawing of chicken skeleton. Invite children to place matching bones on drawing.
Blocks Put out bendable plastic action figures.	**Blocks** Ask children to describe motions of figures.	**Blocks** Watch how children move and talk about figures.	**Blocks** Encourage children to draw pictures of their figures and their block structures.	**Blocks** Challenge children to think of other ways to move the figures.

FIGURE 5–4 Sample week of a thematic unit plan for kindergarten or grade 1

to allow for basic exploration of the environment and getting to know each other beforehand will make it easier for everyone to concentrate more on the theme. This also provides time for an idea for a thematic unit to grow naturally from the children.

The initial event. Once an interest has been identified and a theme selected, plan an initial event that will be stimulating and provocative. It should focus everyone's attention on the theme and be full of images, ideas, and feelings. The event may be one that takes the children beyond the walls of the room, such as a walk or field trip, or it may involve bringing something special to the children, such as a visitor, an animal, or an object. Rearrange the room, and put out new materials and play items that carry through on the theme. The idea is to raise the interest of as many children as possible.

Activity integration. Thematic unit activities should be integrated into each of the learning centers offered but should not replace them. Children need the continuity of knowing that sand, blocks, home-life/dramatic play, and easel painting will be waiting for them every day. Integrate the thematic unit into these areas in small ways such as changing the paint color or texture or the paint tools offered at the easel, providing different containers or toys in the sand, put-

ting out theme-related toys, or providing different dress-up clothes, art to hang, or play food.

Although it may not be possible to integrate theme concepts into every area every time, try to find creative ways to touch as many areas as possible.

Ending a thematic unit. After all the time and effort spent on a thematic teaching unit, it should not be allowed to fizzle away at the end.

Share. It is important to provide time for the children to share what they have learned with each other. Children can show art or projects they have done and tell how they made them. Consider trying a variety of formats. Although having the child stand up in front of the group is a common method, other possibilities include audiotaping or videotaping the child's presentation for sharing with the others. These tapes can then be shared with parents as well.

Display. The children can also make displays that show what they have learned, and the children can circulate among them asking questions and making comments. To keep the group focused on the presentations, provide a simple checklist to mark or coupons to collect to show which displays they visited.

Evaluate. The end of a thematic unit is a time for evaluating what has happened. What were the chil-

Young Artists at Work

Jamil and Corin are hunched over a large sheet of paper, engrossed in their drawing of dinosaurs and actively engaged in a conversation about the color of dinosaurs. As the other children play in the block area, put on dress-up clothes, paint at the easel, or dig in the sand, the boys continue drawing, oblivious to the activity around them. Every once in a while the teacher passes by and, on occasion, makes a comment such as, "Wow, you are working hard. You have drawn so many dinosaurs!" or offers, "Here is a new dinosaur book I just found."

"I'll look for more dinosaurs and see what colors this book shows. You keep drawing," Jamil tells Corin.

"They have been working on that drawing for three days!" the teacher tells a visitor. "We read a book about dinosaurs, and now those two are just so entranced by them."

dren's favorite activities? What do they remember best? What new things did they learn? What do they want to tell others about their experiences? What have the children learned and accomplished?

Celebrate! It takes extra effort, but a celebration of learning or a culminating activity at the end of a thematic unit helps solidify all the learning that has taken place. The culminating activity may consist of special activities that relate to the theme, and/or it may include displays of work and photographs that reflect the activities that have taken place. The entire environment of the room may be changed for the day, and/or visitors may be invited. It should be a party that celebrates the joy of learning.

WHAT IS THE PROJECT APPROACH?

The project approach has many similarities to the use of themes, yet it differs in significant ways. Katz and Chard (2000, p. 2) define a project as "an in-depth study of a particular topic that one or more children undertake." This approach is attracting interest from early childhood educators because of the Reggio Emilia program. Gardner applauds the project approach, as demonstrated at Reggio Emilia, for the way it guides children in using all of their "intellectual, emotional, social, and moral potentials" (Edwards, Gandini, & Forman, 1993, p. xii).

It involves encouraging children to work in small groups of two to five on a project that reflects their personal interests, some of which may be far removed from their everyday experience, and from what the teacher might select. These groups establish a relationship with the teacher in which the teacher not only facilitates but also collaborates in the process directly by supplying the needed skills and direction.

Sylvia Chard (1998, p. 31) makes the following distinctions between the project approach and a thematic unit.

- A thematic unit is planned by the teacher. Projects develop from the children's interests.
- Rather than a theme, project work focuses on a topic. The theme or main idea grows out of the children's investigations.
- Goals for a thematic unit are teacher constructed. In the project approach, children set the goals for their learning.

Purple dinosaur project. Working together with others to build a large project helps children develop independence and self-confidence.

- ⚘ A thematic unit covers a breadth of material. A project goes into greater depth and takes longer.
- ⚘ Thematic activities cover all of the skill areas and are offered to all children. Creating unique projects means that individual children apply and learn different skills.

The Value of the Project Approach

The project approach helps children grow as learners. Katz and Chard (2000) believe the following benefits are best achieved through the project approach.

1. The project approach engages children's intellects by widening their knowledge and skills at their individual levels of understanding. The traditional format of learning through play, while beneficial, lacks intellectual challenge and underestimates children's ability to acquire wider meaning from their experiences. An academic approach, on the other hand, forces children to proceed in a lock-step sequence of learning skills and concepts, whether or not these skills are relevant or appropriate for the individual child.
2. Project work helps children learn in an integrated manner and breaks down the divisions between subjects or play areas.
3. The use of projects challenges teachers to be creative and to devise constructive solutions to educational problems.
4. Project work relies on the children's intrinsic motivation as it allows for a much wider range of choices and independent efforts on a topic of their choice.
5. Children can select work that matches or challenges their skill level.
6. Children can become expert in their own learning. They are in charge of finding information and using it in new ways.
7. When children reflect on and evaluate their contribution to a project, they become accountable for their own learning.

Initiating Projects

The project approach starts with a topic drawn from the interests of the children and about which all have a story or experience to tell. For example, the teacher

Activities that grow out of children's interests and experiences help children create more meaningful art.

might begin by telling a story about a time she lost her shoe. Then the children talk about and draw pictures of their experiences with shoes.

Facilitating learning. Based on what the children say and draw, learning activities are planned that relate to the individual child's ideas and questions. These activities should allow open-ended exploration of topic-related ideas, encouraging the child to observe, sense, explore, and experiment, both individually and with others. For example, after several children participating in a project on plants comment that all leaves are green, a variety of plants are put on display alongside containers of different green materials for collages. These activities are then available as a choice for any child to investigate.

Small group work. One of the key features of the project approach is the importance of working with children in small groups. Teachers meet on a regular basis with small groups of children. Together they discuss the initial experiences and pursue questions and ideas that lead into a variety of independent investigations or projects. Small group projects can range from writing a book to making puppets and putting on a puppet show. Children are limited only by their imaginations.

As they work on their projects, the teacher offers guidance, provides requested materials, directs the children to sources of information, and teaches specific skills as needed.

Discussion/representation. Time is set aside to talk about and share the children's ideas daily. These can be recorded by the teacher in various ways—in charts, graphs, and dictation and through audio-taping. The children's changing ideas can also be documented through their drawings and constructions and through photographs and videotapes made of their activities. This is a very important part of the process; it is the way the different groups' learning is made visible to all of the children.

Culminating Projects

As with a thematic unit, projects need to be recognized in a special way. Concluding activities need to be carefully designed. One of the main dangers with the project approach is the temptation to focus on the finished product and to ignore the thought and process that went into it. Plan ways to share the children's work through displays of not only the project but also all of the documentation of the process that went into it. (See chapter 12 for display ideas.) There also needs to be a time for the same kind of assessment as is done for thematic units.

Projects and Themes in Combination

Although these two approaches have been discussed separately, they are not mutually exclusive. Within the presentation of a thematic unit, small groups of children can initiate independent projects. These projects may relate to the theme or may go in a different direction. On the other hand, a project initiated by a small group of students can grow into a thematic unit if it attracts the interest of the other children.

Whether used separately or in combination, both of these approaches integrate art into the total learning of the child. Art provides the graphic medium through which children can express what they have observed and thought about. Drawings record how a dinosaur was built. Paintings record color experiments. Prints show the child's understanding of pattern. But these artworks do not stand alone. They are richer and more intense because they are part of a total experience.

CONCLUSION: MAKING THE CONNECTION

Let the main ideas which are introduced into a child's education be few and important, and let them be thrown into every combination possible.

—Alfred North Whitehead (1929, p. 2)

Art, as a way of learning and communicating about the world, can enrich every aspect of an early childhood program. Presented with activities that are unified by a common theme, children learn to see and react to the world as an interconnected place. When

---

Teacher Tip

Drawing and the Project Approach

Sylvia Chard recommends that drawing to record information plays an important role in project work. Drawing can be incorporated in the following ways.

1. The first stage in a project is to draw upon the children's existing knowledge and experience. To begin a project, tell a story that relates to the topic to be studied, and then ask children to share their own stories. For example, if the topic is shoes, tell the children about a special pair of shoes and how you felt when you wore them. Follow storytelling by having the children draw memory pictures about their shoes.

2. In the second stage, children do fieldwork to learn more about the topic. In this stage, they can make drawings from direct observation, such as taking off their shoe and drawing it. They can make sketches on field trips, such as to the shoe store, by attaching a few sheets of paper to a clipboard or to a piece of cardboard with a pencil attached.

children's interests provide the starting point for designing art activities, the children see them as meaningful. Self-initiated projects help children develop independent thinking and working skills.

Setting up these kinds of opportunities takes a great deal of work and effort on the teacher's part. There is no published thematic unit or project list that will work with every group of children every time. Each class is unique in its interests and skills, and the units teachers create must be customized accordingly. It is well worth the effort. When children's interests are aroused, when they are full of enthusiasm, and when they know they have a choice, they respond by thinking more deeply. They care more about what they are doing, and they understand the world better. Integrating art into the curriculum also means that all learning becomes more meaningful.

FURTHER READING

Cecil, N. L., & Lauritzen, P. (1995). *Literacy and the arts for the integrated classroom: Alternative ways of knowing.* White Plains, NY: Longman.
There are many ways to integrate art into children's learning. Cecil and Lauritzen present a wide variety of ideas to inspire teachers.

Chard, S. (1998). *The project approach: Making the curriculum come alive.* New York: Scholastic.
This book details ways to initiate projects in the classroom.

Edwards, C., Gandini, L., & Forman, G. (1993). *The hundred languages of children: The Reggio Emilia approach to early childhood education.* Norwood, NJ: Ablex.
This book describes the philosophy of the project approach as practiced in the Reggio Emilia Preprimary Schools, with examples from both Italy and the United States.

Katz, L. G., & Chard, S. C. (2000). *Engaging children's minds: The project approach* (2nd ed.). Norwood, NJ: Ablex.
This book defends the use of projects in early education and presents ways to institute this approach in the classroom.

Creating Art: Painting

What happens when child, paint, and brush mix?

 ## THE PAINTING EXPERIENCE

There is nothing else quite like it. Long tapered brushes dip into liquid color that flows and falls with abandon across a white rectangle of paper. For a moment, the young artist is alone, focused on the interplay of mind and muscle, action and reaction. Painting provides the sensory link between the childish finger that plays in the spilled milk and the masterly hand that painted the Mona Lisa.

Before beginning a painting exploration with children, take a moment to make a tempera painting. Swirl and spread the paint, and concentrate on the way the brush responds to muscular commands and the visual result that is created. Feel the way the brush glides over the surface, and watch how the wet paint catches the light and glistens. Creating a painting is the perfect way to appreciate the importance of process over product to the young child, for whom painting is first and foremost a sensory experience.

How Children Grow through Painting

Children will develop

1. physically, by using the large and small muscles of the arm to control the paintbrush. (Bodily-Kinesthetic)
2. socially, by learning to take care of the paint so that others will also be able to use it. (Interpersonal)
3. emotionally, by being trusted to control an easy-to-spill, messy liquid. (Intrapersonal)
4. language skills, by learning a painting vocabulary. (Linguistic)
5. cognitively, by observing how paint physically changes when it mixes and dries. (Logical-Mathematical)
6. visual perception skills, by observing the visual effects of their motions and identifying the resulting colors, shapes, and lines. (Spatial)
7. art awareness, by responding to paintings done by many different artists.

 INTRODUCING PAINTING AGES ONE AND UP

Children between the ages of one and three will approach painting completely on a sensory level. Combined with their limited control over hand and arm movements, they often create what to adult eyes is a mess. With careful planning, however, this can be an exciting experience for both adults and children. Older children with special vision or muscle-control limitations require a similar guided introduction to painting.

Group Composition

For an initial painting experience, work with one child at a time. After each child has had some experience with the painting setup, two children can paint at the same time.

Setup

It is important to protect the child's clothing as much as possible, as even the most washable tempera or poster paint can stain some fabrics. Provide a smock for each painter (see Teacher Tip). Provide a low table for the child to stand at or an easel that is the child's height. Cover the work surface with newspaper. If

Classroom Museum

Display artworks that show bold painted shapes in a variety of colors, such as the work of Hans Hofmann, Paul Klee, or Wassily Kandinsky. Have children point to and name the colors they see.

using an easel, put heavy plastic underneath to catch the drips. Use spring-type clothespins to clip the paper to the easel.

Have a bucket, paper towels, and sponges nearby for quick wipe-ups.

Materials

For a child's first painting experience, provide thick-handled, stubby paintbrushes. Provide one or two colors of thick, liquid tempera paint in plastic containers, such as yogurt comes in. (These have tight-fitting lids, so unused paint can be saved for the next day.) Fill them half full. Place one brush in each color. If the containers seem to tip easily once the brush is inside, then put them in a small box or plastic basket. Alternatively, cut a hole the size of the container in an upside-down Styrofoam tray.

Note: It is less expensive to buy the larger sizes of liquid tempera. To make the most efficient use of paint, buy the basic colors, and then mix the other colors as needed. Start with red, yellow, and blue. The next choices should then be white and black. If funds are available, supplement these with green, brown, orange, and purple, in that order. Chapter 11 discusses the importance of having many varieties of skin-colored paint available. These can be purchased or mixed.

If the paint is too thin, add a small amount of flour* to thicken it. It should not drip very much when the brush is taken out of the paint. A small amount of liquid detergent may be added to make hand cleanup easier.

Teacher Tip

Painting Smocks

A good smock that will cover most of the child can be made from a large adult's shirt that buttons up the front.

1. Cut the sleeves very short.
2. Put it on the child backwards, and fasten it together in the back with a spring clothespin.
3. Make sure the child's sleeves are pushed up above the elbows.

Special Needs

Painting Modifications

Visual: Children with limited vision should work on a tilted surface or easel so they may have their eyes closer to the work surface. Choose the colors of paint that they can see best, and add sawdust or sand so they can feel their finished painting. Different scents can be added to the paint to help in color identification.

Physical: Some children with orthopedic handicaps work best if they can lie on the floor when painting. Tape paper to the floor or other work surface so that it does not move while they are working. Wrap foam around the handles of the brushes to make them easier to grip. Use wide, low-sided containers for the paint, such as cut-down margarine or frosting containers. If necessary, use tape to hold paint containers in place.

Keep the paint thick, and make sure all children have ample working space, so if there are involuntary movements or lack of control, paint does not splatter on the paper or clothing of other children. (See chapter 11 for more information.)

Warm-Up

Paint is naturally appealing to young children. Introduce the idea of painting by giving the children small buckets of water and brushes and then going outside to paint on walls or pavement. Mime painting while singing a song about painting or color mixing. Share a Big Book about painting such as *Mouse Paint* (Walsh, 1989). When children eventually paint with the liquid tempera, their interest level will be high.

What to Do

When children first begin to paint, they may hold the paintbrush awkwardly and have difficulty staying within the confines of the paper. This is normal and reflects the child's lack of control over the arm and hand muscles. Toddlers will use the whole arm stiffly to move the brush in up-and-down and circular strokes reminiscent of the first scribbles. As children gain muscular control, they will be able to stay on the paper and control the movement of the brush more effectively.

Stay near the child for the first few painting experiences. Give a few simple directions in the beginning. Otherwise, do not interrupt the painting process until the child is done.

Do not worry if children mix up the paint colors. With practice, they will learn to keep the brushes separate. It is sometimes helpful to label the brushes with the same color tape.

What to Say

Keep initial direction very brief, and let the children discover the joy of painting on their own. Interfere

Toddlers use their whole arms when painting.

only if children put the paintbrush up to their mouths or try to leave the table still holding it.

Vocabulary to use during painting explorations includes paint, brush, handle, color names, mix, mixing, drip, dripping, wipe, smooth, and wet.

The comments teachers make should focus on the effects of color mixing and the kinds of lines the child has made.

"Look what happened when the blue touched the yellow!"

"You made a thick green line with the brush."

"That yellow line goes from the top to the bottom of the paper."

Transition Out

Children are usually delighted with the effect they can create using colorful paints. Let them paint until they feel they are finished, then guide them to the place to wash their hands. Put the painting out of the way to dry. It is best if it can dry flat, to minimize drips. If space is a problem, however, paintings can also be hung on a low, wash-line-style drying rack, available from art suppliers. Instructions to make a homemade drying box are presented in figure 5–5.

More to Do

Once the children have experienced painting, try to offer the opportunity to paint on a regular basis. Have the paint table or easel set up and ready before the

Safety Note

Glitter

Commercial glitter is not recommended for young children, as it sticks to their hands and can be accidentally ingested or rubbed into the eyes. However, paint with glitter already mixed in can be purchased commercially and provides an exciting painting experience for young children.

1. Select a box that is slightly larger than the paper children usually use.

2. Draw lines two to three inches apart on opposite sides of the box.

3. Cut halfway in on each line.

4. Cut "shelves" (from cardboard) that are four inches longer than the box. Measure in two inches from the edges and draw lines.

5. Cut halfway in on each line on the shelves.

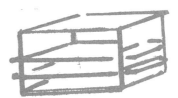

6. Slide each shelf into the corresponding slots.

FIGURE 5–5 Making a paint-drying box

children arrive. Since most toddlers spend only two to five minutes painting, there is usually plenty of time for all of them to make a painting if they wish. There are many ways to vary the basic painting exploration and still allow the children to practice the basic skills.

Use different brushes. Provide different types of brushes, such as wide, house-painting brushes, foam rubber brushes, and long-handled vegetable brushes.

Try new ways to apply paint. Make paint design scrapers. Cut notches in the edge of a sanitized Styrofoam tray, and pull it through wet paint. Try foam rollers and daubers, pattern painters, and fingertip design makers. (See appendix A for sources.)

Offer more colors. Once the child understands painting procedures, offer three colors at the regular paint setup. There is no rigid formula for selecting the colors. Choose from the ones that are available. The primary colors of red, yellow, and blue are good choices to start with, because these three colors provide exciting color mixes. As the children gain experience, increase the number of colors offered to include four or five colors—either brown, green, purple, orange, black, or white.

Use theme-related colors. Sometimes the colors may relate to the theme of the program. If the sea is the theme, try deep blue, green, turquoise, and white.

Teacher Tip

Guide to Mixing Colors

The primary colors. The primary colors are red, yellow, and blue. Primary colors, when mixed, make the secondary colors: (See accompanying figure)

    Red + Yellow = Orange
    Blue + Yellow = Green
    Red + Blue = Purple

Adding white. White plus any color makes a lighter or more pastel tint. Even a small amount of a color will change white. Add the color little by little until the tone is just right. More white will probably be used than any other color, so purchase double the amount of white.

    Red + White = Pink
    Orange + White = Peach
    Blue + White = Pastel Blue
    Purple + White = Lavender
    Green + White = Mint Green
    Brown + White = Tan

Adding black. Black plus any color makes it darker and duller. It takes only a small amount of black to change a color. Mix it in sparingly.

    Black + White = Gray

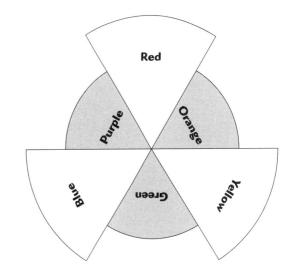

    Black + Yellow = Olive Green
    Black + Red = Brown

Other combinations.

    Orange + Yellow = Gold
    Red + Purple = Magenta
    Red + Green = Brown
    Blue + Purple = Deep Blue (Indigo)
    Blue + Green = Turquoise
    Yellow + Green = Chartreuse

Skin tones. Skin tones can be made by mixing different combinations of black, brown, yellow, red, and white. Always start with the lighter colors, and add the darker ones.

Celebrate a color. Offer the featured color and related colors at the paint setup. On purple day, for example, put out purple, lavender, and white paint.

Add textures to the paint. A variety of materials can be mixed into the liquid paint to give it a different feel.

- The simple addition of a little more water makes a thinner paint and changes the sensory response of the brush as it moves across the paper.
- Detergent, liquid starch, and corn syrup* added to the paint will make it spread differently.

- To make the paint thicker, add sand, sawdust, cornmeal,* flour,* oatmeal,* dry cereal,* or soap flakes.
- Salt* added to the paint will produce a bubbly effect.
- Salt* and Epsom salts sprinkled on the paint produce a glittery effect.

Offer a variety of papers. In addition to the large newsprint, vary the painting surface by providing colored paper, cardboard, and smooth shelf paper. Cut the paper into a variety of large rectangles and squares, or occasionally into a triangle or circle.

EXPLORING PAINTING AGES THREE AND UP

As the child develops more control over the fluid medium of paint, offer a wider variety of activities. In addition to the basic painting activities that are suitable for toddlers, offer more colors and kinds of paint.

Group Composition

Once children can keep the paint within the confines of the paper, can return the brush to the right color fairly consistently, and know how to clean up after themselves when done, they can paint in groups of three and up.

Setup

Provide a ratio of one easel for every five children (i.e., if there are 20 children, have four easels set up), or a table on which four children can paint at one time. Side-by-side easels provide the most opportunity for the children to interact. Cover the table and easel surface with newspaper, and put a piece of heavy plastic under the easel.

Have available a quantity of predampened paper towels, sponges, and a bucket for cleanup. The children should be shown how to wipe up any drips from the floor and how to move to the hand-washing area without touching anything. Children must wear smocks (as described for toddlers). Teach them how to help each other put the smocks on.

Materials

Provide four or five colors of thick tempera paint. Fill stable cups that have tight-fitting lids about half full. Offer large sheets of newspaper or manila paper at the easel. If easels are unavailable, place paper and paint cups, set in trays to prevent tipping, on a newspaper-covered table.

Warm-Up

Most children love to paint, but teachers still need to make them aware of the availability of the paints and the many possibilities they offer. An easel setup is ideal, because it is clearly visible to the children as something different from anything else in the room. A paint table can be marked or labeled in some special way to attract attention.

Classroom Museum

Display and discuss paintings by artists from different times and cultures. Children respond well to the Nonobjective Print Set (Take 5), which features work by Hofmann, Jenkins, Klee, Merida, and Mondrian. See if children can figure out how the artists made the different colors.

Introduce the area by showing a paint brush and inviting the children to mime painting during circle time. Tell a story about a famous painter, or read a book about painting, such as *A Painter* (Florian, 1993), which explains what a painter does in a simple, sensitive text.

Once their interest is aroused, it may be necessary to set up a way for children to take turns. Because painting is an intensely sensory and personal experience, offer it as often as possible; every day is best. Children should awaken each day knowing that they will have blocks and toys and books and paints to explore.

What to Do

Preschoolers and primary school students still spend a great deal of time exploring the sensory qualities of paint. They may paint simple lines and shapes or cover the whole paper with one color. They may start out making symbols for faces or houses and then, fascinated by how the colors accidentally mixed, paint over their initial symbols. In painting, the process is always more important than the product.

This does not mean, however, that the child is not interested in what happens to the finished painting. Because of its large size and bright colors, a painting becomes a very visible product of the child, even more so than a drawing. Children can be very possessive and proud of their paintings, and they will demand that care be taken in handling their pictures.

- **Keep painting open ended.** It is very important to have a hands-off policy in regard to children's painting. Other than a few simple rules based on safety and cleanliness (such as "keep paint away from the face," and "keep the brushes in the paint containers"), children should be allowed to explore any way they wish.

- **Allow color mixing.** Let children mix colors as they desire, even if the brush gets "dirty." Gently model how to hold and wipe the brush.

- **Accept exploration.** Adults must be careful not to show disappointment if the child paints over something they thought was a great picture. This freedom to explore allows the child to grow in self-confidence and creativity. In this way, the child becomes familiar with the possibilities and the control needed to paint richer and more detailed pictures.

- **Foster concentration and reflection.** Encourage children to spend time on their paintings. If they always seem to rush through painting, ask questions that will inspire them to add to their work, such as, "What do you think might happen if you used the smaller brush now?" A painting can also

Boxes provide multiple surfaces to paint.

be put away overnight. The next day, ask if children wish to add to it with paint or with other art materials, such as markers or chalk.

What to Say

Use the painting experience to help the children focus on the art elements and the way that the paint functions. Remember not to interrupt children when they are absorbed in the painting process. Wait for them to look up, or save conversation for later, when helping to take the paper off the easel or returning the dry painting to take home or put in a portfolio. Sample questions include the following:

"How did you make this color?"
"Which brush did you use to make this line?"
"Why do you think the paint dripped like this?"

Transition Out

Children know best when they are finished. They often announce this fact, with a great deal of satisfaction, to no one in particular. Show the children how to take off their smocks, where to hang them, and how to move to the sink to wash up. After a few times the children should be able to do most of this on their own. In situations in which the paintings will be placed on the floor to dry, most children can be shown how to take their own paintings to that place. To prevent accidents when moving their artwork, remind them to keep their smocks on until this chore is done.

More to Do

Use other forms of paint. In addition to liquid tempera, children can try other kinds of paint (see the Artist's Tool Box for ideas).

Provide different sizes of paper. Older children can begin to use smaller sizes of paper, but continue to offer large sheets as well. They continue to need to use their whole arm as part of the painting process, just as adult artists do. Many of the paintings adults are familiar with from small reproductions are in reality quite large. Many of Monet's "Water Lilies," for example, are over five feet long.

A drying box provides a convenient way to store paintings and other wet projects.

Try other surfaces to paint on. The painting surface adds another sensory component to the painting process. Although newsprint offers the most economical choice, try to have other kinds and colors available as well.

Try painted collage. Children can make their own textured painting surface by gluing textured materials such as sand, fabric, and ribbon pieces to a sheet of construction paper on one day and then painting over it the next.

Try monoprints. A sheet of Plexiglas, heavy plastic, or a bare, smooth tabletop can be used to paint on. Then press a sheet of paper over the painting to save it as a monoprint—a one-of-a-kind copy of the painting.

Artist's Tool Box

Types of Paint

In addition to liquid tempera, other types of paint can be offered on occasion. Most of these will work better if used on a table rather than at the easel.

Tempera blocks. This paint comes in dry cakes that fit in special trays. The children must wet the brush to dampen the cube for use. Choose the larger sizes in basic colors and fluorescents (see appendix A for sources). Some adults like the fact that these do not spill. However, the colors and texture of the block paints are not as exciting as liquid tempera paints, so these should never be the only type of paint the children use but, rather, an interesting addition to the program.

Paint "markers". These small plastic containers have felt tips. Fill the container with tempera paint, and use like a marker. The stubby shape of the bottles fits well in little hands, and the paint flows out easily. Keep them tightly capped in a resealable plastic bag when not in use (see appendix A for sources).

Watercolors. The small size of the individual watercolors in a set, even in the larger half-pan size, makes them suitable only for children with well-developed fine-motor control. Watercolors are also more likely to stain clothing than tempera paint. Before giving watercolors to the children to use, wet the color pans and let them sit a short time to soften the paints. Watercolors produce interesting effects when used on wet paper or on top of crayon drawings. Paper can be dampened with a sponge or paintbrush before painting.

Artist's Tool Box

Surfaces for Painting

Brown paper. Brown kraft paper (or a cut, flattened paper bag) provides an absorbent surface with a color that contrasts well with the lighter colors that are often lost on white paper. Try it with pink, yellow, and white paint. Try wrinkling the paper and then smoothing it again to create a bumpy texture that is fun to paint on too.

Colored paper. Colored construction paper in dark colors also offers a good contrast for light-colored paints.

Fabric. Burlap or fabric glued to a cardboard base serves as a challenging texture for painting. The book *The Mud Family* (James, 1994) features illustrations done using this technique. This would be a good choice for a thematic unit on textures.

Paper products. Paper placemats, shelf paper, and thick paper toweling offer different textures for painting.

Wood and stone. The varying texture and absorbency of wood scraps and stones provide an interesting contrast to flat paper.

Try chalk over paint. Encourage children to use chalk to add more details to their dry paintings.

Explore other ways to apply paint. Paint can be applied with all of the following items:

- branches and twigs
- feathers and feather dusters
- housepainting brushes
- paint rollers
- sponges
- sponge brushes
- squeeze bottles (such as empty mustard or shampoo containers)
- craft sticks with cloth taped to the end

Making Connections

Language. Provide a time when children can share their paintings. Encourage them to use color words and comparatives, such as lighter and darker. Ask them to describe how they moved the brush. Read books about children painting, such as *No Good in Art* (Cohen, 1980) or *Peter's Painting* (Moss, 1995).

Math. Count the number of colors used and shapes painted. Compare the amount of paint in the cups before and after painting.

Science. Time how long it takes for different paints to dry. Look through prisms, and then paint the colors seen.

FINGER PAINTING
AGES 2 AND UP

No early childhood art experience would be complete without finger painting. If painting with brushes is an intense sensory experience, then painting with the fingers is the ultimate. For some children, however, finger painting is at first a very confusing activity. These children have often been taught to keep their hands clean, or they may have taken to heart the directions to always wash the paint off their hands. The idea of putting paint on their hands on purpose is bewildering. Never force a child to finger paint. Plenty of others are quite willing to dive in; often a reluctant child, after seeing the others' fun, will tentatively join in. Teachers can help such children by offering light colors of finger paint and showing them that adding detergent to it helps it wash off better.

A great deal of the "messing" that children seem to do when they finger paint is not because finger painting in itself is such a messy medium, but because it is offered so rarely to children. Most children never get beyond the initial exploration. Imagine what the quality of finger paintings would be like if children finger painted as often as they drew with crayons!

Finger paint provides a wonderful sensory experience for young children.

Group Composition

Keep the number of children working at one time very small: one or two toddlers at a time or three to four older children. Remember, they will need to be supervised at the sink or wash-up area. Never have more children working than can fit at the sink.

Setup

Finger painting works best when children work standing at child-height tables. Finger painting may also be done on the floor. This gives the child the opportunity to make large hand and arm movements; however, there is also the chance that the child will kneel in the paint. Floor painting works best if the children are wearing shorts so they do not get paint on the knees of their clothing. In warm weather, try finger painting outdoors, and then let children hose off. Always place newspaper under painting surfaces.

It may help to have a bucket of soapy water for children to soak their hands in before rinsing in the sink. Have available plenty of damp paper towels to wipe paint smears.

Materials

Paint. Commercial finger paint provides vibrant color in a smooth, easy-to-clean formula and should be the main finger paint used. For other finger paint explorations, try shaving cream or whipped soap flakes and liquid starch colored with a small amount of food coloring or tempera paint.

Paper. Commercial finger paint paper is heavy, with a smooth, shiny surface. Although relatively expensive, children should occasionally have the opportunity to finger paint on this paper. Freezer paper and shiny shelf paper can also be used. Paper may be dampened with a wet sponge to make the paint spread more easily.

Teacher to Family

Sample Letter to Families about Painting

Dear Family,

Painting is an important part of our art program, and the children will be painting almost every day. In order for your child to have a wonderful time painting, please dress him or her in clothing that is easy to wash. It is important that sleeves can be pushed up above the elbows to prevent them from dragging in the paint.

Children will be wearing smocks when painting. However, accidents do happen. The water-based tempera paint we use will come out of most fabrics if it is washed in the following way:

1. Apply detergent to the spot and rub.

2. Wash normally.

3. If the spot still shows, repeat rubbing and washing.

4. Line dry. Do not put in the dryer until the spot is gone, as the heat will set the color.

5. It may take several washings to remove the stain completely.

Painting activities help your child grow in many ways, as he or she learns to control the paintbrushes and other painting tools. Please help your son or daughter enjoy painting without the worry of getting paint on clothing.

Your child's teacher,

Other surfaces. Finger painting can also be done directly on smooth-surfaced tabletops or on a piece of Plexiglass. Pictures can be saved by placing a paper over the artwork and rubbing to create a monoprint.

Warm-Up

Have children do "finger exercises" and create an invisible finger painting in the air. Read books that describe wet and unusual textures, such as *Icky, Sticky Gloop* (Matthews, 1997) and *Muddigush* (Knutson, 1992).

What to Do

1. Before starting, make sure the child's sleeves are pushed up over the elbows and the smock sleeves are short enough not to drag in the paint.
2. Place about a quarter of a cup of paint on the paper. Add another quarter cup of water.
3. Encourage the child to mix and spread the paint.
4. Show how to use different parts of the hand to make marks.

What to Say

Use words that describe the feel of the paint, such as cold, wet, or sticky. Encourage children to think of other things that feel the same. Describe the different movements of their hands.

"You moved your hand up and down."
"You wiggled your fingers."

Transition Out

As the finger paint dries, it will become harder for the child to make marks, and the activity will naturally stop. Guide the child to the sink or wash-up area. Remove paintings from the newspaper to dry, or they will stick in place.

More to Do

Mix colors. Give the children several colors, and encourage them to mix them together to make new ones.

Place colors. Instead of putting the paint directly on their paper, put the finger paint on the newspaper next to the paper or in a disposable tray. Let the children dip their fingers in and apply paint where they want it. This encourages a more thoughtful placement of colors.

Wet on wet. Wet paper with a sponge before starting.

Teaching in Action

A Preschool Teacher's Project Log

The Store Project: The First Two Weeks

Monday 10/7. We took a walk to the store on the corner to buy the ingredients for our fruit salad snack. When we got back, I noticed that the children in the dramatic play area were pretending to go to the store.

Tuesday 10/8. I brought in some shopping bags and empty cereal boxes to add to the dramatic play area. Some of the children asked me to help them make a store. We sat in a small group and talked about what we might need in a store. I listed their ideas. They had a pretty good idea about the need for shelves and a cash register. When I asked what we should sell in the store, they had a lot of disagreements.

Later I thought about this and decided we needed to take another trip to the store.

Wednesday 10/9. I called the market and made sure we could visit. Then I asked some parents if they could come on Friday for our trip to the market. I announced our trip at meeting and explained that some children wanted to make a store in our classroom. I read them the book *On Market Street* (Arnold Lobel, 1989, New York: Mulberry).

Thursday 10/10. At meeting we talked briefly about our trip and what we might see. Later, I met with small groups and made lists of what they thought they would see. I gave them stapled "journals" to record what they did see, and they wrote their names and decorated the covers with their ideas about the store. Today we read *Tommy at the Grocery Store* (Bill Grossman, 1991, New York: HarperCollins). They loved the rhymes in this book.

Friday 10/11. We visited the market early in the morning when there was hardly anyone else there. The children loved talking to the produce manager, cashiers, and the butcher and drawing in their journals. The store gave us paper bags and hats. When we got back, we shared about the trip. We listed all of the products we saw being sold. Many children drew more pictures in their journals. Now everyone wants to help make our own supermarket.

Monday 10/13. Wow, such enthusiasm. I shared the photos from our trip, and the children helped me write labels for them. We hung them on the bulletin board. I read the book *Something Good* (Robert Munsch, 1990, Toronto: Annick).

We talked about where our store should be and what kind of furniture we needed. Later, some children helped me clear out the area. There are now lots of shoppers in the dramatic play area.

Tuesday 10/14. Today I read the book *Not So Fast Songololo* (Niki Daly, 1989, New York: Aladdin), and we talked a little about how people shop in different places. We made a list of different types of stores. We talked about what we wanted our store to look like. Tom, Inga, and Monica drew the front of the store on a large paper. Then several other students helped them paint it. Other students made a big sign. Henry and Aaron cut out "cookies" from paper. I sent home a note asking for empty food boxes for the foods on our list.

Wednesday 10/15. Anna's mom came in and helped four children make fruit by covering balls of newspaper with papier-mâché. A parent also donated a printing calculator to use as the cash register. I put it out for the children to explore.

continued

Teaching in Action *continued*

Thursday 10/16. It's starting to look like a store. Several children arranged the boxes on the bookshelf. The papier-mâché fruit was finally dry, and the group painted their fruit very brilliant colors and patterns. Children are very busy making play dough cakes, pies, hot dogs, and tacos to sell. The best thing was when Susi announced that she was making books to sell in the store. Two other girls and she started a book factory. They spent over an hour folding paper into booklets and drawing pictures inside. I recorded them talking about what to draw in the books so that they would sell . . . such entrepreneurs!

At meeting we talked about how people buy things at the store. The topic of money came up. The children shared about their allowances and times when they lost money. I quickly decided to read the book *Bunny Money* (Rosemary Wells, 1997, New York: Dial).

Friday 10/17. I put out a bin of plastic coins for the children to explore and sort at the math center. I hung up some oversized coins nearby. The coins quickly ended up at the store. Some children spent a lot of time cutting out paper dollar bills and drawing "presidents" on them. Then they had a great time counting them. We put them in a box by the cash register.

I had brought in a price stamper and some labels. Several children were fascinated with these and made labels for the boxes in the store. I spent some time with them and asked them how they knew the price. They had some interesting ideas about what made something more valuable. Gina thought that the lasagna should cost more than the spaghetti because the noodles were bigger. Michael thought the papier-mâché fruit should be very expensive ($1,000,000) because it was hard to make. Luis said we had the best store because we just could make the money when we wanted to buy something. Michael thought about that and noted that it would take a long time to make a million dollars to buy his fruit. Many children spent time buying things at the store.

Next week I can see we will spend quite a bit of time on money. This will be great for practicing counting skills.

Studio Page 17

DESIGNING CROSS-CURRICULUM WARM-UPS

Design a warm-up for each of the following art activities that combines art and another curriculum area, such as math, science, or language.

1. Mixing white with other colors of paint at the easel

_____

_____

_____

_____

2. Drawing with chalk on wet paper

_____

_____

_____

_____

3. Painting with twigs

_____

_____

_____

_____

4. Using chalk over a dried painting

_____

_____

_____

_____

5. Drawing on small, smooth stones

_____

_____

_____

_____

Studio Page 18

THEMATIC PLANNING WEB

Language Objectives *Students will*	Cognitive Objectives *Students will*	Emotional Objectives *Students will*	Social Objectives *Students will*
Verbal/Linguistic Activities	**Mathematical/ Logical Activities**	**Intrapersonal Activities**	**Interpersonal Activities**

Theme Question:

Theme Concepts:

Musical/Rhythmic Activities	Visual/Spatial Activities	Naturalistic Activities	Bodily/Kinesthetic Activities
Music Skill Objectives *Students will*	**Art Skill Objectives** *Students will*	**Environmental Skill Objectives** *Students will*	**Physical Objectives** *Students will*

Studio Page 19

OBSERVATION: LOOKING FOR CONNECTIONS

Observe a group of children in a child care or school setting for at least two hours. Note how the guiding adult introduces the different activities planned for the day.

Date of observation: _____ **Length of observation:** _____

Ages of children: _____ **Size of group:** _____

What to Observe

1. What introductory experiences are used? (Reading a story, movement, questioning, and so on.) Which ones seem to be part of the daily routine?

   _____
   _____
   _____
   _____
   _____
   _____

2. How do individual children respond to the introduction?

   _____
   _____
   _____
   _____
   _____

3. Are themes or projects being used in this program? Describe some of the activities. If not, how are learning activities connected for the children?

   _____
   _____
   _____
   _____
   _____
   _____

Studio Page 20

ANALYSIS: MAKING THE CONNECTION

Based on your observations, write a response to the following questions:

1. How many different types of introductions were used?

   _____

   _____

   _____

   _____

2. Which introductions were the most effective?

   _____

   _____

   _____

   _____

3. What role do you think routine played in making activities go smoothly?

   _____

   _____

   _____

   _____

4. Did any child not respond to an introduction? What was the adult's response?

   _____

   _____

   _____

   _____

5. Was learning effectively integrated in this program? Why or why not?

   _____

   _____

   _____

   _____

 For additional information on teaching art to young children, visit our Web site at http://www.earlychilded.delmar.com

Making Art Safely

Questions Addressed in This Chapter:

- ✿ Why are art hazards a concern?
- ✿ How are safe art materials selected?
- ✿ What are some child-safe alternatives?
- ✿ How can safe behavior be promoted?
- ✿ How can teachers set limits?
- ✿ Is it food or art?
- ✿ What recipes work?

Young Artists at Work

Eric takes a piece of play dough and puts it in his mouth. "It tastes salty," he says in surprise.

Sallie picks up a cup of water in which a paintbrush has been rinsed and takes a sip. "It looked like chocolate milk," she whispers sheepishly.

Darlena takes a scissors and snips off a piece of Maria's bangs. She says smugly, "I'm a beauty parlor lady, and I'm making her beautiful."

WHY ARE ART HAZARDS A CONCERN?

What are the limits to a young child's exploration of art materials? Does allowing children to be creative entitle them to do anything that comes into their minds with everything that they find? Common sense tells us definitely not. Young children need our protection. We do not let them put a hand in the fire to discover how hot it is. We do not leave poisons in places where young children will find them. Children are unaware of the dangers in their environment. Guiding adults must take responsibility for the safety of the children in their care.

The adult working directly with children must create a safe environment that they can explore without danger. Selecting safe art materials, organizing a secure work space, and establishing limits on how tools and materials are used will allow children to create freely without endangering themselves. Caregivers and teachers cannot rely solely on outside authorities to make the daily safety decisions that are required when interacting with active and creative young children. We are the ones offering the materials directly to the children, supervising the work space, and enforcing safe behavior among the children. The information in this chapter is designed to provide the information needed to create the safest environment possible for young artists.

Art stores and art catalogs offer a multitude of media for artists. Some have been used for thousands of years, such as chalk. Others are brand new, such as pinking shears for kids. Not all of these wonderful materials, however, are safe to use with young children. Other dangers to children may come from nontraditional materials that are used for artwork, from bacteria-contaminated supplies, and from inexperienced or uncontrolled behavior.

Risk Factors for Children

Because of their physical makeup, and because of the way they explore their environment, young children's health is more vulnerable than adults' or older children's.

Metabolism. Young children are in a period of rapid growth. They have a higher rate of metabolism than adults and therefore absorb toxic materials more rapidly into their bodies. Many toxic materials particularly affect the growing brain and nervous system of the young child.

Body size. Young children have smaller bodies so that the same amount of toxic material will be more concentrated in a child's body than in an adult's. Children's smaller lungs are more likely to be affected after breathing in only a small amount of a toxic or an irritating substance. Children have proportionately shorter torsos and larger heads than adults, so that when sitting they are closer to the work surface. Their mouths and noses also are closer to the art materials and any toxins, bacteria, or irritants that might be present.

Muscular control. Young children may not have sufficient muscular control to handle certain materials safely. Children who are frustrated by a glue top that does not open may decide to open it with their teeth. If children cannot get a scissors to cut, they may push so hard that they not only cut the paper but a finger as well. Children with special needs often have difficulty handling art materials in safe ways because of limited physical control.

Behavior. The wonderful creativity of young children also puts them at risk. In exploring all of the possibilities of using art materials and tools, they often come upon ways that are dangerous to themselves or others. They are fascinated by interesting shaped bottles and containers containing unusual liquids or powders and by brightly colored materials or things that have interesting textures or smells.

Eating. Toddlers are particularly at risk because their sensory exploration of their surroundings includes putting everything in their mouths. Although children can be taught not to do this, they still tend to suck or lick their hands and fingers or chew their fingernails, regardless of what they have last touched. Young children are still relatively inefficient at washing their hands well after touching and using art materials.

Sniffing. Children of all ages often put their noses into things that they should not. Mists and powders floating in the air are quickly sniffed. Powders are shaken for the purpose of creating a cloud. Dust-covered hands are clapped so that they can see the dust rising. Unknown odors are fully investigated. Many children have not yet learned to identify certain smells with toxic substances.

Following directions. Even with the most careful instruction, young children cannot be trusted to follow the best precautions consistently. They can easily become so immersed in an investigation that they forget the directions, or they may not be able to generalize a safety instruction from one very similar material to another. It is easy for them to become confused, especially if the materials seem the same but are handled differently, such as when they are given edible play dough one day and inedible play dough the next. It takes a great amount of experience with an art material, even for adults, before safe handling becomes automatic.

Environmental factors. Beyond the immediate exposure to unsafe art materials, several environmental factors affect the level of danger.

Health factors. All children bring with them a unique set of factors that will determine their susceptibility to

Enthusiastic exploration often puts children at risk.

toxin exposure, including their previous health history; for example, a child who suffers from asthma will be very sensitive to any level of dust exposure. In addition, solvents can induce epileptic fits in some sensitive children.

Exposure. Another factor is the child's frequency and duration of exposure to a material. Working with firing clay on a daily basis is more health threatening than using it once a year. The conditions of exposure are also important. Using dusty materials outside is less dangerous than using them in an enclosed, unventilated room.

Body burden. Previous exposure to toxins that are stored in the body may be a hidden factor. A child who already has a high lead level may be more severely affected by a visit to a stained glass workshop than a child who has a low lead level. Children whose parents smoke cigarettes may be more affected by irritating inhalants as well.

Routes of Entry into the Child's Body

There are three routes of entry for toxins: the skin, lungs, and mouth.

Skin. Although the skin has a protective layer made up of a waxy coating, keratin, and dead skin cells, there are now many common chemicals in our environment and in art materials that can destroy this layer, causing reactions such as burns or rashes on the skin. Some substances may produce allergic reactions only after several exposures. Some of the more common skin irritants include ammonia, chlorine bleach, methyl alcohol, peroxide, turpentine, and most other solvents. Some of these chemicals, such as turpentine, toluene, benzene, and methyl alcohol, can even penetrate through the skin and enter the bloodstream.

In addition to chemical hazards, skin can also be injured in other ways. Sharp, jagged, and pointed objects are always a danger to young children.

Lungs. Inhaling toxins can cause respiratory diseases, asthma, and allergies. If the toxin or irritant affects the upper respiratory system, bronchitis can result. If it reaches the lungs, it can cause pneumonia. Allergies and chronic lung diseases are also possible results. Dusts, vapors, gases, smoke, and fumes can result from many art activities.

Aerosol sprays, airbrushes, and spray guns increase the likelihood of a toxin being inhaled, either by the person using it or by other people in the vicinity and pose great danger to young children.

Substances that can affect the respiratory system include: ammonia, cotton, and fabric dusts, firing clays, fabric dyes, glazes for clay, lead, zinc, model glues, plaster dust, overheated waxes, formaldehyde, melted plastics and Styrofoam, sawdust, and solvents of all kinds—alcohols, benzene, toluene, resin solvent, lacquer thinner, paint and varnish remover, plastic solvents, rubber cement thinner, mineral spirits, turpentine, and kerosene. None of these should be used by young children.

Mouth. Chemicals and bacteria can enter the body through the mouth directly or by contact with contaminated hands, food, work surfaces, and art tools. Dusts that are inhaled may also be swallowed. Young children who still put things into their mouths may be endangered by the chance of choking on small objects. Art materials that can be mistaken for food may also be eaten accidentally.

HOW ARE SAFE ART MATERIALS SELECTED?

In order to allow young children the freedom to explore, so necessary for their creative growth, the first step must be to make sure that any supplies offered are the safest possible. Every material must be chosen

Art supplies should be as safe as possible.

with great caution. Unfortunately there is no sole authority or one comprehensive list of safe or unsafe art supplies for young children. There are no legally mandated standards or labeling required for art materials, and some chemicals that are regulated in the workplace are not regulated in art materials. Medical research is constantly finding new hazards in the environment. New art materials are designed and sold. Materials long considered safe are found to be dangerous. The following guidelines are suggested, against which every material should be evaluated before being offered to children.

Read the Label

Study the ingredients in art supplies by reading the label or doing some research.

Nontoxic means that the material will not cause immediate death or severe injury, but it may be quite toxic over time, or it may cause nonfatal disabilities, especially to a young child.

The Art and Craft Materials Institute has a voluntary labeling program. The *AP Seal* stands for a product certified to contain insufficient quantities of any material that is toxic or injurious to humans or that will cause acute or chronic health problems. The *CP Seal* means that the product meets manufacturing

standards. However, not all of these products will be suitable in an early childhood art program. The labeling is designed for children of all ages and does not take into account the behavioral characteristics of children under age eight.

Any product that is labeled "Keep out of reach of children," "Flammable," "Avoid breathing vapors," "Do not take internally," or "Use in a well-ventilated area" should not be used by children, *ever*!

Research Unlabeled Products

If an art product is not labeled, write to the manufacturer for a Materials Safety Data Sheet that will list the ingredients and health effects. Schools are required to have copies of these kept on file.

If the ingredients of a material are unknown, do not use it.

Choose Children's Art Supplies

Use only art products specifically designed for young children. Art materials intended for use by adults often contain permanent pigments that are not safe for young children.

Use tools sized for a small child's hands.

To handle them safely, adult supplies may require

Teacher Tip

Material Safety Checklist

Examine the material and circle "yes" or "no" for each question:

1. Is there a high probability that it will be ingested?
   yes   no

2. Is there dust produced?
   yes   no

3. It is difficult to wash it off skin and surfaces with water?
   yes   no

4. Will spray, vapor, smoke, or fumes be produced?
   yes   no

5. Are the ingredients unknown?
   yes   no

6. Is it intended for adult use?
   yes   no

7. Will it be difficult for children to handle it safely?
   yes   no

Avoid any product that has one or more "yes" answers.

more skill than a small child has, such as opening the containers, controlling dusts, or cleaning them up.

Products that are labeled for specific ages should be used only by children at that age. Items that do not meet the standard choke test are required to be labeled for restricted use (children ages three and up). A simple device to check the size of objects can be purchased from most school supply catalogs and stores. A general rule is that objects shorter than two inches in length and less than one inch in diameter should not be used by children under age three.

When working with mixed age groups, all art materials available to the children should be suitable for use by the youngest child in the group. This also applies if a child with special needs or allergies would be endangered by any particular art material.

Avoid Old Art Supplies

It is not unusual to find or be given stockpiles of art materials that have been stored away for a long time. But standards for children's art supplies have changed dramatically in the last 10 years, so teachers should discard any supplies that are dated, or that do not have current labeling, even if they still look usable. It is not worth any amount of money saved to risk young children's health.

Analyze Material Usage

After determining that the ingredients are safe, determine whether the material will be safe in use. Many materials can be used in a variety of ways, some of which will be more injurious to the children than others.

For example, chalk designed for children is safe if it is used on dampened paper or dipped in water first. But if it is used dry, the chalk dust easily becomes airborne and can irritate children's respiratory passages.

Painting with poster paint using a paintbrush is safe; blowing bubbles in the paint with a straw is not. There is too great a chance that young children will suck instead of blow, or put the painted end in their mouths, risking ingestion of the paint.

When looking for art activity ideas in books on art for children, remember that many ideas that are suitable for older children are not safe for young children who are just beginning to have physical control over art tools such as scissors and materials such as clays. Always try out the art activity before introducing it to the children.

WHAT ARE SOME CHILD-SAFE ALTERNATIVES?

There are many possible substitutions for unsafe materials or methods for young children.

Solvents

Solvents are found in oil-based paints and paint thinners, varnishes and varnish removers, printing inks and lacquers, rubber cement and its thinners, epoxy, instant and model airplane glues, and permanent felt-tip markers. For example, one tablespoon of turpentine can kill a child if swallowed, and two tablespoons of methyl alcohol (found in shellac) can blind a child. All of these materials are also flammable and extremely dangerous to children's health. Keep these in locked storage away from children, and do not use them when children are present.

Child-Safe Alternative: Use only washable paints, printing inks, and markers. Make sure that they are labeled *water-based* or *watercolor*. Use only school paste, white or gel glues, and homemade pastes.

Aerosol Sprays

Do not use spray glues, spray paints, or chalk fixatives that can be inhaled.

Child-Safe Alternative: Use liquid white and gel glues and water-based paint. To decrease chalk dust, cover chalk drawings with a piece of paper, and rub off excess chalk dust. Then place the drawing in a folded piece of newspaper to keep the dust from rubbing off on the child on his or her way home. Chalk drawings also look beautiful if laminated or covered with clear contact paper.

Toxic Pigments

Toxic metals are found in colored pigments made from cadmium, lead, manganese, cobalt, and chromium. These pigments are found in artist-quality oil, watercolor, and acrylic paints, artists' pastels, and glazes for firing clays. They are also used in copper enameling. As with sprays and solvents, these materials should not be used by children, nor used in places to which children have access. If you must use them, wear a mask and work in a well-ventilated area, preferably outside, where children are not present.

Child-Safe Alternative: Use only water-based poster, tempera, and watercolor paints and colored chalk intended for children. Although a teacher could glaze a firing-clay piece for a child, it is more creative to allow children to paint their clay with watercolor or tempera paints.

Copper enameling is not safe for children to do. Chapter 11 presents ideas for safe jewelry making for young artists.

Dusts

Many art materials create hazardous dusts. Extreme care must be taken to avoid having children breathe in these dusts and to ensure that dust does not accumulate on surfaces accessible to children. Specific suggestions for commonly used art supplies follow.

Firing clay. Clay use produces a fine dust that is easily airborne and inhaled. It settles on surfaces and remains in the environment. Some clays containing talc may be contaminated with asbestos.

Child-Safe Alternative: Air-dried clay should never be handled by young children. Have children use only wet, talc-free clay. They must be taught to keep their hands damp and away from their faces. Wipe all surfaces when done, or use outdoors. Do not eat in the same room that is used for clay work.

Glazes. Many glazes contain toxic pigments such as lead, copper, and cobalt. The dry glaze dust is very fine and easily airborne. The dust settles on all surfaces in the environment.

Child-Safe Alternative: Have the children paint their fired clay with tempera or watercolors. If a more natural effect is desired, use different-colored clays to make designs. If glazing is necessary, it should be done by an adult. Choose only liquid, lead-free glazes. Never allow children to handle unfired, glazed clay pieces.

Plaster. Plaster creates a very irritating dust; in addition, there have been cases of skin being burned when children have been casting body parts in setting plaster.

Child-Safe Alternative: Plaster should be mixed only by the teacher, wearing a dust mask, outdoors or in a well-ventilated room away from the children. Choose activities that do not involve the children in handling dry plaster, carving, or scraping molded plaster, or in casting hands or other body parts. Safe plaster activities include

- making casts by pouring plaster into depressions made in sand.
- pouring plaster into a plastic bag and allowing it to harden (these odd forms can then be painted).
- pouring plaster into dishes of various sizes and shapes, to a depth of three-quarters to one inch (when set, it can be painted with tempera or watercolor paint).

Powdered tempera paint. Dry, powdered tempera paint should never be used by children. Avoid all activities that suggest that children work directly with the powder. Some colors, especially in older paints, may contain toxic pigments.

Child-Safe Alternative: Mix powder paint away from the children, and always wear a dust mask. Liquid tempera and poster paint are safer alternatives.

Fabric dyes. Fabric dyes of all kinds can cause bladder cancer and severe allergic reactions. Artists who use dyes wear organic vapor filter masks. Never use over-the-counter, multipurpose dyes intended to dye both cotton and wool.

Child-Safe Alternative: Dye cotton fabric and wool yarn using dyes made from natural plant materials or food-quality dyes. See chapter 8 for safe dye activities.

Fumes and Toxic Gases

Harmful gases may be released when ordinary materials are heated. Avoid exposing children to these fumes in the following ways.

Waxes. Natural waxes such as beeswax and paraffin are not hazardous by themselves, but when heated, they can vaporize into strong lung irritants such as acrolein and formaldehyde. Avoid activities that have young children working with melted wax (such as batik) or crayons (an old favorite—ironing crayon shavings between two sheets of wax paper).

Child-Safe Alternative: If wax must be melted, do

so in a well-ventilated area not used by children. Never let it get so hot that it smokes. Always melt the wax over hot water (in a double boiler), and never directly on a heat source.

Instead of batik, children can decorate cloth with natural dyes or glue on felt and fabric shapes.

Instead of melting crayons between sheets of wax paper, use a marker or crayon on tracing paper to produce a similar translucent effect.

Plastics. Plastics are safe when used as found. However, heating and sawing them will release toxic gases. Plastic glues contain solvents that actually melt the plastic together, creating fumes.

Child-Safe Alternative: Attach plastics by punching holes in them and tying them with yarn, pipe cleaners, or wire. Attach Styrofoam pieces with toothpicks.

Bacterial Contamination

Several kinds of bacterial contamination can be a problem in art materials.

First is the danger of contamination from reusing Styrofoam and plastic food containers that have held meat, fish, dairy products, or eggs.

Child-Safe Alternative: Rinse containers and their lids in hot, soapy water. Soak for one minute in a disinfectant solution of three-quarters of a cup of chlorine bleach per gallon of water. A final rinse in warm water is necessary to remove the bleach solution. Cover clothing and protect hands from the bleach by wearing rubber gloves. Do not allow children to use this disinfectant solution.

A second form of bacterial or viral contamination can occur when young children touch their mouths, eyes, or noses and then touch modeling materials that are shared.

Child-Safe Alternative: If necessary, older children can be asked to wash their hands or use a tissue. For toddlers and young preschoolers, a good solution is to give the children their own pieces of modeling dough and their own storage containers or resealable bags.

Sharp Objects

A surprising number of materials can cut the skin or injure the eyes of children. While it is impossible to eliminate all of the small injuries of childhood, and children need to learn to handle small risks, do check that the art supplies offered are as safe as possible.

The following items can cause injury: cut or jagged edges on pieces of plastic, broken shells, sharp sticks, adult-sized scissors, unsanded wood, pins, needles, staples, and the ends of pipe cleaners. The younger the children, the more carefully the supplies must be selected.

Allergies

Many children are allergic to common materials used in art. Affected children may be so allergic that they may have a severe reaction if they just touch a surface that has come into contact with the allergen. Some allergens can also become airborne and may cause reactions if inhaled. It is important to find out if a child has any allergies before offering any art materials. The family should be asked about allergies, or a letter should be sent home as soon as possible requesting this information.

Common food allergies include milk and milk products, eggs, peanuts, tree nuts, soy, and wheat. Some children also may be allergic to latex. These ingredients may be found in homemade play dough,* macaroni* used in collage, and pudding* finger paint as well as in some commercial art products. Be sure to obtain and read the Material Data Safety Sheets for all materials used with children. Nonallergenic alternatives should then be substituted.

HOW CAN SAFE BEHAVIOR BE PROMOTED?

Being an adult does not make a teacher impervious to art hazards. It is as important to protect oneself from the dangers that have been discussed as it is to keep children safe. First and foremost, a teacher needs to preserve her or his own health. A sickly, ill teacher does not have the enthusiasm to inspire young artists. One of the important ways that children learn proper behavior is by imitating adults. If a teacher practices unsafe behavior, then she or he is showing the children that safety standards are not really important.

Guidelines for Safe Teacher Behavior

1. Any room or space used by children must be totally free of hazardous materials.
2. When there is a choice, buy the least hazardous art material that will meet personal needs. For example, choose the following:

   Water-based markers instead of permanent markers

   Liquid paint instead of spray paint

   White glue instead of rubber cement

   Tacky craft glue instead of epoxy

3. Keep all hazardous materials in a locked metal cabinet.
4. Do not use any hazardous art supply in front of children. For example, do not use rubber cement while the children use safe white glue.
5. When working with dusty materials, wear a dust mask.
6. When working with skin irritants, wear rubber gloves.
7. When working with solvents or hazardous fumes, wear an approved face mask with the proper filters. This is essential when using fabric dyes or doing stained glass.
8. Adequate ventilation means the outdoors. Unless there is a sealed glove box that is ventilated to the outside, never use hazardous materials at home or in the classroom, even if children are not present. An open window is not sufficient. Fumes and dusts can remain in the air or collect on surfaces and contaminate the children or teacher days later.
9. Handle sharp, dangerous tools with care. Pass scissors to children in a safe way. Store the paper cutter where children cannot see or touch it.

Teacher to Family

Sample Letter to Families: Child Safety Information

Dear Family,

All of the art materials used in our program have been carefully selected to be safe for young children. Some children, however, have special sensitivities. To help us select the safest art materials for your child, please answer the following questions:

1. Is your child allergic to anything?   yes   no

   If yes, please list:

2. Does your child have any respiratory problems?   yes   no

   If yes, please explain:

3. Is your child's skin sensitive to anything?   yes   no

   If yes, please list:

4. Are there any art materials that your child should not use?   yes   no

   Please list and explain.

Thank you for taking the time to complete this form. Together we can make sure that your child will have a safe and fun time creating art.

Your child's teacher,

HOW CAN TEACHERS SET LIMITS?

Creativity doesn't mean doing whatever you want, it means finding new ways to work within a structure.

—*Fred Rogers (1982, p. 4)*

Even the safest art material can be dangerous if it is used in the wrong way. A key element to providing a safe environment for young artists is to teach the children to use the materials in a safe way. "Be Safe" should be the first rule for the young artist's exploration of art materials. All children need to learn that they are ultimately responsible for their own personal safety and for the safety of others.

It is important to remember that most unsafe behavior is not intentional but reflects the child's developmental level and unfamiliarity or inventiveness with the art material or tools. Toddlers taste play dough because they naturally want to use all of their senses, not because they want to do something dangerous. The best way to foster safe behavior is to understand how children at different developmental stages act and to set up activities so that safe behavior is promoted.

Ways to Promote Safe Behavior

There are three ways to foster safe, creative behavior: prevention, redirection, and removal.

Prevention.

1. Offer only those materials and tools appropriate for the child's developmental level.
2. Keep materials and tools not on the child's developmental level out of reach and out of sight.
3. Provide each child with adequate space in which to work. Dangerous behavior often happens when children accidentally bump or push each other.
4. Provide sufficient supplies to prevent the children from grabbing for that one special item.
5. Closely supervise the children while they work, especially during initial explorations of new materials and tools.
6. Keep group sizes small until the children know how to work safely with a particular material or tool.
7. Keep supplies and tools orderly so children do not have to dig or grab for what they want.

Children need to know what behavior is safe and acceptable.

8. Model safe handling of tools and supplies at all times.

Redirection.

1. If a child begins to use a tool or supply unsafely, gently state the safe way to use it, and model correct use if necessary. For example, if the child puts play dough up to her mouth, say, "Play dough is not food, we use it to make art."
2. If two children want the same supply or tool, provide other similar ones.

Removal.

1. When a child's behavior is developmentally appropriate and not unsafe, but annoying to the other children, such as when a toddler draws on other children's papers, gently move the child to a place closer to the others but too far away to reach their materials. Put the move in a positive light by saying, "You will have more space to draw over here."
2. If a child persists in unsafe behavior, redirect her or him to another activity that is more appropriate for that behavior. For example, if a child is snapping the scissors open and closed, explain that the scissors are too sharp to be used that way, but that she

3. When it is obvious that the tools or materials are inappropriate for the developmental level of the children, redirect them to another interesting activity, and then remove those supplies. Just because a particular activity may be recommended for children of a certain age or has been successful for others does not mean that it will be perfect for these particular children. It is better to say that this is not working and clear it away then to set up a potentially dangerous situation or one that will cause children to misbehave.

IS IT FOOD OR ART?

A controversial issue in art for young children is the use of food and food products in art activities. People have strong feelings on either side of this issue. Teachers need to decide where they stand so that they can defend their choices of art materials to parents and to other educators. It is not a clear-cut issue. While both viewpoints are based on concern for what the children are learning, each is based on a different set of values concerning the role of food.

Pro: Why Food Can Be Used for Art

- Many traditional adult art materials, such as egg tempera and casein paint, are made from food products.
- Some modern art materials, such as play dough and white glues, are made from food products.
- It is easier to determine the ingredients in food products than in real art supplies.
- Food items are readily available at the supermarket. Sometimes it is hard to find safe art supplies.
- There is no need to worry if children put their hands into their mouths after using food-based art materials.
- Art activities that use food products provide a multisensory experience in which children can use all of their senses in a safe way.
- Children learn to appreciate the aesthetic qualities of the foods such as the pattern inside of an apple.

- Food used as art can be utilized to relate the activity to the theme of the class, such as making apple prints when reading about Johnny Appleseed.
- Children are motivated by food and have a lot of fun doing these activities.

Con: Food Should Never Be Used in Art Activities

- Many children are severely allergic to some food items, such as milk, wheat, soy, eggs, and peanuts.
- Most traditional art materials are not food based, such as crayons, chalk, and paper.
- Food products used in commercial art supplies are usually inedible residues, such as sour milk or whey.
- With a little research, teachers can determine the ingredients of all art supplies.
- Safe, commercial art supplies for children are widely marketed in department stores and drugstores, and through catalogs. Also, many free, "found" items can be used.
- Children become confused when they are told that they can eat one art material but not another one that seems similar.
- The aesthetic qualities of food should be investigated in cooking activities, not art.
- Food is expensive and should not be wasted.
- Many food/art projects involve sugary foods and reinforce poor eating habits.
- People are hungry in our country and all over the world. Many children do not have enough to eat. It is cruel to have them make projects with food that could have fed them.
- Some ethnic groups are offended if food that is valued by them is used for play and not shown respect.

Making a Choice

The decision to use a food should not be made lightly. Those who feel strongly that it is morally wrong to use any food will have no trouble making their decision. Others are more comfortable if they base their decision on the appropriateness of the activity for the children, taking into account all of the serious implications of food use. They are not willing to

Is homemade play dough an acceptable art material?

nated hands and fingers into their mouths. As those who are opposed to using food in art point out, using edible and inedible materials in similar ways is not a good way to teach children safe behavior. It is confusing for a toddler to be told that she can eat her "candy dough" one day but not her "play dough" the next. One way to develop the basic safety skill of keeping art materials away from the mouth is by helping children learn how to discriminate between edible and inedible substances. In order to strengthen this health-preserving skill, present art activities in such a way that children can clearly identify what food is and what art is.

Ways to help children distinguish food from art supplies.

1. Avoid art materials that closely resemble foods or smell like foods.
2. Completely separate the areas that are used for food and art.
3. If the children will be making something from a food and eating it, it should be called "cooking" and done in the cooking area.
4. Never eat on tables that have been used for art projects. If tables must be used for both purposes, give the children trays on which to do their art, or cover the tables with plastic tablecloths when eating on them.
5. Enforce the rule that no art material is ever tasted, eaten, or drunk.
6. Supervise children, and do not let them put their fingers into their mouths when working with art materials, or before they have washed them.
7. Mix and store art materials in containers that are visually different from those used for food. If a food container is being reused, cover the outside with a label, or paint it.
8. Insist that children wash their hands after they finish using art materials and before they work with foods.

Avoiding food waste. Before selecting an activity, consider what kind of attitude toward food is being modeled and whether or not what the children will learn can be learned only in that way. In a world where there are people who are hungry, we must consider what message we send children when they see

forgo making homemade play doughs just because they are made from flour. They feel that modeling a soft, pliable material is important for the child's growth, and that play dough can be safely handled by the children as an inedible art material.

Some food-based art materials are less objectionable than others. Throughout this book, food-based art materials have been marked with an asterisk(*). Consider the suggested approaches to dealing with the safety and waste issues before choosing to use food in an art activity.

Is It Safe to Eat It?

One of the main ways that children put themselves at risk from hazardous art materials is by ingesting them. This can occur either directly, by eating or tasting an art material, or indirectly, by putting their contami-

TABLE 6–1	Substitutions for Foods in Favorite Art Activities
ACTIVITY	**SUBSTITUTE**
Vegetable or fruit printing	Sponge or block printing
Collages made with macaroni, rice, cereal, and so on	Pebbles, sand, buttons, and so on
Seed/bean mosaics	Pebble, shell mosaics
Edible doughs made from sugar, flour, cornmeal, and so on	Nonhardening modeling clay, purchased play dough
Cereal for stringing a necklace	Cardboard tube pieces, cut straws
Pudding finger paint	Purchased finger paint, detergent or soap finger paint

edible food used in art activities and then often thrown away. The children themselves may be hungry and not understand why they cannot eat the foods intended for an art activity. Children who have been taught not to waste food may be dismayed and confused when asked to paint with a banana or to sprinkle their favorite cereal on their collage. As one little boy said as he looked in a wastebasket full of fruits that had been used in a printing lesson, "Why did we mess up so much good food?" Before using any food product in an art activity, consider whether or not a nonfood item will accomplish the same learning goals. See table 6–1 for suggested substitutes.

WHAT RECIPES WORK?

Most homemade art materials are pale imitations of the real thing. Before cooking up a batch of finger paint or paste or any other art material, determine the cost, effort, and learning advantage of the homemade supply. Ready-made products are often cheaper and more attractive to children.

A few recipes have become traditions in early childhood art. These tried-and-true recipes have stood the test of time for several reasons. In some cases, the recipes are cheaper than the commercial products. They use easily obtained ingredients that are safe for young children, and they are quick and easy to make. Most of these recipes are made from food products,

but the resulting art material does not resemble food, nor is it designed to be eaten. These recipes are often mentioned in the Creating Art sections of this book, and appendix A lists some basic recipes for homemade art materials.

There are hundreds of recipes in books and articles on art for young children. Teachers can make their own pastes, paints, and modeling doughs of all kinds. It is fun to mix up small batches of these just to see how they work. Remember that recipes, particularly those involving flour, may not consistently turn out the same. The particular set of ingredients, the cooking temperature, or the weather may all affect the results. Before making up a large amount for the children to use, experiment with the material in the way the children will.

For example, young children like to squeeze modeling materials very tightly in their fists. Surprisingly, some doughs that model well when gently patted and rolled turn into a sticky mess when squeezed or pressed hard. Also consider the work surface. Some homemade glues cause paper to wrinkle up; some play doughs will stick to a newspaper covering but work fine on a smooth, bare tabletop. Cleanup is something to consider as well. Many concoctions, especially ones that involve flour, leave a residue that must be scrubbed off of the work surface.

Start a collection of recipes that have been tried, and document how much the materials cost, any difficulties in making the recipe, and how successfully the children used it. Once the basic elements of the recipes are familiar, experiment with original ideas. Who knows? Maybe a new art material will be discovered that will become another child art tradition.

CONCLUSION: BALANCING FREEDOM AND SAFETY

Teaching about the hazards of art materials and how to work safely should occur when students first learn art techniques.

—Michael McCann (1985, p. 6)

It is a challenging task to create a safe environment in which children will be free to be artists. Young children have more energy and more inventiveness than

Making a homemade art supply can be an unpredictable experience.

can be imagined. Adults are ultimately responsible for the health and safety of the children in their care, and it is easy to become overcome with guilt. A child cuts herself seriously with a scissors and requires stitches. A child has an allergic reaction to the scent of an art material, goes into shock, and becomes unconscious. An article is published that says an ingredient in an art supply that teachers have used with the children for the last 10 years has been found to cause cancer.

The longer we work with children, the more likely something unfortunate will occur. But if the children are closely supervised, and if teachers have enforced safe behavior and provided the safest art materials based on the best information they can obtain, then they should not bury themselves in guilt. When an accident occurs, take time to analyze why it happened, and correct the situation so it will not be repeated. If an art supply is suddenly deemed unsafe, stop using it. Read, listen, and learn from others. All teachers can benefit from sharing experiences with other people who work with children.

Art experiences encourage children to explore freely. Children are ultimately responsible for creating their own learning. Although direct experience is a wonderful teacher, some experiences are simply too dangerous for children. The teacher has to be their *guiding* adult—caring, watchful, thoughtful, knowledgeable, and always prepared to gently redirect children who are endangering themselves or others.

FURTHER READING

The following books will provide more detailed information on the health hazards in art.

McCann, M. (1985). *Health hazards manual for artists.* New York: Nick Lyons Books.
This book provides a simple outline of health hazards in art.

Qualley, C. A. (1986). *Safety in the art room.* New York: Davis.
This book is specifically directed to teachers of art and contains detailed information on making the art environment hazard free.

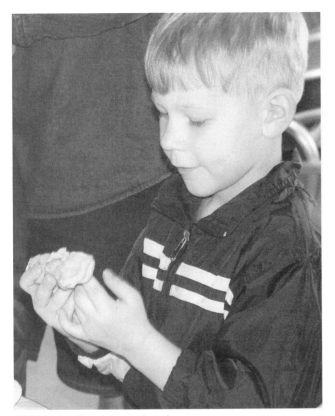

Children's safety is in our hands.

Recipes for art materials can be found in many books. Choose recipes with care. Some that can be used with young children may be found in these books and articles.

Kohl, M. F. (1989). *Mudworks: Creative clay, dough, and modeling experiences*. Bellingham, WA: Bright Ring. This book contains hundreds of recipes for all kinds of art supplies. Some are familiar, and some are surprising. Not all of them are safe or appropriate for children under eight. Select them with care.

Miller, S. A. (1994). *Learning through play: Sand, water, clay & wood*. New York: Scholastic.
This book provides basic information on using modeling materials with young children.

Pinkerton, S. (1989). Concoctions: Creative mixtures to make and enjoy. *Day Care and Early Education, 17*(2), 25–29.
This article describes the fun of inventing new recipes and provides several sample ones to try.

Creating Art: Modeling

Poke it. Pat it. Squoosh it. Modeling provides a tactile experience.

THE MODELING EXPERIENCE

Modeling, or working with three-dimensional pliable materials, is one of the great joys of early childhood. Soft, smooth clays and play doughs are just waiting to be squeezed and poked, to the great delight of the young artist. By giving children the opportunity to eplore a material that has many sides, that can be turned over and around and looked at from different points of view, teachers strengthen children's understanding of the spatial realm in which they exist. Three-dimensional art forms call upon different perceptual modes and different areas of skill development than do drawing, painting, and other two-dimensional activities.

When children draw or paint, there is a strong visual response to the marks they make on the paper. In working with modeling materials, although the visual element is still there, the children respond first to the tactile qualities of the forms as they create them. Young children working with play dough or clay will often manipulate the material vigorously while focusing their eyes on something else or staring off into space.

There is also a great deal of talking and noise-making that goes on as children explore clay. Children working on drawings or paintings will perhaps make a comment or two while they work or add a special sound effect, but many at the clay table will pound and slap and talk incessantly. Modeling materials will provide an opportunity for children to practice their social skills as they respond to each other's actions and exchange pieces of clay or tools.

How Children Grow through Modeling Activities

Children will develop

1. physically, by using the large muscles of the arm and the small muscles of the hand to manipulate the modeling material. (Bodily-Kinesthetic)
2. socially, by working alongside others and sharing materials and space. (Interpersonal)
3. emotionally, by learning that they can control this material and use it to release energy, tension, and emotion. (Intrapersonal)
4. visual perception skills, by exploring three-dimensional forms from differing viewpoints and learning that pliant forms change shape. (Spatial)

5. language skills, by learning a vocabulary for concepts of size, shape, form, comparison, and relationship. (Linguistic)

6. cognitively, by observing cause and effect as their manipulation changes the nature of the form. (Logical-Mathematical)

7. art awareness, by examining three-dimensional modeled forms, such as pottery, that have been created by people from many times and places.

MODELING: A DEVELOPMENTAL VIEW

As in drawing, children go through modeling modes that mirror their physical and cognitive growth. The sorts of forms that children can produce are determined by the amount of control they have over their arms, wrists, hands, and fingers, by their mental ability to imagine a form and then produce it, and by their previous experiences with the material (see table 6–2).

Initial Exploration

When first confronted with a modeling material, children often approach it with a caution that quickly turns to abandon. They push their fingers into it, pat it, pick it up and put it down, drop it, and squeeze it until it oozes out between their fingers. They may lick it and taste it, rub it on their faces, and stick it up to or into their noses for a good whiff. They will bang it with fists, peel it off their arms when it sticks, and throw it, if not stopped. There is no attempt to make

"Man." Nonhardening clay—*Nick, age 5*

TABLE 6–2	The Development of Modeled Forms
MODE	**CHILD'S BEHAVIOR**
1. Initial Exploration	Manipulates material using all of the senses; uses large motions of arm and hand
2. Controlled Exploration	Begins to make basic forms—pancake, worm, and ball; uses palms and fingers
3. Named Forms	Gives names and labels to modeled forms; begins to use them in symbolic play; uses fingers for shaping
4. Symbolic Forms	Plans the forms that will be used; can attach forms; can pull a form out of a larger piece of modeling material; can use fingers to create small details

the clay or dough into something but only a pure, multisensory exploration of this exciting material.

This purely exploratory behavior is seen in the youngest children, those between the ages of one and three, and it corresponds in some ways to scribbling in drawing. However, it is often seen in older children as well, especially as they first start to handle a new or an unfamiliar modeling material.

For toddlers, the behavior reflects their lack of small motor control, their reliance on large motor movements of the arm and hands, and their sensory approach to learning about their environment. For older children, this initial exploratory behavior reflects an attempt to understand the material's possibilities and limits. Even adult artists spend time working freely with a medium in order to assess its parameters before beginning to create a sculpture in earnest.

Controlled Exploration

After the initial explorations of the modeling medium, children will begin to explore the clay or dough in a more systematic way. At this stage the children may flatten the clay into pancake-like forms using the palm of the hand. With their fingers, they may poke a series of indentations into the surface or pull off small pieces and flatten them. They may stick the pieces back together or create a stack of them. One of the first forms that they can make due to the increasing control over their hands is a long, thin cylinder created by rolling a piece of clay between the palms of their two hands.

One of the later forms that develops, sometimes in the fourth or fifth year, is the sphere or ball created by rolling the clay between the palms or between the table and one palm. This is a much more complex skill, as it requires the child to move the hand in a circular motion and is often preceded by much experimentation. Once the ball is perfected, it often becomes the object of much manipulative play; it may be rolled across the table, or several may be lined up in a row.

For children who have had many opportunities to use clays, *controlled exploration* reflects their increasing control over hands and fingers. Older children and adults may also repeat these same manipulations as part of their preliminary explorations of modeling media.

Named Forms

The difference between a *named form* and controlled exploration is not one of form or physical control. It relates instead to the *cognitive* development of the child. The long, thin cylinder becomes a "snake," the poked pancake becomes a "face," the clay balls become "snowballs." This naming of the modeled forms correlates to the naming of scribbled drawings and reflects the child's developing language skills and the growth of mental imagery.

The very manipulative nature of modeling materials allows children at this stage of development to pursue symbolic play in a way that they cannot with two-dimensional art media. Young children "cook" play-dough bits in the pots on a toy stove. They offer a "taco" to taste. They make mommy snakes and baby snakes that hiss and wiggle around the room and then turn into bracelets wrapped around active wrists. They "bowl" with their clay balls.

Although the child's creations may take on a life of their own, they still are, to a large extent, the result of unplanned manipulation. Once made, they are then "seen" to resemble or represent something. As in drawing, children will repeat these behaviors as they perfect the skills needed to create the basic forms of sphere and cylinder at will.

Developing Three-Dimensional Symbols

In the final mode of modeling development, children are able to plan the forms that they will need to create an object. Instead of using the clay solely as a vehicle for sensory sensation and the release of feelings, the modeling material now becomes a means of self-expression for internal images. These images can be formed in several ways. Some are created by bending, flattening, or distorting one of the basic forms, for example, making a "nest" by poking a hole in a clay ball. Others may be produced by joining simple or distorted basic forms, as when a child creates a person from a clay ball and four flattened cylinders. As with the graphic symbols of drawing, the children are not trying to create actual representations of these objects but rather the idea of the object. Once created, they assume a major role in the symbolic play of the child. Airplanes fly and drop bombs; animals eat clay bits from the clay bowl; birds sit on eggs in the nest and then fly off to find clay worms.

"Cookie and stick." Play dough—*Ross, age 3*

The kinds of images that are produced will depend upon the amount of control the child has developed over the particular modeling material. All modeling materials are not the same; they differ in pliancy, stickiness, and rigidity. A child who has had a lot of experience with only one kind of clay or dough is often frustrated by trying to produce with a new one and may engage in purely sensory exploration instead of creating symbols. Regardless of their age, children who have had few experiences working with three-dimensional modeling materials may also need to spend time repeating the processes of each of the earlier modes before they can work on a symbolic level.

Using Modeling Materials for Emotional Release

The creation of modeled forms is often accompanied by children's enthusiastic destruction. Pliant modeling materials give children the power to control a small part of their environment. Clay and play doughs are regularly used by children to release strong feelings in an acceptable way. Clay, unlike other children, bossy adults, or precious belongings, can be hit and smashed, slapped, pinched and poked, and torn apart and put together again. Children who are having difficulty controlling their social behavior benefit from redirecting this behavior to the forgiving clay.

INTRODUCING PLAY DOUGH AGES ONE AND UP

Most toddlers need many opportunities to freely explore soft, pliant modeling materials. The modeling material offered to toddlers must be one that contains no injurious ingredients because of the risk of ingestion. These young children still need to be closely supervised while they are working.

Group Composition

The first exploration of a modeling material should be limited to one or two toddlers. Like paste and glue, modeling materials are quite often tasted or eaten. Provide constant close supervision until children have learned not to eat the material.

Setup

A low, smooth-topped table that is easily washed makes the best working surface. There should be plenty of space for each child. If the tabletop is not appropriate for modeling, or when working at home in a kitchen area, provide each child with a large tray to be used whenever he or she models or does other artwork. The low sides of the tray will help keep some of the pieces from falling to the floor.

There will be less mess on the floor if the children remain seated while working, so provide child-size

Classroom Museum

Display a handmade clay bowl, and supervise the children handling it, or use the bowl to hold a snack.

chairs. However, children can use more of their upper arm motion when standing, so occasionally allow them to stand while working.

Materials

The safest, most pliable modeling material for toddlers is play dough. Use a commercial brand, or produce a homemade version. Many recipes are available in books on art for children, or consult appendix A: Recipes.

For the child's initial exploration, the dough should be a nonfood color and have a nonfood scent. A homemade dough has the advantage of being able to be made without scent for the first few explorations. Use only one color of dough for the first experience so the child can concentrate on the tactile qualities of the materials.

Provide each child with a baseball-size piece of the modeling dough. If the dough will be reused, offer separate, tightly lidded containers or resealable plastic bags, clearly labeled with each child's name.

Warm-Up

Offer the children a lump of play dough, and show them where to use it. Explain that it is not food but something with which to play. Let the children see it, smell it, and touch it.

What to Do

Children will react differently to the stimulus of the play dough. Some will dive right in; others will approach cautiously. Some will pat and poke gently; some will squeeze it tightly in their hands. Often the first response is to try to taste or smell it.

1. Sit at the table with the children.
2. Squeeze and poke a piece of the play dough too, but do not show children how to use it.
3. Avoid making forms such as balls and snakes, which are beyond children's developmental level.
4. Only interfere with children's exploration for safety reasons. Be ready to stop them from putting the dough into their mouths. Remember that it is important from the start to emphasize that art materials are never put into the mouth.

What to Say

Use this activity to talk about the tactile qualities of the play dough. In an excited voice, use words such as

Special Needs

Children who have limited vision love the tactile nature of modeling materials. Provide a large tray with slightly raised sides for the child to work on—it will make it easier to find small pieces of the modeling material.

Music Box

Modeling Chants

1. Push and mush.
   Pull and tug.
   Roll around,
   And mash it up.

2. Poke it. Pat it.
   Make it flat.
   Pick it up
   and put it back.

3. Today I play,
   With sticky clay.
   First I squeeze,
   Then I pat.
   Now I've made it
   nice and flat.

4. First I played
   Now I've stopped.
   In goes my play dough.
   On* goes the top.

(*If using a resealable plastic bag, substitute "zip" goes the top.)

soft, squooshy, pat, poke, push, pull, sticky, press, squash, and flatten. Modeling is a wonderful time to chant or sing with toddlers. Make up some modeling chants to accompany this wonderful activity (see Music Box).

Transition Out

Let the children spend as much time as they wish exploring the nature of the dough. When they lose interest, show them how to gather up the play dough and put it into its storage container. Show them where the containers will be stored, and tell them that it will be there for them to use again.

More to Do

Once children are familiar with safe ways to use play doughs, the activity can be varied in many ways.

Color and scent. Toddlers love using play dough over and over. Vary this experience first by offering a different color each time. Later provide colors that they can mix. Once they have learned not to taste the dough, add nonfood scents. (See chapter 7 for a list of possible scents.)

Textures. Find a recipe for homemade play dough that has a different texture, or add a material to commercial play dough to provide a different tactile experience. Make sure whatever is added is safe if ingested.

Provide tools. The majority of a child's modeling experiences should be done with the fingers only. Manipulating the play dough directly is the best way to develop hand and finger strength. On occasion, provide some very simple tools. Little children love to cut up play dough. A plastic knife provides a safe way for the child to feel grown up and trusted. A small wooden or plastic rolling pin is another tool that children enjoy, and one that helps them develop hand-eye coordination.

Teacher Tip

Tools to Avoid

Avoid giving the children cookie cutters to go with the rolling pin, however. Although these are commonly used in early childhood programs, in many ways they are similar to giving the children precut paper patterns on which to draw. They tell the children that adults do not think the forms they create on their own are as good as the commercial cookie-cutter designs. Cookie cutters also reduce the wonderful three-dimensionality of the play dough to two dimensions and so do not help develop the child's spatial abilities.

Cookie cutter use is another case of trying to make children's artwork more pleasing to the aesthetic sense of adults. Unfortunately, once cookie cutters are introduced, many children abandon their own creative exploration of the clay to develop their skill in making the perfect cutout.

EXPLORING PLAY DOUGH
AGES THREE AND UP

Children who have had some experience using modeling doughs are ready for a larger variety of activities.

Group Composition

Modeling activities lend themselves to both individual and group pursuits. One child can work alone at a small table. Large tables allow groups of six to eight to enjoy the social interaction that usually accompanies modeling.

Setup

Play dough should be available at all times. Store it in child-accessible covered containers or resealable plastic bags so children can help themselves.

Materials

Preschoolers and primary-age children can be given several colors of play dough at a time, which they will mix with great enthusiasm. Try to pick colors that when combined form attractive new ones, such as red and yellow to make orange, or blue and yellow to make green. Both commercially made and homemade play doughs can be used.

Warm-Up

One way to introduce play dough is to have children sit in a circle. Pass around an "imaginary" lump of clay. Have each child pretend to make it into something, and then tell the group what each child made. Use this time to introduce the rules for using play dough.

What to Do

Show children where the containers or plastic bags are stored. Model how to select one, and take it to the designated table. Make it clear where it can be used and where it cannot. For example, play dough should not be used on a rug or in a book area.

What to Say

Encourage children to describe what they are making, and engage in pretend play with them. Use words that describe the forms they are making, such as cone,

Classroom Museum

Share the sculptures of Henry Moore. His gently rounded human forms are appealing to young children. Compare them to work by other sculptors. If possible, visit a sculpture in the neighborhood, and study and sketch it from different sides.

cylinder, and sphere. Introduce the word *coil* to describe the long snakes children love to roll out. Ask them to tell you how they made certain forms and how they were able to attach them.

Transition Out

By this age, children should be expected to put away their play dough and clean up their work space. Respond positively to independent behavior. If a child wishes, finished sculptures can be displayed temporarily for classmates and families or shared at meeting time. Another way to preserve the experience is to take photographs during creation and after the project is done. Create a display of the photographs in the art area, or include them in the child's portfolio.

"Person." Play dough—*Melody, age 4*

Teacher Tip

Cautions about Baked Play Dough

Try to avoid instances in which all of the children are required to make something permanent, such as making gifts of baked play-dough paperweights. Many young children lack the skill to make something that will dry or bake well. Their pieces may be too thin, not well attached, or more often so thick that they dry poorly, if at all. If teachers tell them they have to change what they have made to be bakable, then they may feel this is a criticism. Remember, if teachers have to personally "fix" children's artwork so that it can be baked, then this is not a creative developmental art activity for young children.

A better alternative is to prebake simple round pieces of dough that the children can then use as a base on which to paint or glue pieces of collage items in their own creative ways.

More to Do

Play with color. Let the children color their own dough by squeezing a drop or two of food coloring or liquid tempera paint onto uncolored, homemade dough and then mixing the color with their hands. (Homemade play dough recipes are in appendix A: Recipes.)

Make salt-flour dough. Children can also mix their own play dough. A salt-flour dough is the easiest for children to do on their own. Note: Salt may cause a burning sensation or irritate any small cuts or scrapes that children have on their hands. Check the children's hands first. If children complain about burning, let them wash their hands right away.

1. Work with a small group of three or four children that can be closely supervised.
2. Give each child a bowl, and help each child measure and pour one cup of flour and one-quarter cup of salt. Add one-quarter cup of warm water, and let them knead it together.
3. If the dough is too dry, add some drops of water. If it is too wet, add more flour.
4. Show excitement and interest as the children respond to the changing tactile quality of the mixture. Children can add liquid tempera or food coloring to the dough as well.

Try baked dough. Several of the homemade doughs are suitable for air drying or baking. In general, children are much more involved in the process of using the modeling material than in creating a finished work. Usually it is best to save children's sculptures only when they request it. If the piece is sturdy enough, put it in a safe, dry place to air dry, or bake it according to the directions of the recipe.

Suggest "stick" sculptures. Another way that play dough can be used is for children to use a lump of air-drying dough as a base in which to insert materials such as sticks, toothpicks, pipe cleaners, cardboard strips, craft sticks, beads, buttons, drinking straws, and nature materials, such as pinecones, acorns, shells, dried grasses, and twigs. When the dough has dried, the objects will be securely fastened to the base.

Try impressions. Give the children objects with interesting textures to press into the dough. Try berry baskets, plastic food trays, plastic forks, potato mashers, and any other washable items.

EXPLORING NONHARDENING CLAY AGES THREE AND UP

Nonhardening clay is an oil-based modeling material, also called plasticine or modeling clay. These do not dry out when exposed to the air. They are more rigid than play dough and are suitable for older children who have more developed finger strength.

Group Composition

Nonhardening clay, like play dough, is suitable for individual or large group work. Modeling clay should not be ingested. It is not appropriate for children who still try to taste or eat modeling materials.

Setup

These clays work best on a smooth, washable surface such as a plastic laminate tabletop, a plastic placemat or tray, or even a laminated piece of construction paper. Do not use it on newspaper, as it picks up the ink.

Materials

Very brightly colored modeling clays are available. Provide each child with a baseball-size piece or several smaller pieces in different colors.

Warm-Up

Put clay in a fancy box. Use guided discovery to introduce nonhardening clay. Then read *The New Baby Calf* (Chase & Chase, 1984). The illustrations in this book

"Flower and nest." Nonhardening clay—*Heather, age 5*

Classroom Museum

Display brightly colored Mexican figurines of roosters and other common animals. Talk about why artists might use color on some sculptures and not on others. Also share handmade pottery pieces. Have a potter visit and demonstrate making a pot, or visit a potter's studio. Use handmade pottery to serve snacks.

are created from modeling clay. Have the children try to figure out how the different textures were made.

What to Do

Modeling clay needs to be softened by warming it in the hand. This naturally fits the pattern of young children's behavior, as it encourages free exploration before the expression of ideas. Show children how to

Teacher Tip

Using Food Coloring

- Some food coloring will stain the hands the way lollipops stain the mouth, but the stain does not last long. Parents and children, however, may be upset by the stain, particularly if they do not know what caused it.
- When adding food coloring to dough, always add a few drops at a time. Fold dough over the color rather than putting hands directly in it.
- There may be some children who are sensitive to food dyes; check with families before using them.

warm the modeling clay in their hands and slowly begin to knead it. If the room is chilly, it is sometimes helpful to break the clay into smaller pieces and then warm them. Oil-based modeling compounds will hold sharper detail, will remain more upright, and will stay quite flexible when rolled into extremely long, thin "snakes"—much to the delight of young children. Soft play doughs often sag and crack when rolled thin, and their details slowly soften and fill in.

However, children who have used the much softer play dough often do not want to work harder to create something out of modeling clay. In order to encourage children to develop the finger strength needed, modeling clay should be offered exclusively for a period of time.

More to Do

It is well worth the effort to present modeling clay to young children who are able to create symbolic forms.

Explore forms. Children can be much more expressive with this flexible but strong modeling material and can develop more sophisticated forms to work with, such as cubes (made by tapping a sphere on the table to create the sides) and slabs (flat, rectangular "pancakes"), which can be used in building structures.

Safety Notes

- Make sure that the modeling clay colors that are chosen do not come off on the hands and are specifically designed for children.
- Look for safety labeling.
- Modeling clay should not be ingested. It is not suitable for children who still try to taste or eat modeling materials.
- Make sure children do not put their hands into their mouths while working, and wash their hands well when they are done.
- Check that they do not have clay under their fingernails. Modeling clay will wash off in soapy water but may require a bit of soaking or scrubbing.

Make impressions. Textured objects, such as coins and keys, can be pressed into the clay and will leave clear impressions.

EXPLORING FIRING CLAY
AGES THREE AND UP

Firing clay is the real clay that comes from the earth and from which pottery is made. It has been used for thousands of years by people around the world. The china dishes we use every day are made from this substance. Although strongly advocated in many books on art for young children because of its mudlike, tactile qualities, firing clay has lost its popularity in many early childhood programs.

There are a number of reasons for this. One of the main ones is the health hazard related to the use of firing clay. Another is the need for constant supervision as the children work and the difficulty cleaning up the resulting "mess."

In general, commercial and homemade play doughs and modeling clays can provide plenty of wonderful modeling experiences for young children and meet all of the same growth objectives. They should form the backbone of any three-dimensional art activity program. Firing clay, although not essential to a well-rounded program, can offer a special experience for older children. This is particularly true if it is related to a child-initiated interest in pottery, developed either through a visit to a pottery studio, from a guest potter, or from observation of handmade pottery dishes and bowls from different cultures. However, if a safe environment is not available for firing clay activities, then do not offer them.

Group Composition

The fewer children who work with the clay at a time, the more closely they can be supervised. Try to work with no more than four children at a time. The ideal situation is to have one adult work directly with one or two children. It may be possible to arrange for a local potter or parent to provide this close attention. The adult can work with clay beside the child to offer assistance and encouragement as needed and help the child focus on the tactile qualities of the clay.

Setup

Children create the least mess when they work standing at a table covered with several layers of newspaper.

- Use wet firing clay outdoors, if possible.
- Provide the children with buckets of water in which to rinse their hands as soon as they get dusty.
- Never use firing clay in any multipurpose room or where food is eaten. Clay use produces a fine dust that settles on all surfaces.
- If a pottery studio is used, it should be damp mopped, and all surfaces should be wiped down daily.

Cleanup. The clay-covered newspaper will need to be folded up slowly to not spread the dust.

- Wash all tools and wipe down all surfaces to eliminate dust.
- Use buckets for the initial hand and tool rinsing so the clay-filled water can be dumped outside on the ground where it will not clog the sink drain.

Materials

Purchase only talc-free, moist clay (see appendix A for sources). Avoid all powdered or dry clay mixes. Figure one pound of moist clay per child. A 25-pound bag will serve 25 students. Each child will need a baseball-size piece. Store unused clay in double plastic bags that are tightly closed and placed inside a covered plastic can. When used clay is returned to the bag, add a half-cup of water per piece to replace evaporated moisture. Clay will keep a very long time this way.

Warm-Up

Visit a pottery studio, invite a guest potter, or share a special ceramic bowl or dish. An excellent book to share with children, either before or after experience with the clay, is *The Potter* (Florian, 1991). If you wish, make an original Big Book about firing clay. Discuss how clay changes when it is baked at a hot temperature, and show examples of unglazed, baked clay and glazed, fired clay. Compare how the firing clay differs from the other modeling materials the children have used.

What to Do

Children who have had a lot of experience using play dough and nonhardening clay have great difficulty adjusting to firing clay. Unlike these soft, elastic materials, firing clay is stiff, cold, and damp. It makes the hands feel very dry. It dries out and cracks when handled and turns to mud when too much water is added. Before beginning, show children how to add small amounts of water by dipping fingertips into a small, shallow water cup.

1. Present the firing clay to the children as an exploration. Encourage them to try different ways of using it, and let them explore on their own. Do not expect them to produce a finished product.

2. Show children how to return the clay to its storage container when they are done.

3. Two pieces of clay will not join and stay together when dry without special preparation:

- To join: apply slip—a watery clay mixture—to each piece.
- Press together.
- Smooth joint so it cannot be seen.

4. The more the clay is handled, the more it dries out. Overly dry clay cracks and will not stay together. Small amounts of water should be added as needed. It takes a lot of experience to know just how much water to add. Children will quickly learn that too much water reduces the clay to a mud pile. Use this experience to help children see cause and effect. Help them learn to add just a little at a time.

Art Words

Working with Clay

Bisque
Unglazed clay that has been fired in a kiln. It is hard and porous.

Coil
A long rope of clay made by rolling it on a flat surface with the palms moving outward.

Firing
Slowly heating clay in an insulated oven called a "kiln."

Firing clay
Modeling compound formed from earth that dries out in the air and becomes hard when fired in a kiln.

Glaze
A finely ground mixture of minerals that when fired to a high temperature forms a glassy coating on clay.

Greenware
Clay that has air dried. It is very brittle and easily broken.

Handwedging
Kneading clay to bend it and remove pockets of air.

Kiln
An oven made from fire brick in which clay can be fired to temperatures over 1000°F.

Leather hard
Clay that is still damp but no longer flexible. It can be cut and carved.

Nonhardening clay
Modeling compounds that never harden but stay soft and pliable.

Scraffito
Using a stick or pointed tool to scratch designs into the surface of the clay.

Slab
A flat piece of clay made either by pressing with the palms or by using a rolling pin.

Slip
Liquid clay made by combining clay with water to form a thick, custardlike substance. It is used to join clay pieces.

Wedging
Kneading and pressing clay to remove air pockets and to create an even texture.

More to Do

Make clay tiles. Most creations by young children are too fragile to survive firing in the kiln. Again, they are best saved through photography. If, however, a kiln is available, a wonderful, cooperative culminating activity for the firing clay exploration is to make clay tiles.

1. Make one or several large flat squares of clay, about one-half-inch thick, and four to six per side. Children can help roll out the clay using rolling pins.
2. Have the children take turns drawing an original design or picture on the tiles using pencils or craft sticks. Caution children not to press too hard.
3. Alternatively, wet the clay surface and have children attach small pieces of clay, such as flattened balls and skinny snakes, combined to make a picture. Keep the height under one inch.
4. Poke holes in the top of the tiles so they can be hung up after firing.
5. Air dry completely—at least one week.
6. Low-fire the tiles in the kiln (1100°–1500° F).
7. After firing, the tiles can be painted with watercolors or tempera paint or left natural.

Make wind chimes. Clay slabs can also be made into wind chimes. Have children make flat pancakes with the clay, and then cut them into three or four different shapes. Impress designs in the clay, or draw in the clay with a pencil. Poke a hole in the top of each piece. Suspend with yarn or leather thongs from a tree branch or dowel. A group wind chime can be made by having each child contribute one shape.

Make pinch pots. After many opportunities to explore clay, introduce older children to basic pottery techniques, beginning with the pinch pot. Start with a ball of clay, and demonstrate how to make a hole in the center using the thumb. Make the hole wider by pinching the sides of the bowl between the thumb and fingers. Emphasize the need to keep the walls of the pot about the same thickness. For comparison, have children examine the sides of pottery bowls and mugs. Sometimes the walls get too thin and start to crack. This can be remedied by wetting the clay well and then folding over the edge.

Safety Notes

Using Clay Wisely

- Have children wear smocks to prevent dust from collecting on clothing. Wash smocks after use.
- Remind children to keep their hands away from their faces and to dampen them when they are dusty and dry. Children must never put their hands into their mouths or touch their faces when using the clay. They must clean under their fingernails as well as clean their hands when they are done. Do not allow children to clap their hands together, raising dust.
- Kilns must be located in areas far away from where children are working. They must be fully ventilated to the outside. Never use a kiln that does not meet these requirements.

Make coil pots. Show children how to roll out ropes of clay using the palms of their hands. Make a base by cutting a circular shape from a slab of clay. Attach a thick coil to the outside edge of the base using slip. Smooth the inside so that no joints show.

Make animals. Children love making animals from clay but often have difficulty making the legs and necks strong enough to support the body and head. Talk about how large animals need strong legs. Offer the idea of attaching the animal to a slab base or making it sitting or lying down. Emphasize the importance of using slip to attach limbs and details, and make sure the child smoothes joints. Share the illustrations of child-made clay animals found in *The Sweet and Sour Animal Book* (Hughes, 1994). If clay animals will be fired in a kiln, make sure to hollow out any thick bodies so that they will dry better and be less likely to crack during firing.

Use movement. Have children imagine that they are lumps of clay. Call out different forms and objects, and encourage the children to mold themselves into those shapes.

Making Connections

Language. Share books that describe what clay is, such as *Clay* (Dixon, 1990) or *A Ball of Clay* (Hawkinson, 1974). After using the clay, have children make their own Big Book about the experience.

Science/math. Make two equal lumps of clay. Wrap one in plastic. Fire the other one. Have the children compare the two pieces and describe how they are different. Use a balance scale, and see which one is heavier. Discuss why.

Teacher Tip

Firing Clay

The following guidelines will help make the firing experience more successful.

1. Work to be fired should be fairly uniform in thickness so that it dries evenly.
2. Place clay pieces to be dried in a location where they cannot be handled by the children. Greenware is very brittle.
3. Clay should dry slowly. The location needs to be away from sun and heaters.
4. Check pieces daily, and gently turn them, if necessary, to allow drying on all sides.
5. Work can be fired only when it is completely dry. Damp spots will cause the piece to crack during firing. Damp clay feels cold to the touch. Dry clay feels room temperature and has a chalky texture.
6. Allow plenty of time. It usually takes one week for clay work to dry completely, but this depends on the weather. It is better to wait longer before firing to be sure, rather than to rush the process and risk a ruined project and a disappointed child.
7. Stack unglazed pieces in the kiln with the heavier ones on the bottom.

Teaching in Action

A Day with Clay: A Teacher's Notebook Entry

My friend Julian, who is an art student at the local college, came today and showed the children how he makes a clay pot. We set up a table out on the grass by the playground fence. We all gathered around and watched. Outside was perfect. It was very informal and open. The children would watch awhile, go play, and then wander back.

All the while Julian worked he kept describing how it felt. He said things such as, "This is bumpy; I must make it smoother." He also described what he was doing, as in, "I am pushing the clay with my fingers." He was so patient and answered all of the children's questions. He let them touch the clay and the pot he was making too.

When Julian was done, he invited the children who were standing around him to make pots also. He gave them each a piece of clay and guided them in making it rounded and pushing a hole in the middle with their thumbs. When they were finished, a few others came over and made some pots. Several just wanted to pound the clay flat. Julian showed them how to press sticks and stones into the clay to make impressions. Some children decided to do that to their clay pots. He carved the child's name on each one and took all of the projects to fire in his kiln. He said he thought they would turn out fine. I had a bucket of water for the children to rinse their hands in, and then they went inside to wash up at the sink.

I took lots of photographs. I can't wait to get them back. Then we can make a class book about our Clay Day!

Studio Page 21

SAFETY SEARCH
Art Health Hazards in Your Environment

How safe are your home and workplace? Conduct an inspection using this worksheet. Check off any potential art hazards that you find.

	Home	Work		Home	Work
SOLVENTS			**GLUES**		
benzene	○	○	epoxy	○	○
carbon tetrachloride	○	○	model cement	○	○
lacquer thinner	○	○	plastic cement	○	○
mineral spirits	○	○	rubber cement	○	○
paint remover	○	○	super glues	○	○
paint thinner	○	○			
resins/resin solvents	○	○	**DUSTS**		
shellac solvent (methyl alcohol)	○	○	artists' pastels	○	○
silk-screen solvents	○	○	dyes	○	○
turpentine	○	○	firing clays	○	○
			glass powders (enameling)	○	○
AEROSOL SPRAYS			glazes (clays)	○	○
fixative	○	○	plaster	○	○
spray glue	○	○			
spray paint	○	○	**OTHER**		
			lead solder	○	○
PAINTS			permanent markers	○	○
enamels	○	○	silk-screen inks	○	○
latex paint	○	○			
oil paint	○	○			
varnishes	○	○			

Using your checklist, answer the following questions:

1. Are all items that you checked in locked metal cabinets?   yes   no

2. Are these items used only in areas that are not used by children?   yes   no

3. Are there dust masks available?   yes   no

4. Is there a face mask with proper filters for safe solvent use?   yes   no

5. Are surfaces and floors in areas where these items are stored and used kept clean and orderly?   yes   no

6. Which environment is safer for children, your home or work space?

_____

_____

Studio Page 22

RECIPE RECORD SHEET

Art Material:

Source of Recipe:

Ingredients:

Directions:

1. What was the cost of the ingredients in this recipe? Is this homemade material more or less expensive than a similar commercial one?

   _____

2. How much did it make?

   _____

3. How many children would it serve?

   _____

4. Where can the ingredients be found?

   _____

5. Is the material aesthetically pleasing and fun to use?

   _____

6. Is this material easily confused with food? Should it be a cooking activity or an art activity?

   _____

Studio Page 23

FOOD VERSUS ART
Where Do You Stand?

Where do you stand on this issue?

_____

_____

_____

_____

_____

What art materials do you think are appropriate for young children?

_____

_____

_____

_____

Using what you have learned in this chapter, justify your position on this issue.
Explain why you would or would not have the children do the following:

1. Use homemade play doughs

_____

_____

2. Finger paint with pudding

_____

_____

3. String cereal necklaces

_____

_____

4. Use vegetables for printmaking

_____

_____

Studio Page 24

OBSERVATION: USING A MODELING MATERIAL

The purpose of this observation is to allow you to study how a child approaches three-dimensional modeling activities.

Setup

- Observe an individual child in a home or school setting.
- Provide a safe modeling material you think will be suitable for this particular child. Do not provide tools.

Observation

1. What does the child do first with the material?

_____

_____

_____

2. How does the child move his or her hands?

_____

_____

_____

3. What forms does the child make?

_____

_____

_____

4. What does the child say?

_____

_____

_____

5. Based on your observations, at which developmental level of modeling does the child seem to be?

_____

_____

_____

For additional information on teaching art to young children, visit our Web site at http://www.earlychilded.delmar.com

Awakening the Senses

Chapter 7

> ❝ *It was the most imaginative, rich childhood you could ever want. That's why I have so much inside me that I want to paint.* ❞
>
> —Andrew Wyeth
> (Merryman, 1991, p. 21)

Questions Addressed in This Chapter:

- ✧ What is beauty?
- ✧ How does an aesthetic sense develop?
- ✧ What are the elements of art?
- ✧ How is sensory perception developed in young children?
- ✧ How can music, movement, and art be integrated?

Young Artists at Work

"What a beautiful painting!" exclaims the preschool teacher, as she takes the dripping painting off the easel. Three-year-old Michelle smiles and runs off to the sand table, while the teacher carries Michelle's large sheet of newsprint covered with wiggly lines of lime green and black to the storage shelf. Soon Michelle's parents arrive to take her and her painting home. They too declare the painting beautiful and proudly hang it on the refrigerator door in the kitchen. When Michelle is eighteen and getting ready to study art in college, she finds her preschool painting. "Why did they save this old thing?" she chuckles.

WHAT IS BEAUTY?

Is this painting really beautiful? Why was it hung on the refrigerator instead of over the living room couch? Why does grown-up Michelle no longer think it is beautiful?

Webster's Collegiate Dictionary defines beautiful as "delighting the senses or mind." When we judge something beautiful, we are describing its effect on our sense of sight, touch, smell, taste, and/or hearing—its aesthetic quality. But there are many other factors that determine what impact a piece of art will have on our senses. No two people make identical judgments about art. People find beauty in different styles of painting or other art media because of their personal beliefs, knowledge, or experiences. The preschool teacher thinks Michelle's painting is beautiful because she knows that it represents an initial experi-

"My house." Tempera paint—*Mercedes, age 4*

ment with crossing wet lines of paint. Michelle's parents think it is beautiful because it was their beloved child who created this new visual image. However, they will not hang it over the sofa, because the colors do not "go" with their beautiful living-room color scheme of rose and blue. Eighteen-year-old Michelle laughs, because she thinks her current art is so much more mature and, therefore, more beautiful than her childish beginnings.

HOW DOES AN AESTHETIC SENSE DEVELOP?

Aesthetics refers to a person's ability to sense and gain beauty and wonder from his environment. It can be done with any or all of a person's five senses as well as his imagination.

—*Mary Mayesky, Donald Neuman, & Ronald J. Wlodkowski (2002, p. 11)*

Children are not born knowing what is beautiful. If that were true, then every human being would have the same standards of beauty. However, children are born with a sense of wonder that makes them curious about their surroundings. As they explore with their senses, they learn to identify pleasing experiences with beauty. At first children may discover what the important people around them think is beautiful. Parents, siblings, grandparents, and peers may express a personal view of beauty to the young child in statements such as, "Look at that beautiful sunset!", "Isn't that a gorgeous vase?", "There are wonderful designs on this sweater", and "Feel the beautiful quilt Grandma made you."

As children grow they are also influenced by the environment around them. The natural and human-made objects they encounter can provide pleasing or interesting sensory experiences that will shape their view of what is beautiful. Things that feel familiar, comforting, or exciting become incorporated into an aesthetic belief about what is beautiful.

The Importance of Culture

Many ideas about beauty are held in common with other people with whom the child shares a similar heritage. When a group holds the same ideas about

the beauty of some object or experience, this represents a cultural aesthetic or style. Style can be based on shared lifestyle, history, or experience. Styles can be handed down from one generation to another, as in the Amish tradition of making quilts from only solid-colored fabrics. Style can also denote artwork that is based upon a common aesthetic belief, such as the style of Realism, in which artists try to represent real objects as they look to our eyes, or Surrealism, in which objects are shown as they look in our dreams and fantasies.

Although childhood experiences and cultural styles form the core of an individual's aesthetic philosophy, each person's definition of beauty is always changing. Some cultural styles change over time. Eighteenth-century European men felt beautifully dressed when wearing long, curled, and powdered wigs. Sometimes one group of people or an individual will copy or adapt a style from another group, such as when non–Native Americans wear T-shirts decorated with traditional Native American symbols. Children are constantly bombarded with often conflicting ideas about beauty from books, television, and in movies and commercials. These too are added to their internal brew of aesthetic experiences and judgments. Taken together, all of these diverse influences form a personal aesthetic philosophy that determines what they think is beautiful and what they like.

Art and Beauty

Liking a piece of art, however, is not the same as understanding and valuing it. The word *beautiful* is not a simple adjective but also a word of judgment. Not all art is beautiful. Some art assails the senses with distorted or unpleasant images or strong emotional statements, which makes it difficult to separate how we personally feel about a piece of art from its aesthetic value. Sometimes it is hard to separate our feelings about an artwork from its value as a creative statement by an artist. We may not like every piece of artwork done by every child with whom we work, but we can appreciate, and we can help children appreciate, the aesthetic elements in that piece of art by developing their sensitivity to the elements of art around them.

Guiding adults need to be aware of how they influence children's perception of beauty and the development of their aesthetic philosophy and judgment. This impact can be felt in two ways. One way that adults can affect young children's aesthetic perceptions is by creating a pleasing environment with carefully selected, beautiful objects. The other way is to expand children's definition of beauty by pointing out the aesthetic and sensory qualities in their art and environment, and by providing experiences that foster sensory awareness. The goal should be to help children grow into adults who love beautiful things, who value all kinds of art, and who can still find wonder in the beauty of the world.

WHAT ARE THE ELEMENTS OF ART?

When looking at a beautiful piece of artwork or a wonderful part of nature, we are overwhelmed by the total effect. But to recreate this experience for someone who has not seen it, we must describe it in terms of the artistic ingredients of which it is composed. These ingredients, or *elements* of art, are the building blocks of the artist. Line, color, texture, shape, pattern, form, and space are found to varying degrees in almost every piece of art and throughout nature. When we react to something aesthetically, our senses are being affected by the way these elements have been brought together at that moment in time.

The creation of art is the process of playing creatively with these elements and arranging them in an aesthetically meaningful way. This is what young children are doing when they explore art media. However, they also need to learn how to identify and describe these elements so that they can talk about, understand, and make aesthetic judgments about artistic works.

The following descriptions of the art elements will increase the educator's ability to describe children's artwork and talk about natural forms. Each element is followed by suggestions for activities that help children focus on these elements in art and in their environment.

Line

A line is a mark made by a tool moving across a surface. It can be curved or straight or zigzag or wiggly.

Lines can be thick or thin or long or short and are used by artists to make shapes and symbols and by writers to form letters, words, and numbers. Lines can show direction—horizontal, vertical, or diagonal. Lines are present in artwork of all media, and in the environment. Lines are the mainstay of children's earliest drawings and will continue to remain an important element in all of their art.

Playing with lines. Have fun with the children looking for different kinds of lines. Find straight lines between the tiles on the floor, curved lines hanging from the electric poles, and zigzag lines in the cracks of a frozen puddle.

Have the children line up one behind the other, and make a line that moves, wiggles, and sways as they walk in an open space or around furnishings.

Making connections.

Language. Read some of the many children's books that feature lines, such as *You're a Genius BLACKBOARD BEAR* (Alexander, 1995), then put out blank booklets for the children to draw their own "line" stories.

Math/Science. Compare the length of different lines in the children's artwork or line examples from nature. Lay pieces of yarn along a drawn or painted lines, and cut to length. Use them to make a graph. Tape all of the yarn pieces on a sheet of paper; label with the source.

Color

The world is full of color. The white light from the sun is made up of a spectrum of colors. As light bounces off different objects, some of the color rays are absorbed, and others are reflected into the eyes. When there is no light, there is no color. Young children love the bright colors red, yellow, and blue. When given a choice, they will often choose the brighter color paint or paper, but they also like strong, saturated colors, such as deep purple, vivid pink, rich turquoise, and black. Make sure children always have access to media in a wide range of colors.

Playing with color. Take time every day to notice the colors in the environment. Comment on the color of the clothing children are wearing and the color of the grass, leaves, and sky. Use descriptive or comparative words to identify a color. For example, "Your sweater is as green as the leaves on our tree," and "Today the sky reminds me of the color of a robin's egg."

Children love to mix colors. Finger painting with two or three colors is a very tactile way to combine colors, as is mixing several colors of play dough together. Colors also get mixed intentionally or unintentionally when painting and printing. Mixing new colors gives the child a sense of power. It is wonderful to be able to make such a noticeable change in the characteristics of an object in this simple way. Never discipline or show frustration with a child who is exploring what happens when colors come together.

Art Words

Design

⚙ **Art elements**
The basic visual and tactile qualities of an artwork—line, color, shape, texture, form, and space.

⚙ **Color**
The surface quality of an object or a substance as revealed by the light that reflects off it and that is seen as a hue in the spectrum.

⚙ **Composition**
The arrangement of the art elements into a whole.

⚙ **Form**
Form has two meanings. First, it can refer to the whole of a work of art. Second, it is used to refer to the three-dimensional equivalent of shape that has the qualities of mass and volume.

⚙ **Hue**
A color, such as red, or yellow.

⚙ **Intensity**
The brightness or dullness of a color.

⚙ **Line**
A continuous stroke made with a moving tool. A boundary between or around shapes.

⚙ **Pattern**
A repeated, recognizable combination of art elements.

⚙ **Primary colors**
The three basic colors from which all other colors are derived and which cannot be mixed from the other colors. In painting, these are red, yellow, and blue. In colored light, they are magenta, cyan, and yellow.

⚙ **Secondary colors**
The colors created by mixing two of the primary colors.

⚙ **Shape**
A two-dimensional area or image that has defined edges or borders.

⚙ **Space**
An open or empty area in an artwork.

⚙ **Symmetry**
Equilibrium or balance created by placing art elements equally on both sides of a central axis.

⚙ **Texture**
The tactile or visual surface quality of an object or artwork.

⚙ **Three-dimensional**
Having height, width, and depth.

⚙ **Tint**
A color lightened by the addition of white.

⚙ **Tone**
The relative lightness or darkness of a color.

⚙ **Two-dimensional**
Having height and width, but no depth.

⚙ **Value**
The range of lights and darks of the colors.

Not everyone sees colors in exactly the same way. Children who are color blind need to be identified so that they do not feel uncomfortable during color activities and games. Art materials can be scented to help children with visual difficulties. To help children understand that colors can appear differently, tape red or yellow cellophane over a hole cut in an index card. Looking through this window will make all of the colors look a little bit different.

Making connections.

Language. There is an incredible number of books about color for young children. A must is the old classic *Hailstones and Halibut Bones* (O'Neill, 1961). This book of poems, each about a different color, provides perfect introductions to color activities. For the very young, read the book *White Rabbit's Color Book* (Baker, 1994), which depicts a beautifully drawn rabbit playing in paint and discovering new colors. At the end of the book, the rabbit covers himself with all of the col-

Music Box

Colors

(*To the tune "A Hunting We Will Go"*)

Red is the color
Red is the color
Red is the color of Michael's shirt.*

(*Substitute any name and item.*)

ors and turns into a beautiful brown rabbit. It is a charming way to teach color mixing and help children appreciate the color brown. Use the book to introduce color-mixing activities.

Math/Science. Provide premeasured amounts of different colors of paint, let children mix them and then have children compare the results. For example, measure out a quarter cup of white to mix with a teaspoon of red, and vice versa. Make a labeled chart of the resulting colors, and then use them to paint with at the easel.

Music. With the children, make up songs about the different colors using a familiar tune (see Music Box).

Texture

Texture is the way something feels to the touch. Surfaces can be hard or soft, rough or smooth, or bumpy or jagged. Texture is found in all artwork and is an especially important element in collage and modeling activities.

Playing with texture. Invite the children to compare the textures of different items in the classroom or in the collage offerings. Ask, "Is it soft or rough?" and, "Which is stickier: the paste or the glue?" Use words that describe textures as the children play. There are many more texture activities in the touch and kinesthetic sections that follow.

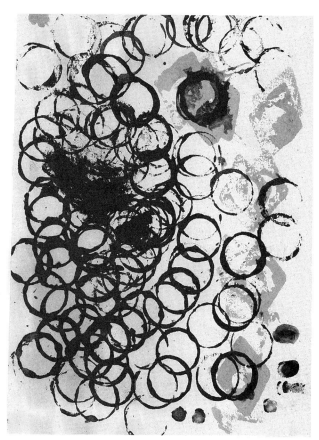

"I made circles and diamonds." Object print—*Shane, age 4*

Making connections.

Language. Toddlers will enjoy any of the books available that contain actual textures to touch. In *The Petting Zoo* (Hanna, 1992), animals are covered with pieces of cloth that approximate how the animals actually feel. Children love identifying the different textures in the collages that illustrate *Smoky Night* (Bunting, 1994) and *Snowballs* (Ehlert, 1995).

Math/Science. Invite younger children to sort pieces of material with different textures. Glue them on a chart, or make them into a class book. Older children can find magazine pictures of things that have different textures, such as clippings of a dog (furry) or a pillow (soft), and can then make a similar chart or book.

Music. See Music Box for an example of a texture-play song.

Shape

Everything has a shape. A two-dimensional shape has height and width and may be geometric, organic, symbolic, or free form.

- Geometric shapes follow mathematical principles, such as squares, rectangles, circles, and triangles.
- Organic shapes come from nature, as in the shape of a leaf or butterfly.

Special Needs

Color blindness

Children who are color blind often have difficulty with color-related activities. These children quickly learn to try to hide their color discrimination difficulties, especially if they are laughed at by other children when using a color the wrong way, such as drawing a purple tree. Often adults mistakenly think the child does not know the colors yet and will try to force the child to learn them. It is important to identify these children as early as possible.

Once identified, help these children by using scented crayons and markers and adding scents to paints. It also helps to always have the colors in the same order at the easel and to line up the markers and crayons in the same color order. When doing color games and activities, have these children work with the colors they can identify.

Music Box

Touch–It Song

(To the tune "Go In and Out the Windows")

Let's go find something soft.*
Let's go find something soft.
Let's go find something soft.
Something soft to touch.

(*Substitute any texture words.*)

While the children sing, one child may find and touch something with that texture before the song ends.

- Symbolic shapes have a special meaning, such as that of letters or numbers.
- Free-form shapes are invented shapes that follow no rules.

Each of the four categories of shapes may contain some shapes that are symmetrical. If a straight line is drawn through the center of a shape, it will be exactly the same on both sides. Squares, butterflies, the letter "A," and hearts are all symmetrical shapes. All of these shapes will be found in children's artwork and in the classroom environment.

Playing with shapes. Play games with the children that involve finding shapes. Talk about the qualities of these shapes. Are they big or small, short or tall, or colored or textured? There are hundreds of art activities that use shapes. Many will be described throughout this book.

Making connections.

Language. Almost any children's book can be used for a shape hunt. Name a shape that is used in one of the illustrations, and then ask the children to look for it as they listen to the story. *My Very First Book of Shapes* (Carle, 1974) provides an excellent way to introduce the names of the shapes to toddlers.

Children who are using graphic symbols love *A Wing on a Flea* (Emberly, 1961) and *The Secret Birthday Message* (Carle, 1972), in which a secret message is made up of shapes.

Math/Science. Let children sort shapes by size or the number of sides. Make charts or books about the characteristics of shapes. Ask children to count the number of shapes they used in their artwork.

Music. Display pictures of different shapes. Use a different clap or vocal sound to go with each one. Point to the shapes in varying order, and have the children make that sound. Give children a chance to make up the sounds and point to the shapes. The "Touch-It Song" can also be used with shape names.

Pattern

A pattern is a design made from repeated shapes, lines, and colors. Patterns occur naturally, as in the designs on a leopard's skin, or are invented by artists. Children should be encouraged to see the patterns they create in their art explorations.

Playing with pattern. Encourage children to find examples of pattern in the environment. Comment on patterns found on the clothing they are wearing. Help children see that a pattern is made up of smaller elements. Find the shapes, lines, and colors in the patterns. Patterns are important not only in art; being able to find and understand patterns is also the basis of mathematical understanding.

Making connections.

Language. *Dots, Spots, Speckles, and Stripes* (Hoban, 1987) is a fun book for toddlers. After sharing the book, go on a pattern hunt. For children with longer attention spans, try stories that are filled with different patterns. Challenge them to find all of the patterns in books such

as Polacco's *Rechenka's Eggs* (1988b) and *Thundercake* (1990) and Ringgold's *Tar Beach* (1991).

Math. Invite children to use an object to make a repeated print. (See Creating Art: Printmaking, on p. 215.) Count the number of prints on each child's paper. Order the prints from smallest to largest in a class book.

Science. Look for patterns in nature, such as on butterfly wings, leaves, and flowers. Children who are ready for responsive art activities can record the organic patterns in their drawings.

Music. Listen for patterns in the words, melody, and rhythm of favorite songs. Chart the patterns using colors or shapes. For a responsive art activity, suggest that children record the song's pattern using art media.

Form

Form is the three-dimensional quality of objects. Forms have height, width, and depth. There are spheres, pyramids, cubes, cylinders, and rectangular solids. Children need lots of exposure to a wide variety of forms. Most objects in our world are three-dimensional. Children's early physical handling and examination of many forms allow them as adults to recognize the nature of forms just by looking at them.

Playing with form. Forms are complex. They are not always the same in back or on the bottom as they appear from the front. Block play and modeling activities are excellent ways for children to explore form. Construction activities and papier-mâché involve three-dimensional forms. Creative movement activities also help children learn to judge spatial elements in their environment.

Making connections.

Language. Many of Tana Hoban's books are ideal for introducing the idea of form. The clear photographs help focus on the form rather than the use. Try *Round! Round! Round!* (1974) and *Of Colors and Things* (1989). Use these to teach the different words that describe geometric forms. Children can find pictures of objects with different forms and create a class book.

Math. Order forms such as balls from smallest to largest. Make a collection of boxes, and stack them in size order. Use blocks to compare different forms. Look at the number and shape of the sides. Play a form-finding game. Name the shape of one side of a solid, then find the matching block, such as circle = cylinder, triangle = pyramid.

Science. Fill hollow forms of different sizes and shapes, such as boxes, oatmeal containers, and bottles, with sand or Styrofoam packing material. Have children predict which holds the most and which the least. Empty and measure to find out.

Music. Look at the forms of different musical instruments. Compare how they look to how they sound. Challenge the children to think about why instruments such as a bass and violin sound different even though they have similar forms.

Space

Artists do not just see shapes and forms; they also see the space that surrounds them. This may be the empty space of the paper, or the open spaces in a sculpture. Young children find this space when they look through a tube and see the view in a circle or look through a hole poked in play dough.

Playing with space. To help young children see space in their artwork, make comments such as, "You have left a rectangular space in the middle of your painting," or "You have made round spaces in your play dough. Can you see through them?" Cut differently shaped holes in pieces of poster board or cardboard covered with contact paper for durability. Encourage children to look through them at anything in the environment, including their artwork and block buildings.

Making connections.

Language. Children love books with cutout windows through which to glimpse parts of the next picture. Two particularly clever ones are *Opposites* (Felix, 1992) and *Color Zoo* (Ehlert, 1989). (See appendix C for more.)

Math. Ask children to count the spaces in their block buildings.

Science. Take two equal pieces of play dough, and poke holes in one. Have children compare the weights using a balance scale. Let them experiment with this idea by letting them weigh things that are full and empty and solid and poked with holes.

Music. Point out that silent moments in a song (rests) are like holes or spaces. Listen for them in different pieces of music.

HOW IS SENSORY PERCEPTION DEVELOPED IN YOUNG CHILDREN?

We know that children learn in active, not passive, ways. The sense of belonging to the environment is part of each one. It is only later that children learn that it is often a do-not-touch, do-not-see, do-not-hear, do-not-taste world.

—Larry Kantner (1989, p. 45)

It is through the senses that we learn about the world. Research (cited in Bruner, 1979, pp. 142–143) indicates that early sensory deprivation in animals prevents them from developing an adequate model of the world in which they will eventually live. In the same way, children need to have the opportunity to experience many sensory activities in order to develop not only their

Young Artists at Work

"The sand is singing," says Bruce as he pours the sand into a pail with a soft whir.

Mariah looks at the teacher through a tube. "I made you round," she remarks.

Allen lies down on the grass and says quietly, "I smell the grass growing."

aesthetic beliefs but also their cognitive map of the world. A child who has never seen, touched, smelled, heard about, or tasted ice cream will not have a concept of what ice cream is, will not be able to understand stories, poems, or songs about ice cream, and certainly will have no basis upon which to develop a symbol to represent ice cream in an artwork.

It is easy for adults to forget what it is like to focus entirely on a sensory stimulus. In our busy lives, it is rare to take a moment to focus completely on the aesthetic qualities of objects—the many greens in a lawn of grass, the rough texture of a concrete block wall, the smell of rain on hot pavement, the sound of the refrigerator humming, and the taste of our toothpaste in the morning. But in order to guide young children's aesthetic growth, adults need to be able to become aware of these qualities again with childlike wonder.

Sensory awareness is not something that can be put out on a table like crayons and paper. Daily interactions with young children should be peppered with statements and questions that show the wonder and value of the sensory qualities of the environment. Adults cannot verbalize these qualities to the children if they do not experience them themselves. Like an artist who reminds us of the colors of a beautiful sunset or the texture of sand through a painting, adults must bring that same focus to what they say to children.

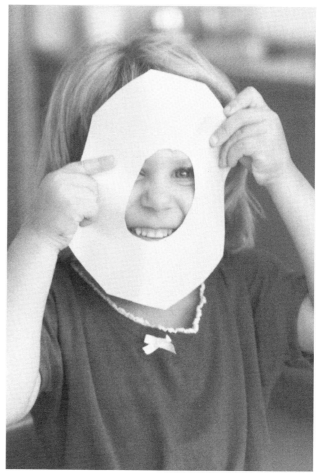

Visual elements invite playful peeking at new views of the world.

A drawing in sand holds a moment of awareness—the damp sand, the soft, grainy feel beneath the hand, and the warm sun forming a shadow.

There is a sensory element in every activity in which children are involved. Instead of seeing blocks, see shapes and forms; instead of glue, notice stickiness. Listen and learn from children.

Young children do not hesitate to invite us to "feel this" or "smell that," and we must do the same with them. Find a sensory element, and express it.

"Look at how the light is shining on your wet paint!"
"Oh, the sand is so cool and damp today!"
"These flowers smell like a summer day!"

And, of course, lavish the young artists with comments about the sensory quality of their work.

"That red and green look beautiful together!"
"Your clay ball feels so wonderfully round!"

Developing Sensory and Visual Perception

In addition to finding and celebrating the sensory qualities of children's ordinary activities, adults need to provide extraordinary and unexpected sensory experiences for them. These explorations often cross the boundaries of particular subject areas, providing not only artistic and aesthetic growth but also cognitive growth in the linguistic and logical-mathematical domains, as well as the bodily-kinesthetic and musical intelligences through the manipulation of a wide variety of objects and materials. For this reason, these kinds of activities should be part of all early childhood programs. The following "Teaching in Action" section provides only a partial listing of a multitude of possible sensory activities. These can be used as springboards for designing original activities.

The ones presented here have been selected for their close relationship to art activities and are grouped by the sensory mode that is their main focus. Many are multisensory. It is almost impossible to eliminate the input from all senses but one, without placing great limits on the freedom of exploration of the child. In fact, many young children dislike being restricted from using any of their senses. They want to peek over blindfolds and taste things before being told to do so. They should never be punished for such natural curiosity. Instead, take care in setting up these experiences, so that peeking and bold explorations are part of the fun.

Children often seem to spend only a short amount of time investigating these sensory activities before dashing off to something else. Remember that time for a young artist is not the same as time for an adult, and that the value of an experience cannot be measured by the clock. Even a minute or two of investigating an unusual texture or visual perception, or challenging the senses in a new way, is of utmost benefit to a child's cognitive growth. The child's new information about that exploration will enrich her or him in a way that constant exposure to familiar and everyday objects will not.

It is well worth the effort to spend time preparing

Teaching in Action

Visual Perceptual Activities

Tube viewfinder. At its simplest, a viewfinder can be a plain cardboard tube rescued from the trash. Set out an attractive basket or container full of long and short tubes, and encourage the children to look through them and describe what they see. Give them an attractive name such as "viewscopes" or "looking tubes." For another experience, prepare some tubes ahead of time by taping colored cellophane to one end. Try taping black paper over an end, and poke several small holes in it. The children can use art materials to decorate their viewscopes.

Cardboard windows. Make viewfinders with differently shaped openings by cutting holes in stiff cardboard cards. The holes can be made small, for one-eye viewing, or large enough for the child to use both eyes. If possible, laminate these for durability, or cover them with clear package sealing tape. Vary this activity by taping colored cellophane over the openings. Try overlapping several colors of cellophane in strips across the opening for another unusual effect.

Picture frames. Prepare a set of construction paper or cardboard "frames" with varying sizes, shapes, and placement of holes cut out of them. These can also be laminated for durability.

continued

Teaching in Action *continued*

Children can use these to cover a piece of artwork, an illustration in a book, magazine pictures, or even games and puzzles for the thrill of seeing the detail of a small part. Young children love the peek-a-boo effect they can create and like turning the frame in different ways to see how the effect changes. On occasion, add colored cellophane to these as well, or create frames with multiple openings for a different experience.

Envelope holes. Cut out magazine pictures and mount them on heavy construction paper or poster board. Wildlife and nature magazines provide excellent sources of interesting scenes, animals, and people. The mounted pictures should be slightly smaller than an 8½-by-11-inch brown mailing envelope. Study the picture, and cut a hole in the envelope in a location where an interesting detail will show, such as an eye, a mouth, or a flower. Place the picture in the envelope. Children can study the detail and try to imagine the rest of the picture before pulling it out of the envelope.

Book of holes. To make a book, create "frames" by cutting holes in pieces of construction paper. Place two mounted magazine pictures back to back, then a frame, then two more back-to-back pictures and another frame. Add a front and back cover, both with well-placed holes, and staple the book together. Place the holes in creative and interesting ways, or try using more than one frame between pictures. Several beautiful children's books, such as *Look Again!* (Hoban, 1971) and *Go Away Big Green Monster* (Emberly, 1992), use this same idea and can inspire teachers to make a masterpiece of their own.

Look-about table. Set out, at the children's level, an object that encourages looking in new ways. Possible items include smooth and crinkled aluminum foil mounted on cardboard, crystals, Fresnel lenses, magnifiers, kaleidoscopes, fly's-eye viewers, liquid crystals, mirrors, optical lenses, colored Plexiglass, sunglasses, color paddles, holographic metallic papers, prisms, nonbreakable mirrors, transparent colored or textured plastics, plastic water globes, or even a small fish bowl, complete with fish.

Color lights. Set up a small table lamp in one corner of the room. Vary the color of the lightbulb, and encourage the children to look at their familiar toys, book illustrations, and artwork in a "new" light. *Color! Color! Color!* (Heller, 1995) uses color acetates between pages to create similar effects.

To change the total room environment for a special occasion, cover overhead lights or windows with loosely draped, colored tissue paper.

these explorations. Offer them regularly, and change them often. Do not be afraid to repeat an exploration at a later date. Young children grow quickly and will experience these activities differently at later stages of development. With careful planning and construction, many of the sensory materials mentioned here can be reused many times over the years.

Presenting Visual and Sensory Experiences

In planning how to present these visual and sensory experiences, it is important to consider how to capture the children's attention. Some tubes sitting in a basket cannot compete with a bright and shiny toy, unless the teacher adds that special touch, perhaps an intriguing comment, to attract the child. Place the sensory table in a highly visible place where there is frequent traffic, perhaps near the door so it is one of the first things the children find when they arrive. Make a comment about it as children arrive: "Look, we have a beautiful conch shell from Florida on the Look-About Table today!"

These items can also be introduced at circle time and then placed on the observation table, drawing center, or other selected location. For example, show an "envelope with holes" to the group, and have the children take turns describing what they see. Then show them where there are more envelopes in a basket for them to explore. To introduce a conch shell, read *Bimwili and the Zimwi* (Aardema, 1985), a tale about a conch shell in an African setting.

Do not overwhelm the children with too many choices. Put out only one sensory exploration at a time. The key is to change the displays and items often, but repeat them regularly with slight changes or in new combinations. The more these kinds of experiences are offered, the more comfortable teachers become using the language and formulating the right questions. Teachers owe it to the children to offer these special experiences that allow them to touch, taste, smell, listen, and see in new ways.

Vision

We begin with the sense of sight. Through our eyes we sense the art elements of line, shape, color, pattern, value, form, and space. All art activities can be experienced through visual input. Refer to the art elements when describing children's artwork:

> **"You used bright colors."**
> **"You made a pattern when you pressed the potato masher into the clay."**

The visual images that enter the brain become the basis for the mental images we create. Children need a wide variety of challenging and enriching visual experiences. Seeing familiar things in a new light or a new way prepares children to be more accepting of the unfamiliar images they will encounter in life. Learning to discriminate between different colors or different shapes helps children see the world with more definition and meaning.

Playing with visual elements. A window gives freedom to see through a wall and yet at the same time limits us to seeing only a part of the total view beyond the wall. The following activities do the same. They force the child to see only a small, selected part of something. In doing so, that part becomes important—it becomes a whole, like a picture framed in a camera's viewfinder. Children have this same type of "photographic" experience by looking through child-size window frames or viewfinders.

Touch

The tactile sense is very powerful. The entire surface of the human body is sensitive to pressure and temperature, as well as to the textural qualities of the matter that makes up the world. Young children rely heavily on tactile exploration to acquire knowledge about the characteristics of individual materials and objects and to develop an understanding of how things are spatially arranged. The environment and activities offered to young children should provide continuous opportunities to touch.

A touch box helps children focus on the tactile qualities of objects.

Teaching in Action

Tactile Perceptual Activities

Touch blocks. Glue different textures to each outer side of a box or cardboard cube. Cubes can be made from six square pieces of corrugated cardboard taped together at the edges. (Use clear, package-sealing tape.) Use textured items that are fairly flat, such as a variety of fabrics, carpet, and sandpaper. Make several. Children can use these for stacking and matching activities.

Touch boxes. Touch boxes encourage children to feel an object without using the sense of sight. Cut a hole large enough for a child's hand to fit inside of a box (shoe boxes work well). Cut the hole in the smaller side. Cover the hole by taping a piece of cloth over the top of the hole on the inside to form a flap. Glue an object with an interesting texture to the bottom of the box, put the top back on, and close with a rubber band. Encourage children to reach inside to feel the object first and then peek inside to see it.

Make the box more versatile by cutting pieces of cardboard the size of the box bottom and gluing a different object to each. Change the objects regularly by simply lifting out one cardboard and putting in another. A beautifully decorated touch box can become a regular stop for children as they explore the environment that has been prepared for them.

Objects for touch boxes should be at least the size of the palm and durable enough to take a great deal of handling. Use both natural and human-made objects that have a variety of forms and textures. Check that objects do not have sharp or jagged edges. Some suggested objects include aluminum foil ball, block, bone, box, candle, coral, cotton, crumpled paper ball, fabric (especially velvet and corduroy), pinecone, plastic lid, plastic toy, polyester stuffing, netting, rubber ball, rug piece, screwdriver, shell, spoon, stone, twig, and wax (canning). To use an item that spoils or is hard to glue, such as an apple, a lemon, an orange, or a potato, place it in the box without glue. The children may need help holding the box while they find the object, as it will roll around easily. Use creativity to find objects that will make the touch box a wonderful experience for each child.

Stuff bins. Partially fill a basket, dishpan, or large, clear plastic storage container with "stuff," through which the children can move their hands. Items for wet and dry stuff bins are listed in table 7–1 on p. 206.

Please-touch table. Set up a small, low table on which to display one or a few items. Select these natural and human-made items with care. They should be individually beautiful items that are less familiar to the children and will attract their interest. To encourage a relaxed exploration, make sure the items are not very valuable and will stand the children's inexpert handling. Possible items might include a large conch shell, a piece of brain coral, a large rock with fossil impressions, a large gear from an old machine, the inside of a clock, a carved Peruvian gourd, a feathered mask, an African wood carving, or an intricately woven basket. Invite children and parents to contribute items to this table too. Encourage children to make tactile observations of these items by asking questions such as the following:

continued

Teaching in Action
continued

"What part feels smooth?"
"Is it cold to your touch?"
"Are there places you can put your fingers?"
"Does it feel differently on the bottom?"

Nature scavenger hunt. Take the children for a walk outside to find objects with interesting textures. Ask toddlers to find objects with just one texture, such as something smooth, shiny, or wet. Alternatively, say, "Find me all kinds of objects with different textures or that are interesting to touch." When they find items, describe the texture to them: "Oh, you found a bumpy rock!" "What a shiny cap you found."

Three-year-olds can look for two contrasting textures such as something hard and something soft. Older children can find several objects and then sort and group them. Remind the children not to damage any living plants. Look over the area before taking the children out to make sure it is safe and to get an idea about what kinds of objects they might find. It may be necessary to limit the area of the search to just the grass or playground. Even in a small area, many interesting textures can be found, such as a rough piece of bark, a bottle cap with bumpy edges, or a smooth, shiny candy wrapper. Collect all of the objects the children find, and bring them inside to use in their collages.

Texture cards. Glue pairs of sample textures to large cards made of heavy poster board or cardboard. If possible, try to use textured items that are similar in color. A variety of fabrics will work well. The children can try to match cards while closing their eyes and feeling the textures. Oversize dominoes with textures glued onto them instead of numbers can also be made.

Sand. Few children can resist the tactile qualities of sand. Dry sand runs through the fingers; wet sand sticks. Sand is a material that young children feel that they can control. They can make their own textures in the sand by pushing and pulling and patting and pressing. They can pour it and mold it. A sand table or covered outdoor sandbox is an essential piece of aesthetic equipment for young children.

To increase the children's tactile exploration of sand, vary the equipment and dampness of the sand. Remove the traditional sand toys occasionally and substitute more unusual items, such as natural objects (seashells, stones, twigs), large kitchen tools (slotted spoon, potato masher, spatula, turner), tools (screwdriver, mallet, wrenches, large bolts), cardboard (boxes of different sizes, strips, and squares of corrugated cardboard), and caps and lids of all kinds.

To introduce sand play or to accompany it, read one of these delightful books about sand: *Story in the Sand* (Myrus & Squillance, 1963) or *The Sand Lady* (Reed, 1968). Children will also enjoy *At the Beach* (Lee, 1994), in which cut-paper collages illustrate a story about children learning to write Chinese characters in the sand. If there is a beach nearby, take the children there to experience play in a giant sandbox. Encourage them to create bold sand drawings and collages inspired by these experiences.

TABLE 7–1	Ideas for Stuff Bins

Dry Stuff Bins

cardboard squares	grass	pebbles	sawdust
cornmeal*	gravel	pennies	short pieces of yarn
cotton balls	leaves (green or dry)	plastic caps	or string
craft sticks	lids (plastic, metal, juice)	plastic "Easter" grass	shredded paper
crumpled white tissue	macaroni*	polyester stuffing	Styrofoam packing
paper	marbles	popcorn*	material
excelsior	metal washers	raffia	tiles
fabric scraps	nylon netting	ribbons and bows	wood shavings
flowers	oatmeal*	rice*	

Note: After being explored in the stuff bin, these materials can be added to the collage choices. (Remember, if working with children under age three, to use only items that pass the choke test.)

Wet Stuff Bins

bubble mixture (dish detergent and water)

cornstarch slurry* (heat while stirring: one part cornstarch to five parts water until creamy; let cool)

goop* (mix one part cornstarch to one part cold water)

shaving cream

unflavored gelatin mixture*

water (vary the temperature)

whipped soap (beat with hand mixer: two parts soap flakes to one part water)

Note: Food coloring may be used to color these materials to excite the visual sense. After initial explorations, cups, containers, and other tools for the children to use in manipulating the material may be added.

Playing with touch. Most art activities involve input from the tactile sense. Finger paint, modeling dough, textured collage materials, and sticky glue are explored with sensitive fingers. Art tools such as brushes and scissors, printmaking objects, and smooth-gliding drawing tools are felt both texturally and through the pressure that is sent back and forth from hand to object as they are used.

As children explore art media, teachers should increase their awareness of these tactile qualities through what they say. Use texture words such as silky, soft, smooth, squishy, metallic, bumpy, and rough. Refer to the temperature of the materials: "Oh, this finger paint feels cold!" or "The play dough is warm from your hand." Make them aware of the pressure they are using: "You pressed hard with your crayons," "You

are using effort to push your scissors through the paper," or "You touched the paintbrush to your paper very lightly."

Smell

The sense of smell is also involved in the creation of art. The waxy odor of crayons, the minty smell of paste, and the ammonia-like scent of white glue are an integral part of art exploration. Although the sense of smell is often less valued than the other senses, it is a very powerful one. A whiff of a familiar odor from the past can bring back a memory. The scent of school paste can make adults feel like they are in kindergarten again. Opening a box of new crayons can bring to mind a drawing made at age five. The smells that surround the children as they do artwork will be associated with art for the rest of their lives.

Make sure the classroom itself is always clean and fresh smelling. Check for allergies, and then select an air freshener, potpourri, or a disinfectant that leaves a pleasant odor. Open the windows in fair weather.

As the children explore the art activities, make comments about the smells of the materials they are using, such as:

"The paste smells so fresh and clean!"
"This play dough smells minty."
"The yellow paint smells like a field of flowers."

Try to associate the smells with pleasant experiences, but avoid references to foods that might cause the children to try to taste the material.

Sound

Some art activities are very quiet; others are quite noisy. A young child painting at the easel is a model of quiet. That same child actively exploring play dough bangs and slaps with glee. The sounds that surround art activities rise and fall as children enter the creative state of immersion or chatter happily with their friends. There are many activities that will encourage children to interrelate art and sound.

Taste

Taste is the only sense that children should not use when they are engaged in art experiences. Instead, emphasize the aesthetic qualities of food as it is served and eaten. Describe the visual and textural appearance of different foods, such as the rich pink and

Teaching in Action

Olfactory Perceptual Activities

Add scents. Scents can be added to homemade materials or paints. Choose scents such as different shampoos, dish detergents, potpourri, and scented oils. Food-related spices can also be used—cinnamon, allspice, nutmeg, cumin, coriander, thyme, marjoram, cloves, savory, and the mints. These strong-smelling scents are not as likely to be tasted.

Scented materials. Scented crayons and markers are available, but they should be used with great caution. The scents are too exciting for most children. They smell like candy, tempting young children to taste them, and they cause a problem when children stick them in their noses or someone else's for a better whiff. For children with limited vision, however, the scents help them identify the colors.

Scent jars. Scent jars can be used as a focused exploration on the sense of smell. Prepare cotton balls by sprinkling each one with a liquid scent. Another method is to glue powdered spices to a piece of paper. Place the scents in plastic containers, such as yogurt cups or icing containers, that have tight fitting lids. Cut a small hole in the lid, and tape the lid onto the container. The scents will remain strong for several days. Ask the children if the smells remind them of anything.

As an extension, mark each container with a different symbol. Make a chart with the children of the smells they liked the best. Use the most popular smells to scent paints or homemade recipes. Another variation on this activity is to make pairs of scents and have the children try to match the pairs.

green of watermelon, the circle shape of a sliced orange, and the bumpy surface of a chocolate-chip cookie.

HOW CAN MUSIC, MOVEMENT, AND ART BE INTEGRATED?

Combining art, music, and movement in early childhood programs makes sense. Movement and music come naturally to young children, just as art does. Although music and movement activities address different sensory and perceptual modes than art activities, they contribute to children's growth in similar ways.

The Importance of Music and Movement

As with visual art, music and movement can positively affect health and brain development and can enhance growth in the physical, social, cognitive, and language areas.

Music, movement, and the brain. Music and movement have also been shown to enhance long-term memory. Long-term memory is always forming and reforming interconnections with the information being absorbed (Caine & Caine, 1994). Adding music and movement to learning activities helps establish memories more quickly and firmly. Physical movement increases oxygen to the brain, which produces enhanced cognitive functioning (Sousa, 2001, p. 230). According to Jensen (2001, p. 94), academic achievement is better in schools that offer frequent breaks for physical movement.

Music, movement, and well-being. According to Jensen (2001, pp. 37, 95), listening to music and moving creatively will lower levels of the stress hormones, affect the heart rate, and increase antibodies in children. Research has shown that when premature babies were exposed to music daily, they grew faster and went home earlier than those who were not (Sousa, 2001, p. 223).

Music, movement, and the developmental areas. Physical development occurs when children listen and sing to music. Music stimulates and develops a child's auditory perception. Moving creatively and making music with hands and instruments foster the control and coordination of large and small body movements. Socially, music and movement draw groups together in song, performance, and dance. Cognitively, music and movement allow children to investigate patterns, contrasts, sequencing, and cause and effect. Language is developed as children compose their own rhythms and songs and dramatize and use mime to express their ideas. Listening skills increase as children pay attention to the music they hear and follow the lead in dance.

How Children Develop Musically

Music development starts very early. Infants respond to music by turning their heads and making sounds and movements. Young toddlers can repeat sounds, move to rhythms, and start to learn simple songs. By age three, children are able to make up their own songs, hold a beat, and match body movements to it. They also start to sing in a group.

At ages four and five, children can learn to match and classify sounds, can play singing and movement games, and can reproduce musical patterns. Five-year-olds are the perfect age to start a musical instrument such as the piano. Between ages six and eight, children improve in their ability to sing in tune and in large groups.

Making music with children is an ideal way to develop physical coordination and listening and social skills.

What is Drawing?

Drawing is a language ▶
in which children can
combine what they
know with what they
imagine to represent
their dreams.

"They want to go
to the stars. I made
a ladder for them"
Marker
—Steven, age 5-1/2

Drawing expands ▶
and enriches the
first words.

"It's my birthday!"
Crayon and pencil
—Serena, age 6

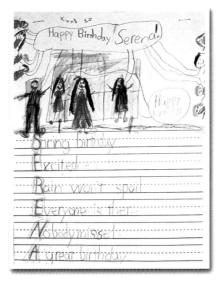

The same motions ▶
that make images
also form letters.

"There's a fire in the
house. These red
lines are the flames."
Marker
—Joey, age 3

◀ Drawing can provide a way to
record what is familiar and to
express personal stories.

"This is my neighborhood. My
house has a fence around it.
My friend is on the other
side of the creek."
Pencil, marker, oil pastel,
glued paper
—Brittany, age 8

What is Printmaking?

◀ Printmaking gives children a new way to see familiar objects.

"Look at the shape the lid makes!"
Gadget print
—Shannon, age 4

◀ The repetitive quality of printmaking provides the perfect opportunity for children to work together.

"Rainbow fish."
Carved Styrofoam and sponge prints
—Emma, Mackenzie, Jason, and Jack, ages 7 and 8.

When used in collages, ▶ previously made exploratory prints compel children to reexamine their work from a new perspective.

"A snake, bear, and turtle are friends"
Carved clay and gadget print collage
—Emily, age 5

What is Collage?

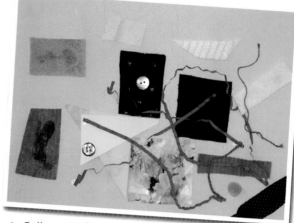

▲ Collage creates opportunities to talk about the relationships of shape, size, texture, color, and position.

"I like buttons the best. They are on top."
Precut paper, yarn, fabric, and buttons —Jori, age 4

◀ Planning, visualizing, and cutting out a shape develop eye-hand coordination.

"This is me dancing." Cut paper collage
—Tierra, age 6

Because collages are not ▶ expected to be realistic, children are more likely to try unusual combinations of images and ideas.

"The mouse is playing by his house all day and all night."
Paper, fabric, and stones
—Erika, age 8

What is Painting?

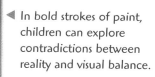

▲ Painting at the easel develops physical control over the arm and hand, and unpredictable paint.

"My rainbow." Tempera —Katie, age 3

Through painting, children can express not only their creativity but also what they have learned. ▶

"He has four arms. That's funny."
Tempera —William, age 5

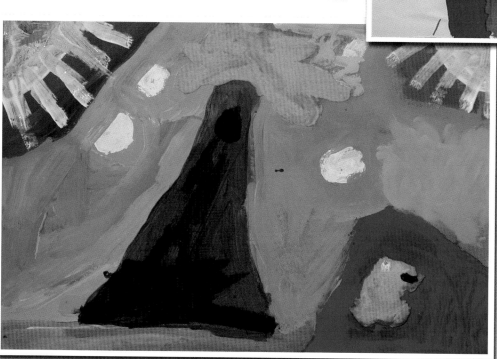

◀ In bold strokes of paint, children can explore contradictions between reality and visual balance.

"It's a tree and frog in a pond." Tempera —Sarah, age 7

What is Modeling?

Working in clay challenges children to convert two-dimensional graphic symbols into three-dimensional ones.

"Flower." Modeling clay
—Emma, age 6

"Clay basket and eggs."
Firing clay
—Cheryl, age 4-1/2

"Mouse." Modeling clay
—Colin, age 4-1/2

Clay asks children to join together ▶
the parts that create the whole.

"Bugs." Homemade play dough
—Danita, Georgie, Nathan, ages 5 to 7

"Black cat." Modeling clay
—Hughie, age 4-1/2

What is a Mural?

Making a mural asks children to share common experiences while respecting the space of others. Here children create their own wild things after reading Maurice Sendak's book, *Where the Wild Things Are,* and discussing their dreams.

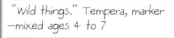

"Wild things." Tempera, marker
—mixed ages 4 to 7

Wild animals in our neighborhood.	
Animal	How we know it lives here.
Rabbit	Kayla sees them in her yard.
Squirrel	We see them in trees by school.
Deer	They eat plants in Michael's garden.
Fox	Keris saw one that was hit by car on the road.
Frog	William caught one. Steven has some tadpoles
Turtle	Mrs. Koster helped one cross the road. It was a snapping turtle!
Skunk	Rachel, Zack, Erika, and Sarah have all smelled them! Tyler saw a dead one. It still smelled!
Groundhog	Alex has a groundhog hole in his backyard.
Coyote	Dana hears them howl at night.

◀ Making a mural can connect experiences. Caring for abandoned rabbits and thinking about wildlife they have seen will begin the process for these children.

"Wild animals in our neighborhood." Tempera
—Keris, William, Zack, Carolyn, Sabrina, Tyler, Alex, Mackenzie, Jenna, Taylor, Erika, and Dana, ages 6 to 8.

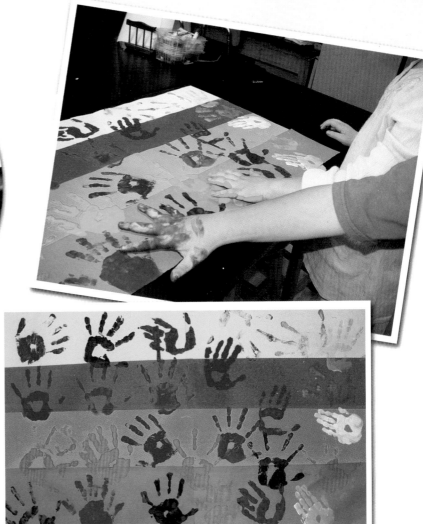

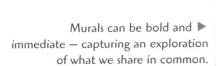

Murals can be bold and ▶
immediate — capturing an exploration
of what we share in common.

"Our handprints are the same
and different."
Tempera
—mixed ages 3 to 5

◀ Murals can culminate in a
thematic unit or research
project — summarizing
visually what children have
learned.

"Pond study mural."
Cut paper and crayon
—mixed ages 5 to 6

What is Creativity?

◀ When children can choose their own shapes, colors, and stories, creativity can flourish.

"Our stick puppets."
Paper, marker, buttons, fabric
—Damon, Michael, and Emily, ages 3, 4, and 5

◀ "Can you guess who we are?"
Grocery bag masks, tempera paint
—Edgar and Allison, ages 6 and 7

▼ Creativity is creating something that has a life of its own.

"Hello everyone."
Paper bag puppet, mixed media
—Samantha, age 4

▼ "My tiger cat goes grr."
Stick mask, mixed media
—Brianna, age 6

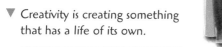

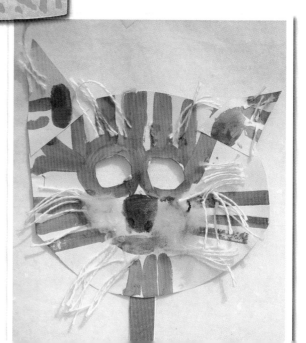

Approaches to Teaching Music

Music is organized sound. One of the tasks of teaching music is to introduce children to the different ways in which music plays with and orders sound. Listening, rhythmic activities, singing, and playing instruments form the basis of creative music.

Rhythmic activities. Rhythm is fundamental to life. Each of us carries our own natural rhythm in our heartbeat. Develop children's sense of rhythm, and introduce them to ways to create sound patterns by providing safe, simple objects for them to shake and tap, such as spoons, margarine containers, and wooden dowels. Set up a sound center where children can explore the sound and rhythms they can make. Provide older children with a tape recorder so they can play back their rhythms. Carry around a small drum or tambourine to catch and mirror the rhythms of the children. For example, as children paint at the easel, tap out a rhythm that matches the movement of their arms.

Playing and making instruments. Rhythmic activities naturally grow into explorations of musical instruments. First experiences with musical instruments should allow children to explore the different sounds they can make. Expand the sound center into a music center, and provide simple, durable sound makers, both homemade and purchased. Drums can be made from plastic, lidded cans and wooden spoons. Fill containers with tightly fitting lids or folded and stapled paper plates with different materials, such as rice,* gravel, sand, and beans,* to make shakers. Make rhythm instruments from dowels and wooden blocks. Provide art materials so children can add distinctive designs to their sound makers.

It is also important for children to experience real instruments. Maracas, tambourines, sand blocks, bells of all kinds, clappers, triangles, and finger cymbals are durable and inexpensive. Add instruments from other cultures as well. The addition of xylophones allows children to invent and play their own melodies.

Help children learn to identify the instruments by name. Ask them to describe the shape and sound of each. Make a tape of each instrument's sound, and place it in the sound center so children can explore timbre, the quality of the sound, by matching the mystery sound to its instrument.

As children gain skill and confidence, stage impromptu parades and concerts. Add child-created sounds to a favorite story or poem. Always remember to keep these activities open ended and flexible. Performances that require hours of rehearsal and create stress are inappropriate for young children and steal away the child's natural affinity for making music.

Singing with children. Children sing spontaneously from as early as age two. They often make up little tunes based on simple, repetitive words while playing. However, it may take longer for them to become comfortable singing with others. Use the following guidelines when planning a song to sing.

- Choose songs that are short, are easy to sing, have a steady beat, have lots of repetition, and have a limited range. The majority of children will sing most comfortably from middle C to A. Nursery rhymes and folk songs are often in this range.
- When introducing a new song, sing it in its entirety.
- Have children join in the chorus or last line first. Adding movement also helps children remember the words better, as do open-ended songs to which children can add their own words.
- If children cannot match the pitch of a song, try to match their pitch. Most young children only begin to sing in tune in the primary grades.

Listening to music. Listening to music is much like looking at artworks by others. On one level, children can listen for pure enjoyment, just as they get pleasure from looking at a painting. Playing calm music while children work and play can create a peaceful, relaxing environment. However, we also want to develop perceptive listening. Just as children can find the elements of art in a picture, they also can find music elements in the music they hear.

Introduce children to a wide variety of music. Ask questions that help them focus on the rhythm, timbre, melody, and **dynamics** (changes in volume) that they hear. Children can also be asked to identify the mood of certain musical pieces. Painting, drawing, or moving to music can help focus attention on these elements.

Teaching in Action

Musical Activities

Rhythm instruments. Collect containers with tight-fitting lids. Let the children fill them with different small objects such as sand, rice,* beans,* or pebbles. Then put on the lids, shake them, and listen to the sounds they make. Use tin cans and cardboard tubes for different sound effects. Cover the open ends with a piece of paper, and affix them with package-sealing tape. Children can decorate with paint, crayon, marker, paper, and/or collage materials.

Responding to music. Set up a tape recorder while children are working in the easel area or at the drawing table. Music can also accompany some of the group mural activities described in chapter 10. Play tapes that feature a variety of sounds and rhythms from many cultures and traditions (see table 7–2). Let the children respond to the music in their own ways. When they are done drawing or painting, ask them how the music made them feel. At other times, let the children choose the kind of music they want to hear while working.

TABLE 7–2	Suggested Music for Art Explorations
ARTIST	**TITLE**
Africa Fete 3	*Selections*
Benedictine Monks of Santo Domingo De Silos	*Chants*
Claude Debussy	*The Snow Is Dancing, Play of the Waves*
Hamza El Din	*The Water Wheel*
Edward Grieg	*Peer Gynt*
Ferde Grofé	*Grand Canyon Suite*
Ronan Hardiman	*Lord of the Dance*
Gustav Holst	*The Planets*
Tokeya Inajin	*Dream Catcher*
Inti-Illumani	*Imagination*
Modest Petrovich Mussorgsky	*Pictures at an Exhibition*
Michael Oldfield	*Tubular Bells 1 and 2*
Nikolai Andreyevich Rimsky-Korsakov	*Scheherazade*
Rumillajita	*Wiracocha*
Camille Saint-Saens	*The Swan*
Igor Stravinsky	*Petrushka*
Bob Zander	*Almost Oriana*

These are just a few of a multitude of musical selections that can inspire young children as they create art.

Invite children to paint a line that follows the melody, or to make different movements to match the soft and loud parts, different instruments, or rhythms that they hear.

When selecting music to play for children, choose pieces that complement the children's mood and activity level. A peppy song can help children clean up with vigor. A lullaby can help children relax at nap time. Be sure to introduce music from many other cultures as musical preferences are established at a young age. Table 7–2 provides some interesting musical pieces to share with children.

Learning to Move

Young children learn with their whole bodies. The movement of their arms as they move a brush across the paper or stamp a print develops coordination and muscle strength. Bending and reaching as part of a creative movement activity will develop flexibility and balance. Mirroring the actions of another will develop body awareness. As children practice these movements, they develop control over their own bodies. In creative movement activities, children are asked to use their bodies to solve open-ended problems that allow them to move at a level that is comfortable for them, but one that challenges them to add new motions.

Movement activities are also powerful motivators and make wonderful transitions into other activities. In addition they can stand on their own as integral experiences for young children.

Designing Movement Activities

Some of the best creative movement activities are based on spur-of-the-moment reactions to the needs of the children and the teacher's own kinesthetic sense and do not require any special preparation.

For example, imagine reading a book about a bird to a group of young preschoolers, but a few of them are having trouble sitting still. As they hear about the bird flapping its wings, ask the children to flap their arms like the bird. Continue to encourage the children to imitate the actions of the bird during the story and end by asking them to fly slowly to an activity of their choice. By bringing into play the kinesthetic sense we add more meaning to the words and to what the chil-

Movement activities are powerful motivators.

dren are hearing, and at the same time channel the healthy bodily energy of wiggly children.

Use the following guidelines when designing creative movement activities:

- **Explore.** Begin by asking children to move at different levels, in different spaces, and at different speeds. Use your assessment of what these particular children can do easily and what is challenging for them to build further activities.
- **Practice movement control.** Ask children to change direction, start, and stop. To maintain control establish special signals for starting and stopping that are used regularly.
- **Provide open-ended starter ideas.** The best responsive movement activities start by having children observe movements in nature or in the community around them. Then instead of directing them to move in a certain way, ask questions

that allow open-ended exploration of an idea, such as, how would it feel to be an animal? What animal would you be? How would it move if it were hungry? Ask children to imagine being a growing flower, a tree in a storm, a flying insect, a heavily loaded truck, or a digging machine.

- **Move together.** Encourage children to combine their movements with those of others. Say, "Let's make a parade of animals. How would your animal march?" Become a garden of flowers bending in a breeze or bees buzzing inside of a busy beehive.

- **Add a rhythmic accompaniment.** Tap on a drum, shake a tambourine, or play related music.

- **Add props.** Children can make masks or puppets or a hat to wear.

- **Add complexity.** While it is important to repeat popular movement activities regularly to develop confidence, try to enrich each movement session by adding one or more new movements to try.

Combining Music, Movement, and Art

The arts make a powerful combination. Instead of separating them, look for ways to intertwine them. When planning any activity, from reading a story to taking a walk in the park, ask the following questions:

- Is there something we can draw, paint, or sculpt?
- Can we find any art or music elements?
- Is there a song we can sing that relates to this topic, or can we add new words to a familiar song?
- Is there music for listening?
- What creative movement can be added?

The following activities provide examples of some of the ways the arts can be combined.

Shape trail. Outside on a paved area, paint or draw with chalk a series of crisscrossing trails of foot-sized shapes. Use one repeated shape for each "trail." Challenge the children to follow a trail by stepping on only one kind of shape.

Body shapes. Ask the children to lie down on the floor and make their bodies into a shape such as a circle or triangle. Be accepting of all their creative re-

Music Box

The Body Shape Song

(*To the tune "Mary Had a Little Lamb"*)

Now I am a circle, circle, circle.*
Now I am a circle
Lying on the floor.

(*Repeat with different shapes.*)

sponses. Sing a song such as "The Body Shape Song" (see Music Box).

Body viewfinders. Ask children to create differently shaped "windows" to look through using parts of their bodies. They can try touching the fingers of one or both hands together in different ways, or putting a hand on another part of the body and looking through the opening.

Picture pose. Invite children to look at a photograph, poster, or fine-art print of a person and try to imitate the position or expression of the pictured person. For a variation, use a picture of an animal.

People mirror. Have each child work with a partner. One child is the model, the other the mirror. The model strikes a pose and the mirror tries to imitate it. Then have them reverse roles. An adult or older child can partner with a toddler.

People camera. Have each child work with a partner. One child is the camera, the other the photographer. The camera closes its "shutters" (eyes), and the photographer slowly turns the camera around to face a view. When the photographer says, "Click," the camera opens the "shutters" for a moment, looks at the view, and closes them again. Then they may reverse roles.

Indoor texture hunt. This simple game can be used to assess the children's identification of different textures. Start with the children in a circle. Ask them to find something in the room that is smooth. When they find it, they are to put their hand on it and stay there until everyone has found something. Encourage them to help each other and remind them to walk safely. When all the children are touching something, call out another texture for them to find and touch. Do not correct children who touch the wrong texture, but make a mental note to introduce more activities that involve that one. This game can also be played outdoors. To add to the fun, ask the children to "move smoothly to a smooth object," "walk bumpily to a bumpy one," or "take rough steps to a rough one." Be inventive and the children will too! (*Note:* This game can also be played with shapes, kinds of lines, or colors.)

My textures. Ask the child or children to touch different textures on their bodies or clothes as they are named. For example, if "soft" is the word, they might touch their hair or skin. "Bumpy" could be the bottom of their shoes. After the teacher names a few, each child can take a turn calling out a texture. (*Note:* Colors, shapes, or kinds of lines can be substituted for textures in this activity as well.)

Music Box

Music words

Dynamics. Changes in volume from loud to soft and the accenting of certain tones.

Harmony. A sequence of tones that enriches a melody.

Form. The structure that organizes the elements of music.

Melody. A sequence of tones that changes or repeats.

Mood. The way a particular combination of music elements affects the listener.

Pitch. How high or low a sound is.

Rhythm. Time-based patterns that order sounds.

Timbre. The unique quality of a sound.

Rhythmic lines. Have a small group of children sit around a large piece of paper. Let each one choose a crayon or marker. As them to make their lines "dance" to the rhythms or sounds that they hear. Tap a rhythm on a small drum or even a covered margarine container or coffee can. After a few seconds change the rhythm. A set of bells or a child's xylophone can be used to add pitch. The children can also take turns making the sounds for each other. Music can also be used but they need to be very short bits of a variety of musical pieces. Prepare a tape of short selections ahead of time.

This activity can be done with the children using finger paint or paint and brushes, and with play dough. When using play dough, encourage the children to pat and poke the dough according to the rhythm they hear.

CONCLUSION: THE SENSITIVE TEACHER

Fifty percent of a child's learning capacity shuts off when made to sit still.

—Clyde Gillespie (Turner, 1990, p. 243)

All of us have treasured memories of something exceedingly beautiful. Perhaps it was a sunrise we saw driving to work or the image of our mother's face. Our children, too, deserve such memories. It is up to the adults who work with young children to help create these images. Some suggestions include

- sharing beautiful objects from nature and artists' hands.
- teaching children to see the elements of line, shape, color, form, space, texture, and pattern in the world around them.
- providing activities that develop children's sensory perception skills.
- providing opportunities for children to use their imaginations in new ways.
- pointing out the sensory, kinesthetic, and aesthetic elements in the children's own work and in the artwork of others.

The sensory and kinesthetic activities presented in this chapter may seem different than more "traditional" art activities for young children. Some of them may cross into other curriculum areas; others do not use the expected art materials. Nevertheless, these explorations form the basis of what art will mean to young artists and upon which they will make aesthetic judgments about the world.

The guiding adults of early childhood are the most important ingredients in forming a child's initial opinion about art. It is only when children feel safe and confident that they are able to learn aesthetically. It is the teacher's job to create an environment that is open to exploration, that is full of wonderful experiences that allow the children to gain pleasure as they use their senses, and that rewards children for using their natural learning style.

Teachers must bring excitement and enthusiasm to the classroom daily. Adults must be open to the aesthetic wonders that surround them—the pattern of the raindrops on the windowpane, the rainbow in the spilled oil in a puddle, the warm fur of a kitten—and share these with children. Every experience can be an aesthetic one. Learn to see with the eyes of an artist and the heart of a poet. Anyone can walk on the ceiling, fly with a bird, or dance on the ocean floor through the power of imagination. Teachers must visualize themselves as enthusiastic nurturers of young artists' sensory and kinesthetic development and know that their style of interaction and the environment they create will make every day special for a young child.

Sensory awareness cannot be put on a table like a box of crayons. It must be found in the world around us.

FURTHER READING

Bender, S. (1989). *Plain and simple: A woman's journey to the Amish.* San Franciso: HarperCollins.
  Bender describes how she learned to see beauty in simplicity from making quilts with the Amish.

Cameron, J. (1992). *The artist's way: A spiritual path to higher creativity.* New York: G. P. Putnam's Sons.
  This book discusses the meaning of art and provides methods of enhancing aesthetic and creative self-awareness.

McDonald, D. T. (2001). *Music in our lives: The early years.* Washington, DC: National Association for the Education of Young Children.
  A detailed overview of a developmentally appropriate music curriculum for young children.

Pica, R. (2004). *Experiences in movement: Birth to age 8* (2nd ed.). Clifton Park, NY: Thomson Delmar Learning.
  This book provides a foundation for teaching creative movement to young children.

Creating Art: Print-making

Creating an object print helps a child focus on the characteristics of the object.

THE PRINTMAKING EXPERIENCE

Printmaking is any art form that involves making a copy of something. Some printing techniques can produce multiple prints, others only one copy (monoprint). Printmaking can provide another way for young children to explore the sensory characteristics of objects. Before offering printing activities to young children, it is important to understand the nature of the technique and how young children approach this art form.

How Children Grow through Printmaking

Children will develop

1. physically, by using the large and small muscles of the arm to apply paint to an object and then move the object on the paper. (Bodily-Kinesthetic)
2. socially, by sharing the printing tools and paint trays. (Interpersonal)
3. emotionally, by learning to enjoy making prints as a means of self-expression and by seeing themselves as competent people who can control "messy" paint. (Intrapersonal)
4. visual perception skills, by exploring new ways to arrange print marks on a paper and by matching an object to the shape of its print. (Spatial)
5. language, by learning a vocabulary of printing words and by describing their prints. (Linguistic)
6. cognitively, by learning that different objects and materials make different print marks, depending on their texture and shape. (Logical-Mathematical)
7. art awareness, by becoming familiar with prints used in book illustrations and other artwork.

To provide satisfying printmaking activities for young children, teachers need to consider the children's physical control and experience when selecting or designing printing activities. Once an activity has been presented, teachers need to allow the children to use the printing tools freely and creatively, even if they are not making true "prints." It is the sensory experience of printmaking that is of most benefit to the children. The following explorations and practice activities emphasize this objective of printmaking.

EXPLORING PRINTMAKING AGES TWO AND UP

Printmaking is another way that young children can use their senses in a kinesthetic way to learn more about objects. The children use their sense of touch as they handle the object and apply pressure to make the print. They can compare the stiffness of the object with the slippery wetness of the paint. The print provides a visual image of the texture, pattern, and shape of the object, and the stamping process often creates a rhythmic sound. Printmaking is also a very active art form that requires the children to move their arms with vigor and apply pressure sensitively.

Group Composition

For initial printmaking explorations, limit the group to one or two toddlers or four older children. Once the children are familiar with the technique and can work more independently, the group size can be increased for the practice activities.

Setup

Provide a low table that the children can work at while standing. Children usually only spend a few minutes making prints and can do so standing up. This also enables them to reach the trays of paint and objects more easily. Cover the table with newspaper. Have all materials set out before inviting children to begin. Place the trays between the papers or down the

Classroom Museum

Look for silk-screen prints by Native American artists of the Northwest coast, such as Tim Paul, Bill Reid, Tony Hunt, and others. Also seek handprinted fabric from India and Africa. Indian wood blocks, used for printing the cloth, can be found in import stores.

middle of the table, depending on the size and shape of the table. Have smocks ready for the children to wear. (See chapter 5 for a discussion of smocks.)

Materials

- Paint: Choose several colors of very thick tempera paint or finger paint. Make sure that the paint colors will not stain hands. White is always a safe choice, as are pastels that are mixed using white and a few drops of a color. If the paint is thin, it can be thickened by adding flour. Paint thickened in this way must be used up quickly or it will spoil. Place a small amount of paint in each tray.

- Trays: Put the paint in low-sided trays. Use Styrofoam or plastic food trays that have been sanitized (see chapter 6), and ensure that sides are no higher than half an inch, or try paper plates.

- Printing tools: For the first exploration, provide the children with large, easily grasped objects that they can dip in the paint, such as a variety of potato mashers or long, cardboard tubes. Place one tool in each tray.

- Paper: Use paper in the 9-by-12-inch size range. Larger paper makes it difficult for the children to reach the trays and objects without leaning into their prints. Have plenty of extra paper so that children can make more than one print if they wish.

- Drying rack: A cardboard-box drying rack (figure 5–5) or other wet project storage unit placed near the printmakers will provide a quick place for the prints to dry while still supervising the children. With experience, the children can put their own prints away.

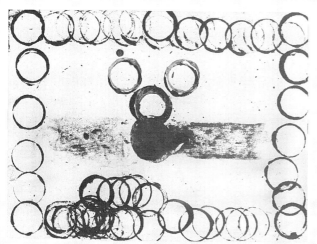

"This is a circle picture. I kept making more and more circle prints. It was fun." Print—*Shawnee, age 4*

Warm-Up

Have the printmaking materials set out on the table. Ask the children what kind of mark they think the object will make if it is dipped into the paint. Invite some of the children to try to make a print.

What to Do

Many children will begin their exploration very hesitantly. They may study the paint-covered end or the resulting print. Once they have an idea of the result of their actions, they may try other ways of moving the object on the paper.

During the initial explorations, do not interfere except for safety reasons. Allow the children to investigate this technique in any way they wish.

What to Say

When children are done, comment on the shapes they have made: "Look, you made circles," or, on the way they moved the tool: "You moved the tube up and down." Or, relate the mark to the object: "Which mark did the tube make? What made this mark?" When

Music Box

Printing Chant

Stamp, stamp, stamp.
Press, press, press.
Printing.
Printing.
It's the best!

children say a paper is finished, ask if they wish to make another.

Use a vocabulary that describes the marks made by the objects and the actions the child has used. Words to use include shape (and all of the shape names), pattern, texture, repeated, lift, press, stamp, hold, move, and place. Say a printing chant with toddlers, and mime it with older children.

Printmaking allows children to explore how shapes can be put together in new ways.

217

Transition Out

As the children finish, help them put their prints in a place to dry. Then guide them in removing the smocks and washing their hands. After the printmaking experience, set up a matching activity in which the child matches a print with the object that made it. Older children can match the object with its print in their artwork. Talk about how the print is different from, but similar to, the original tool that made it.

More to Do

After the exploratory activity, offer printmaking on a regular basis. Vary the printing tools, combining new ones with familiar ones. Toddlers need larger print-making tools than three- to eight-year-olds, but no matter what their age, children find small objects messier than larger ones.

Sponge prints. Sponges make great printing tools. Cut the sponge into simple geometric shapes. Avoid precut stereotyped shapes such as dinosaurs, rabbits, or letters. Although these may give "meaning" to the artwork for the adult viewer, such shapes have little meaning for the child who benefits more from sensory experiences with the basic shapes. Attach a clothespin to the top of the sponge shape, or, using craft glue, attach a spool "handle" to the sponge.

"Rubber" stamps. Commercial rubber stamps are too small for little hands to grasp, but larger ones are easy to make. Cut out simple geometric shapes—

Safety Note

Avoiding Food Items for Printmaking

Many books recommend using fruits and vegetables for printmaking. Consider carefully the message children receive when told to put food in paint and then see the food thrown away. Although a carefully made print of a sliced orange or an apple may make a beautiful print that allows the shape of the fruit to be seen in a new way, young children do not have the skill to create such a print. This is not an aesthetic experience for children. (See chapter 6 for further discussion on this topic.) Table 7–3 offers plenty of ideas for printing explorations that do not use foods.

square, circle, triangle, rectangle, oval, and so on—from heavy Styrofoam trays. Use craft glue to affix these shapes to sanded wooden blocks.

Roller prints. Wrap and glue string, yarn, or rick-rack to cardboard tubes or juice cans. When dry, roll the decorated cylinder in paint, and then roll it on the paper. This is a very messy but exciting exploration.

"Gadget" prints. Almost any object can make a print. When selecting objects for young children, look

TABLE 7–3	Printmaking Objects

Berry baskets	Forks	Shells
Blocks (building or interlocking)	Garlic press	Shoes
Bristle blocks	Hands	Sponge ball
Cans (with smooth edges)	Juice cans	Sponges (in simple geometric shapes, not pictorial)
Corks	Lids and tops	
Corrugated cardboard (cut into rectangular pieces)	Ornamental corn	Spools
	Pinecones	Toy trucks
Erasers	Plastic cups and containers	Tubes
Feet	Potato masher	Wooden blocks
Film cans	Rocks	

for ones that will be easy for the child to grasp, and ones that have smooth edges and an interesting texture. Toddlers require objects that can be grasped with the fist and that are very sturdy.

Big Books. Make a Big Book about pattern, using prints made from the same objects the children have used, and share it with them.

Printing plates. Cut fairly flat objects, such as corrugated cardboard, sandpaper, and burlap, into interesting shapes, and glue on a cardboard base. When the glue is dry, paint over the entire cardboard surface using a brush. Press a piece of paper over it to make a print.

Styrofoam prints. Cut out flat pieces from the bottoms of sanitized food trays (see chapter 6). Use a pencil to draw on the tray. Roll water-based printing ink over the drawing, and place a piece of paper on top. Rub well to produce a print.

Making Connections

Language. Have children try to figure out what was used to make the prints in books such as *Swimmy* (Lionni, 1963) and *I Was All Thumbs* (Waber, 1975). Invite them to cut their prints into shapes and paste them into a booklet. If they wish, they can then add drawings and a story to go with them.

Math. Together with the students, discover patterns in their prints, or create patterns by lining up several prints. Count the number of different shapes children make in their prints. Make a graph showing the results. Display it with the prints.

Science. Practice making predictions. Have children look at printing objects, and draw or describe the print they might make. Then estimate how many prints can be made from one dip in the paint. Which object makes the most prints with a single dip? Why? Experiment with different thicknesses of paint. Does the thickness of the paint make a difference in the number of prints possible on one dip?

Social studies. Many cultures decorate their textiles with prints of different types, such as an African mud cloth and Indonesian batiks. Create printed cloth banners and lengths of fabric by stamping on designs using different printing objects.

Teacher Tip

Understanding the Process

To make a clear handprint, children have to first put paint on the hand either by dipping or spreading it on. Then they must press it down, hold it still, and lift it up again off the paper. It is this pressing down, holding still, and lifting up pattern of action that is the key to printmaking.

Often children do not press, hold, and lift; instead, they treat the printing object as a paintbrush and smear the paint over the paper.

Physical development explains this behavior. Toddlers who do not yet have wrist control will find the press, hold, and lift action difficult to accomplish.

Children who draw scribbles will naturally move their arms in circular or up-and-down motions across the page. Toddlers and younger preschoolers will want to explore the nature of the paint rather than focusing on the nature of the object that is used to apply the paint. They do not yet have enough art experience to differentiate between a brush and some other paint applicator, or between a printing tool and an object with which to paint.

Young children also have difficulty understanding the idea of making multiple copies of something. They are concerned with the process, not the product. They see little reason to make duplicates of something when they could be creating something new and different. Often they will make one stamp with a printing tool and consider themselves done. Encourage further exploration by asking questions.

Teaching in Action

Printing a Mural: An Interview

Q: Have you ever done any printmaking with your child care children?

A: Yes. One of the best experiences I ever had was one of those spur-of-the-moment things. There was only a half day of school, and I ended up with eight children, ranging in age from one to eight. I didn't want them all just fooling around in front of the TV, so I looked around and I happened to have some paper plates, some tempera paint, and a roll of brown kraft paper, so I decided to try a printed mural.

Q: Do you always have art supplies like that?

A: I have found that art is something that will get everyone involved. Even the littlest ones can have a part. I try to keep some paint in the cupboard along with other basic supplies.

Q: How did you get them started?

A: It was a beautiful day, so I took everyone out to the yard, and I began by playing a game of shape tag. I called out a shape and they had to touch something with that shape.

Q: How did the toddlers participate?

A: I had the older children hold hands with the one-year-old and the two-year-old and find a shape together.

Q: How did you transition into printmaking?

A: I had brought out my box of printing objects. There were cardboard tubes and potato mashers and wooden blocks and sponges—big things even the little ones could handle. I dumped out the box and asked them to choose an object they thought would make an interesting shape. Then I put a small amount of paint on the paper plates and showed them how to dip an object into the paint and press it to make a shape. I used a piece of newspaper for my demonstration, and then I let them try their shapes on it. I asked the older children to work with the toddlers.

Q: How did you get the mural going?

A: Well . . . while they were experimenting on the paper, I rolled out the mural paper on the picnic table and held it down with stones. Then I said, "Who is ready to make a shape trail with their printing tool?" Those who were ready—there were about four—came over, and I told them to start a trail on one edge and make it end on another edge. I challenged them to see how long they could make it. I told them they could cross each others' trails but not cover them up. When they finished, they rinsed their hands in a bucket of water and went to play on the swings and in the sandbox, while the rest came over and finished. The two little ones were in the second group, and I could give them the attention they needed.

Q: How did you end the activity?

A: When everyone had made their shape trail, we went inside and washed up, and then I gave them some crackers for a snack. We talked about the shape of the crackers. It was neat. Some even made a shape trail with their crackers on their plate. Meanwhile, the mural was drying quickly in the sun. When snack was done, we went out and checked. It was dry, so we brought it inside, and the children had fun counting the shapes in their trails and seeing whose was the longest, whose had the most shapes, whose curved the most, and so on. Then three of the preschoolers played driving their cars along the shape trails. They had a lot of fun with it for many days afterward, and they learned more than if they had spent that time watching TV.

Studio Page 25

WHAT IS YOUR PERSONAL SENSE OF BEAUTY?

Make a list of things that you think are beautiful. Next to each item, record whether it is from nature or human-made. Also note how you decided it was beautiful and from whom you learned to appreciate its beauty.

Item of Beauty	Source	Why It Is Beautiful

Review your list. Can you find any relationships among these items? What senses do you use in experiencing these beautiful things? What has been the greatest influence on your personal sense of beauty?

_____

_____

_____

_____

_____

_____

_____

_____

Studio Page 26

REVIEWING THE ART ELEMENTS

Draw an illustration for each of these art elements.

Line	Shape
Color	**Texture**
Pattern	**Form**
Space	**Symmetry**

Studio Page 27

DESIGNING A BIG BOOK ABOUT ART

A Big Book is the perfect size to read to a group of small children. The large pictures can be easily seen by everyone. The appendix at the end of this book suggests many commercial Big Books you can use. However, you will not find books on every topic you may need, nor will the books exactly fit your chosen activities. The ideal solution is to use your creativity and make your own!

Guidelines for Creating a Big Book on an Art Topic

1. Select a topic based on one of the art elements or senses.
2. Limit the book to five or six one-sided pages.
3. Use just a few words.
4. Illustrations should be made from the same materials that the children will have to use.
5. Illustrations should be large, bold, and simple. Avoid cute, stereotypical, or cartoonish drawings.
6. Plan the book so the children can interact with it. For example, include pockets that contain hidden shapes or holes to look through.
7. Make the pages from heavy oaktag, poster board, or corrugated cardboard. Join the pages with metal, looseleaf rings.

Suggested Ideas for Your Big Book

Topic: Color. Feature a different color on each page. For each color, cut out a variety of shapes from different kinds of paper in that color. Write the color names in crayon and marker in that color. At the back of the book, attach an envelope containing shapes in each color. Have children find the correct page for the "lost" shapes.

Topic: Pattern. Use gadget or sponge prints to illustrate the following concepts:

- All patterns are made of repeated shapes.
- Some patterns are made from one repeated shape.
- Some patterns are made with two repeated shapes.
- Some patterns are made with three or more repeated shapes.
- Some patterns are made in only one color.
- Some patterns have lots of colors.
- Some patterns are made of different-size shapes.

Use yarn to attach samples of the objects used to make the prints to the book. Invite children to match them to the patterns.

Topic: Line. Use marker, crayon, or paint to draw different kinds of lines on each page. Some lines to include are straight, curved, zigzag, jagged, thick, and thin. Try to have each line be a continuation of the one on the previous page. On the last page, put all of the different lines together in a wild line "party."

Studio Page 28

OBSERVATION: A SENSORY EXPERIENCE

Choose one of the senses, and design a sensory experience for children. Present the activity to two or three children, and record what the children do.

Date of observation: _____   **Length of observation:** _____

Ages of children: _____   **Size of group:** _____

1. Describe the sensory experience.

   _____

   _____

   _____

   _____

2. What is the first thing the children do? How long do the children investigate the activity?

   _____

   _____

   _____

   _____

3. What do the children and you say?

   _____

   _____

   _____

   _____

4. Analysis: Using the information in this chapter and what you learned from the observation, defend the inclusion of sensory art activities in an early childhood setting.

   _____

   _____

   _____

   _____

 For additional information on teaching art to young children, visit our Web site at http://www.earlychilded.delmar.com

Introducing the World's Art

" A picture lives only through him who looks at it. "

—Pablo Picasso
(cited in Bruner, 1979, p. 22)

Questions Addressed in This Chapter:

- What do children learn from the art of others?
- How should artworks be selected?
- Why should the program include art from other cultures?
- What do children learn from multicultural art examples?
- How can teachers build their collections?
- How are artworks, prints, and artifacts used with children?
- How can community resources be used?
- How can children's literature be used to teach art?

Young Artists at Work

"What are those things?" Brian whispers.

"I think they're spaceships," his friend Allen replies.

"No, silly, can't you see they're whirlies?" says Shannon.

"What's a whirly?"

"That's when you take a brush and whirl it all around."

"Oh," says Michael thoughtfully, "I do that when I paint too."

"Well," says the teacher, coming up behind the children, "I see you have discovered our new print, Van Gogh's *Starry Night*. Come over to the rug, and I'll read you a story about the artist. It's called *Camille and the Sunflowers*" (Anholt, 1994).

WHAT DO CHILDREN LEARN FROM THE ART OF OTHERS?

Fine taste in the arts, or in any other aspect of life, cannot be specifically taught nor suddenly acquired. It develops slowly and subtly as a result of frequent exposure to examples which various cultures and generations have recognized as significant.

—Aline D. Wolf (1984, p. 21)

The aesthetic experiences that teachers present to children sensitize them to the qualities of objects in their environment. In selecting those objects, we must look not only to nature but also to the artwork and artifacts that express our cultural and historical roots. The graphic images and human-made objects that surround children when they are young will have an impact on how they will judge other artwork they encounter throughout life. People tend to like those things with which they feel comfortable and to reject the strange and unfamiliar. It is a basic principle of good advertising to bombard customers' senses until the product is so familiar that they choose it almost automatically. Educators must decide what they would like the objects in their children's environment to advertise.

Expanding the Child's Definition of Art

Children absorb many meanings from the objects in their environment. The illustrations in the books teachers select to read, the pictures they hang on the wall, and the knickknacks on the shelf all show what artistic images those teachers personally value. Do not think children are too busy playing to notice. Watch what happens if they are told not to touch something that has been sitting "unnoticed" in the room for several weeks, or an "ignored" picture that has been hanging on the wall for two months is now turned upside down.

Through the display of carefully selected artworks, children learn that art is more than just "messing around for fun." The children learn that art is not just what they do when they paint at the easel or draw with crayons. They learn that when they are exploring art forms they are participating in a long chain of human creativity. Young children naturally create art as part of their way of interacting with and learning about the world. Exposure to the art of others helps them understand why art is created, who is an artist, and how art is a part of their everyday environment.

Participating in the process of making art is only one facet of a total art experience. Surrounding children with exciting artworks to explore with all of the senses provides them with the impetus to practice the cognitive skills of describing and responding to art.

How Do Young Children Perceive the Art of Others?

Initially, children respond to artwork in a sensory way, seeing colors, shapes, and textures. They consistently prefer the brightest colors and are strongly attracted to colorful artwork (Parsons, 1987; Winner, 1982). Although children as young as two years old can identify pictures as representations of objects (Winner, 1989), they often prefer abstract artwork. They like to free-associate imaginary ideas or memories from the picture's image (Parsons, 1987). When viewing representational artwork, young children tend to prefer simpler and more direct pictures, whereas adult "art experts" would select more complex and intricate ones (Gardner, 1973). Young children tend to have "favorites," works that are personally pleasing. They

judge artwork as good based on whether or not they like it (Parsons, 1987). Although they cannot readily identify different art styles, children recognize that art can show imaginary subjects (Gardner, Winter, & Kircher, 1975).

Children also have many misconceptions about art. Even though they themselves may have made art from similar media, many children may not be able to identify how an artwork they did not witness being made was created. They also may not be familiar with museums and what kind of artwork is exhibited there (Gardner, Winter, & Kircher, 1975).

Educators can utilize young children's initial attraction to colorful graphic images to attract them to look at a wide variety of artworks. The artworks themselves will invite them into conversation about the qualities of the pieces. The ability to understand artworks extends far beyond seeing the subject of the piece. Teaching children to notice the way different artists have used the elements of art—line, shape, color, texture, pattern, form, and space—sets the stage for a more sophisticated understanding of art.

"Soopr.man." Crayon—*Laurel, age 5*

HOW SHOULD ARTWORKS BE SELECTED?

If young children delight in looking at picture books of bunnies, babies, and bears, why not paintings such as Da Vinci's "Mona Lisa," Van Gogh's "Starry Night," Renoir's "Girl with a Watering Can," or Chagall's "Peasant Life"?

—Joyce Mesrobian (1992, p. 19)

In order to select the best art images to share with children, teachers must rely on more than their own personal values about what kind of art is pleasing to them. Children already bring with them the aesthetic values of their family and culture. Teachers must expand their knowledge of art so children will be exposed not only to the style of art with which their heritage and upbringing have made them comfortable, and the art that reflects their background, but also those works that allow them to experience a wide range of artistic inventiveness.

 Art Words

Major Styles of Western Art

☼ **Abstract Expressionism**
Art having no recognizable subject, with a focus on color and media, often applied in a kinesthetic way. *Artists:* Willem De Kooning, Hans Hofmann, Jackson Pollock, and Wassily Kandinsky

☼ **Abstraction**
Art that is based on real images but uses them as design elements. *Artists:* Constantin Brancusi, Lyonel Feininger, Paul Klee, Henry Matisse, Henry Moore, and Joan Miró

☼ **Cubism**
Art that represents three-dimensional objects as if made of geometric shapes and forms. *Artists:* Paul Cézanne, Georges Braque, and Pablo Picasso

☼ **Expressionism**
Art that focuses on showing emotions. *Artists:* Paul Gauguin, Edvard Munch, Vincent Van Gogh, and Georges Rouault

☼ **Folk Art**
Art done by people who have not had formal training in art, or who use nontraditional art media. *Artists:* David Butler, the "Tin Man," Grandma Moses, and Henri Rousseau

☼ **Impressionism**
Art that focuses on capturing the effect of light. *Artists:* Mary Cassatt, Edgar Degas, Claude Monet, and Pierre Auguste Renoir

☼ **Kinetic Art**
Art that moves or has moving parts. *Artist:* Alexander Calder

☼ **Nonobjective**
Art based on geometric and organic shapes and forms. *Artists:* Piet Mondrian, Hans Hofmann, and Franz Kline

☼ **Op Art**
Art based on visual illusions and perceptions. *Artists:* Frank Stella and Victor Vaserly

☼ **Pointillism**
Art that uses small dots of different colors that the eye blends together. *Artists:* Georges Seurat and Camille Pissarro

☼ **Pop Art**
Art that is based on images from everyday life and popular culture, such as soup cans, clothespins, and cartoons. *Artists:* Jasper Johns, Roy Lichtenstein, Claus Oldenburg, and Andy Warhol

☼ **Realism**
Art that focuses on showing reality. *Artists:* John Audubon, Leonardo DaVinci, Winslow Homer, Edward Hopper, Georgia O'Keeffe, Maxfield Parrish, Rembrandt Van Rijn, Grant Wood, and Andrew Wyeth

☼ **Romanticism**
Art that attempts to make everything look more beautiful and wonderful than in reality. *Artists:* Albert Bierstadt, William Blake, John Constable, John Copley, Eugène Delacroix, Jacques David, and William Turner

☼ **Surrealism**
Art that focuses on fantasies or dreams. *Artists:* Marc Chagall, Salvadore Dalí, and Frida Kahlo

Criteria for Selection

It should be the goal of every guiding adult to help children value the very essence of artistic creation, regardless of the artist or the origin of the work. By exposing children to a wide range of art forms, we prepare them to be accepting of others' creativity wherever they encounter it, throughout their lives. As Gardner (1991, p. 101) states, "models initially encountered by children continue to affect their tastes and preferences indefinitely, and these preferences prove very difficult to change."

Selected artworks should illustrate the following concepts:

1. People of many different ages create art.
2. Art has been made by people from many places and times.
3. Art tells us about the lives of other people.
4. Art is made from a wide variety of materials that reflects the environment and choice of the artist.
5. There are many ways or styles of doing art.
6. Art is found in many places in our environment.

Sources of Information about Artworks

Teachers must take the time to learn all that they can about the history and stories that relate to each piece of art that they present to children. The more they know about the art, the more confidently they will be able to present it to children. There are many wonderful children's books on artists and types of art that can be consulted. They can provide interesting facts to share about the selected pieces. Refer to appendix B for specific books about artists and their art. Become familiar with the major styles of Western and non-Western art and the different subject matter and media that artists have used.

Starting a Collection

Every adult who works with children should have a personal collection of art prints and artifacts. This collection can be supplemented with some works provided by a school, another teacher, or even borrowed from an artist, but most of it should consist of individually selected pieces that have been chosen because they relate to what the teacher wants to share with particular children and meet the criteria stated earlier. The collection does not have to be large, although over the years it will slowly grow as new pieces are found that speak to the teacher and to the children.

Start with one or two pieces of art that are interesting, perhaps some prints or artifacts, and learn about them. Then pick a piece that is unfamiliar, perhaps disconcerting, and find out why it causes those feelings. To start, use the list of art in table 8–1. Strive for a balanced collection of artworks representing different subject matter, art media, styles, and places of origin. As prints and artifacts are added to the collection, research each one. Slowly, expertise will develop. Teachers do not have to become art historians overnight, just experts on one piece of artwork at a time.

Make sure that each piece is engaging for young children. It does not matter if it is a great masterpiece, represents an important culture, or is a favorite artwork; it will not interest children if the subject matter or meaning is too complex for them to understand. No matter what style is used, children relate best to pictures that have subjects that they can identify with on a very basic level, such as faces, children, and people involved in activities, animals, nature scenes, and places. This does not mean that the pictures can only show familiar subjects, but they should have something on which children can base their understanding. Children who have never seen a red poppy can relate to the flower element of Georgia O'Keeffe's *Red Poppy*. They do not have to have lived in the sixteenth century to identify with the child in Rembrandt's *Girl with Broom*. They will also enjoy abstract and nonobjective works that resemble their own artwork, and works such as René Magritte's *Raining Cats and Dogs* that involve visual puns or tricks.

WHY SHOULD THE PROGRAM INCLUDE ART FROM OTHER CULTURES?

How can we teach the essence of a people—
Native American people, for instance? We can't,
but we can do better than bows and arrows.

—Patty Greenberg (1992, p. 30)

TABLE 8–1	**Engaging Art Posters for Young Children**

These exemplify the type of artwork that appeals to young children. Most are readily available from the sources listed. Addresses are listed in appendix A.

TITLE	ARTIST/CULTURE	DESCRIPTION	SOURCE
The Acrobat	Marc Chagall	Floating man	Modern Learning
Banjo Lesson	Henry O. Tanner	Boy learning banjo from grandfather	Modern Learning/ Dale Seymour Portfolios: African-American Artists
Beasts of the Sea	Henri Matisse	Cut-paper collage of sea life	Take 5: Collage
Blue Boat	Winslow Homer	Fishermen in blue canoe	Boston Museum
California	John Outterbridge	Sculptural assemblage of car	Take 5: African-American Art
Cat and Bird	Paul Klee	Abstract cat with a "hidden" bird to find	Metropolitan
Children at Beach	Mary Cassatt	Two toddlers dig in sand	National Gallery
The Circus	Georges Seurat	Pointillistic circus scene in pastels	Metropolitan
Decorated Eggs	Ukranian	Psyanky hand-dyed eggs	Dale Seymour
Diamond in Red, Yellow, and Blue	Piet Mondrian	Geometric design	National
False Face Mask	Iroquois	Carved wooden mask	Mask Set: Crystal
Girl with Watering Can	August Renoir	Impressionism— young girl in garden	Metropolitan
Going to Church	William H. Johnson	Black family goes to church	African-American set: Crizmac
Goldfish	Henri Matisse	Colorful abstract of fish in a glass jar	Metropolitan
Hilltop Farm	Maxfield Parrish	Blue-toned evening winter landscape	Boston Museum
Hope Street: Church Mothers	Marie Johnson-Calloway	Black women dressed for church	MAPS Set: Crystal
Hopi-Tewa Vessels	Nampeyo	Pottery bowls	Take 5: Native American
Improvisation 31	Wassily Kandinsky	Pastel nonobjective	National Gallery
Reclining Mother and Child	Henry Moore	Stone sculpture	Take 5: Sculpture

TITLE	ARTIST/CULTURE	DESCRIPTION	SOURCE
Red Horses	Franz Marc	Three red playful horses	Boston Museum
Red Poppy	Georgia O'Keeffe	Giant close-up of red poppy	Boston Museum
Robinson Garcia Laguna	Kuna People of Panama	Mola of appliquéd cloth showing two boxers	Folk Art Set: Crystal
Soap Bubbles	Jean-Baptist Chardin	Realistic view of boy blowing bubbles	Take 5: Children
Standing Bison	Douglas Mazonowitz	Prehistoric cave art reproduction	Modern Learning
Storyteller	Pueblo	Folk art: pottery sculpture of storyteller with children	Print Set: Crystal
Sunflowers	Vincent Van Gogh	Thickly textured, yellow-toned still life	Modern Learning
Tar Beach	Faith Ringgold	Black family group	Take 5: Urban Environments
Tropical Forest with Monkeys	Henri Rousseau	Imaginary jungle scene	National Gallery
War Wolf Helmet	Tlingit	Carved wood headpiece	Mask Set: Crystal
Water Lilies	Claude Monet	Impressionistic view of water	Boston Museum

Note: Some prints are available only in sets. Other prints in the sets may also be useful with young children.

Art communicates more than stereotypes or bald facts. Children learn more about a culture and its people from looking at its art, about how and why it was made, and coming to understand the use or importance of artwork in that culture than they do from making stereotypical symbols of that culture. It is important when selecting pieces for a personal art collection to include examples of artwork from diverse cultures.

When children see that the art of their culture and the art of other cultures contain many similarities, that culture becomes less strange and more appreciated. A simple woven basket from Botswana can link a small African village where baskets are used for carrying and storing grains, fruits, and peanuts to a preschool where similar baskets are used to hold some of the art supplies. African masks can be compared to those worn by people on Halloween, by characters on TV, and in plays and movies. All over the world artists have created art for the same purposes—to beautify their homes, to make everyday things distinctive, to make a personal statement, to tell their stories or record their history, and to express their spiritual beliefs. Art unites all of humankind.

WHAT DO CHILDREN LEARN FROM MULTICULTURAL ART EXAMPLES?

The art of a people can introduce the sense of pride in one's own heritage that is so badly needed by so many minority children. It can also introduce respect for others' achievements, which is equally needed by all children.

—Elaine Pear Cohen & Ruth Straus Gainer
(1976/1995, p. 223)

When children see the art of their heritage displayed and honored, they feel valued as people. When they see the art of others treated with respect, they learn to value people who are different. Children model their behavior on adults' behavior. As teachers add pieces to their collection of artworks, they must consider the message of their selection and how the discussion of them will affect the children. Before we can teach children to relate to the art of the world, we ourselves must come to love and understand the art of others. We will always have our personal favorites, just as the children will, but as we live and work with each piece, it will become an old friend from which we will not wish to part.

In selecting artwork for the collection, make sure that it is representative of the art of everyone, and that each piece is accorded respect and understanding.

1. Examples of multicultural art should be displayed in our rooms every day. Do not trivialize the artwork of others by showing it only in the context of a particular holiday or art project.
2. Strive for balance. Do not collect most of the examples from one racial or ethnic group.
3. Respect the integrity of the artwork and the particular time, place, and person who created it. Do not disconnect the artwork from its creators by having the children copy the symbols or the design of the work. Making a paper copy of an African mask in a school setting is not the same as the ritualistic carving of a wooden mask by the African artist.
4. Avoid stereotypes. Collect artwork that shows different racial and ethnic groups involved in all kinds of common activities. Make sure that the examples are not just from the past, but include art that was made by living artists.

Art Words

Art Media

Acrylic
A painting made from acrylic polymer paints.

Collage
A picture containing glued-on objects or paper.

Drawing
A picture made from any linear art material: pencil, marker, charcoal, pen and ink, and so on.

Fresco
A painting made in wet plaster.

Mixed Media
A picture or sculpture made from a combination of materials, such as paint, paper, wire, and fabric.

Mobile
Three-dimensional art that moves.

Monoprint
A picture made using a technique that produces only one print.

Oil
A painting done with oil-based pigments.

Pastel
A drawing made from soft, colored chalks.

Print
A picture made using any one of the printing techniques that produce multiple copies, including woodcut, serigraph (silk screen), etching, and lithography.

Sculpture
A three-dimensional artwork. Sculpture can be made from a limitless variety of materials, including wood, stone, clay, metal, found objects, papier-mâché, fabric, plaster, wax, and resins.

HOW CAN TEACHERS BUILD THEIR COLLECTIONS?

Children feel a certain magic about the real thing. You hear their breath draw in, see their eyes widen, hear their respect and wonder. . . . Nothing really substitutes for this experience.

—Jo Miles Schuman (1981, p. 1)

There are several types and sources of art examples from which teachers can build a collection. Try to include pieces of each kind so that children will experience a breadth of art media in a variety of formats.

Original Artwork

Children need to see and touch "real" pieces of art. They need to feel the texture of an oil painting, the flowing form of a stone carving, and the exhilaration of blowing on a mobile. They will have many of these experiences in the context of creating their own art. They also need, however, to see that it is not just little children, in this room, at this time, who make art. There are many art media and forms that are not safe for or within the skill level of children but that they can experience on an aesthetic level, such as a welded metal sculpture or a piece of stained glass. Original art forms can be obtained as follows.

Other children. The teacher's personal collection of children's art can provide pieces for the current group of children to study. Permanently mounted in public spaces such as the hall and lobby, group-produced pieces such as clay tiles (see chapter 6) or mobiles provide a tie to the children who have come before.

Artists in the community. Every community has wonderful artists who work in all kinds of art media. Most of these people are willing to lend or donate a piece of art. A donated oil painting or wood carving has an advantage over borrowed pieces, in that the children can handle as well as look at the piece. The piece does not have to be the artist's most cherished or even completed. An unfinished painting or sculpture can be more interesting for young children to explore than an elaborately framed artwork that they cannot touch. Children are concerned with process, and unfinished works mirror their own approach to art.

Art Words

Art Subjects

- **Abstract**
  A picture emphasizing shapes, colors, lines, and texture over subject matter.

- **Cityscape**
  A representation of a city.

- **Interior**
  A picture showing the inside of a room.

- **Landscape**
  A representation of the outdoors.

- **Portrait**
  A picture of a person.

- **Seascape**
  A representation of the sea.

- **Still Life**
  An arrangement of objects on a surface.

Teachers' artwork. If teachers have done original art of their own, they may have a piece to share with the children. It could be a picture drawn as a young child or a piece of pottery made in a workshop. Sharing a piece of our own artwork is quite different from providing a model we have made and expect the children to copy.

Display the art, and discuss it with the children. Do not then have the children do an art exploration with the same materials, as that would be too much like providing a model. Remember that as educators we have a unique relationship with children. There are many things that we do teach by modeling. We expect children to copy the correct shapes of letters and numbers. We want them to copy our manners and the way we are sensitive to others. We do not want them to copy our art.

What teachers can do when sharing their artwork is model how artists share their creative efforts. Children learn that people they know and care about create art. Share how it felt to make it, why it is special, and where it is kept at home. By being proud of our own work, we model self-confidence. Use this experience to lead into a discussion about what the children might like to share about their own art.

Fine Art Posters

In recent years, inexpensive but high-quality prints of artworks from around the world have become widely available. Posters have the advantage of being large enough for a group of children to experience at one time and durable enough to take many years of handling. Sources for art prints and suggested titles that appeal to young children are listed in table 8–1 and appendix A. Fine art prints can also sometimes be borrowed from libraries.

Medium-size prints. Smaller art prints can be obtained inexpensively from some of the many beautiful calendars that feature artworks of all kinds, and from a variety of magazines and catalogs. These prints are too small for large group study or public display but are perfect for use with small groups of three or four children.

Mini art prints. Museum postcards and pictures clipped from museum catalogs and mounted on tag board can be used for a variety of activities by one or two children. These prints are just the right size for small hands, and the freedom they have to handle them makes them very popular with children.

Art Books

There are many books written especially for children that contain numerous examples of art. Books are best used for sharing the art with one or two children at a time, or for a child to use independently. Children gain nothing from observing the small prints in a book when it is shared with a large group. Showing a group of children a picture of an African mask from a heavy adult art book, and then expecting them to show appreciation for this art form, is ridiculous. For a child, the miniature picture in the book has no rela-

tionship to the powerful, life-size piece of art it represents.

When reading a book about an art form to a group of children, try to have a related large print or artifact to share with them as well as the illustrations. Otherwise, share the book with just a few children at a time, or put it in the reading area for children to enjoy on their own.

Art Artifacts

An artifact is a handmade, three-dimensional, cultural art form. Examples of artifacts include baskets, quilts, and wood carvings. They are often unsigned and made for daily use, and they may be considered a form of collective folk art. They are not usually one-of-a-kind pieces but are representative of a class of articles from the everyday life of a people. These are the cultural art forms that represent the ethnic heritage of a group of people. They are often handed down from one generation to another and carry the family's story with them.

Children need many opportunities to experience the art of others. The intricate pattern of a *mola* fascinates a child.

In American culture, examples of contemporary artifacts include handmade quilts, weavings, and pottery. Although they may not be considered fine arts because of the element of repetition of traditional forms and designs, high-quality handmade artifacts retain the creative touch of the artist. They are not made from precut or purchased patterns, but represent a creative variation on a piece that follows a cultural tradition.

When selecting artifacts, choose those that reflect the artist who created it. Each handmade and designed artifact will have a different color, form, and perhaps decorative element from the others. Artifacts are made from materials that are found in the locality in which they were made. A quilt might be made from a family's old clothing or a weaving from the neighbor's sheep wool.

Sources of art artifacts. These items are intended for home, community, or ritual use, not for public display outside of the culture. Teachers may have some artifacts that belonged to their own families, or that they have made themselves and can share with the children. If teachers are willing to share personally valued artifacts, such as grandmother's patchwork quilt, then others are more likely to do so. The families of the children may wish to bring in a special artifact to show the group. If friends have traveled widely or are collectors of a specific type of artifact, then they may be willing to let the children see one or two pieces or might invite the children to visit the collection. (See the following section on using community resources for specific guidelines.) Sharing cultural artifacts is an excellent way for people of different heritages to bond.

On occasion, a particular artifact may be purchased that will either expand the cultural experience of the children or relate to an activity. For example, share an Indonesian shadow puppet before making shadow puppets with the children. If cultural artifacts are being sold, then the sale should benefit the family or community that made them. Beware of items made for the "souvenir" market. Especially on imported items, look for labels that indicate the country of origin. Avoid those that look like they were mass-produced. Before buying an artifact, research its culture to find out if the item is one that is used in the daily life of the people. Artifacts of all kinds are available from many sources, such as department stores, importers, charitable organizations, and craft fairs. Charitable organizations are a good source, because they usually provide information about who made the item and how the money will be used to help the artisans. Craft fairs provide the opportunity to buy directly from the creator and collect the story that goes with the piece.

Many artifacts are relatively low cost and durably made. After all, they are intended to survive the wear and tear of a normal household. Children will especially benefit from being able to touch and perhaps even to use the artifact, such as using an African basket to serve crackers for snack, eating soup from a hand-thrown tureen, or sitting under a handmade quilt for story time. Try to have a few such usable artifacts in the collection. Table 8–2 suggests some of the types of artifacts that teachers might seek. Appendix A provides a list of artifacts and their sources.

HOW ARE ARTWORKS, PRINTS, AND ARTIFACTS USED WITH CHILDREN?

There are activities in a developmentally appropriate curriculum that can take art to another level, one of discussion and understanding.

—*Marjorie Schiller (1995, p. 38)*

How a piece of art is presented is as important as the selection process that went into obtaining it. Hanging a Van Gogh print on the wall or displaying a piece of Burmese lacquerware is just a start. If teachers do not focus the children's attention on the artwork and relate it to their lives and artistic heritage, then it will have no more meaning than the cartoon characters that decorate so many classrooms. Teachers must engage children in the process of looking, questioning, and thinking about each piece. The following activities will provide models that can be expanded to accompany any artwork selected for a collection.

Setting Up a Masterpiece Corner

Select a prominent place in the room in which to display a featured piece of artwork on a regular basis. The

TABLE 8–2 | **Multicultural Artifacts**

Banners	Baskets
Beads	Beadwork
Calligraphy	Cloth, hand-painted, hand-dyed, or hand-printed
Cornhusk items	Crocheted items
Decorated eggs	Dolls, handmade
Embroidery	Ethnic clothing
Figurines, modeled clay, stone, wood	Furniture, handmade
Games, hand-carved or modeled	Glassware, hand-blown
Gourds, carved	Handmade papers, also cast paper
Jewelry, handmade	Inlays, wood or stone
Knitted items of original design	Lacquerware
Masks	Mats, woven fiber
Mosaics	Musical instruments
Papier-mâché	Pottery, hand- or wheel-built, not slip cast
Puppets	Quilts
Sand painting	Scrimshaw
Straw designs	Tapestries
Tinware	Weavings
Wrought iron	Yarn paintings

area should be free of distractions such as toys, competing signs, and other wall decorations and should be in a "clean-hands" area. Store related fine-art manipulatives, art books, and prints on nearby shelves. There should be room for several children to gather. Like the sensory table, a good location is near the entrance to the room where it will attract the children's attention as they enter with fresh eyes each day.

It is important to place the print or artifact at the children's eye level. Leave one artwork on exhibit for a length of time. If the subject corresponds to a theme focus, leave it up during that thematic unit.

After several days of display, or if several children become very interested in the piece, involve the children in one of the following suggested art appreciation activities.

Using a Puppet or Stuffed Animal

The key to engaging the children's interest in a piece of artwork is in the way we express our personal enthusiasm and interest in the work. Our voices need to be full of energy and excitement as we discuss the art-

work with the children. Some people find it helpful to use a puppet or stuffed animal. Just like children, adults often feel less inhibited when having "Rembrandt Bear" or "Art, the Aardvark" talk to the children.

Convert a simple stuffed animal or purchased puppet into an "art expert" by adding a few small details such as a beret and a smock (with paint splotches, of course) and by sewing a crayon or paintbrush onto a "paw." An original puppet can be created using a sock, papier-mâché, or cloth. It helps if the "arms" can be moved so more expression can be added to the presentation. The "art expert" should be constructed durably, as it will prove a popular friend to the children, who will often model the teacher's art discussions in their play. Make sure to give it a personal history that tells how it came to be so expert in art.

Questions to Ask

Although the specific questions will depend upon the particular piece that has been selected, the following will offer some ideas to get started.

What does it tell you about? These questions focus on the subject matter or the story of the artwork.

- What is the season? Weather? Time of day?
- What kind of place is this?
- What is happening in this picture?
- Who is this person? Who are these people? What are they doing?
- What is this animal? Tree? Plant? Building?
- What objects in the picture do you know? Use? Are there any you do not know? Use?

How was it made? These questions help children learn about the different art media.

- How do you think the artist made this? How can you tell?
- Does this look like it was made with any art materials that we use?
- What do you think the artist used to put the paint on her painting?
- How did the artist make this texture? Color? Line? Shape? Pattern?
- How did the artist carve this hard stone? Wood?

Can you find? These questions give the children practice in using art vocabulary.

- Can you find a line? Shape? Color? Texture? Pattern? (Be specific, for example, red rectangle, rough texture.)
- Can you trace with your finger a line? Shape?
- Can you touch or point to a line? Shape? Color? Texture? Pattern?

How does it make you feel? Young children are not always able to express their feelings verbally. Be accepting of any responses that the children make to these questions. Trying to imagine how the people in the artworks, particularly portraits, and the artists feel helps children become more sensitive to the feelings of others.

- If you were in this place, how would you feel?
- How does the person in this picture feel?
- How was the artist feeling when she made this?
- How do you feel when you look at this?
- Do you ever feel that way when you paint? Draw? Model?

What comes next? These questions challenge children to make predictions based on the visual clues they see and allow them to practice creative visualization. In designing these questions, make sure there are enough clues to give direction to the child, but that there is no one right answer. Be accepting of all responses.

- What do you think will happen next? Happened before?
- What do you think this person (animal) will do next? Did before?
- What will the weather be later?
- Who do you think lives in this building?
- What is inside this building? Box?
- What is behind this tree? Building? Fence? Curtain? Door?

How many? Questions can also relate to other curriculum areas, such as math, language arts, social studies, and science.

- How many red circles (blue squares, etc.) can you find? (math)
- Tell me a story about this picture. (language arts)
- Why are these houses made from reeds? (social studies)
- Do these clouds look like rain clouds? (science)

Can you do? Asking children to respond through creative movement to art helps them develop their mental imaging skills and allows them to become more involved in the artwork. There are no right answers to these questions; accept all of the children's responses.

- Can you make your face look like this one?
- Can you stand (sit) in the same position as this person? How would this person walk?
- Can you imagine you are climbing this tree? (Mime climbing up a tree.)
- Can you imagine opening and closing this door? Looking in this window? (Mime.)
- Can you imagine you are touching this animal? (Mime.)

What is the same or different? These questions encourage the children to develop skill in visual comparison. For very young children, keep the comparisons

There are many ways to share fine art with young children. Showing just a tantalizing part of an artwork adds an element of surprise. "Rembrandt Bear" helps introduce the print *Goldfish* by Matisse, using a peekaboo window.

general and obvious. Older children will enjoy trying to solve trickier ones.

In a single artwork:

☼ In this picture, which person (house, animal) is bigger? Older? Younger? Smaller?

☼ Can you find the biggest (smallest) square (triangle)?

☼ Can you find the longest (shortest, thickest, thinnest) line?

☼ Can you find the brightest (dullest, lightest, darkest) color?

Comparing two artworks:

☼ In which picture is there a person? A house? An animal? A rectangle? The color pink?

☼ Which picture looks more real?

☼ Which artwork is round (three-dimensional)? Which is flat?

☼ Which artwork makes you feel happy? Sad?

☼ Which artwork have we seen before?

Personal taste. These questions allow children to express their personal reaction to an artwork based on their aesthetic response of the moment. Asking children to pick their favorite is a good way to spark interest in an artwork. It is a useful assessment technique to ask children for their personal opinions when first displaying an artwork, and then again after it has been on display awhile and discussed. Notice if negative initial reactions have changed or become tempered as children become more familiar with the piece. Be accepting of all responses.

Do not tell children that they must like something, but do make them justify their response by asking "Why?" Young children may not be able to express verbally why the piece elicits a certain personal response and may respond with "Because" or "I don't know, I just do." However, asking "why" sets up a pattern in which children learn that a feeling about an artwork is always based on something. Some of the sophisticated justifications that young children can make are quite surprising, especially after they have looked at and discussed several artworks.

- Do you like this? Why?
- Which of these is your favorite? Why?
- Would you like this artwork to hang in your home? Bedroom? Why?
- Would you like to meet this artist? Why?
- Would you like to make an artwork like this? Why?

Presenting Artwork from Another Culture

When presenting an artwork from another culture, have the children focus on its universal artistic qualities first so that it is clearly identified as a piece of art. Ask a selection of questions from any of the art categories before asking about the cultural element. Questions should focus on finding similarities with familiar art forms and investigating possible uses.

- How is this artwork similar to the one we use? Make?
- How do you think it is used?

Remember that young children under age eight have a minimal knowledge of the world. They do not know specific geographical information. They respond best when descriptions of how something is made and used in another place are embedded in a story. Children can identify with common human themes such as family, food, and homes; they love stories that contain animals. Consult appendix B for some suggested storybooks, or write an original story.

Designing a Big Book about Artworks

If a children's book about the specific artwork to be presented cannot be found, the teacher can make a Big Book for the children. In designing such a book, try to find photographs in magazine articles or calendar illustrations, or draw simple pictures or make collages that show the steps in making the artwork. If

possible, glue on real samples of the materials used to make the artwork, such as wool and yarn for a book about weaving, or palm leaves for a book about basket making. Many craft stores carry art materials from around the world. When presenting an artwork from another culture, research details such as children's names, customs, and daily life so that the story will be accurate.

Children like repetitive and cumulative textbooks. Here is a sample of a repetitive text based on information about basket making in Botswana from *Native Artists of Africa* by Reavis Moore (1993):

Nangura of the Mbukushu goes to the river,
To get the palm leaves,
For a basket to store her grain in.

Nangura of the Mbukushu collects the bark
To dye the palm leaves,
For a basket to store her grain in.

A cumulative text is an excellent format for describing the creation of artwork that is done in a series of steps, and the repetition of each step helps children learn the sequence of how the article was made. Hand or body motions can be designed that mime the process to go along with the text. Using the same information as was used in the repetitive sample, here is a brief sample of a cumulative text.

Nangura of the Mbukushu goes to the river,
[Mime walking.]
To collect the palm leaves, [Mime reaching up for leaves.]
For a basket to store her grain in. [Mime holding a basket.]

Nangura of the Mbukushu goes to the forest,
[Mime walking.]
To collect the bark to dye the palm leaves, [Mime pulling bark.]
For a basket to store her grain in. [Mime holding basket.]

Nangura of the Mbukushu fills up the kettle,
[Mime pouring water.]
To boil the dye, from the bark she collected, to dye the palm leaves, [Mime stirring a hot kettle.]
For a basket to store her grain in. [Mime holding basket.]

Small, hand-size prints entice young children to look closely and make comparisons as they sort and group them.

Nangura of the Mbukusku gathers up the dyed leaves [Mime gathering leaves.] that were boiled in the dye, from the bark she collected, to dye the palm leaves, [Mime stirring the kettle.] For a basket to store her grain in. [Mime holding basket.]

Engaging Children with Art Prints

The following activities are designed to help a small group of toddlers or a larger group of older children become engaged with an art print.

Using a peekaboo window. This activity can be done with a large print (12-by-18 inches or larger) that has been on display or one that the children have never seen. From a sheet of paper the same size as the print, cut out a "window" in any shape that corresponds to a particularly interesting part of the picture. For example, in a painting such as Matisse's *Goldfish*, highlight one of the fish. In a portrait or mask, accent an eye, a mouth, or a decorative element. In a nonobjective artwork, choose a shape or a color. Place the window paper over the print, and fasten it securely at the top so it lifts easily. Then ask a series of thought-provoking questions about that part and what might be in the rest of the picture.

If they have seen the print before, ask children questions that challenge their memories.

- Do you remember what this _____ was a part of?
- What other_____ are in this artwork? (colors, shapes, lines, details, textures, animals, people, plants, or any other visual element that relates to the artwork)
- What is special about this one part of the artwork?

If it is new to them, ask children questions that entice them to predict.

- What do you imagine this _____ is part of?
- What else do you think might be in the artwork?
- What other _____ do you imagine are in this artwork? (colors, shapes, lines, details, textures, animals, people, plants or any other visual element that relates to the artwork)

It is not necessary to ask a lot of questions. If the children are very excited about seeing the rest of the artwork after only one or two questions, then end the questioning by saying: "Let's look at the artwork and see what the artist chose to do." The children will respond by comparing what they see to what they thought. This is an excellent way to develop mental imagery skills. Often children like to raise and lower the window several times. They also like to be able to touch the artwork. Leave the print covered for a while after the session so children can explore the window effect on their own.

Envelope (or book) of holes. Medium-size prints (about 8-by-10 inches) can be used in the same kind of cutout envelope or window book that was described in chapter 7. Medium-size prints are easy to find. There are many calendars that contain reproductions of art, and people are happy to donate them when the year runs out. Magazine pages are just the right size, and a wide range of art is found in magazines such as *The Smithsonian* and *Natural History*. The National Gallery also sells inexpensive prints in this size.

Art to hang. Laminate or cover four or five medium-size prints with clear contact paper. Punch two holes in the top of each print, and attach a string or piece of yarn. Hang a child-height hook in the home life area or play corner, and let the children select and change the displayed art at will. If possible, try to get copies of the larger prints that have been discussed with the group, making sure the assortment represents a variety of art forms. Store the prints in an attractive basket or a box decorated with a collage of mini art prints. On occasion, substitute or add a new print.

A blank wall or divider in one area of the room can be turned into a "museum" by providing a group of varied medium-size prints and a row of child-height hooks. Large blocks can be used as bases for any three-dimensional artworks that are durable enough for the children to handle, such as baskets, weaving, and tinware.

Two books to share with the children as they explore the museum area are *Matthew's Dream* (Lionni, 1991), in which a young mouse decides to become an artist after visiting a museum, and *Visiting the Art Museum* (Brown & Brown, 1986).

This area can also become a gallery or crafts fair. Children can "buy" new art to hang in the home life area, or they can select favorite pieces to take home to share and enjoy for several days. The yarn hanger makes it easy for parents to display the print on a doorknob or other convenient hanging place. Attach a brief history of the artwork, the artist's name, and any special facts about it to the back of any artwork that is sent home.

Art bags. Sew simple cloth bags with a handle, or decorate sturdy paper bags with mini-print collages. In each bag, place a medium-size print or a durable, inexpensive artifact along with a book that relates to the artwork and a toy, game, clothing, or food item that relates to the theme (see table 8–3). It is important to select artwork from a variety of heritages, so parents as well as children become familiar with the world of art.

Children can take a bag home for a special treat such as a birthday or holiday. Set up a sign-out system. Make sure that the artwork is labeled, and provide a notebook in which parents can write their comments before they return the bags.

Living portraits. After sharing several prints of portraits, place an empty, unbreakable picture frame in the area where the dress-up clothes are kept. Children can take turns "posing" behind the frame. Keep a camera handy so as not to miss some of these creative portraits.

I see a . . . Play a game modeled on "I see a color . . . ," in which one child names a detail in a print, and others have three guesses to find it. The one who finds it goes next. If it is not found, the same child goes again. Encourage the children to select art elements such as "I see a red square," or "I see a zigzag line." An exciting variation is to give each child a cardboard "looking" tube to use while playing this game.

Puzzles. Glue an inexpensive, medium-size print to a piece of corrugated cardboard. Laminate or cover with clear contact paper. Cut it into a few simple shapes that follow the shapes in the picture. Make a frame for the pieces with two sheets of cardboard slightly larger than the print. In one piece, cut a window the size of the print. Glue the window frame to the base, and fit puzzle pieces inside (see figure 8–1).

TABLE 8–3	Suggestions for Art Bags

Artwork:	*Still Life with Apples on a Pink Tablecloth* by Henri Mattisse
Book:	*What am I? Looking through Shapes at Apples and Grapes* by Leo Dillon and Diane Dillon (1994)
Item:	Apple wrapped in a pink piece of cloth
Artwork:	*Girl with a Watering Can* by Auguste Renoir
Book:	*Planting a Rainbow* by Lois Ehlert (1988)
Item:	A packet of flower seeds and a toy watering can
Artwork:	*Key West, Hauling Anchor* by Winslow Homer
Book:	*Sail Away* by Donald Crews (1995)
Item:	A toy sailboat
Artwork:	*Peaceable Kingdom* by Edward Hicks
Book:	*The Land of Many Colors* by Klamath County YMCA Preschool (1993)
Item:	Animal finger puppets
Artwork:	Native American basket
Book:	"Mandan Gardeners" in *Children of the Earth and Sky* by Stephen Krensky (1991)
Item:	Cornmeal chips
Artwork:	Wood carving of an elephant from Kenya
Book:	*I Am Eyes * Ni Macho* by Leila Ward (1978)
Item:	Peanuts
Artwork:	*Diamond Painting in Red, Yellow, and Blue* by Piet Mondrian
Book:	*Color Zoo* by Lois Ehlert (1989)
Item:	Set of colorful blocks

Note: All prints mentioned are available in 11 × 14 inch sizes from the National Gallery of Art.

Sorting activities using postcard-size prints.
Postcard-size prints can be purchased; alternatively, glue small copies of prints from art magazines, calendars, and museum catalogs to postcard-size tagboard. If possible, have them laminated for durability. Aline Wolf, in her book *Mommy, It's a Renoir!,* explains how to prepare special folders to store sets of mini-art prints, and how to create sorting activities for children that increase in difficulty as the children become more familiar with the artworks. Sorting sets can consist of two to four pairs of miniprints that feature contrasting features.

For example:

- pairs of duplicate pictures
- pairs that are predominately the same color, such as two mostly blue artworks and two mostly yellow
- pair a print that features mostly one color with a card bearing a shape in that color
- pair a print of an artwork that has a basic shape—round, square, and so on—with a matching-shape card
- pairs of different subjects, such as two portraits, two still lifes, and two landscapes

- pairs that show different art forms, such as two African masks, two Navajo weavings, and two Kuna Indian molas
- pairs that show the same art form created by different cultures, such as two baskets from Kenya, two Micmac baskets, and two American willow baskets
- pairs that show the same subject, such as a sun or face, done in different media, styles, or cultures

Sorting sets are most appropriate for children ages three and up. Three-year-olds will probably enjoy just looking at the miniprints and doing the simplest matching activities. Older children will enjoy working alone or in pairs trying to match the more challenging sets. Place the sets in attractive folders, clear plastic page protectors, small baskets, or decorated card boxes, and keep them in the "clean-hands" area. To make the sorting activity self-checking, place matching symbols on the back of each pair of prints. When children think they have a match, they can peek on the back to check themselves.

Sorting game board. A variation on this sorting activity is to create a game board by glueing six miniprints on a piece of cardboard and laminating it or covering it with clear contact paper. The board can be decorated to resemble a museum with different wings, such as painting, sculpture, Asian art, and so on. For an easy level, provide duplicate miniprints for the children to match with the ones on the board. For a more advanced level, provide miniprints that are similar to the ones on the board. Glue a sturdy envelope on the back of the board to store the cards.

Hot and cold. Postcard-size prints can be used to play the traditional game of "Hot and Cold." Instead of using a piece of colored paper, a child places a miniprint in plain view somewhere in the room, while one or more children leave the room or cover their eyes. Then they try to find the print, while the other children tell them if they are getting warmer (closer to the print) or colder (farther from the print).

Print match. If several miniprints that match large or medium prints are available, then play this matching game. Hang the large or medium prints on the wall, and have the children sit in a circle in front of them. In the center of the circle, place the miniprints face down in a basket. Place all of the children's names in a basket, or use choosing sticks. (Choosing sticks are craft sticks with the child's name written at one end. Place the sticks name-end down into a small

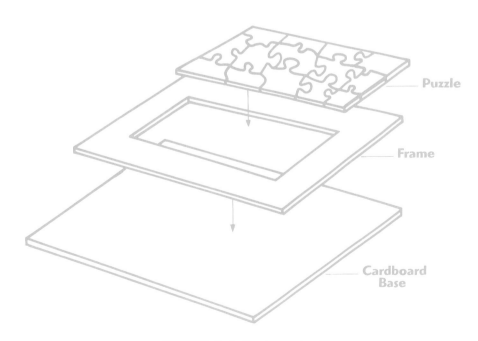

FIGURE 8–1 Puzzle construction

Puzzle

Frame

Cardboard Base

container. Pull a stick to choose a child.) The chosen child picks a miniprint and tries to match it to the larger print.

This game provides an excellent opportunity to explain to the children that prints are photographs of real artworks that are in museums. Demonstrate this by showing a real basket and a print of a basket or some similar artwork, or if there are prints that match some of the artifacts, play the Match Game and have children match the print to the real object. To demonstrate enlargement, show a snapshot-size photograph of something familiar to the children (such as themselves) and an 8-by-10-inch photograph of the same subject. Matching commercial Big Books with the regular versions is another way to reinforce the concept of enlargement. Give the children plenty of time to explore these examples. These are new and difficult concepts for many young children, especially if they have not had much experience with photography.

Miniprint collections. Encourage the children and their families to begin collections of art postcards.

Start them off on a lifelong hobby by giving each child a miniprint in a folder that she or he can decorate. Postcards are widely available, and families can add to their collection when they travel or visit museums. Provide an information sheet for the family about why and how they should create the collection, so it is clear that the postcards should show artwork and not views or local-interest pictures. Provide time for the children to share their collections, and interest them in playing sorting games with their own card sets.

Miniprint gifts. Another way to bring the art of the world into the children's lives is to give them gifts that feature great art. Birthday cards and bookmarks can be made by glueing reproductions of prints clipped from magazines and catalogs onto various sizes and types of paper. Very small prints can be glued to heavy tagboard and made into magnets by sticking magnetic tape on the back. If there is access to a badge maker, make art pins for gifts as well. Whenever giving a print as a gift, be sure to label it with the artist or culture that made it.

Field trips provide children with rich, sensory experiences that add meaning to their art.

HOW CAN COMMUNITY RESOURCES BE USED?

Trips . . . give children an opportunity to see for themselves something they will learn more about later in pictures or in books or through conversation.

—*Rhonda Redleaf (1983, p. 3)*

One way for children to learn about other art forms and the role of art in adult life is for them to meet working artists and to see art in the community. Because most young children have short attention spans, these kinds of activities need to be carefully planned. Although a bad experience can do more harm than no experience, it is not difficult to organize a successful artist visit, art-related field trip, or museum trip. The key is to design the experience so it meets the attention level of the particular children.

Guest Artists

The guest artist can be a friend, a colleague, or a family or community member who creates original art that is relatively portable and not injurious to the children's health. It would not be a good idea to have someone oil paint in the children's room or solder stained glass. The person should genuinely like young children and their infinite curiosity. When inviting artists to visit, make sure to prepare them for the particular group of children, and explain clearly what they should share and say.

It is a good practice to have an information sheet prepared ahead of time to give to families and artists who will visit the class. The information sheet should list the times of the various daily activities, the number of children, their ages, and any particular information about items, such as special needs. There should also be a brief outline on how to design a program for children this age.

Presenting to toddlers. Toddlers respond best to artists who create fairly large pieces that change appearance quickly. Basket making, painting, drawing, pottery, weaving, and sewing quilt squares together are examples of this kind of art activity.

Setup. Squirmy toddlers respond better if the teacher announces the visitor's arrival and directs the artist to

Teacher Tip

It is well worth the effort to create an information sheet to send to guests before they visit. A sample follows:

Guidelines for Guest Artists

1. Bring an unfinished piece to work on and samples of your artwork at various stages.
2. Avoid dangerous tools if possible. If you must bring anything sharp or hot, make sure you have a childproof container for it.
3. Children are more sensitive to toxic materials than adults. Do not bring any solvents, permanent markers, solvent-based glues, oil paints, varnishes, sprays, or dusty materials.
4. Bring only one or two finished pieces that you feel will appeal to young children. Consider how you will display them safely.
5. Bring samples that the children can touch.
6. If possible, bring a "souvenir" of the process that the children can take home.
7. Keep your presentation simple. Prepare questions about your art that you could ask young children, since they have short attention spans. Plan for no longer than 15 minutes.
8. You may also wish to write a letter telling families about your demonstration for the children to take home.

a quiet corner, rather than having the visitor offer a group program. The artist then sets up and begins to work on a sample piece of art. This kind of presentation mirrors Gardner's "skilled master" model (1991, p. 204).

What the guest should say. Toddlers can gather around to watch and ask questions. The visitor should be prepared to answer the children's questions in a simple, understandable way without talking down to them.

Samples. The visitor should bring sample materials and child-safe tools that can be touched by the toddlers. Any dangerous tools should be put away out of sight after each use or, if possible, not used during the demonstration. For example, a quilter could substitute small, blunt scissors for sharp shears when cutting threads.

Presenting to three-year-olds and up. Children ages three and up can benefit from a slightly longer and more complex visit. Before the guest arrives, tell the children about the visit, and ask questions to find out what they already know about this art form. Relate the visit to any explorations or art activities that the children have done by asking intriguing questions such as, "Mrs. Kahn will be showing us how she paints landscapes today. I wonder if she will use an easel like you do when you paint?", or "Mr. Chang will be showing us Chinese calligraphy today. Calligraphy means beautiful writing. Do you think he uses a paintbrush or a pencil?"

Setup. When visitors arrive and have set up their work, gather the children around and introduce them. Let the guests explain what they do, and give a brief demonstration if the art form is suitable for a large group to see clearly, such as working on a large painting or making a good-size basket. The toddler format can be used for demonstrations that are best viewed by small groups of children at a time. If the process is very long, the guest might bring several samples in various stages of completion and then work on one that is just about complete.

Artists should limit the number of displayed fin-ished pieces to only one or two. More than that is too overwhelming for the children. If the pieces are fragile or breakable, then they will need to be displayed in a location where the children cannot touch them. The artist should bring a sample of materials that the children can touch as well. For example, a calligrapher could let the children touch the brush and the ink stone instead of the finished calligraphy.

What the guest should say. Rather than a lecture, the guest should be prepared with interesting questions to ask the children. For example, a quilt maker might ask, "How many pieces do you think are in one square?", or "How big do you think this quilt will be when I have sewn these six squares together?" A calligrapher might ask, "Do I hold the brush the same way you do?" A basket maker might say, "What do you use baskets for?" Teachers may want to offer possible questions to the guest ahead of time.

The guest or teacher may want to read a children's book that relates to the visit, or visitors may have interesting stories to share about when they were young, or how they became artists.

Samples. Just like toddlers, older children need to be able to use their sense of touch as much as possible. Encourage guests to bring a small sample the children can take home with them. A quilter could offer a scrap of cloth that matches the quilt, a basket maker a piece of reed, and a weaver some yarn. Painters can apply paint that matches the painting to a piece of paper; when dry, they can cut it into simple shapes and sign them for the children.

Concluding the visit. Prepare a brief letter to send home to families about the child's experience. This helps families understand the child's new knowledge. The child's "souvenir" can be attached to the letter as well so that it will have a context of meaning once it is home.

After the guest has left, have children participate in making a thank-you card. A nice thank-you is a photograph of the visit. Also take photographs to keep in a scrapbook so children can "read" and remember the experience.

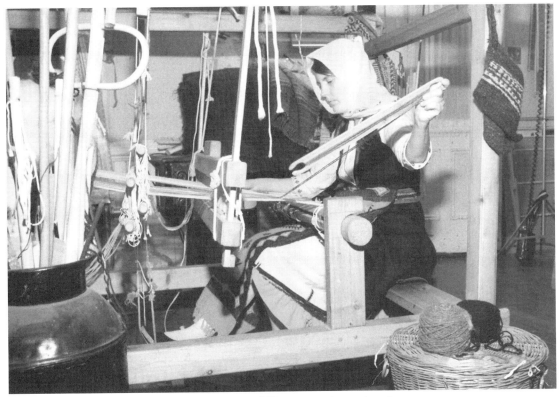

Visits from guest artists teach children that many different people create art.

Visiting an Artist's Studio

Taking a group of young children to an artist's studio can be a major undertaking and is most suitable for older children or a small, mixed-age group with ample supervision. The advantages of such a visit are that artists are often more comfortable working in their own surroundings with all of their supplies on hand. The children also get to see the working environment that the artist has created.

The disadvantages are numerous. The work space may not be large enough or safe enough for young children, and there may be many items that they cannot touch. In cases where artists use materials that are hazardous for young children, a visit to the studio is not advised unless those materials can be cleaned up and put away. The workplace of a painter, an illustrator, a calligrapher, a weaver, a spinner, a basket maker, a quilter, a woodcarver, and a stone sculptor should be relatively safe, with minor adjustments. A printing studio, stained glass studio, pottery studio, or metal workshop may need to be carefully cleaned up, certain processes not demonstrated, and the children closely supervised.

In considering such a field trip, always visit the artist's work space ahead of time. Check for the following features:

1. **Space.** Is there a space large enough for all of the children to gather and observe the artist, or must they take turns? What can the children who are waiting their turn look at or do?

2. **Safety.** Are there any dangers that cannot be removed? What areas does the artist need to clean up? What parts of the process are dangerous for the children?

3. **Preparation.** What do we need to tell the families and children so they will be prepared? Do they need special clothing? What should they look for and point out to the children?

Make sure there is ample supervision for children. Families and other supporting adults should be invited to come and oversee one or two children each. Use the guidelines for guest artists to plan the actual presentation.

Visiting Museums

Most museums are not set up to deal with groups of young children. The "look-but-don't-touch" nature of the displays usually means that the children cannot use their natural learning impulses and thus spend the visit constrained and unhappy, leaving them with a dislike for museum going that may last all of their lives. The exception is the children's museum, of which numerous versions have sprung up around the country. These museums are set up to engage children of all ages in activities that involve the arts and sciences. If such a museum is in the vicinity, do take advantage of the wonderful features it offers. Again, make sure to visit the site ahead of time, and arrange for adequate supervision.

Other Places to Visit

Young children may also enjoy a visit to a piece of public sculpture if there is an example within walking distance. Public sculptures are often found in parks or near government and university buildings. Outdoor sculpture gardens attached to museums may also make a good experience. When visiting these locations, go prepared with a list of questions to focus the children on the visual elements of the pieces, and find out something about the artist who made it. Because these sculptural forms are separated from the artist and very different from their own art, children often have difficulty recognizing them as art and treat them more like unusual playground equipment. Expect such visits to be brief, and perhaps tie them in with a trip to another location.

Reconstructions of older historical homes or farm sites may demonstrate traditional handicrafts from earlier times, such as wool spinning or candle making. These places are usually set up to handle groups, and they may shorten and customize their presentation for young visitors. There is often a real story to make the place come alive for children.

HOW CAN CHILDREN'S LITERATURE BE USED TO TEACH ART?

Even if teachers do not own any art prints, do not know any artists, or live far from suitable museums, they can still introduce children to great art. The picture books that teachers read to children are also pieces of art. For many children it is the picture that first entices them to the world of books, and books for the very youngest children are often wordless. In selecting books to share with young artists, always consider the importance of the pictures, not just as illustrations of the story but also as aesthetic statements.

Picture books can be chosen on the same basis as artworks. Make sure that a variety of artistic media, styles, and cultures is represented in the books that are offered. Specific descriptions of a multitude of children's books are found in appendix B. Make sure to have some examples from the following categories to introduce to the children.

1. **Caldecott Winners.** The Caldecott award is given each year to an outstandingly illustrated children's book. Select those that are on the children's level (see appendix B).
2. **Media.** Look for books that illustrate some of the less common art techniques, such as *Red Leaf Yellow Leaf* (Ehlert, 1991), which uses natural materials in collages to create three-dimensional images. *Sing a Song of Sixpence* (Reid, 1987) has illustrations made from plasticine, *Draw Me a Star* (Carle, 1992) uses painted and printed papers in collage, and *Bitter Bananas* (Olabye, 1994) features chalk over cut-paper collages.
3. **Multicultural.** Include books that feature art forms from other cultures, such as *Totem Pole* (Hoyt-Goldsmith, 1990), which tells how a totem pole is made, and *Abuela's Weave* (Castaneda, 1993), which tells how weaving fits into the life of a girl and her grandmother in Guatemala.
4. **Big Books.** For group sharing, have several Big Books in which the children can easily see the illustrations. More and more books are now available in this format. Appendix B indicates books that are available as Big Books.

Sharing Books with Children

It is not necessary to read every word or the whole book. If the children are wiggly, simplify the text. Talk about the pictures. Point to objects, and say their names. If there are unfamiliar objects in the pictures, introduce them slowly—only a few at a time. Compare them to familiar things that the children know.

Children enjoy books with repetitious and rhythmic text. After several readings, they will read along. Use an expressive voice. Change the tone for different characters. It is not necessary to read a book as written. Use the illustrations to inspire storytelling and different uses for the book. Ask children to predict what will happen next, before the page is turned.

CONCLUSION: BECOMING AN ARTIST

When children are surrounded by artworks, photographs, collections of beautiful things—and all their own attempts are encouraged—they will begin to value art.

—Gaelene Rowe (1987, p. 5)

Children need to experience a wide variety of art forms. Bringing the art of the world to our children enriches us all.

Art is much more than the physical act of manipulating art materials. Art is also looking at, talking about, and appreciating the art of others. Teachers dedicated to educating the whole child must provide children with opportunities not only to explore the process of art but also to experience a broad range of artwork. In doing so, they introduce children to the artistic heritage of humankind and the long continuum of creativity that it represents.

It will take effort on the teacher's part to do this. Putting markers out on a table is simpler and more immediate than learning about a piece of artwork and the culture that created it, and then designing a way to explain it to young children. But adults who work with children must never stop learning. We must dedicate ourselves to becoming as knowledgeable about art as we can be. Our lives will be richer, as will the lives of the children we touch. Together we will approach the crayons on the table, the play dough on the tray, and the paint at the easel with a new respect and sense of purpose.

FURTHER READING

Brooks, S. W., & Sentori, S. M. (1988). *See the paintings!* Rosemount, NJ: Modern Learning Press.
This book is a guidebook to presenting reproductions of paintings to children. Although it is directed to elementary-level students, many of the ideas can be adapted to younger children as well.

Mesrobian, J. (1992). Rediscovering the Ninja Turtles' namesakes. *Day Care and Early Education, 20*(1), 18–19.
A practicing teacher describes how she introduced fine art prints to her preschoolers.

Parsons, M. J. (1987). *How we understand art.* New York: Cambridge University Press.
Based on his research, Parsons presents the way children at different ages respond to different types of paintings.

Wolf, A. D. (1984). *Mommy, it's a Renoir!* Altoona, PA: Parent Child Press.
This book presents a systematic approach to introducing children to fine art through the use of art cards.

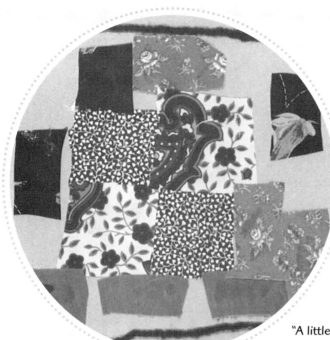

Creating Art: Fiber Art

"A little quilt. I used the scraps from my mom's big quilt."
Fabric collage—*Susan, age 5*

THE FIBER ART EXPERIENCE

Fiber art refers to any art form that involves the use of yarn, cloth, or the raw materials that are used to make them. Because fabric plays such an important role in everyday life in terms of clothing and furnishings, it is often seen as a functional object rather than an art form. Yet even the most simple piece of clothing bears the mark of unnamed artists who determined the shape of its pieces, the drape of the fabric, and its texture and pattern.

Introducing fiber art to children helps them appreciate this often "hidden" and ancient art, which has found unique expression and form throughout time and across cultures. It is an excellent example of an art medium that can serve as a unifying theme for young children. Fiber activities can be used as part of the thematic study of texture, line, pattern, and growing things.

How Children Grow through Fiber Art Activities

Children will develop

1. physically, by using hand-eye coordination and small muscles in repetitive patterns. (Bodily-Kinesthetic)
2. socially, by working with others to create fiber art, and by sharing materials. (Interpersonal)
3. emotionally, by using fiber art materials in an expressive way. (Intrapersonal)
4. visual perception skills, by working with patterned space in three-dimensional fiber materials. (Spatial)
5. language, by learning fiber art terms and by talking about the fiber art of their own creation and that of others. (Linguistic)
6. cognitively, by observing and analyzing changes in raw materials as they are processed, and by learning to identify and create patterns. (Logical-Mathematical)
7. art awareness, by gaining knowledge about the art of others, through touching and talking about different examples of fiber art.

EXPLORING FIBER PREPARATION
AGES TWO AND UP

Children enjoy seeing raw fiber change as it is cleaned and prepared.

Group Composition

Pairs or a small group of three to six children.

Materials

- ✿ One-half pound raw wool (Raw wool can be obtained from a sheep farmer, or consult the sources in appendix A.)
- ✿ Three dishpans
- ✿ Detergent
- ✿ Fabric softener

Setup

1. Fill each pan with warm water.
2. Add one-quarter cup detergent to first two pans.
3. Add a capful of softener to last pan.
4. Place pans in row on table, low counter, floor, or outside.
5. Children will move from pan to pan down the row.

Warm-Up

If possible, visit a sheep farm, or observe sheep at a zoo. Watch a video of sheep and shearing. Compare shearing to cutting hair. Children are often concerned that shearing hurts the sheep. Fill the room with pictures, toys, and models of sheep and examples of wool yarn and clothing.

What to Do

1. Have child take a small handful of wool.
2. Place in first pan and pull it apart.
3. Squeeze gently, and move it to second pan.
4. Pull it apart and move it gently in water until clean.
5. Rinse in last pan.
6. Place near heater or in sun to dry. Turn often.
7. When dry, fluff by pulling it apart. Use it in collages, in a stuff bin, or for dyeing and spinning.

Classroom Museum

Display and discuss a handwoven woolen garment or piece of fabric.

What to Say

Ask: "Why does the wool change color when it's washed?", and "How does it feel before and after it is washed?" Words to use: wool, fleece, fiber, and grease.

Making Connections

Language. Read *Charlie Needs a Cloak* (dePaola, 1973). Even the youngest children love the delightfully mischievous sheep in this simple story of converting wool to a cloak.

Math. Measure the temperature and/or quantity of the water used for washing the wool.

Science. Experiment with different temperatures of water and amounts of detergent. Which combination produces the cleanest wool?

Social Studies. Talk about the different articles of clothing that can be made from wool, such as sweaters, socks, and hats. Bring in examples from different places in the world, and look for similarities and differences.

EXPLORING DYEING
AGES TWO AND UP

This activity can directly follow the washing of the wool or can be done after it is spun into yarn.

Group Composition

Small groups of three to six children.

Materials

- ☼ Washed wool or yarn (Cotton fabric can also be used. Results will be paler and less permanent. Cut the fabric into four-inch squares.)
- ☼ Dye materials: unsweetened, dry packaged soft drink mix* such as Kool-Aid, or natural plant materials (see table 8–4)
- ☼ Crock-Pot (Set up on a counter where children can see the process but not touch the pot when it is hot.)
- ☼ Water
- ☼ Wooden spoon or tongs
- ☼ Rubber gloves
- ☼ Dishpan

Warm-Up

Transition into this activity by going for a walk and collecting some plant materials that produce dye.

Classroom Museum

Set out a basket of yarn that has been dyed in natural colors, or display hand-dyed fabrics from around the world, such as tie dye, batik, and ikat.

Serve drink mix for snack, and encourage children to wonder about the color. Create a chart showing the children's predictions about which color the different dyestuffs will make on the wool or cloth.

What to Do

1. Have children place a small amount of wool, yarn, or a cotton square in Crock-Pot.
2. Cover with water.
3. Sprinkle one or more flavors of drink mix over the materials, or add the plant materials. Allow children to select colors or plant matter.
4. Move the Crock-Pot to the counter, turn on high, and cover.
5. Stir plant dyes occasionally. Do not stir drink-mix dyes.
6. Heat until it simmers. Check color. If saturated enough, remove and place in dishpan, using rubber gloves and spoon or tongs. If it needs to cook longer, turn Crock-Pot to low, and simmer until color is deeper.
7. Once removed, rinse in cool water. Let dry near heater or in sun.
8. Make a chart showing a piece of the plant material and then a sample of the dyed wool, yarn, or cloth, and then put the dyed materials in a collage or stuff bin, or use in another fiber activity.

What to Say

Ask: "How long do you think it will take to change color?", and "What color will it be?" Words to use: dye, dyed, color names, hot, and cool.

TABLE 8–4	Safe, Natural Dye Sources for Young Children

PLANT	COLOR PRODUCED
Apple leaves	Green, yellow
Blackberry shoots	Green, yellow
Carrot tops	Green, yellow
Dock (edible weed)	Yellow
Grape leaves	Yellow
Indian corn (the black kernels; also blue corn)	Blue, gray
Onion skins	Orange
Tea	Brown, orange
Walnut hulls	Brown

More to Do

Try tie dye. Using cloth, create a tie-dyed effect by wrapping sections of the cloth with tightly wound rubber bands.

Quilt it. Dyed cloth pieces can later be sewed or glued to create a quilt or wall hanging.

Making Connections

Language. Read the dyeing sections in *Songs from the Loom: A Navajo Girl Learns to Weave* (Roessel, 1995, pp. 34–36). If necessary, simplify the story for younger children. Then have children make their own books about dyeing the yarn, illustrating them with draw-ings, photographs, and samples of dyed plants and dyed yarn and cloth.

Math. Time how long it takes for the wool to change color.

Science. Identify the different plant parts used for dyeing: leaves, stems, skin of root (onion), and seed case (walnut).

Social Studies. Compare colors of hand-dyed yarn and cloth to that worn by children. Which are more colorful? Why do people like wearing colorful cloth-ing? Look at photographs of crowds of people from different places in the world or at different kinds of celebrations. Are certain colors of clothing more com-mon than others?

PICKING AND CARDING WOOL AGES TWO AND UP

Before wool can be converted into yarn and cloth, it must be cleaned. Picking is the process of removing debris from the fleece. Carding is like combing hair to remove tangles.

"I liked playing with the wool, except when it stuck to my fingers. We made it blue with that drink mix stuff." Fleece collage—Susan, age 5

Group Composition

Whole group or small group. Have children sitting in a circle or around a table.

Materials

- Hair combs
- Washed and/or dyed wool
- Hand cards or dog combs

Warm-Up

Give each child a hair comb, and let the child comb her or his own hair. Then demonstrate how wool is combed before spinning, and let each child compare the two processes.

What to Do

Following washing of the wool:

1. Demonstrate how to pull it apart to make it fluffy, and pick out any large pieces of hay or other veg-etable matter.
2. Give each child a small piece of wool to "pick."
3. Place picked wool in center of table or circle.
4. Demonstrate how to card the wool by pulling it across the teeth of the cards or combs to straighten the fiber.

5. Pass cards or combs around the circle. Invite children to take pieces of picked wool from center and try carding. Colors may be mixed to create new blends. Other children can continue picking while waiting a turn to card.

What to Say

Ask: "How is this like combing your hair?", and "How does it feel before and after carding?" Words to use: wool, carders, and picking.

More to Do

Make collages. Use picked and carded wool for collages, stuff bins, or spinning.

Make a chart. Attach wool in different stages of preparation to a wall chart.

Record the process. Have children draw pictures of the carding process.

Making Connections

Language. Children age four and up enjoy the story *A New Coat for Anna* (Ziefert, 1986). The story's theme of cooperation can be compared to how the children cooperated in carding the wool.

Math. Glue carded fibers to cardboard, and then have children measure their length. Are they all the same, or do they vary?

Teacher Tip

Determining Group Composition

The number of children who can participate at one time in many of these activities will vary, depending on their age and skill. Fiber art activities are particularly successful with mixed-age groups. Some of the activities here may be too complicated for toddlers or younger preschoolers to do on their own, but they may be able to do a part of the activity when paired with older children or adults. The activities in this Creating Art section have been labeled suitable for a whole group (15 to 25), a small group (4 to 6), and pairs.

Science. Experiment with different kinds of cards or combs. Which works fastest? Which is easiest to use?

Social Studies. Compare wool carders and combs to the hair combs used by the children. Make a display of different kinds of combs and brushes. Look at comb designs from different cultures. Invite children to invent their own comb designs and draw pictures of them.

EXPLORING SPINNING AGES THREE AND UP

Hand spinning is an ancient process. In cultures where hand spinning is still done, children learn at very young ages. Successful spinning requires the repetition of a simple movement pattern. Children are thrilled when they see fluffy fiber turn to yarn.

Group Composition

Pairs. This activity works extremely well with mixed ages, such as a five-year-old and a three-year-old. Have children sit opposite each other at a table.

Materials

- Spindles: Screw a cup hook into the end of a 12-inch length of a quarter-inch diameter dowel.
- Spindle whorls: A whorl is the weight that goes at the end of the spindle. Stick a potato or an apple on the end. (This is a traditional practice in South America and Europe.) A wheel from a toy vehicle or a plasticine ball can also be used. If firing clay is available, spindle whorls can be made by flattening a ball of clay and poking a dowel-size hole in the center. Making clay whorls to use for spinning is a good project for children ages four or older. Have children draw designs in the whorls and then fire them unglazed.
- Washed and carded wool, stretched out into thin pieces, each about 12 inches long (or use commercial roving)

Warm-Up

Transition into this activity by inviting a spinner to demonstrate, or use an activity from the Making Connections section.

What to Do

1. Demonstrate how the wool can be twisted into yarn with the fingers, then let the children try it.
2. Attach finger-twisted yarn to hook of spindle by wrapping it around several times.
3. Tell the children that one will be the "pincher" and the other will be the "spinner." Later they can switch roles so both get a turn at each job.

Classroom Museum

Display and discuss skeins of hand-spun yarn and/or a garment or cloth made from hand-spun yarn.

4. The pincher will pinch the wool about one inch above the hook. The other child holds the top of the spindle while resting the bottom on the table. The spinner then turns the spindle five or six turns.
5. The spinner stops the spindle, and the pincher slides his or her fingers up about an inch. The pincher must never let go completely or the wool will untwist. Then the spinner spins again.
6. Repeat this pattern—pinch wool, turn spindle, stop spindle, slide fingers up—until a length of

Spinning yarn is a wonderful partner project. Children are fascinated to see the fluffy wool turn to yarn.

yarn has been spun. It helps if the children chant, "Pinch. Turn. Stop. Slide," as they work.

7. At this point, if the children are very young, remove the yarn from the spindle. For older children, demonstrate how to remove the yarn from the hook, wrap the wool around the spindle, and re-attach the end to the hook. Then holding the end and a new piece of roving, give it several turns to attach the new piece.

8. The yarn will tend to untwist when removed from the spindle. Put the two ends together, and let the yarn twist into a "two-ply" yarn.

What to Say

Ask: "How does the wool change?", and "Which way is it stronger, before or after spinning?" Words to use include pinch, spin, yarn, thick, thin, fast, slow, lumpy, smooth, and twist.

More to Do

Use the yarn in a collage or for weaving.

Making Connections

Language. *The Goat in the Rug* (Blood & Link, 1980) is another appealing story about fiber processing for young children. It introduces angora goats.

Math. Measure or compare the finished lengths of yarn.

Science. Tie weights to the spun yarn to test its strength. Is thick yarn stronger than thin yarn? Does it make a difference how tightly twisted it is?

Teacher Tip

The following simplified steps can be repeated until the pattern is learned. It usually takes children about five to ten minutes to learn to work independently.

Spinning Steps

Help child wrap carded wool around hook. Then say as you guide:

- Pinch (Pinch wool above hook.)
- Spin (Turn spindle.)
- Hold (Hold spindle still while partner slides finger up about an inch.)
- Pinch (Pinch wool again.)

To continue spinning, repeat the steps pinch, spin, and hold. To make yarn longer, unwrap from hook and wind around spindle. Reattach end to hook. Hold wool and yarn end together, and spin several times.

Social Studies. Make a display of different fiber plants, fiber samples, and yarns such as silk, cotton, linen, and ramie. Discuss why some fibers are better for warm climates and others for cold climates.

✋ EXPLORING WEAVING AGES THREE AND UP

Many young children have difficulty with weaving activities that require them to go over and under in a regular pattern. The following activities allow children to see how the weaving process is done but are open ended enough so that all of the children can participate successfully.

Group Composition

Pairs.

Materials

- ☼ Yarn, ribbon, shoe laces, or string
- ☼ Commercial vertical floor or table loom (see figure 8–2 and see also appendix A), or
- ☼ Large frame with fine chicken wire or yarn stretched across it and mounted vertically on floor or table. If using chicken wire, make sure rough edges are covered with tape.

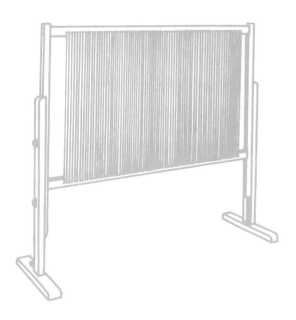

FIGURE 8–2 Partner loom

Classroom Museum

Display and discuss handwoven fabrics. Guatemalan, Mexican, and South American textiles are available from many sources (see appendix A).

Warm-Up

Transition into weaving by inviting a weaver to bring a small loom for the children to see and try operating, or pull apart a piece of cloth (burlap works well) to see the yarn from which it is made.

What to Do

1. Set up the loom. Chicken wire is easier for the children than the yarn. The activity may be introduced with the chicken wire first and then later set up with yarn.
2. Have two children face each other with the loom between them. One child pushes a piece of yarn or other material through the holes in the chicken wire or between the stretched yarns. Then the other child takes the end and pushes it back through to the partner. If necessary, wrap tape around the ends of the yarn. Use the song "Go in and out the Windows" to reinforce the pattern. Children may weave in any direction.
3. As the weaving grows and changes, take time to talk about the patterns that form.

What to Say

Ask "What is the texture of the weaving?", "How do the different yarns change how it feels and looks?", "What patterns do you see?" Words to use include over, under, back, front, yarn, and weave.

More to Do

Weave in other ways. Plastic berry baskets can be used for weaving by individual children.

Sing and move. Play "In and out the Window." Have all children but one stand in circle holding hands. Children lift their arms as the child weaves in and out between them as the song is sung. Continue until all children have had a turn to "weave."

Making Connections

Language. Share *The Rug Makers* (Allen, 1991), which describes in simple language a day in the life of a young boy from India.

Math/Science. Compare different lengths and kinds of yarns.

Teacher Tip

When Are Children Ready to Do Fiber Art Activities?

Most fiber art activities require specific fine motor and visual perception skills. In order to be successful at most of these activities, the children need to have certain abilities. They should be able to

1. pick up or grasp small objects with thumb and index fingers.
2. rotate an object in one direction at a constant speed.
3. push and pull small objects with thumb and index fingers.
4. identify top and bottom, front and back, and inside and outside.
5. repeat a patterned motion.

EXPLORING STITCHING AND SEWING AGES THREE AND UP

Sewing two pieces of cloth together is too difficult for many young children. The following activity helps them develop skills that can later be used with cloth.

Group Composition

Small group.

Materials

- Sanitized Styrofoam trays
- Large-eyed, three-inch plastic needles
- Yarn

Warm-Up

Children do not often notice how clothing is put together. Have an embroiderer, a seamstress, or a tailor visit and demonstrate sewing work, or wear an embroidered garment or point out one a child is wearing. Take an old garment apart at the seams to see how it is put together. Have children find seams and stitches on their own clothing.

What to Do

1. Thread a large number of needles with different colors of yarn, in 12-to-16-inch lengths. Double the yarn, and make a large knot at the end.
2. Demonstrate: Show children how to punch holes in the Styrofoam or paper with the needle and how to pull the yarn through from one side to the other.
3. Invite children to select a threaded needle, and push it in and out of the tray. Do not expect children to make neat stitches. For most, this will be an exploration. It will take many stitching explorations before a child understands how to go from front to back in a patterned way. If children are to acquire this skill, they need many opportunities to practice it.
4. When the yarn is used up, cut off needle and tape end to back of tray.

What to Say

Ask, "How many stitches have you made?", and "Look how the yarn makes lines." Words to use include in, out, front, back, needle, stitch, and yarn.

Classroom Museum

Hmong embroidered and appliquéd pieces can be displayed and discussed. Embroidery is also used in the traditional dress of many cultures such as Ukrainian, Greek, Chinese, and Indian.

More to Do

Provide other surfaces. Pre-punch holes in a piece of cardboard for children to use.

Draw lines. After children have had time to practice stitching through the tray, invite them to draw some lines on the tray with a pencil, and then try following them with stitches.

Try cloth. When children understand how to stitch from front to back regularly, introduce an open-weave cloth such as burlap that a needle will pass through easily. Start with free stitching, and then invite children to draw some lines to follow.

Make a wall hanging. Join the children's cloth stitchery to create a large group piece, or have children take turns working on a large piece of burlap.

Move creatively. Have children hold hands in a line. The first child is the needle and threads through the line, ducking under the uplifted arms. Still clasping hands, the others follow.

Making Connections

Language. Read *Nine-in-One, Grr! Grr!* (Xiong, 1989), a folktale of the Hmong people of Southeast Asia. This book is illustrated with stitched and appliquéd story cloths, traditional Hmong narrative needlework.

Math. Measure items in a room using equal-length pieces of yarn. Create a pictograph.

Science. Experiment with other ways to join cloth, such as glue, staples, and tape. Which is strongest?

EXPLORING APPLIQUÉ
AGES TWO AND UP

Appliqué is an art form in which cloth shapes are sewn on top of other cloth pieces.

Group Composition

Small group.

Materials

- Precut felt pieces (in a variety of colors and shapes)
- Glue
- Heavy paper, cardboard, or felt base (about 9-by-9 inches, or larger)

Warm-Up

Invite an appliqué artist to visit, or wear an appliquéd garment or point out one worn by a child. Talk about how one piece of cloth is put on top of another. Identify shapes found in an example of appliqué.

What to Do

1. Place materials at a table.
2. Encourage exploration of how different pieces look when placed over and under others.
3. Glue down into a collage.

What to Say

Ask, "Which shapes are on top?", "Which are underneath?", and "What textures do you feel?" Words to use include under, over, overlap, shape names, and texture words.

More to Do

Try different cloth. Vary the activity by offering other types of materials, such as cottons and velvets.

Try a different base. Glue cloth pieces onto burlap or heavy cotton.

Classroom Museum

Display and discuss examples of appliqué—in a handmade quilt, in Hmong needlework, or in a mola from Panama (see appendix A).

Add stitches. If children have mastered basic sewing, use burlap as a base for glued-down shapes. Then have children add simple stitching to their works.

Hang it up. Glue a strip of heavy cardboard to the top back of the children's projects. Attach yarn to each end to hang it.

Explore the sewing machine. Bring in a sewing machine. Have children imagine how it works, and then draw their ideas. Next, open it up and examine the working parts. Draw it again. Use the machine to sew the top edges of the children's projects, and insert a dowel to hang them up.

Making Connections

Language. Read *Mole's Hill* (Ehlert, 1994). This book features traditional Native American appliqué designs.

Math. Have children sort felt shapes by color, size, or shape before using them in their appliqué.

Science. Explore opaque, translucent, and transparent materials. What happens when they overlap?

Social Studies. Display and talk about the inlaid appliqué molas made by the Kuna Indians of Panama.

MAKING YARN PICTURES AGES TWO AND UP

Because of the linear nature of yarn, it can be used to create a "drawing." Yarn can be difficult for young children to handle. Use short lengths of heavy yarn in the beginning.

Group Composition

Small group.

Materials

- Yarn (different colors and thicknesses, 4 to 12 inches long)
- Contact paper (stapled sticky side up to a paper or cardboard base), or
- Paper (on which white glue has been spread)

Warm-Up

Collect short pieces of yarn, and put them in a stuff bin. Invite the children to explore the way they can bend and twist the yarn together. Have children imagine that they are pieces of yarn that are stretched, bent, folded, twisted, and so on. Have them join hands to form longer pieces of yarn, and then wrap around furniture in the room or trees and playground equipment outside.

What to Do

1. Demonstrate: Show children how to press the yarn onto the contact paper or glued surface.
2. If using the glued surface, provide damp paper towels to wipe fingers so yarn does not stick to them.

What to Say

Ask, "How did you get the yarn to stay there?", "Did you put the glue on the paper first?", and "Do any pieces of yarn cross other ones?" Words to use include

Classroom Museum

Display and discuss Huichol yarn paintings (see appendix A). Find lines, shapes, symmetry, and patterns.

line descriptions; thick, thinly stretched, bend, and folded.

Transition Out

Have children wipe their fingers on the paper towel before rinsing at the sink. Put clear wrap over the contact paper pictures for protection. Tape around to the back. Place glued yarn pictures in drying box or on table to dry.

More to Do

Use yarn in other activities. Give children practice glueing yarn by encouraging them to add yarn to their collages, puppets, and masks.

Glue yarn to cloth. Once children are skilled in gluing yarn to paper, challenge them to create yarn pictures on felt and burlap backgrounds.

Making Connections

Language. Read sections from "Mariano Valadez of the Huichol Tribe" in *Native Artists of North America* (Moore, 1993b), or create your own Big Book based on this information.

Math. Measure each child's height using a piece of yarn. Invite children to use the yarn to find other things that are about the same height.

EXPLORING QUILTING
AGES TWO AND UP

Because quilt making involves creating a whole from parts, it is an ideal art form for cooperative activities. Quilts often represent family traditions and cultural heritage. A rich body of children's literature features quilts.

Group Composition

Whole group.

Materials

- Squares of cloth (have each child bring in a 9-inch square).
- Glue, or
- Invite someone to sew it together.

Warm-Up

Have a quilter visit, or share a handmade quilt with the children. Read a story about quilting. Point out the patterns in the quilts.

What to Do

1. Have children stand in a circle with their quilt squares.
2. Invite them to take turns placing their square on the floor so that it touches the other ones.
3. Describe the patterns that are created.
4. Challenge the children to place their squares so that a rectangle is formed.
5. Have children retrieve their squares, and then create a new arrangement. This can be repeated several times in a row, or on different days. Use this opportunity to develop two concepts: (1) a whole is created from its parts, and (2) a pattern is created from the repetition of an element.
6. After several rearrangements, ask the children to make a final arrangement for the finished quilt. If the quilt will be glued together, put out a large sheet of paper. As children place their squares, apply glue to the paper in those spots. Emphasize that each piece must touch another.
7. If the quilt will be sewn, arrange the pieces on the floor, and then gather them up by rows. Have a parent or volunteer sew the pieces together during

Classroom Museum

Display and discuss quilts of all kinds, such as the work of Harriet Powers, Faith Ringgold, Michael Cummings (MAPS: African-American), Amish quilts, early American quilts, and more. Create quilt matching cards from catalogs and calendars.

class time, so the children can participate in the excitement of seeing the quilt grow together. The quilt top can be left as it is and used for dramatic play, or it can be stuffed and finished, destined to become a favorite spot to cuddle. Or give it as a gift to a nursing home or other needy group with which the children have a relationship.

What to Say

Ask, "Can you count the squares?", "How many are in a row?", and "What patterns do you see?" Words to use include quilt, pieces, pattern, row, repeated, stitch, and bind.

More to Do

Make a crayon quilt. Have children use white or light-colored cloth squares, and draw on them with crayons. Iron the crayoned cloth (not in the same room as the children because of the fumes) to make it permanent.

Vary the pieces. Use equilateral, triangle-shaped cloth pieces.

Dye the pieces. Use fabric squares that have been tie-dyed in tea.

Print the pieces. Use fabric squares that have been printed by the children.

Making Connections

Language. There are many books about quilt making. *The Boy and the Quilt* (Kurtz, 1991) features a little boy making his first quilt. Young children will enjoy his delightful independence. *Eight Hands Round: A Patchwork Alphabet* (Paul, 1991) presents different quilt patterns and their history.

Math. Offer pattern blocks and color tiles with which to make sample quilt patterns.

Have children line up in an alternating pattern, based on their clothing, such as light and dark, or long sleeves and short sleeves.

Science. Look for patterns in nature—on a turtle's back, a tiger-striped cat, on insects, and more.

Art Words

Fiber Art

Appliqué
A design made by attaching pieces of cloth to a fabric background.

Basket
A container woven from twigs, reeds, or other sturdy fiber.

Carding
Brushing wool fibers to straighten them.

Dye
Any substance that changes the color of a material.

Embroidery
A design made with thread on cloth.

Fiber
A fine, threadlike material.

Fiber art
Art forms that use fibers or materials created from fiber such as weaving, appliqué, and embroidery.

Hand spun
Yarn that has been made by hand.

Loom
A frame or machine on which yarn is stretched for weaving cloth.

Natural dye
A dye obtained from plant materials, such as flowers, leaves, or bark.

Quilt
A fabric design created by piecing together smaller bits of fabric.

Spindle
A stick used to twist and hold yarn as it is spun.

Spinning
The process of turning fiber into yarn.

Stitchery
A design made with yarn or cloth.

Story cloth
Appliquéd and embroidered textiles, made by the Hmong people of Southeast Asia, which record traditional folktales and personal life stories.

Table loom
A loom small enough to be used on a table.

Textile
A woven fabric.

Tie-dye
A design made by tying parts of a cloth together and then dying it.

Vertical loom
A loom on which the yarns for weaving (warp) are held vertically to the ground.

Weaving
The process of creating fabric by interlocking threads and yarns.

Whorl
A weight on the end of a hand spindle.

Teaching in Action

Thematic Unit Ideas:
Why Do We Wear the Clothes We Do?

The type and kind of clothing worn daily is an important facet of a young child's life. Getting into and out of complicated clothing, bundling up in cold weather or dressing lightly in the heat, and feeling comfortable or irritated by the fit or texture of a garment all directly influence how a child feels. Begin the thematic study by building on this interest. There are many ways to do this. One way is to wear an unusual handmade garment, or comment on a new outfit that a child is wearing, and then follow up with any or all of the following:

- Compare this piece of clothing with that worn by other children. Notice the colors and textures in the different garments.

- Make charts and pictographs of the clothing children are wearing.

- Make a web of all of the different items of clothing children can name.

- Ask children how they think clothing is made and how it is colored, and record their ideas on a KWL (what we Know; what we Wonder about; what we want to Learn)chart to return to later in the unit.

- Have children draw pictures of themselves wearing different types of clothing in different settings, such as in school, at night, on a cold day, or at the swimming pool or beach.

Initial Event

Follow up these activities with a visit by a fiber artist, such as a weaver, a knitter, an embroiderer, a quilter, or a dressmaker. Try to have this visitor come over a period of several days, and make a complete garment from beginning to end, so children can see the entire process. A small piece of clothing for one of the children's dolls or stuffed animals would be particularly motivating for children. Document the visit by taking photographs or making a videotape of the visitor at work, and have the children record what they see by drawing in theme journals.

Follow up this event by having the visitor and parents work with small groups of children doing some of the different fiber art activities described in this Creating Art section.

More to Do

Supplement the fiber art activities with ones selected from the Making Connections sections. Also try the following:

- Visit a children's clothing store. Have children make drawings of the clothing displays. Older children can put together an outfit and calculate the cost.

- Put out long pieces of wildly printed and richly textured fabric, such as velours and taffetas, and encourage children to make up new outfits for the dramatic play area.

continued

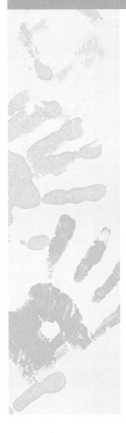

Teaching in Action   *continued*

- Investigate special clothing worn for different occupations. Have a firefighter, football player, ballet dancer, or construction worker come and explain why he or she dresses the way he or she does.

- Invite children to wear certain colors or types of clothing on special days, such as sweatsuit day or beach day. Plan special activities to go with the clothing. Sweatsuit day, for example, could focus on exercising activities.

- Cut out simple vest shapes from brown paper grocery bags, and have children decorate them with printed designs or drawn symbols representing possible future careers.

- Make an attractive display of cloth scraps, laces, ribbons, and trims, arranged by color and texture, for the collage area.

- Display paintings showing people from different times and places wearing a variety of clothing styles. For example, introduce some of the following (all from the National Gallery): *The Hobby Horse* (Anonymous), *Anne with a Green Parasol* (Bellows), *Little Girl in Lavender* (Bradley), *White Cloud* (Catlin), *Italian Girl* (Corot), *Marchesa Brigida* (Rubens).

- Explore different ways clothing is fastened—zippers, buttons, laces, and hook-and-loop tape. Add buttons to the collage offerings.

- Extend the study to include footwear, jewelry, hairstyles, and masks.

Studio Page 29

ARTWORK STUDY

Select an original piece of art, a print, or an artifact that interests you. Record the following information:

Title _____

Artist/Culture _____

Media _____

Description/Story _____

_____

_____

Based on this artwork, write an example of each type of question you could ask children.

1. What does it tell you about?

    _____

2. How was it made?

    _____

3. Can you find? (art elements)

    _____

4. How does it make you feel?

    _____

5. What comes next?

    _____

6. How many? (related curriculum question)

    _____

7. Can you? (kinesthetic response question)

    _____

COMPARING ARTWORK

Select two pieces of artwork with some similarity, such as subject, media, colors, artist, or culture. Describe each piece.

ARTWORK 1:   Title _____

Artist/Culture _____

Media _____

Description/Story _____

ARTWORK 2:   Title _____

Artist/Culture _____

Media _____

Description/Story _____

Write three questions that would help children focus on the similarities in the artwork.

1. _____

2. _____

3. _____

Write three questions that would help children focus on the differences in the artwork.

1. _____

2. _____

3. _____

Studio Page 31

SELF-EXPLORATION: MY ARTISTIC HERITAGE

What is your cultural background?

_____

_____

What artwork did you have in your home when you were growing up?

_____

_____

As a child, did you know anyone who was an artist?

_____

_____

As a child, did you visit museums?

_____

_____

As a child, did you have any favorite piece or type of art?

_____

_____

As a child, was there any artwork you hated?

_____

_____

In your home now you have the following pieces of artwork:

_____

_____

Do these pieces reflect your artistic heritage, another family member's, and/or choices made based on what you have learned about art as an adult?

_____

_____

Studio Page 32

SELF-EXPLORATION: MY VIEW OF ART NOW

I think it is important to learn about art created by others because:

_____

_____

_____

_____

_____

_____

_____

I would like to learn more about the art of:

_____

_____

_____

_____

_____

_____

_____

_____

If I could own any piece of artwork ever created, I would choose:

_____

_____

_____

_____

_____

_____

_____

For additional information on teaching art to young children, visit our Web site at http://www.earlychilded.delmar.com

Creating a Place for Art

Questions Addressed in This Chapter:

- ❍ What kind of environment is needed for art?
- ❍ How should the art environment be arranged?
- ❍ How should art supplies be organized?
- ❍ How is an aesthetic environment created?

Young Artists at Work

Michael takes his paper and crayons and crawls under the table. Lying on his stomach, he draws and draws and draws.

Katina slowly looks through the plastic bins on the shelf. Carefully she selects a piece of ribbon, a gold button, and a piece of shiny silver paper. Then she carries her treasures to the table, eager to make her collage.

Suddenly it grows dark, and rain starts hitting the windows. The children stop what they are doing and run to the window. One boy puts his finger on the window and traces the path of the raindrops.

WHAT KIND OF ENVIRONMENT IS NEEDED FOR ART?

A site for art needs to encompass bold energetic expression and studied, time-consuming precision, solitary work, and social kibitzing.

—*Jim Greenman (1988, p. 162)*

Environment is anything that surrounds us and exerts an influence over us. It consists of space and furnishings, time, and organizing elements. Environment affects our social and emotional sense of well-being. We change to fit different environments. We relax in our living rooms and feel anxious in the doctor's waiting room. Children run and leap in open spaces and huddle under beds. In designing an environment in which young artists will work, it is important to consider how the surroundings, organization, and supply storage systems will affect these children.

Defining the Instructional Space

The instructional environment is the total space available for the children's use and how it is arranged. It includes the contiguous outdoor areas as well as any entranceways or hallways that the children will pass through or use. The actual space is less important than its design. It does not matter if the art program is provided at home, in a mixed-age preschool program in a large room such as a church basement, or in classrooms designed especially for young children. Almost any space can be effectively arranged to provide an excellent experience for young artists.

Jim Greenman (1988) identifies the following characteristics as important elements of environments that surround young children: comfort, softness, safety and health, private and social space, order, time, mobility, and the adult dimension. Each of these can be viewed as essential to the presentation of art activities.

Comfort. Children feel comfortable when they can use their whole bodies and all of their senses as they explore and learn. Creative movement and sensory experiences require open and, preferably, carpeted spaces where children can move their bodies in many ways. Tables for art activities should be low enough for small children to kneel, sit, or stand at comfortably. Small, foot-high play tables that straddle the children's legs, picnic benches, and coffee tables all provide toddler-size work surfaces.

Softness. There need to be places where the child can curl up and cuddle, handle plants and animals, and use soft, pliable art materials. Art media provide the important elements of wetness, mushiness, malleability, and stickiness, which toddlers and preschoolers need to have in their daily environment.

Safety and health. The children must be provided with a space that is safe and healthy, but with small risks allowed so that they have the opportunity to learn to manage themselves safely. By handling carefully selected art materials, children learn to deal with such small challenges as water cups that spill, paint that drips, and scissors that are sharp.

Privacy and social space. There need to be places where children can work in large groups, as well as small, private spaces where one or two children can work on a special project. Art activities should not be limited to the "art table." There should be times and places for children to take their crayons and paper and work off by themselves. The floor is always available as an artwork surface. Private spaces can be found under tables or beside a piece of furniture. "Drawing boards" (small chalkboards work well) can provide a drawing surface in a carpeted area. Obviously some art media need to be confined to areas that are easy to wipe up or near a sink, but even these spaces can be arranged to provide more privacy for the young artist. Tables for a group of four can be mixed with tables for one or two. Low dividers or storage units can provide a sense of privacy around the easels or modeling areas and at the same time contain these messier materials in a limited space.

Order. More than anything else, order—the structuring of space, time, and materials—reflects the educational goals of the teacher. If children are expected to work independently, then the materials and space need to be arranged so children can self-select. If there are materials that children are not to use without adult supervision, such as firing clay (see chapter 6), then these need to be placed where children cannot reach them.

Order is especially important in art pursuits. Children need to understand where materials and tools are kept, how they are to take them, where to use them, and how they are to be returned. This order cannot be introduced all at once to children; it must be built up over time, slowly adding new materials and tools as children gain competence in handling each new addition. For example, one drawing material should be introduced and used for a period of time, and then the next added, and so on, until the children have access to a variety of drawing materials. They can then use the materials in combinations of their choosing. They should be able to obtain supplies, take them to the designated work areas, and return them when they are done. This leads to much richer art possibilities than having crayons put out on a table for one week, markers the next, chalk the next, and so on.

Time. Time is also a part of the environment, and art explorations, in particular, require a different sense of time than other activities. Some art activities take just a few minutes, while others take days. Some children will spend long periods at an art activity, while others doing the same activity are done in a flash. Creating art requires a flexible time schedule. It needs to be part of a group of activities so that there are other choices for children who are ready to move on, and provisions must be made for the storage of unfinished work to be completed another day.

Mobility. Children need space to move in active ways within the environment. Outdoor areas are often underused for art activities. Children need to feel that they can move their arms boldly and bounce around while painting, modeling, or constructing. Everyone feels bolder outdoors, and there is less concern about damage. The outdoors is a good place for large projects such as murals and refrigerator-box constructions, and for wet, messy projects such as papier-mâché and wet clay.

Mobility also refers to the furnishings. It is important that many elements of the environment be as flexible as possible to allow teachers to adjust the arrangement to suit the needs of particular children at specific times.

The adult dimension. Children are not the only ones occupying the environment. Attention needs to be given to the adults who work there as well. There should be places where teachers can sit comfortably when they are talking to children about their art, and where they join children when they too are creating art. There should be room for teachers to move as boldly as the children, and viewpoints from which they can see everything that is going on at once. Teachers need to feel comfortable in this space that they have created.

HOW SHOULD THE ART ENVIRONMENT BE ARRANGED?

The consideration of the children's own needs and rhythms shapes the arrangement of space and physical environment.

—*Lella Gandini (Edwards, Gandini, & Forman, 1993, p. 147)*

Layout

Art activities should not be arranged independently of the other uses of the room. In some cases the art activities will overlap areas used for other activities. Some equipment, such as easels and computers, requires exclusive locations, away from the flow of traffic. Some art activities, such as painting a mural or refrigerator box, require large, temporary locations (outdoors in good weather).

Instead of thinking in terms of the traditional activity areas such as blocks, dramatic play, art center, and so on, teachers need to view the total environment, consider its inherent qualities, and design flexibility into the layout. There should be a quiet, relaxed area with soft furnishings where children can enjoy beautifully illustrated books and study art prints and interesting artifacts, an open space for kinesthetic movement and group activities, and an uncarpeted area for creative and constructive activities, such as block building and collage making. Wet and messy activities, whether art or science or cooking, need to center around the sink or water source. In a home setting, bear in mind that such work areas might be located in a living room, a playroom, a workshop, or a kitchen.

Adequate Space

Plan enough space for children to move from one area of the environment to another and to spread out and work comfortably. Younger children need more space than older ones. Allow at least four square feet or more of artwork surface for each toddler, and at least three square feet for each older child.

Traffic Pattern

Consider how the children will move in the room. Will the activity areas attract them? Will there be sufficient room for children to gather around an interesting exploration? How many children can work in an area at a time? The more flexible the room arrangement, the easier it will be if several children all want to work together. There should be ways to add more chairs, push two tables together, or even move all of the furniture out of the way to accommodate children who wish to explore an art activity on the floor.

Water Requirements

Art activities that require water need to be located near a water source. The dirtier the children's hands get, the closer they need to be to a sink or washing area. Finger

Environments for children should provide a variety of activity areas.

painting and printmaking in particular require an easy, clear passage to the sink. Dishpans and buckets of water can provide a preliminary rinse-off area when working outside or at a distance from a sink.

Separate Art Activities from Food Areas

In all situations, art activities and cooking activities must be kept separate. As detailed in chapter 6, children need to learn from the beginning that art materials are never eaten, and separating these two activities is one way to do this. In a home situation, when the weather does not allow outside artwork, the kitchen may provide the only location for art activities requiring water. One way to separate art from food activities is to have a special low table, tray, or mat that is used only for art activities. If tables must be used for both food and art, then put down a special covering for one of the activities, such as a plastic tablecloth for eating or an old shower curtain for art.

HOW SHOULD ART SUPPLIES BE ORGANIZED?

How art supplies are arranged in the environment is more than just a convenience. Carefully considered storage not only provides a more appealing appear-ance but also teaches. The art materials and tools should be displayed and stored so that children learn how to get what they need and put an item back by themselves. Categorizing the materials by their unifying qualities teaches children visual perceptual skills as they learn to group similar items together. Toddlers do best with broad categories of storage units with easily distinguished appearances, while older children can handle more complex storage systems. The order in which materials are arranged also teaches, as when materials used in a particular sequence are ordered from left to right.

Location

Not all work spaces for art need to be at tables, nor do all art activities need to be done in the same work space. Easels, for example, create a special place just for painting. Try to set them up in such a way that brushes and bottles of paint are beautifully displayed nearby.

Drawing has a far wider range of suitable places than some other, messier activities. Carpeted areas and durable pillows can entice children to sit and lie quietly while drawing. Places to crawl under and draw allow children private moments with their art. Encourage children to expand drawing activities by making small, portable containers of markers and crayons and by placing drawing materials in many areas of the room, such as by an aquarium or near a plant. Drawing

Places for art should encourage children to share.

Teacher Tip

Activity Requirements

Drawing. Standing-height work surface or a child-size table and chair. Alternatively, the floor, a drawing board, or an easel may be used.

Painting. An easel or other raised, slanted surface works well. Otherwise, a wall can be used, or a low table. The area must be near water. Protect surfaces.

Printing. Low table without chairs, close to water. Protect surfaces. Have a place to store wet prints near the work area.

Modeling. Low table with chairs, close to water. Special mats or trays can be provided to confine the material to a limited area.

Collage and construction. Low table with or without chairs, or, for larger projects, the floor. Close to supply storage and water and by a place convenient to store drying projects.

Mural making. Wall or floor or blackboard area. Can be done outdoors if it is not windy. Protect surfaces when using paint or glue.

Computer use. Child-height table and chair, far from water areas, paint, modeling, and sand. There should be no glare from windows or lights on screen.

should not be an occasional choice at the art table. Rather, it should be ever present throughout the room—available to record children's ideas and thoughts throughout the day.

Supplies should be stored as close to the area of use as possible. Materials stored close to each other will tend to be used together. Paper, scissors, and drawing materials stored by the block area will increase the likelihood that children will make signs, maps, and other additions to their block creations.

Display

Supplies that are freely available to the children should be placed at child height and attractively displayed in sturdy, clearly labeled containers. When supplies are carefully arranged, children are encouraged to treat them more respectfully. Children will, for example, carefully consider which piece to take when cut-paper shapes are ordered in containers by shape and color, but they will root and grab from a box of mixed-up scraps.

Although supplies should be ample, avoid putting out huge amounts of any material. When children see large amounts of a material, whether paper or buttons, they are more likely to use the supply wastefully. It is better to display fewer supplies and refill the containers more often.

Labels can be a way to introduce children to the printed word and should include both the word and a picture or sample of the object. Even though labeled, containers should be low enough and wide enough so that children can easily see what is inside from their low vantage point. Clear plastic containers work well for many supplies, as do low baskets, cut-down cardboard boxes, and dishpans.

Storage

Closed storage, such as closets, cupboards, or boxes, is essential. Whatever children see and ask for, they should be able to use, as this encourages creative growth. When there are insufficient supplies of a popular material, or when an item is not safe for children of that age, then those materials should not be offered to that particular group of children and should be stored completely out of their sight.

Storing Finished Work

Before selecting any activity, consider carefully how the finished products will be handled. There is nothing more frustrating than trying to find space for items such as 25 dripping wet, papier-mâché-covered boxes, or a 3-by-10-foot freshly painted mural.

Try to plan multiple-use areas. Tables can be used

for working on during the session and for storing projects at the end of the day. The area under tables or on top of shelves can also be used. It is often better to leave wet projects to dry where they are rather than risk damaging them. If projects must be moved, have the children work on trays or pieces of sturdy cardboard.

Cubbies or individual boxes for each child make a good place to store small projects, drawings, dry paintings, and collages. Placed close to the door, they help remind families to pick up their child's work. If cubbies cannot be used, a table by the door can hold work ready to go home.

HOW IS AN AESTHETIC ENVIRONMENT CREATED?

A teacher as an artist thinks and designs the classroom differently from a teacher as a researcher or a teacher as an administrator.

—*Renate Nummela Caine &*
Geoffrey Caine (1974, p. 123)

There is more to designing a space for living or working than arranging the furniture in a functional way.

Clear containers help children find supplies quickly and easily.

This is particularly true of work spaces for children. In selecting the individual elements that make up the children's learning environment, we must consider the ways in which these elements will enrich the children's perceptions and thereby influence their aesthetic experience. Although people have different aesthetic senses, and room designs will reflect the uniqueness of personal experiences, the following guidelines, based on principles of color, design, and children's behavior, are intended as an initial direction from which teachers can create a beautiful work space for children.

Guidelines for Establishing an Aesthetic Environment

Whether the work space is a large, formal classroom or a corner of a family room or kitchen, the basic guidelines that follow can be used to provide an aesthetic place for children to create art.

Floor and walls. The floor is an important working area of the room. Carpeted areas provide softness and absorb sound. Tiles and linoleum areas are easy to clean up when wet or sandy and make a good surface for block building. Area rugs provide the most flexibility and can be used to divide areas visually and texturally.

The walls are also a major teaching area. They provide a place for wall-mounted activities such as easels and mirrors, as well as a display space for the children's work. But very often the walls are overused. When they are plastered with signs and artwork and garish commercial bulletin board displays, they overload the senses and make the room a tiring place.

Wall displays need to be carefully selected and hung at the child's eye level. It is an eye-opening experience to lower ourselves to the children's height occasionally and see the environment we have prepared from their vantage point.

Color and texture. View the walls and floor as background for the objects that will be displayed in the room. Bright or strongly colored walls or floors are limiting, especially if we consider that most children's toys and clothes are brightly colored. Bright colors make a room seem smaller and are tiresome after a while. Light, neutral colors such as white, off-white, or soft gray will allow the color scheme of the room to be varied simply by changing the colors in the displays and will allow the colorful toys to stand out from the background. To add a brightly colored area, put up a temporary covering of colored paper.

Consider the textures and patterns of the various materials on the floors and walls of rooms as well. It is good to have a variety, but to prevent the effect from being overwhelming, keep the colors of these items closely related. Here again, neutral earth colors, including beiges, grays, and browns, will provide an unobtrusive background for brightly colored toys and art materials.

Work surfaces. Light, neutral-colored backgrounds not only increase the aesthetic quality of a room but also make the space seem larger. They provide an unobtrusive foil to the children's own choice of colors in their artwork. Avoid the overuse of bright and saturated colors and patterns in areas where children are creating art. Although initially attractive, they quickly tire the senses and make it hard for children to concentrate on their own color use in their art.

Tables that the children work on should be neutral colors, such as beiges, browns, or grays. When covering tables with protective coverings, select plain ones when possible. Even newspaper, although certainly necessary for many activities, can prove wearing on the senses after a while. Try to avoid having surfaces constantly covered with it, and substitute plain white newsprint or brown kraft paper on occasion.

Storage items. Wood has a warm, neutral color and will blend into most color schemes. Baskets are art forms that provide a beautiful way to store many items. Take the time to paint or cover any cardboard boxes that are used for storage. Choose a color that goes with the color of other items in the room. When using purchased plastic bins or containers, try to get them in similar colors, such as all blues or white. Clear containers are the most versatile and allow the children to quickly see the contents. Use labels to create a color-coded sorting system. Clear, package-sealing tape works especially well for attaching labels to a variety of containers (see appendix A).

Displays. Rather than overloading a child's senses, place only a few carefully selected items on display at a time, and change the displays often. Young children quickly lose focus if surrounded by too many things.

They will jump from one thing to another with barely a glance. Select a special place for displaying each type of item. Less effort is needed in setting them up and keeping them orderly and neat when small displays are set up in limited areas. Use areas outside of the children's learning zone, such as hallways and entrances, for large and/or permanent displays of children's art (see chapter 12, Creating Art).

Art prints. Choose a visible location, and put up only one large fine art print at a time. Make sure it is at the children's eye level. (See chapter 8 for ways to encourage children to become familiar with the print.) "Cute" wall cutouts, stereotypical seasonal and holiday decorations, and purchased bulletin board items will not contribute to developing aesthetic awareness in young children and should be avoided. Small fine art prints can be displayed in a housekeeping corner or the reading area.

Art artifacts. Put out one three-dimensional artifact at a time. Provide a special display base, such as a small low table or large painted box, on which it can rest. (See chapter 8 for suggested artifacts and how to present them.)

Beautifully illustrated books. Display a small selection of books by standing them upright on a low shelf or facing forward on a book rack so that children can easily see and handle them. Provide a cozy reading area that has carpeting or small rugs for the children to sit on. Pillows and large cushions can add to the sensory quality of this area and appeal to children who like to curl up in cozy areas. The "clean-hands only" reading area could be separated with a beautiful screen, hanging streamers, or low bookcases containing attractively arranged puzzles and games, in addition to books.

Nature objects. Adding live plants, aquariums, terrariums, and other displays of natural objects can also enrich the aesthetics of the environment. Set up slowly changing displays of natural objects, such as shells, leaves, or rocks. Arrange the objects by size, texture, or color, and provide magnifying glasses or a Fresnel lens so children can study them more closely. Quantities of small natural objects, such as acorns, seeds, and pebbles, can be displayed on a shelf or windowsill. Use clear plastic jars and containers that allow light to pass through and are safe for children to turn, shake, and study how the objects move and reform.

Children's artwork. Classroom displays of children's artwork are often overwhelming. To avoid having to put up everyone's work all of the time, select one child to be "artist of the week," and put up a few pieces of child-selected artwork. It will make that one child's piece of work much more special and will eliminate the urge to compare the work of one child to another. Make sure the works are displayed at a child's height, and in a location where they will not be damaged by splashing water or wandering hands. A good location is the "clean-hands" area.

Theme-related displays of children's artwork can be incorporated into the children's activities. For example, children's drawings of fish can be displayed by the aquarium, along with fish books and photographs of fish, or made into a book about fish. Children should participate in creating these displays and deciding how they will look and where they will be placed.

Details. As much attention should be paid to the small details as to the larger objects in the room. In the play corner, are the dress-up clothes and the dolls' clothes and bedding made from cloth that looks and feels beautiful? Is there a variety of textures? Do the dishes and tableware match? Are the blocks carefully arranged by size and shape? Are the puzzles, games, and toys displayed so that each one is separate and clearly visible instead of piled indiscriminately in a basket or box? It is better to put out a limited selection of toys and games at a time and rotate them when the children begin to lose interest. Remember to remove and replace worn and broken items frequently.

Expressing Personal Taste

Our environments mirror who we are. The colors, shapes, and patterns that appeal to one person may be different from what appeals to another. What teachers consider the ideal environment for children may change as they learn new teaching approaches or visit other classrooms. In fashioning environments in which children will create art, there are unlimited possibilities. All of the earlier suggestions are starting points, not unbreakable rules. No two early childhood environments need to be alike, nor should they remain static. The environment should change as the children's interests and activities change, or as teachers explore new ways to create the ideal environment for children. The key element is flexibility. When flexibility is built into the room, teachers can create the best environment for their particular children at that particular moment.

Children need safe, comfortable spaces in which to learn.

CONCLUSION: CREATING A SENSE OF PLACE

The space has to be a sort of aquarium that mirrors ideas, values, attitudes, and cultures of the people who live within.

—Loris Malaguzzi (Edwards et al., 1993, p. 149)

For many years the emphasis on places for children has been on ease of cleaning and efficient functioning. This has been the model for most public schools in the United States. One large space is intended to serve all purposes. It is not surprising that in such an environment, art activities are limited to a multipurpose table that has to be cleared off at snack time, some boxes of junk, and perhaps a lonely easel. Cooking and art often go on at the same sink. In order to create an environment that is conducive to art creation, some major changes must occur in how we build and equip the basic room.

The key to an enticing, functional place for children to create art is an environment where children can focus on the activities and supplies available, work independently, and clean up when done. Guiding adults want an environment that is safe and functional and in which children can learn. But most of all the space should show that adults value the role of art not as a playtime activity but as an important way that children show us what they are thinking.

Although every space is unique, with careful planning it can meet these requirements. It is well worth the effort.

- ۞ Children behave better in environments that consider their needs.
- ۞ Space that is arranged so that teachers can move about easily and find needed supplies quickly helps them become more relaxed and attentive to the children as they create art.
- ۞ Beautiful work spaces inspire both adults and children to create their best work.

On the whole, our society suffers from a lack of aesthetic vision. Many homes are decorated with an accumulation of well-liked things that do not relate to each other. Our educational settings mirror this. Adults often feel that children need all of these things to use and learn from. But do they?

Sandboxes are filled with so many shovels and containers that there is no room for a child to just play with the sand. Styrofoam trays, wrapping paper, strips of carpet remnants, and some old yarn bits are shoved in a cardboard box, and then children are expected to make something beautiful from them. Children are overwhelmed; they do not learn to focus in such an environment. Adults need to teach them that there is beauty in each part, and that each part relates to the others to make the whole.

FURTHER READING

Church, E. B., & Miller, K. (1990). *Learning through play: Blocks*. New York: Scholastic.
This book is a comprehensive guide to using blocks with young children.

Greenman, J. (1988). *Caring spaces, learning places*. Redmond, WA: Exchange Press.
This sensitive book provides a picture of how to plan the total environment for young children and should be read by anyone planning a place in which to teach.

Seefeldt, C. (1995). Art—Serious work. *Young Children, 50*(3), 39–45.
This article describes the way art is valued and presented in the Reggio Emilia Preprimary Schools of Italy.

"My house is flying." Marker—*Brittany, age 5*

Creating Art: Sculpture

Blocks allow children to create their own environment.

THE SCULPTURE EXPERIENCE

The smooth shape of the blocks gave me a sense that never left me—of form becoming feeling.

—*Frank Lloyd Wright (Willard, 1972, p. 7)*

Children, too, are builders. They create environments. They are the architects of the spaces they inhabit, often creating complex arrangements of toys and furnishings indoors and shelters of sticks and grass outdoors. Frank Lloyd Wright (Willard, 1972, p. 7) attributed his interest in architecture to the gift of a box of Froebel blocks from his mother. But there is more in a box of blocks or in any three-dimensional art form than a possible future as an architect.

How Children Grow through Three-Dimensional Art Activities

Children will develop

1. physically, by using large muscles in moving blocks and boxes, by using the small muscles of the hand and arm in controlling the placement of smaller three-dimensional objects, and by using eye-hand coordination to effect careful placements. (Bodily-Kinesthetic)
2. socially, by sharing space and materials with others and by working cooperatively on large constructions. (Interpersonal)
3. emotionally, by gaining confidence through building substantial structures. (Intrapersonal)
4. visual perception skills, by learning to see three-dimensional structures from a variety of viewpoints—inside and outside, top and bottom, and front, sides, and back, and by using their eyes to measure spaces to be filled with other three-dimensional parts. (Spatial)
5. language, by learning a vocabulary for concepts of size, form, shape, location, and relationship, and by describing the nature of the structures through conversation. (Linguistic)
6. cognitively, by sorting objects by categories, by organizing them into patterns, by counting them, and by observing cause and effect as they try different solutions to problems. (Logical-Mathematical)
7. art awareness, by gaining an understanding of sculpture and architecture.

 **EXPLORING BLOCKS AGES ONE AND UP**

Much has been written on the importance of block play for young children (Church & Miller, 1990; Gelfer, 1990; Hirsch, 1974). In this section, the focus will be on the art learning that is developed in block play.

Group Composition

The number of children who can be in a block area will be determined by their ages and the size of the area. Two toddlers can work side by side if there are enough blocks and space. If there are only a few blocks in a small, enclosed area, then bumping and grabbing may result. Preschoolers and primary children, who may become involved in cooperative building projects, often can work in larger groups, but attention must always be paid to each child having enough room to move around and get more blocks without knocking over someone else's structure. Other factors that affect the group size are the size of the blocks and the floor surface.

Setup

A flat, low-pile carpet makes a good surface as it muffles the blocks when they fall. It is also more comfortable for the children to sit on while working. A smooth wood or tile floor, however, provides a slightly more stable base on which to work and allows smooth motion for wheeled vehicles. A well-designed block area should include both types of surfaces. Use masking tape to mark off a distance from the shelves in which building is not allowed, so that children can get blocks off the shelves without knocking someone's structure down.

Materials

Try to offer several different sizes of blocks. Toddlers need plenty of large ones. Older children enjoy smaller, more intricate shapes.

Warm-Up

Most children need little introduction to block play. Sit with children in a circle. Have each child select a block, and add it to a group block structure. Review

Classroom Museum

Display a print of one of Frank Lloyd Wright's buildings. Tell the children about how he loved to build with blocks. If possible, visit a piece of public sculpture, or have a sculptor visit the children.

the rules as children do so. The book *Changes Changes* (Hutchins, 1972) can be shared before introducing the block area.

What to Do

Introduce the children to the layout of the block area and where the blocks can be used. Show them how the blocks are to be put away when they are finished. Discuss safety, and set a height limit using a yardstick. Have children find where it comes to on their body as a guide.

Safety Note

Like other supplies, blocks need to be arranged aesthetically and safely. Low shelves are essential. Blocks stored higher than the child's waist can fall and cause injuries. On the shelves, the blocks should not be stacked more than several high, and each type of block should have its own location. Create a label for each location by tracing the shape of the block on paper and then attaching it to the correct shelf. Put the heaviest blocks on the bottom. Use the top of the shelves for accessories stored in clear plastic bins.

What to Say

Block play elicits conversations about form, space, shadow, balance, symmetry, top view, and side view.

Offer description. Say: "You are making your tower symmetrical. See, you have the same blocks on each side." "You have made lots of spaces in your structure. Look, here's a square one." "Your house is balanced. You put a tall brick at each end."

Provide direction. Ask: "What size block will you use next?" "How can you make the base stronger?" "Which block goes next in the pattern?"

Give encouragement. Suggest to children that they include art in their building projects. Ask: "From which view will you draw a picture?" "Can you make a roof with this cardboard?" "Do you want to make some signs for your road?"

More to Do

Blocks and boxes introduce children to the world of architecture. It is natural for young children to build structures that mirror the buildings they inhabit and see around them. Encourage this connection by pointing out the relationships between the basic forms and their architectural counterparts (see figure 9–1).

Take a walk. Explore the neighborhood, and find cylindrical columns, triangular roofs, rectangular bricks, arches, and more. Note how doorways are created by placing a crosspiece over two vertical supports (post and lintel), and point out similar constructions in children's block buildings.

Ask an expert. Invite an architect or architecture student to come and share his or her sketches, plans, and models of buildings. Such a visit will inspire the children to draw "blueprints" of their own. (See chapter 8 for visitor guidelines.)

Design a personal space. Plan a day for older children to each be given a small section of the room in which to build her or his own private place using blocks, moveable furnishings, and other delineating materials to form the walls. Share the story *Roxaboxen* (McLerran, 1991) as the perfect complement to this activity.

Sphere

Pyramid

Rectangular Solid

Triangular Solid

Cube

Cone

Cylinder

Arch

FIGURE 9–1 Basic three-dimensional forms

Artist's Tool Box

Kinds of Blocks

Large blocks. Made of plastic, wood, cardboard, or foam, large blocks allow children to build structures they can sit on or inside. They are excellent for dramatic play and for balancing towers. They provide a fun way to discover spatial relationships by building walls to peek over, through, and around.

Boxes. Child-decorated cardboard boxes stuffed with newspaper can be used as temporary building units as well. Empty cardboard boxes provide spaces to build within. Boxes with holes or the bottom cut out can be used for tunnels or structures to build through.

Pattern blocks. These small, flat, colored blocks of wood or plastic demonstrate many mathematical relationships. They are excellent for developing ideas of symmetry and pattern, as well as for inventing creative designs and patterns.

Unit blocks. These blocks are usually wooden and come in a variety of geometric and architectural forms. They represent mathematical concepts, such as two triangles aligning to form a rectangle the same size as the rectangular unit block. This offers the children an excellent opportunity to investigate symmetry and geometric relationships.

Making Connections

Language. Books to read that provide a link to architecture include *This Is My House* (Dorros, 1992), *Houses and Homes* (Morris, 1992), and *Building a House* (Robbins, 1984). *Architecture Colors* (Crosbie & Rosenthal, 1993) is particularly suitable for toddlers and can be read and then followed by a walk in the neighborhood to find and name the same forms.

The book *What It Feels Like to Be a Building* (Wilson, 1969/1988) provides many ideas for kinesthetic activities that relate to architectural forms. Children can hold hands and form arches, windows, and doors for others to pass through. They can also mime constructing imaginary buildings with "invisible" blocks.

Math. The following books can be used to teach basic geometric forms: *Brown Rabbit's Shape Book* (Baker, 1994a), *Round! Round! Round!* (Hoban, 1974), and *Of Colors and Things* (Hoban, 1989). (See appendix B for other suggestions.) Children can also count the blocks in their buildings.

Art Words

Architectural Structures

☼ **Arch**
A curved structure supporting the weight of part of a building.

☼ **Beam**
A long, straight piece of solid material, such as wood or metal, that supports the weight of some of the building.

☼ **Column**
An upright support.

☼ **Post and lintel**
Two upright supports (posts) that hold up a horizontal piece of solid material (lintel), such as wood, stone, or metal, to create an opening such as a door or window.

Teacher Tip

Adding Art to the Block Corner

Art materials can be added to the block area to increase the dramatic and architectural possibilities.

- **Paper, markers, and crayons** for making maps, and drawing pictures of the buildings
- **Blue paper and white pencils or crayons** to make "blueprints"
- **Cardboard pieces, tubes, and scissors** for the construction of roofs, signs, ramps, and more

- **Fabric pieces** to use for rugs and furnishings in houses
- **Nonhardening clay** to make people and animals
- **Bottle caps and thread spools** to add decorative patterns
- **Aluminum foil** to cover blocks for a sparkling effect

Note: These materials should be slowly added to the block area, so that children have time to investigate the possibilities of each before being overwhelmed by too many choices.

EXPLORING BOXES
AGES ONE AND UP

Boxes of all kinds inspire the imagination of children. Small boxes can become homes for beloved stuffed toys. Appliance boxes can be turned into spaceships or submarines. Boxes can be glued together to create animals, cities, and more.

Group Composition

Depending on the sizes of the boxes and the purpose, box activities can range from individual projects to large, cooperative ones. Two children can work together painting a small box. Four can work on a larger one.

Setup

Although small boxes can be used at a table, most box activities will require open floor space. If painting and gluing are to be done, then the floor should be uncarpeted and covered with a protective covering, such

Classroom Museum

Share the box assemblages of Duchamp and Nevelson, such as Nevelson's *Case with Five Balusters* (Take 5: Collage & Assemblage).

as an old plastic shower curtain. Newspaper can be used, although it sometimes slides or moves under the boxes when children handle them energetically.

Materials

Boxes of all types can be used separately or together.

Warm-Up

Create an intriguing arrangement of boxes, or put smaller ones inside of bigger ones. Ask children to suggest things that they could do with the boxes. Expand on their ideas by asking questions, such as "What would happen if we put a string on the box, or if we painted it?" Then try out these ideas.

What to Do

Always have a supply of small- and medium-size boxes available for children to use as they desire. Provide supplies for gluing them together, painting them, or using them with papier-mâché. (See papier-mâché section.)

On occasion, provide large- and giant-size boxes, and create an open area for children to explore and use them. Let children play with the boxes—stacking them, pushing and pulling them, and crawling in and out of them—before offering art materials for children to use with them. This gives them time to experiment with these larger forms without seeing them as just surfaces to "decorate."

What to Say

As children play with the boxes, draw their attention to art elements and spatial relationships. Describe the different forms. Say: "This box is rectangular." "This box is a cylinder. That one is like a cube." Describe location, size, and position. Say: "This box is on top. That one is on the bottom." "You crawled into that box." "This one is smaller than that one."

Transition Out

When children finish working on their boxes, point out what they did on each side. Large boxes are best left to dry where they are. Smaller boxes can be placed in an open space, a hallway, or under a table.

More to Do

Add on. Provide precut pieces of flat cardboard that can be glued onto the boxes in various ways.

Find boxes. Take a field trip to the local grocery store, and have each child select a carton to bring back. Find out what the store does with the empty cartons.

Make it move. Attaching a string turns a box into a vehicle. Art can be created inside of the box as well as outside.

Artist's Tool Box

Kinds of Boxes

Tiny boxes. Jewelry or pudding mix boxes can be used to make miniature houses to be arranged in a model of the neighborhood or town. They can also be made into homes for tiny toys or special treasures, or glued together into unique, three-dimensional structures.

Medium boxes. Shoe boxes and cereal, pasta, and oatmeal containers can also be made into houses, homes for treasures, and creatures of all kinds. Attach a string to turn a box into a vehicle. Art can be created inside of the box as well as outside. Holes can be cut so viewers can peek inside. Boxes can also be the base of puppets and masks (see chapter 11).

Large boxes. Corrugated cardboard boxes can be used singly or glued together to create large, elaborate structures. This kind of box activity is most suitable for pairs or small groups of children, to encourage them to work together.

Giant boxes. Giant boxes are instantly appealing to young children, providing an immediate sense of privacy and drawing forth imaginative play. Painting larger boxes provides large motor movement for young children. Adding other boxes, cardboard pieces, paper, cloth, and other art elements can enhance the children's imaginative play.

Change it. Decorate the inside with artwork. Cut holes so viewers can peek inside.

Make a puppet. Boxes can also be turned into hand puppets (see chapter 11).

Making Connections

Language. The following books feature boxes used in different ways: *Boxes! Boxes!* (Fisher, 1984), *The Trip* (Keats, 1978), and *The Gift* (Prater, 1985). Have children make up titles, signs, and labels for their box constructions.

Math. Have children count the number of boxes and the number of sides. Discover similarities and differences in the boxes. Group them by size and shape.

Science. Using Styrofoam packing material or blocks, figure out which box holds the most and which the least.

Social Studies. Explore the different ways items are packaged. Which other materials beside cardboard boxes are used? Study how baskets, bags, and boxes are used by people from different places.

EXPLORING PAPIER-MÂCHÉ AGES THREE AND UP

Papier-mâché is a wonderfully sticky material that dries hard and paintable. It is the best way to convert flimsy cereal boxes into sturdy constructions.

Papier-mâché should be seen as a medium to be used when children have a specific problem or project in mind. For example, if children are frustrated because paint will not stick to the box they are painting, suggest papier-mâché. If some children want to build a box robot and the boxes will not stick together, suggest papier-mâché. Avoid doing papier-mâché as a whole-group activity. It takes a preconceived goal to motivate children to work through the difficulties of the medium and to see the end result over the intermediate newspaper-covered mess.

Classroom Museum

Share prints of or actual papier-mâché artifacts, such as masks from Mexico. (See appendix A for papier-mâché artifacts and mask prints.)

Group Composition

Children are ready to do papier-mâché when they can stay in one place while working. Younger preschoolers can work in pairs on individual projects. Older children can work on large, oversized structures if they take turns working in groups of three or four.

Setup

Have children work at a low table covered with several thicknesses of newspaper and without chairs if doing individual projects. Large projects should be set up on a sheet of plastic or an old shower curtain on top of which are several layers of newspaper.

It is essential that the work area be located very close to water. If necessary, use a bucket for an initial rinse. Nothing is as slippery and dangerous as wet papier-mâché paste on the floor. Outdoors is always a good choice if the weather cooperates.

Materials

Paste container. Each child needs his or her own individual container for the paste. It should be wide mouthed, such as a three-pound margarine container.

Papier mâché paste. This is also called "art paste." (See appendix A.) It is effective to use thinned white washable glue as well.

Papier-mâché challenges children to control a wet, sticky material and create three-dimensional projects.

can cover a cereal or spaghetti box, left open at one end so that it will turn into a puppet form to fit over their hand. A small group of children can make a stack of graduated boxes into a snowperson. A tray can be used to make a masklike shape. But regardless of the intended end, while the children are using the paste and paper, they cannot help being involved in pure sensory exploration.

What to Do

1. Demonstrate how to dip a strip of paper into the paste, and then place it on the box or tray.
2. Children should keep their hands over their paste buckets, which should be set directly in front of them in order to catch drips.
3. Encourage the children to cover the box or tray completely, so that nothing shows. One layer is usually sufficient for the first papier-mâché experience. In future experiences, children can be encouraged to put on more layers to make the base sturdier.
4. Place finished projects on a sheet of plastic to dry. They will stick to newspaper. Place them in a safe, dry place near a heater or in the sun to speed drying time.
5. When the papier-mâché is dry, the form can be painted and/or collaged.

What to Say

Use this experience to direct the children's attention to the different sides of the form. Children commonly miss sides and are surprised to find how many there really are on a cereal or cardboard box. Encourage them to look from different vantage points. For example, say: "Did you put papier-mâché on the top?" "Did you look at the other side?" "How can you put that strip on to cover that place?"

More to Do

Celebrate mess. Read books that feature characters enjoying wet, messy things, such as *Muddigush* (Knutson, 1992).

Base. A structure to cover, such as a cereal box, cardboard box, or Styrofoam tray. Avoid curved objects such as balloons and tubes. Children need to build skill in applying the papier-mâché on stable objects before they can handle an object that must be held while the paste is applied.

Newspaper. Pretorn into two-inch strips.

Warm-Up

Papier-mâché activities can be related to a variety of occurrences. A walk to view buildings could lead to a project for some children who want to make buildings. A pair of children who want to make puppets

Teaching in Action

Spaceship Command Center: A Box Project

The following excerpts from a teacher's journal show how the project approach was used in a prekindergarten class to correlate children's interests in space with art, science, and language studies.

Week 1

Day 1: The idea: Mike, Bobby, and Jeff arrived all excited. It seems there was a show about space on TV last night. At meeting, all they wanted to do was talk about the spaceship. At blocks, they built a launch pad and used cardboard tubes as rockets.

Day 2: Discovering the depth of interest: Today I decided to read Ezra Jack Keats's *Regards to the Man in the Moon* (1981). Then I asked: "What do you think we would need for a trip into space?" What ideas! I couldn't write them down fast enough on the chart. Toby said she has a cousin who went to NASA Space Camp. I wonder if she could come for a visit? I must get in touch. I noticed that many of the paintings and drawings were about space today.

Day 3: What do we already know? Today I asked: "What do we know about space?" I made a huge web of children's ideas. I can see they have heard about stars, planets, and the sun, but not much else. There was a discussion about aliens and *Star Wars.* I must find some factual books about space. Not surprisingly, everyone was building a launch pad today at blocks!

Day 4: Building on the interest: I found out about a space exhibit at the discovery center. I called and arranged for a visit the end of next week. That gives me time to plan the busing and the parent volunteers. We will use this time to read more about space and make a list of questions. I put a sheet up labeled "Our questions about space" in the meeting area. I put up a big poster of the solar system. Then I pretended I was the sun and the children were the planets, and they had a grand time circling around me to the music of *The Planets* by Gustav Holst. I will try to read another two pages and do a movement activity each day at morning meeting.

Day 5: Small groups begin: At small group time, I started off by having my group of children look at a picture of the space shuttle and then figure out what the different parts were. I wasn't surprised when Mike, Bobby, and Jeff asked if they could build a spaceship. Everyone started to call out ideas. I said, "Why don't we draw some pictures of our ideas?" Boy, did they work on those pictures! So much detail!

Carol [the aide] had her group looking at photographs of each of the planets and talking about the sizes, colors, and names. Some children in her group wanted to make a mural about space.

Week 2

Day 6: Group work continues: We found a huge roll of black paper. I hung it on the wall, and the children sat in front of it, and we tried to imagine the blackness of space. I gave them each a tube to look through and turned off the light. It was very effective. At group time we continued to work on sketches for the spaceship. We put out gold and silver tempera paint at the easel, and the children had a grand time painting stars and comets of all kinds to paste on the mural. The spaceship group made tons more sketches. Carol's group made planets.

continued

Teaching in Action *continued*

Day 7: Finding direction: I read Gail Gibbons's *Stargazers* (1992, New York: Holiday House). I simplified the text a bit. Then I passed around a telescope for children to look through. They cut out and pasted their stars on the mural. They even made a Milky Way! I can't believe they had such patience to cut out even their little tiny stars. We had so many we even hung some from the ceiling. Then we sat in front of the mural and sang "Twinkle, Twinkle Little Star" and made wishes. Suddenly someone said, I think it was Jeff, "Why don't we make our spaceship in front of the mural so we will be heading into space . . . like we could have a big window. The captain and his mates could sit here and look out."

Day 8: Building begins: Toby's cousin couldn't come, but she sent in a videotape of the training. We watched it twice. The second time we looked for ideas for our spaceship. We added seat cushions and seatbelts to the parent wish list by the door. We decided to move a table in front of the mural, and I cut open a large cardboard box. The children drew big windows, and I cut them out. Then they painted it. Now I have taped it to the table, and it looks great! They have already set up three chairs and sit there counting down.

Day 9: Our trip—What did we learn? It was wonderful! The children were so well behaved. I could see that all of our preparations made a big difference. They had a space shuttle model the children could go inside. When we got back, the first thing they wanted to do was make the control panel like the one at the museum. But I got everyone together first, and we wrote down the answers on our question chart. Then I got out some boxes, and everyone helped paint them. It was a good release after being so controlled all morning at the museum.

Day 10: The command center: It's done! I can't believe the children had such a great idea. We put some low boxes on the table and the bigger ones on the floor around it. Catie had the idea of using bottle lids for the dials. I attached them with chenille stems so they turn. Then the best idea of all was Louie's. He said, "Why don't we put the computer here?" At the museum, there was a computer in the spaceship. So we did! Some parents even brought in cushions and belts for the chairs. We all took a turn sitting in the command seats. Wow! Next week I will put out paper bags with precut openings so they can make helmets if they wish. But the funny thing was when my colleague Joanne poked her head in and said, "What book gave you that neat idea for a computer center?" "It's not in a book," I said. "It grew in the children's imaginations."

BECOMING SENSITIVE TO OUR ENVIRONMENT

The following activities are designed to provoke thought about the environments in which we exist and the effect they have on our feelings and behavior.

1. Make a list of places where you feel most relaxed. Categorize them as soft or hard, open or closed, private or social.

    _____

    _____

    _____

    _____

    _____

    _____

    _____

2. Make a list of all of the different environments you spend time in each day, such as the bedroom, kitchen, classroom, bus, and so on. Describe your behavior in each environment in terms of how you move, talk, and dress, and whether you feel comfortable or not.

    _____

    _____

    _____

    _____

    _____

    _____

    _____

3. Based on what you wrote above, describe the perfect environment for you.

    _____

    _____

    _____

    _____

    _____

    _____

    _____

Studio Page 34

OBSERVATION: AESTHETICS OF AN ENVIRONMENT

Choose a room in a home or school where children do artwork. Examine this room's aesthetic effect. Use the information in this chapter as a guide.

1. What are the background colors in this room?

   Walls: _____

   Ceiling: _____

   Floor: _____

   Floor coverings: _____

2. What is displayed on each wall? Be specific. Make a sketch if necessary.

   Wall 1: _____

   Wall 2: _____

   Wall 3: _____

   Wall 4: _____

3. Are there any sensory displays? If yes, describe them.

   _____

   _____

   _____

4. How are toys, games, and books displayed?

   _____

   _____

   _____

5. What is the total aesthetic effect of this room? Is there anything you would change to make it more aesthetically pleasing for children?

   _____

   _____

   _____

6. Do you think the room encourages or discourages children's artistic behavior? Is there anything you might change? Draw sketches of your ideas.

   _____

   _____

   _____

DESIGNING THE ENVIRONMENT

Keeping in mind what the children will be learning about art, design an ideal environment.

1. On this graph paper is outlined a room 14-by-20 feet. (Scale is one square equals one foot.)

2. Trace the scaled pattern pieces on Studio Page 36, or design your own.

3. Cut them out, and try several possible arrangements to create an environment that would be ideal for young artists.

4. Plan areas for wet and messy activities, quiet, comfortable ones, creative and dramatic play, and kinesthetic movement.

5. Consider all of the different art activities that could take place in each area, and then indicate where supplies would be located.

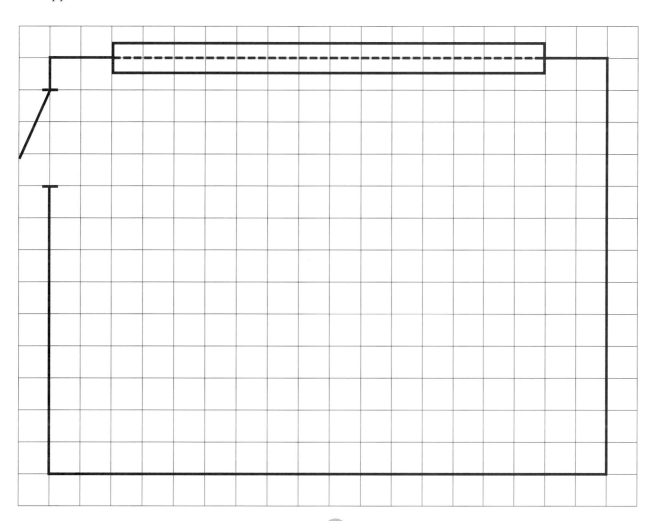

Table

Table

Table

Low Shelf

Low Shelf

Low Shelf

Round Table

Round Table

Half Round Table

Child's Chair

Low Sink

Counter with Storage Below

Rocking Chair

Double Easel

Single Easel

Play Kitchen

For additional information on teaching art to young children, visit our Web site at http://www.earlychilded.delmar.com

Cooperative Art Activities

> 66 *Working in a group can help you produce something more, to think more widely, to enrich you.* 99
>
> —Tiziana Fillipina (Goleman, Kaufman, & Ray, 1992, p. 85)

Questions Addressed in This Chapter:

- ♡ What is cooperative art?
- ♡ How can children be encouraged to work together?
- ♡ What is involved in cooperative art activities?
- ♡ How can young children use the computer to create art?

Young Artists at Work

"Your monkey has real long legs."

"So does yours."

"That's because he's trying to climb up this tree."

"My person is up in the air. He's jumping. You need long legs to do that."

"Yep. My monkey is going to jump when he gets to the top of the tree."

"Oops, the paint is dripping."

"Hurry. Catch it before it runs over Sari's picture."

"Sari will be mad if the paint drips on her dog."

"You are working hard on your paintings for our mural," says the teacher. "I see that you have used two different sizes of brushes."

"Yes, I used Mandie's little brush to paint the buttons, and she used my big brush to paint the long, long legs."

"See," says the teacher, "When we share things, we have more choices of things to use in our art."

WHAT IS COOPERATIVE ART?

Creative actions celebrate the individual, even when the actions are part of a group effort.

—Clare Cherry, Douglas Godwin, & Jesse Staples
(1989, p. 133)

The traditional view of the artist is that of a socially inept loner, creating in isolation. In actuality, most art that has been produced over the span of human history, from the Egyptian wall paintings to the environmental art of Christo, has involved the cooperative efforts of groups of artists with different skills and interests. Cooperative art is art that is created by two or more people. The individuals explore the art media in their own personal way, but they also act and react to the exploration of their cooperative partners. The artists may work at the same time, in series, or on different sections. Well-designed cooperative art activities allow children at different ages and skill levels to work together to create something uniquely different from what they would create on their own. When carefully planned, adults can even participate in many

of these activities. There is great satisfaction in feeling a part of a successful group art activity.

Children need to learn that art is not always done by just one person. This is best learned by participating in many group art experiences. The most common cooperative art activity is the mural. This chapter will also describe many other ways for young artists to cooperate.

HOW CAN CHILDREN BE ENCOURAGED TO WORK TOGETHER?

At two they will play in parallel, but by three they will play together.

—Dorothy Einon (1985, p. 79)

Toddlers

Children begin life totally self-centered. Infants know when they are hungry and demand to be fed. Toddlers see a toy they want and nothing short of physical restraint will prevent them from grabbing it. Children between birth and age two perceive themselves as the center of the universe. Toddlers work best in situations where they can pursue their own explorations under the watchful eyes of caregivers. Adults can promote social growth by providing activities in which toddlers can work alongside others. Setting up activities in which two toddlers or a toddler and an older child are painting at the same table or are smashing play dough together helps toddlers learn that they can do artwork in close proximity to other children.

As toddlers work beside each other, they begin to become aware of each other's actions. One child will begin to pound the clay, and another child will imitate the same action. One child will see another using scissors and will demand a pair too. Imitation is one of the ways that children learn skills and behaviors. Adults and other children can serve as artistic role models for the young child.

Three- and Four-Year-Olds

Many three- and four-year-olds can work together on all kinds of projects, from building a block city to painting a mural. They become enraptured by the excitement of the collective moment and yet are interested in and "see" only the part they personally created. Cooperative activities for these children, therefore, do not have the same meaning as those designed for older children and adults, in which ideas are arrived at jointly and the project is viewed as a whole. Young preschoolers work best on projects that do not have definite end goals but instead allow each child to play an individual part in the process.

Five-Year-Olds and Up

When children gain the ability to value and differentiate their own products from those of others, they can start to see that each contribution is a part of something larger—a whole—which is different from each small part but which is still partially theirs. Teachers can tell when children reach this stage, because they start to notice the artwork of the other children and will comment, "That is my friend's painting," or "That is Cheri's," when referring to a piece of art they see. They use the terms "we did" instead of "I did" when referring to group projects. They can identify who did the different parts of a project. When children reach this stage, they are ready for more complex group activities.

These children are able to plan ahead of time which part of the project they will work on, and they enjoy working on projects that involve a common idea, such as building a castle out of blocks or building

"All my friends are playing jump rope." Section of mural, marker—Joanne, age 4

a box robot together. They may, however, still need adult guidance in learning how to incorporate the ideas of each member in a gracious way.

How Many Children Can Work Together?

Group size is a critical factor in determining if children will work together successfully or come to blows. At the Reggio Emilia preprimary schools they have found that different group sizes create different dynamics. Pairs of children can engage in intense social and cognitive interactions. The addition of a third child can produce solidarity but also conflict. Groups of four and five have other dynamics (Edwards, Gandini, & Forman, 1993).

In many overcrowded, understaffed early childhood programs, it is difficult to set up opportunities for the children to work together in small groups. Teachers cannot expect small groups of children to work together on their own without careful adult observation and interaction. Teachers need to be there to teach resolution skills when two children both want to put the tower on the castle, or both children want to make the robot's head. A caring adult is needed when a two-year-old paints wildly across a four-year-old's carefully done mural painting. A strategic question can make the difference in how the children decide to carry out an idea. In order for group work to be meaningful for young children, it needs to be carefully thought out, adequately supervised, and based on the interests and needs of the children.

Promoting Cooperative Behaviors

Learning how to work with others will make people more successful in life. Young children can gain skill in small behaviors that will help them grow to be more effective group members. Working on group art projects will help children grow socially by

1. developing the ability to concentrate on a task in the presence of others.
2. developing the ability to wait for a turn.
3. developing the ability to share materials with others.
4. gaining the knowledge that working with others is a pleasant, joyful experience.

Teachers can encourage the growth of these preliminary cooperative skills in a number of ways.

Toddlers.

1. Provide opportunities for two or three toddlers to work at the same table. Make sure they each have plenty of space for bodily movement without interfering with each other.
2. Place supplies in a common container from which children must select their pieces. Provide sufficient amounts of the supply so that children can have as much as they wish. Encourage children to take one item at a time.
3. Have children take turns working in pairs on a mural or a drawing or on painting a box. Make sure each child has plenty of space in which to work.

Three- to five-year-olds.

1. Have children work in groups of four to six at the same table or work space.
2. Have pairs of children share some supplies such as glue or hole punches.
3. Offer supplies in common containers, and encourage children to develop the independent behavior of taking only a few items at a time. This can be encouraged by giving children small trays on which to place their selections.
4. When a supply is limited, ask children to share fairly, such as having the children check that each has a red paper square or a similar supply of blocks.
5. Plan activities to which each child can contribute, such as the mural suggestions that follow.

Five- to eight-year-olds.

1. Provide opportunities for children to work independently in teams of three to five to accomplish a set goal. Start with simple tasks such as painting a box or sorting paper scraps by color. After the children learn to work together successfully, advance to more complex activities, such as making a poster, putting on a puppet show about a book they have read, or building a papier-mâché sculpture out of boxes.
2. When working on group projects, always have the children meet and plan ahead of time what part each child will do. Teach children that in a team

each member can contribute in different ways. Have children assume roles within their team. In a group of four, one child could be in charge of getting supplies, the second could be assigned to returning the supplies, the third could record the group's accomplishments—either by writing or making illustrative drawings—and the fourth could report orally to the class. There is a large body of literature on teaching cooperative group skills to children age five and up. (See Further Reading at the end of this chapter.)

3. Children at these ages are also ready to participate in large group cooperative behaviors. Have the whole class participate in deciding how the art materials should be cared for and organized. Then have individuals or pairs of children assume responsibility for taking care of a specific supply.

Mixed-age and ability groups. Groups that contain a range of ages actually offer one of the best settings in which to develop cooperative art behaviors. The older children and adults can model respect for each other's artwork and at the same time supervise the more impulsive little ones.

1. Select activities that each individual, no matter what his or her ability level, can participate in fairly equally. Most of the activities in this chapter are suitable for mixed groups and can be used in child care situations, in family groups, or for child-parent art workshops.

2. Have members of the group take turns working in pairs or in groups of three. The older members should help the younger ones find a place to work and supplies to use.

3. Allow the youngest group members to go first, as older members will be able to work around one another's artwork, whereas the young children may not "see" the work already there and may work on top of it.

In mural making, children contribute in their own unique ways to create a marvelous whole.

Mural making provides the perfect opportunity to practice sharing materials and space with others.

Enjoying Working Together

Always include an element of fun when working together. Songs, laughter, and excitement should all be part of the experience. It is the group experience that is important, not the finished product. Avoid the trap of planning an end use for the cooperative project before it is started. Do not be a boss, telling people to do this or work on that so that a beautiful piece of artwork results. That is not a model for cooperative art. The teacher's role is to be the guide. Provide the location, the materials, the excitement, and the beginning of an idea, then let the participants take over. Teachers can even participate themselves! The result will be a true expression of each individual's creative moment as a part of that group, at that time, and in that place.

WHAT IS INVOLVED IN COOPERATIVE ART ACTIVITIES?

Well-designed group art activities can provide an excellent way to introduce children to working in a group. Children can make group art using a variety of media, from drawing to collage, and they can work on walls, tables, floors, and windows.

It is important that children be familiar with the medium to be used in the project and have had many practice experiences with it. A group activity is not the place to explore a material for the first time but instead provides an opportunity to take pride in using a skill and creating something that requires a level of control. It is important that these projects be designed as open-ended activities, so that every child can participate fully.

The Common Experience

In order to produce a collective artwork, all of those involved need to share an experience. This common experience will combine the ideas and actions of each child. The experience should be one in which children participate directly, otherwise they come to rely on stereotypes and teachers' examples rather than thinking on their own.

The common experience forms the basis for planning and carrying out murals and group sculptures. For example, after a trip to the zoo, children share what they saw, and the teacher makes a class chart of their observations. That chart then becomes the source of ideas for what children will put on their zoo mural.

The common experience can be the following:

- a field trip
- an event that occurs, such as rain, snow, or a parade
- observation of something real, such as nature objects, animals, machines, or a store
- reading a story or poem together
- a class theme or project topic

The Mural

The word **mural**, although technically defined as a "wall painting," in literature on children's art usually refers to a very large, two-dimensional piece of artwork created by a group of children. That is the definition used here. There are four types of murals: collage, painted, printed, and thematic.

The collage mural. This type of mural is an excellent initial group art activity. Because the children are attaching objects rather than creating original artwork directly on the surface, they can concentrate on how they will place the object in relationship to the others. This mural teaches two important concepts. First, a mural is an artwork made up of many parts; second, each artist must respect the work of the others and take care not to cover up any parts that other people have already put on the mural.

The painted or printed mural. In these types of murals, the children paint or print directly on the same piece of background paper. Depending on the experience of the children and the location available, the children may take turns or work in larger groups. A long, narrow paper hung on a wall, with open space around it, can have more children working on it than can a wide piece of paper laid out on a table or the floor. If a table is used, a good guideline is to work with no more than the number who usually would fit at that table. Make sure there is ample space for children to move their arms and reach the supplies as they work.

Printmaking in particular lends itself to a shared surface. All of the printmaking activities presented in chapter 7 can be used to create a mural. More specific ideas are presented in the Creating Art section.

These murals give children the opportunity to use large, muscular motions that are in sharp contrast to the movements made in the more constrained areas where they usually work. Be sure to provide plenty of space for children to extend their arms out to full range. Murals are best done with the paper affixed to a wall but can also be done on a table or the floor. Position the paper so the children have to extend their arms full length to paint near the top. Tape up newspaper extending beyond all of the edges to catch the inevitable stray strokes.

There is a wonderful element of spontaneity to this type of mural, and they are very popular in early childhood programs. They work best when they grow directly out of the interests and activities of the children,

Young Artists at Work

Marc and Terry, deep in conversation, huddle together at the computer in the corner of the room, ignoring the active play of the other children.

"Put a yellow line there."

"Make it go that way."

"Cover it all up with green."

"Wow, look at that; those lines are thick."

"Should we make rainbow lines again?"

"Oh look, the line just got thinner."

"Now I will make a circle."

and when time is spent planning with the children what part each one will do. These murals use very basic art supplies that are usually on hand and can therefore be set up quickly.

Thematic murals. Murals can provide a way for children to express what they have experienced and learned in a thematic unit. A thematic mural starts with the common experience of the children. It provides an opportunity for children to talk with each other about what they know about the subject and then work together to produce a unified presentation of the theme. The Creating Art section that follows contains suggestions for creating successful thematic murals.

The Group Sculpture

When many hands contribute to an artwork, incredible energy results. Group sculptures make lively activities for mixed-age groups. Even the youngest child can be helped to place a part on a group sculpture. Group sculptures can be simple and immediate. For example, children on the playground can collect stones or sticks and arrange them into a design on the pavement. Wood scraps collected as part of a visit to a carpenter's shop can become an amazing structure. Other sculptures, such as those described in the Creating Art section, can result in beautiful artworks to display in the classroom.

HOW CAN YOUNG CHILDREN USE THE COMPUTER TO CREATE ART?

Very sophisticated conversations about art happen not only at the art table but also between children working at the classroom computer. Computers have found their way into the hands of the very young, and they are providing an interactive medium unlike any other art form. Like collage, computer graphics provide an avenue of art exploration that challenges both child and teacher to accept new ways of thinking and work-

Computers challenge children to think about art in new ways.

The computer provides the perfect place for an art conversation.

ing with the elements of art. This section will look at how the use of computers can enhance the art program offered to children.

The Computer As Art Medium

When the computer is viewed as an art medium rather than as a teaching tool, the logic of its inclusion in any art program involving children becomes apparent. A computer loaded with a simple graphic "paint" program is another way to create lines and shapes. The monitor screen is the "paper," and the mouse is the tool for applying the lines and shapes and colors. The child manipulates colored light rather than pieces of paper, paintbrushes, or glue, but the artistic decisions are the same.

Using the Computer for Art Activities

In this technologically sophisticated society, even very young children are often familiar with computers. The similarity of the computer monitor to the ever-present television makes children feel quite comfortable with a medium that sometimes intimidates adults. Being able to create their own "television" picture makes children feel independent and powerful. With the increasing number of computers in the home, home-based child care programs may be even more likely than more formal programs to have a computer available for children to use. Properly selected and set up, computer art software provides a wonderful way to introduce children to the computer, beginning a pattern of comfort and success with this technology that will play such a large role in children's futures.

The computer can be viewed as another component of the art program, just like easels and collage centers. It is neither more nor less important than any of the other art activities offered to children. Like the other activities, the computer allows children to play with the art elements in a creative way. Opportunities to work at the computer can be offered as one of the children's daily play choices.

Selecting Art Software

The computer software discussed in this section is of one type only. These are often called "paint," "graphic," or "drawing" programs and may come as part of the initial software on the computer, may be the graphic part of "works" programs that combine word processing, spreadsheets, and data processing or may be purchased in special versions designed just for children. Because specific software programs that are available change rapidly, use the following general guidelines for making sure that the one selected will work well for young artists. (See appendix A for some specific examples of excellent computer art programs.)

1. There should be a large, open work space of white or black on which to draw.
2. The cursor should be large and easy to see.
3. The menu of color, shape, and line choices should be visible at all times, either at the side or top of the screen.
4. Menu choice boxes should be large, with logical symbols for line types, shape, and fill options.
5. The program should have a limited number of menu options. Children do not need such things as multiple pages, graduated colors, and inversions.
6. Programs that load quickly are most convenient. If the only one available requires a complicated loading procedure, be sure to load the program before the children arrive. Turn the monitor off until it is time for the children to work.
7. The ability to save and print the children's pictures allows the children to review what they have done or to put on a computer art show. Some programs save groups of pictures with a "slide show" feature.
8. Most importantly, the program should be open-ended. It should not have predrawn coloring-book-style pictures to color, nor should it involve the manipulation of shapes or pictures on an already drawn background. Just because the words "draw," "paint," "picture," or "art" are in the title of a program does not mean it is a true art program. Always preview a program before offering it to children.

Locating the Computer

The computer should be located away from heavy traffic and in a "clean-hands" location. There must be an electrical outlet capable of handling the necessary power, preferably with a surge protector. Make sure the computer area will be visible from all parts of the room so that assistance can be offered when needed.

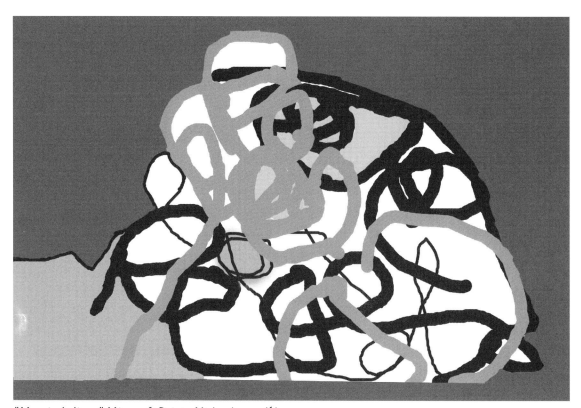

"My wiggly lines." Microsoft Paint—*Michael, age 4¹⁄₂*

"Houses and sun." Microsoft Paint—*Dreana, age 8*

Choosing Equipment

Consider the following equipment when setting up a computer art program.

Computers. Any computer that runs the appropriate software can be used. Many child-appropriate art programs can be used on older, lower-powered machines. If the right combination of a program and an older machine can be found, then one computer can be dedicated to art exploration.

Printers. A black-and-white or color printer is a nice addition, as it provides a way to capture the children's work, but it is not essential. For young computer artists, just as in all of the other art forms, process is more important than product, and the printed versions of children's art are often pale imitations of the glowing images on the screen anyway. For many children, part of the fun seems to be making their pictures disappear when they are done.

Input devices. A mouse is the best way for young children to draw on the computer. Joysticks can also

be used. A cordless mouse provides more freedom of movement.

Try to put the keyboard out of the way so that the child can focus on the mouse and the screen. On some computers, the keyboard can be placed on top of the monitor, or it can be removed and the mouse plugged in directly. If the keyboard is not removable, then it is essential to cover the keys with a protective skin (see appendix A). This will keep sand and other deleterious items out of the keyboard. The keyboard can also be covered with a cardboard box when children are using the mouse to draw.

CONCLUSION: COOPERATIVE ART UNITES PEOPLE

In this society, art is all too often seen as something a person does alone. Yet some of the most joyful art experiences children can have are those in which they work in a group to create something massive—a mural, a box robot, or a wall of boxes. Working together for a common purpose forges children into a group. It becomes "our mural," "our robot," or "our wall." It is not surprising that so many of the "class-building activities" of cooperative learning programs are art based. It is easy to incorporate the ideas and skill levels of each individual into an art activity. Using themes and providing opportunities for projects are other ways to increase group bonding.

Peers Model Skills

Imitation is one way that children learn new skills. Slightly more advanced peers provide better models for young children than adults, whose skills may be far greater than children need or are capable of imitating. Working together on a mural or at the computer provides the perfect opportunity for children to learn from one another.

Coming Together

Educators also benefit from working alongside their peers. Teaching, like art, is often seen as an individual affair. Teachers need to meet often with peers to share ideas and frustrations. Thematic units are easier to

plan when there are two or three minds brainstorming. Teachers need to involve parents as partners in their programs. Foot painting and nature collages are easier to manage when there are extra hands. Everyone needs to come together in order to grow together. The program will be richer, and the young artists will show more growth.

FURTHER READING

For ways to help young children cooperate, read:

Janke, R. A., & Peterson, J. P. (1995). *Peacemaker's A, B, Cs for young children*. Marine on St. Croix, MN: Growing Communities for Peace.

This book presents a well-organized, thoughtful program for teaching children to take an active role in getting along peacefully with others.

Kagan, S. (1994). *Cooperative learning*. San Juan Capistrano, CA: Resources for Teachers.

A systematic program for developing cooperative group behavior is presented in this comprehensive manual. There are special suggestions for introducing cooperative skills to children age five and up.

Creating Art: Group Art

CREATING ART TOGETHER

Cooperative art projects can take many forms. From painting a mural to sitting side by side at the computer, working with others gives children a chance to talk about art in a way that is different from individual artistic pursuits. There must be a common vocabulary. "Should we put aqua on the fish?" There must be collaboration. "Shall we color the tree trunk gray or brown?" And there must be cooperation. "I'll hold the paint for you, and then you can hold it for me."

The result is more than the sum of its parts. Cooperative art activities turn *me* into *we* and unite individuals.

How Children Grow through Creating Art Cooperatively

Children will develop

1. physically, by exercising the small and large muscles of the arm, wrist, and fingers to manipulate art material and by using hand-eye coordination to follow the lines and shapes created by others and joining to them. (Bodily-Kinesthetic)
2. Socially, by sharing materials and space with others. (Interpersonal)
3. emotionally, by feeling independent and powerful in being allowed to use a complex and valuable machine. (Intrapersonal)
4. visual perception skills, by associating the movement of the hand with the placement of shapes within a boundary. (Spatial)
5. cognitively, by learning how to combine ideas with those of others to solve problems.
6. language, by interacting verbally with a partner while creating art. (Linguistically)

EXPLORING COMPUTERS AGES ONE AND UP

Children approaching the computer for the first time explore in the same way that they explore crayons or markers or paint. Unlike adults, who often have difficulty knowing in which direction to move the mouse, children quickly learn, sometimes in as little as one or two moves, how to control the direction of their lines as they watch the screen. Control over the computer image develops in the same way in both young children and adults encountering a free-drawing software program for the first time.

1. There is an initial fascination with how the rhythmic movement of the hand and mouse creates lines of colored light on the screen. Toddlers and adults alike fill the screen with linear designs reminiscent of the first scribbles of childhood.
2. Next, the computer artist becomes fascinated with the choice of colors, line types, and shapes. One

colored line or shape is placed over another again and again.

3. When the user, child or adult, is familiar with the options, deliberation sets in. Lines are carefully placed, shapes positioned, and symbols created. Because there is no preset notion of how computer art must look, just as with collage, all artists can find their own ways of creating with the computer medium.

Group Composition

Computer art can be created by children of all ages. Very young toddlers, sitting on an adult's lap, enjoy moving the mouse and seeing what happens. Three-year-olds and older children like to work in pairs with a buddy of the same age or older. The computer seems to elicit more verbalization about the art elements than other art forms. Children often converse, help each other, or work together on the same screen image. Watching the visual images appear on the screen is intriguing enough to hold the attention of one child, while the other one operates the mouse.

Setup

The computer should be placed on a low table at which two children can comfortably sit or stand. One computer can service about 10 children working in pairs on a daily basis. If only one computer is available for a larger number of children, then the children may have to take turns. It is important to make sure that girls have equal access to the computer. Research shows that when computer access is limited, boys often get more opportunities at the computer than girls (Davidson, 1989, p. 23).

Art Words

A Guide to the Computer

○ **Clicking**
Pressing the button on the mouse to select an item on the menu.

○ **Cursor**
A blinking line or shape that indicates where the first mark will appear on the screen. It is controlled by the mouse.

○ **Disk**
Contains the program.

○ **Disk drive**
Reads information from the disk.

○ **Hardware**
The physical equipment used—computer, mouse, printer.

○ **Icon**
The symbol representing a menu option.

○ **Joystick**
A hand-held device with a stick that can be moved in different directions to control the movement of the cursor on a computer screen.

○ **Menu**
A list of choices available in a computer program. Items are selected by placing the cursor on the icon and by clicking the mouse.

○ **Mouse**
A hand-held device, which, when rolled along a surface, controls the movement of the cursor on the screen.

○ **Mouse pad**
A soft foam pad on which a mouse is moved.

○ **Printer**
A machine that produces a paper copy in black and white or in color of what is visible on the screen.

○ **Software (or programs)**
Sets of instructions, stored on disks, that tell a computer how to perform a particular task.

Set up a system so that the children know that they will each get a turn to work for as long as they wish.

Have the program loaded and the computer on but the screen off. Preset the program to draw with a thick, straight line in a bright color, rather than the thin black line of the initial setup.

Materials

Besides the computer, mouse, and software program, a mouse pad is required. Purchase the largest size available to allow for the larger arm movements of young children.

Optional, but highly recommended, is a cover for the keyboard.

Warm-Up

Children are naturally fascinated by a computer. When introducing it, the many operations to create a picture need to be explained. Several children can be instructed one-on-one at the computer, and then they can be paired with novices as "teachers."

What to Do

Children are far more accepting of the computer as an art medium than adults. They quickly learn how to move the mouse. Depending on their age and fine motor control, some will need more monitoring.

- If the child is having difficulty holding the button down continuously, check hand position. Some young children do better if they use two fingers (the index and middle fingers) on the button.
- If the child is constantly hitting the menu bars and losing the line setting, reset the menu and remind him or her gently to keep the cursor on the white or black screen part. Children usually self-correct for this after a few times, because it is no fun waiting for an adult to come and reset the machine.
- Accidentally hitting menu choices may also be the way children discover other menu options independently.
- In the beginning, some children will need help changing the color. When they ask, slowly demonstrate how to do it, or pair the child with another who already knows how to do it.

Special Needs

Peripherals

There are many peripheral devices available that allow children who cannot use their hands to work on the computer. In some cases, a joystick will work better than a mouse. There are also touch screens and tablets (see appendix A for sources).

What to Say

It is important to use the correct computer terminology. This early experience with the computer will set the stage for later computer literacy. Words to introduce include: screen, mouse, menu, and cursor. Computer art, by its very nature, engages children in a discussion of art elements; line qualities, geometric shapes, and basic colors must be chosen from the menu. Verbalize these choices: "You are making wide, yellow lines, now," or "What shape will you choose to use now?"

Transition Out

When children finish, take a moment to describe what they did, such as "You covered the screen with so many straight lines!" or "Look at all the colors you used!"

If the work will be saved, consider having one work disk or folder for each child. This makes it easier to find the work when reloading. Label the disks with colorful stickers, covered with clear package-sealing tape, to make it easier for the children to find their own.

More to Do

Make prints. Printing out a picture is exciting. Children love to watch the picture slowly appear. It is possible to teach children how to save and then print out their own work.

EXPLORING COLLAGE MURALS AGES TWO AND UP

Collage murals are ideal group projects for children and adults of all ages. They can either be carefully planned, or they can be created on the spot in response to an exciting experience.

Group Composition

Any number of children can contribute to a collage mural as long as the background is big enough. Do not hesitate to add on to the background or to create several murals at the same time, if necessary.

Setup

Hang the background on the wall, on a bulletin board, or lay it across several table tops or the floor. Outdoors, try using clothespins to attach it to a fence, or roll it out on a sidewalk. Have small bottles of white glue nearby. If working indoors, keep a damp sponge ready to wipe up glue drips.

Materials

Brown kraft paper makes an excellent background for most murals. Rolls of paper suitable for murals are also available in a wide range of colors. If the objects to be attached are very heavy, cardboard cut from cartons can be glued together to form a sturdy base. If the pieces are small and heavy, such as pebbles, try using a wooden board or a piece of plywood.

Use white glue rather than paste to attach the pieces. For very young children, have an older child or adult help apply the glue. Because glue is slow drying, the item may need to be held in place for a while before it is affixed to a vertical surface.

Introduction

Each type of collage mural should begin with a common experience that gets everyone excited about the project. A few of the many possibilities follow.

Examples of collage murals.

Nature collage. Take a walk in the woods or park. Provide each participant with a bag in which to collect leaves, pebbles, flowers, and so on.

Special Needs

Adapting Mural Making

Mural making is a group process. All children need to be able to participate fully. Mural paper should be hung so that children have the opportunity to use large muscular motions. Provide plenty of room for them to extend their arms out full range. Accommodate children in wheelchairs by hanging the mural on the wall and at a height that allows them to work comfortably. If necessary, attach brushes or drawing tools to a dowel to extend the child's reach.

Note: These extended tools can be very useful in mural making and should be available for all children.

Color collage. Hold featured color days. Ask everyone to wear something in a specific color. Fill the room with objects in that color. Read a book about that color (see appendix B). Put out a collection of objects and art papers and materials in a specific color or, for a higher-level activity, have children find objects in that color for the mural.

Shape mural. Play a game about shapes (see chapter 6). Offer precut paper in one basic shape (circle, square, etc.) in an assortment of sizes and colors, or let children cut the shapes for the mural. The children can glue the shapes directly onto the mural. More experienced children may create a piece of artwork on their shape before attaching it. They can draw, paint, or make collages or prints. If using printing, offer items that create prints in the featured shape.

Textures. Invite children to find examples of a specific texture in the room, or play a sensory game from chapter 6. Put out objects that have that texture. For a higher-level activity, have children select that texture from an assortment.

Faces. Talk about facial features, and put out mirrors for the children to look in. Have a face hunt, and clip magazine pages that have faces on them. Then have children tear or cut out the eyes, noses, and mouths to make their own faces on construction paper shapes.

When done, have children sit in a circle and share their faces. Talk about places where crowds of people are seen, such as at a sporting event, at a show, or in a class. Then have each child in turn glue the face to the mural.

Mosaic collage. Take a walk and collect rounded or flat pebbles or stones. Toddlers should collect stones two to three inches in diameter; older ones should find smaller pieces about one-half inch to one inch in diameter. Have students glue the stones on a heavy cardboard or wood base. (Variation: Have students paint or color on them first, or use small blocks of wood, bottle caps, or seashells instead of stones.)

What to Do

1. After children have collected their objects or made their pieces, sit in a semicircle in front of the mural background.
2. Have children discuss what they have collected or made, and then decide together where to glue them on the mural paper.
3. Have each child come up and glue it on the mural.

What to Say

As children place their pieces, talk about leaving room for others and not covering up someone else's part. With each new addition, enthusiastically describe how well it looks with the other shapes already there.

Transition Out

Make sure all of the pieces are securely attached, and then place the mural flat to dry. Make a point of complimenting the group for working well together in creating a work of art.

More to Do

Celebrate it. Display the mural in an area where the group gathers, and refer to it often, reminding children of the joy of the experience.

Enhance the environment. Use the mural to provide a backdrop for thematic studies or a related learning center. For example, a nature collage could be hung in a science area. A pebble mosaic could hang in a math area accompanied by pictographs of the different sizes and colors of pebbles used.

Join with others. Invite another group to add on to the mural or make a companion piece.

Share with others. Hang the mural in a public place such as a hallway, lobby, or local business.

Teach with it. Murals can be used for lessons in language, math, and science.

Move creatively. Depending on the objects, invent matching movements. For a leaf mural, have the children move like falling leaves. For a shape mural, have them make their bodies into those shapes.

Making Connections

Language. Read books that relate to the theme of the mural. For example, introduce an ocean mural by reading Leo Lionni's *Swimmy* (1963). Have children write and draw about the experience. (See appendix B for books that relate to themes.)

Math. Sort, count, measure, and graph the objects used in the mural.

Science. Identify nature objects, and make labels for them or create a key. Sort objects into living and non-living.

Social Studies. Learn the names for the objects or shapes in another language. Study how people in other places use the same objects or shapes in their art.

Perception. Fill stuff bins with similar objects, textures, or shapes. Blindfold children, and let them try to identify objects on the mural using only touch.

INTRODUCING PAINTED MURALS AGES THREE AND UP

Helping children paint directly on the same background paper requires careful organization and attention to detail. However, it is well worth the effort. A painted mural truly reflects cooperation among all of the participants.

Group Composition

Painted murals require that children already have experience handling brushes and paint. More experienced children can work in larger groups, as they will need less assistance handling the materials. Even so, it is always better to keep groups as small as possible. Three to four younger children usually work well together. At the primary level, four to six make a good group size. Try to set up other related activities for children to do while they wait their turn to paint.

Setup

Hang the mural paper on the wall or bulletin board, or lay it across a table or the floor. Outside, use clothespins to attach it to a fence, or lay it on a sidewalk or paved area. Place newspaper extending beyond the edges to catch drips and misses.

Materials

There are several ways to distribute the paint. If children will need only one color at a time, paper or plastic drinking cups filled one-quarter full work well. Trays of cups to choose from can be set up near the mural.

If children need several colors, try placing teaspoons full of thick tempera on a sturdy paper plate. The cake size works well for little hands.

Avoid washing brushes unless it is absolutely necessary. Wet brushes make the paint runny and often cause drips. Set up a brush cleaning area away from the mural, and make sure there are paper towels or newspaper for blotting the brushes dry before reuse. If possible, have an older child or a parent supervise this area.

Classroom Museum

Display examples of Diego Rivero's murals, and read the book *Diego* (Winter, 1991), which tells about his life.

Warm-Up

Murals that do not require a painted background, such as the examples that follow, can be painted directly without preliminary sketching and are a good introduction to the painted mural. More involved thematic murals may need to be preplanned. (See Thematic Murals in this chapter.) Always provide a common experience that leads directly into the mural activity.

Examples of warm-ups for painted murals.

Paint drops. Rain is running down the windowpanes. It is a perfect day for drip painting! Add water to tempera paint so that it drips slowly. (Try it out first.) Hang a long sheet of paper on a wall, and be sure to put newspaper on the floor. Show the children how the paint drips, and encourage them to make many raindrops on their own.

Clouds. Lie on the grass and watch clouds floating in a blue sky. Give out white paint, and paint cloud shapes on a blue background paper.

Flower garden. Walk in a garden, and talk about the colors and shapes of the flowers. Then invite children to paint flowers on a green background paper.

Bubbles. Blow bubbles with the children. Talk about their colors, sizes, and shapes. If possible, use a giant bubble wand. Have the children think about ways bubbles could be shown in paint. Combine soap, water, and some tempera paint for color, and mix it to make it frothy. Then paint bubble shapes on the mural. (Remember, not all bubbles are round.)

What to Do

1. Provide constant supervision as the children paint. Help them find a space and, if necessary, mark it out for them with chalk.
2. Enlist the aid of older children and parents to help refill paint.
3. Wipe up spills immediately.

What to Say

As the children work, emphasize cooperative behavior. Compliment children when they respect the work of others and use their materials carefully. Watch for children having trouble controlling the paint, and offer suggestions such as, "Did you remember to wipe your brush?", or challenge them to solve the problem: "I see your paint color is running into Sue's. What could you do to prevent that?"

Transition Out

Help children put away supplies and clean their hands. Encourage them to look at what they have painted from a distance so they can see how it is part of the whole mural.

More to Do

Follow up. After painting a mural, take time to talk about the experience, any difficulties that had to be solved, and what was learned.

Find colors. Have children identify the colors used in the mural. If they mixed colors, have them tell how they made their colors, or have others try to guess.

Display it. Find a special way to incorporate the mural into the classroom. A sky mural could be hung on the ceiling or suspended over a reading area. Murals can be mounted on cardboard panels and folded into a low, freestanding screen to divide two learning areas.

Making Connections

Language. Read books that relate to the subject of the mural. Have children record their ideas about the experience in their journals. Make a Big Book about the mural project illustrated with pictures of the mural in progress.

Math. Measure different elements in the mural. For example, in the paint drop mural, which drip was the longest? The shortest?

Science. Time how long it takes the mural to dry. Do some colors dry faster than others? Why might that be?

Social Studies. Look at examples of mural and wall paintings done by people from other times and places. How are they similar to or different than the children's mural?

Teacher to Family

Asking for Help

Group art projects are hard to handle alone. Do not hesitate to invite family members to help. Plan ahead to make the experience a joy for all.

Ways Family Members Can Help

- Supervise the supply area, and help children get paint, glue, and so on.
- Assist a child with special needs.
- Help supervise washing up at the sink or cleaning up the work space.
- Monitor children who have finished working or who are waiting a turn.

EXPLORING PRINTED MURALS AGES ONE AND UP

Printmaking provides an ideal medium for cooperative art activities. Prints are easier than paint to contain inside of a designated area. The printed mural enables children of different levels and abilities to work together successfully.

Group Composition

As with painting, more experienced children can work in larger groups. One toddler can work with an older child or adult. Preschoolers can work in groups of three and four. Primary students can work in groups of four to six. A mural is not the place to experiment. All participants should have had the opportunity to print with similar materials individually before doing so on the mural.

Materials

- Objects for printing (See table 7–3 for suggestions.)
- Thick tempera paint in small shallow trays or water-based printing ink
- Mural paper

Warm-Up

Printmaking activities can be set up very quickly. This is the ideal medium for a mural that captures a sudden interest or an experience, as the following examples illustrate.

Examples of warm-ups for printed murals.

Snowflakes. Create this mural on a snowy day. Have the children play outside in the snow, and then come in and share how it felt. Invite them to recreate the feeling of snow in a mural. Put out sponge balls or other objects to print with and white paint in trays to make snowflake prints. Have each child decide where to put his or her snowflake print in relation to the others.

Shoe prints. Collect some old shoes in different sizes, from baby shoes to high heels. On a day when a child arrives in brand-new sneakers and the conversation naturally turns to comparing shoes, make a shoe-print mural. Bring out the paper and shoes, put colorful paint in several trays, and take the shoes for a walk across the paper.

Handprints. Use this activity to unite groups and become comfortable with their differences. Compare the size and color of everyone's hands. Have each child mix up paint to match skin tone. (See Teacher Tip: Guide to Mixing Colors in chapter 5.) Then have the children paint their hands and make handprints across a long sheet of kraft paper. Parents and visitors can be invited to add their handprints to the mural as well. If desired, label below the handprints with the child's name.

Suggestions follow:

1. Add liquid detergent to the paint to simplify cleanup.
2. Paint can be applied by placing a small amount in a shallow pan and then pressing the hand in it.
3. Hands can also be painted with a brush. The feel of the brush on the sensitive nerves of the palm is an indescribable sensory experience that every young child and adult should experience.
4. Provide a dishpan of warm, soapy water for cleanup.

Footprints. This mural can follow activities such as dancing barefoot, studying body parts, or discovering animal tracks in the mud or snow. It works best if there are two people, one to supervise the children putting on the paint and walking across the mural, and the other to help the children wash and dry their feet. This is a great outdoor, warm weather activity. Follow these guidelines:

1. Have children remove their shoes and socks, and then sit on a low chair placed at one end of a long piece of kraft paper.
2. Fill a shallow baking pan with a small amount of paint, and have children press both of their feet into the paint.
3. Help children stand and walk across the paper to the other end. Wet paint is slippery, so supervise closely. Encourage children to make an original track of their own. Play some music to accompany gentle dancing, or try some tiptoe prints.

4. Have a bucket of warm, soapy water and towels at the other end of the mural, and help children clean the paint off their feet.

Wheels. Relate to children's interest in wheeled vehicles by closely examining a truck or visiting a tire store and then organizing a wheel mural. Read *Wheels Around* (Rotner, 1995, New York: Houghton Mifflin).

Place a large sheet of paper on the table or floor. Make sure each child has plenty of room, as this is a very active activity. Fill several shallow trays with a small amount of paint. Place a variety of toy vehicles with different types of tire treads in the trays. Children will love driving their vehicles and leaving colorful tracks behind.

When the mural is dry, let children try to match the vehicles with their tracks. For variation, use small plastic animals and people instead of vehicles to make footprints, or draw roads first and then drive the cars on them.

What to Do

1. Place printing objects and trays of paint on a table near the mural. Have an older child or adult supervise this area and distribute more paint when needed.

2. Show each child where to work, and delineate her or his space on the paper.

3. Provide scraps of paper so children can try out printing the object before using it on the mural.

What to Say

Look for patterns created, and describe them for children. Ask questions that help children solve problems or work more effectively. For example, if the print is not clear, ask: "Have you tried it on the scrap paper to see just how much paint works best?"

More to Do

Search for patterns. See if the children can find places where the same print reappears.

Combing methods. Add printed elements to collage or painted murals, or add painted areas or collage items to a printed one.

Making Connections

Language. Read books that relate to the mural experience. Make a matching Big Book that features prints made from the same objects as the mural.

Math. Count and graph the different printed shapes.

Teacher Tip

Selecting Relevant Experiences

Experience with the real thing is absolutely essential. Art symbols created from direct experience are richer and more meaningful than those created secondhand. Teachers who want to expand their students' horizons need to discover ways to make the ordinary extraordinary rather than trying to create artificial experiences for their students. Making murals about daily happenings, such as the weather, the environment, and class events, is one way to do this.

Murals created without a direct experience must unfortunately rely on stereotypes and teachers' examples and do not allow children to create their own understanding of the subject. Snow murals, for example, should only be done in regions where it snows, and then only when it is snowing. They have little meaning for children who have never experienced snow. Video, stories, and teacher-created examples cannot replace the experience of feeling snowflakes stick to one's eyelashes, melting flakes on one's tongue, or making snow angels in a drift.

CREATING THEMATIC MURALS AGES FOUR AND UP

Thematic murals are the most complex but also one of the most rewarding group projects. A thematic mural builds on the children's existing knowledge and is best done as a culminating activity after the children have had many opportunities to explore not only the art medium but also the concepts and ideas that will be expressed in the mural.

Group Composition

A thematic mural should be the result of planning by the entire group, although small groups of three or four may work on individual parts. To be successful, the children should be experienced with the chosen art materials and should be able to participate in large group discussions.

Setup

The creation of a thematic mural may require many days of work. Select a location where there is plenty of space for small groups to work and that is convenient to the art materials. Hang the backing paper vertically 316in a visible location to keep interest high.

Warm-Up

Sitting with the whole group, create a list of all of the items related to the theme. Ask the children to describe the colors, textures, and patterns as well. If desired, look back at book illustrations, artwork, photographs of trips, artifacts, and other unit materials that might help children visualize the theme better.

Decide on the base colors for the background, and have children choose which details they want to include.

What to Do

Background. Begin by painting the background. Provide small paper cups or plates, and encourage children to mix their own paint color for the background using a ratio of two tablespoons of the base color mixed with several drops of a supplementary one. See chart below for ideas.

Have small groups take turns painting areas of the background. Encourage them to blend their colors into each other so that the whole paper is covered.

Foreground. While the paint is drying, children should return to the list and select the items they would like to include in the mural. Younger children can be given paper on which to draw or paint their selection and then cut it out. Older children can be asked to sketch their ideas.

When everyone is ready, call the group together and share the artwork or sketches. Discuss where each might be best placed on the mural. For example, a turtle might be at the bottom of a pond and a fish swimming near the surface.

Have the children take turns gluing their pictures to the mural. Older children can redraw their sketch directly on the mural surface, and then paint it.

SUBJECT	BASE COLOR	SUPPLEMENTARY COLORS
Water	Blue	White, green, purple, brown
Grass, forest, or garden	Green	White, yellow, brown
Sky	Blue	White, lavender
Snow	White	Gray, blue, purple
Fall	Orange	Red, yellow, brown
Beach	Beige	Yellow, white, tan, brown

Special Needs

Keeping Group Art Activities Open Ended

It is important to design mural activities so that every child can make a contribution no matter what the level of artistic skill. Never choose subject matter so limiting that there is no role for the child who is still scribbling or at early symbolic stages to participate in the project. Often this can be accomplished simply by paying careful attention to how the subject is worded. Instead of saying, "Let's make airplanes in the sky," say, "Can you make things that fly?"

Both cutout drawings and painted artwork can be enhanced with glued-on collage materials. Nature objects can be added as well. For example, real shells collected at the beach could be attached to a beach theme mural.

What to Say

Throughout the process, take time to sit as a whole group and discuss the progress being made. Compliment children who have worked well with each other, and discuss difficulties that occurred and how they were addressed.

Locating objects on the background invites discussion about perspective. Discuss how things that are bigger and lower down look like they are closer. Let children tape items in several different locations on the mural to help them decide where they want to put them.

Transition Out

Culminate the mural activity by holding a group meeting to review what was done and to assess the result. Invite each child to share a special memory about making the mural.

More to Do

Other backgrounds. Instead of painting the background, use sidewalk chalk or a paper collage, or try sponge painting it.

Add dimension. Glue small pieces of cardboard behind objects to raise them slightly above the surface and create dimensionality.

Create panels. Instead of making one large mural, have children work in small groups to create panels illustrating different aspects of the topic. For example, if the thematic unit is "Where does our food come from?" then separate panels could feature the farm, the factory, the supermarket, and the kitchen. Panels could also show a sequence of events, such as the metamorphosis of a butterfly.

Making Connections

Language. Encourage children to return to books they read, stories they wrote, and their journal entries to check facts and research ideas for the mural.

Math. Calculate the sizes of the different objects. Will they be life-size representations in the mural?

Science. Thematic murals are the ideal format in which to visually capture science concepts. Murals can show what children have learned about the water cycle, constellations in the night sky, and more.

EXPLORING GROUP SCULPTURES AGES ONE AND UP

Group sculptures are three-dimensional versions of the mural and can take many forms.

Group Composition

Both small and large groups can successfully build a sculpture. Toddlers may need assistance in attaching their parts.

Setup

Although dependent on the nature of the project, most group constructions require a large, open space in which the children can work.

Materials

Group sculptures can be built from any easily handled and joined three-dimensional material. Try boxes, paper bags stuffed with newspaper, chenille stems, straws, wooden blocks, corrugated cardboard, telephone wire, or Styrofoam packing material.

Warm-Up

Just like murals, constructions need to grow out of a special experience. For example, visit a sculpture garden, and then come back and build a class sculpture out of corrugated cardboard. Follow up a trip to the lumberyard by using wood scraps to build a tower or building. If children are using straws or toothpicks in a math counting activity, culminate with having the children glue them together into a linear sculpture using a piece of Styrofoam for a base.

What to Do

1. Have children prepare their contributions to the construction. This could involve painting it, giving it a shape, or glueing on pieces.
2. Toddlers can be helped individually to place their pieces. For older children, have the group sit in a circle around the work space. In turn, invite them to come and place their parts.
3. Together, decide how best to attach the pieces, while considering stability and other safety factors.

What to Say

Encourage children to consider how their part will go with the rest. Describe the work as it changes with each addition: "Look, it's getting taller." Respond positively to each child's contribution: "Your piece helps make it stronger."

Transition Out

Compliment the group's effort, and emphasize how each part contributes to the total effect of the whole. If desired, go around the circle and have each child express how she or he feels about what was accomplished.

More to Do

Build a box display. To introduce this activity, place a series of boxes from largest to smallest, one inside of the other. Put a tiny treasure in the smallest box. Have children take turns opening the boxes until they reach the treasure. Talk about the different ways boxes are used. Explain that each child will be making his or her own special box that will be joined with others to create a wall of treasures. Have ready a collection of small boxes such as jewelry, shoe and cereal boxes that are similar in size. Cut open on one of the larger sides. Tape the other sides closed if necessary. If the box is gray inside, have the children paint the inside. When the box is dry, children can place "treasures" inside—nature or other small objects that are special to them, or two-dimensional or three-dimensional pieces of their own artwork. Glue the boxes together, open side facing out, to create a wall or tower. Invite children to change their displays often.

Build a village. Walk through the neighborhood and identify the different types of buildings. In the classroom, draw and label several of the local streets on a sheet of paper covering a large table. Next, give the children blocks of wood or boxes of various sizes and shapes. Encourage them to create buildings for the class neighborhood.

Create a colored light quilt. Visit a building that has stained glass windows. Then give children colored cellophane and tissue paper. Explore what happens when light passes through these materials. Have children arrange the materials in small plastic bags. Use clear packing tape to tape the bags together.

Hang the "light quilt" in a window. (Variation: Place lightweight nature objects such as twigs, leaves, and shells in bags, with or without the colored papers.)

Make it move. Invite children to design paper shapes, and suspend them from strings. Then hang them from a curtain rod. Alternatively, make the shapes from sanitized Styrofoam trays, and hang them outside from a tree branch.

Draw it. Encourage children to make drawings showing the sequence of steps in building the sculpture. Display these near the piece.

Making Connections

Language. Tape-record children as they work. Replay the tape, and have children try to identify the speaker. Display selected quotes next to the finished piece. Record the children's description of what they did on an experience chart. Use the sculpture as a focal point for dramatic play.

Math. Measure the height and width of the sculpture as it is under construction. Record on a chart next to the time.

Science. If the piece is located in a sunny spot, point out the shadow and how it changes.

Social Studies. Look for similarities and differences in each child's contribution. Talk about how the sculpture would be less interesting if every part was exactly alike.

Teaching in Action

Putting a Group Project Together: Our Neighborhood Mural, Grade 1

An Interview with Mrs. Petersen

Q: How did you begin?

A: My first-grade class was very involved in the thematic unit *Where do we live?* We had done so many individual activities, that I wanted to do a group project that would allow children to work together.

Q: What were some of the individual activities?

A: Well, for one thing, we began by learning about where each child lived. The children drew pictures of their houses and shared them with the group. We talked about who lived in the house and the things they did there. Some children brought in photographs of their homes, and we shared them. Then they wrote about their homes in their journals. Everyone had to learn to write their own address and phone number, and we displayed it with each child's house drawing. We emphasized differences a lot. I read the children the book *The Big Orange Splot* (Pinkwater, 1977), and we talked about the ways each of their houses is different.

We also went for a walk around the school and looked at the houses and stores. I told the children to look for different geometric shapes. Then when we got back we made a list of what they noticed and drew pictures. By now, houses were a popular subject at the easel and in the block corner. I was pleased to see that the children weren't just making the same old stereotypical house shape either, and they were getting very colorful.

continued

Teaching in Action *continued*

Q: How did you get them started on the mural?

A: Well . . . I drew the streets we had taken on our walk on a large piece of paper. I traced our walk on the roads on the mural and explained that it was like a map. Then I asked children to imagine our walk and to name the different stores and houses we had passed. I had them use their journals and our chart to help them remember. But it really was amazing how much of the walk they could describe. Next, the children each chose a building to make out of paper. They cut out the shapes and used crayons for the details.

Q: Why did you have them cut their buildings out of paper rather than painting them?

A: First, I wanted to tie in a review of the basic shapes. As the children worked, I had them name the shapes that they were using. Also, I wanted them to have more experience in cutting. My goals for them were to identify and cut out rectangles, squares, and triangles. We hadn't done much before that. Second, I thought that since it was our first mural of the year, a collage-type mural would let them see better how we all contributed a part to the whole.

Q: Describe how you had the children put the mural together.

A: I hung the mural paper out on the bulletin board in the hall. That was the only place I had that was big enough. Then we all sat in front of it with the children holding their buildings. I started at the beginning of our walk, and as I moved my finger along the road, I asked what building we would see along the way. The child with that particular building would then come up. I didn't want glue dripping in the hall, so I gave the children a piece of tape, and they taped it in place. I thought that that would make it go faster, so they wouldn't lose interest. But I also discovered that using the tape let the children adjust the position of their buildings. Sometimes we had to move one to make sure another would fit without covering up the others.

Q: Did you leave it taped?

A: No, later I put it flat on the floor in the classroom and had each child glue down her or his building.

Q: What do you think the children learned in making this mural?

A: They learned which houses and buildings are in the neighborhood of the school, and they were introduced to some beginning mapping. They learned that buildings can be made of many geographic shapes joined in different ways, and that this helped them make more accurate representations of houses and buildings. The children also learned how to work together in creating the mural. I will build on this concept now by introducing how people need to work together to create a community in which all are safe and healthy, and where their rights are respected.

Studio Page 37

WORKING IN GROUPS

Think of one or more open-ended group art activities that could be done in response to the following experiences.

Experience	Activity Idea
A walk in the neighborhood	
A trip to a shoe store	
Watching clouds	
A quilter's visit	
Studying shapes	
Setting up a classroom fish tank	

Studio Page 38

Choose an age group, and write an activity plan for a group art activity that will help children learn to work cooperatively.

Group Composition: _____

Group Size: _____

Time Frame: _____

Objectives:

Physical _____

Social _____

Emotional _____

Perceptual _____

Cognitive _____

Art awareness _____

Setup: _____

Materials: _____

Procedure:

Introduction _____

What I will do _____

What I will say _____

Transition out _____

OBSERVATION: CHILDREN WORKING TOGETHER

Observe two groups of two or three children playing together or working on a common project. Group A should be children under three years old. Group B should be children four years old and up.

Group A Composition:

Child A: Age: Sex:

Child B: Age: Sex:

Child C: Age: Sex:

Group A Observation:

1. In what activity were children involved? _____

2. How long did children work together? _____

3. What did children say to each other? (A tape recording can be used.) _____

4. Which child/children imitated the actions of another? _____

5. Which child/children initiated group actions? _____

6. How often did an adult intervene, if at all? _____

Group B Composition:

Child A: Age: Sex:

Child B: Age: Sex:

Child C: Age: Sex:

Group B Observation:

1. In what activity were children involved? _____

2. How long did children work together? _____

3. What did children say to each other? (A tape recording can be used.) _____

4. Which child/children imitated the actions of another? _____

5. Which child/children initiated group actions? _____

6. How often did an adult intervene, if at all? _____

Studio Page 40

ANALYSIS: DEFINING COOPERATION

Based on your observations, defend or oppose the following statement:

> When working in the same room or at the same table, each child speaks for himself, even though he thinks he is listening to and understands the others. This kind of "collective monologue" is really a mutual excitation to action rather than a real exchange of ideas.
>
> —*Jean Piaget (1967, p. 29)*

_____

_____

_____

_____

_____

_____

_____

_____

_____

_____

_____

_____

_____

_____

_____

_____

_____

_____

_____

_____

_____

_____

For additional information on teaching art to young children, visit our Web site at http://www.earlychilded.delmar.com

Dealing with Differences

Questions Addressed in This Chapter:

- How can teachers create a climate in which art can flourish?
- How can art be used in anti-bias activities?
- How are children with special needs included in the art program?
- What is the role of holidays in an art program for young children?
- What is art therapy?

Young Artists at Work

Timothy:	The man in that painting is ugly.
Teacher:	Why do you say that?
Timothy:	His face is painted all black.
Teacher:	It is unfair and hurtful to say someone is ugly because of his skin color. In our classroom we respect how everyone looks. Why do you think the artist used black paint for the skin tone of this man?
Timothy:	Some people have black skin.
Teacher:	What color paint would an artist use to show your skin? Let's go mix some paint to match your skin color.

HOW CAN TEACHERS CREATE A CLIMATE IN WHICH ART CAN FLOURISH?

In offering art to young children, teachers need to be sure that the choice of activities creates an environment in which children from all backgrounds feel comfortable and can be creative in their artwork. Children differ in their racial, religious, cultural, and ethnic backgrounds. Research shows that children begin to be aware of these individual differences by age two, and that between the ages of three and five they develop a sense of who they are and how they differ from others (cited in Derman-Sparks & the A.B.C. Task Force, 1989, p. 1). Before children can feel free to relax and express themselves in creative art activities, they need to feel valued for who they are, not for how they look, talk, and behave. They need to be treated fairly and have their differences seen as strengths that enrich the learning of all of the children.

The visual and tactile nature of art allows children, regardless of their differences, to explore and learn together. Children who speak different languages can learn by observing each other as they create with the art materials. Because art is common to all cultures, it can be a vehicle through which cultural differences can be explored.

Creating an Art Environment That Celebrates Differences

It is not differences in themselves that cause the problems, but how people respond to differences.

—Louise Derman-Sparks & the A.B.C. Task Force (1989, p. 6)

Teachers must take action to encourage the development of an anti-bias atmosphere among children. They need to consider the materials they choose to supply and the pictures they display. Activities should be provided that foster discussion and the elimination of the misconceptions that are the basis of many prejudicial beliefs held by young children. There are a variety of ways that art can be used to support an anti-bias curriculum.

1. Provide art materials that reflect the wide range of natural skin tones. Paints, papers, play doughs, and crayons in the entire range of skin colors need to be regularly available, along with the other colors.
2. Mirrors should be available at all times for children to study themselves.
3. Images of people who represent the racial and ethnic groups found in the community and in the larger society need to be displayed. There should be a balance in the images so that there is no token group. It is recommended that about half of the

Children need to feel comfortable in order to express themselves through art.

images should represent the background of the predominant group of children in the class. The remainder of the images should represent the rest of the diversity found in society (Derman-Sparks & the A.B.C. Task Force, 1989).

4. When selecting artworks, look for pieces that show a range of people of different ages, sexes, sizes, colors, and abilities, people who are involved in activities that depict current life. Many prints are available that reflect this diversity, including those depicting art from Haitian, African, African-American, Native American, Mexican, and Asian sources. (See chapter 8 for suggestions and appendix A for sources.)

5. Artworks should also represent artists of diverse backgrounds and time periods, including the present. This is particularly important for Native Americans.

6. Illustrations in the books read to the children and available for them to use should also reflect society's diversity.

7. Stereotypical and inaccurate images should be removed from display in the room and used only in discussions of unfair representations of groups of people. Avoid so-called "multicultural" materials such as bulletin-board kits and patterns that depict

people from around the world wearing traditional clothing from the past. These materials leave children with the impression that, for example, all Native Americans wear leather and feathers, all Japanese wear kimonos, and all Africans wear dashikis.

Talking to Children about Differences

When art materials that reflect skin differences and images of a variety of people are introduced to young children, occasions will arise in which biased or unkind remarks will be made, and a response will be required by the teacher. A child may not want to handle black play dough because it is "ugly," or another may say, "My skin-color paint is prettier than yours." Whether it is during an art activity, or at any other time of the day, children's discriminating behavior must be addressed. Such comments, even by very young children, must not be ignored or excused, nor is the teacher's personal discomfort in dealing with difficult subjects a reason not to act. The following suggestions may help:

1. Immediately address the child's negative response. A response to the aforementioned statements

might be: "All colors are beautiful. Why do you say that?" If the comment is directed to another child, say: "That is a hurtful thing to say. Why do you say that?"

2. Help children figure out why they are uncomfortable.

3. Explain what remarks are hurtful, and give examples of things the child might say or do instead.

HOW CAN ART BE USED IN ANTI-BIAS ACTIVITIES?

Art activities can be used to help children express their feelings about individual differences. They provide an opportunity for teachers to initiate a dialogue to correct mistaken beliefs and model respect for others.

Sample Activities

The following examples provide models of these kinds of activities, suitable for children age two and up. They use a variety of materials and approaches. Most are designed for small groups or one on one.

Mixing my special color. Read a book about skin color, such as *All the Colors We Are* (Kissinger, 1994). Help children mix paint that matches the color of their skin. Place the paint in a labeled container that closes tightly. Give the color a beautiful name. Explain that whenever children want to paint a picture of themselves, they may use their own special color of paint.

Valuing children's unique colors. Read the book, *We Are All Alike . . . We Are All Different* (Cheltenham Elementary School Kindergarten, 1994). Collect a variety of paint-chip samples from a paint store. Have children sort them into groups. Then have them find the ones that match their hair, skin, and eye color. Make a graph or chart of the different range of colors in the group.

Make sure that there are skin-color paints available at the easel. Then when children use the paint color that is closest to their skin color, hair color, or eye color, make a comment about the beauty of that color and express its relationship to the children's coloring, such as: "You are painting with a beautiful almond brown (rich peach, soft beige, deep brown, etc.). It is the same color as your skin (hair, eyes)."

"Friends." Crayon—Laurel, age 4

1. Invite a child to lie down on a sheet of kraft paper cut to her or his length, and trace around her or him. (Do not force a child to participate. This activity makes some children feel uncomfortable.)

2. Cut out the tracing for toddlers and preschoolers who have beginning cutting skills. More adept cutters can cut their own.

3. Help children select the color of paint or crayons that best matches their skin, hair, eyes, and clothing, so they may color in their "Me Persons."

Color awareness collages. Transition in by reading *Black Is Beautiful* (McGovern, 1969). Have children find or make a list of all of the beautiful black or brown things that they know. Take a neighborhood or nature walk and look for brown or black things. Put out the collage items, exclaiming over the beautiful color of each material.

Open-ended art activities are suitable for all children.

Washing up. This interaction can occur following any messy activity in which the children's hands get covered with an art material, such as finger painting, printing, clay work, or painting.

When children are washing up at the sink, say, "What do you think might happen to the color of our skin when we wash the paint off? Look, it stays the same color. Our skin color doesn't come off, only the paint." Also provide opportunities for children to wash dirt off dolls that have different skin colors.

"It is me." Read *Bodies* (Brenner, 1973). Develop awareness of body parts and names by calling out a body part and a way to move it, such as, "Shake your arm up and down. Wiggle your toes. Put your hands on your head." Develop a rhythmic pattern, and repeat the actions several times. Another way to develop awareness is to encourage children to touch the different body parts on their finished silhouettes. Create life-size renderings of each child.

HOW ARE CHILDREN WITH SPECIAL NEEDS INCLUDED IN THE ART PROGRAM?

Most important to remember is that they are children first, and they can learn.

—Linda McCormick & Stephanie Feeney
(1995, p. 16)

Because of the open-ended nature of well-designed art activities, children with special needs can participate fully in most art programs, often without many modifications. If necessary, changes can be made in the tools and environment to allow active participation. The other children also need to be encouraged to accept and support those with special needs.

Defining Special Needs

Children with special needs are a tremendously diverse group. Some have obvious disabilities, and others have disabilities that cannot be seen by the casual observer. The Individuals with Disabilities Act (P.L. 94–142) has identified 10 categories of children who can receive special education services. These include children with learning disabilities, speech and language impairments, mental retardation, emotional disturbance, multiple disabilities, autism, hearing impairments, visual impairments, orthopedic impairments, and other health impairments.

In addition, the law mandates that children with disabilities be educated in the least restrictive environment. As a result of this law, many children with disabilities will be found in regular educational settings (Heward, 2000). This has led to many inclusion programs for young children where special provisions are made so that all children can achieve success.

Meeting Special Needs

Because children with special needs have unique developmental paths, inclusive early childhood programs need to focus on ways to help them become engaged in learning and in interacting socially with peers. Exploratory art activities, which entice children with colors, textures, and unexpected results, and which can be done alongside peers who are also exploring, can be vital to this process. Art activities also provide an opportunity for children to apply skills needed for further development. Grasping a marker or paintbrush prepares a child for holding a pencil for writing. Pushing and pulling play dough strengthens hand and arm muscles.

Adjusting interactions. However, in order to be successful, adjustments in teacher interaction level may need to be made. For example, research indicates that when a child talks more, language skills improve (Hart & Risley, 1995). For children with speech delays and impairments, the teacher may encourage verbalization by asking targeted questions and by responding to nonverbal child-initiated interactions by soliciting a verbal response. Talking about the child's art process and work provides a nonthreatening environment in which to do this.

Children with developmental delays need more time and practice to accomplish goals. Every minute that the child is in an educational setting must focus on the basic skills and behaviors that the child needs to obtain. Teachers can facilitate needed development by joining the child in an art activity and using the time to focus on general instructional goals. For example, if the goal for a particular child is to learn to ask for things rather than pointing, then as part of a

collage activity, the teacher may sit beside the child and place some intriguing collage materials to the far side in order to elicit a request from the child.

Adjusting the activity. The teacher may also need to do a task analysis and break down art activities into small steps so the child can achieve success. These steps can then be modeled and verbalized for the child, either one by one or in a series based on the child's needs. For example, an exploratory printmaking activity might be broken down into several parts. First, the child selects a printmaking tool from a tray containing several. Second, the child dips it into the chosen paint color. Third, the child presses the tool onto paper that is taped to the table. Last, the child puts the tool back into the tray. The steps are then repeated until the print is completed. At each of these steps, the guiding adult should give verbal and visual cues. With each succeeding repetition, the adult can withdraw some of the support until the child can carry out the tasks independently.

Getting help. An important part of working with children with special needs is obtaining information and assistance from the child's family. Families play a major role in caring for the child, and they understand much about the child's needs and capabilities. They can share what interactions and modifications of the environment have been successful for them. In addition, an early intervention team or professionals with expertise in the child's area of need can also offer needed assistance.

General Modifications for Art

All children with special needs are individually unique in terms of how they cope with art materials. The following list provides some general ideas. Specific suggestions are also found in the Creating Art sections throughout the book.

Meeting needs for muscular control.

1. Put trays across wheelchairs.
2. Provide wheelchair-height table.
3. Use pillows to position child to better manipulate materials.
4. Art tools such as crayons, markers, pencils, brushes, and pens can be wrapped in foam hair curlers to

improve grip. Velcro pieces can be attached to a cotton glove and the art tool.

5. Attach drawing tool or paintbrush to arm, prosthesis, foot, or headgear. Some children without the use of their arms use their mouths. Drawing tools can be taped into cigarette holders, or a special holder can be made or purchased. Remember, children do not draw with their hands, but with their minds.

6. If necessary, provide a rotary cutting wheel and a cutting mat instead of scissors.

7. Use no-spill paint containers and thickened paint. Choose brushes in a size that best matches the child's muscle control. Short, stubby brushes may work better than long-handled easel brushes. Foam brushes may make the paint easier to control.

Meeting visual needs.

1. Place a screen or textured surface under the paper to add texture to drawn lines.

2. Use a fabric tracing or marking wheel to create a raised line. Place pads of newspaper or rubber mats beneath lightweight paper.

3. Use scented crayons and markers; add scents to paint and glue (see chapters 6 and 7).

4. Provide many tactile materials.

5. Place supplies in the same locations every time, and attach tactile, identifying symbols on supply containers. For example, attach an actual piece of each collage material to collage storage bins. This will allow children to develop independence in obtaining their own supplies.

6. If the child has some vision, find out which colors are easiest to see, and provide many materials in those colors. For example, fluorescent colors and reflective safety tapes may appeal to some children.

Other assistance.

1. Some children who have visual or motor difficulties may need hand-over-hand assistance. Place a hand over the student's to assist with such skills as dipping the paintbrush into the container and then onto the paper, or dipping a finger into paste and then applying it to the object to be glued.

2. Some children may need their base paper taped to the table to keep it from moving or wrinkling when they work.

Behavioral and emotional needs.

1. Select activities that have few steps and instant results, such as modeling, painting, and print-making. Expect lots of exploration and physical expression of feelings.

2. For children who are easily distracted, provide work areas that allow plenty of space and that seem separate from the rest of the room.

3. Select and arrange art supplies carefully to help limit distractions as well.

Helping Other Children Accept Those with Special Needs

1. Do not criticize children for expressing curiosity. When children notice and ask questions about disabilities and special equipment, answer matter-of-factly with a simple and an accurate reply. It is important to be honest when answering. Use correct terminology whenever possible.

Child: "Why does Jared need a special holder for his crayons?"

Teacher: "Jared uses a holder because he has trouble holding small objects tightly. Jared likes to draw like you do, but he has muscular dystrophy, so we figured out a way that he could do it."

2. Do not deny differences, but help children see their shared similarities.

Child: "Maya just messes with the paints."

Teacher: "Maya likes to paint, just like you do. She has learned how to do many things. Now she is learning how to hold the brush."

3. Children need to become familiar with special equipment and devices but also need to learn to respect the equipment of a child with special needs. If possible, rent or borrow a variety of equipment for children to explore, but make it clear that they must respect the personal equipment of the child who must use it.

4. If a children are comfortable doing so, have them explain how their special equipment helps them create art and why it is important to take care of it. If they cannot do this on their own, then have them demonstrate how the equipment is used while an adult explains.

5. Invite artists with disabilities to share their art. Make sure they are prepared for the sometimes bold questions of children.

WHAT IS THE ROLE OF HOLIDAYS IN AN ART PROGRAM FOR YOUNG CHILDREN?

The overuse of holiday units interferes with a developmental approach to curriculum as too many "canned" activities take the place of activities tailored to the needs of specific groups of children.

—Louise Derman-Sparks & the A.B.C. Task Force (1989, p. 86)

In many early childhood programs, holidays have become a major focus for the creation of art. Art activity books abound that purport to deliver exciting new ways to create holiday art and decorations. We all like to celebrate, but we need to take a deeper look at the effect that this focus has on the child's view of the purpose of art. Holidays are fun; they create rituals, which build a sense of solidarity; they are part of a society's cultural life, but there are dangers in relating art creation so closely to holidays.

Fairness

First of all, how do teachers select which holidays to celebrate and which symbols the children will make? Not all holidays are celebrated in the same way by everyone. The holidays of all children in the group must be presented with equal emphasis. One holiday should not receive more time and attention than another. Holiday activities are often seen as one way to teach children about other cultures. However, for young children, they are best set in the context of the daily life and culture of specific children and their families in order to avoid creating stereotypes.

"Snowman." Tempera paint—*Jessica, age 6*

"Whirly lines." Tempera paint—*Tyler, age 5*

Presenting Multicultural Art beyond the Holiday

Presenting artwork that relates to that culture throughout the year rather than just in the context of the holiday helps prevent children from associating the art and culture with only the holiday. For example, Native American art and culture should be displayed and discussed in many art contexts—when making masks, working with beads, creating with clay, learning to spin and weave, and examining baskets—not just at Thanksgiving.

Avoiding Stereotypical Symbols

One of the hardest things to avoid when dealing with holiday-related art activities is the stereotypical images related to holidays. These images limit children's creativity and visual imaginations, and they often undermine their artistic self-confidence as they quickly learn that they cannot replicate the commercial perfection of a holiday symbol.

The perfect Christmas-tree shape, for example, is impossible for young children to make successfully without resorting to patterns or step-by-step copying, and the image becomes so ingrained that many upper-level art teachers find that they have to take their students on nature walks just to prove that all pine trees are not symmetrical, and that they can be represented in many other ways in their art. Hearts, egg shapes, bunnies, turkeys, and pumpkins all become bland, perfect symbols instead of reflecting the infinite variety of their actual forms.

It is hard to avoid these symbols, as they permeate the markets and media of this society. However, guiding adults need to consider carefully which images they want to surround the children in their care. Teachers can take the following actions to expand children's artistic imaginations and fight the prevailing stereotypes.

1. Avoid all holiday-related shapes in art activities. Do not give children cutouts of Christmas trees, turkeys, pumpkins, hearts, or other holiday shapes, or holiday coloring pages or stickers for the children to paint, draw, or make into collages.
2. Do not give children holiday-shaped cookie cutters to print with or to use with play dough. Instead, use simple geometric shapes from which they can build their own versions of these symbols if they wish.

3. Do not limit color choices of materials to only those of the prevailing holiday.

4. Instead of displaying stereotypical holiday images, provide aesthetic experiences with a collection of pumpkins, piles of pine boughs, a display of turkey feathers, a basket of eggs, or a cage of real rabbits, so the children can see and touch them and discover similarities and differences on their own.

WHAT IS ART THERAPY?

The art therapist functions as an educator who modifies art activities to meet the emotional needs of troubled children. All children find emotional release through the expressive nature of art activities, and some children may use art to work through traumatic experiences. For example, a child who has experienced a natural disaster may draw pictures of houses and trees that are then scribbled over or "destroyed," as happened in the disaster. Gradually, such pictures decrease as the child comes to terms with the occurrence.

For some children, however, art can be used to release otherwise unexpressed feelings and thoughts that may require adult help. A child whose pet was killed in an accident may draw increasingly bloody pictures, indicating that the incident is still very disturbing and that there is a need to work through these deep feelings.

Qualified art therapists work with a team of professionals to interpret the child's art, based on many samples. They then provide healing art activities. Art therapy is a distinct field of study that requires expertise in both art and psychology.

It is dangerous for untrained observers to make judgments about a child's emotional state based on just one or a few pieces of artwork. The constant use of one color of paint may simply reflect what color was available or closest to the child. Research indicates that many young children often use paint colors in the order that they are arranged at the easel (Winner, 1982, p. 151). Pictures of family members may reflect attempts by children to control their world. The parents may be shown small and the child huge, a new baby may be left out, or divorce and remarriage may not be

Dramatic play using artwork of their own creation draws all children closer together.

reflected at all in the child's "family" portrait. On the other hand, the arrangement of images may just indicate how well the child controls the art medium.

The educator's role should be to allow children to use art as a personal way to express their thoughts and emotions—a safe place to show their feelings and, incidentally, give adults a peek inside of an often otherwise private world.

CONCLUSION: CARING FOR EACH OTHER

Art is an outlet that lets children convey what they might not be able to say in words.

—Diane Dodge & Laura Colker (1992, p. 161)

The graphic symbols of art can often be used to express thoughts and feelings that are hard to put into words. Teachers need to be sensitive to the personal needs and beliefs of their students. Children can and should talk about the differences among them, but actually painting with different skin tones and working on the same art projects with those who are different helps children form tangible links. The art activities that teachers choose can help children broaden their perspectives in ways that will make them more successful participants in the future.

This chapter has offered ideas that challenge the educator to address sometimes controversial issues. Overheard comments could be ignored. Black and brown play dough could be avoided, because it makes some children uncomfortable or makes them act silly. Teachers could focus on the more readily available "old masters" instead of looking for the harder-to-locate artwork of African Americans and Latinos and those of other cultures. Teachers could give into the pressure to make commercialized holiday "art," or they can make the other choice, the one that takes a little more effort. They can make a commitment to do what is best for the children, knowing that change happens not all at once but a little bit every day.

FURTHER READING

The following references will help guide the development of an anti-bias program:

Derman-Sparks, L., & the A.B.C. Task Force. (1989). *Anti-bias curriculum: Tools for empowering young children.* Washington, DC: National Association for the Education of Young Children.
Using realistic examples, this book provides many positive ways that teachers can address bias in the classroom.

Gonzalez-Mena, J. (1993). *Multicultural issues in child care.* Mountain View, CA: Mayfield.
Often teachers do not realize that common practices and beliefs about child care are culturally determined. Gonzalez-Mena helps educators analyze their own behavior from a cultural viewpoint.

Thomson, B. J. (1993). *Words can hurt you.* New York: Addison-Wesley.
Many activities suitable for children under age eight are presented in this program designed to help children accept individual and cultural differences.

For detailed information on modifying activities for children with special needs, see the following references:

Art Educators of New Jersey. (1976/1995). *Insights: Art in special education.* Cherry Hill, NJ: Art Educators of New Jersey.
This comprehensive book on art for children with special needs, from preschool to grade 12, represents the combined experience of many teachers. It is full of invaluable, detailed suggestions.

Rodriquez, S. (1997). *The special artist's handbook.* Palo Alto, CA: Dale Seymour.
This book is directed more toward children over age five, but it still has many usable ideas for the early childhood classroom.

To learn more about art therapy, see the following works:

Malchiodi, C. A. (1998). *Understanding children's drawings*. New York: Guilford
This book looks at the different interpretations that can be made based on children's drawings, and it presents therapeutic ways to use drawing with children.

Ross, C. (1997). *Something to draw on: Activities and interventions using an art therapy approach*. London: Jessica Kingsley.
This book presents activity ideas for teachers to use with children who are experiencing emotional difficulties.

Puppets come to life in children's minds.

Creating Art: Art for Dramatic Play

ART FOR DRAMATIC PLAY

Masks, puppets, and a variety of other three-dimensional art forms provide children with an opportunity and impetus to actively engage in social interactions. Of all of the art forms, these call forth dramatic, imaginative play. Putting on a mask can allow children to transform themselves into new creatures. Speaking through a puppet, children can invent a new persona. Wearing a special hat can change the way a child walks. Shy children become bold. Loud children speak in tiny voices. These are truly magical creations. Puppet and mask making activities can be done with small groups working on individual projects at a table, or by individual children who need to create a puppet or mask to meet some particular requirement of their own self-selected play activities. These art forms are also ideal for the project approach, in which pairs or very small groups of older children plan a dramatic activity based on an experience and then create the needed props.

The activities that follow may seem simple. There are no tricky moving parts or multiple steps, but the children will add the magic—their own imaginations.

How Children Grow through Puppetry and Mask Making

Children will develop

1. fine motor skills, through the manipulation of a wide variety of materials to create three-dimensional art. (Bodily-Kinesthetic)
2. socially, by using masks and puppets to interact with other children through dramatic play. (Interpersonal)
3. emotionally, by being able to express feelings through the puppet or mask art form. (Intrapersonal)
4. visual perception skills, by using a wide variety of materials in new combinations and by solving a variety of three-dimensional construction problems.
5. language, by using vocabulary to describe three-dimensional forms and by developing literacy skills through the use of the puppets and masks to tell oral stories. (Linguistic)
6. cognitively, by observing cause and effect as their actions effect motion and reaction from peers. (Logical-Mathematical)
7. art awareness, by gaining familiarity with masks and puppets from many times and places.

EXPLORING STICK PUPPETS
AGES ONE AND UP

A puppet is really any inanimate object brought to life through the active manipulation of a child's hand. The addition of art materials fleshes out the child's conception. Most young children do not truly see the actual puppet but rather the imaginary being it becomes through their play.

The transition into puppet activities is important. Making a puppet should not be a one-time activity but something the child will return to again and again in order to create a character or persona with which to face the world. Introduce children to the world of puppets by including purchased or adult-made puppets as regular visitors to the program. Puppets can share secrets, read stories, and play with the children. They allow the adult to enter the child's world. Many of the most successful early childhood television programs, such as *Mr. Roger's Neighborhood* and *Sesame Street*, depend heavily on the use of puppets.

After introducing the puppet-making supplies, they should be available on a regular basis for whenever a child wants or needs to create a puppet. This is another reason to keep the design of the puppets quite simple, and within children's ability to create independently, without step-by-step instruction.

Group Composition

Independent or small group.

Setup

Puppet-making supplies should be available at all times. Create a puppet center. Place sticks, tubes, and cloth on a special shelf or small table near other art supplies. Display several child-made samples alongside them. A sectioned bottle box, kept in the same location, can be used to store unfinished and completed puppets.

Materials

- Strips of corrugated cardboard (1-by-12 inches) and/or paper towel tubes
- Precut construction paper in geometric shapes: circles, squares, triangles. (Do not provide patterns or elaborate precut shapes that predetermine what the puppet will be.)
- Drawing materials: crayons, markers
- Collage materials: fabric, yarn, Styrofoam packing material, and so on
- White glue
- Scissors (optional)

Classroom Museum

Introduce children to Balinese shadow puppets (see appendix A).

Warm-Up

A stick puppet consists of a shape mounted on a sturdy stick. It can be as simple as a face drawn on a circle or as elaborate as an animal complete with moving legs operated with supplementary sticks. Make several simple stick puppets ahead of time. These should simply be different shapes glued to the end of the cardboard strip or tube. Make up a story to tell with them, such as "Where is the missing triangle?" or use them as part of a shape activity. Show children where the puppet supplies are, and invite them to make their own stick puppets any time they want. Suggest ways of using the collage materials. Children may want to make puppets to interact with the sample ones. Leave the samples out for them to play with.

Be open to all of the children's versions of this activity. Even if it is just a scribble drawing attached to the end of the tube, in the child's mind, it is a persona. Interact with the children and their puppets to find out their intent.

What to Do

1. Select a large shape.
2. Glue the stick or tube to the back of the shape.
3. Add details: draw on features, glue on other

shapes for "limbs," and attach collage materials for hair, clothing, and so on.

What to Say

Encourage the children to find their own solutions to their problems. Ask: "How could you make the stick hold better so that the paper doesn't bend?"

If necessary, give a hint: "How could you move or add on to the stick or tube to make it hold the paper up?" Cardboard strips can be doubled up over each other to make them extend to the top.

Transition Out

Provide a place for children to keep their puppets, such as a box decorated as a house. When it is time to transition to another activity, have the children put their puppets to sleep.

More To Do

Create mini puppets. Children with well-developed fine motor skills can make smaller stick puppets using craft sticks as the support.

Make shadow puppets. Stick puppets can be used as shadow puppets. For toddlers and young preschoolers who prefer to see the effect they are creating, use an overhead projector or unshaded lamp to cast a light on a wall, in front of which they can play.

Stick puppets can be made independently by young children.

Build a shadow theater. Older children who understand that they can create an effect for others to see can use a shadow theater. Place a piece of white paper over the puppet theater opening. Use an overhead projector or a lamp to cast a light from the back.

Make them move. Moving parts can be made by using paper fasteners. Because most preschoolers will need an adult to help use them, offer them as an option, not a requirement.

Add cloth. Have the child place a wad of polyester stuffing in the center of a 9-by-12-inch square of plain-colored cloth. Gather it together over a cardboard stick or tube. Help the child wrap a piece of yarn around it several times and tie it tightly. Provide markers, small felt pieces, and yarn for creating features. The stick can also be wrapped with a piece of cloth to form a hand-concealing cape.

Make a set. Older children can draw a background scene on a sheet of paper and hang it on a wall or bulletin board to create a backdrop.

Making Connections

Language. Make a class Big Book. On each page, have a different child draw a scene. Then share the book with the whole group. Have children come forward and animate their puppet in front of their page.

Use a small tape recorder to record children's puppet plays. Share the recording in the listening center.

Math. As children count items, let them touch each one with their puppet.

Science. Go outside at different times on a sunny day, and have children observe their shadows as they move their puppets. Why do the shadows change?

Kinesthetic. Play puppet shadow tag on a sunny day. Have children try to make their puppet's shadow touch someone else's.

Sensory. Place colored cellophane or acetate on an overhead projector, and project it onto a white wall. Move the puppets in front of the light, and observe the colored shadows that result.

EXPLORING STRING PUPPETS AGES ONE AND UP

Children are enthralled by anything on a string. It seems almost magical the way the object responds to their pulls and tugs.

Group Composition

Individual or small group.

Setup

Have string or yarn precut into one-, two-, and three-foot lengths and stored over a peg or hook or laid out on a counter.

Materials

- Construction paper
- Scissors
- Paste or glue
- String or yarn
- Hole punch
- Optional: collage materials, drawing materials, paint

Warm-Up

String puppets can be made as part of a thematic unit on flying things, during which children have observed the different ways familiar things fly, such as a bee, fly, butterfly, kite, plane, and so on. They can also relate to themes concerning weather (wind), seasons (falling leaves, snowflakes), birds, vehicles, fish, and insects. Another way the idea could be initiated is through showing a piece of string and asking carefully placed questions, such as, "What do you think might happen if you put a string on what you made? Would you like to find out?" String puppets may also be a child-initiated activity; many times if the string and hole punch are available, children will come up with the idea of putting a string on their artwork all by themselves.

What to Do

1. Have children cut out a large shape of their own design. Depending on the initiating activity, this

Classroom Museum

Introduce the work of Alexander Calder, the inventor of the mobile. Children enjoy hearing about the miniature circus he made and then used to put on performances for his friends, and about how he made the world's largest mobiles by painting jet planes with original artwork. (Print available: *Fish Tail and Lobster Trap* [Take 5].)

may either be in response to the idea of creating something that can fly or it can be a cutting activity done for its own sake.

2. Children may paste on other shapes or collage materials. The shapes may also be folded or bent.

3. Children can punch their own holes in the shapes but may need help attaching the string. (Hint: A quick and easy way to attach the string is to put it through the hole, double it up, and tie an overhand knot at the end.)

4. Children can then experiment with making their art form fly in different ways. If the weather is pleasant, this is fun to do outside.

More to Do

Make mobiles. Particularly in response to themes concerning flying objects, artwork on strings can be suspended from the ceiling to float on the air currents.

Create vehicles. Strings can be attached to "vehicles" made from shoe, cereal, and gift boxes, which can then be pulled along the floor. Even older children who may have "outgrown" pull toys enjoy playing with ones they have made themselves.

Making Connections

Science. Observe how the different shapes fly. For older children, create a chart of the different motions, such as spinning, low flying, dipping, and so on. Ask

1. Select a very large box that is wider than it is deep. A box 12-by-24-by-36 inches makes a theater big enough for three or four children to play in at once.

2. Cut off flaps.

3. Cut opening in bottom of box.

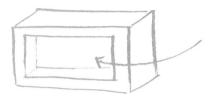

4. Cut up corners.

5. Poke holes in corner joints. Fasten with wire or chenille stems.

6. Make a curtain from filmy material, and put it on a dowel. Attach the curtained dowel to the inside of the stage opening. Affix with chenille stems through holes in the cardboard.

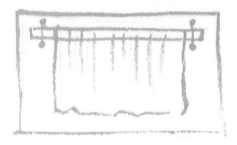

7. Paint front of theater, if desired.

8. To use: place on a table with the back edge even with the edge of the table. For string puppets, place it on the floor, and have children stand behind it with their puppets suspended below.

FIGURE 11–1 Folding puppet theater

questions that make children think about the relationship between the size of the shape and its weight and the resulting motion. For pulled-box projects, have children pull them over different surfaces, such as a smooth tile or wood floor and various rugs and mats. Compare how differently the vehicle moves. Objects of various weights can be put into the boxes, and children can compare the difference in how much effort is needed to pull them.

Music and movement. Play music such as *The Flight of the Bumblebee* (Rimsky-Korsakov), and have children move with their puppets in relationship to the sounds they hear. A tape of vehicle sounds could accompany a parade of pulled-box vehicles. Allow plenty of space for these activities.

EXPLORING HAND PUPPETS AGES ONE AND UP

Hand puppets come in many different forms. Children love the action and reactions they get from manipulating these simple creations.

Group Composition

Individual or small group.

Setup

Material for hand puppets can be put out with those for stick puppets. Display child-made hand puppets next to the supplies.

Materials

- Hand covering: sock, lunch bag, short tube, cereal box, or juice can. (The item should be able to fit over the child's hand or several fingers.)
- Paste or glue
- Scissors
- Construction paper
- Optional: collage materials, drawing materials, paint

Warm-Up

It does not take much to spark children's interest in hand puppets. Slipping a hand into a box or putting a

Classroom Museum

Invite a puppeteer to visit, and put on a show. After the show, ask the puppeteer to show how the puppets work.

tube over the fingers and saying, "Can you make me into someone to play with?" can inspire great feats of imagination. Creating hand puppets for a show of their own creation also makes an excellent small group project for children.

What to Do

1. Have the child figure out how the object best fits the hand or fingers, and what will be the front and back.
2. Place the object front-side up on the table.
3. Add cut-paper shapes, collage items, drawings, and/or paint to create the character.
4. Let dry before doing the other side (optional), or before using it. Waiting is the hard part for children. Fast-drying glue is a help.

What to Say

Encourage children to make up special voices for their puppets. Talk about how voices sound different when expressing various emotions.

Transition Out

If possible, provide small boxes for children to put their puppets to sleep in when it is time to stop using them. Hand puppets can also be stored or displayed on empty cardboard yarn cones.

More to Do

Finger puppets. Fold three-inch-wide strips of felt in half lengthwise, and sew up along outer edge. Cut resulting tube into three-inch sections. Children can slip these on their fingers. Use marker, small assorted

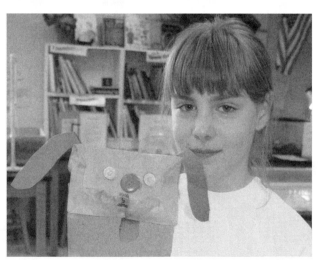

A paper bag can quickly be turned into a new creation using a child's imagination.

felt shapes, or small collage items (yarn, buttons, etc.) to create the puppets. Cut an opening out of the bottom of a shoe box, and glue on fabric curtains to make a mini-theater.

Making Connections

Language. Invite children to use their puppets to retell a favorite story in a new way. Encourage them to be inventive with the characters.

Math. Have children use their hand puppets to count and sort math manipulatives.

Science. Have children observe an object or event closely, and then explain it to their puppet.

Music and movement. Have children move their puppets to the rhythm of a variety of musical pieces.

EXPLORING MASK MAKING
AGES THREE AND UP

Masks allow children to express themselves in ways that they might not otherwise. Behind a mask, children feel like they are someone else; they may try acting in a new way or attempt things that might be too frightening barefaced. Like puppets, mask making should be available at all times for children to create as they feel the need, such as when dramatic play activities inspire children to turn themselves into particular characters, or when a child has a deep emotion to express but needs to do so from behind a mask. Again, simple masks that children can do independently make the best mask-making activities.

Group Composition

Individual or small group.

Setup

Create a mask-making center by putting out mask bases and associated art supplies near the dramatic play area. Display several child-created masks at the center.

Materials

- ☼ Mask bases: construction paper, tagboard, or cardboard face-size rectangles or circles with eye holes precut

Classroom Museum

Display prints or actual masks from many cultures, such as Native American, African, and Asian.

- ☼ Paste or glue
- ☼ Scissors
- ☼ Colored paper, collage materials, drawing materials, and/or paint

Warm-Up

Mask-making activities can be initiated in several ways. Interest can be aroused by showing a mask and then studying masks from other cultures, putting mask prints or handmade masks on display, or reading a book such as *Who's in Rabbit's House* (Aardema, 1967). This Masai tale from Africa is illustrated with pictures of people wearing masks, representing the characters in the story. Masks fit into thematic units on the face, senses, and body. If precut mask bases are available, then children will also self-initiate mask making as part of collage-making, painting, or drawing activities.

Paper-bag masks combine imaginative peeking and hiding.

What to Do

1. Glue on paper and collage items, paint, or draw on the mask base. Mask bases can be clipped to an easel for ease in painting.
2. If glue or paint is used, let the mask dry.
3. Masks can be used in several ways. Most simply, they can be held up to the face with the hands, or they can be attached to a handle made from a tube or cardboard strip. This is the preferred method, because most children can attach the handle themselves. It also works best for children who wear glasses or have hairstyles that prevent tying the mask on well. Masks with handles are easy for the child to take on and off. Some children, however, may want their masks tied on. Yarn or string can be used on tagboard or cardboard but tears paper too easily. For paper masks, cut a strip of paper about two inches wide, and staple or glue it to the sides of the mask so it fits the child when resting on top of the ears.
4. Provide a delineated space where children can move about safely as they act out their characters' actions.

What to Say

Encourage children to make up sounds and voices to go with their masks. Join the fun. Put on a mask, and interact with them.

Transition Out

Give children an opportunity to share their masks with each other before taking them home. For children's safety, they should not wear the masks when they take them home. Provide a bag in which to carry the mask.

More to Do

Make half masks. Some children may not want their full faces covered or may want to make goggles. Have available rectangular pieces, about four by nine inches, with precut eye holes. These will need to be worn with a paper strip fastened around the back of the head. Goggles can be made into an aesthetic experience by taping colored cellophane on the inner side of the eye holes.

Encourage dramatic play. Try to encourage the children not to take their masks home right away. That way they will be able to develop richer dramatic

Teacher Tip

Preparing Mask Bases

The requirement for all mask-making activities is to have available paper, cardboard, or bags in which eye holes have already been cut. Few young children can manage to locate eye holes in a usable place and then poke a scissors into the paper to cut them out. It is also important that the eye holes be large enough to provide safe visibility for children. Eye holes should be circles, not eye shapes, at least two inches in diameter, and separated by half an inch. Make a cardboard template to use on a regular basis.

play through interacting with the other children. By using their mask ideas, teachers can find related literature and themes to expand their play. For example, if several children have made animal masks and others have made monsters, then an interesting zoo or circus could result. A group of robots could lead into dramatic play about outer space.

Making Connections

Literature. Read *Dancing Masks of Africa* (Price, 1975), which, in beautiful, simple language, describes how African masks are used.

Math. Create simple math problems using the children's masks. Have them count the total eyes, ears, mouth, and so on.

Science. Study the different parts of the face and their functions (eyes, nose, mouth, teeth, tongue, ears). Match them to the features on the masks. Compare how they are similar or different.

Music and movement. Move to music while wearing masks.

Special Needs

Dealing with a Fear of Masks

Young children are often frightened by adults or strangers wearing masks. Mask-making activities help them deal with this fear. To reassure children who are easily frightened, adults should

- make their own masks using the same materials available to the children.

- avoid masks that show gruesome features.
- always put the mask on and take it off in front of the children.
- play peekaboo games with simple masks.

Children may also be frightened or uncomfortable when their own faces are tightly covered by masks. Allow them to hold masks up to their faces. Only tie them on when requested. Always keep eye holes very large, and provide plenty of helmet and goggle mask bases for more reluctant children to use.

EXPLORING HATS
AGES ONE AND UP

Making hats, jewelry, and other body decorations is another way that art and dramatic play interact. Wearing hats and jewelry makes children feel that they are grown-ups.

As with puppets and masks, body-wear items should be simple enough for children to make on their own. Creating original hats provides them with an opportunity to use a variety of art materials in three-dimensional form.

Group Composition

Individual or small group.

Setup

Place premade hat bands and hat bases close to the art supply area, or set up a hat-making center by the dramatic play area. Display child-made hats in this center.

Materials

- ✪ Premade hat bands: Use two-inch-wide strips of tagboard glued into circles large enough to fit over the children's heads and rest on their ears
- ✪ Paper cones: Bring the two corners of 12-by-18-inch paper rectangles together to form a conelike shape; glue or tape together. This hat form can be worn in several ways. It may need to be tied on to keep it in place.

Safety Note

Avoid Staples

Do not use staples, as they can get caught in children's hair.

Classroom Museum

Look at and discuss paintings that show people wearing hats, such as *Sunday in the Park,* Seurat (Modern Learning) or *Hope Street: Church Mothers,* M. Johnson-Calloway (Take 5).

- ✪ Alternatively, use paper plates with string attached on opposite sides.
- ✪ Drawing and collage materials
- ✪ Scissors
- ✪ Paste or glue

Warm-Up

An interest in hats can be sparked by observing some unusual ones, studying the hats of different workers in the community, and then reading a book such as *Hats! Hats! Hats!* (Morris, 1993). Suggest that children make thinking hats, reading hats, or hats for dancing. Hat making also relates to themes that involve parades and circuses. Hats can be used to enrich dramatic play and storytelling.

Keep a collection of hats to wear when reading related stories, such as a sunbonnet for a book about gardens or a ski cap for a winter story.

What to Do

1. Have children attach collage materials or shapes that they have cut out and perhaps drawn onto the hat base.
2. Let glue dry before wearing.
3. Attach strings to tie under chin for cone hats, if necessary.

What to Say

Hat making provides an ideal time to talk about different careers that are identified by special uniforms and hats. Name the different kinds of hats in books and in photographs of family and friends.

Transition Out

Create an attractive place for children to store their hats so they can use them in their dramatic play. Cut the flaps off the top of several large cereal boxes. Tape them together with the open tops facing out, and cover with self-stick paper covering.

Making Connections

Language. Share the charming story, *Jennie's Hat* (Keats, 1966), about a little girl with a fantastic hat.

Make a Big Book, or write a poem about the children's hats.

Math. Measure the size of each child's head, and then make each child a measuring tape to use when creating hatbands.

Science. Examine a hard hat and a bike helmet. How do they protect one's head? Design a protective wrapping for a favorite stuffed toy. Then drop it from different heights. What happens?

Music and movement. Play music and have children parade while wearing their hats.

EXPLORING JEWELRY MAKING
AGES ONE AND UP

Jewelry can take many forms. Necklaces, bracelets, pins, and badges can all be simple enough for children to make independently. For example, strips of paper can be decorated, glued into circles, and worn as bracelets, armbands, or watches. These activities provide an excellent way to work with the art element or theme of pattern.

Group Composition

Individual or small group.

Setup

Create a jewelry-making center near the dramatic play area. Put items to string in low trays. Notch a piece of cardboard, and place a precut, taped piece of yarn in each notch.

Materials

- ☺ Items to string: cut cardboard tubes (half- to one-inch sections), paper shapes with holes punched in them; small pieces of Styrofoam cut into shapes

Classroom Museum

Look at and discuss patterns in the beadwork of Native American and African people.

with punched holes in the center, straight macaroni,* child-made soda-clay beads (see appendix A: Recipes). (*Note:* Items for children under age three must pass choke test.)

- ☺ Yarn or heavy string: Wrap tape around one end for easy stringing. Tie a large piece of folded paper or a cardboard tube section to the other end to prevent strung items from falling off.

Warm-Up

Arouse children's interest by pointing out someone wearing unusual jewelry or by having a jewelry craftsperson visit the class. Jewelry making may be initiated through dramatic play.

What to Do

1. Assemble items to string in small trays. Prepare many measured pieces of yarn, with taped tips and paper ends. Lay them out on a table or counter so children can help themselves without tangling them.

2. Have children string items in a pattern of their own design.

3. Remove tied-on paper when done, and use an overhand knot to tie ends together.

What to Say

Stringing beads provides the ideal time to focus children on patterns. As they choose items to string, describe what they have done. For example, describe a pattern: "First you used a square piece, next a round one . . ." Make them think about their choices: "What will you put on next?" Use words such as pattern, repeated, first, second, third, and so on.

Transition Out

Have children describe any patterns that they have made. Record the pattern on a chart using color or shape symbols. Felt boards or magnet-backed paper shapes work well for this.

More to Do

Use smaller beads. Children with more developed fine motor control can string the larger sizes of pony beads sold commercially (see appendix A: Supplies). These mix well with handmade soda beads.

Make strip jewelry. Provide a wide assortment of paper strips to make necklaces, bracelets, wristbands, and headbands. Show children how to join the ends, add glue, and then hold together several seconds until the glue holds. Encourage children to draw patterns on their strips before glueing or to attach collage items after they are glued.

Making Connections

Language. Read *My Painted House/My Friendly Chicken* (Angelou, 1994) or the section on wampum in *The Story of the Dreamcatcher and Other Native American Crafts* (Lord, 1995).

Math. Look for patterns created as children string the beads. Ask them to find the patterns.

Teacher Tip

Selecting Open-Ended Activities

In this section, activities are presented that allow children to create original artwork with which they can play. Most of these activities provide a simple base upon which children work their own magic. Unfortunately, there have been many puppet, mask-making, and other related projects suggested for children that provide detailed patterns or elaborate, precut pieces. These do not allow the children to express themselves or solve construction problems on their own. Often this is due to an attempt to have young children make projects that are too complex for their skill level, such as paper-bag puppets with talking mouths or masks in sophisticated shapes.

In selecting activities, teachers must make sure that they are open ended and allow the children to make the most of their artistic decisions. They should build on the child's experiences and on thematic curriculum ideas, but they must not limit the child's expression.

Teaching in Action

Puppets: Transcript of a Student Observation

When I entered the three- and four-year-olds' room, I saw the teacher's aide working with a small group of children. They were sitting on a rug, and the aide was using a puppet made of a cardboard tube and a piece of round paper with a simple face on it. She was using a funny little voice and singing a song that described something about each child. When she said the child's name, she would lightly touch the child's hand with the puppet. The children seemed delighted. They giggled whenever the puppet touched them. Then she asked them if they would like to make a puppet too. The children seemed very excited by the idea.

She had paper circles in a basket, and she let the children each choose a circle and gave them each some markers in a small tray. The children drew a face for their puppets. I noticed that some of them were already talking in little, high-pitched puppet voices as they drew. When they were done, they went to a table and glued a cardboard tube to the back of the face. The aide had moved to the table and assisted them by asking if they had put on enough glue and reminding them to hold the paper to the tube until it was stuck.

Next the children began to have their puppets talk to each other. Two of them took them to the housekeeping area and fed them and pushed them in the carriage. Several others joined the aide in singing the song again, this time using their own puppet to touch a friend. When it was time to go home, the teacher asked the children to put their puppets to sleep in the puppet house [a decorated box that looked like a house]. I thought it would be hard to get them to leave the puppets, but the way she said "Tomorrow you can wake them up to play again" seemed to fit with how the children thought about the puppets—like real playmates—so they all came over and carefully laid their puppets in the box to sleep. When their families picked them up, some children took family members over to see the puppets sleeping. They were so cute. They would say, "Shhh . . . Don't wake them up."

Studio Page 41

MODIFYING AN ART PROGRAM

Imagine that you have just been told that a four-year-old girl with limited vision will be joining your group of preschoolers.

What modifications would you make in how art activities are offered?

_____
_____
_____
_____
_____
_____
_____
_____
_____
_____
_____
_____

How would you rearrange the environment to accommodate her needs?

_____
_____
_____
_____
_____
_____
_____
_____
_____
_____
_____
_____
_____

Studio Page 42

DEALING WITH DIFFICULT SITUATIONS

Consider each of the following situations, and decide what you would say and do.

1. A parent picks up her son's painting and says, "Another painting all in black! Why don't you use some pretty colors when you paint?"

_____

_____

_____

_____

2. A little girl refuses to touch the brown play dough. "It's yucky!" she declares.

_____

_____

_____

_____

3. Michael, age five, draws only faces with blood coming out of their mouths.

_____

_____

_____

_____

4. An aide shows the children how to trace their hands to make turkeys.

_____

_____

_____

_____

5. A child with muscular dystrophy is having trouble holding her crayon.

_____

_____

_____

_____

OBSERVATION: BIAS IN THE ENVIRONMENT

Visit a school or child care center when children are not present, and observe the following:

1. Are there crayons, paper, plasticine, play dough, or paints available in a variety of skin colors?

   _____

   _____

2. Are there child-height mirrors?

   _____

   _____

3. Are there images or artworks that depict people of different racial and ethnic groups?

   _____

   _____

4. Are predominant groups represented by the majority of the images or artworks?

   _____

   _____

5. Is society's diversity represented by the images or artworks displayed?

   _____

   _____

6. Are books available that reflect society's diversity?

   _____

   _____

7. Are there any stereotypical or inaccurate images representing certain groups, such as Native Americans?

   _____

   _____

8. Are there any commercial or stereotypical holiday artworks on display?

   _____

   _____

ANALYSIS: ELIMINATING BIAS

Based on what you observed, would you judge this a bias-free environment for young children?

_____
_____
_____
_____

If yes, write a letter to the director telling him or her what you especially liked about what the program offers young children. (Optional: This letter may be mailed to the director, if desired.)

_____
_____
_____
_____
_____
_____
_____
_____
_____

If no, make a plan of action that could be used to eliminate bias in the environment. Include cost, time frame, and personnel necessary to accomplish this task. Remember, change occurs bit by bit.

_____
_____
_____
_____
_____
_____
_____

For additional information on teaching art to young children, visit our Web site at http://www.earlychilded.delmar.com

Assessing Growth

> *Growth itself contains the germ of happiness.*
>
> —Pearl S. Buck ("To the Young," To My Daughters with Love, 1967)

Questions Addressed in This Chapter:

- What is authentic art assessment?
- How can children's artistic growth be assessed?
- What daily observation methods can be used?
- How can portfolios be used for long-term assessment?
- What can be learned by looking at a child's art?
- How do teachers share with families?
- How do teachers assess themselves?

Young Artists at Work

"Come see my bear!" my daughter shouted happily. She grabbed my hand and pulled me down the hall. It was the kindergarten open house, and the school was crowded with families. She looked carefully at each painting and drawing hung in neat rows on both sides of the hall.

"Is it this one?" I kept asking.

She shook her head no. Finally after several trips up and down the hall she said dejectedly, "It's not here."

"We'll ask your teacher where it is," I said encouragingly.

"Why, it's right here," said the teacher, pointing to a group of brown finger paintings that had been cut into identical teddy-bear shapes, each trimmed with a colorful bow at the neck.

"Here's yours," I said, showing her the one with her name on it.

My daughter studied it carefully. "No, that's not mine. I made a bear."

"This is a bear," said the teacher. "Don't you remember we made finger paintings, and then I cut them into bear shapes?"

"That's not mine," my daughter insisted stubbornly.

The teacher rolled her eyes and said, "These little ones never remember what they make."

The teacher turned to talk to another family, and my daughter scampered off to greet a friend. I turned back to the finger painting and studied it closely. Yes, although parts were missing, I could see that there had been a bear there, carefully drawn with a little finger—a childish bear, now brutally cut in order to fit the adult image of a pleasing bear shape.

As I turned away to join my daughter, I heard a family behind me exclaiming, "Oh, what cute little bears! The teachers here always have the children make such charming art. The children are fortunate to have such a great kindergarten program!"

WHAT IS AUTHENTIC ART ASSESSMENT?

Nobody sees a flower—really—it is so small it takes time—we haven't time—and to see takes time, like to have a friend takes time.

—Georgia O'Keeffe (Cameron, 1992, p. 22)

Art, unlike many other pursuits of young children, produces a tangible product. It is easy to fall into the trap of assessing the child, the teacher, and even the total program based on that product. How teachers view a child's artwork, and what they choose to do with it, will reflect the strength of their philosophy about child art. It takes a strong and dedicated educator to withstand the natural inclination to judge children by the art they produce, and to combat the pressure to dress up the program with parent-pleasing art.

This does not mean that teachers should not assess their art programs, but that they need to do so on the many components that enable children to produce art. Assessment is evaluating the progress that children and educators have made toward the goals they have set. Authentic assessment consists of looking at this progress in many different ways, using a variety of assessment tools. Properly done, such an assessment allows teachers to constantly improve the program so that they can provide the richest art experiences to young children.

HOW CAN CHILDREN'S ARTISTIC GROWTH BE ASSESSED?

Portfolios, collections of the child's work, and written observations are becoming an accepted method of documenting the child's progress. Written observations, which are thorough, objective, regular, and done in the natural classroom environment, are accurate measures of a child's progress.

—Barbara Nilsen (2001)

Watching children is an essential component of good teaching. Teachers can learn many things from how children behave and react artistically.

Observing the Individual

Individual behavior patterns can give us information about the following growth areas:

1. Physical: The child's physical control of the art media
2. Social: The child's ability to work with others in art activities
3. Emotional: The child's comfort level with art media and the art of others as expressed in art activities
4. Spatial: The child's visual perception skills
5. Symbolic language: The child's skill in relating graphic images and oral language
6. Cognitive understanding: The child's ability to express art concepts graphically and through oral language

Observing Group Dynamics

No child functions alone. Teachers must also place the child in the context of the group. Children learn as much from interacting with their peers as they do from adults. Every group has a unique dynamic, and no two groups react in the same way to the art activities that teachers offer. Observations of the behavior

"The Artists." Crayon—Laurel, age 4

of groups of children can help teachers see each child more broadly. Group behavior patterns can provide the following information:

1. The suitability of the art experience for the particular group
2. The interests of the group
3. The role of the child within the group

WHAT DAILY OBSERVATION METHODS CAN BE USED?

Working with very young children requires teachers to constantly interact with one or more children throughout the day. Every interaction and casual observation becomes stored in teachers' memories, and becomes what is often characterized as their "feeling" about a child or the group. If, day after day, a child builds with blocks, then the teacher feels the child must like blocks more than the other activities. If some children refuse to use finger paint, then teachers conclude they must not like to get messy and probably come from a home that stresses cleanliness. Teacher intuition is one of the basic forms of assessment.

Memories are far from perfect, however, and teachers are more likely to remember the unusual occurrences than the everyday behavior that is more reflective of an individual child and group. Past experiences also influence how teachers process their observations.

There is no way to record in memory every single behavior of a child. There will always be only partial images. That is why it is so important to have a system for recording behavioral observations in a systematic way. The crucial factor is always time. Teachers want to spend their time interacting with children, not writing about them. Systems for recording assessment information must be quick and simple.

Checklists

Checklists strategically placed around the children's environment can provide a convenient way to record behavior. Design a checklist by first creating a brief list of desirable behaviors in each art area. Then develop a simple symbol for each behavior, such as the initial letters or a shape. Choose symbols that directly relate to the behavior. Although it may take a while to learn them, eventually their use will become automatic. Make a list of the children's names, and then hang it at the easels, by the blocks, near the collage supplies, and so on. Use Velcro to attach a pencil near each list.

Throughout the day, mark the lists with symbols to indicate that a child is in a particular area and what behavior is being observed. Done on a regular basis, these checklists will provide a better picture of the child's daily behavior and skill development than memory alone. (See figures 12–1 and 12–2).

Anecdotal Record Keeping

Anecdotal records provide an ongoing picture of the child's behavior at set times in specific settings. They can be made at the time of the observation or soon after the event. To be useful, the record should document the setting of the event, including the time, the children involved, and any other related information. Anecdotes should be objective, recording only observed behaviors and direct quotes of the children, not the teacher's opinion about the reason for that behavior.

Sample Behaviors and Checklist Symbols

1. Works independently	I
2. Asks for help	H
3. Cleans up after self	Cl
4. Interacts positively with others	↕
5. Controls tools	T
6. Cuts with scissors	Cts
7. Stays on paper	Sp
8. Verbalizes about work	V
9. Identifies art elements	ID
10. Includes alphabet letters in work	ABC
11. Includes numerical information	123
12. Uses materials in a new way	*
13. Observes cause and effect	C&E
14. Observes similarities and differences	S/D
15. Shares materials	→

FIGURE 12–1 Sample behaviors and checklist system

AT THE EASEL AREA

Child's Name	Observation
Michelle	I ID Sp
Nick	T I → ↕
Stan	123 V H
Berette	V Cl
Jared	I ID Sp
Lin	H Cl

FIGURE 12–2 Sample checklist

Brief anecdotal records. Simple anecdotal notes can be made in checklist style by adding a space for date and comments. Next to the child's name on a behavioral checklist, simple notations can be recorded at the same time that other behavior is observed (see figure 12–3).

Detailed anecdotal records. More detailed observations may need to be recorded for a variety of purposes. Listing the steps a child went through to create a piece of art may show how the child was able to solve a problem. A description of the creation of a painting

DATE: March 4

Child's Name	Behavior
Rosario	Cts (heavy board)
Henry	↕ (worked on project with Bill)
Marcia	123 (counted squares on collage)
Bill	↕ (initiated collage with H.)
Ronnie	V "Look at my elephant!"

FIGURE 12–3 Sample checklist with anecdotal notes

Mario 2/4

At easel 10:04 to 10:10.
Started by making yellow line.
Then used blue. Touched where made green.
Put finger up to eye. Smiled.
Then took brush and smeared the colors together.
I asked, "What color is that?"
He said, "Green."

Susan 2/4

Drawing/cutting 10:50 to 11:05.
Took markers and went to block area.
Made a sign for building.
Said, "This is a supermarket."
Then drew rectangles and got scissors and cut them out.
Called them food.

FIGURE 12–4 Sample anecdotal records

may be used in an art display or to make the child's art more meaningful for the families. An ongoing record of how a group project evolved may become an integral part of the learning process when it is shared with the children and their families (see figure 12–4).

If possible, teachers should try to write one detailed anecdote about a child daily. To make it easier, prepare forms with the children's names and date already on them. Having the names on them prevents children from being missed. Index cards work well, as they can be carried in a pocket. Some teachers are more comfortable using clipboards or notebooks with one page

divided into sections for each child. Another method is to write on large, self-stick labels. They can then be peeled off and attached to the child's portfolio.

Recording project work. Project work can be recorded on a specially designed sheet that allows input from the children. A large sheet of paper can be divided into days. Each day the group can dictate its accomplishments. Children can also be encouraged to record on the sheet in their own way. Alternatively, each day's work can be recorded on separate sheets that are later bound to create a book about the project.

Process Folios

A process folio (figure 12–5) is a collection of materials that records how a piece of artwork or a series of art-works was accomplished. Process folios might be made for a group project such as the dinosaur described in figure 12–6, or for a group of easel paintings done over a week's time. Folios contain information from the checklists for the particular child or group of children, anecdotal records, related sketches, or notes

---

CONTENTS OF A SAMPLE PROCESS FOLIO: DINOSAUR PROJECT

Calendar showing days and time project was worked on

Child-dictated anecdotal records (figure 12–6)

Teacher's anecdotal records

Photos of dinosaur being built

Photos of finished dinosaur and everyone who worked on it

Class graph comparing heights of dinosaur and children in class

Michelle's drawings of finished dinosaur

Frank's story about the dinosaur (dictated and illustrated)

Margo's and Toma's story about the dinosaur (recorded on audiotape)

Sheet of comments about dinosaur written by families and visitors to program

FIGURE 12–5 Contents of sample process folio: Dinosaur project

Our Dinosaur Project

Day 1: We have decided to build a dinosaur. Michelle is making a head out of a box. Frank is making a big tail.

Day 2: Michelle's mom gave us a big box for the body.

Day 3: We decided to paint our dinosaur purple. We painted the head today.

Day 4: Toma and Mark helped us paint the body and tail. Michelle made neat teeth out of a Styrofoam tray.

Day 5: We tried to put our dinosaur together today. First we tried glue, but it fell off. Then Michelle thought we should use tape. So we taped it, but when Mrs. Denal moved it so we could have reading time, the head fell off. Everyone laughed. Frank was upset. He went and played with the blocks.

Day 6: Mrs. Denal showed us how to use wire to attach the parts of our dinosaur. She made the holes, and we pushed the wire through. Now our dinosaur is really strong. His head even moves because of the wire.

Day 7: We named our dinosaur "Purple." Margo wrote the name for us, and we hung it on a string around his neck. We measured him, and he is four feet high. He is taller than we are. We pretended he was wild, and Kate, Toma, and Frank built a pen for him out of the big blocks. Then we knocked it down and let him out. He is really friendly and will guard our room when we aren't here.

FIGURE 12–6 Sample project record

done by children, and audiotapes, photographs, and/or videotapes of the work in progress. Materials should be placed in the folio on a daily basis.

The process folio becomes an integral part of the artwork and serves to reproduce the multimedia process of creating graphic art. If the artwork is to be shared with families or displayed in an exhibit, then the process folio materials can be used to give meaning to the work.

Depending on the nature of the materials being collected about the artwork, process folios can be as simple as a file folder or large brown envelope, or as complex as a bound looseleaf notebook or child-decorated box.

Photography

Photography provides many opportunities for discovering and developing space-time concepts and relationships. A photograph freezes both space and time.

—*Lydia A. Gerhardt (1973, p. 165)*

Anyone working with children should always have a camera close at hand. It does not have to be a fancy one, but it should be simple and foolproof to operate. Automatic focusing, a light sensor, and a built-in flash are essential and generally available on even lower-priced cameras. If the camera is convenient to use and nearby, then it is more likely to be picked up at opportune moments.

To save costs, consider asking each family to donate a roll of color print film. Explain how the photographs will be used, and make sure to distribute the photographs to families at the end of the session.

The uses of photos are multitudinous.

1. Photographs of block structures, sculptures, and other three-dimensional projects can be displayed long after the originals are gone.
2. Photo albums of children's art, field trips, and special events can be kept in the book area.
3. Photographs of children working can be saved in process folios and portfolios as a visual way to remember how something was done.
4. Photographs of class members, families, friends, and visitors, as well as the children's homes and family events, can be used in portrait lessons and family studies.
5. Photographs of familiar objects shown from unusual viewpoints can challenge children's visual perception.
6. Photographs can be used to record art activities, setups, and child interactions for teachers to later review their teaching methods.

Photography tips. In the beginning, children are sometimes silly when photographs are taken. The more photographs are taken, the more accustomed children will become to the process. If necessary, walk around taking pictures with an empty camera. This also offers an opportunity to learn the best locations from which to capture activities in the different areas. Other suggestions follow:

- Try to get down to the children's level when taking photographs so all of the pictures do not reflect an adult's perspective.
- If using a flash, check the distance from the subject to avoid washed-out pictures. Consider using high-speed film instead.
- Do not shoot against a bright background, such as a window.
- Consider using an instant (or a digital) camera, if one is available, for situations in which there is not enough time to return developed pictures.

Videotaping

The availability of camcorders has made it possible to truly record the multimedia process of child art production. If a camera is available on a regular basis, it can be used to create a time record of a child's artistic growth. Have each family donate a videotape for their child's record. Label the tape with the child's name and the dates, and then, at regular intervals, videotape the child creating art. At the end of the term, return the tape to the family, who will then have a treasured record of their child's artistic growth.

Videotapes can also be made to record projects, as part of portfolios, and as a way to assess teaching style.

Videotaping tips.

- Built-in microphones tend to be very sensitive to background noise. Make sure that there is no banging or moving of furniture while taping. A directional microphone will produce better results.
- Do not film with a window behind the child. The light meter will adjust to the window's brightness, and the child will be in a shadow.
- Before filming, practice using the camcorder. The tape may rewind slightly when it is stopped. Before starting the next taping session, wind it forward slightly.

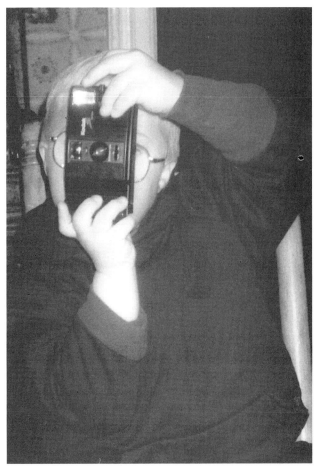

Children see their surroundings differently through a camera. (Photo credit: Kenneth Rozek)

- It is a good idea to start each taping with a view of a placard on which is written the date and the art experience being filmed. Some camcorders have an automatic date and time display feature as well.

Obtaining releases. Before taking any photographs or making a videotape, it is essential to obtain a signed release from all families. Many institutions have parents fill out such forms upon enrollment. However, if special use is going to be made of the pictures, such as a public display in an exhibit or at a workshop presentation, then a more specific release should be obtained (see figure 12–7). If a family refuses to sign a release, then that request must be respected. When shooting photographs, be careful to avoid taking pictures of children without releases, except when shot from the back.

Sample Model Release

The undersigned hereby grants _____ the right to make and have made, publish, reproduce,
Photographer's name

use, and reuse photographs or likenesses of my child _____ , in which my child appears,
Child's name

with or without his or her name, and to circulate and use the same for educational purposes. I further agree to hold

_____ harmless from any claim action and damages based on a violation or alleged violation
Photographer's name

of these representations. All photographs, negatives, prints, transparencies, drawings, reproductions, and sketches

made by _____ shall be the exclusive property of _____ .
Photographer's name   *Photographer's name*

Parent's or legal guardian's signature _____

_____   _____
Witness   *School official*

_____   _____
Date   *Title*

FIGURE 12–7 Sample model release

HOW CAN PORTFOLIOS BE USED FOR LONG-TERM ASSESSMENT?

A portfolio is a collection of artwork and related materials made over a period of time. It may contain all of the same items as a process folio, as well as completed process folios and child-created books about their art. Each child should have an art folder in which completed or unfinished artwork is stored, along with any other art-related materials. The child and her or his family should know where the folder is kept and be able to look through it at will.

Introducing Portfolios

Young children often do not seem to want to part with their artwork. This is partly a function of their wanting something tangible to share with their families at the end of the day, and partly a function of how art programs are run. A "make and take" view of art education encourages children and their families to feel that children must walk out the door clinging to a dripping painting or a gluey, paper-bag puppet. However, if children are introduced to the idea of an art folder or a portfolio on the very first day, if they participate in choosing the color of the paper or decorating the folder, and if they see where it will be kept, then they will be far more willing to leave their artwork behind. Families also need to be informed about the portfolio from the beginning and invited to look through it whenever they wish.

Constructing the Portfolio

The portfolio can be simply made from a very large piece of paper folded in half, or from two sheets taped together. If it will be used only for a short time, then this will suffice. If the folder will be used over a long period, such as a year or two, then it can be made sturdier by using clear packing tape to protect the edges, or it can be made from two corrugated cardboard pieces taped together along one side to form a hinge. The portfolio must be as large as the largest paper used by an individual child.

Small or bulky items such as videotapes and audiotapes can be stored separately in shallow gift boxes labeled with the child's name. These boxes can be sent home for the family's enjoyment on a regular basis.

Teacher Tip

Making a Portfolio

Materials

- Two pieces of corrugated cardboard, cut to the size of the finished portfolio (A), 24-by-36 inches, will hold all but the very largest pieces
- Two sheets of paper at least 2 inches larger in both directions than the cardboard (B) and two sheets the same size (C)
- Two pieces of fabric, 4 inches wide and the length of the folding edge of the portfolio (D)
- Six lengths of ribbon, about 12 inches each (E)
- White glue
- Scissors

What to Do

1. Before beginning, select matching paper, fabric, and ribbon colors.

2. Glue together the sheets of paper (B).
3. Place both sheets of cardboard (A) side by side on top of the paper, as illustrated. Leave an even amount of paper projecting on all sides. Leave a 2-inch space between the boards in the center.
4. Place a small line of glue on the outside edges of the boards. Flip and glue down.
5. Cut off the corners, as shown.
6. Fold over and glue down the flaps.
7. Attach ribbons, as shown.
8. Glue the sheets of same size-paper (C) over the glued-down flaps and ribbon ends.
9. Glue a strip of fabric (D) on the inside and outside of the folded edge. Make sure glue is only on edges of fabric to maintain flexibility when folded.
10. Use your creativity to decorate the outside of the portfolio. Attach a pocket made from a large envelope to the inside to store a table of contents.

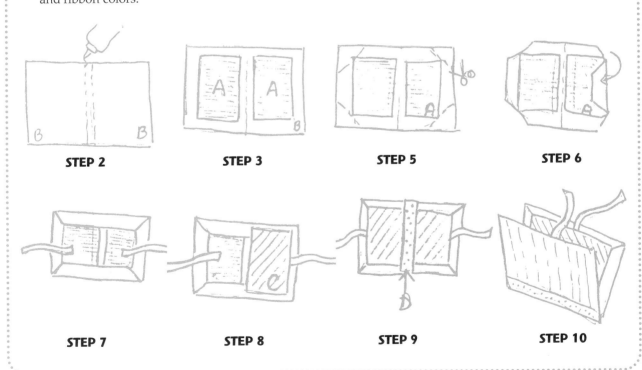

STEP 2   STEP 3   STEP 5   STEP 6

STEP 7   STEP 8   STEP 9   STEP 10

Storing the Portfolio

One of the reasons educators hesitate to initiate the portfolio is the problem of storing it and still retaining easy access. A pile of large floppy papers is unsightly and heavy. It becomes almost impossible to remove folders on the bottom without handling all of the folders above.

One solution is the commercially made, vertical, divided storage boxes that are used to store art prints (see appendix A). Another is to construct a giant drying box (see figure 5–4) with one-inch separations between the shelves, to store one portfolio on each shelf.

Labeling the Portfolio

For easy access to children and families, the folder must be clearly labeled (see figure 12–8). An index card stapled to the folder provides a sturdy tab. Cards placed at varying locations across the top of each folder allow individual children to locate their folders more easily. Color-code or mark the cards with special symbols as well as names to quickly locate folders.

Selecting Work for the Portfolio

Having a portfolio does not mean that every piece of artwork is put into the folder forever. Once children have been introduced to the portfolio, they should be asked daily if they wish to put their artwork into the folder. If artwork is three-dimensional, ask if they would like a photograph taken for the portfolio. The teacher can also select pieces for the folder (see figure 12–9). Children are more willing to part with art if they know why it is being selected, as in, "This paint-

---

Portfolio Label

Name: _____

Date completed: _____

Title or comment by child: _____

FIGURE 12–8 Portfolio label

What to Include in an Art Portfolio

Artwork
- ○ In a wide range of media
- ○ Done at different times

Photographs
- ○ Of three-dimensional projects
- ○ Of group projects such as murals
- ○ Of child doing art

Videos
- ○ Of child doing art

Checklist summaries
- ○ Of time spent at different activities
- ○ Of common art activity choices

Anecdotal materials
- ○ Child generated
- ○ Teacher generated
- ○ Family generated

Dictation
- ○ Child's ideas written down by teacher
- ○ Audiotapes of child talking about art

Interviews
- ○ Record of what child learned and observed about own art

Attitude lists (see figure 12–10)
- ○ Favorite art activities
- ○ Favorite art prints and artifacts
- ○ Favorite artists
- ○ Favorite book illustrations
- ○ Home art activities

Process folios
- ○ For projects
- ○ For a series of works

FIGURE 12–9 What to include in an art portfolio

Attitude toward Art

Conduct interviews at spaced intervals to assess changes in attitude toward art.

1. What is your favorite art material or activity?
2. What do you like best about creating art?
3. What art print or artifact do you like to look at?
4. Who is your favorite artist?
5. Which book has the best pictures?
6. Do you ever do artwork at home? Tell me about it.

FIGURE 12–10 Attitude toward art

ing shows how you have learned to make orange and brown. Let's put it in your portfolio. Would you like me to write anything about it to go with it?"

Time Line for Collecting Work

The portfolio should represent a natural time line, such as one session, three months, or a half year. The time period should be long enough to show growth, but not so long that the collection becomes unwieldy. Each piece in the portfolio should be labeled with the date. At the end of the time period, the work should be ordered by date to highlight the child's growth or changing interests. If the program is long term, extending over a year or more, then a few pieces from older portfolios can be selected to begin a new one.

When sending the work home, always send it in the portfolio itself, and create a new one to use for the next time period. This provides families with a unified presentation of the artwork rather than a hodgepodge of papers and keeps these simply constructed folders from becoming dog-eared. It is also beneficial for children to reestablish ownership of the portfolio concept through the creation and decoration of a new folder on a regular basis.

Preparing Artwork for the Portfolio

Artwork placed in a portfolio does not have to be mounted but should not be wrinkled. Each piece should be labeled with name, date, and any comments by the child. A simple preprinted form can be filled in and affixed to the back.

Using the Portfolio

The portfolio system allows art experiences to be richer and deeper in many ways.

- The child, teacher, and family can look through the portfolio individually or together, to review past progress (see figure 12–10 and figure 12–11).
- The child can decide to store a piece of artwork to be worked on another day.
- The teacher can suggest reworking a piece of artwork, such as using chalk over a painting or painting over a crayon drawing.
- Work can be collected, categorized, and made into work logs, booklets, or series showing growth in skill or knowledge or variations on a theme (see chapter 2).
- Work for display can be selected from a range of work rather than on the spur of the moment.
- At the end of the session, the portfolio can be sent home as a marvelous record of the child's artistic growth.

Self-Reflection on Portfolio Contents

1. Which artwork took the longest to make? The shortest?
2. Which artwork shows something new you learned?
3. Which artwork has the most colors? Lines? Patterns? Shapes?
4. Which art material did you use the most?
5. Is there any work you want to add more to?
6. Is there any work you would like to make into a book?
7. Is there any work you want to make a story about?
8. Which is your favorite piece?

FIGURE 12–11 Self-reflection on portfolio contents

WHAT CAN BE LEARNED BY LOOKING AT A CHILD'S ART?

Once teachers understand how children create art, they can also look at the individual artworks themselves as a means of assessing how a child is learning and thinking. Engel (1995) identifies two approaches to evaluating child art. One describes the individual piece and what it says about how the child is communicating through art. The other is developmental—it looks at the work's commonalities with the work of other children at the same level and uses this to place the child's work in perspective. By combining the two evaluative approaches, teachers can create a summary statement of a child's growth in art.

The Descriptive Approach

Engel suggests that starting with a basic description of the visual elements in a piece of artwork forces teachers to look carefully before making interpretive statements. She offers a continuum of questions to ask about the piece, from the most to least objective.

1. What is it made from? When and where was it made?
2. What are the basic art elements used? What lines, shapes, colors, patterns, forms, and textures can be seen? What art techniques did the child display (such as using the point or side of a crayon, or varying pressure to make different-size lines with the same brush)?
3. What, if anything, does the artwork represent? Is it a picture of a face or a house, or is it unidentifiable?
4. What is the organization of the picture? Where are different elements placed? What was done first? Last? Is the piece symmetrical or unbalanced?
5. What is its purpose? Was the child experimenting? Does it tell a story?
6. Where did the idea for the piece come from? Is it a response to an experience? Does it reflect the child's interests? Has it been influenced by TV or other cultural factors?

The Developmental Approach

Although each piece of child art is unique, it also reflects the graphic mode in which the child is operating. As described in chapter 3, children's art can be characterized as random marks, consciously controlled lines and shapes, action symbols, object symbols reflecting spatial and numerical understandings, and story pictures showing the use of notation. By looking at a particular work and knowing something

Children's art tells us many things.

of the conditions under which it was created, teachers can compare it to these artistic modes in order to place it in the general context of children's art.

1. Are the marks random or controlled?
2. Do the marks represent an action (such as driving a truck or going to grandma's)?
3. Do the graphic symbols show spatial understanding?
4. Do the graphic symbols show numerical concepts?
5. Are the graphic symbols understandable to other observers from the same culture?
6. Does the piece use any of the conventions common to the art of this culture, such as foreground and background, relative size, realistic shape and detail, shading, and overlap of things in front of others? (*Note:* Most of these would be found only occasionally in self-initiated work by young children.)
7. Does the piece communicate the child's knowledge of the media or subject? Does it express how the child feels about the media or subject?

Composing a Summary Statement

Using the responses to the aforementioned questions and, if possible, combining it with anecdotal notes and what the child says about the work, teachers can create a meaningful summary of the piece. Such a summary (see figure 12–12) can be used as part of the portfolio presentation, as part of the display of an artwork, in reports to families, and for the teacher's own records.

HOW DO TEACHERS SHARE WITH FAMILIES?

Creating art which reminds children of what they enjoy about school, then displaying the art in a prominent place at home positively reinforces a child's independence.

—*Simone Alter-Muri (1994, p. 5)*

Families have a very different relationship with their children than do teachers and other caregivers. Children look to their families for exclusive attention and ultimate acceptance as capable people. When children show their artwork to a family member and say, "Look

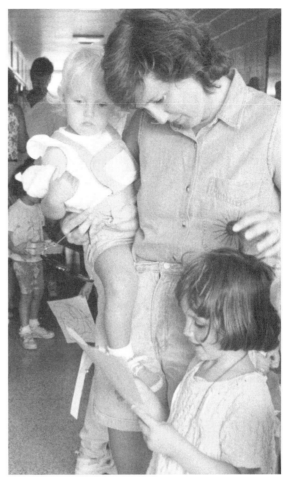

Families need to know how to respond to their children's art.

what I made!" they want more than a tepid "That's nice" or an ordinary "Good work." They definitely do not want criticism from this all-important person whom they wish to please. Children really want to know that their families have taken the time to acknowledge their efforts and joy.

Unfortunately, families are far less equipped to give the deep response that children are seeking than are teachers and other trained caregivers. Where the educator sees exploration and creative experimentation, the families may see only what they think is a visible (and perhaps an uncomplimentary) reflection on the quality of their children and their family.

Helping Families Appreciate Their Children's Artwork

It is the teacher's job to educate families about their children's artwork. Remember, unless teachers make

Four-year-old Heather's painting of a cat is typical of her work over the last three months. It was done in tempera paint on smooth tagboard. She used a stiff bristle brush and three colors of paint—red, yellow, and blue. Heather demonstrated that she has learned how to make green by putting yellow paint over the blue to make the green grass. She controlled the paint well, using the brush to keep the line size uniform throughout the picture.

She began by painting the sky and the grass. Then she made the cat's face. The shape of the head shows her spatial understanding that the ears are part of the cat. The cat is facing toward us, and the lack of a body may represent her inability to show it from the front, or her attempt to show that the body would be covered up by the head if viewed up close. Heather's number concept is strong. She shows three whiskers on each side, two ears and two eyes. The addition of the second sun represents a need to maintain the strong symmetry of the picture, rather than a lack of knowledge.

We can tell from the picture that Heather is familiar with and likes cats. Her cat and sun symbols are easily recognizable to the viewer. Heather's work is characteristic of early childhood art that uses simple, but recognizable, symbols to tell a story. As she learns to control the size of her painted line, we would expect that Heather will refine her symbol for a cat, using thinner lines for the whiskers and experimenting with views that would show more of the body. With time, she may also add more details to her painting to expand her visual stories.

FIGURE 12–12 Sample summary: Heather's cat

an effort to record children's process, family members will make judgments based only on children's products.

Ways to help families appreciate their children's art process. These general suggestions are accompanied by specific Teacher to Family samples.

- Provide many opportunities for families to review process folders and portfolios.
- When talking to families about their children's art

activities, emphasize process and growth rather than the project, and then help family members see this in the artwork. Checklists and anecdotal records will prove invaluable in remembering the specific actions of the children. Instead of saying, "Mary made a painting today," say, "Mary used paint today and learned how to make pink. See the pink spots in her painting." Instead of saying, "Arturo made a collage today," say, "Arturo cut many shapes from a piece of paper today. He used them in his collage. He made these triangles by cutting the corners off the paper."

⚙ Schedule "Art Happenings" throughout the year at which families are invited to create art together. This is a good time for group projects, such as murals, in which everyone can participate (see chapter 10). Watching families interact also gives teachers a better idea of their attitude toward their children's artwork.

⚙ Attach simple, prepared descriptions of art processes to artwork being sent home.

⚙ Send home letters, or, better yet, institute a regular newsletter that describes the children's art activities along with other class activities, in terms of process and growth.

⚙ Prepare an attractive booklet, illustrated with children's drawings, that briefly explains the goals of the art program, what children learn through art, and what kinds of art experiences will be offered.

⚙ Send home suggestions for setting up a simple art center in the home. It should not be project based but rather should provide a few basic art supplies that are always available, such as crayons, markers, paper, glue, scissors, and a modeling material such as play dough that children can use in their own ways. Help families by suggesting ways that they can contain messes, such as by setting up a small area as an art studio, providing an "art table," or, if space is limited, designating a plastic tray as the art spot.

⚙ Use a home art survey to find out the artistic background and experience of individual children.

Ways to help families understand artistic development. Families often do not have other children's artwork with which to compare their children's artwork, and so they cannot tell if what their children bring home is appropriate or not. Teachers need to help families understand the process of artistic development and have them come to understand that scribbling and exploring are a natural part of

Teacher to Family

Art Note (Attach to paintings going home)

This painting was done at the easel using tempera paints and a variety of brushes. Painting helps children grow in many ways.

- They learn to use large and small muscles as they reach and stretch to make colorful strokes.
- Their hand–eye coordination improves as they move the brush from the paint container to the paper and back again.
- Their visual perception increases as they see how new colors are made as one color mixes with another.

Take time to enjoy this painting with your child. Some things to say include:

- You made many colorful lines.
- You made some interesting colors with the paint.
- Can you show me a yellow (or other color) line you made?
- Is there a story to go with your picture?

Through sharing this painting, you can discover what your child has learned and thought about today.

Your child's teacher,

every child's art. It is the teacher's job to assure families that their children are performing in ways that are to be expected. There are a variety of ways to do this.

- Display many examples of artwork of all kinds, by children of all ages, either in the public areas where parents congregate or through exhibits and open houses.
- Hold family workshops in which examples of child art and process folios are shared, and concerns about artwork are discussed.
- Send to families, on a regular basis, summaries of children's art detailing what children have accomplished (see figure 12–12).
- Families gain a better appreciation for the process of art if they participate in workshops that allow them to draw, paint and use play dough and other supplies available to their children.

HOW DO TEACHERS ASSESS THEMSELVES?

Probably the most important assessment teachers can do is of themselves. Without self-assessment, teachers cannot grow and improve. Teaching is not a static profession with only one right way to get the job done. The most exciting educators are those who constantly tinker with their programs, who try new methods, and who are willing to take risks. Those educators must have methods of assessment to help them know what is working and what is not.

Since program self-assessment is done privately for ourselves, it is tempting for teachers to skip this crucial activity when they are exhausted from a busy day with energetic and challenging youngsters. Preplanned, easy-to-use assessment methods make it more likely that teachers will take the time to assess the programs they deliver. The following methods are suggested as ways to accomplish this task. Each provides a different viewpoint; when used in combination, they give an overall view of how teachers are doing.

Checklists

Checklists can be designed to quickly survey almost any area of the program. They provide objective information on the frequency of particular behaviors and the areas that may require attention. Checklists do not work if they are buried on a desk or in folders. They

Teacher to Family

Checklist: Home Art Experiences

1. What kind of artwork does your child do at home?

   _____

2. Where in your home does your child do artwork?

   _____

3. Where in your home is your child's artwork displayed?

   _____

4. Is there artwork by other people displayed in your home?

   _____

5. Has your family recently visited children's museums, craft shows, or other places where art is displayed?

   _____

6. Would you be interested in sharing any artwork that you or family members have done, or could you demonstrate an art technique to the children?

   _____

Teacher to Family

Sample Newsletter

Dear Family,

This week we have been observing water—a perfect activity for such a wet, rainy week. We began by experiencing a variety of water activities. We put ice in the water on the water table, and the children had fun seeing how long it took for the ice to melt. We boiled water and observed the steam rising. Then we used the boiling water to make some delicious mint tea. At the easel, some children experimented with what happens when water is mixed with paint. Tuesday we went outside and splashed in the puddles on the playground. We observed the various ways water looked when it moved.

We talked about different ways to remember what we observed. Some children decided to make charts. Others made drawings of what they saw. Several decided to make books and used each page to draw pictures of different kinds of water. The children used creativity in inventing symbols to represent ice, steam, and water. They also had to decide which colors to use to represent water.

Please take time to talk to your child about what he or she learned about water as you enjoy the water projects that are coming home.

Your child's teacher,

need to be strategically placed where they will be seen daily and, once filled in, acted upon and then filed with program planning materials so that the information will be used in future planning. Checklists can be created for assessing the environment, activities, and teaching methods (see figures 12–13 to 12–16).

Teachers need to know how they are doing and how they can improve.

Assessing the Physical Art Environment

Area Observed | Condition: Acceptable/Needs Attention[1]

	Organization	Safety	Upkeep	Cleanliness	Aesthetics
Art Print Displays					
Artifact Displays					
Blocks					
Book Displays					
Bookmaking					
Child Art Displays					
Collage					
Computer					
Dramatic Art					
Drawing Supplies					
Easel					
Modeling					
Painting					
Printing					
Sand					
Sensory Items					
Sink					
Storage					

[1]If an area needs attention, take action as soon as possible:

- Organization: Areas that need major straightening up daily after the children leave require reorganization.
- Safety: Places where children were injured or nearly injured need to be checked for hazards.
- Upkeep: Items that look worn or broken should be removed or fixed.
- Cleanliness: Dirty areas need to be looked at for ways to make them easier to clean during use.
- Aesthetics: Cluttered areas may be distracting. Too many colors may assault the senses. Materials may need to be rearranged to improve appearances.

FIGURE 12–13 Checklist: Assessing the physical art environment

Feedback from the Children

The checklists and anecdotal records that have been suggested for assessing the children can also be used for program assessment. These checklists reveal which activities attract interest and which are ignored. They document how many children choose to work in certain areas, how long they stay there, how much they interact, and what skills they are exhibiting. They also capture some teacher interaction with the children and provide a picture of what teachers have said.

Personal Art Notebook

Create a notebook in which to keep all of the materials generated in formulating the art aspect of the total program. The notebook serves as a tangible memory of the form and nature of the program. Keep copies of

Analyzing the Social Art Environment

Category	Observation (check applicable description)
SPACE:	⭕ Children have plenty of space for art activities.
	⭕ Children interfere with each other during art activities.
	⭕ Furniture constantly has to be moved to make room for art activities.
PRIVACY	⭕ Many children utilize private art spaces.
	⭕ Few children utilize private art spaces.
COMFORT	⭕ Children are quiet and calm in art areas.
	⭕ Children are noisy and irritable in art areas.
	⭕ Children avoid art areas.
SOCIAL INTERACTION	⭕ Many positive interactions take place in art areas.
ADULT USAGE	⭕ Many adult-child interactions take place in art areas.
	⭕ Few adult-child interactions take place in art areas.

FIGURE 12–14 Checklist: Analyzing the social art environment

plans, anecdotal records of how the activities went, checklists, and notes on actions taken to deal with difficult or unusual situations. Keep copies of all letters sent home to families. Looking back over this material will be invaluable in making better plans the next time.

Reflective Teaching Journal

A reflective journal provides a place for teachers to record their inner feelings about their work. Teachers need to set aside a time once a week, such as when the children are resting, to write a few reflective sentences on how they personally feel about what has been happening in this program of their creation. One way to approach this task is to respond to these sentence starters:

This week I felt competent when . . .
This week I felt frustrated when . . .
This week I felt exhilarated when . . .

"Terrific Me" Folder

Place a file folder labeled "TM" in a strategic place. Whenever complimentary notes from parents, children, or others are received, place them in this folder. Also include copies of materials from workshops attended or given, extra work done, notes about major accomplishments, and any other positive materials and activities. It is human nature to remember the negatives. Reviewing the materials in this folder every few months will provide not only an uplifting experience but also a more rounded view of one's accomplishments.

Children's art can be viewed in many ways. It speaks to us all.

Art Experience Assessment

Art experience: _____

Date(s): _____

Group composition: _____

ASSESSMENT AREA	CHECK IF PRESENT
Physical Growth	
• Required the use and control of large muscles	○
• Required the use and control of small muscles of the hand	○
• Required hand-eye coordination	○
• Required the use of more than one sense	○
Social Growth	
• Allowed children to work alongside others	○
• Required sharing of supplies	○
• Fostered positive peer interaction	○
• Fostered positive child-adult interaction and dialogue	○
Emotional Growth	
• Allowed children to work independently	○
• Allowed children to express personal feelings	○
• Provided time for introspection and concentration	○
Cognitive Growth	
• Encouraged children to verbalize about their work	○
• Fostered development of new graphic symbols	○
• Provided opportunities to use the vocabulary of art	○
• Enabled children to observe: Change	○
Cause and effect	○
Pattern	○
• Enabled children to make comparisons	○
• Provided experience with spatial concepts	○
• Required children to make artistic decisions	○
• Required children to order the sequence of their actions	○
Creativity	
• Utilized and challenged existing skills and knowledge	○
• Children were motivated to try activity	○
• Provided sufficient time for immersion	○
• Encouraged children to combine familiar elements in new ways	○
• Required children to solve challenging problems	○
Integration	
• Utilized knowledge from other curriculum areas	○
• Enhanced knowledge of other curriculum areas	○
• Enabled children to find connections among areas	○
Art of Others	
• Included opportunities to view art of others	○
• Included opportunities to discuss art of others	○
Reflection	
• Allowed children to talk about their own work	○
• Allowed children to decide what to do with their work	○
• Allowed children to participate in presenting the work	○

Note: Few art experiences include all of these areas. The more areas checked, however, the better designed and the more worthwhile that art experience is for children.

FIGURE 12–15 Checklist: Art experience assessment

Teacher Self-Assessment

Art experience: _____

Date(s): _____

Group composition: _____

ASSESSMENT AREA	CHECK IF PRESENT	ASSESSMENT AREA	CHECK IF PRESENT
Personal Behavior		I initiated artistic dialogue using questions based on:	
I showed confidence in my art ability.	○	• art elements	○
I avoided terms of self-deprecation.	○	• process	○
I expressed enthusiasm for the activity.	○	• artistic decisions	○
I wore art-related clothing.	○	• predictions	○
I participated in the activity by modeling process and/or technique.	○	• cause and effect	○
		• connecting events	○
Nonverbal Responses		• curriculum extension	○
My face mirrored my words.	○	I elicited stories.	○
I lowered myself to the child's level.	○	I took dictation.	○
I shared my feelings.	○	**Responses to Problems**	
I allowed wait time.	○	I gave encouragement when needed.	○
I made eye contact before speaking.	○	I provided comfort when needed.	○
		I provided direction when needed.	○
Verbal Responses		I fostered children's self-confidence by avoiding patterns and models.	○
I used descriptive statements.	○		
I used paraphrasing.	○		
I made interpretive statements.	○		

FIGURE 12–16 Checklist: Teacher self-assessment

CONCLUSION: A VISION TO GROW ON

We make sure to give children materials that will take any child's imprint and rejoice with the children over the beauty and differences in their creations.

—*Sydney G. Clemens (1991, p. 5)*

Art is a way of learning and communicating about the world that can enrich every aspect of an early childhood program. Teachers must constantly strive to offer a rich and thoughtful art program to young artists. No program is perfect. Although we do our best, we all make mistakes and fall into ruts. We do not always have the leisure or energy to choose our words with care, to clean up unsightly clutter, to read every beautifully illustrated book, to place each artwork carefully in a portfolio, to snap the perfect picture, or to select the most appropriate art experience for that moment in time. In the midst of a real-life, early childhood program surrounded by paint-covered hands, broken crayons, and too many unpredictable children, teachers need to keep before them a vision of a thoughtful art program as a worthwhile goal toward which to strive.

The Program

A thoughtful art program

- provides opportunities for verbal communication.
- is rich in sensory, kinesthetic, and multicultural experiences.
- helps children experience the art of others.

- provides a way to deal with individual and cultural differences.
- allows time for immersion, creativity, reflection, and self-assessment.

The Teachers

Excellent early childhood teachers

- are self-confident and enthusiastic.
- are creative and knowledgeable.
- are willing to take risks and try new approaches.
- choose words and behaviors that foster artistic dialogues with children.
- constantly assess their programs and themselves, and strive for improvement.

Step by Step

Change does not occur all at once. Teachers need to set small goals for themselves, working to improve one component of the program at a time. If in our hearts we truly care about the children, if we are amazed by the meaning they create through art, then improvement will follow. We will greet each smiling face and each "Look what I made!" with a heartfelt response, and our program will be as rich as we can make it.

FURTHER READING

To learn more about assessment methods, see the following:

Genishi, C. (1993). Art, portfolios, and assessment. *Early Childhood Today, 8*(2), 67.
This article details various assessment methods using art and portfolios.

Nilsen, B. (2001). *Week by week* (2nd ed.). Clifton Park, NY: Delmar Learning.
This book provides a comprehensive system of assessment methods, in all growth areas, for the practicing educator.

Paced, M., & Black, J. (1994). *Authentic assessment of the young child: Celebrating development and learning.* New York: Macmillan.
This book provides a detailed analysis of and uses for a wide variety of assessment methods.

Creating Art: Displaying Art

Displays can have many purposes.

SHOWING RESPECT FOR CHILDREN'S ART

It's important to keep in mind that how you handle children's art when it is finished says a lot about how much you value their efforts.

—*Diane T. Dodge & Joanna Phinney (1990, p. 175)*

No matter how much teachers recognize that process is more important than the finished product, at the end of each day they will be faced with many tangible art products that will require attention. Toddlers, who are immersed in explorations, may care little about what happens to these products and may not even remember making them. Older children will have many different attitudes to their work, depending on their purposes. Some, like toddlers, may care little for exploratory pieces. Others may cherish every piece they have touched. Work that expresses a particular feeling or subject may be highly valued. Art that the child intends as a "gift" will be viewed differently than art that is done just because the materials are there and the mood struck. For many children, of all ages, who use art as an emotional release, the artwork is viewed as

an extension of themselves. Its treatment is taken personally.

Adults may have a difficult time ascertaining how a child feels about a particular piece of artwork. Often this is not verbalized by the child. It is always best if the adult treats all children's artwork with respect. This models for the children how deeply adults value them and the work they produce.

Handling Artwork

Teachers need to keep track of their students' artwork and handle it with care.

Put on names. Strive to put names on the back of all pieces of work. Attach pencils or markers to walls with Velcro so that they are always handy. Develop a shorthand code, or use initials if pressed for time. If there are different sessions in the program, consider using a different-color marker for each session. For example, all of the green names might belong to the A.M. group, and all of the orange ones to the P.M. group. Label a shelf, cubby, or floor space with each child's name, and teach children to put their projects in their spots. Holding up children's artwork and saying "Whose is this?" tells the children that the teacher

Teacher Tip

Mounting Two-Dimensional Artwork

Supplies Needed:

colored construction paper
scissors
stapler or white glue

METHOD 1: Single Mount

1. Select a piece of construction paper slightly larger than the artwork. If the paper is the same size as the largest piece of construction paper, then overlap two sheets to make the mount larger. Artwork can be trimmed to make neater edges or so a smaller mount can be used. Trim up to one inch around the edges, as long as no part of the artwork is being cut off. Never cut off any major part of the work, such as turning rectangular paintings into circles or bear shapes. Standard paper sizes can be mounted on the next size up (8½ by 11 inches on 9 by 12 inches, 12 by 18 inches on 18 by 24 inches, and 18 by 24 inches on 24 by 36 inches.)
2. Center the artwork. If desired, the bottom border can be slightly larger than the top.
3. Staple or glue the artwork to mount. If gluing, place a small line of white glue around the very edge of the work. Never put glue in the center of the work, as it can cause wrinkles or discoloration.
4. Attach child's name to the mount using a self-stick label, or staple on a piece of paper.

METHOD 2: Double Mounts

1. Cut a piece of white or black paper so that it is one inch longer and wider than the artwork on all sides.
2. Center artwork and white/black mount on a larger piece of colored construction paper, and glue or staple.

Other Methods:

1. Commercial mats are available to fit standard sizes of paper. They give a finished look to the artwork and can be used for exhibits or special works (see appendix A).
2. Small pieces by the same child or several children can be mounted on one large backing paper.
3. Glue a corrugated cardboard strip or dowel to the back upper edge of the artwork. Punch holes in each end of the cardboard, and attach a piece of yarn for hanging. This works well for projects done on cloth.
4. Purchase several glass or Plexiglas frames in a size that fits most artwork produced. Tape a selected piece into the frame. Change the framed artwork on a regular basis. This system works well for work displayed in offices and bathrooms.
5. Avoid using trash items, such as Styrofoam trays, that trivialize the artwork.

did not care enough to notice what art they were making that day.

Do not fold artwork. If artwork is too large to fit in a space, then roll it up. Folded artwork can never be mounted properly. If stored for a period of time, it will tear at the folds. Art portfolios need to be large enough to hold the largest-size paper that individual children use.

Never throw away artwork in front of children. There will always be a few pieces of artwork that remain unidentified, no matter how hard teachers strive to label them all. If artwork must be discarded, do so discreetly. When children see artwork in the trash, they worry that the same thing may happen to theirs. Make sure parents are taught to do the same thing. Many children become disillusioned about creating art, because "it will just get thrown away at home."

Prepare work attractively. Make sure that all artwork that goes home or is displayed is properly labeled and presented.

Do not change it. Never cut off pieces of an art-work, or draw or work on it to make it "better." This is insulting to the child artist and reflects a lack of self-confidence on the part of the educator.

Sending Artwork Home

Artwork that is not being put into a portfolio will need to be sent home, but how it is sent will often make a difference in how the child and family come to value the art. Ideally, each work that goes home should be labeled, accompanied by an explanatory note and neatly mounted on a backing paper or stapled into a booklet labeled with the child's name and comments. In reality, such care for the individual works is impossible unless two things are done.

Encourage effort. Children need to be encouraged to spend time on their work. Rather than creating six drawings in five minutes, they need to learn how to spend ten minutes on one drawing. Encouraging children to spend more time on their art does not mean forcing them to do so. Toddlers and young preschoolers will usually spend less time on their art than older children because of their shorter concentration spans. However, concentration on an art project can be fostered in many ways.

- Provide quiet, private spaces for art to eliminate the distraction of other beckoning activities.
- Instead of putting out piles of paper at the table from which children help themselves with abandon, store paper out of the way so they have to get up and select another piece.
- Ask extending questions: "What other lines (shapes, patterns, flowers) can you add to your drawing?" Or, "Are you sure you are finished? Have you used all of the colors that you wanted to?"
- Provide reassurance: "There is plenty of time for you to work some more on your picture and then go play in the sand."

Create a presentation center. An area must be set where artwork is prepared to go home or to be put into the portfolio. This area can be a small table or shelf containing a stapler, colored paper in various sizes, markers, and preprinted labels.

When children finish a drawing or another dry project, or on the following day for projects that have been left overnight to dry (such as paintings, prints, and collages), the artwork is brought to the table. Ask the child to select a color for the background mount. Staple the artwork on the mount along with the label and any art notes for the family. The child then takes the work to a designated storage place or portfolio. If a child does produce a series of artworks on one day or over several days, they can be stapled together between two mounting sheets to form a book of art.

DISPLAYING ARTWORK IN THE CLASSROOM

In the classroom itself, teachers need to carefully consider their purpose in displaying the children's artwork. Some teachers do it as a form of self-flattery rather than as a way to educate the children. Hanging everyone's paintings or collages at the same time creates an overwhelming display—fine for a special occasion but hard to live with day after day. It does not take long for the art to be treated as just a colorful background.

Selecting Work

Teachers need to limit classroom displays to a selection of works that illustrates the theme or learning that is going on or to acknowledge the artistic accomplishment of one or a few children at a time. Remember that despite this seemingly limiting suggestion, each day the room will still be filled with art—art that is in the process of being made—paintings at the easel, sculptures of play dough on the table, and puppets on the stage.

Artist of the Week

One way to create a purposeful display is to establish an artist of the week or month. With that child, select a piece from the portfolio for display. Accompany the piece with a photograph of the artist, a transcribed interview, and/or dictation about the piece. Take time to introduce the child and the art to the group. Discuss it with a group in the same way a print would be discussed (see chapter 8). Hang the artwork in a place of honor. Because the artist is present, in addition to descriptive questions and statements, questions about technique can be answered:

"What kind of brush made this line?"
"What did you do to make this color?"

This same approach can also be used to present a group project.

Thematic Displays

Another method is to create a display of thematically related art that adds to or creates a unique environment and elicits the creation of more art. For example, for an underwater theme, turn one corner of the room into an aquarium with sea creatures hanging from the ceiling. Hang an undersea mural on the wall. Drape fishnets and shells on the shelving, and place sea-theme sculptures among them. Place the sand or water table in the center, or use the area to display and read books about the sea.

PUBLIC DISPLAYS OF CHILDREN'S ARTWORK

The purpose of public exhibits of children's art is different from home and classroom displays. The public arena is used to present the program to people who have not participated directly in the children's art process. Depending on how they are approached, public exhibits can destroy or benefit an art program.

Teacher Tip

Mounting Three-Dimensional Artwork

Wall Mounts
For work that is relatively lightweight, such as papier-mâché or cardboard sculptures, bulky but lightweight collages, small modeled sculptures, and fiber projects.

1. Straight pins: Use to mount bulky or thick items in showcases or on bulletin boards outside of classroom areas where art is displayed to the public. If the pins are hammered into the cork, they will remain very secure and should pose no danger to young children.
2. Wire or chenille stems: Use to attach lightweight sculptures to a heavy paper or cardboard base, which can then be stapled to the wall.
3. String or yarn: Tie to sculptures, and then suspend from pins, nails, or thumbtacks.
4. Boxes: Staple to small boxes to a wall, or join a group of boxes together with glue, wire, paper fasteners, or chenille stems. Paint the boxes a neutral color such as white or gray. Place small sculptures in each box.

Ceiling Mounts
For lightweight, three-dimensional projects, particularly those made of paper, tagboard, tubes, and fiber, such as mobiles.

1. Depending on the ceiling composition, use straight pins, staples, or hooks. Suspend artworks from strings so that they are just above the children's reach and out of the path of traffic, such as over tables or shelving. If the ceiling is high, consider attaching clips to the ends of suspended strings so work can be quickly hung without resorting to a ladder.
2. String wires across the room, from which projects can be suspended using clothespins.

Floor Mounts
For heavy, large, and/or delicate sculptures.

1. Raise work to child's eye level by using cardboard boxes of various sizes, painted in neutral colors.
2. Place oversized work on a piece of large paper, a cloth, or a rug to set it off from the rest of the floor.

What Is the Purpose of the Display?

Teachers must begin by analyzing why they are creating a public display in the first place. When the sole purpose of presentations of child art is to boost the egos of the children or the educators, then they can create pressure situations that are detrimental to the art process. Fearful of being judged by families or outsiders, educators exhort the children to do their best because their families are going to see it, or they select pseudo-art projects for the children to do that they hope will make a good impression. Teachers may display work that they think is most adult pleasing and reject work that looks out of control or unpleasant. Some teachers think, "I can't show this. Their families will be so disappointed in them. They'll think I'm not teaching anything."

Competitions and judged art shows also do not belong in early art education programs. They emphasize adult-pleasing products and foster the attitude that certain types of art are better than others. Such events may have a positive effect on the winners but can cause the losers to give up on art creation entirely.

There are, however, several positive functions that the public presentation of child art can serve, which also enhance an art program. All depend on having a portfolio/process folio system in place. Presentations with such carefully considered purposes will ultimately lead to more genuine ego building than those that have "ego boosting" as their main purpose.

Positive Public Presentations

Educational. Carefully designed exhibits can help families and friends learn more about how and why young children create art. They can also teach about art concepts and techniques and other curriculum areas, and they can help introduce adults to art created by people from other places and cultures.

Promotional. A well-put-together public display can introduce a program's best aspects. It can be a multimedia glimpse into the children's daily pursuits.

Celebratory. A public display can be a culminating experience for a theme unit or set of group projects. It is a way of sharing what the children have accomplished and learned.

Teacher Tip

Guidelines for Classroom Displays

- Avoid clutter.
- Display only one or a few pieces of art at a time.
- Change displayed artwork frequently.

Locating the Display

Depending on their purpose, these kinds of public displays can be located in a variety of places.

Walls outside of the children's work space are convenient for educational and promotional displays. Lobbies, hallways, stairwells, doors, offices, bathrooms, and any other space that is visited on a regular basis by the public can be used.

Celebratory presentations will require much more space, as they involve more than a static display of artwork. Auditoriums, cafeterias, hallways, the outdoors, or, if necessary, the entire classroom, cleared of its normal furnishings, can be used.

Educational Displays

A multitude of ideas exists for educational displays.

Artistic growth. To show artistic growth, display a series of works done by one child over a period of time. Accompany the display with photographs of children's hands illustrating different grips on art tools or anecdotal descriptions of how the works were created.

Art elements. To illustrate art elements, display a series of works by different children illustrating the use of line, shape, color, texture, form, or pattern. Accompany the display with bold graphics representing the art element and children's descriptions of the element in their artwork. Photographs of children exploring sensory experiences related to the particular element can be included, as can children's books about the element.

Techniques. To demonstrate a particular technique, select artworks done using that technique, such as papier-mâché puppets, clay bowls, or dyed-wool collages. Accompany the artworks with step-by-step photographs of how the children made them and their dictated or written explanations.

Multidisciplinary. Learning from other curriculum areas can be displayed by hanging charts and graphs, sample experiments, child-created comments and stories (experience charts), and photographs accompanied by any illustrative artwork the children created.

Art experiences. Experiences with artwork from other cultures can be shown by displaying artifacts or prints of the featured pieces, accompanied by descriptions of the culture and how they were made, along with children's art that reflects a related concept. For example, combine printed cloth from India with children's prints, or Mexican clay pottery with children's clay forms.

Promotional Displays

A promotional display should give a feeling for the art experiences in which the children participate. Select one or more pieces of artwork showing a range of techniques and approaches. Accompany the works with photographs of children creating similar art and/or children's comments or explanations. Label displays with bold signs that attract attention, such as "Our Artists at Work" or "The Wonderful World of Paint." Examples of the range of promotional presentations include brochures and calendars, showcases and bulletin boards, and badges and T-shirts, all featuring children's art.

Celebratory Presentations

Celebrations are more than just art exhibits, and as such, they involve far more elements and preparation, including any or all of the following:

- artwork—with descriptions (by children or adults)
- banners
- demonstrations—of technique and/or of art forms
- dramatic performances (children, adults, mixed groups, professional)
- guest performers—artists, musicians, dancers (children or adults)
- interactive exhibits (viewers are asked to respond to a question or survey, or to decide which tool or method was used to make an artwork)
- invitations
- participatory displays (such as a mural to which every guest contributes something)
- photographs
- posters
- process folio materials
- videotape

Celebrations of art are an ideal way to include families in their children's learning and to educate them about children's art. Invite families to help prepare and present the different activities.

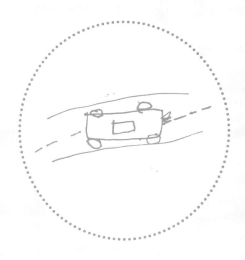

Teaching in Action

Sample Plans for a Celebratory Presentation

Festival of Lines: A Celebration for Toddlers and Their Families

An Introduction to Our Art Program

Location: The playground

Time: 2:00 to 4:00 P.M.

Welcome Table: Program and map; painted or paper streamer lines for visitors to follow to the different activities.

Art Display: Children's drawings and paintings with associated dictation.

Photography Display: Photographs of children creating art.

Interactive Art Display: Children's paintings with a set of brushes hung on string. Participants are invited to match the lines in the painting with the brush that created them.

Participatory Art Activity 1: Large sheet of mural paper, baskets of colorful markers, and an invitation to add some original lines.

Participatory Art Activity 2: Partner loom (see figure 8–2) is set up with a basket of colorful yarn and an invitation to weave a line.

Art Element Display: Children's paintings are interspersed with bold graphics showing different kinds of lines. Participants are asked to find the total number of each kind of line visible in the paintings. A box and coupons are provided for the guesses. At the end of the celebration, names will be drawn to receive door prizes.

Puppet Show: Put on by family volunteers, the show features a simple tale about a magic string, based on the book *Billy and the Magic String* (Karnovsky, 1995).

Demonstration 1: High school student volunteers demonstrate and teach about string figures from around the world.

Demonstration 2: Professional spinner demonstrates how wool is turned into yarn. She gives pieces of yarn to participants to use on partner loom.

Demonstration 3: Basket weaver creates willow baskets, surrounded by a display of photographs showing examples of lines in nature.

Demonstration 4: Washtub instrument. Participants can try making different tones by changing length of strings.

Measurement Table: Volunteers measure a length of string that is the height of each participant and tape it to a graph.

Musical Entertainment: Harp player and/or string players.

Refreshments: Foods that resemble lines (pretzel sticks, licorice sticks, breadsticks, carrot sticks and curls, spaghetti).

ANECDOTAL RECORDS

Based on the following anecdotes, describe the areas of growth demonstrated by each child as you would explain them to the child's family.

Lien 10/3 Age 3

Approached easel. Stirred paint in each container. Dipped brush into green and made a green line. Then dipped brush in red and smeared it over the green line. Exclaimed, "I made brown!"

_____

_____

_____

Salvo 11/9 Age 4

At collage center. Took tray and filled it with buttons. At table began to place buttons in rows. I suggested that he glue the row on a piece of paper. Shook head no. Five minutes later was still playing with the buttons. Cam approached and began to join in sorting. Together they made a row of buttons from one end of the table to the other. Very animated discussion about which button should come next in row. Cam invited me to see their "pattern."

_____

_____

_____

Wendy 3/24 Age 2½

Wendy was standing in front of the African mask print. I asked her what shapes she saw in the print. She pointed to the eyes and said, "Circles."

_____

_____

_____

Loren 4/12 Age 5

Loren sat under the table and worked on her book for all of the free time. Used crayon and marker. Worked very slowly and kept hesitating before selecting a color. Did not want to talk about it when I came by, so I left her alone. Later I noticed she was "reading" her book to Valerie in the book nook.

_____

_____

_____

Studio Page 46

ART NOTES FOR FAMILIES

Compose a general art note that could be attached to artwork going home that would explain

- what the art experience is.
- what the child learns by doing it.
- what the family might say about it.
- how the family might display it.

For your simple note, choose one of the following art areas: drawing, collage, printmaking, puppet making, or box sculpture.

_____

_____

_____

_____

_____

_____

_____

_____

_____

_____

_____

_____

_____

_____

_____

_____

_____

_____

_____

_____

_____

_____

Studio Page 47

DISPLAYING CHILDREN'S ART

Sketch a plan for an educational display of children's artwork. Include supplementary graphics (headings, labels, explanations, questions) as well as commentary about the art itself.

LAYOUT:

GRAPHICS:

Heading:

_____

Explanation:

_____

Questions:

_____

_____

Commentary on art:

_____

_____

_____

_____

_____

Studio Page 48

PLANNING A CELEBRATION OF ART

Select a topic or a theme, and plan a celebratory presentation.

Title:

_____

Welcome:

_____

_____

Educational Art Displays:

_____

_____

Dramatic Performances:

_____

_____

Musical Performances:

_____

_____

Interactive Exhibits:

_____

_____

Participatory Displays:

_____

_____

Demonstrations:

_____

_____

Graphic Elements (invitations, brochures, posters, signs, banners):

_____

_____

For additional information on teaching art to young children,
visit our Web site at http://www.earlychilded.delmar.com

Teacher Resources

 ART SUPPLIES SOURCES

Boxes, for storing large prints, Big Books, portfolios (chapters 4, 12)

> Calloway House (cardboard storage boxes and units)
> 451 Richardson Dr.
> Lancaster, PA 17603-4098
> http://www.callowayhouse.com

Package sealing tape, clear (chapter 5)

> Reliable
> Suite 300 West
> 1501 Woodfield Road
> Schaumberg, IL 60173
> 1-800-735-4000
> http://www.reliable.com

> National Bag, Inc.
> 2233 Old Mill Rd.
> Hudson, OH 44236
> 1-800-247-6000
> http://www.nationalbag.com

> Quill Office Products
> 100 Schelter Rd.
> Lincolnshire, IL 60069-3621
> http://www.quillcorp.com

Paint daubers (chapter 5)

Paint markers, refillable (chapter 4)

Paint scrapers and fingertip painters (chapter 5)

Papier-mâché paste (chapter 5)

Pony beads, large (chapter 11)

Precut mats (chapter 12)

Tempera blocks (chapter 5)

Vertical floor loom (chapter 8)

These items are all available from many art supply companies, including:

> Dick Blick
> P.O. Box 1267

> Galesburg, IL 61402-1267
> 1-800-447-8192
> http://www.dickblick.com

J. L. Hammett Co.
P.O. Box 9057
Braintree, MA 02184-9057
1-800-333-4600
http://www.hammett.com

Lakeshore Learning Materials
2695 E. Dominguez St.
Carson, CA 90749
1-800-428-4414
http://www.lakeshorelearning.com

NASCO
901 Janesville Ave.
Fort Atkinson, WI 53538-0901
1-800-558-9595
http://www.enasco.com

Sax Arts and Crafts
P.O. Box 51710
New Berlin, WI 53151
1-800-558-6696
http://www.saxarts.com

Triarco
14650 28th Ave. No.
Plymouth, MN 55447
1-800-328-3360
http://www.triarcoarts.com

Wool (chapter 8)

> Earth Guild
> 33 Hayward St.
> Asheville, NC 28801
> 1-800-327-8448
> http://www.earthguild.com

> Apple Hollow Fiber Arts
> Sturgeon Bay, WI 54235
> 888-324-8302
> http://www.applehollow.com

ARTIFACT SOURCES

Art Institute of Chicago
The Museum Shop
Michigan Avenue at Adams St.
Chicago, IL 60603
1-800-621-9337
http://www.artic.edu
Huichol yarn painting and beadwork; Guatemalan
weaving

Art.com
10700 World Trade Blvd.
Suite 100
Raleigh, NC 27617
800-952-5592
http://www.art.com

Davis Publications
50 Portland St.
Worcester, MA 01608
1-800-533-2847
http://www.davis-art.com
African artifact kit

Global Crafts
300 B Flagler Avenue
New Smyrna Beach, Florida 32169
1-866-468-3438
http://www.globalcrafts.org
Wide assortment of baskets from Africa, Asia, and the
Caribbean, as well as other artifacts

Jas. Townsend & Son, Inc.
133 N. First St.
Pierceton, IN 46562
1-800-338-1665
http://www.jastown.com
Colonial American: pierced tinware, large assortment of hats,
wool, spinning supplies

Mola Lady
Janet Gruver
8500 Creek Side Dr.
Bismark, ND 58504
1-800-880-6677
Molas made by the Kuna people of Panama (sales go toward
providing health care)

Museum of Modern Art
11 W. 53rd St.
New York, NY 10019-5401
1-800-447-6662
http://www.moma.org
Chinese Brush Painting Workstation with book on Chinese
brush painting by I. Ching Hsu

Oxfam America
P.O. Box 821
Lewiston, ME 04240
www.oxfamamerica.org
Handmade items from India, Africa, Indonesia, South and
Central America: weaving, pottery, carvings, masks, shadow
puppets, baskets

Save the Children
P.O. Box 166
Peru, IN 46970
1-800-833-3154
http://www.savethechildren.org
Carvings, masks, and other handmade artifacts from Africa
and Asia

SOURCES OF PRINTS AND POSTERS

Art Image
P.O. Box 160
Derby Line, VT 05830
1-800-361-2598
http://www.artimagepublications.com

Art Institute of Chicago
The Museum Shop
Michigan Avenue at Adams St.
Chicago, IL 60603
1-800-621-9337
http://www.artic.edu
Prints and postcard reproductions from
their collection

Art with Heart
Syracuse Cultural Workers
P.O. Box 6367
Syracuse, NY 13217
1-315-474-1132
Contemporary posters and postcards, many featuring
African-American and Native American artists

Cherokee Publications
P.O. Box 430
Cherokee, NC 28719
http://www.cherokeepub.com
Native American books, posters, kits, and music

Crizmac
P.O. Box 65928
Tucson, AR 85728-5928
1-800-913-8555
http://www.crizmac.com
Individual and sets of prints, including Take 5, of Native
American, Haitan, African, and other art from many times
and places

Davis Publications
50 Portland St.
Worcester, MA 01608
1-800-533-2847
http://www.davis-art.com
Sets of large, laminated reproductions on many topics,
including the art elements and multicultural art

Dover Publications
31 E. 2nd St.
Mineola, NY 11501
http://store.doverpublications.com
Postcards and inexpensive books that can be cut apart to use

as prints: Native American, African, Asian, Central and South American

Knowledge Unlimited
P.O. Box 52
Madison, WI 53707-0052
1-800-356-2303
http://thekustore.com
Sets of (Take 5) prints: Native American, African-American, women artists, and others

Metropolitan Museum of Art
255 Gracie Station
New York, NY 10028-9998
1-800-468-7386
http://www.metmuseum.org
Print and postcard reproductions of artwork in their collection

Museum of Fine Arts, Boston
P.O. Box 244
Avon, MA 02322-0244
http://www.mfa.org
Prints and postcard reproductions from their collection

Museum of Modern Art
11 W. 53rd St.
New York, NY 10019-5401
1-800-447-6662
http://www.moma.org
Prints and postcards from their collection

Nasco Arts and Crafts
901 Janesville Ave.
Fort Atkinson, WI 53538-0901
1-800-558-9595
http://www.enasco.com
Caraway book series on world art forms, Take 5 and many other print series, and famous artists postcard sets

National Gallery of Art
2000B South Club Dr.
Landover, MD 20785
http://www.nga.gov
Postcards and medium-size prints of works in their collection

Print Finders
15 Roosevelt Pl.
Scarsdale, NY 10583
1-914-725-2332
Print Finders will try to locate a particular print and its size, cost, and availability, and then will order it.

Sax Visual Arts Resources
P.O. Box 51710
New Berlin, WI 53151
1-800-558-6696
http://www.saxarts.com
Print sets reproducing African-American, African, Native American art and more

Southwest Indian Foundation
P.O. Box 86
Gallup, NM 87302-0001

1-505-863-4037
http://www.southwestindian.com
Native American artifacts from the Southwest United States

Unicef
P.O. Box 182233
Chattanooga, TN 37422
1-800-553-1200
http://www.unicef.org
Contemporary cards featuring multinational artists, silk boxes from Bangladesh, and handmade paper from Nepal

COMPUTER SUPPLIES AND SOFTWARE

Art Software

The following CD-ROM software is for both Macintosh and Windows platforms. Consult programs for specific computer requirements.

Blue's Art Time Activities by Humongous MAC/WIN

Flying Colors by Magic Mouse Productions MAC/WIN

Kid Pix 3 by Broderbund MAC/WIN

Kid Works Deluxe by KNA Multimedia MAC/WIN

Magic Artist Studio Disney MAC/WIN

Sesame Street Elmo's Art Workshop by Learning Company MAC/WIN

Please note: Some of these programs contain coloring-book types of activities. These are not creative art. Use only the free draw sections that allow the child to start with a blank screen and draw lines and shapes.

Suppliers

Educational Resources
1550 Executive Dr.
Elgin, IL 60123
1-800-624-2926
http://www.edresources.com

Smart Kids Software
P.O. Box 590464
Houston, TX 77259
888-881-6001
http://www.smartkidssoftware.com

TAD Distribution Family Software
949-581-6368
http://www.surpluscdrom.com

Input Devices

Computer Interactive Art Pad: Cool-icam/IBM/MAC

Creation Station: WIN/MAC
Drawing tablet with cordless pressure pen in two sizes, 4" by 5" or 12" by 12", produced by CalComp

Light Pen WACOM Graphire: WIN/MAC
A pencil-like device that is hooked to the computer and "draws" directly on the monitor. Produced by KidBoard Inc.

SketchBoard: KB Gear WIN/MAC
> Large six-by-eight-inch drawing surface and pressure-sensitive pen, produced by KidBoard Inc.

Touch Window: Edmark/MAC/WIN
> Attaches to computer screen and allows drawing with a finger

Keyboard Protective Covers (Safeskins)

Reliable
Suite 300 West
1501 Woodfield Rd.
Schaumberg, IL 60173

 **RECIPES**

Modeling Doughs

Play dough*
Ingredients:

> 1 cup water
> food coloring (optional)
> ¼ cup of salt
> 1 tablespoon vegetable oil
> 1 tablespoon alum
> 1 cup flour

Directions:

1. Bring water to a boil.
2. Add salt and food coloring.
3. Remove from heat.
4. Add the oil, alum, and flour.
5. While it is still hot, mix and knead for five minutes.

Makes 2 cups

Note:

1. This is a pliant play dough that stays soft for a long time.
2. It can be stored in a tightly closed container or plastic bag for several weeks.
3. Add cornmeal, sawdust, coffee grounds, sand, or other grainy items to change the texture.

Uncooked baking dough*
Ingredients:

> 1 cup flour
> ½ cup salt
> ½ cup warm water
> food coloring (optional)

Directions:

1. Combine all of the ingredients in a bowl.
2. Mix and then knead until smooth.
3. Add more flour if too sticky, more water if too dry.

Makes 1 cup

Note:

1. This dough does not keep. Use it in one day.
2. Add 1 teaspoon alum as a preservative if you want to use it longer.
3. This dough can be baked at 300°F until hard—approximately 20 to 60 minutes, depending on the thickness of the pieces.

Soda Clay for Beads*

Children can make bead shapes from dough made from the following recipe. They must be made a day or two before stringing.

Ingredients:

> 1 cup baking soda
> ½ cup cornstarch
> ⅔ cup warm water
> food coloring or tempera paint (optional)

Directions:

1. Mix ingredients and heat until thick as mashed potatoes.
2. Pour on a cool surface, and knead when cool.
3. Add coloring, if desired, during kneading process.
4. Store in plastic bag until ready to use.
5. Shape beads.
6. Use a drinking straw to make holes (holes made with toothpicks are too small for young children to thread).
7. To speed drying, bake 10 minutes at lowest oven setting or 30 seconds in a microwave on medium setting.

Makes 1 cup

(Suggestion: Make several batches in different colors.)

Homemade Pastes

Recommended homemade pastes

Flour paste: Recipe—Add water to flour until it reaches a thick but spreadable consistency.

> *Advantages:* This is a quick and handy recipe. It is easily made from ingredients found in most kitchens in any amount needed. It works very well on most kinds of paper. It is safe and does not stain clothing. The texture is very different from school paste and provides an interesting change for children. This is one of the few pastes that children can make themselves.

> *Disadvantages:* Flour paste cannot be stored and should be used when it is first made. It wrinkles thinner papers and provides a relatively weak bond so it cannot be used with collage objects. (See chapter 6 for a discussion about using food items for art supplies.) It washes off easily when wet but requires soaking and scrubbing if allowed to dry on surfaces.

Cornstarch paste: Recipe—Mix one part cornstarch to three parts cold water in a saucepan. Add two tablespoons of sugar and one tablespoon vinegar for each part of cornstarch (¼ cup cornstarch and ¾ cups water will make about half a pint). Stirring constantly, slowly heat the mixture until it clears and thickens. Cool before using. Paste can be stored in the refrigerator several weeks, if kept in a tightly sealed container.

> *Advantages:* Cornstarch paste has a very pleasant texture and is not too sticky. It is a safe, almost colorless paste that dries clear and washes out of clothing. It forms a stronger bond than flour paste and can be used for lightweight items, such as fabric, yarn, ribbon, rice, and thin cardboard.

> *Disadvantages:* This is probably one of the better homemade paste recipes in terms of strength, but because it must be cooked, it has to be prepared ahead of time. It is also hard to remove from surfaces when dry, requiring soaking and scrubbing.

Children's Literature on Art

There are many excellent annotated bibliographies on children's art books (Depree & MacKinnon, 1994; Ivy, 1995). In recent years, there has been a great increase in children's books about art, and it is hard to keep any bibliography up to date. This list is not intended to be comprehensive; instead, the books here have been specifically selected for their effectiveness with children age eight and under. Where appropriate, those books especially appealing to toddlers have been noted. There is a mix of recent publications and classics, all of which have been child endorsed. A number in brackets (e.g., [1]) indicates the chapter in which uses for the book have been mentioned. An asterisk highlights Caldecott winners. For each book, the main focus has been indicated under the following headings:

Art Awareness: Books that describe the lives and work of artists, past and present.

Art Elements: Books focusing on the basic elements of art—color, form, line, pattern, shape, space, and texture. If a book features one particular element, that is also listed.

Becoming an Artist: Books expressing the kinds of feelings artist have and the decisions they make when creating art.

Child Art: Books that provide examples of children's art.

Developing Understanding: Books using art to help children learn to appreciate individual differences and the importance of caring about each other.

Media: Books describing how different art media are used or illustrated in a particular art medium.

Multicultural: Books featuring the art and cultures of people from all over the world.

Museums: Books that introduce the concept of a museum to young children.

Sensory Perception: Books that increase children's sensitivity to the aesthetic elements in the world around them.

Aardema, V. (1967). *Who's in rabbit's house?* New York: Dial Books. **(Media: masks; Multicultural: Africa) [11]**
The characters in this tale from the Masai of Africa are shown as people wearing masks. Four and up.

*Aardema, V. (1976). *Why mosquitos buzz in people's ears.* New York: Dial Books. **(Art Elements: shape, pattern; Multicultural: Africa)**
A mosquito's teasing leads to a chain of events that leaves a baby owlet dead. In punishment, the mosquito is condemned to make its presence known by buzzing. Aardema illustrates this African folktale with subtly colored shapes and patterns. Four and up.

Aardema, V. (1985). *Bimwili and the Zimwi.* New York: Dial Books. **(Multicultural: Africa) [7]**
A delightful tale of how a young African boy uses a conch shell to save his garden. Follow a reading of the story by presenting a conch shell as a sensory experience. Four and up.

Alexander, M. (1995). *You're a genius BLACKBOARD BEAR.* Cambridge, MA: Candlewick Press. **(Art Elements: line; Media: chalk drawing) [7]**
A chalk-drawn bear comes to life and draws the parts of a spaceship. Together, he and a little boy build the ship, but then they chicken out of traveling to outer space. Four and up.

Allen, C. (1991). *The rug makers.* Austin, TX: Steck-Vaughn. **(Media: weaving; Multicultural: India) [8]**
A young boy from India explains how Oriental carpets are made in his village. Illustrated with many photographs. Four and up.

Angelou, M. (1994). *My painted house/My friendly chicken.* New York: Clarkson-Potter. **(Art Awareness: architecture; Media: bodywear; Multicultural: Africa) [11]**
In a child's voice, the painted houses of the Ndebele of Africa are described. Photographs illustrate the beautiful costumes and jewelry of the women. Toddler and up.

Anholt, L. (1994). *Camille and the sunflowers.* Happauge, NY: Barron's Educational Series. **(Art Awareness) [8]**
This simply told story presents the art of Vincent Van Gogh through the eyes of Camille, a young boy in one of his paintings. Richly illustrated with actual paintings and scenes based on his paintings. Four and up.

Anholt, L. (1996). *Degas and the little dancer.* Happauge, NY: Barrons.

Anholt, L. (1998). *Picasso and the girl with a ponytail.* Happauge, NY: Barrons.

Anholt, L. (2000). *Leonardo and the flying boy.* Happauge, NY: Barrons. **(Art Awareness)**
The books by Anholt are fictionalized stories about famous artists, told through the experiences of a young child who befriends them. Four and up.

Anno, M. (1989). *Anno's faces.* New York: Philomel Books. **(Art Awareness: portraits; Media: mask making)**

Transparent plastic pages turn pictures of fruits and vegetables into faces that smile and frown. Toddler and up.

Anonymous. (1997). *A is for artist: A Getty Museum alphabet.* Los Angeles: J. Paul Getty Museum. **(Art Awareness)**
Details from seventeenth- and eighteenth-century paintings are matched to each letter of the alphabet. Toddler and up.

Arai, T. (Ed). (1997). *Just like me: Stories and self-portraits by fourteen artists.* Chicago: Children's Book Press. **(Art Awareness; Becoming an Artist)**
This book features brief autobiographies, accompanied by self-portraits by 14 artists well known for their children's book illustrations. Six and up.

Asch, F. (1978). *Sand cake.* New York: Parents Magazine Press. **(Art Elements: texture; Media: sand)**
Asch's lovable bear character makes a cake out of sand after receiving much advice from his friends. After reading this book, place different containers for molding the sand at the sand table or in the sandbox. Toddler and up.

Asch, F. (1981). *Bread and honey.* New York: Parents Magazine Press. **(Becoming an Artist; Media: painting)**
Ben paints a picture of his mother in school. On the way home, he shows his picture to his friends, each of whom make a suggestion on how he can "improve" his artwork. By the time he arrives home, the painting no longer resembles his mother, but she "likes it just the way it is." Toddler and up.

Asch, F. (1985). *Bear shadow.* New York: Simon & Schuster. **(Sensory Perception)**
A little bear tries to get away from his shadow. This is a good book to use with toddlers and younger preschoolers to accompany shadow activities. Toddler and up.

Asch, F. (1994). *The Earth and I.* New York: Harcourt Brace.

Asch, F. (1995). *Water.* New York: Harcourt Brace **(Media: watercolor; Sensory Perception) [10]**
In these two books, soft, rainbow-hued watercolors illustrate simple texts about our world. Following the reading of either of these books, provide the opportunity for the children to paint on wet paper and to create their own blended rainbows. Four and up.

Ata, T., & Moroney, L. (1989). *Baby rattlesnake.* San Francisco: Children's Book Press. **(Art Elements: pattern, shape; Multicultural: Native American)**
This Native American folktale features traditional symbols and patterns in the borders around each painted illustration. Four and up.

Baker, A. (1994a). *Brown rabbit's shape book.* New York: Larouse Kingfisher. **(Art Elements: form) [9]**
A large package arrives, containing smaller parcels in various forms, such as a cylinder and a cube, inside of which are balloons. The rabbit blows up the balloons and describes their forms. Follow up reading this book with a surprise package of forms inside of forms, or blow up balloons of different sizes and forms. Four and up.

Baker, A. (1994b). *White rabbit's color book.* New York: Larouse Kingfisher. **(Art Elements: color; Media: paint) [7, 10]**
Through simple text and charming illustrations, a white rabbit dips himself in different paint pots with predictable results. On his last dip into green and red, he turns into a brown rabbit. A good book for toddlers and preschoolers to lead into a discussion of browns. Toddler and up.

Baker, J. (1987). *Where the forest meets the sea.* New York: Greenwillow Books. **(Art Elements: texture, Media: mixed collage) [4]**
A visit to the Australian rain forest is illustrated with three-dimensional, found-object collages. This is a perfect book to use in conjunction with a nature walk to find materials for collages. Also available as a Big Book from Scholastic. Toddler and up.

Baker, J. (1991). *Window.* New York: Puffin Books. **(Art Elements: texture; Media: mixed collage) [4]**
Three-dimensional collages of windows show an increasingly urban environment. Children enjoy identifying the different materials used in the pictures. Toddler and up.

Barrett, P., & Barrett, S. (1972). *The line Sophie drew.* New York: Scroll Press. **(Art Elements: line; Media: drawing) [3]**
Using a black line, Sophie draws pictures that take her on all kinds of adventures. This book can be used when introducing children to the element of line. Four and up.

Barrows, A. (1996). *The artist's model.* Minneapolis, MN: Carolrhoda. **(Becoming an Artist)**
A young girl models for her father. The book follows his artwork from sketch to final book illustration. Four and up.

Barrows, A. (1997). *The artist's friends.* New York: Lerner. **(Becoming an Artist)**
A young girl and her father visit his artist friends to learn about different careers in art. The work of a portrait painter, computer graphics designer, sculptor, caricaturist, and art director is illustrated. Four and up.

Bartalos, M. (1995). *Shadow Willie.* New York: Viking Press **(Sensory Perception)**
Bold, black shadow shapes illustrate a story about a boy playing with his shadow. Use this book as part of a kinesthetic activity involving shadow play. Toddler and up.

Blizzard, G. S. (1992). *Come look with me: Exploring landscape art with children.* Charlottesville, VA: Thomasson-Grant. **(Art Awareness)**
Twelve landscape paintings are presented, with information on the artists and thought-provoking questions suitable for preschoolers. Part of a series that also includes *World of Play, Animals in Art,* and *Enjoying Art with Children.* Toddler and up.

Blood, C. L., & Link, M. (1980). *The goat in the rug.* New York: Four Winds Press. **(Media: fiber art; Multicultural: Native American) [8]**
An angora goat tells how her hair is processed into a blanket. A fun way to introduce the steps of fiber preparation, including spinning, dyeing, and weaving, to children. Four and up.

Blos, J. W. (1984). *Martin's hats.* New York: Morrow. **(Media: hats)**
A boy has imaginary adventures while wearing different hats. This is an excellent book to tie into hat-making activities. Toddler and up.

Bouchard, D. (1993). *The elders are watching.* Golden, CO: Fulcrum. **(Art Awareness; Multicultural: Native American)**
An ecological message is interwoven with artwork by Northwestern Indian artist Roy Henry Vickers. Various sections can be used to relate to nature walks and art activities. Six and up.

Brenner, B. (1970). *Faces.* New York: Dutton. **(Art Awareness: portraits; Media: mask making**
Photographs show eyes, noses, mouths, and ears reacting to pleasant and unpleasant sensations. Toddler and up.

Brenner, B. (1973). *Bodies.* New York: Dutton. **(Sensory Perception) [11]**

Photographs show different body parts in action. Relate this book to kinesthetic activities of all kinds. Toddler and up.

Brown, L. K., & Brown, M. (1986). *Visiting the art museum.* New York: E. P. Dutton. **(Art Awareness; museums) [8]**

This cartoonlike book depicts a humorous family outing to the art museum. It includes photos of actual paintings. Younger children will not understand all of the humorous parts. Read selected sections that will enhance their understanding of a museum visit. Four and up.

Brown, M. (1979). *Listen to a shape.* New York: F. Watts. **(Art Elements: shape)**

The basic shapes of the square, the circle, and more are introduced using simple poetry and examples from nature. A good introductory book for toddlers and preschoolers who are just learning shapes. Toddler and up.

*Brown, M. (1982). *Shadow.* New York: Macmillan. **(Media: masks; Multicultural: Africa; Sensory Perception)**

A mystical view of shadows, set in Africa and featuring African dance and masks. A perfect book to accompany children's mask-making activities. When their masks are done, turn off the overhead lights, set up a spotlight, and let the children create their own shadow dance. Four and up.

Brown, M. (1984). *There's no place like home.* New York: Parents Magazine Press. **(Art Awareness: architecture; Media: construction)**

Simple rhymes describe the many varieties of places where people and animals live. A good introduction for toddlers and preschoolers to the different kinds of buildings in which people live. Toddler and up.

Bulla, C. R. (1996). *What makes a shadow?* New York: HarperCollins. **(Sensory Perception; Media: puppets)**

Simple drawings and text explain what a shadow is. It includes directions for making shadow puppets. Toddler and up.

*Bunting, E. (1994). *Smoky night.* New York: Harcourt Brace. **(Art Elements: texture; Media: collage) [7]**

A fire in the night drives a young African-American boy from his apartment during the 1992 Los Angeles riots. He overcomes cultural differences to help his Asian neighbors. Illustrated with paintings framed with textured collages that give a feeling for the chaos and scariness of the riot. This Caldecott-winning book will give children ideas for ways they can "frame" their artwork. Six and up.

Burke-Weiner, K. (1992). *The maybe garden.* New York: Beyond Words Publications. **(Becoming an Artist)**

A boy plants a garden of fantastic colors and shapes while his mother plants a real one. Use this book to show how artists can imagine the real world in their own fantastic way. Four and up.

Bush, T. (1995). *Grunt, the primitive cave boy.* New York: Crown. **(Art Awareness; Media: drawing)**

A tongue-in-cheek story about a prehistoric boy who loves to draw animals. Somehow his pictures always seem to attract the animal he draws, making him very popular with the hunters of his clan. Explains, on a simple level, the idea that prehistoric artists might have believed that drawing had magical powers. Six and up.

Cabrera, J. (1997). *Cat's colors.* New York: Dial Books. **(Art Elements: color; Media: paint)**

Boldly painted illustrations and a simple text make this an ideal book for introducing colors to toddlers. A playful kitten asks "What is my favorite color?" as he explores his surroundings. Toddler and up.

Carle, E. (1972). *The secret birthday message.* New York: HarperTrophy. **(Art Elements: shape) [7]**

A message, made from shapes, follows cutout pages that repeat the shapes. An excellent book for older preschoolers who are beginning to use graphic symbols. Four and up.

Carle, E. (1974). *My very first book of shapes.* New York: Harper & Row. **(Art Elements: shape) [7]**

The presentation of differently sized and shaped objects helps children become aware of the shapes found in the environment. Use this book to introduce the basic shapes to toddlers and younger preschoolers. Toddler and up.

Carle, E. (1977). *The grouchy ladybug.* New York: HarperCollins. **(Media: cut-paper collage) [4]**

An aggressive ladybug challenges other creatures, regardless of their size. A clever book design shows the different sizes of the animals, who are illustrated with cut-paper collage. After reading this book, provide many different sizes and textures of paper in the collage area. Toddler and up.

Carle, E. (1984). *The mixed-up chameleon.* New York: Crowell. **(Art Elements: shape; Media: collage) [4]**

A chameleon wishes he could be other animals. Shapes are put together to make new creatures. Different shapes also form the borders of the pages. This book will inspire children to create their own creatures by combining cut-paper shapes. Toddler and up.

Carle, E. (1987). *The tiny seed.* Natick, MA: Picture Book Studio. **(Media: cut-paper collage, printmaking)**

Collages of paint-splattered papers illustrate how a seed grows. Follow this book with kinesthetic activities that involve growing plants. Invite the children to make painted and printed paper to use in their collages. Also available as a Big Book from Scholastic. Toddler and up.

Carle, E. (1992). *Draw me a star.* New York: Philomel Books. **(Becoming an Artist; Media: drawing) [8]**

Painted-paper collages illustrate the story of how the author learned to draw a star. This book is most suitable for older children, as drawing a star can be a very frustrating experience for many younger children. Emphasize that there are many ways to draw a star. Shift the focus of the book to how (and from whom) we learn to do different things. Invite children to invent their own ways to draw a star and then to "teach" a friend their original method. Six and up.

Carle, E. (1998). *Hello, red fox.* New York: Simon & Schuster. **(Art Elements: color; Media: collage)**

A playful exploration of the effect of complementary colors on afterimages is beautifully integrated into a story of a frog inviting his friends to a party. It introduces the color wheel to young children. Toddler and up.

Carlstrom, N. W. (1992). *Northern lullaby.* New York: Philomel Books. **(Art Elements: pattern; Media: drawing; Multicultural: Native American) [3]**

A simple text about sleep draws on Native American symbols and patterns. A perfect read-aloud for a quiet time. Six and up.

Castaneda, O. S. (1993). *Abuela's weave.* New York: Lee & Low. **(Media: fiber art; Multicultural: Central America) [8]**

A young Guatemalan girl and her grandmother grow closer as they weave beautiful cloth to sell at the market. This book helps children understand why some artists sell their work. Six and up.

Catalonotto, P. (1995). *The painter.* New York: Orchard Books. **(Becoming an Artist)**

An artist and his young daughter share time together doing many different activities, including painting side by side. Four and up.

Chapman, C. (1994). *Snow on snow on snow.* New York: Dial Books. **(Media: painting) [5]**

Flat paintings that show the brush strokes illustrate a story of an African-American boy who loses and then finds his dog in the snow. Toddler and up.

Charles, O. (1988). *How is a crayon made?* New York: Simon & Schuster. **(Media: drawing) [3, 7]**

Colorful, sharp photographs show the complete process of making crayons. Children love learning how those mysterious and ever-present crayons are really made and may be inspired to reinvestigate their artistic possibilities. Four and up.

Chase, E. N., & Chase, B. (1984). *The new baby calf.* New York: Scholastic. **(Art Elements: texture; Media: modeling clay) [6]**

A simple story about a baby calf is special because of the textured illustrations made from modeling clay. This book will inspire young children to create picture stories from their modeling clay. Toddler and up.

Cheltenham Elementary School Kindergarten. (1994). *We are all alike . . . We are all different.* New York: Scholastic. **(Art Awareness: portraits; Child Art; Developing Understanding) [11]**

Children's drawings illustrate this book about how people are the same and different. Also available as a Big Book from Scholastic. Toddler and up.

Chocolate, D. M. N. (1994). *Imani in the belly.* New York: Bridgewater Books. **(Media: cut-paper collage; Multicultural: Africa)**

A West African folktale is boldly illustrated with cut-paper collages made of bright solid colors. This is an excellent book to accompany children's collage activities. Four and up.

Clayton, E. (1996). *Ella's trip to the museum.* New York: Crown. **(Museums)**

In this bouncy, lively book, Ella imagines herself as part of each artwork she sees. Use this book to introduce children to the excitement of imagining themselves inside of a painting. Four and up.

Cohen, M. (1979). *Lost in the museum.* New York: Greenwillow Books. **(Museums)**

Although this book describes a trip to a museum of natural history, the message "stay together" is an important one for any field trip. Share this book before taking children on any art-related trip. Four and up.

Cohen, M. (1980). *No good in art.* New York: Greenwillow Books. **(Becoming an Artist; Media: painting)**

Inappropriate comments by the kindergarten art teacher make a child afraid to paint. The first-grade art teacher encourages him with positive comments. A must-read for anyone teaching art to young children. Four and up.

Cohn, J. (1995) *Why did it happen?* New York: William Morrow. **(Developing Understanding; Media: drawing)**

A young boy uses drawing to work out his feelings of anger and fear after his friend, the neighborhood grocer, is killed during a robbery. It includes information for parents and teachers on ways to help children cope with violence. Four and up.

Collins, D. R. (1990). *Country artist: A story of Beatrix Potter.* New York: Carolrhoda Books. **(Art Awareness)**

A simple biography about Beatrix Potter and her wonderful stories for children. Four and up.

Collins, P. L. (1992). *I am an artist.* Brookfield, CT: Millbrook Press. **(Sensory Perception; Media: painting)**

In simple, poetic language, this book shows children that responding aesthetically to beautiful things is part of being an artist. A good read-aloud for a quiet time. Toddler and up.

Crews, D. (1978). *Freight train.* New York: Greenwillow Books.

Crews, D. (1983). *Parade.* New York: William Morrow. **[11]**

Crews, D. (1986). *Flying.* New York: William Morrow.

Crews, D. (1995). *Sail away.* New York: Greenwillow Books. **(Art Elements: color, pattern, shape) [8]**

Crews's illustration style of airbrushed shapes provides a perfect way to introduce the concept of pattern as repeated shapes. All of these books feature repeated images of objects, creating visual patterns. Help children see the different repetitions in each book, and point out how the repetition makes the objects seem like they are moving. These books can also be used in related thematic units. Toddler and up.

Crimi, C. (1995). *Outside inside.* New York: Simon & Schuster. **(Art Elements: space; Media: cut-paper collage; Sensory Perception) [10]**

Cut-paper collages show opposing pictures of what a young girl is doing inside compared to what is happening outside. Toddler and up.

Crosbie, M. J., & Rosenthal, S. (1993). *Architecture COLORS.* Washington, DC: Preservation Press. **(Art Awareness: architecture; Art Elements: color, form) [9]**

This board book illustrates each color with a photograph of an architectural feature on a home or building opposite the word for the color and the feature. This is a good read-aloud for toddlers and a read-it-myself book for preschoolers. Follow up reading this book with a walk through the neighborhood, looking for the colors and architectural features mentioned in the book. One of a series published by the National Trust for Historic Preservation that also includes *Architecture SHAPES, Architecture COUNTS,* and *Architecture ANIMALS.* Toddler and up.

Davis, W. (1996). *From tree to paper.* New York: Scholastic. **(Media: paper)**

Photographs show the process by which a tree becomes a sheet of paper. Use this book when introducing different kinds of paper for collages. Four and up.

Day, N. R. (1995). *The lion's whiskers: An Ethiopian folktale.* New York: Scholastic. **(Media: mixed collage; Multicultural: Africa) [4]**

Beautiful textured-paper collages illustrate a story about how a stepmother won the love of her stepson. Ideal for sharing when children are involved in collage activities. Four and up.

Deeter, C. (1998). *Seymour Bleu.* New York: Simon & Schuster. **(Becoming an Artist)**

An artistic cat overcomes artist's block by visiting different places and friends. Use this book to help children discover ideas for their art. Six and up.

Demarest, C. L. (1995). *My blue boat.* New York: Harcourt Brace. **(Art Elements: color)**

Using her imagination, a little girl sits in her little boat and pictures a sea voyage. Beautifully illustrated with watercolors. Use this book when studying the color blue or to relate to a thematic unit on the sea. Four and up.

Demi. (1980). *Liang and the magic paintbrush.* New York: Henry Holt. **(Media: painting; Multicultural: China)**

A Chinese boy is given a magic paintbrush that can make his pictures come alive. Six and up.

de Paola, T. (1973). *Charlie needs a cloak.* Englewood Cliffs, NJ: Prentice Hall. **(Media: fiber art) [8]**

Charlie is a shepherd who needs a new cape to wear in the winter. In simple language, the story describes the basic processes of turning wool into a finished garment. At each step, the sheep "help" Charlie. This book is an excellent introduction to fiber processing for all children, who particularly love the antics of the delightfully illustrated sheep. Toddler and up.

de Paola, T. (1988). *The legend of the Indian paintbrush.* New York: G. P. Putnam's Sons. **(Media: painting; Multicultural: Native American)**

This retelling of a Plains Indian tale of the origin of the flower "Indian paintbrush" explains the role of painting in the life of the Plains tribes. This book relates well to painting activities involving different types of paintbrushes or using natural materials such as twigs and grasses to apply paint. Also available as a Big Book from Scholastic. Four and up.

de Paola, T. (1989). *The art lesson.* New York: Trumpet Club. **(Becoming an Artist; Media: drawing)**

This book tells the autobiographical story of how young Tomie was frustrated by an overly directive art teacher and how he finally reached an unsettling compromise with her. It provides a model of poor art teaching in the school setting, as well as a model of good parenting, and it should be read by all adults who work with young children. Six and up.

Desimini, L. (1994). *My house.* New York: Henry Holt **(Art Elements: texture; Media: mixed collage) [4]**

Wonderful collages using all kinds of materials show a simple house in changing weather, providing children an opportunity to see the same subject done in a variety of media. Toddler and up.

Dewey, A. (1995). *The sky.* New York: Green Tiger Press. **(Art Elements: shape, texture; Media: chalk; Sensory Awareness)**

A simple, subtle text and soft, pastel-colored chalk drawings show different views of the sky. Toddler and up.

Dillon, L., & Dillon, D. (1994). *What am I? Looking through shapes at apples and grapes.* New York: Blue Sky Press. **(Sensory Perception: space; Developing Understanding) [8]**

Cutout windows highlight luscious photographs of fruits and vegetables. The book ends with a rainbow of hands in many shades. Looking through the windows helps children focus on the details of these everyday objects. Precede or follow up a reading of this book by putting out view tubes or viewfinders or, alternatively, tie the book into a sensory experience with fruits or vegetables. Toddler and up.

Dixon, A. (1990). *Clay.* New York: Garrett Educational Company. **(Media: firing clay) [6]**

This book shows how clay is dug from the ground and then used to make many useful objects, including drainpipes, dishes, and china figurines. Use this book with older preschoolers and primary children when introducing firing clay to them. Four and up.

Dixon, A. (1994). *The sleeping lady.* Anchorage, AK: Alaska Northwest Books. **(Art Elements: shape, pattern; Multicultural: Native American)**

Beautiful paintings with borders illustrate a Native American folktale about the origin of the mountains. Six and up.

Dobrin, A. (1973). *Josephine's 'magination.* New York: Scholastic **(Media: collage, construction, puppets; Multicultural: Haiti) [11]**

A Haitian girl uses her imagination to create a doll from one of her mother's broken brooms. The text is overly long for very young children but can be read in sections or retold. The story can be related to using collage or construction materials in a new way or in puppetry. Four and up.

Dodds, D. A. (1989). *Wheel away.* New York: Harper & Row. **(Media: painted paper collage, murals) [10]**

Cut-paper collages with splatter-paint designs illustrate a wheel as it goes over, under, and around. This is a perfect book to accompany printmaking, paintings, and murals done using toy trucks and cars. Follow a reading of the book with kinesthetic activities in which children can also "wheel" over, under, and around. Also available as a Big Book from Scholastic. Toddler and up.

Dorros, A. (1992). *This is my house.* New York: Scholastic. **(Art Awareness: architecture; Media: three-dimensional construction) [9]**

Drawings and a rhythmic text present different houses from around the world. A good introduction to the different ways homes are built. Also available as a Big Book from Scholastic. Toddler and up.

Downes, B. (1996). *A stitch in rhyme.* New York: Knopf. **(Media: fiber)**

Traditional children's rhymes are illustrated by embroidered pictures. Use this book in conjunction with explorations of stitchery. Toddler and up.

Druscher, H. (1983). *Simon's book.* New York: Lothrop, Lee, & Shepard. **(Media: bookmaking, drawing) [3]**

A boy starts a drawing of a monster and then goes to bed. During the night, the pen, the ink, and the monster come alive and finish the drawing, with surprising results. The simple, animated text enchants children of all ages and can be used to lead into a discussion of how a book is made. Four and up.

Ehlert, L. (1988). *Planting a rainbow.* Orlando, FL: Harcourt Brace Jovanovich. **(Art Elements: color; Media: cut-paper collage) [4, 8]**

A simple text, with boldly colored cut-paper illustrations, presents the planting of bulbs in a garden. The plants that grow are grouped by colors. Pages are cut so that a rainbow is formed. An excellent book to use in conjunction with a sensory display of forced spring bulbs. Also available as a Big Book from Scholastic. Toddler and up.

Ehlert, L. (1989). *Color zoo*. New York: HarperCollins. **(Sensory Perception: space) [7, 8]**
Layered openings in the book form abstract animals that change shape as the page is turned. The wordless book appeals to children of all ages and inspires them to create their own book of "holes." Toddler and up.

Ehlert, L. (1991). *Red leaf yellow leaf*. New York: Harcourt Brace. **(Art Elements: texture; Media: mixed collage) [8]**
Collages of paper and objects illustrate autumn and the seasonal cycle of a tree. Toddler and up.

Ehlert, L. (1994). *Mole's hill*. New York: Harcourt Brace. **(Art Elements: pattern; Media: paper collage; Multicultural: Native American) [4, 8]**
Based on a Native American folktale, the story is illustrated with paper collages inspired by Woodland tribe beadwork and ribbon appliqué. Toddler and up.

Ehlert, L. (1995). *Snowballs*. New York: Harcourt Brace. **(Art Elements: texture; Media: mixed collage) [7]**
Collages of corn, raisins, cloth, and buttons are used to decorate cut-paper snowmen of different shapes. From page to page, a cut-paper bird "snacks" on the goodies. Toddler and up.

Ehlert, J. (1997). *Hands*. New York: Harcourt Brace. **(Becoming an Artist; Media: collage)**
A child who dreams of being an artist watches her father's hands build and her mother's hands sew and then uses the scraps from each to make a collage. Four and up.

*Emberly, B. (1968). *Drummer Hoff*. New York: Prentice Hall. **(Art Elements: pattern)**
Bright colors and patterns make this Caldecott winner attractive to young children. The repetitive rhyme is easy for beginning readers to follow. Use this book to transition into pattern activities. Toddler and up.

Emberly, E. (1961). *A wing on a flea: A book about shapes*. Boston: Little Brown. **(Art Elements: shape) [7]**
Shapes are found in parts of everyday objects. Toddler and up.

Emberly, E. (1992). *Go away big green monster*. New York: Little Brown. **(Art Elements: shape, space; Sensory Perception) [7]**
In this delightful book, holes are cut out of each page. As the pages turn, the holes form pictures that end up as part of a monster's face. Use it as a model for a "book of holes" of your own design or to inspire children to look at their own art through holes of different shapes. Toddler and up.

Ernst, L. (1983). *Sam Johnson and the blue ribbon quilt*. New York: Lothrop, Lee, & Shepard. **(Developing Understanding; Media: quilting)**
A farmer becomes fascinated with making quilts, and much to everyone's astonishment, he joins his wife's quilting club. This book combats the stereotype that only women like to sew and make quilts. Six and up.

Everett, G. (1991). *Li'l sis and Uncle Willie*. New York: Hyperion Books. **(Multicultural: African American) [5]**
The art of African-American artist William H. Johnson is used to create the story of his life. Six and up.

Falk, A. (1964). *Matthew blows bubbles*. New York: McGraw-Hill. **(Sensory Perception)**
A simple story about bubbles to read when involved in bubbly art activities, such as whipped-soap finger paint or when creating a bubble mural. Toddler and up.

Fanelli, S. (1995) *My map book*. New York: HarperCollins. **(Child Art; Media: drawing) [3]**
Maps drawn by a young child, who has lived in Italy and England, show her room, home, face, and more. These will inspire children to draw their own maps of special places. Four and up.

Feelings, M. (1974). *Jambo means hello: Swahili alphabet book*. New York: Dial Books. **(Media: clay, wood; Multicultural: Africa)**
Using the alphabet, Feelings illustrates many things from life in Africa, including the art forms of pottery and wood carving. Four and up.

Felix, M. (1992) *Opposites*. Mankato, MN: Creative Editions. **(Sensory Perception: space) [7]**
A mouse chews out differently shaped windows in blank white pages. As the windows open, opposing pictures appear, such as a rainy day and a sunny day. Use with activities that involve looking through openings. Wordless. Toddler and up.

Felix, M. (1993a). *Colors*. Mankato. MN: Creative Editions. **(Art Elements: color) [5]**
This small, wordless book features beautifully detailed drawings of a mouse who opens tubes of red, yellow, and blue paint and then creates green, orange, purple, and black. Toddler and up.

Felix, M. (1993b). *House*. Mankato, MN: Creative Editions. **(Art Awareness: architecture; Sensory Perception)**
The same little mouse begins by chewing a heart shape out of the page. It then gnaws out a paper shape, underneath which a detailed drawing of grass and plants appears. At the end, the paper is shown folded into a house. The heart shape becomes a window for the mouse to peek through. Wordless. Toddler and up.

Fine, J. (1979). *I carve stone*. New York: Thomas Y. Crowell. **(Art Elements: form; Becoming an Artist)**
Excellent photographs and a sensitive text explain how a woman sculptor carves stone sculptures. Four and up.

Fisher, A. (1971). *Feathered ones and furry*. New York: Thomas Y. Crowell. **(Media: printmaking)**
Charming poems about a variety of animals are illustrated with simple linoleum cuts by Eric Carle. Use Styrofoam printmaking to get a similar effect. Four and up.

Fisher, L. E. (1984). *Boxes! Boxes!* New York: Viking Press. **(Art Elements: form; Media: box construction) [9]**
Differently sized and shaped boxes are used to hold a variety of items in a child's room. Four and up.

Fleming, D. (1993). *In the small, small pond*. New York: Henry Holt. **(Art Elements: texture; Media: paper) [5]**
Bright collages of nature and animals show a variety of textures. An excellent choice to accompany texture walks. Toddler and up.

Florian, D. (1991). *A potter*. New York: Greenwillow Books. **(Media: firing clay) [6]**
A simple text tells how a potter creates works from clay. Use this book when introducing firing clay. Toddler and up.

Florian, D. (1993). *A painter*. New York: Greenwillow Books. **(Becoming an Artist)**
Using simple text, who a painter is and what a painter does and feels is explained. Use this book with young children before introducing a piece of adult art. Toddler and up.

Fox, M. (1989). *Shoes from Grandpa.* New York: Orchard Books. **(Art Elements: texture; Media: mixed collage)**
Torn tissue and other paper are combined with real buttons, lace, and more, illustrating a cumulative story of a little girl who receives a pair of shoes from her grandfather and then gets too many pieces of clothing to go with them. Toddler and up.

Fox, M. (1997). *The straight line wonder.* New York: MONDO. **(Art Elements: line)**
Tired of being straight, a line explores curves and points. Although his friend warns him against being different, his difference eventually makes him a success. Four and up.

Frasier, D. (1991). *On the day you were born.* Orlando, FL: Harcourt Brace. **(Art Elements: shape; Media: cut-paper collages)**
Cut-paper collages are used to illustrate people's place in the universe. The bold, bright colors and shapes are appealing to young children, and the heartwarming text makes everyone feel special. An ideal book to share on birthdays and other special days. Toddler and up.

Freeman, D. (1959). *Norman the doorman.* New York: Viking Press. **(Becoming an Artist; Museums)**
This is a wonderful book for introducing the idea of a museum to young children. A little mouse lives in a suit of armor in a museum and enjoys giving tours to art-loving creatures. Using the wire from mousetraps, he makes a sculpture and enters it in an art contest with great success. Four and up.

Freeman, D. (1966). *A rainbow of my own.* New York: Puffin Books. **(Art Elements: color; Sensory Perception)**
A little boy imagines that a rainbow is his friend. Toddler and up.

Freeman, D. (1976). *The chalk box story.* New York: J. B. Lippincott. **(Art Elements: line; Media: chalk) [3]**
Pieces of colored chalk draw a story about a boy who is stranded on an island and then rescued by a turtle. Four and up.

Garland, M. (1995). *Dinner at Magritte's.* New York: Dutton. **(Art Awareness)**
A bored little boy spends a day in the surreal world of René Magritte and Salvador Dalí in which metaphors become visual fantasies. A delightful romp for the imagination, and a fun way to introduce the style of surrealism. Four and up.

Garza, C. L. (1990). *Family pictures/Cuadros de familia.* Chicago: Children's Book Press. **(Art Awareness; Multicultural: Mexican American)**
Paintings by Mexican-American artists tell the story of a child growing up in a Hispanic community in Texas. Four and up.

Geiss, T. (1997). *Puzzle gallery: Children.* New York: Knopf. **(Art Awareness)**
Twelve-piece puzzles of artworks are accompanied by a brief description and things to find. Other books in the series include *Games, Pets,* and *Food.* Six and up.

Gerstein, M. (1984). *The room.* New York: Harper & Row. **(Media: mural; Sensory Perception)**
Detailed drawings and a simple text show how an apartment is successively lived in by several different people including some artists who paint the walls with bold colors. Have children compare how the appearance of the room changes when the walls are decorated differently. Six and up.

Gibbons, G. (1983). *Paper, paper everywhere.* San Diego: Harcourt Brace. **(Media: collage)**
Simple text describes how paper is made and used. Six and up.

Gibbons, G. (1998). *The art box.* New York: Holiday House. **(Becoming an Artist; Media: drawing, painting)**
Collage and drawn illustrations show the tools and materials used by artists for drawing and painting. Four and up.

Gilchrist, E. S. (1997). *Madelia.* New York: Dial Books. **(Becoming an Artist; Media: watercolor)**
An African-American girl listens to her father preach the Sunday sermon and finds inspiration for a watercolor painting. This is a wonderful introduction to the way artists find ideas for their art. Four and up.

Gilliland, J. H. (1995). *Not in the house, Newton!* New York: Clarion. **(Media: drawing)**
Using a magical red crayon, Newton fills his house with drawings turned real. Use this book when focusing on the color red. Four and up.

Gilman, P. (1992). *Something from nothing.* New York: Scholastic. **(Media: collage, construction)**
A story of a little boy who as a baby is given a blanket made by his grandfather. As the years go by, the blanket wears out, and the grandfather makes it into something new. When that item wears out, the clever grandfather again makes something else from it. An excellent story to tie in with reusing items for art activities. Also available as a Big Book from Scholastic. Four and up.

Grifalconi, A. (1986). *The village of round and square houses.* New York: Little Brown. **(Art Awareness: architecture; Multicultural: Africa)**
A story about why the villages in Cameroon have round and square houses. This book can be used to lead into a discussion of why buildings are certain shapes. Four and up.

*Hall, D. (1980). *The ox-cart man.* New York: Viking Press. **(Art Awareness; Art Elements: pattern; Media: fiber art)**
Folk-art-style paintings illustrate how in the past a subsistence farm family's chores changed with the seasons. Use this book to teach children how food and fiber are part of the cycle of life. Toddler and up.

Hanna, J. (1992). *The petting zoo.* Garden City, NY: Doubleday. **(Art Elements: texture; Media: collage) [7]**
In this book, designed for toddlers, pieces of differently textured cloth are used to illustrate how different wild animals might feel. Toddler.

Haskins, J. (1989). *Count your way through Mexico.* Minneapolis, MN: Carolrhoda Books. **(Media: papier-mâché; Multicultural: Mexico)**
Mexican life is presented using the numbers one to 10 in Spanish. Presents the use of papier-mâché masks on the Day of Three Kings. Four and up.

Hathorn, L. (1998). *Sky sash so blue.* New York: Simon & Schuster. **(Developing Understanding; Media: fabric collage)**
Fabric collages illustrate the story of the remarkable creativity and resilience of a slave family in the Old South. Four and up.

Hausmann, G. (1992). *Turtle Island ABC.* New York: St. Martin's Press. **(Media: chalk drawing; Multicultural: Native American)**
Each letter of the alphabet is illustrated with a Native American symbol, such as an arrow for "A" and a buffalo for "B." The

meaning and importance of each symbol is beautifully explained. The illustrations are rendered in monochromatic chalks. Toddler and up.

Hawkinson, J. (1974). *A ball of clay.* Chicago: Albert Whitman. **(Media: firing clay) [6]**

A book about clay—what it is, where to find it, and how to prepare and use it. Select relevant parts to share with older preschoolers and primary children who want to know more about clay. Four and up.

Heller, R. (1995). *Color! Color! Color!* New York: Grosset & Dunlap. **(Art Elements: color) [7]**

With rhythmic language, Ruth Heller presents a multitude of concepts about color. The book includes color acetates that overlap to show color mixing. A good book to share with one or two children so they can investigate the complex illustrations. Six and up.

Hoban, T. (1971). *Look again!* New York: Macmillan. **(Sensory Perception; Art Elements: space) [7]**

This book uses differently shaped windows to focus on interesting parts of photographs.

Hoban, T. (1974). *Round! Round! Round!* New York: Macmillan.

Hoban, T. (1978). *Is it red? Is it yellow? Is it blue?* New York: William Morrow.

Hoban, T. (1979). *Circles triangles squares.* New York: Macmillan.

Hoban, T. (1986). *Shapes shapes shapes.* New York: Greenwillow Books.

Hoban, T. (1987). *Dots, spots, speckles, and stripes.* New York: Greenwillow Books.

Hoban, T. (1988). *Look look look.* New York: Greenwillow Books.

Hoban T. (1989). *Of colors and things.* New York: Greenwillow Books.

Hoban, T. (1995). *Colors everywhere.* New York: Greenwillow Books. **(Art Elements: color, form, shape, pattern, texture) [4, 7, 9]**

Hoban, T. (1998). *So many squares. So many circles.* New York: Greenwillow Books.

Hoban's wordless books of magnificent photographs entice children's eyes to see the details of color, shape, form, and pattern in everyday objects. These are excellent books for toddlers and preschoolers to study on their own. They can also be used to introduce sensory activities involving the art elements. *Of Colors and Things* and *Look Look Look* are also available as Big Books from Scholastic. Toddler and up.

Howe, J. (1987). *I wish I were a butterfly.* New York: Harcourt Brace. **(Sensory Perception)**

This simple story of a cricket who thinks he is ugly and wishes he were a beautiful butterfly can be used to introduce a discussion of beauty. Four and up.

Hoyt-Goldsmith, D. (1990). *Totem pole.* New York: Scholastic. **(Art Awareness; Media: wood carving; Multicultural: Native American) [8]**

Photographs illustrate the contemporary life of a boy whose father is a totem pole carver of the Tsimshian tribe of the Pacific Northwest. The text may need to be simplified for younger children, but the pictures are excellent for discussion. Four and up.

Hudson, C. W., & Ford, B. G. (1990). *Bright eyes, brown skin.* Littleton, MA: Sundance. **(Developing Understanding) [11]**

Illustrated with pictures of four African-American children enjoying typical preschool activities (including drawing), this poem celebrates physical appearance. A perfect book for toddlers and young preschoolers. Four and up.

Hughes, L. (1994). *The sweet and sour animal book.* New York: Oxford University Press. **(Child Art; Media: modeling)**

Lively two- and three-dimensional artwork by children illustrates Langston Hughes's alphabet book of poetry. Very suitable to share with children of all ages. Four and up.

Hughes, L. (1995). *The block.* New York: Metropolitan Museum of Art. **(Art Awareness: collage)**

The cut-paper collages and photomontages of African-American artist Romare Beardon illustrate selected poems of Langston Hughes in this beautiful book. Four and up.

Hughes, S. (1986). *All shapes and sizes.* New York: Lothrop, Lee, & Shepard. **(Art Elements: shape)**

A rhythmic text describes the shape and size of familiar objects. Toddler and up.

Hutchins, P. (1972). *Changes changes.* New York: Macmillan. **(Art Elements: form; Media: blocks) [9]**

A wordless story (appealing to toddlers) is told using brightly colored blocks and two wooden figures. Children will enjoy making up their own "block" stories after reading this book. Toddlers.

Isadora, R. (1985). *I touch.* New York: Greenwillow Books. **(Art Elements: texture) [5]**

This board book for toddlers features a simple text describing different textures, such as a sticky lollipop. Toddlers.

Isom, J. S. (1998). *The first starry night.* Waterown, MA: Charlesbridge. **(Art Awareness; Developing Understanding)**

An orphan befriends Vincent Van Gogh, and together they form a warm, supportive friendship. Four and up.

James, B. (1994). *The mud family.* New York: Putnam's. **(Art Elements: texture; Media: painting; Multicultural: Native American) [5]**

A young Native American girl of the prehistoric past makes a family from mud (clay) to help bring rain to the parched Southwest. Wonderfully illustrated with paintings done on textured fabric. Four and up.

Jenkins, S. (1995). *Looking down.* New York: Houghton Mifflin. **(Media: collage; Sensory Perception)**

Starting with a view of the earth, each collage illustration moves in closer and closer, ending with a close-up of a ladybug. Use this book to introduce the concept of enlargement. Follow up by displaying a poster-size print and a postcard-size reproduction of the same artwork. Four and up.

Johnson, A. (1997). *Daddy calls me Man.* New York: Orchard Books. **(Becoming an Artist)**

Four short poems about a young African-American boy whose parents are artists are illustrated with the parents' paintings. The last page shows all the paintings hanging in the parents' art studio. Four and up.

Johnson, C. (1955). *Harold and the purple crayon.* New York: Harper & Row. **(Media: bookmaking, crayon drawing) [3]**

Using a purple crayon, Harold draws himself an adventure. This classic remains a child-pleaser. A good book to introduce the idea of drawing a story that continues from one page to the next when children begin "writing" their own books. Toddler and up.

Johnston, T., & de Paola, T. (1985). *The quilt story.* New York: G. P. Putnam's Sons. **(Media: quilting)**
A treasured quilt provides comfort to two little girls from different times. Also available as a Big Book from Scholastic. Four and up.

Jonas, A. (1987). *Reflections.* New York: Greenwillow Books. **(Sensory Perception)**
This book features paintings that when turned upside down become different pictures. This book can inspire activities using mirrors and is a good companion to walks on which children study reflections in puddles and ponds. Six and up.

Jonas, A. (1989). *Color dance.* New York: Greenwillow Books. **(Art Elements: color; Sensory Perception)**
Three children dance with transparent cloth that overlaps to create new colors. Follow up by giving children transparent or translucent materials, such as cellophane, sheer cloth, or tissue in a variety of colors to explore in sensory activities. Toddler and up.

Jonas, A. (1994). *The quilt.* New York: Puffin. **(Media: quilting)**
An African-American girl sleeps beneath a quilt made by her mother and father and has fantastical dreams. Toddler and up.

Kalan, R. (1978). *Rain.* New York: Greenwillow Books. **(Sensory Perception)**
This book focuses on the sensory elements of rain as it falls on people everywhere. Toddler and up.

Karnovsky, S. (1995). *Billy and the magic string.* New York: Troll. **(Art Elements: line)** [5, 12]
This book features a little boy and his adventures with a magic string that can become anything he chooses. Following the reading of this book, give each child a piece of yarn, and let her or him make "magic" string pictures on the floor or table. Four and up.

*Keats, E. J. (1962). *The snowy day.* New York: Viking Press. **(Media: painted paper collages)** [4]
In this Caldecott winner, painted cut-paper collages illustrate the experiences of an African-American boy as he explores the snow. Also available as a Big Book from Scholastic. Toddler and up.

Keats, E. J. (1966). *Jennie's hat.* New York: Harper & Row. **(Media: mixed collage, hats)** [11]
Jennie does not like her new hat. Delightful collages show her "improving" the hat. Toddler and up.

Keats, E. J. (1978). *The trip.* New York: Mulberry Books. **(Media: box construction)** [9]
In this story, a lonely boy makes a simple diarama in a shoe box and then imagines himself inside. The story ends with the boy making friends with children dressed in costumes for Halloween. Four and up.

Keats, E. J. (1981). *Regards to the man in the moon.* New York: Macmillan. **(Media: construction, murals)** [9]
Children paint a space mural, build spaceships out of junk, and then take an imaginary trip through space. Four and up.

Kent, J. (1975). *The Christmas piñata.* New York: Parent's Magazine Press. **(Media: papier-mâché; Multicultural: Mexico)**
Told from a view of a broken clay pot, this book details how a piñata is made and used in a Mexican village for Los Posadas. Four and up.

Kesselman, W. (1980). *Emma.* New York: Doubleday Books for Young Readers. **(Becoming an Artist)**
An elderly woman takes up painting to surround herself with the joyful memories of her life. A wonderful way to introduce children to the idea that art brings personal joy and can be created by artists of any age.

Kissinger, K. (1994). *All the colors we are.* St. Paul, MN: Redleaf Press. **(Developing Understanding)** [11]
Beautiful photographs illustrate this book that explains simply why people have different-colored skin. Use this book to accompany mixing skin-toned paints. (Bilingual: Spanish) Four and up.

Klamath County YMCA Preschool. (1993). *The land of many colors.* New York: Scholastic. **(Art Elements: color; Developing Understanding)**
A small child settles a conflict between the purple, blue, and green people. This book was written by preschoolers and speaks to them in their own language. Four and up.

Knutson, K. (1992). *Muddigush.* New York: Macmillan. **(Media: painted paper collage)** [4, 9]
Children love the descriptive words and patterned and marbled paper collages that show a child's joy in playing in the mud. Toddler and up.

Krauss, R. (1953). *A very special house.* New York: Harper & Row. **(Media: drawing)** [3]
In joyful rhyme, a small boy draws and imagines a house full of excitement and fun. This classic book, illustrated by Maurice Sendak, celebrates the ability of imagination to create new worlds, on a level appropriate for toddlers and preschoolers. Toddler and up.

Krensky, S. (1991). *Children of the earth and sky.* New York: Scholastic.

Krensky, S. (1994). *Children of wind and water.* New York: Scholastic. **(Media: firing clay, weaving, wood; Multicultural: Native American)** [8]
These two books consist of short stories about a Hopi painter and a Navajo weaver. The second introduces a Tlingit carver. Four and up.

Kroll, V. (1992). *Wood-Hoopoe Willie.* Watertown, MA: Charlesbridge. **(Art Elements: pattern; Media: fiber art; Multicultural: Africa)**
A young African-American boy saves a Kwanza celebration by playing the drums when the adult drummer is incapacitated in a car accident. The book describes and illustrates many African instruments. Richly patterned African cloth is featured throughout the book. Four and up.

Kurtz, S. (1991). *The boy and the quilt.* Intercourse, PA: Good Books. **(Media: quilting)** [8]
A little boy collects fabric squares of many colors and sews his own crazy quilt. It shows, step by step, how the quilt is made and combats the stereotype that only girls make quilts. Four and up

Kuskin, K. (1965). *Sand and snow.* New York: Harper & Row. **(Art Elements: texture; Media: sand; Sensory Perception)**
This book uses poetry to compare the beach in the heat of summer and the snow in the cold of winter. Accompany this book with modeling doughs to which sand has been added, or provide sensory bins of sand and snow. In winter have a "Beach Day" complete with towels, pails, sunbonnets, and, of course, sand art activities. Toddler and up.

Kuskin, K. (1994). *Patchwork island.* New York: HarperCollins. **(Art Elements: pattern, texture; Media: quilting)**

A mother makes an "island" quilt for her son. There are many patterns in this book for children to find. Four and up.

La Coccinella. (Eds.). (1994). *Shadow magic.* New York: Universe. **(Sensory Perception)**

This board book features cut-out pages that are designed to be placed in front of a light source to create interesting shadows. Children enjoy working in pairs to create the shadows using a flashlight. Four and up.

Laden, N. (2000). *Robert, the insect architect.* San Francisco: Chronicle. **(Media: architecture, collage)**

A termite who loves to play with his food becomes a philanthropic architect. The book is illustrated with fantastic collages made from unusual materials. Four and up.

Lawson, J. (1992). *Kate's castle.* New York: Oxford University Press. **(Art Elements: texture; Media: sand)**

This cumulative text follows the construction of a mighty sand castle and is illustrated with softly colored pictures. A good read-aloud for kindergarten and primary children who may want to write a cumulative book about their own sand constructions. Four and up.

Leaf, M. (1987). *Eyes of the dragon.* New York: Lothrop, Lee, & Shepard. **(Media: painting; Multicultural: China)**

An artist paints eyeless dragons on the city wall. When the artist is ordered by an official to put eyes on them, the dragons come alive and break loose from the wall. Use this book to make children think about why artists include some things and leave other things out of their artwork. Six and up.

Lee, H. V. (1994). *At the beach.* New York: Henry Holt. **(Media: cut-paper collage; Multicultural: China) [7]**

In this story, children learn to write Chinese characters in the sand on the beach. The pictures are made of intricate cut-paper collages. Following a reading of this story, children may want to "write" in sand or sensory bins. Four and up.

Le Ford, B. (1995). *A blue butterfly: A story about Claude Monet.* New York: Doubleday. **(Art Awareness) [5]**

A simple text and soft, impressionistic watercolors present the life of one of the great Impressionists. A good read-aloud for all ages. Four and up.

Leigh, N. K. (1993). *Learning to swim in Swaziland.* New York: Scholastic. **(Media: drawing; Multicultural: Africa)**

A child's view of the South African country of Swaziland, illustrated with photographs and the child's crayon drawings. Four and up.

Lepschy, I. (1992). *Pablo Picasso.* Happauge, NY: Barron's Educational Series. **(Art Awareness; Becoming an Artist)**

This biography of Picasso focuses on his difficulties as a young child, both at home and at school. It demonstrates how artistic creativity in young children is often hard to recognize. This is a must-read for both teacher and parents. The text may need to be shortened and simplified for preschoolers. This book is part of a series called "Children of Genius." Six and up. Another book in the series is *Leonardo da Vinci* (1984).

Lercher Bornstein, P. (1997). *That's how it is when we draw.* New York: Clarion. **(Becoming an Artist)**

A young girl experiences different feelings as she draws monsters, people, flowers, and animals. She draws a bad time by scribbling everyone away and draws exuberant lines for a rainbow. This is an excellent book to foster the understanding that one child's art can have many meanings. Four and up.

Lessac, F. (1987). *My little island.* New York: HarperTrophy.

Lessac, F. (1989). *Caribbean alphabet.* New York: Tambourine Books. **(Art Awareness; Multicultural: Haiti)**

Brilliantly colored folk art paintings illustrate the life and culture on a Caribbean Island. Four and up.

LeTord, B. (1999). *A bird or two: The story about Henri Matisse.* Grand Rapids, MI: Wm. B. Erdmans. **(Art Awareness)**

Lighthearted watercolors and a simple text create an appreciation for the art of Matisse. Four and up.

Lewis, S. (1991). *African-American art for young people.* Worcester, MA: Davis. **(Multicultural: African American)**

Twelve African-American artists are discussed on a simple level, and an example of their artwork is reproduced. The work of Powers (quilting), Barthe and Lewis (sculpture), Tanner, Hunter, Hayden, Johnson, Jones, Bearden, Lawrence, and Catlett (painting), and Butler (found-object constructions) is presented.

Lionni, L. (1959). *Little blue and little yellow.* New York: Mulberry Books. **(Art Elements: color; Media: torn-paper collage) [5]**

A delightful tale about color mixing, illustrated with torn-paper circles and other simple shapes. A classic to be shared with children. Four and up.

Lionni, L. (1961). *On my beach there are many pebbles.* New York: Mulberry Books. **(Sensory Perception; Media: drawing)**

Beautiful pencil drawings of pebbles, both real and amazing, show children how to look at simple things and see beauty. A quiet time read-aloud to accompany sensory art activities involving collecting, observing, and using pebbles and stones. Toddler and up.

Lionni, L. (1963). *Swimmy.* New York: Alfred A. Knopf. **(Developing Understanding; Media: printmaking) [7]**

A fish learns how to cooperate with others in this book illustrated with simple prints. Also available as a Big Book from Scholastic. Toddler and up.

Lionni, L. (1975). *A color of his own.* New York: Alfred A. Knopf. **(Art Elements: color, pattern; Media: printmaking)**

A lizard tries out many colors until he finds one just right for him. A favorite read-aloud. Also available as a Big Book from Scholastic. Four and up.

Lionni, L. (1982). *Let's make rabbits.* New York: Alfred A. Knopf. **(Media: collage, drawing) [4]**

Two rabbits, one drawn and one cut out of paper, get a taste of real life. Use this book to help children see the difference between two-dimensional drawings and collages and three-dimensional forms. Four and up.

Lionni, L. (1991). *Matthew's dream.* New York: Alfred Knopf. **(Becoming an Artist; Museums) [8]**

A visit to an art museum inspires a young mouse to become a painter, against the wishes of his family. Four and up.

Littlechild, G. (1993). *This land is my land.* Emeryville, CA: Children's Book Press. **(Art Awareness; Media: painting; Multicultural: Native American)**

Native American artist George Littlechild discusses each of his paintings in terms that children can understand. In doing so, he also explains a lot about Native American history, culture, and the people's hopes and dreams. Choose a selection that relates to what the children already know about Native American life and read only one section at a sitting. Six and up.

Locker, T. (1994). *Miranda's smile.* New York: Dial Books for Young Readers. **(Art Awareness: portrait; Becoming an Artist; Media: painting)**
An artist tries to paint his daughter's portrait with her special smile. Illustrated with several different portraits of the girl, this book is a wonderful way to introduce portraits to children age three and up. Four and up.

Lopez, A. (1972). *Celebration.* Garden City, NY: Doubleday. **(Art Awareness; Media: drawing, painting; Multicultural: Native American)**
Native American dances and games are presented through a simple text illustrated with reproductions of fine art drawings and paintings of many different tribes. An excellent book to help introduce toddlers and preschoolers to Native American culture. Also available as a Big Book from Sundance. Toddler and up.

Lord, S. (1995). *The story of the dreamcatcher and other Native American crafts.* New York: Scholastic. **(Media: beadwork, masks; Multicultural: Native American)** [11]
This book tells, in simple language, a little bit about several Native American crafts, including the dreamcatcher, beadwork, and mask making. It is illustrated with color photographs of examples of these art forms. Four and up.

MacDonald, S. (1994). *Sea shapes.* New York: Harcourt Brace. **(Art Elements: shape; Media: cut-paper collage)** [4]
Opposite each intricate cut-paper seascape are three shapes for the children to find in the picture. Share with one or two children, or let one child explore independently. Four and up.

Mallat, K., & McMillan, B. (1997). *The picture that Mom drew.* New York: Walker. **(Media: drawing)**
This cumulative textbook tells how a colored pencil drawing of a beach scene is made. It introduces the terms "line," "shape," and "form." Each is shown using a close-up of the drawing. Four and up.

Martin, B. (1996). *Brown bear, brown bear. What do you see?* New York: Henry Holt. **(Art Elements: color)**
In this classic, repetitive tale, illustrated by Eric Carle, each page introduces an animal in a different color. An excellent book about color for toddlers and preschoolers. Toddler and up.

Matthews, M. (1997). *Icky, sticky gloop.* New York: Troll. **(Media: play dough)**
Join the fun as Benjamin Franklin Bunny invents gloop and then help children mix up their own batch of play dough. Toddler and up.

Mayhew, J. (2002). *Katie and the sunflowers.* New York: Orchard. **(Art Awareness; Museums)**
A young girl visits the museum and travels into famous impressionist paintings, including those by Van Gogh, Gauguin, and Cezanne. Four and up.

McDermott, G. (1993). *Raven: A trickster tale from the Pacific Northwest.* New York: Harcourt Brace. **(Art Elements: shape, pattern; Multicultural: Native American)**
This Native American story is illustrated with pictures based on the traditional art forms and patterns of the Northwest coastal tribes. Four and up.

McGovern, A. (1969). *Black is beautiful.* New York: Scholastic. **(Art Elements: color; Developing Understanding)** [11]

This book celebrates the color black. Use it to help children become more comfortable using black art materials. Toddler and up.

McLerran, A. (1991). *Roxaboxen.* New York: Lothrop, Lee, & Shepard. **(Art Awareness: architecture; Media: construction)** [9]
On the edge of the desert, a group of neighborhood children build "houses" out of stones, sticks, old pottery, and crates. Using their imaginations, a town is created. Four and up.

Metropolitan Museum. (2002). *Museum ABC.* New York: Little, Brown **(Art Awareness; Museums)**
Each letter of the alphabet is illustrated with details from famous works of art. Toddler and up.

Micklethwait, L. (1994). *I spy a lion: Animals in art.* New York: Greenwillow Books. **(Art Awareness; Sensory Perception)**
Readers are asked to find animals and other details in a variety of famous artworks. A good book to share with one or two children or for older children to investigate on their own. One of an extensive series. Four and up.

Micklethwait, L. (1995a). *Spot a cat.* New York: Dorling Kingsley.

Micklethwait, L. (1995b). *Spot a dog.* New York: Dorling Kingsley. **(Art Awareness)**
Toddlers and preschoolers will enjoy looking for cats and dogs in a wide selection of famous artworks. Toddler and up.

Moncure, J. (1982). *The touch book.* Chicago: Children's Book Press. **(Art Elements: texture)**
A wide variety of textures is presented in this rhyming text. Toddler and up.

Moon, N. (1994). *Lucy's picture.* New York: Dial Books for Young Readers. **(Becoming an Artist; Media: mixed collage)** [4]
Lucy wants to make a gift for her grandfather, but a painting is just not right. She decides to make a collage of things she collects inside and outside the schoolroom. A perfect read-aloud for young children. It emphasizes that the element of artistic choice is an important part of the art process. Four and up.

Moore, R. (1993a). *Native artists of Africa.* Santa Fe, NM: John Muir. **(Multicultural: Africa)** [8]
Interviews with contemporary African artists provide information about their work. Readers are introduced to a Berber rug weaver, a painter, and a basket weaver. Text will need to be simplified for young children. Photographs show the artists at work. Six and up.

Moore, R. (1993b). *Native artists of North America.* Santa Fe, NM: John Muir. **(Multicultural: Native American)** [8]
In the same format, contemporary Native American artists provide information on how and why they create their art. Artists introduced include Valdez (Huichol yarn painting), Teters (painter), and Rahr (beadwork and cornhusk dolls). Six and up.

Morris, A. (1992). *Houses and homes.* New York: Mulberry Books. **(Art Awareness: architecture; Media: construction)** [9]
Photographs show homes from many different places in the world. Toddler and up.

Morris, A. (1993). *Hats hats hats.* New York: Mulberry Books. **(Media: hats)** [11]
All kinds of headgear from around the world are shown in vividly colored photographs. A perfect book to accompany hat-making activities. Toddler and up.

Moss, S. (1995). *Peter's painting.* Greenvale, NY: MONDO. **(Becoming an Artist; Media: painting) [5]**

This book expresses the multimedia nature of child art in a beautifully expressed story of a little boy whose simple "scribble" paintings transport him into the world of his imagination. It is illustrated with richly colored paintings of Peter painting in his bedroom, which with each page has more and more paintings hanging on the walls. A perfect book to share with toddlers and preschoolers who love to paint. Have children find each painting he makes on the walls on the next page. Toddler and up.

Munsch, R. (1992). *Purple, green, and yellow.* Toronto: Annick Press. **(Media: drawing) [3]**

In this delightfully illustrated book, a little girl gets bored with using washable markers. She then uses permanent markers to color herself and her dad. The splendid drawings do not wash off, but after applying a special marker, they both look good as new—as long as it does not rain. Although the book is obviously fantastic, some children may be tempted to write on themselves after reading the book. It is most suitable for older children and should be accompanied by a discussion of safe ways to use markers. Six and up.

Myers, W. D. (1995). *The story of the three kings.* New York: HarperCollins. **(Art Elements: pattern; Multicultural: Africa)**

A folktale, set in an African setting, features jewel-like paintings with intricate patterns. A good companion to pattern activities for primary-age children. Four and up.

Myrus, D., & Squillance, A. (1963). *Story in the sand.* New York: Macmillan. **(Art Elements: texture; Media: sand) [7]**

A visit to the beach is illustrated with photographs of patterns and textures made with footprints, and drawings in the sand detailed with shells and beach finds. Four and up.

Neitzel, S. (1989). *The jacket I wear in the snow.* New York: Greenwillow Books. **(Media: fiber art)**

Pictures show the different articles of clothing a little girl wears to go out in the snow. This book is a good introduction to a thematic unit on clothing. Also available as a Big Book from Scholastic. Toddler and up.

Nicholson, N. (1998). *The little girl in the red dress with cat and dog.* New York: Viking Press. **(Art Awareness)**

Inspired by a folk art painting in the Museum of American Folk Art, this story tells how the painting was created from the viewpoint of the little girl. It describes the arrival of the itinerant painter and how the painting came about. The illustrations mirror the folk art style of the original painting. Four and up.

Nikola-Lisa, W. (2000). *A year with Grandma Moses.* New York: Henry Holt. **(Art Awareness)**

The words and paintings of folk artist Grandma Moses illustrate this book about the seasons. Toddler and up.

Olabye, I. (1994). *Bitter bananas.* Honesdale, PA: Boyds Mill Press. **(Media: chalk, collage; Multicultural: Africa) [8]**

Cut-paper and chalk collages illustrate a simple tale of an African boy who figures out a way to save the bananas from the baboons. This book can be used to introduce the idea of combining collage and drawing materials. Four and up.

O'Neill, M. (1961). *Hailstones and halibut bones: Adventures in color.* Garden City, NY: Doubleday. **(Art Elements: color) [8]**

Beautiful poems describe each color in terms of the things that come in that color. Includes purple, gold, black, brown, blue, gray, white, orange, red, pink, green, and yellow. Toddler and up.

O'Neill, M. (1969). *Fingers are always bringing me news.* Garden City, NY: Doubleday **(Developing Understanding; Art Elements: texture) [10]**

Each poem in this book describes different people's fingers and what they touch and feel. Use these poems to relate to activities involving the sense of touch. Toddler and up.

Osofsky, D. (1992). *Dreamcatcher.* New York: Orchard Books. **(Media: chalk drawing; Multicultural: Native American)**

Soft pastel drawings and a simple text tell the tale of a sleeping child and a dreamcatcher. A wonderful book to read aloud when sharing a dreamcatcher as an artifact. Four and up.

Parton, D. (1994). *The coat of many colors.* New York: HarperCollins. **(Media: quilting)**

Based on the song of the same name, this book tells the tale of a poor child and a special patchwork coat. Four and up.

Paterson, B. (1990). *My first animals.* New York: Thomas Y. Crowell. **(Art Elements: shape; Media: torn-paper collage)**

Familiar animals are illustrated with torn-paper shapes in this simply written book, suitable for toddlers.

Paul, A. W. (1991). *Eight hands round: A Patchwork Alphabet.* New York: HarperCollins. **(Art Elements: pattern; Media: quilting) [8]**

Traditional American quilt patterns are presented along with actual or fanciful explanations for their origins. Can be read in short sections. Six and up.

Peek, M. (1985). *Mary wore her red dress.* New York: Houghton Mifflin. **(Art Elements: color)**

Traditional children's song about colors of clothing helps teach colors using movement. Toddler and up.

Pfister, M. (1992). *The rainbow fish.* New York: North-South Books. **(Developing Understanding) [1, 5]**

The most beautiful fish in the ocean discovers that by giving of himself he can find friendship and happiness. The scales on the rainbow fish that he shares with the other fish in the sea are made with real reflective foil. A powerful book to use to teach children the values of cooperation and sharing. Toddler and up.

Phillip, N. (Ed.). (1995). *Songs are sung.* New York: Orchard Books. **(Art Element: texture; Media: painting; Multicultural: Native American)**

Inuit poetry is illustrated with paintings rendered with bold strokes of paint on a textured canvas background. Six and up.

Pinkwater, D. M. (1977). *The big orange splot.* New York: Scholastic. **(Becoming an Artist; Developing Understanding) [10]**

An exuberant story about a man who paints his house in his unique way, much to the initial distress of his neighbors. Children love the colorful language and exaggerated happenings in this book, which extols creativity. Follow up the story by encouraging children to paint a box or picture in their own way. Four and up.

Pitmann, H. C. (1998). *Still-life stew.* New York: Disney. **(Media: still life, modeling)**

A joyful artist gathers luscious vegetables from her garden, creates a still life, and then chops the vegetables up for stew. This book is a delightful way to introduce the term *still life* to children. The illustrations are made of modeling clay. Four and up.

Polacco, P. (1988a). *The keeping quilt.* New York: Simon & Schuster. **(Media: quilting)**

Four generations of a Jewish family are linked by a handmade quilt. Each generation treasures the quilt but uses it in different ways. This book can be used with children to start them thinking about why people keep artworks instead of discarding them. Four and up.

Polacco, P. (1988b). *Rechenka's eggs.* New York: Philomel Books. **(Art Elements: pattern; Multicultural: Ukranian) [7]**

Patterns are everywhere in this engaging story of a magic goose and some beautifully decorated Pysanky eggs. An excellent book to encourage children to find patterns in illustrations. Four and up.

Polacco, P. (1990). *Thunder cake.* New York: Putnam & Grosset. **(Art Elements: pattern) [7]**

Clothing and quilts are covered with patterns in this simple story of a grandmother who helps her granddaughter learn to be brave during a thunderstorm. After reading the book, have children find patterns on their clothing as well. Four and up.

Prater, J. (1985). *The gift.* New York: Viking Press. **(Media: box construction) [9]**

In this wordless book, a gift arrives in a big box. Children in the book then use the box to transport themselves on an imaginary trip. Toddler and up.

Price, C. (1975). *Dancing masks of Africa.* New York: Charles Scribner's Sons. **(Media: maskmaking; Multicultural: Africa) [11]**

An enthusiastic text and bold illustrations present a variety of African masks, in the context in which they are used. Information on the sources of the different masks is provided at the back of the book. This is an excellent introduction to African masks for children age three and up. Enrich the images of the book with large reproductions of similar masks or actual masks, if possible. Three and up.

Reed, G. (1968). *The sand lady.* New York: Lothrop, Lee, & Shepard. **(Art Elements: texture; Media: sand) [7]**

A young girl makes a mermaid from her beach combings. The mermaid comes to life and gives her a special message. Four and up.

Reed, M. (1990). *The button box.* New York: Dutton. **(Art Elements: pattern)**

A young boy plays with the family's button collection, sorting and making patterns. Use this book to accompany sensory activities using buttons, or when using buttons in collages. Four and up.

Reed, M. (1997). *A string of beads.* New York: Dutton. **(Media: beads; Multiculural)**

The history of beads is told in this simple story of a girl and her grandmother making and stringing beads. Beads from many cultures are illustrated. Four and up.

Reid, B. (1987). *Sing a song of sixpence.* New York: Scholastic. **(Art Elements: texture; Media: modeling clay) [8]**

Traditional Mother Goose rhymes are illustrated with dimensional modeling clay pictures. Also available as a Big Book from Scholastic. Toddler and up.

Ringgold, F. (1991). *Tar beach.* New York: Random House. **(Multicultural: African American; Media: quilting) [7]**

This autobiographical story about growing up in Harlem incorporates many African-American traditions. Faith Ringgold is an artist who works in painted and quilted fabrics. The book is illustrated with paintings done on textured canvas and based on her "Woman on the Bridge" series. The quilted border is from the actual quilt and the quilt, is shown at the end of the book. Also available as a Big Book from Scholastic. Four and up.

Roalf, P. (1993). *Looking at painting: Children.* New York: Hyperion Books. **(Art Awareness)**

Each double-page spread shows a reproduction of a painting featuring children, followed by a brief discussion about the artist and the painting. One of an extensive series by this author that includes the subject of cats, the circus, dancers, landscapes, families, and seascapes. Four and up.

Robbins, K. (1984). *Building a house.* New York: Four Winds Press. **(Art Awareness: architecture) [9]**

Using clear black-and-white photos, this book details the complete construction of a house. It includes not only putting up the foundation and walls but also installing electricity, water, and more. Children will be fascinated by these pictures. If possible, visit a house being built and compare it to the information in the book. Four and up.

Robenberg, L. (1991). *The scrap doll.* New York: HarperCollins. **(Becoming an Artist; Media: puppets)**

A little girl transforms a plain rag doll into a beautiful one by painting on a face and making new clothes for it. Use this book to show children how plain or ordinary things can be converted into special ones, such as turning a bag into a puppet, through imagination. Four and up.

Rockwell, A. F. (1993). *Mr. Panda's painting.* New York: Simon & Schuster. **(Art Elements: color; Media: painting)**

In this simple book for toddlers, Mr. Panda runs out of paint, buys some more, and then makes a painting with each new, brilliant color. Toddlers.

Roessel, M. (1995). *Songs from the loom: A Navajo girl learns to weave.* Minneapolis, MN: Lerner. **(Art Awareness; Media: fiber art; Multicultural: Native American) [8]**

Ruth Roessel, a Navajo weaver, teaches her granddaughter how to spin, dye, and weave. The text is too complicated for younger children, but the story and activities can be retold while showing the excellent photographs. Six and up.

Rosetti, C. (1992). *Color.* New York: HarperCollins. **(Art Elements: color)**

Poetry introduces colors to very young children. Toddlers.

Ross, D. (1993). *The serpent shell.* Happauge, NY: Barron's Educational Series. **(Sensory Perception)**

Pastel watercolors combined with crayon illustrate a fanciful tale of how a sea serpent is saved by a young boy and a marvelous conch shell. Following this story, put a conch on the sensory table. Four and up.

Rotner, S. (1994). *Faces.* New York: Atheneum. **(Multicultural: portraits)**

Photographs and a minimal text show children from around the world involved in everyday activities. An excellent book to use with anti-bias activities portraiture. Toddler and up.

Rotner, S. (1996). *Colors around us.* New York: Little Simon. **(Art Elements: color)**

Photographs depict a range of each of the basic colors. Flaps lift up to reveal a color name or color riddle. Toddler and up.

Rylant, C. (1988). *All that I see.* New York: Orchard Books. **(Becoming an Artist)**

A shy boy befriends an artist through an exchange of artwork. Use this book to show how different artists have their own vision of the world. Four and up.

Say, A. (1996). *Emma's rug.* New York: Houghton Mifflin. **(Becoming an Artist)**

An Asian-American girl finds artistic inspiration in her beloved "security" rug. When her mother washes it, she becomes distraught and can no longer paint until she discovers inspiration in the world around her. Four and up.

Schick, E. (1987). *Art lessons.* New York: Greenwillow Books. **(Becoming an Artist; Media: drawing)**

An eight-year-old boy takes drawing lessons from a neighbor, who provides a model of positive art teaching and teaches him how to observe beauty. It is a must-read for all adults who teach art to young children. Six and up.

Schwartz, A. (1983). *Begin at the beginning.* New York: Harper & Row. **(Becoming an Artist; Media: painting)**

A young girl who is making a painting for the second-grade art show does not know where to begin. This book helps children think like artists. Six and up.

*Sendak, M. (1964). *Where the wild things are.* New York: Harper & Row. **(Art Elements: line) [8]**

This children's classic about a little boy who does not want to eat his supper provides the perfect transition into making "wild things," whether drawn, painted, or modeled. Have the children notice how Sendak used lines to add detail to his drawings. Toddler and up.

Serfozo, M. (1988). *Who said red?* New York: Macmillan. **(Art Elements: color; Media: watercolor painting)**

A simple text about colors is illustrated with softly toned watercolor paintings. Toddler and up.

Shalom, V. (1995). *The color of things.* New York: Rizzoli International. **(Art Elements: color; Sensory Perception)**

Colors are drained from a town, and children paint them back again. This thought-provoking book helps children see how important color is to our world. Six and up.

Shasta, M. (1994). *The hall of beasts.* New York: Simon & Schuster. **(Media: murals)**

A grandfather and his grandson go see a mural of animals that is in a building ready to be torn down. Before their eyes, the animals come free of the wall and leave. Use this book to introduce the idea of a mural. Six and up.

Shaw, C. G. (1988). *It looked like spilt milk.* New York: HarperTrophy. **(Art Elements: shape)**

Free-form shapes turn into ordinary objects. A fun book for all young children. Also available as a Big Book from Scholastic. Toddler and up.

Showers, P. (1991). *The listening walk.* New York: HarperCollins. **(Sensory Perception: sound)**

This simple text describes a "listening" walk as a child walking outside hears different sounds in his environment. Use this book to accompany activities focusing on the sense of hearing. Toddler and up.

Siberell, A. (1982). *Whale in the sky.* New York: Dutton Children's Books. **(Media: printmaking; Multicultural: Native American) [4]**

Woodcut prints are used to illustrate this retelling of a traditional Northwest Coast myth. The book also explains in a simple way how and why totem poles were made, and it describes the tools and paints that were used. Six and up.

Simon, S. (1985). *Soap bubble magic.* New York: Lothrop, Lee & Shepard. **(Sensory Perception)**

This science book for children presents the fun and excitement of bubble making while explaining why bubbles do the things they do. Six and up.

Skofield, J. (1984). *All wet! All wet!* New York: Harper & Row. **(Sensory Perception) [5]**

A boy and the animals of the woods enjoy the sights, smells, and sounds of a rainy day in the summer. A perfect book to accompany a walk in the rain. Toddler and up.

Sweeney, J. (1996). *Once upon a lily pad: Love in Monet's garden.* New York: Chronicle Books. **(Art Awareness)**

A playful view of Monet and his garden from the point of view of two frogs who live in a pond that he loves to paint. It includes a foldout reproduction of *Waterlilies.* Six and up.

Sweeney, J. (1998). *Bijou, Bonbon and Beau: The kittens who danced for Degas.* San Francisco: Chronicle Books. **(Art Awareness)**

Three kittens are born in a Paris theater, where they become favorites of the ballet dancers of Degas, who includes them in his sketches. It includes a foldout reproduction of *Rehearsal on the Stage.* Six and up.

Sweeney, J. (2000). *Suzette and the puppy: A story about Mary Cassatt.* Haupauge, NY: Barrons. **(Art Awareness)**

A fictional story about the young girl in Cassattt's painting, *The Girl in the Blue Armchair,* which delightfully introduces children to the world of the French Impressionists. Four and up.

Testa, F. (1982). *If you take a paintbrush.* New York: Dial Books. **(Art Elements: color)**

This book compares the colors of a variety of objects.

Thompson, B. (1995). *The magic quilt.* Littleton, MA: Sundance. **(Art Elements: color; Media: chalk drawing)**

Beautiful chalk drawings illustrate a simple story of a young African-American girl who is afraid to sleep at night while her mother is away. Together, she and her grandmother make a quilt of many colors, using her mother's clothing, which helps her feel her mother is near. The simple text is perfect for toddlers and preschoolers. The colors yellow, gold, pink, green, and purple are integrated into the story. Toddler and up.

Tripp, V. (1987). *The penguins' paint.* Chicago: Children's Book Press. **(Art Elements: color; Media: painting)**

Penguins find some buckets of paint and have fun painting everything in new colors. A lighthearted approach to color mixing for toddlers and young preschoolers. Toddlers and up.

Vaughan, M. (1995). *Hands hands hands.* New York: Greenvale. **(Sensory Perception)**

This book celebrates all of the wonderful things that hands can do. Toddler and up.

Vazquez, S. (1998). *The school mural.* Milwaukee, WI: Raintree. **(Media: mural)**

Colorful cut-paper illustrations show how a class plans and makes a mural to commemorate the school's 50th anniversary. Six and up.

Venezia, M. (1991). *Paul Klee.* Chicago: Children's Book Press. **(Art Awareness)**

This child-appealing biography of Klee tells the story of his life, starting in childhood, and it is illustrated with reproductions of his artwork and with Venezia's humorous cartoons. The text is simply worded but is rather long and contains difficult concepts for preschoolers. Read selected passages and retell other parts. This book is one of a series by this author called *Getting to Know the World's Greatest Artists.* Other books in the series include *Rembrandt* (1988), *da Vinci* (1989), *Hopper* (1989), *Monet* (1989), *Cassatt* (1990), *Michelangelo* (1991), *Botticelli* (1992), *Bruegel* (1992), *Pollock* (1992), *Goya* (1993), and *O'Keeffe* (1993). Six and up.

Waber, B. (1975). *I was all thumbs.* New York: Houghton Mifflin. **(Media: printmaking) [7]**
A laboratory octopus escapes and has to learn how to live in the dangerous but beautiful freedom of the ocean. Use this book to accompany printmaking activities, especially with sea-related thematic activities and murals. Four and up.

Waber, B. (1996). *"You look ridiculous," said the rhinoceros to the hippopotamus.* Boston: Houghton-Mifflin. **(Media: printmaking)**
Bold prints illustrate this humorous tale, making it an excellent accompaniment to printmaking activities. Four and up.

Walsh, E. S. (1989). *Mouse paint.* New York: Trumpet Club. **(Art Elements: color; Media: painting) [5]**
A delightful story with a simple text about mice who play in some paint and discover color mixing. It is an excellent read-aloud for toddlers. Also available as a Big Book from Scholastic. Toddler and up.

Walsh, V. (1997). *Going to the Getty.* Los Angeles: J. Paul Getty Museum. **(Art Awareness; Museums)**
Photographs and reproductions from the Getty Museum accompany a simple text about what to look for in art. Six and up.

Walter, M. P. (1995). *Darkness.* New York: Simon & Schuster. **(Art Awareness; Art Elements: color)**
Bold, sweeping paintings by an African-American artist illustrate the beauty of dark colors through pictures of eruptions, night, and more. Sharing this book is a wonderful way to focus on the often-ignored deep, rich, dark colors of our world. Four and up.

Ward, L. (1978). *I am eyes * Ni macho.* New York: Greenwillow Books. **(Art Elements: pattern; Multicultural: Africa) [8]**
In simple text and patterned pictures, an African boy observes his world. A good companion for pattern activities. Also available as a Big Book from Scholastic. Four and up.

Waters, K. (1990). *Lion dancer.* New York: Scholastic. **(Multicultural: China)**
This book follows a young boy from Chinatown as he gets ready to celebrate the Chinese New Year. Also available as a Big Book from Scholastic. Four and up.

Williams, K. L. (1990). *Galimoto.* New York: Lothrop, Lee, & Shepard. **(Becoming an Artist; Media: construction; Multicultural: Africa) [5]**
An African boy collects a variety of discarded materials to build a toy car. This is an excellent book to use with children to inspire them to be "inventors." Four and up.

Williams, K. L. (1998). *Painted dreams.* New York: Lothrop, Lee, & Shepard. **(Becoming an Artist; Media: drawing, painting: Multicultural)**
A young Haitian girl uses materials she finds, such as broken bricks and charcoal, to draw pictures on the cement walls of her house. When she decorates her mother's market stall, she attracts customers and recognition. Use this book when exploring different ways to draw and paint. Four and up.

Williams, L. E. (1995). *The long silk strand.* Honesdale, PA: Boyds Mills Press. **(Media: mixed collage; Multicultural: China)**
Real silk thread and cut-paper collages illlustrate this Chinese folktale. Ask children to think of ways they could use a thread in their collages. Four and up.

Wilson, F. (1969/1988). *What it feels like to be a building.* Washington, DC: The Preservation Press. **(Art Awareness: architecture) [9]**
Simple people shapes illustrate an analogy of how buildings are constructed. Beside each simple drawing of an architectural feature, such as a column or an arch, are illustrations that show how the stress and strains would feel if the structure were built out of people. Very sophisticated ideas are made easy to understand, and children of all ages will learn more about building from this book. Follow up with a walk to find examples of these forms in the neighborhood, and try some kinesthetic activities inspired by the book. Six and up.

Winter, J. (1991). *Diego.* New York: Random House. **(Art Awareness: murals; Multicultural: Mexico) [10]**
This Spanish/English biography of Mexican muralist Diego Rivera focuses on his childhood and youth. Six and up.

Winthrop, E. (1988). *Shoes.* New York: Harper & Row. **(Media: murals, printmaking)**
This book illustrates shoes from around the world and then delightfully concludes that bare feet are the best. A perfect book to accompany a shoe or footprint mural. Toddler and up.

Witte, E., & Witte, P. (1992). *Touch me book.* Racine, WA: Western. **(Art Elements: texture)**
Pieces of real wood, cloth, and other textured materials illustrate this board book about textures. A fun book for toddlers to explore on their own. Toddlers.

Wolff, R. J. (1968a). *Feeling blue.* New York: Charles Scribner's Sons.

Wolff, R. J. (1968b). *Hello yellow.* New York: Charles Scribner's Sons.

Wolff, R. J. (1968c). *Seeing red.* New York: Charles Scribner's Sons. **(Art Awareness: color; Sensory Perception) [10]**
These outwardly simple books present sophisticated concepts of color that help children see more than basic red, yellow, and blue. Four and up.

Wolkstein, D. (1992). *Little mouse's painting.* New York: Morrow Junior Books. **(Becoming an Artist; Media: painting; Sensory Perception)**
A little mouse creates a painting that looks different depending on the viewer's distance. This book introduces the idea that the appearance of a piece of art can change depending on how one views it. Follow up the story by having the children stand at different distances from a selected print or piece of art, and then ask them to describe what they see. Four and up.

Xiong, B. (1989). *Nine-in-one, grrr, grrr.* Emeryville, CA: Children's Book Press. **(Media: embroidery; Multicultural: Southeast Asia) [8]**
A simple folktale from the Hmong people of Southeast Asia is illustrated with traditional embroidered story cloths. Four and up.

Yabuuchi, M. (1985). *Whose footprints?* New York: Philomel Books. **(Media: murals, printmaking) [10]**
Footprints are matched with the animal that made them. Use this book to initiate or accompany murals that feature foot painting. Also available as a Big Book from Macmillan. Four and up.

Yenawine, P., & the Museum of Modern Art. (1991). *Colors.* New York: Delacorte Press. **(Art Awareness; Art Elements)**
Artwork from the Museum of Modern Art illustrates this simple art concept book suitable for toddlers and young preschoolers. One of a series, including *Lines, Shapes,* and *Stories.* Toddler and up.

*Yolen, J. (1988). *Owl moon.* New York: Philomel Books. **(Art Elements: color; Media: painting)**
Beautiful prose poetry describes how a young boy and his father go for a walk on a snowy moonlit night. The illustrations can be used to help children see that artists use more than just white when painting snow. Four and up.

Young, E. (1991). *Seven blind mice.* New York: Philomel. **(Sensory Perception)**
Based on the tale of the blind men and the elephant, seven blind mice use their senses to investigate an elephant. Also available as a Big Book from Scholastic. Toddler and up.

Ziebel, P. (1989). *Look closer!* New York: Clarion. **(Sensory Perception)**
Close-ups of objects are followed by a full view of each object in use. A favorite for increasing the visual awareness of toddlers. After reading the book, provide magnifying glasses of various types with which the children may explore. Toddler and up.

Ziefert, H. (1986). *A new coat for Anna.* New York: Alfred A. Knopf. **(Media: fiber art) [8]**
During World War II, a mother trades a watch for wool and makes her daughter a coat from scratch. The process of spinning, dyeing, weaving, and tailoring requires many people to cooperate to produce Anna's new coat. Six and up.

Teacher References

BOOKS

These books will help teachers learn more about the world of visual art.

Baird, B. (1965). *The art of the puppet*. New York: Macmillan.
Puppets from ancient to modern times and from around the world are shown in beautiful illustrations.

Batterberry, A. (1975). *The Pantheon story of art for young children*. New York: Pantheon Books.
Overview of art history presented in simple language.

Baumann, H. (1954). *The caves of the great hunters*. New York: Pantheon Books.
This book tells the story of the discovery of the cave paintings of Lascaux, France. Use it to create a retelling of the story that will fascinate young children.

Caraway, C. (1981). *The mola design book*. Owings Mills, MD: Stemmer House.
This book tells the history of molas as made by the women of the San Blas Islands off the coast of Panama. It includes many black-and-white drawings of mola designs.

Chan, A. (1990). *Hmong textile designs*. Owings Mills, MD: Stemmer House.
This book provides a brief history of the Hmong people of Southeast Asia, the role of textile needle art in their culture, and current directions of the art form as practiced by recent Hmong immigrants in America. Black line drawings illustrate many Hmong pieces.

D'Alleva, A. (1993). *Native American arts and cultures*. Worcester, MA: Davis.
Native American art from the past and present is organized by region and tribe. Art is clearly described in the text, accompanied by black-and-white and color photographs.

Depree, H., & MacKinnon, L. (1994). *Art, books, and children*. Bothell, WA: Lands End.
This beautifully illustrated book provides many ideas for relating poetry and stories to children's art activities. It contains lists of children's books organized by topic.

Glubok, S. (1964a). *The art of the American Indian*. New York: Harper & Row.

Glubok, S. (1964b). *The art of the Eskimo*. New York: Harper & Row.

Glubok, S. (1965). *The art of Africa*. New York: Harper & Row.

Glubok, S. (1966). *The art of ancient Peru*. New York: Harper & Row.

Glubok, S. (1973). *The art of China*. New York: Macmillan.
These are beautifully illustrated books with simple, clear descriptions.

Greenfeld, H. (1990). *First impressions: Marc Chagall*. New York: Harry N. Abrams.
The story of Chagall's childhood and development as an artist illustrates the kinds of choices artists make in their lives.

Ivy, B. (1995). *Children's books about art*. Palo Alto, CA: Dale Seymour.
This annotated bibliography of children's books about art also provides a range of activities using these books.

Janson, H. W., & Janson, A. F. (1987). *The history of art for young people*. New York: Harry E. Abrams.
This overview of art from prehistoric times to the present will provide a source of background information on changing art styles and practices.

Lyons, M. E. (1993). *Stitching stars: The story quilts of Harriet Powers*. New York: Charles Scribner's Sons.
This beautifully written book tells the story of how former slave Harriet Powers created her two unique "story quilts." Illustrated with beautiful photographs and set against the background of the history and beliefs of African Americans, this book provides information that will enrich any discussion of American quilt making. (Part of a series titled "African-American Artists and Artisans.")

Rodari, F. (1991). *A weekend with Picasso*. New York: Rizzoli.
Intended for older children, this book uses facts from Picasso's life to create a fictional weekend spent with the artist. Illustrated with photographs and Picasso's artwork, it provides a rich source of information to share with young children.

Saccardi, M. (1997). *The art in story*. North Haven, CT: Shoestring Press.
This book is an invaluable teaching resource containing original stories to tell children about the art of the world. It covers both ancient and modern art, including Egypt, Greece, Asia, Africa, the Middle Ages, the Renaissance, Impressionism, and computer art. In addition, it provides ideas for related activities and a comprehensive bibliography of both children's and adult books.

Schuman, J. M. (1981). *Art from many hands*. Worcester, MA: Davis.
Although most of the art projects presented in this book are too advanced for children under age eight, the information about the different folk-art forms is invaluable and can be used to create simple books about multicultural artwork. The bibliography is excellent.

Stewart, H. (1979). *Looking at Indian art of the Northwest Coast.* Toronto: Douglas & McIntyre.

An excellent guide to both the past and contemporary art of the Northwest Coast tribes. This book discusses the meaning of the different symbols and forms, with many illustrations of totems, carvings, garments, and paintings.

Turner, R. M. (1993). *Faith Ringgold.* New York: Little, Brown.

A beautifully illustrated biography of African-American quilt-maker Faith Ringgold, this book provides background information to share with Ringgold's children's book *Tar Beach.*

Ventura, P. (1984). *Great painters.* New York: G. P. Putnam's Sons.

A cleverly illustrated overview of European painting from the Renaissance to Picasso, this book provides a general overview of the milestones of art history.

CD-ROMS

The following CD-ROMS can be used as a source of information about art of many kinds. Some of the reproductions of artwork can be shared with young children.

Sources include Crystal Publications, 1-800-913-8555, and Sax Arts and Crafts, 1-800-522-4278.

Electronic Library of Art (Sony)

Exploring Modern Art: Tate Gallery (Microsoft)

History through Art Series

History and Cultures of Africa (Queue)

Look What I See! (Metropolitan Museum of Art)

Microsoft Art Gallery (Microsoft)

National Museum of American Art (Smithsonian)

Picasso (Grolier)

The Ultimate Frank Lloyd Wright: America's Architect (Microsoft)

With Open Eyes: Art Works from the Chicago Institute of Art (Chicago Institute)

VIDEODISCS

Videodiscs allow access to individual pieces of information and pictures. Selected pieces of artwork can be shared with children as an occasional alternative to prints, especially in cases where a print is unavailable.

All of the following are available from Crystal Publications, 1-800-913-8555. Other sources include Sax Arts and Crafts, 1-800-522-4278, and Quality Computers, 1-800-777-3642.

American Art from the National Gallery

Ancient Egypt

Art of the Western World Series

Great Artist Series

In a Brilliant Light: Van Gogh at Arles

The National Gallery of Art

Van Gogh Revisited

With Open Eyes: Art Works from the Chicago Institute of Art

WORLD WIDE WEB

Search Engines

The following site is a good starting place for finding information about art for children on the Web:

http://www.yahooligans.com

Museums

Information on art can be obtained directly from museums around the world. In some cases it is possible to take a virtual tour of parts of the museum or to see works from a current exhibit. Some museums have extensive illustrated listings of their art holdings on line. Here are just a few possible sites to "visit."

Exploratorium, San Francisco	www.exploratorium.edu
Guggenheim Museum, New York City	www.guggenheim.org
J. Paul Getty Museum, Los Angeles	www.getty.edu
Louvre, Paris	www.louvre.fr
Metropolitan Museum of Art, New York City	www.metmuseum.org
Museum of American Folk Art, New York City	www.folkartmuse.org
Museum of Modern Art, New York City	www.moma.org
National Museum of American Art, Washington, DC	www.nmaa.si.edu

References

Alter-Muri, S. (1994). Art eases the process of attachment and separation. *Day Care and Early Education, 22*(1), 4–11.

Amabile, T. (1983). *The social psychology of creativity.* New York: Springer-Verlag.

Arieti, S. (1976). *Creativity: The magic synthesis.* New York: Basic Books.

Arnheim, R. (1969). *Visual thinking.* Berkeley, CA: University of California Press.

Art Educators of New Jersey. (1976/1995). *Insights: Art in special education.* Cherry Hill, NJ: Art Educators of New Jersey.

Ayres, W. (1995). Teaching is an act of hope. *Teaching Tolerance, 4*(2), 22–25.

Becker, J., Reed, K., Steinhaus, P., & Week, P. (1994). *Themestorming.* Beltsville, MD: Gryphon.

Bender, S. (1989). *Plain and simple: A woman's journey to the Amish.* San Francisco: HarperCollins.

Biber, B. (1984). *Early education and psychology development.* New Haven: Yale University Press.

Boden, M. A. (1990). *The creative mind.* New York: Basic Books.

Bos, B. (1978). *Don't move the muffin pans.* Roseville, CA: Turn-the-Page Press.

Brandt, R. (1995). Punished by rewards? A conversation with Alfie Kohn. *Educational Leadership, 53*(1), 13–16.

Bredekamp, S. (Ed.). (1987). *Developmentally appropriate practice in early childhood programs serving children from birth through age 8.* Washington, DC: National Association for the Education of Young Children.

Brooks, S. W., & Sentori, S. M. (1988). *See the paintings!* Rosemount, NJ: Modern Learning Press.

Bruner, J. (1979). *On knowing: Essays for the left hand.* Cambridge: Harvard University Press.

Bry, A. (1978). *Visualization: Directing the movies of your mind.* New York: Harper & Row.

Buck, P. S. (1967). "To the young." *To my daughters, with love.* New York: John Day.

Burn, J. R. (1989). Express it with puppetry—an international language. In S. Hoffman & L. L. Lamme (Eds.), *Learning from the inside out* (pp. 29–34). Wheaton, MD: Association for Childhood Education International.

Caine, R. N., & Caine, G. (1994). *Making connections: Teaching and the human brain.* New York: Addison-Wesley.

Cameron, J. (1992). *The artist's way: A spiritual path to higher creativity.* New York: G. P. Putnam's Sons.

Carey, J. (Ed.). (2002). *Brain facts* (4th ed.). Washington, DC: Society for Neuroscience.

Catlin, C. (1994). *Toddlers together.* Beltsville, MD: Gryphon.

Cecil, N. L., & Lauritzen, P. (1995). *Literacy and the arts for the integrated classroom: Alternative ways of knowing.* White Plains, NY: Longman.

Chapman, L. (1978). *Approaches to art in education.* New York: Harcourt Brace Jovanovich.

Chard, S. (1998a). *The project approach: Making the curriculum come alive.* New York: Scholastic.

Chard, S. (1998b). *The project approach: Managing successful projects.* New York: Scholastic.

Chenfeld, M. B. (2000). *Teaching in the key of life.* Washington, DC: National Association for the Education of Young Children.

Cherry, C. (1990). *Creative art for the developing child.* Carthage, IL: Fearon Teacher Aids.

Cherry, C., Godwin, D., & Staples, J. (1989). *Is the left brain always right? A guide to whole child development.* Belmont, CA: David S. Lake.

Church, E. B., & Miller, K. (1990). *Learning through play: Blocks.* New York: Scholastic.

Clemens, S. G. (1991). Art in the classroom: Making every day special. *Young Children, 46*(1), 4–11.

Cockerton, T., Moore, S., & Norman, D. (1971). Cognitive test performance and background music. *Perceptual and Motor Skills, 85,* 1435–1438.

Cohen, E. P., & Gainer, R. S. (1976/1995). *Art: Another language for learning.* Portsmouth, NH: Heinemann.

Colbert, C., & Taunton, M. (1992). *An NAEA briefing paper: Developmentally appropriate practices for the visual arts education of young children.* Reston, VA: National Art Education Association.

Costello, R. (Ed.). (1995). *Webster's College Dictionary.* New York: Random House.

Cox, M. V. (1993). *Children's drawings of the human figure.* Hove, UK: Erlbaum.

Crary, E. (1984). *Kids can cooperate.* Seattle, WA: Parenting Press.

Davidson, J. I. (1989). *Children and computers together in the early childhood classroom.* Clifton Park, NY: Delmar Learning.

Dennis, W. (1966). Goodenough scores, art experience, and modernization. *Journal of Social Psychology, 68,* 213–215.

Depree, H., & Mackinnon, L. (1994). *Art, books, and children.* Bothwell, WA: Lands End.

Derman-Sparks, L., & the A.B.C. Task Force. (1989). *Anti-bias curriculum: Tools for empowering young children.* Washington, DC: National Association for the Education of Young Children.

Dewey, J. (1958). *Art as experience.* New York: Capricorn Books. (First published in 1934.)

Di Leo, J. H. (1970). *Young children and their drawings.* New York: Brunner/Mazel.

Dissanayake, E. (1995). *Homo aestheticus: Where art comes from and why.* Seattle, WA: University of Washington Press.

Dodge, D. T., & Colker, L. J. (1992). *The creative curriculum.* Washington, DC: Teaching Strategies.

Dodge, D. T., & Phinney, J. (1990). *A parent's guide to early childhood education.* Beltsville, MD: Gryphon.

Edwards, B. (1979). *Drawing on the right side of the brain.* Los Angeles: J. P. Tarcher.

Edwards, B. (1986). *Drawing on the artist within.* New York: Simon & Schuster.

Edwards, C., Gandini, L., & Forman, G. (1993). *The hundred languages of children: The Reggio Emilia approach to early childhood education.* Norwood, NJ: Ablex.

Edwards, L. C. (1990). *Affective development and the creative arts.* New York: Macmillan.

Edwards, L. C. (1993). The creative arts process: What it is and what it is not. *Young Children, 48*(3), 77–81.

Einon, D. (1985). *Play with a purpose.* New York: Pantheon Books.

Eisner, E. (1972). *Educating artistic vision.* New York: Macmillan.

Eisner, E. (1976). *The arts, human development, and education.* Berkeley, CA: McCutchen.

Eisner, E. (1983). *Beyond creating.* Los Angeles: Getty Center for Education in Art.

Elkind, D. (1974). *Children and adolescents.* New York: Oxford University Press.

Engel, B. S. (1995). *Considering children's art: Why and how to value their works.* Washington, DC: National Association for the Education of Young Children.

Engel, B. S. (1996). Learning to look: Appreciating children's art. *Young Children, 51*(2), 74–79.

Feldman, E. B. (1970). *Becoming human through art.* Englewood Cliffs, NJ: Prentice Hall.

Fein, S. (1984). *Heidi's horse.* Pleasant Hill, CA: Exelrod Press.

Fein, S. (1993). *First drawings: Genesis of visual thinking.* Pleasant Hill, CA: Exelrod Press.

Finn, C. (1986). *What works: Research about teaching and learning.* Washington, DC: United States Department of Education.

Gardner, H. (1973). *The arts and human development.* New York: John Wiley & Sons.

Gardner, H. (1980). *Artful scribbles: The significance of children's drawings.* New York: Basic Books.

Gardner, H. (1982). *Art, mind, and brain.* New York: Basic Books.

Gardner, H. (1983). *Frames of mind.* New York: Basic Books.

Gardner, H. (1990a). *Art education.* An invitational address at the Conference for the National Art Education Association, Kansas City, MO.

Gardner, H. (1990b). *To open minds.* New York: Basic Books.

Gardner, H. (1991). *The unschooled mind.* New York: Basic Books.

Gardner, H. (1993). *Multiple intelligences: The theory in practice.* New York: Basic Books.

Gardner, H. (1995). Reflections on multiple intelligences: Myths and messages. *Phi Delta Kappan, 77*(1), 200–209.

Gardner, H., Winter, E., & Kircher, M. (1975). Children's conceptions of the arts. *Journal of Aesthetic Education, 9*(3), 60–77.

Gelfer, J. (1990). Discovering and learning art through blocks. *Day Care and Early Education, 17*(4), 21–24.

Genishi, C. (1993). Art, portfolios, and assessment, *Early Childhood Today, 8*(2), 67.

Gerhardt, Lydia A. (1973). *Moving and knowing: The young child orients himself in space.* Englewood Cliffs, NJ: Prentice Hall.

Goleman, D. (1995). *Emotional intelligence.* New York: Bantam.

Goleman, D., Kaufman, P., & Ray, M. (1992). *The creative spirit.* New York: Dutton.

Golomb, C. (1981). Representation and reality. *Review of Visual Arts Education, 14,* 36–48.

Gonzalez-Mena, J. (1993). *Multicultural issues in child care.* Mountain View, CA: Mayfield.

Goodenough, F. L. (1926). *Children's drawings as measures of intellectual maturity.* New York: Harcourt Brace Jovanovich.

Gratz, R., & Boulton, P. (1993). Taking care of kids: A director's concerns about environmental hazards. *Day Care and Early Education, 21*(2), 29–31.

Greenberg, P. (Ed.). (1972). *Art education: Elementary.* Washington, DC: National Art Education Association.

Greenberg, P. (1992). Teaching about Native Americans? Or teaching about people including Native Americans? *Young Child, 47*(6), 27–30.

Greenfeld, H. (1990). *First impressions: Marc Chagall.* New York: Abrams.

Greenman, J. (1988). *Caring spaces, learning places: Children's environments that work.* Redmond, WA: Exchange Press.

Guilford, J. P. (1977). *Way beyond IQ.* Buffalo, NY: The Creative Education Foundation.

Guilford, J. P. (1986). *Creative talents: Their nature, uses, development.* Buffalo, NY: Bearly.

Harris, D., & Goodenough, F. L. (1963). *Children's drawings as measures of intellectual maturity.* New York: Harcourt, Brace & World.

Hart, B., & Risley, T. R. (1995). *Meaningful differences in the everyday experiences of young American children.* Baltimore: Brookes.

Hart, K. (1994). *I can paint!* Portsmouth, NH: Heinemann.

Hart, L. (1983). *Human brain, human learning.* White Plains, NY: Longman.

Haugland, S. W. (1993). Are computers an important learning resource? *Day Care and Early Education, 20*(3), 30–31.

Haugland, S. W., & Shade, D. S. (1990). *Developmental evaluations of software for young children.* Clifton Park, NY: Delmar Learning.

Hendricks, G. (1981). *The centered teacher.* Englewood Cliffs, NJ: Prentice Hall.

Herefore, N., & Schall, J. (Eds.). (1991). *Learning through play: Art.* New York: Scholastic.

Herman, G. N., & Hollingworth, P. (1992). *Kinetic kaleidoscope.* Tucson, AZ: Zephyr Press.

Heward, W. L. (2000). *Exceptional children* (6th ed.). Upper Saddle River, NJ: Merrill.

Hirsch, E. S. (Ed.). (1974). *The block book.* Washington, DC: National Association for the Education of Young Children.

Hohmann, C. (1990). *Young children and computers.* Ypsilanti, MI: High/Scope.

Hymes, J. L. (1989). *Teaching the child under six.* West Greenwich, RI: Consortium Press.

Ivy, B. (1995). *Children's books about art.* Palo Alto, CA: Dale Seymour.

Janke, R. A., & Peterson, J. P. (1995). *Peacemaker's A,B,Cs for young children.* Marine on St. Croix, MN: Growing Communities for Peace.

Jansen, H. W. (1962). *History of art.* New York: Harry N. Abrams.

Jensen, E. (1998). *Teaching with the brain in mind.* Alexandria, VA: Association for Supervision and Curriculum Development.

Jensen, E. (2001). *Arts with the brain in mind.* Alexandria, VA: Association for Supervision and Curriculum Development.

Johnson, G. (1991). *In the palaces of memory: Explorations of thinking.* Albuquerque, NM: University of New Mexico Press.

Kagan, S. (1994). *Cooperative learning.* San Juan Capistrano, CA: Resources for Teachers.

Kamii, C., & DeVries, K. (1993). *Physical knowledge in preschool education: Implications of Piaget's theory.* New York: Teachers College Press.

Kantner, L. (1989). Beginnings: Children and their art. In S. Hoffman & L. L. Lamme (Eds.), *Learning from the inside out* (pp. 44–51). Wheaton, MD: Association for Childhood Education International.

Katz, L. G., & Chard, S. C. (2000). *Engaging children's minds: The project approach.* (2nd ed.). Norwood, NJ: Ablex.

Kellogg, R. (1969). *Analyzing children's art.* Palo Alto, CA: National Press Books.

Kellogg, R. (1979). *Children's drawings/children's minds.* New York: Avon Books.

Kindler, A. (Ed.). (1997). *Child development in art.* Reston, VA: National Art Education Association.

Kindler, A., & Darras, B. (1994). Artistic development in context: Emergence and development of pictorial imagery in the early childhood years. *Visual Art Research, 20,* 1–3.

Kohl, M. F. (1985). *Scribble cookies.* Bellingham, WA: Bright Ring.

Kohl, M. F. (1989). *Mudworks: Creative clay, dough, and modeling experiences.* Bellingham, WA: Bright Ring.

Kohn, A. (1993). *Punished by rewards.* New York: Houghton Mifflin.

Lay-Dopyera, M., & Dopyera, J. E. (1992). Strategies for teaching. In C. Seefeldt (Ed.), *The early childhood curriculum* (pp. 16–41). New York: Teacher's College Press.

LeeKeenan, D., & Nimmo, J. (1992). Connections: Using the project approach with 2- and 3-year-olds in a university lab school. In C. Edwards et al. (Eds.), *The hundred languages of children* (pp. 251–267). Norwood, NJ: Ablex.

Leeper, S. H., Dales, R. J., Skipper, D. S., & Witherspoon, R. L. (1974). *Good schools for young children.* New York: Macmillan.

London, P. (1991). *No more secondhand art.* Boston: Shambhala Press.

Lowenfeld, V., & Brittain, W. L. (1987). *Creative and mental growth.* New York: Macmillan.

Luvmour, J., & Luvmour, S. (1993). *Natural learning rhythms.* Berkeley, CA: Celestial Arts.

Malchiodi, C. A. (1998). *Understanding children's drawings.* New York: Guilford.

Marshall, H. H. (1995). Beyond "I like the way . . ." *Young Children, 50,* 25–28.

Mayesky, M., Neuman, D., & Wlodkowski, R. J. (2002). *Creative activities for young children* (7th ed.). Clifton Park, NY: Thomson Delmar Learning.

McCann, M. (1985). *Health hazards manual for artists.* New York: Nick Lyons Books.

McCormick, L., & Feeney, S. (1995). Modifying and expanding activities for children with handicaps. *Young Children, 50,* 10–16.

McDonald, D. T. (2001). *Music in our lives: The early years.* Washington, DC: National Association for the Education of Young Children.

McFee, J. (1961). *Preparation for art.* San Francisco: Wadsworth.

McFee, J. (1978). *Visual literacy and art education.* Invitational address at the Conference for the National Art Education Association, Kansas City, MO.

McFee, J., & Degge, R. M. (1981). *Art, culture, and environment: A catalyst for teaching.* Dubuque, IA: Kendall/Hunt.

McWinnie, H. J. (1992). Art in early childhood education. In C. Seefeldt (Ed.), *The early childhood curriculum* (pp. 264–285). New York: Teachers College Press.

Merryman, R. (1991). *First impressions: Andrew Wyeth.* New York: Harry N. Abrams.

Mesrobian, J. (1992). Rediscovering the Ninja Turtles' namesakes. *Day Care and Early Education, 20*(1), 18–19.

Miller, S. A. (1994). *Learning through play: Sand, water, clay, & wood.* New York: Scholastic.

Mogelon, A. (1969). *One hundred ways to have fun with an alligator.* Blauvelt, NY: Art Education.

Montessori, M. (1967). *The absorbent mind.* New York: Holt, Rinehart & Winston.

Nachmanovitch, S. (1990). *Free play.* Los Angeles: Jeremy P. Tarcher.

National Association for the Education of Young Children. (1986). Position statement on developmentally appropriate practice in early childhood programs serving children from birth through age 8. *Young Children, 41*(6), 3–9.

New, R. S. (1990). Excellent early education: A city in Italy has it. *Young Children, 45*(6), 4–10.

Nilsen, B. (2001). *Week by week* (2nd ed.). Clifton Park, NY: Thomson Delmar Learning.

Noyce, R. M., & Christie, J. F. (1989). *Integrating reading and writing instruction.* New York: Allyn & Bacon.

Olson, J. L. (1992). *Envisioning writing.* Portsmouth, NH: Heinemann.

Ormrod, J. E. (2003). *Educational psychology: Developing learners* (4th ed.). Upper Saddle River, NJ: Merrill.

Paced, M., & Black, J. (1994). *Authentic assessment of the young child: Celebrating development and learning.* New York: Macmillan.

Parsons, M. J. (1987). *How we understand art.* New York: Cambridge University Press.

Parsons, M. J. (1994). Can children do aesthetics? A developmental account. *Journal of Aesthetic Education, 28*(1), 33–45.

Paulsen, G. (1991). *The monument.* New York: Dell.

Piaget, J. (1959). *The child's conception of the world.* (J. Tomlinson and A. Tomlinson, Trans.). Savage, MD: Rowman & Littlefield. (Original work published 1929.)

Piaget, J. (1967). *Six psychological studies.* (A. Tenzer, Trans.). New York: Random House. (Original work published 1964.)

Pica, R. (2000). *Experiences in movement with music activites and theory.* Clifton Park, NY: Thomson Delmar Learning.

Pinker, S. (1997). *How the mind works.* New York: Norton.

Pinkerton, S. (1989). Concoctions: Creative mixtures to make and enjoy. *Day Care and Early Education, 17*(2), 25–29.

Prescott, E. (1978). Is day care as good as a home? *Young Children, 33,* 13–19.

Qualley, C. A. (1986). *Safety in the art room.* New York: Davis.

Read, H. (1956). *Education through art.* New York: Pantheon Books.

Redleaf, R. (1983). *Open the door: Let's explore: Neighborhood field trips for young children.* Mt. Rainer, MD: Gryphon.

Rodriguez, S. (1997). *The special artist's handbook.* Palo Alto, CA: Dale Seymour.

Rogers, F. (1982). *Talking with families about creativity.* Pittsburg, PA: Family Communications.

Ross, C. (1997). *Something to draw on: Activities and interventions using an art therapy approach.* London: Jessica Kingsley.

Rowe, G. (1987). *Guiding young artists.* South Melbourne, Australia: Oxford University Press Australia.

Rubin, W. S. (1968). *Dada and surrealism and their heritage.* New York: Museum of Modern Art.

Saracho, O. N., & Spodek, B. (Eds.). (1983). *Understanding the multicultural experience in early childhood education.* Washington, DC: National Association for the Education of Young Children.

Schaefer-Simmern, H. (1950). *The unfolding of artistic ability.* Berkeley: University of California Press.

Schiller, M. (1995). An emergent art curriculum that fosters understanding. *Young Children, 50*(3), 33–38.

Schirrmacher, R. (1986). Talking with young children about their art. *Young Children, 41*(5), 3–7.

Schirrmacher, R. (2002). *Art and creative development for young children* (4th ed.). Clifton Park, NY: Thomson Delmar Learning.

Schuman, J. M. (1981). *Art from many hands.* Worcester, MA: Davis.

Sciarra, D. J., & Dorsey, A. G. (2003). *Developing and administering a child care center* (5th ed.). Clifton Park, NY: Thomson Delmar Learning.

Seefeldt, C. (Ed.). (1992). *The early childhood curriculum.* New York: Teachers College Press.

Seefeldt, C. (1995). Art—Serious work. *Young Children, 50*(3), 39–45.

Shade, D. D. (1991). Integrating computers into the curriculum. *Day Care and Early Education, 19*(1), 45–47.

Shectman, A. E. (Ed.). (1995). *Insights: Art in special education.* Cherry Hill, NJ: Art Educators of New Jersey.

Smith, N. R. (1979). How a picture means. *New Directions in Child Development* (3), 59–72.

Solomon, K. (1989). Bringing the outside in: Craftspeople share. *Day Care and Early Education, 16*(4), 26–27.

Sousa, D. A. (2001). *How the brain works* (2nd ed.). Thousand Oaks, CA: Corwin.

Stallings, J. (1975). Implementation and child effects of teaching practices in follow-through classrooms. *Monographs of the Society for Research in Child Development, 40*(Serial No. 163).

Stone, J. G. (1969). *A guide to discipline.* Washington, DC: National Association for the Education of Young Children.

Sylwester, R. (1998). *Student brains, school issues: A collection of articles.* Arlington Heights, IL: Skylight.

Szekely, G. (1991). *Play to art.* Portsmouth, NH: Heinemann.

Thompson, C. M. (1995). Transforming curriculum in the arts. In S. Bredekamp & T. Rosegrant (Eds.), *Reaching potentials: Transforming early childhood curriculum and assessment* (pp. 81–96). Washington, DC: National Association for the Education of Young Children.

Thomson, B. J. (1993). *Words can hurt you: Beginning a program of anti-bias education.* New York: Addison-Wesley.

Torrance, E. P. (1963). *Education of the creative potential.* Minneapolis: University of Minnesota Press.

Torrance, E. P. (1970). *Encouraging creativity in the classroom.* Dubuque, IA: William C. Brown.

Turner, T. (1990). *Whole language planning.* Transitions: SDE Sourcebook. Peterborough, NH: The Society for Developmental Education.

Tzu, Lao (1963). *Tao Te Ching.* (D. C. Lau, Trans.). New York: Viking Penguin.

Vygotsky, L. S. (1978). *Mind in society.* Cambridge: Harvard University Press.

Whitehead, A. N. (1929). *The aims of education.* New York: Macmillan.

Willard, C. (1972). *Frank Lloyd Wright.* New York: Macmillan.

Williams, R. A., Rockwell, R. E., & Sherwood, E. A. (1987). *Mudpies to magnets.* Mt. Rainer, MD: Gryphon.

Winkur, J. (1992). *Friendly advice.* New York: Penguin Books.

Winner, E. (1982). *Invented worlds: The psychology of the arts.* Cambridge: Harvard University Press.

Winner, E. (1989). Children's perceptions of aesthetic properties in art. *British Journal of Developmental Psychology, 4,* 149–160.

Winner, E., Blank, P., Massey, C., & Gardner, H. (1983). Children's sensitivity to aesthetic properties in line drawings. In D. R. Rogers & J. A. Sloboda (Eds.), *The acquisition of symbolic skills* (pp. 86–96). London: Plenum.

Wolf, A. D. (1984). *Mommy, it's a Renoir!* Altoona, PA: Parent Child Press.

Wolf, D. (1979). *Early symbolization.* San Francisco: New Directions for Child Development.

Wolf, D., & Perry, M. D. (1989). From endpoints to repertories. *Journal of Aesthetic Education, 22,* 17–34.

Zavitkovsky, D. (1994). *Docia's stories.* Redmond, WA: Child Care Information Exchange.

Glossary

A

abstract—In art, a work that emphasizes formal elements over subject matter.

Abstract Expressionism—Artistic style in which art has no recognizable subject, and which focuses on color and media, often applied in a kinesthetic way.

Abstraction—Art that is based on real images but uses them as design elements.

acrylic—A painting made from acrylic polymer paints.

acrylic paint—A synthetic, resin-based paint that dries quickly and permanently. Not suitable for use by young children.

appliqué—A design made by attaching pieces of cloth to a fabric background.

arch—A curved structure supporting the weight of part of a building.

art elements—The basic visual components of artworks—line, shape, color, form, texture, value, and space.

art therapy—The use of art to help children and adults express their feelings as they work through problems.

artifact—A handmade, three-dimensional cultural art form.

B

baker's dough—A modeling compound made from flour, water, and salt, which can be baked in a household oven.

basket—A container woven from twigs, reeds, or another sturdy fiber.

beam—A long, straight piece of solid material, such as wood or metal, that supports the weight of some of the building.

bisque—Unglazed clay that has been fired in a kiln.

bodily-kinesthetic intelligence—In Howard Gardner's theory of multiple intelligences, the ability to use the body to solve problems or to make things.

bogus drawing paper—A heavyweight (80 lb.) gray paper with a rough-textured surface that provides contrast to the smoothness of most other paper.

C

carding—Brushing wool fibers to straighten them.

cellophane—A thin, transparent film.

chenille stems—Fiber-covered wires, also called pipe cleaners.

cityscape—A representation of a city.

classroom—The inside area of a location used by the children.

clay—Any soft modeling compound, but especially that formed from earth.

clicking—In computer use, pressing the button on the mouse to select an item on the screen.

coil—A long rope of clay made by rolling it on a flat surface with the palms moving outward.

collage—A picture containing glued-on objects or paper.

color—The surface quality of an object or a substance as revealed by the light that reflects off of it and that is seen as a hue in the spectrum.

column—An upright support in a building.

composition—The arrangement of the art elements into a whole.

construction paper—A medium-weight paper that comes in a wide variety of colors.

contrast—An unlikeness in quality.

copper enameling—A process in which copper pieces are covered with melted glass. It is not a safe activity for young children.

craft—Any art form that produces a usable product, such as a fabric, container, or puppet. Often based on traditional techniques, such as basket weaving, embroidery, glassmaking, quilting, pottery, tin work, and weaving.

Cubism—Artistic style in which art represents three-dimensional objects as if they were made of geometric shapes and forms.

cursor—A blinking line or shape that indicates where the first mark will appear on a computer screen.

disk—A small, flexible, plastic disk coated with magnetic material on which data for a computer can be stored.

disk drive—The portal in which a disk is placed in order for its information to be accessed.

drawing—A picture made from any linear art material: pencil, marker, charcoal, ink, chalk, and so on.

dye—Any substance that changes the color of a material.

dynamics—Changes in volume from loud to soft or soft to loud and the accenting of certain tones.

embroidery—A design made with thread on cloth.

Expressionism—An artistic style focused on showing emotions.

fabric dye—Any substance that permanently colors cloth. Not all dyes are safe for children to use.

fiber—A fine, threadlike material.

fiber art—Art forms, such as weaving, appliqué, and embroidery, that use fibers or materials created from fiber.

firing—Slowly heating clay in an insulated oven called a "kiln."

firing clay—A modeling compound formed from earth that dries out in the air and becomes hard when fired in a kiln.

fixative—Any substance that affixes chalk permanently to paper. Fixatives are not safe to use around children.

folk art—Art done by people who have not had formal training in art, or who use nontraditional art media in ways that reflect their culture.

form—The whole of a work of art; also, the three-dimensional equivalent of shape that has the qualities of mass and volume, or the structure that organizes the elements of music.

free-form—An irregular shape.

fresco—A painting made in wet plaster.

geometric—A shape that conforms to mathematical principles.

glaze—A finely ground mixture of minerals that when fired to a high temperature forms a glassy coating on clay.

goal—A statement of the kind of growth in a child's behavior that would be expected over a period of time and after many explorations.

greenware—Clay that has air dried.

guiding adult—The person who selects and prepares the supplies, maps out the possible routes, and provides encouragement along the way.

hand spun—Yarn that has been made by hand.

handwedging—Kneading clay to bend it and remove pockets of air.

hardware—Computer equipment, including a monitor, mouse, keyboard, system board, and hard drive.

harmony—A sequence of tones that enrich a melody.

hue—Color, such as red or yellow.

I

icon—The symbol on a computer screen representing a menu option.

Impressionism—A style of art concerned with capturing the effect of light.

intelligence (multiple intelligences theory)—A conception of human cognition, proposed by Howard Gardner, that recognizes seven different realms of intellectual capability within each individual. The intelligences are linguistic, logical-mathematical, spatial, musical, bodily-kinesthetic, interpersonal, and intrapersonal.

intensity—The brightness or dullness of a color.

interior—In art, a representation of the inside of a building.

interpersonal intelligence—In Howard Gardner's theory of multiple intelligences, the ability to understand and work with others.

intrapersonal intelligence—In Howard Gardner's theory of multiple intelligences, the ability to understand oneself.

joystick—A hand-held device with a stick that can be moved in different directions to control the movement of the cursor on a computer screen.

kiln—An oven made from fire brick in which clay can be fired to temperatures over 1000°F.

kinetic art—Art that moves or has moving parts.

kraft paper—Medium-weight brown paper similar to grocery bags, often sold in rolls. Sturdy enough for drawing and other art activities.

landscape—A representation of the outdoors.

leather hard—Clay that is still damp but no longer flexible.

line—A continuous stroke made with a moving tool. A boundary between or around shapes.

linguistic intelligence—In Howard Gardner's theory of multiple intelligences, the ability to manipulate the symbols of language.

logical-mathematical intelligence—In Howard Gardner's theory of multiple intelligences, the ability to manipulate numerical patterns and concepts.

loom—A frame or machine on which yarn is stretched for weaving cloth.

mandala—A circular design with radiating straight lines.

manila paper—A medium-weight, inexpensive, and durable paper in a pale golden beige with a slight texture.

medium—Any art material. Plural: media.

melody—A sequence of tones that changes or repeats.

menu—A list of choices available in a computer program, from which the user can select options using the mouse or keyboard.

mixed media—A piece of sculpture made from a combination of materials, such as paint, paper, wire, and fabric.

mobile—Three-dimensional art that moves.

monoprint—A printing method that produces only one copy of the original.

mood—The way a particular combination of music elements affects the listener.

mosaic—A picture made from small pieces, such as stones, seeds, or paper bits.

mouse—A hand-held device, which, when rolled in different directions along a surface, controls the movement of the cursor on the screen.

mouse pad—A soft, foam pad on which a mouse is moved.

mural—A large group artwork, usually hung or painted on a wall.

musical intelligence—In Howard Gardner's theory of multiple intelligences, the ability to manipulate rhythm and sound.

natural dye—A dye obtained from plant materials, such as flowers, leaves, or bark.

naturalistic-environmental intelligence—In Howard Gardner's theory of multiple intelligences, the ability to sense and make use of the characteristics of the natural world.

newsprint—A lightweight, inexpensive, slightly gray paper.

nonhardening clay—Modeling compounds that never harden but stay soft and pliable.

Nonobjective—Art based on geometric and organic shapes and forms.

objective—A statement describing a behavior that can be accomplished within the time frame of the activity.

oil—A painting done with oil-based pigments.

Op art—Art based on visual illusions and perceptions.

outdoor area—A contiguous play area outside the classroom.

papier-mâché—A mixture of paper and paste that can be used to cover objects or formed into shapes and allowed to become dry and hard.

pastel—A drawing made with chalk composed of ground pigments.

pattern—A repeated, recognizable combination of art elements.

pitch—How high or low a sound is.

Pointillism—A painting style in which the painter uses small dots of different colors.

Pop art—Art that is based on images from everyday life and popular culture.

portrait—A representation of the outer and inner characteristics of a being.

post and lintel—Two upright supports (posts) that hold up a horizontal piece of solid material (lintel), such as wood, stone, or metal, to create an opening such as a door or window.

pottery—Fired clay.

primary colors—The three basic colors from which all other colors are derived, and which cannot be mixed from the other colors. In painting, these are red, yellow, and blue. In colored light, they are magenta, cyan, and yellow.

print—A picture made using any technique that produces multiple copies, including woodcut, serigraph (silk screen), etching, and lithography.

printer—A machine that produces a paper copy of what is visible on the screen.

quilt—A fabric design created by piecing together smaller bits of fabric.

Realism—An artistic style that focuses on representing what our eyes see.

rhythm—Time-based patterns that order sound.

Romanticism—An artistic style concerned with making things look more beautiful than they are.

scraffito—Using a stick or pointed tool to scratch designs into the surface of clay.

sculpture—A three-dimensional artwork. Sculpture can be made from a limitless variety of materials, including wood, stone, clay, metal, found objects, papier-mâché, fabric, plaster, wax, and resins.

seascape—A representation of the sea.

secondary colors—The colors created by mixing two of the primary colors.

shade—A color darkened by the addition of black.

shape—A two-dimensional area or image that has defined edges or borders.

slab—A flat piece of clay made either by pressing with the palms or by using a rolling pin.

slip—Liquid clay made by combining clay with water to form a thick, custardlike substance. It is used to join clay pieces.

software—Computer programs, stored on disks, that enable a computer to perform tasks.

space—An open or empty area in an artwork.

spatial intelligence—In Howard Gardner's theory of multiple intelligences, the ability to visualize the configuration of objects in space.

spindle—A stick used to twist and hold yarn as it is spun.

spinning—The process of turning fiber into yarn.

spinning wheel—A hand- or foot-powered machine used to turn fiber into yarn.

stitchery—A design made with yarn or cloth.

still life—A representation of an arrangement of objects.

story cloth—Appliquéd and embroidered textiles, made by the Hmong people of Southeast Asia, which record traditional folktales and personal life stories.

Surrealism—An artistic style concerned with fantasies or dreams.

symmetry—Equilibrium or balance created by placing art elements equally on both sides of a central axis.

table loom—A loom small enough to be used on a table.

tagboard—A stiff, smooth, bendable board, also called poster board or oaktag.

textile—A woven fabric.

texture—The tactile or visual surface quality of an object or artwork.

three-dimensional—Having height, width, and depth.

tie-dye—A design made by tying parts of a cloth together and then dying the cloth.

timbre—The unique quality of a sound that makes it recognizable.

tint—A color lightened by the addition of white.

toddler—A child between the ages of 18 months and three years.

tone—The relative lightness or darkness of a color.

two-dimensional—Having height and width, but no depth.

value—The range of lights and darks of colors.

vertical loom—A loom on which the yarns for weaving (warp) are held vertically to the ground.

weaving—The process of creating a fabric by interlocking threads and yarns.

wedging—Kneading and pressing clay to remove air pockets and to create an even texture.

white drawing paper—A sturdy paper with a smooth surface.

whorl—A weight on the end of a hand spindle.

young artist (child)—A child between the ages of 18 months and eight years.

Z

zone of proximal development—The point between where a child can work independently and where a child needs total adult assistance. According to Vygotsky, this is where the best learning takes place.

Index